MULTI-PARTY ACTIONS

MULTI-PARTY ACTIONS

by
CHRISTOPHER HODGES
MA (Oxon), FSALS, FICPD

Solicitor of the Supreme Court of England and Wales
Solicitor of the Supreme Court of Hong Kong
Partner, CMS Cameron McKenna, London

OXFORD
UNIVERSITY PRESS

OXFORD
UNIVERSITY PRESS

Great Clarendon Street, Oxford OX2 6DP

Oxford University Press is a department of the University of Oxford.
It furthers the University's objective of excellence in research, scholarship,
and education by publishing worldwide in

Oxford New York

Athens Auckland Bangkok Bogotá Buenos Aires Calcutta
Cape Town Chennai Dar es Salaam Delhi Florence Hong Kong Istanbul
Karachi Kuala Lumpur Madrid Melbourne Mexico City Mumbai
Nairobi Paris São Paulo Shanghai Singapore Taipei Tokyo Toronto Warsaw

with associated companies in Berlin Ibadan

Oxford is a registered trade mark of Oxford University Press
in the UK and in certain other countries

Published in the United States
by Oxford University Press Inc., New York

© Christopher Hodges 2001

The moral rights of the authors have been asserted
Database right Oxford University Press (maker)

First published 2001

Crown copyright material is reproduced with the permission of the
Controller of Her Majesty's Stationery Office

All rights reserved. No part of this publication may be reproduced,
stored in a retrieval system, or transmitted, in any form or by any means,
without the prior permission in writing of Oxford University Press,
or as expressly permitted by law, or under terms agreed with the appropriate
reprographics rights organization. Enquiries concerning reproduction
outside the scope of the above should be sent to the Rights Department,
Oxford University Press, at the address above

You must not circulate this book in any other binding or cover
and you must impose this same condition on any acquiror

British Library Cataloguing in Publication Data

Data available

Library of Congress Cataloging in Publication Data

Data available

ISBN 0–19–829896–X

1 3 5 7 9 10 8 6 4 2

Typeset in Garamond by
Cambrian Typesetters, Frimley, Surrey

Printed in Great Britain
on acid-free paper by
Biddles Ltd, Guildford and King's Lynn

FOREWORD

Our methods of handling group litigation were developed by judges on a pragmatic basis. The essence of the procedure is that a nominated judge takes on the management of a group of claims. The Civil Procedure Rules (1998), as amended in 2000, reflect this system. At the heart is the Group Litigation Order which identifies a cluster of claims as suitable for determination as group litigation. The order provides for case management of claims which give rise to related issues of fact or law. The distinctive feature of this system is discretionary case management by a single nominated judge.

The question is sometimes raised whether this system should be replaced by the far more comprehensive and far-reaching system of class actions as it is known in the United States. There are marked cultural differences. First, the United States tort claims are tried by juries. Subject to narrow exceptions that is not so in England. Secondly, the scale of jury awards in the United States are far higher than awards made by judges in England. Massive awards for injuries, which are not of the most serious kind, would rightly not be tolerated by English public opinion. Thirdly, it is a feature of class actions in the United States that firms of lawyers earn billions of dollars in cases which do not even come to trial and often result in meagre recoveries by individual claimants. This too would be unacceptable in England. Finally, I would say that in England there is a general perception among judges, in this respect reflecting public opinion, that the tort system is becoming too expansive and wasteful. There is also an unarticulated but nevertheless real conviction among judges that we must not allow our social welfare state to become a society bent on litigation. The introduction of United States style class actions cannot but contribute to such unwelcome developments in our legal system.

In my view the newly referred '2000' model of Group Litigation Orders is at present adequate for our purposes. But practitioners and judges need to have expert guidance on how different techniques can be applied in different situations. This book admirably fulfils this purpose. The case histories are a particularly valuable feature. And the comparative survey is most helpful. The book is an indispensable aid to those who have to grapple with problems of group litigation.

I unreservedly commend it.

Johan Steyn
House of Lords

PREFACE

This book could not have been written without the support of a number of people, to all of whom thanks are due. First, my co-authors who have kindly shared the benefit of their experiences by contributing case histories. Secondly, much of the information and many of the ideas presented here have a common origin in the experience of or discussions amongst my colleagues, particularly Ian Dodds-Smith, Gary Hickinbottom, Mark Tyler, and Anthony Barton of CMS Cameron McKenna, and Laurel Harbour and Sarah Croft of Shook Hardy & Bacon. We have lived with this topic for nearly two decades and continue to find it fascinating as it continues to develop. I am grateful to Professor Mark Mildred, both for discussions over several years and for kindly reading an advanced draft of the manuscript and making a number of helpful comments, and also to Charles Gibson for comments, particularly in relation to costs. Responsibility for the contents remains mine. Thirdly, I am grateful for the encouragement and support of a number of clients, particularly those in the pharmaceutical, medical device, cosmetics, tobacco, electronics, and insurance industries. Fourthly, I am very grateful to Lisa Williams for her extremely accurate typing and her ability to decipher incomprehensible and labyrinthine amendments, and support from Elizabeth Harrison and Jodie North. Lastly, I must acknowledge and thank Chris Rycroft of OUP whose advice on the content of the book has been wise, encouraging and invaluable.

Christopher Hodges
Mitre House, 160 Aldersgate Street,
London EC1A 4DD
4 July 2000

CONTENTS—SUMMARY

Tables of Cases	xxiii
Tables of Legislation and Treaties	xxxiii
List of Abbreviations	xli

I INTRODUCTORY

1. Introduction: The Phenomenon of Multi-Party Actions in England and Wales	3

II MANAGING GROUP LITIGATION

2. Basic Principles and Issues	11
3. Initiation	29
4. Investigating, Commencing, and Pleading Claims	47
5. Initial Management of the Group	65
6. Advertising	83
7. Further Management Issues	95
8. Costs	109
9. Other Procedural Mechanisms	121

III FUNDING MULTI-PARTY ACTIONS

10. Legal Expenses Insurance	135
11. Conditional Fee Arrangements	139
12. Public Funding	177

IV MULTI-PARTY RULES IN OTHER JURISDICTIONS

13. Class Actions: An American Perspective	205
14. Class Actions in the Common Law Provinces of Canada	223
15. Multi-Party Actions in Australia	269

V CASE STUDIES

16. Introduction to Case Studies	303
17. Pertussis Vaccine Litigation	319
18. Opren Litigation	327
19. HIV Haemophilia Litigation	341
20. Gravigard IUD	349
21. Myodil Litigation	357
22. Benzodiazepine Litigation	369
23. Lloyd's Litigation	393
24. *Reay v BNFL*; *Hope v BNFL*	405
25. Manufacturing Operations: Mixed Claims *B & ors v X Co*; *D & ors v X Co*	415
26. Docklands Nuisance Class Actions	425
27. Lockton Litigation	437
28. Creutzfeldt-Jakob Disease (Human Growth Hormone) Litigation	445
29. British Coal: Vibration White Finger Litigation	455
30. British Coal: Respiratory Disease Litigation	465
31. Norplant Litigation	475
32. Tobacco Litigation: 1992–1999	489
Appendices	505

CONTENTS

Tables of Cases   xxiii
Tables of Legislation and Treaties   xxxiii
List of Abbreviations   xli

I INTRODUCTORY

1. Introduction: The Phenomenon of Multi-Party Actions in England and Wales   1.01

II MANAGING GROUP LITIGATION

2. Basic Principles and Issues

    A. Judicial Discretion and Flexibility   2.01
    B. Fundamental Management Issues   2.06
    C. The Two Competing Approaches   2.08
    D. Tactical Positions   2.14
    E. Lessons from the Case Histories   2.20
    F. Developments in Practice   2.23
        CJD litigation   2.24
        Norplant litigation   2.25
        Tobacco litigation   2.27
        MMR litigation   2.30
        Human rights considerations   2.31
    G. The Contemporary Approach   2.32

3. Initiation

    A. Overview: Group Litigation Order Issues   3.01
    B. How many Claimants Constitute a Co-ordinatable Group?   3.04
    C. Application for a Group Litigation Order (GLO)
        Who can make an application?   3.07
        Preliminary steps   3.10
        To whom should the application be made?   3.11
        Information to be included in the application   3.14
    D. Certification: Jurisdiction and Court Discretion   3.16
    E. Certification: Experience on Criteria and Discretion   3.24

F.	Effect of the GLO	
	The management court	3.39
	Binding nature of orders and judgments	3.43
G.	Right to Challenge a GLO	3.54

4. Investigating, Commencing, and Pleading Claims

A.	Pre-Action Protocols	4.01
B.	Pre-Action Discovery	4.09
C.	The Group Register: Claimants' Membership of the Group	4.12
	Criteria and verification	4.17
	Financial viability	4.28
	Joining the register	4.32
D.	Particulars of Claim	4.36
	Group Particulars of Claim	4.40

5. Initial Management of the Group

A.	Managing Judge	5.01
B.	Directions	5.03
C.	Preliminary Issues, Lead Cases, and Test Cases	5.09
D.	Representation Issues	
	Lead solicitor	5.24
	Protection of claimants: the independent trustee	5.33
E.	Cut-off Dates	5.39
	Cut-off dates and limitation	5.54

6. Advertising

A.	The Issue	6.01
B.	Regulatory Controls	6.05
C.	Judicial Comments	6.10
D.	Advertising under Part 19.III	6.29

7. Further Management Issues

A.	Leaving the Group	7.01
B.	Documentary Evidence	7.02
C.	Expert Evidence	7.08
D.	Expert Evidence in Personal Injury Claims: Medical Report Attributing Individual Injury to the Product or Negligent Act	7.11

E.	Settlement of Proceedings	7.20
F.	Court may Make Aggregate Award	7.22
G.	Striking Out	7.23

8. Costs

A.	Individual and Common Costs	8.01
B.	Liability of Individuals for Common Costs: Several, not Joint	8.09
C.	Lead Solicitors	8.12
D.	The Issue of Mixed Winning and Losing	8.16
E.	Costs on Joining or Leaving a Group	8.20
F.	Cost-Sharing Arrangements	8.22
G.	Decisions on Costs	8.24
	The *BCCI* case	8.25
	The *Watson Burton* case	8.27
	The *Nationwide* case	8.31

9. Other Procedural Mechanisms

A.	Various Alternatives	9.01
B.	Part 19.II—Representative Parties	9.03
C.	Actions for an Injunction to Protect the Collective Interests of Consumers	
	Overview	9.09
	Qualified entities	9.10
	Powers of qualified entities	9.15
	Courts	9.17
	Remedies	9.19
	The collective interests of consumers	9.25
D.	Proposals on Representative Actions by Organisations	9.27

III FUNDING MULTI-PARTY ACTIONS

10. Legal Expenses Insurance

11. Conditional Fee Arrangements

A.	Background	11.01
B.	Permitted Conditional Fees	11.07
C.	Setting the Uplift	11.13

D.	The Costs Risk and the Insurance Solution	11.18
E.	Risk Assessment under CFAs	11.23
	Risk for the client	11.24
	Risk for the lawyers	11.25
	Risk for insurers	11.27
	Funding of investigation costs	11.29
	Payment of insurance premiums	11.30
F.	Recoverability of Success Fees and Insurance Premiums	11.35
G.	Notification and Challenge	11.43
H.	The Need for Risk Assessment	11.49
I.	Risks of Different Types of Case	11.53
J.	Financial Implications of Different Types of Case	11.55
K.	The Bar and CFAs	11.62
L.	Conflicts between Lawyer and Client with CFAs	11.63
M.	Risk Assessments and CFAs in Multi-Party Actions: The Future	11.73
N.	Economic Impact on Defendants	11.82
O.	The International Context	11.83

12. Public Funding

A.	Public Funding: The Statutory Framework	12.01
	Factors affecting the Funding Code	12.06
	Payments	12.08
	Costs protection	12.09
B.	Funding Service Levels	12.17
C.	Funding Excluded Services	12.28
D.	Multi-Party Action Funding	12.30
E.	MPA Procedures	12.33
F.	Community Legal Service Contracts	12.35
G.	Wider Public Interest Cases	12.37
	No cost-benefit ratio: valuing public interest	12.45
	Public Interest Advisory Panel	12.49
	Financial eligibility	12.52
	Not a public inquiry: consistency	12.53
	Competing interests	12.58
	Possible future restriction on public interest funding	12.62
H.	Representations by Defendants	12.64

IV MULTI-PARTY RULES IN OTHER JURISDICTIONS

13. Class Actions: An American Perspective
- A. Introduction — 13.01
- B. The Theory of Class Actions — 13.04
- C. Class Actions in Practice — 13.14
- D. Conclusion — 13.42

Appendix

14. Class Actions in the Common Law Provinces of Canada
- A. Introduction — 14.01
- B. Certification of a Class Action — 14.05
  - Cause of action — 14.08
  - Size and identification of class — 14.09
  - Common issues — 14.13
  - Preferable procedure — 14.18
  - Class representative — 14.27
  - Examples — 14.29
- C. Notice to Class Members — 14.30
- D. Judicial Control — 14.31
- E. Representation of Class Members — 14.34
- F. Resolution of Individual Issues and Damages — 14.35
- G. Fees and Funding — 14.37
- H. Limitation Periods — 14.46
- I. Conclusion — 14.47

Appendix 1—Ontario
Appendix 2—British Columbia
Appendix 3—Quebec

15. Multi-Party Actions in Australia
- A. Introduction — 15.01
- B. Traditional Mechanisms — 15.08
  - Joinder — 15.09
  - Test cases — 15.13
  - Consolidation — 15.16
  - Representative actions — 15.21
- C. Class Actions under Part IVA Federal Court Act 1992
  - Generally — 15.26

Requirements for a representative action	15.31
Commencement of proceedings	15.34
Identification of the applicants	15.36
Issues common to all the applicants arising from like circumstances	15.40
A claim against the same respondent	15.45
Opt-out procedure	15.46
Further individual or group proceedings	15.49
Order that proceedings not continue as representative proceedings	15.50
Notice provisions	15.56
Determination of non-common issues	15.60
Settlement	15.64
Judgment	15.68
Costs	15.73
D. Representative Actions by the Australian Competition and Consumer Commission	15.77
E. Conclusion	15.80

Appendix

V CASE STUDIES

16. Introduction to Case Studies

A. The Historical Context	16.01
B. The Funding Background: Legal Aid	16.05
C. Underlying Success Rates	16.10
D. The Difficulties in Succeeding in a Pharmaceutical Claim	16.16
E. The Future of Group Litigation?	16.22

17. Pertussis Vaccine Litigation

A. Background	17.02
B. Litigation	17.06
C. The Judicial Review: *R v The Legal Aid Board No 8 Appeals Committee, Ex Parte Angell et al*	17.22
D. The Irish Litigation	17.25
E. Conclusions	17.26

18. Opren Litigation

A. The Product	18.01
B. Background	18.04

C.	The Opren Action Group	18.06
D.	The US Litigation	18.07
E.	The English Litigation—Part 1	18.08
	The timetable	18.11
	Discovery	18.17
	Costs	18.18
	Medical evidence	18.20
	Settlement	18.24
F.	*Randall v Eli Lilly & Ors*	18.27
G.	The Arbitration Report 28 July 1988	18.28
H.	The English Litigation—Part 2	18.30
	The preliminary issue of limitation	18.31
	First trial on limitation—15 October 1990– 2 November 1990	18.34
	The Limitation Act 1980	18.35
	Discretion	18.47
	Second trial on limitation	18.51
	The Court of Appeal	18.53

19. HIV Haemophilia Litigation

A.	Haemophilia	19.01
B.	AIDS	19.03
C.	The Effect of AIDS on UK Haemophiliacs	19.05
D.	First Interlocutory Hearing	19.07
E.	Second Interlocutory Hearing	19.10
F.	Subsequent Interlocutory Orders	19.16
G.	The Court of Appeal Rules on Public Interest Immunity	19.19
H.	Ognall J's Statement	19.21
I.	The Settlement of the Main Action	19.22
J.	The Medical Negligence Cases	19.26

20. Gravigard IUD

A.	The Product	20.01
B.	Assumptions of Guilt through Association: Folklore and Publicity	20.03
C.	The Allegations	20.05
D.	Procedural History	20.06

	E.	Commentary	20.12
	F.	Postscript	20.20

21. Myodil Litigation

	A.	Description of the Parties	21.01
	B.	Description of the Product	21.04
	C.	The General Nature of the Allegations	21.07
	D.	Outline Description of the Litigation	21.11
	E.	Settlement	21.12
	F.	The Relationship between Generic and Individual Proceedings	21.15
	G.	Trial of Generic Issue and Selection of Lead Cases	21.17
	H.	Cut-off Dates and Admittance to the Group: Latecomers and One Group	21.18
	I.	Medical Criteria: A Common Approach to Causation	21.20
	J.	Registration of Plaintiffs	21.22
	K.	The Role of the Legal Aid Board	21.27
	L.	Action Groups/Media	21.29

22. Benzodiazepine Litigation

	A.	The Products	22.01
	B.	The Claims	22.08
	C.	The Approach of the Court	22.13
	D.	The Course of the Litigation	22.19
	E.	Pleadings	22.31
	F.	Medical Evidence	22.35
		Production of documents relied upon by examining psychiatrists	22.36
		Access to medical records and prescribers	22.41
		Attribution of verified symptoms	22.48
	G.	Cut-off Dates	22.54
	H.	Legal Aid, Funding, and Costs Issues	22.60
	I.	Striking Out	22.68
		Individual cases	22.70
		Strike out of prescriber cases	22.74
		Strike out of manufacturer cases	22.79
	J.	Conclusion	22.83

23. Lloyd's Litigation

- A. Background — 23.01
- B. Causes of the Litigation — 23.03
- C. The Syndicate — 23.04
- D. Causes of Action — 23.06
  - LMX spiral cases — 23.07
  - Long-tail cases — 23.08
  - Run-off contract cases — 23.12
  - Reinsurance to close cases (RITC) — 23.13
  - Personal stop loss cases — 23.15
  - Portfolio selection cases — 23.16
  - Central fund litigation — 23.17
  - Other cases — 23.18
- E. The Outhwaite Syndicates — 23.19
- F. Commercial Court Administration — 23.23
- G. Proceedings
  - Writs and points of claim — 23.26
  - Law firm administration — 23.33
  - Limitation — 23.36
  - Points of defence — 23.39
  - Summonses for directions — 23.40
  - Adjournments — 23.46
  - Settlement — 23.48

24. *Reay v BNFL; Hope v BNFL*

- A. Factual Background
  - Sellafield — 24.01
  - Investigation into the plant's effects — 24.02
  - The Gardner Study — 24.03
  - Case facts — 24.04
- B. Procedural History — 24.07
- C. Key Aspects of the Cases
  - Advertising for plaintiffs — 24.08
  - Challenging legal aid — 24.09
  - Selection of plaintiffs — 24.11
  - Pleaded case — 24.14
  - Evidence — 24.18
  - Discovery — 24.26
  - Assigned judge — 24.31
  - The trial — 24.32
  - Follow on cases — 24.34

25. Manufacturing Operations: Mixed Claims
B & ors v X Co; D & ors v X Co

A.	The Background to the Proceedings	25.01
	The TV programme	25.02
	The two incidents	25.03
	The grant of legal aid	25.06
	The scientific studies	25.08
B.	Procedural History	25.12
	Procedural history of the cancer claims	25.13
	Procedural history of the nuisance proceedings	25.15
C.	Key Aspects of the *B* and *D* Proceedings	
	Legal aid	25.17
	The pleaded allegations of nuisance	25.21
	Evidence	25.24
	Costs orders against the plaintiffs	25.30
	Settlement initiatives	25.32

26. Docklands Nuisance Class Actions

A.	Background	26.01
B.	Relevant Considerations	26.05
C.	Subsequent Developments Leading to the Submission of Representations	26.08
D.	The Judicial Review Proceedings	26.14
E.	Proceedings as Issued against LDDC and Canary Wharf Limited (CW), the Successor to O&Y	26.21
F.	Further Representations	26.25
G.	Conclusion	26.28

27. Lockton Litigation

A.	Background to the Litigation	27.01
B.	The Facts	27.03
C.	Proposal for a Group Action	27.06
D.	Selection of Lead Actions	27.11
E.	Costs Issues	27.19

28. Creutzfeldt-Jakob Disease (Human Growth Hormone) Litigation

A.	The Human Growth Hormone Programme 1959–1985	28.01

B.	Prelude to the Litigation	28.06
C.	The Litigation	28.12
D.	The Inadvisability of a Generic Trial and Ignoring the Facts of Individual Cases	28.17
E.	After the Generic Trial	28.20
F.	Litigation after the Generic Trial	28.22
G.	Complications of the Generic Trial Approach	28.34
H.	Costs	28.35
I.	Conclusion	28.40

29. British Coal: Vibration White Finger Litigation

A.	Introduction	29.01
B.	The Group Action	29.02
C.	The Steering Committee	29.06
D.	Pre-Trial Phase	29.08
E.	The Trials and Appeals	29.12
F.	Handling Agreement	29.24

30. British Coal: Respiratory Disease Litigation

A.	Background	30.01
B.	The First Cases	30.03
C.	Steps towards Co-ordination	30.06
D.	Case Management Decisions	30.09
E.	Limitation, Cut-off, and Publicity	30.18
F.	Trial	30.19
G.	Costs	30.20
H.	Comments on Case Management	30.22

31. Norplant Litigation

A.	The Product	31.01
B.	The Pre-Litigation Phase	31.04
C.	Transfer and Court Control	31.14
D.	Directions	31.21
E.	Evidence	31.37
F.	Withdrawal of Funding	31.38

G.	Unresolved Funding Issues	31.39
H.	Some Conclusions	31.42
I.	Aftermath	31.44

32. Tobacco Litigation: 1992–1999

A.	Advertising for Clients	32.01
B.	Applying for Legal Aid	32.05
C.	Legal Advisers Decide to Fund Actions under Conditional Fee Agreements (CFAs)	32.11
D.	Collection of Medical Records	32.13
E.	Issue of Proceedings	32.16
F.	Plaintiffs' Application for Early Assignment of a Judge	32.18
G.	First Draft Master Statement of Claim	32.22
H.	Hearing before the Senior Master	32.24
I.	Issue of Further Proceedings	32.25
J.	Assignment of a Judge	32.27
K.	Selection of Lead Cases	32.29
L.	Further Pleadings	32.34
M.	Debarring Order	32.38
N.	Media Order	32.41
O.	Court of Appeal	32.42
P.	Further Directions	32.48
Q.	Limitation Hearing	32.52

APPENDICES

A	CPR Rule 19.III	505
B	Practice Direction—Group Litigation	507
C	CPR Rule 19.II	511
D	Community Legal Service's Multi-Party Action (MPA) Solicitors' Panel	514
E	Costs Rules Relative to a GLO	516
F	Directive 98/27/EC on Injunctions for the Protection of Consumers' Interests	518
G	Specimen Initial Group Litigation (GLO) Directions	523

H	Legal Services Commission's Multi-Party Action Documents:	529
	Multi-Party Action Panel Arrangements	529
	Multi-Party Action Solicitor's Panel Membership Criteria and Guidance	540
Index		545

TABLE OF CASES

United Kingdom

A Ltd v B Ltd [1996] 1 WLR 665 ....11.69
AB v John Wyeth & Brother Ltd and another [1991] 2 Med LR 341 ....4.45, 5.43, 5.50–1, 5.55–6
AB & Others v John Wyeth & Brother Ltd [1993] 4 Med LR 1, CA 2.02, 4.28, 5.57,
                              6.10–11, 7.24
AB & Others v John Wyeth & Brother Ltd (No 2) [1994] 5 Med LR 149; (1994) PIQR 109,
  CA...2.02, 2.15, 2.26, 3.36, 5.04,
               7.24–6, 7.30, 12.56, 12.64, 16.14, 22.18, 22.75–80
AB & Others v John Wyeth & Brother Ltd (No 3) [1996] 7 Med LR 267; affirmed [1997]
  8 Med LR 57, CA 2.01, 4.17, 4.23–4, 4.28, 5.16, 5.25, 5.44–5,
            5.52, 6.11, 7.24, 7.27, 7.29–32, 16.12, 22.18–19, 22.82–3
AB & Others v Tameside and Glossop Health Authority and another (1997) 35 BMLR 79,
  CA 16.13
Ainsley 18.30
Aitken & Others v Pulbrook & Others 23.38
Albery & Budden v BP Oil & Shell UK (Megaw, Bridge, Cumming-Bruce LJJ, 2 May 1980),
  CA 12.57
Aratra Potato Co Ltd v Taylor Joynson Garrett (a firm) [1995] 4 All ER 695 ....11.01, 11.09
Armstrong & Others v British Coal Corporation 29.01
Arnold v National Westminster Bank plc [1991] 2 WLR 1177, HL 3.47, 3.51
Ashmore v British Coal Corporation [1990] 2 QB 338; [1990] 2 All ER 981, CA 3.51–2, 7.25

B v John Wyeth & Brother Ltd [1992] 1 WLR 168...7.13
B and Foster v Roussel Laboratories Ltd (May J, 30 June 1997) 2.04–5, 2.26, 4.43
B & Others v X Co; D & Others v X Co 2.09, 4.22, 4.26, 7.22, 16.02,
             25.01, 25.15–17, 25.19, 25.25–6, 25.32, 25.38
Baby Drinks Litigation 16.02
Bairstow v Queens Moat House plc and others, unreported judgment of Mr Justice Nelson,
  14 April 2000, QBD 8.06
Bank of Credit and Commerce International Litigation 8.25, 12.30
Bank of Credit and Commerce International SA v Ali and others [1999] 2 All ER 83 ....8.25–6
Bank of Credit and Commerce International SA v Ali and others (No 4) *The Times*, 2 March 2000;
  149 NLJ 1222, 4 November 1999, ChD 8.25
Beale 18.30
Benzodiazepine Litigation 2.07, 2.09–11, 2.13, 2.18, 2.22, 3.34–8, 4.22–4, 4.26, 4.28,
       4.41–2, 5.16, 5.21, 5.25, 5.43–6, 5.51, 6.10, 7.13, 7.24–30, 12.61,
               16.02, 16.11, 16.14, 22.01–85
Berger and others v Eli Lilly & Co and others [1992] 3 Med LR 233; reversed in part [1993]
  1 WLR 782, CA 5.54, 18.51–3
Bevan Ashford v Geoff Yeandle (Contractors) Ltd [1993] 3 Al ER 238, ChD 11.07
Biss v Lambeth Health Authority [1978] 1 WLR 382 ....7.28
Bollinger (J) SA v Goldwell Ltd [1971] RPC 412 ....9.07
Breast Cancer Radiation Injury Litigation 5.35, 6.21, 12.30, 16.12
Breast Implant Litigation 6.14, 16.02

Table of Cases

Bremer Vulkan Schiffbau und Maschinenfabrik v South India Shipping Corporation Ltd [1981]
    2 WLR 141 ....2.02
British Coal: Respiratory Disease Litigation 2.32, 5.49, 16.02, 30.01–24
British Coal: Vibration White Finger Litigation 2.32, 4.42, 5.12, 12.30, 16.02, 29.01–26
British Waterways Board v Norman [1993] 22 HLR 232; *The Times*, 11 November 1993 ....11.01,
    11.10, 11.69
BSE Litigation 12.30, 16.02

Canary Wharf 25.36
Chapman v The Chief Constable of South Yorkshire Police and others; Rimmer v The Chief
    Constable of South Yorkshire Police and others *The Times*, 20 March 1990 ....2.03
Chrzanowska v Glaxo Laboratories Ltd *The Times*, 16 March 1990 (Steyn J, 2 March 1990),
    QBD 7.05, 8.09
Citibank NA and others v Excess Insurance Co Ltd (Transcript), 7 August 1998, QBD 10.09
CJD Litigation 2.23–5, 2.32, 5.20, 5.49, 12.30, 16.02, 28.01–46
Coenen v Payne [1974] 1 WLR 984 ....5.09
Contrast Media—arachnoiditis Litigation 16.02

Dalkon Shield Litigation 6.14, 16.02, 20.03
D'Arcy 24.11
DAS Legal Expenses Insurance Co Ltd v Hughes Hooker & Co (6 November 1995) 10.08
Davies (Joseph Owen) v Eli Lilly & Co [1987] 1 WLR 1136, CA 5.07, 8.09, 27.22, 27.27
Davies v Eli Lilly & Co and Others *The Times*, 11 May 1987 ....18.18
Davies v Eli Lilly & Co and Others (No 2) *The Times*, 23 July 1987 ....2.15
Davies v Eli Lilly & Co and Others [1987] 1 All ER 801, CA; reversing *The Times*, 2 August
    1986 ....18.11, 18.17
Deeny v Littlejohn & Co & Others 23.25
Depo-Medrone Litigation 12.30
DES Litigation 16.02
Docklands Nuisance Class Actions 26.01–30
Dolling-Baker v Merritt [1990] 1 WLR 1205 ....7.03
Duke of Bedford v Ellis [1901] AC 1, HL......................................9.05, 9.07

East Coast Aggregates v Parra-Pagan and others; Ross v Owners of the ship 'Bowbelle' and the
    Owners of the ship 'Marchioness' [1977] 1 Lloyd's Rep 196, QBD
    (Admiralty Ct) 5.27, 6.19, 8.15
EMI Records v Riley [1981] 2 All ER 838; [1981] 1 WLR 923 ....9.07
Equitable Life Assurance Society v Hyman [2000] 3 WLR 529, HL 2.32, 5.13

Femodene and Minulet Litigation 12.30, 16.02
Fluoride products Litigation 16.02
Foster (Caroline) v Roussel Laboratories Ltd (May J: 30 June 1997) 31.19–21
Foster (Caroline) v Roussel Laboratories Ltd (Buckley J: 30 June 1998) 31.27

Geraghty & Co v Awad Awwad (Schiemann LJ, 25 November 1999), CA 11.07, 11.10
Gibson's Settlement Trusts, Re [1981] Ch 179; [1981] 1 All ER 233 ....6.19
Giles v Thompson [1993] All ER 321, HL...11.01
Godfrey v Department of Health and Social Security (25 July 1988) 3.51
Gravigard IUD Litigation 2.04, 2.09, 2.13, 4.10, 4.41–2, 5.49, 11.74, 16.02,
    20.01–21
Group Action Afrika et al v Cape plc (Buckley J, 30 July 1999); affirmed [2000] 1 Lloyd's
    Rep 139, CA 3.06
Gulf War Syndrome Litigation 11.34, 11.73, 12.26, 12.30
Gundry v Sainsbury [1910] 1 KB 645 ....11.10

Table of Cases

Hallam-Eames & Others v Merrett Syndicates & Others 23.37
Hardie & Lane Ltd v Chiltern [1928] 1 KB 663, CA 9.06–7
Hay v University of Alberta Hospital [1991] 2 Med LR 204 .... 5.07
HIV Haemophilia Litigation 2.04, 5.05, 5.21, 16.02, 19.01–27, 22.18
Hodgson v Imperial Tobacco Ltd [1998] 2 All ER 673; [1998] 41 BMLR 1; *The Times*,
    13 February 1998; *The Independent*, 27 January 1998, CA 6.23–6, 6.29, 11.52
Hodgson v Imperial Tobacco Ltd (Wright J, 9 February 1999) 32.10, 32.26, 32.43,
    32.53, 32.56
Hope v British Nuclear Fuels plc 24.04, 24.06–7, 24.11, 24.13–15, 24.24, 24.27,
    24.33–4
Hormone Pregnancy Tests Litigation 16.02
Hormone Replacement Litigation 16.02
Horrocks v Ford Motor Co Ltd, *The Times*, 15 February 1990 .... 2.02, 22.14
Hughes v Kingston upon Hull City Council [1998] All ER (D) 563 .... 11.10
Human insulin—hypoglycaemic unawareness Litigation 16.02
Hunter v Chief Constable of West Midlands police [1982] AC 529 .... 7.25
Hyman and Williams v Schering Chemicals Ltd *The Times*, 10 June 1980, CA 5.13

Infant Drinks Litigation 12.30
Injectable anti-inflammatory steroids Litigation 16.02
Injectable hormonal contraception Litigation 16.02

Jaffray v Society of Lloyds' *The Times*, 4 November 1999 .... 5.47
Janson v Property Insurance Co Ltd (1913) 19 Com Cas 36 .... 9.07

Kinnear 17.09, 17.12, 17.15

L & W v John Wyeth & Brother Ltd (Ian Kennedy J, 6 May 1992) 4.26, 7.13–14
Lariam Litigation 2.25, 12.30, 16.02, 32.48, 32.50
Lion Laboratories Ltd v Evans [1984] 2 All ER 417 .... 12.53
Lloyd's Litigation 5.05, 5.32, 5.47, 7.03, 16.02, 23.01–48
Lockley v The National Blood Transfusion Service [1992] 2 All ER 589 .... 8.17
Lockton Litigation 16.02, 27.01–35
London Association for Protection of Trade v Greenlands Ltd [1916] 2 AC 15 .... 9.04
Longworth v Prescription Pricing Authority (13 February 1998, CA) 7.32
Lort v Thames Water Utilities Ltd (CA, 29 January 1993) 7.16
Loveday v Renton and the Wellcome Foundation Ltd [1990] 1 Med LR 117 .... 5.15,
    17.01, 17.09, 17.12, 17.20, 17.23–4
LSD Litigation 16.02
Lubbe v Cape plc [2000] 1 WLR 1545, HL 1.02, 3.06

McCafferty v Metropolitan Police Receiver [1977] 1 WLR 1073 .... 18.38
Macfarlane v Tayside Health Board (25 November 1999), HL (Scotland) 16.22
Manley v Law Society [1981] 1 All ER 401 .... 16.05
Markt & Co Ltd v Knight Steamship Co Ltd [1910] 2 KB 1021, CA 9.06, 9.08, 15.23–4
Metropolitan Bank Ltd v Pooley (1885) 10 App Cas 210 .... 7.31
Michael (M) Furriers Ltd v Askew (1983) 127 SJ 597, CA 9.07
Mills v Cooper [1967] 2 QB 459 .... 3.46–7
Minocin Litigation 12.30, 16.02
MMR/MR Vaccine Litigation 2.22–3, 4.04, 2.30,
    4.04–9, 5.30, 6.03, 6.27, 7.09, 8.18, 12.30, 16.02, 16.14
Morelli and Coyle v *Sunday Times* Solicitors Journal, 8 January 1999 .... 11.07
Murphy and another v Young & Co's Brewery and Sun Alliance [1997] 1 WLR 1591, CA 10.09
Myodil Litigation 2.09, 4.22, 4.24–5, 4.42, 5.19, 7.05, 16.02, 21.01–29

Table of Cases

N & Others v United Kingdom Medical Research Council and Secretary of State for Health,
'The Creutzfeldt Jakob Disease Litigation' [1996] 7 Med LR 309 ....28.19
Nash and others v Eli Lilly & Co and others [1991] 2 Med LR 169; *The Times*, 13 February
1991 ....5.54–5, 18.34, 18.50–3
Nash and others v Eli Lilly & Co and others [1992] 4 All ER 383 ....18.53
Nationwide Building Society v Various Solicitors (1998) 148 NW 241; 142 SJ LB 78;
The Times, 5 February 1998, ChD 8.31–4
News Group Newspapers Ltd v Society of Graphical and Allied Trades '82 (No 2) [1987]
ICR 181 ....9.07
Norplant Litigation 2.05, 2.13, 2.22–3, 2.25–6, 2.32, 4.43,
5.48, 6.28, 8.18, 12.30, 12.61, 16.02, 16.12, 31.01–44, 32.50
North West Water Authority v Binne & Partners [1990] 3 All ER 547 ....3.48, 3.50, 3.53
Nottingham District Heating Scheme Litigation 12.30
Nur v John Wyeth & Brother Ltd [1996] 7 Med LR 300 ....2.05, 4.26,
5.07, 7.15, 7.18, 7.24, 22.47

Ochwat and Parylo v Watson Burton (a firm) (Transcript: Smith Bernol) 10 December 1999,
CA (Civ Div) 8.27–30
Opren Litigation 2.04, 2.13, 4.41,
5.16, 5.21, 5.37, 5.54, 8.09, 16.02, 18.01–73, 22.18
Oral Steroids Litigation 16.02
Organophosphate Sheep Dip Farmers Litigation 12.26, 12.30, 16.02

Pan Atlantic Insurance Co Ltd and Republic Insurance Co v Pine Top Insurance Co Ltd
[1989] 1 Lloyd's Rep 568 ....9.07
Pancreatic enzymes Litigation 16.02
Persona Litigation 12.30, 16.02
Pertussis Vaccine Litigation 2.04, 2.13, 3.51, 5.15–16, 16.02,
17.01–27
Pesticides—(benomyl)- anophthalmia and microphthalmia Litigation 16.02
Phelps v Hillingdon LBC [2000] 3 WLR 776, HL 4.22
Pozzi v Eli Lilly *The Times*, 1 May 1986 ....18.20
Practolol Litigation 16.02
Prince v Palmer and others (District Judge Diamond, 22 June 1993) 7.16–17
Prudential Assurance Co Ltd v Newman Industries Ltd [1981] Ch 229; [1979] 3 All ER
507 ....9.07

Quantum Claims Compensation Specialists Ltd v Powell *The Times*, 26 February 1998
(Scotland) 11.01, 11.10
R v GD Searle & Co Ltd (Anthony Diamond QC, 9 March 1990) 4.10
R v Legal Aid Board, ex p Belcher (Dyson J, 15 July 1995) 4.29
R v Legal Aid Board, ex p Donne & Co [1996] 3 All ER 1 ....5.29
R v Legal Aid Board, ex p Megarry and Others (Turner J, 25 April 1994) 32.06
R v Legal Aid Board, ex p Owners Abroad (Tour Operator) (Transcript: Smith Bernol,
31 July 1997), QBD (Crown Office List) 12.69
R v Medicines Control Agency, ex p Pharma Nord [1998] 3 CMLR 109 ....12.57
R v The Number 8 Area Committee of the Legal Aid Board, ex p Megarry & Others
(Popplewell J, 1 July 1994) 3.01, 3.22, 32.06
Randall v Eli Lilly & Others *The Times*, 4 February 1988 ....18.27
Reay v British Nuclear Fuels plc [1994] 5 Med LR 1 ....5.15, 24.04–5,
24.07, 24.11, 24.13–16, 24.27, 24.33–4
Roaccutane Litigation 12.30
Rylands v Fletcher 26.22–3

Table of Cases

Sayers (Paul) and others v SmithKline Beecham plc and others (Master Ungley, 3 September 1999) 4.05–6, 6.27, 7.09
Sellafield Litigation 2.10, 5.15, 6.12, 16.02
SESA GOA & A/S Bulk & Silimna (3 December 1997) 11.11
Singh v Observer Ltd [1989] 3 All ER 777 .... 11.69
Smith v Cardiff Corporation [1954] 1 QB 210 .... 9.07
Smolden v Whitworth [1997] PIQR 133; [1997] ELR 249 .... 12.40
Swain v The Law Society [1983] AC 598, HL 11.10

Talbot v Berkshire County Council [1994] QB 290 .... 3.48
Tanner (John Charles) v British Coal Corporation, unreported judgment of 20 December 1989, judgment of 20 June 1999, CA 30.03
TGA Chapman Ltd and another v Christopher and Sun Alliance [1997] 1 WLR 12, CA 10.09
Thai Trading Co (a firm) v Taylor [1998] 3 All ER 65, CA 11.07, 11.09–10, 11.69–70
Thalidomide Litigation 16.02
Thoday v Thoday [1964] 1 All ER 341 .... 3.45
Thrasyvoulou v Secretary of State for the Environment [1990] 2 WLR 1, HL 3.46
Tobacco Litigation 2.04, 2.09, 2.22–3, 2.25, 2.28–9,
 4.22, 4.30, 4.42, 4.44, 5.21, 6.12, 6.23–6, 6.29, 8.18–19, 11.30, 11.52, 11.68,
 11.80–1, 12.30, 12.68, 16.02, 16.05, 16.14, 31.39, 32.01–58
Upjohn Ltd v The Licensing Authority established by the Medicines Act 1968 and others [1999] 1 WLR 927 .... 12.57

Walker v Eli Lilly *The Times*, 3 December 1986 .... 18..20
Wall v Radford [1991] 2 All ER 741 .... 3.48, 3.51, 3.53
Ward v Guinness Mahon plc [1996] 1 WLR 894, CA 8.09, 8.11, 8.22
Wells v Wells, Page v Sheerness Steel Co; Thomas v Brighton Health Authority [1999] 1 AC 345 .... 11.41
Wells and Coles v Barnsley Metropolitan Borough Council; Leeds City Council v Carr, unreported (Kennedy LJ, Jowitt J, 15 October 1999), DC 11.10
Wilkinson v Ancliff [1986] 1 WLR 1352 .... 18.42

TABLE OF CASES FROM OTHER JURISDICTIONS

Australia

Australian Competition and Consumer Commisssion v Chats House Investments Pty Ltd &
    Others (1996) 71 FCR 250; (1996) 142 ALR 177 ....15.65
Australian Competition and Consumer Commisssion v Giraffe World Australia Pty Ltd &
    Others [1998] ATPR 41–648; (1998) 156 ALR 273; (1998) 54 FCR
    512 ....15.53
Australian Competition and Consumer Commisssion v Glendale Chemical Products Pty Ltd
    (1998) 40 IPR 619; [1998] ATPR 41–632......................................15.79
Australian Competition and Consumer Commisssion v Golden Sphere International Inc &
    Others (1998) 83 FCR 424; [1998] ATPR 41–638 ....15.70
Australian Competition and Consumer Commisssion v Internic Technology Pty Ltd and
    Another [1998] ATPR 41–646 ....15.55
Bishop v Bridgelands Securities (1990) 25 FCR 311...15.11
Bolwell Fibreglass Pty Ltd v Foley [1984] VR 97 ....15.17
Bright v Femcare Ltd [1997] FCA 1377 ....15.30

Cameron v McBain [1948] VLR 245 ....15.16–17
Cameron v Qantas Airways Ltd [1993] ATPR 41–251 ....15.39
Carnie v Esanda Finance Corporation Ltd (1995) 182 CLR 398; (1995) 127 ALR 76;
    (1995) 69 ALJR 206 ....15.03–4, 15.24–5
Connell v Nevada Financial Group Pty Ltd (1996) 139 ALR 723 ....15.39

Duke of Bedford v Ellis [1901] AC 1 ....15.22

Emanuele v Australian Securities Commission (1997) 188 CLR 114 ....15.04

Femcare Ltd v Bright [2000] FCA 512, 19 April 2000 ....15.48

Gold Coast City Council v Pioneer & Others [1997] ATPR 44–076 ....15.53
Gui Sen Huang v Minister for Immigration and Multicultural Affairs (1997)
    50 ALR 134 ....15.55

Harjanto v Minister for Immigration & Multicultural Affairs (1998) 88 FCR 411 ....15.72
Harrison v Lidoform Pty Ltd (24 November 1998, Federal Ct of Australia) 15.39
Horwood v British Statesman Publishing Co Ltd (1929) 45 TLR 237 ....15.17

Jenkins v NZI Securities Australia Ltd & Others (1994) 52 FCR 572; (1994) 124 ALR
    605 ....15.71
Johnson Tiles Pty Ltd v Esso Australia Pty Ltd [1999] FCA 1645,
    25 November 1999 ....15.53

Ling, Re; ex parte Ling v Commonwealth of Australia (1995) 58 FCR 129 ....15.16
Lopez v Star World Enterprises Pty Ltd [1997] FCA 104 ....15.64
Lopez v Star World Enterprises Pty Ltd (in liq) [1999] ATPR 41–678 ....15.65

Nixon v Philip Morris (Australia) Ltd [1999] FCA 1107; [1999] ATPR 41–707; (1999)
    165 ALR 515 .... 15.45, 15.48
Payne v Young (1980) 145 CLR 609; (1980) 54 ALJR 448; (1980) 30 ALR 557 .... 15.11
Philip Morris (Australia) Ltd v Nixon [2000] FCA 229; (2000) 170 ALR 487 .... 15.40, 15.45

Ryan v Great Lakes Council and Others (1997) 78 FCR 309; (1997) 149 ALR 45 .... 15.45
Ryan v Great Lakes Council and Others (1998) 154 ALR 584 .... 15.76

Schanka & Others v Employment National (Administration) Pty Ltd (1998) 86 IR 283 .... 15.54
Schutt Flying Academy (Australia) Pty Ltd v Mobil Oil Australia Ltd [2000] VSCA 103, 8 June
    2000 .... 15.30, 15.48
Silkfield Pty Ltd v Wong (1998) 159 ALR 329 .... 15.42
Soverina Pty Ltd v Natwest Australia Bank Ltd (1993) 118 ALR 298; (1993) 40 FCR
    452 .... 15.40
Symington v Hoechst Schering Agrevo and Others (1997) 78 FCR 164; (1997) 149 ALR
    261 .... 15.45

Todd v Jones [1969] VR 169 .... 15.17
TPC v Queensland Aggregates Pty Ltd (1981) 51 FLR 356 .... 15.12
Tropical Shine Holdings Pty Ltd v Lake Gesture Pty Ltd (1993) 45 FCR 457; (1993)
    118 ALR 510; [1993] ATPR 41–283 .... 15.37–8, 15.53

Wong v Silkfield Pty Ltd [1999] ATPR 41–713; (1999) 165 ALR 373; (1999) 15 LegRep 7;
    (1999) 73 ALJR 1427 .... 15.41
Woodhouse v McPhee (1998) 80 FCR 529 .... 15.76
Woodlands & Another v Permanent Trustee Co Ltd & Others (1995) 58 FCR 139 .... 15.75–6

Zhang de Yong v Minister for Immigration, Local Government and Ethnic Affairs (1993) 118 ALR
    165; (1993) 45 FCR 384 .... 15.40, 15.54

Canada

Abdool v Anaheim Management Ltd (1995) 21 OR (3d) 453 (Div Ct) 14.21, 14.26, 14.29
Allen v CIBC Trust Corporation (1998) 39 OR (3d) 675 (Gen Div) 14.17
Anderson v Wilson [1999] 175 DLR (4th) 409 (Ont CA) 14.04, 14.08, 14.15–16

Bendall v McGhan Medical Corporation (1993) 14 OR (3d) 744 (Gen Div) 14.29
Bywater v Toronto Transit Commission [1998] OJ No 4913 (Gen Div) 14.10, 14.26, 14.29
Bywater v Toronto Transit Commission (1999) 43 OR (3d) 367 (Gen Div) 14.30

Campbell v Flexwatt Corporation (1997) 44 BCLR (3d) 343 (BCCA) 14.04, 14.15
Carom v Bre-X Minerals Ltd (1999) 43 OR (3d) 441 (Gen Div) 14.11
Carom v Bre-X Minerals Ltd (1999) 44 OR (3d) 173 (Gen Div) 14.19, 14.21–2, 14.29
Chace v Crane Canada Inc [1997] 44 BCLR (3d) 264 (BCCA) 14.04, 14.29
Chippewas of Sarnia Band v Canada [1996] 137 DLR (4th) 239; supp reasons 138 DLR (4th)
    574 (Gen Div) 14.05
Cooper Industries (Canada) Inc v Adam (Ontario Ct File No B172/95) 14.05, 14.29
Cooper Industries (Canada) Inc v Babin (Ontario Ct File No B173/95) 14.05
Crown Bay Hotel Ltd Partnership v Zurich Indemnity Insurance Co of Canada (1998)
    40 OR (3d) 83 (Gen Div) 14.39

Dabbs v Sun Life Assurance Co of Canada (1998) 40 OR (3d) 429 (Gen Div) 14.32–3

Table of Cases from Other Jurisdictions

Endean v Canadian Red Cross Society [1997] 147 DLR (4th) 158 (BCSC) 14.29

Gagne v Silcorp Ltd (1998) 41 OR (3d) 417 (CA) 14.38

Haney Iron Works v Manufacturers Life Insurance Co [1998] 169 DLR (4th) 565
    (BCSC) 14.32
Harrington v Dow Corning [1996] 22 BCLR (3d) 97 (BCSC) 14.16, 14.29

Mangan v Inco Ltd (1998) 38 OR (3d) 703 (Gen Div) 14.30
Maxwell v MLG Ventures Ltd [1995] OJ No 1136 (Gen Div) 14.29
Monhteros v Devry Canada Inc (1998) 41 OR (3d) 63 (Gen Div) 14.29

Naiken v General Motors of Canada Ltd [1983] SCR 72 .... 14.01
Nantais v Telectronics Propriety Ltd (1995) 25 OR (3d) 331 (Gen Div); leave to appeal denied
    129 DLR (4th) 110 (Gen Div) 14.11, 14.29
Nantais v Telectronics Propriety (Canada) Ltd (1996) 28 OR (3d) 523 (Gen Div) 14.39
Nash v CIBC Trust Corporation [1996] OJ No 1460 (Gen Div) 14.29

Ontario New Home Warranty Program v Chevron Chemical Co [1999] OJ No 2245
    (Gen Div) 14.33

Parsons v Canadian Red Cross Society [1999] OJ No 3572 (OSCJ) 14.33
Peppiatt v Nicol [1998] OJ No 3370 (Gen Div) 14.04, 14.29
Peppiatt v Royal Bank of Canada (1993) 16 OR (3d) 133 (Gen Div) 14.29
Peppiatt v Royal Bank of Canada (1996) 27 OR (3d) 462 (Gen Div) 14.28

Robertson v The Thomson Corporation (1999) 43 OR (3d) 161 (Gen Div) 14.12, 14.26, 14.29

SR Gent (Canada Inc v Ontarion [1999] OJ No 3362 (OSCJ) 14.22

Tiemstra v Insurance Corporation of British Columbia [1997] 149 DLR (4th) 419
    (BCCA) 14.04

Webb v K-Mart Canada Ltd [1999] OJ No 2268 (OSCJ) 14.11, 14.29
Wicke v Canadian Occidental Petroleum (1998) 40 OR (3d) 731 (Gen Div) 14.29
Windisman v Toronto College Park Ltd (1996) 28 OR (3d) 29 (Gen Div) 14.04

Eire

Best (Kenneth) v The Wellcome Foundation Ltd 17.21, 17.25

United States

Agent Orange Product Liability Litigation, Re 818 F 2d 145 (2d Cir 1987); cert denied
    484 US 1004 (1988) 13.22, 13.38, 13.40
Alabama v Blue Bord Body Co 573F, 2d 309 (5th Cir 1978) 3.38
Amchem Prods Inc v Windsor 521 US 591, 117 S Ct 2231 (1997) 13.03,
    .... 13.07, 13.11, 13.13–14, 13.20
American Medical Systems Inc 75 F 3d 1069 (6th Cir 1996) 13.23–8
Arch v American Tobacco Co 175 FRD 469 (ED Pa 1997) 13.32

Table of Cases from Other Jurisdictions

Avallone v American Tobacco Co CA No MID-L-4883-98MT (Sup Ct NJ 13 April 1999) 13.33

Barnes v American Tobacco Corporation 161 F 3d 127 (3d Cir 1998); cert denied 119 S Ct 1760
    (1999) 13.07, 13.32–3
Broin v Philip Morris Cos 641 So 2d 888 (Fla Ct App 1994); rev denied 654 So 2d 919
    (Fla 1995) 13.33
Brooks v Southern Bell Tel & Tel Co 133 FRD 54 (SD Fla 1990) 13.07–8
Brown v American Tobacco Co Case No JCCP-4042, slip op (San Diego Sup Ct 10 April
    2000) 13.33

Califano v Yamasaki 442 US 682 (1979) 13.01
Castano v American Tobacco Co 160 FRD 544 (ED La 1995) 13.31
Castano v American Tobacco Co 84 F 3d 734 (5th Cir 1996) 13.31–3
Chamberlain v American Tobacco Co Case No 196-CV-2005, 1999 WL US Dist LEXIS
    5843 (ND Ohio, 12 April 1999) 13.32
Cipollone v Liggett Group Inc 505 US 504 (1992) 32.01–4
Clay v American Tobacco Co Case No 97-CV-4167-JPG, 1999 WL 688437 (SD Ill, 9 July
    1999) 13.32
Coburn v 4-R Corporation 77 FRD 43 (ED Ky 1977) 13.15
Consentino v Philip Morris Inc NO MID-L5135-97 slip op (NJ Super Ct Law Div
    22 October 1998); recon denied (NJ Super Ct Law Div 11 February 1999) 13.33

East Texas Motor Freight v Rodriguez 431 US 395 (1977) 13.14
Eisen v Carlisle & Jacquelin 417 US 157 (1974) 13.10
Emig v American Tobacco Co 184 F 3d 379 (D Kan 1998) 13.32

Geiger v American Tobacco Co 696 NYS 2d 345 (NY Sup Ct 1999) 13.33
General Tel Co v Falcon 457 US 147 (1982) 13.14
Gentile v State Bar of Nevada [1991] 500 1 US 1030; 111 SCR 2720 ....6.24
Georgine v Amchem Prods Inc 83 F 3d 610 (3d Cir 1996) 13.07–8, 13.11, 13.21

Hanson v American Tobacco Co Case No LR-C-96-881, 1999 US Dist LEXIS 16277
    (ES Ark 21 July, 1999) 13.32
Harding v Tambrands Inc 165 FRD 623 (D Kan 1996) 13.06, 13.11, 13.30

Insolia v Philip Morris Inc 186 FRD 535 (WD Wis 1998) 13.32

Kociemba v GD Searle & Co USDC, District of Minnesota, Third Division, 8–85 CIV 1599
    1988) 20.04
Kurczi v Eli Lilly & Co 160 FRD 667 (ND Ohio 1995) 13.41

Norplant Contraceptive Products Liability Litigation, Re 168 FRD 577 (ED Tex 1996) 13.30

Ortiz v Fibreboard 119 S Ct 2295 (1999) 13.13

Pasternak v The Upjohn Company, 95-CV-5987 (EDNY 19 September 1994) 3.36–8
Philip Morrs Inc v The Honorable Edward S Angeletti Misc No 2, September Term, 1998
    slip op (Md 16 May 2000) 13.33

Reed v Philip Morris Inc 1997 WL 538921 (Super Ct DC 18 August 1997) 13.33
Richardson v Philip Morris Inc No 961450/CE212596 (Baltimore City Cir Ct 28 January
    1998) 13.33
Rhone-Poulenc Rorer Inc, Re 51 F 3d 1293 (7th Cir); cert denied 116 S Ct 184
    (1995) 13.22, 13.34–7

Table of Cases from Other Jurisdictions

RJ Reynolds Tobacco Co v Engle 672 So 2d 39 (Fla App 3d District 1996) 13.33
Ruiz v American Tobacco Co 180 FRD 194 (DPR 1998) 13.32

School Asbestos Litigation, Re 789 F 2d 996 (3d Cir); cert denied 479 US 852 (1986) 13.40
Scott v American Tobacco Co No 96-8461 (Orleans Parish, La, 16 April 1997) 13.33
Selzer v Board of Education 112 FRD 176 (SDNY 1986) 13.14
Small v Lorillad Tobacco Co 679 NYS 2d 593 (NY App Div 1998); aff's 94 NY 2d 43,
    698 NYS 2d 615 (NY 1999) 13.33
Smith v Brown & Williamson Tobacco Corporation 174 FRD 90 (WD Mo
    1997) 13.10, 13.22, 13.32, 13.41
State of Alabama v Blue Bird Body Co 573 F 2d 309 (5th Cir 1978) 13.41

Taylor v American Tobacco Co Inc Case No 97715975 NP slip op (Cir Ct Wayne City Mich
    10 January 2000) 13.33
Thompson v Philip Morris 189 FRD 544 (D Minn 1999) 13.32

Valentino v Carter-Wallace Inc 97 F 3d 1227 (9th Cir 1996) 13.11, 13.29

TABLE OF UK STATUTES

Access to Justice Act 1999 ....12.20, 16.09
    ss 1, 4 ....12.01
    s 5 ....12.01
        (6) 12.07
    s 6 ....12.02
        (6) 12.03
        (8) 12.29
            (a)..12.04–5
            (b)..12.05
    s 7 ....12.06
    s 8 ....12.06
        (2)(g)..12.37
    s 9 ....12.06
    s 10(1), (2) 12.08
    s 11 ....12.32
        (1) 12.09, 12.11
        (2) 12.10
        (3) 12.16
    s 23 ....12.05
    s 27 ....11.07, 11.09–10, 11.15
    s 29 ....10.04, 11.35
    s 30 ....11.36
    s 31 ....11.38
    Sch 2 ....12.03–5, 12.28
        para 1 ....12.29
    Sch 15 ....11.07
Administration of Justice Act 1985
    s 9 ....6.05
Atomic Energy Authority Act 1954 ....24.16

Broadcasting Act 1990 ....6.08

Coal Industry Act 1987
    s 1 ....30.01
Coal Industry Act 1994................................29.24
Coal Industry Nationalisation Act 1946
    s 1(4) 30.01
Consumer Protection Act 1987 ....22.12, 31.10, 31.12
    Pt I 4.11, 12.28, 16.16, 31.07
    s 4(1)(e) 16.21, 20.19
Control of Pollution Act 1974......................26.03
    s 61(5) 26.01
    s 74 ....26.01
County Courts Act 1984..............................31.18

Courts and Legal Services Act
    1990 ....11.18, 11.69
    s 58 ....11.04–5, 11.07, 11.15
        (1) 11.09–11
        (8) 11.13
    s 58A(4)..11.07
Criminal Law Act 1967................................11.01

Human Rights Act 1998 ....12.31, 12.38
    Sch 1 ....2.31

Insurance Companies Act 1982....................10.03
    ss 71, 81 ....10.07

Law Reform (Miscellaneous Provisions) Act
    1934 ....24.05
Legal Aid Act 1988..........................12.64, 16.05
    s 15(3) 4.29
    s 17 ....12.10, 16.05
    s 18(4) 16.05
    s 38 ....12.69, 26.20
Legal Aid Act 1996 ....10.02
Legal Aid and Advice Act 1949....................16.06
Limitation Act 1980 ....4.35, 5.56, 18.13, 30.18, 32.53
    s 11 ....18.66
        (4) 18.35
            (b)..18.36
    s 14 ....18.54, 18.63
        (1) 18.37
            (a)..18.38
            (b)..............................18.42, 18.44
        (2) **18.38**
        (3) 18.39
    s 14A 23.37
    s 33 ....18.63, 18.67, 32.52
        (3) 18.47
Local Government, Planning and Land Act 1980
    s 136 ....26.11

Medicines Act 1968 ....18.01, 20.02, 20.18
Mines and Quarries Act 1954
    s 74(1) 30.01
        (2) 30.01

National Health Service Act 1977 ....19.20

Table of UK Statutes

Nuclear Installations Act 1965 ....24.16

Railway Clauses Consolidation Act 1845
   s 86 ....26.18
Railways Act 1993
   s 122 ....26.18

Solicitors Act 1974
   s 31 ....6.05
Supreme Court Act 1981
   s 51 ....29.19–20
     (6) 11.52, 32.38

Vaccine Damage Payments Act 1979........17.04–6

TABLE OF UK STATUTORY INSTRUMENTS

Access to Justice Act 1999 (Commencement No 3, Transitional Provisions and Savings) Order 2000, SI 2000/774 .... 11.07
Access to Justice Act 1999 (Transitional Provisions) Order 2000, SI 2000/900 .... 11.35
Access to Justice (Membership Organisations) Regulations 2000, SI 2000/693 .... 11.36

Broadcasting (Foreign Satellite Programmes) (Specified Countries) (Amendment) Order 1993, SI 1993/3047 .... 9.27
Broadcasting (Foreign Satellite Programmes) (Specified Countries) Order 1994, SI 1994/453 .... 9.27
Broadcasting (Prescribed Countries) (Amendment) Order 1993, SI 1993/3046 .... 9.27
Broadcasting (Prescribed Countries) Order 1994, SI 1994/454 .... 9.27

Civil Legal Aid (General) Regulations 1989, SI 1989/339 .... 16.05, 24.09
    reg 28 .... 12.64
    reg 82(5) 12.69
Civil Legal Aid (Scotland) Regulations 1987
    regs 7, 8 .... 12.64
Civil Procedure Rules 1998, SI 1998/3132 .... 1.02, 2.03, 2.28, 2.32, 3.04, 4.01, 4.07, 4.34, 7.03, 7.12, 7.20, 8.24–5, 16.09, 22.14, 22.17–18, 22.84, 28.33, 28.45–6
    Pt 1 .... 2.33, 3.18, 4.20
    r 1.1 .... 3.18, 3.28, 11.51
        (2)(a) 8.19
    r 5.4(1) 4.15
    Pt 8 .... 4.05, 4.09
    r 16.4 .... 2.33, 4.36
    Pt 19.II 1.10, 3.10, 3.20, 3.24, 3.27, 3.32, 9.01, 9.03, 9.05, 9.07
    r 19.6 .... 9.03–4
        (4) 9.08
    rr 19.7–19.9 .... 9.03
    Pt 19.III 1.07, 2.04, 2.30, 3.01, 3.06, 3.19–21, 3.54, 4.04, 4.09, 4.12, 4.16, 4.23, 4.25, 4.27, 4.32, 4.33, 6.15, 7.21, 9.01, 9.05, 9.07, 16.02–3
    r 19.10 .... 3.07, 3.09, 3.15, 3.19, 4.15
    r 19.11(1) 3.16, 3.19
        (2)(a) 3.39, 4.13–14
        (b) 3.19
        (3) **3.39**
        (c) 6.29
    r 19.12 .... **3.43**
        (1)(a) 3.44
        (3) 3.54
        (4) 7.07
    r 19.13 .... **5.03**
        (b) 5.10
        (c) 3.10, 5.32, 5.39
    r 19.14 .... 3.40, 7.01
    r 19.15 .... 5.17, 7.21
    Pt 22 .... 4.20, 4.38
    Pt 24 .... 22.68, 22.78
    Pt 31 .... 7.02
    rr 31.5, 31.7 .... 7.02
    rr 35.1, 35.7 .... 7.08
    Pt 36 .... 11.82
    Pts 43–48 .... 2.29
    Pt 44 .... 8.01, 11.15, 11.47
    r 44.3(4)(b) 8.05
    r 44.3B(1)(a) 11.37
        (b) 11.36
        (c) 11.43
    r 44.14(1)(b) 11.69
    r 48.6A 8.13, 8.17
        (2) **8.03**
        (3), (4) **8.08**
        (5) **8.14**
        (6), (7) **8.20**
    Sch 1
        RSC Ord 15, r 6(2)(a) 17.12
            r 12 .... 9.04
        RSC Ord 18, r 7 .... 32.27
            12 .... 22.39
                (1A) 7.12–13, 22.49
                (1C) 7.17, 22.20, 22.37, 22.70
            r 19 .... 22.68, 22.78

RSC Ord 24 ....24.28
    r 2(5), (6).....................................7.03
    r 7A...17.13
    r 14..4.09
    r 14A..19.11
RSC Ord 53, r 5(3)...........................32.06
RSC Ord 62, r 1(4)............................6.19
    r 11...11.52
Community Legal Service (Cost Protection) Regulations 2000, SI 2000/824
    reg 3(1) 12.12
    (4) 12.12–13
    reg 5 ....12.14
    reg 6 ....12.15
Community Legal Service (Costs) Regulations 2000, SI 2000/441
    reg 9 ....12.11
Community Legal Service (Financial) Regulations 2000, SI 2000/516.............12.08
Community Legal Service (Funding) Order 2000, SI 2000/627
    reg 5 ....12.35
Conditional Fee Agreements Order 1995, SI 1995/1674.................11.04, 11.07
Conditional Fee Agreements Order 1998, SI 1998/1860.................11.04, 11.07
Conditional Fee Agreements Order 2000, SI 2000/823....................11.06, 11.13
Conditional Fee Agreements Regulations 1995, SI 1995/1675..11.04
Conditional Fee Agreements Regulations 2000, SI 2000/692
    regs 2, 4, 6...................................11.08
Consumer Credit (Exempt Agreements) Order 1989, SI 1989/869....................9.27
Consumer Credit (Total Charge for Credit, Agreements and Advertisements) (Amendment) Regulations 1999, SI 1999/3177...9.27
Consumer Protection (Cancellation of Contracts Concluded away from Business Premises) Regulations 1987, SI 1987/2117..............9.27
Control of Misleading Advertisements (Amendment) Regulations 2000, SI 2000/914.....9.27
Control of Misleading Advertisements Regulations 1988, SI 1988/915 ....9.27

High Court and County Courts Jurisdiction Order 1991, SI1991/724
    Art 7(5)..31.18

Insurance Companies (Legal Expenses Insurance) (Application for Authorisation) Regulations 1990, SI 1990/1160...............................10.03
Insurance Companies (Legal Expenses Insurance) Regulations 1990, SI 1990/1159...........10.03
    reg 6 ....10.07
    reg 8 ....10.08

Legal Advice and Assistance Regulations 1989, SI 1989/340...12.35
Legal Aid (Prescribed Panels) Regulations 1999, SI 1999/166..11.54

Medicine Act 1968 (Amendment) Regulations 1995, SI 1995/2321..................................9.27
Medicines (Advertising) Regulations 1994, SI 1994/1932..9.27
Medicines (Advertising and Monitoring of Advertising) Regulations 1999, SI 1999/267...9.27
Medicines (Monitoring of Advertising) Regulations 1994, SI 1994/1933 ....9.27

Package Travel, Package Holidays and Package Tours (Amendment) Regulations 1992, SI 1992/3288...9.27
Package Travel, Package Holidays and Package Tours (Amendment) Regulations 1998, SI 1998/1208...9.27

Satellite Television Service Regulations 1997, SI 1997/1682...9.27
Solicitors Rules of Professional Conduct
    r 8 ....11.01, 11.09
Solicitors' Practice Rules 1990 ....6.05–6, 6.15
    r 1 ....11.13
    r 8 ....11.10
    rr 12.14, 14.10...........................11.13

Television Broadcasting Regulations 1998, SI 1998/3196...9.27
Television Broadcasting Regulations 2000, SI 2000/54..9.27
Timeshare Regulations 1997, SI 1997/1081...9.27

Unfair Arbitration Agreements (Specified Amount) Order 1996, SI 1996/3211...9.27
Unfair Terms in Consumer Contracts Regulations 1994, SI 1994/3159..............9.27
Unfair Terms in Consumer Contracts Regulations 1999, SI 1999/2083..............9.27

TABLE OF NATIONAL LEGISLATION FROM OTHER JURISDICTIONS

Australia

Constitution 15.03

Federal Court of Australia Act 1.04, 15.46
   s 22 .... App 15 298
   Pt IVA 15.05, 15.07–8,
        15.21, 15.26, 15.30–1, 15.33, 15.39,
        15.55, 15.59, 15.70, 15.72, 15.81–2
   ss 33A, 33B .... **App 15 291**
   s 33C **15.32**, 15.40,
        15.45, 15.51, **App 15 291**
      (1) 15.43
        (a) 15.37–8
        (c) 15.42, 15.44
   s 33D .... 15.35, 15.45, **App 15 291**
   s 33E .... **App 15 292**
      (1), (2) 15.34
   ss 33F, 33G .... **App 15 292**
   s 33H .... 15.37, **App 15 292**
      (2) 15.36
   s 33J 15.15, **15.47**,
        15.69, **App 15 292**
      (1) 15.56
   s 33K .... **15.49**, **App 15 293**
   ss 33L, 33M 15.50,
        15.67, **App 15 293**
   s 33N 15.54–5,
        15.59, 15.67, **App 15 293**
      (1) **15.52**
   s 33P .... 15.67, **App 15 294**
   s 33Q .... 15.54, **App 15 294**
      (2), (3) 15.61
   s 33R .... **App 15 294**
      (1), (2) 15.62
   s 33S .... **App 15 294**
      (a), (b) 15.63
   ss 33T, 33U .... **App 15 294**
   s 33V .... **15.64**–5, 15.68, **App 15 295**
      (1) 15.65
   s 33W .... 15.56, 15.66, **App 15 295**
   s 33X .... **App 15 295**
      (1) 15.56–7
      (2)–(6) 15.57
   s 33Y .... App 15 295
      (2) 15.58
      (3)–(8) **15.58**
   s 33Z .... **15.68**, 15.70, App 15 296
      (1) 15.70
   s 33ZA .... App 15 296
      (3) 15.57
   s 33ZB 15.48,
        15.54, 15.69, 15.71, **App 15 297**
   s 33ZC .... **App 15 297**
   s 33ZD .... **App 15 298**
   s 33ZE .... 15.15, **App 15 298**
   ss 33ZF, 33ZG .... **App 15 298**
   ss 33ZH, 33ZJ .... **App 15 299**
Federal Court of Australia Amendment Act
   1991 .... App 15 291
Federal Court Rules
   Ord 6, r 2 .... **15.10**
      (a) 15.11
      (b) 15.12
   r 13(1) 15.21
   Ord 10, r 1 .... **15.14**
   Ord 29, r 2 .... **15.17**
   r 5 .... **15.19**

High Court Rules
   Ord 16, rr 1, 7 .... 15.10
      r 12 .... 15.21
   Ord 31, r 7 .... 15.19

Jurisdiction of Courts (Cross-vesting) Act
   1987 .... App 15 292

Trade Practices Act 1974 .... 15.06
   Pt V 15.78
   Pt VA 15.06
   s 52 .... 15.78
   s 75AQ(1), (2) 15.79
   s 87(1), (1A) .... App 15 299
      (1B) 15.78

Australian Capital Territory
Supreme Court Rules
   Ord 19, rr 1, 5 .... 15.10
      r 10 .... 15.21

Table of National Legislation from Other Jurisdictions

Ord 51, r 1 ....15.19

New South Wales
Supreme Court Rules
   Pt 8, r 2 ....15.10
   r 13 ....15.21
   Pt 26, r 1 ....15.14
   Pt 31, r 2 ....15.17
   r 7 ....15.19

Northern Territory
Supreme Court Rules
   r 9.02 ....15.10
   r 9.12 ....15.19
   rr 18.01, 18.02 ....15.21

Queensland
Rules of the Supreme Court
   Ord 3, rr 1, 5 ....15.10
   r 10 ....15.21
   Ord 17, r 13 ....15.19
   Ord 61, r 5 ....15.19

South Australia
Supreme Court Rules
   r 27.01 ....15.10
   r 34.01 ....15.21
   r 73.01 ....15.19

Tasmania
Rules of the Supreme Court
   Ord 18, rr 1, 4 ....15.10
   r 9 ....15.21
   Ord 55 ....15.19

Victoria
Rules of the Supreme Court
   Ch 1, r 9.03 ....15.10
   r 9.12 ....15.19
   r 18.02 ....15.21
   r 18A 15.21, 15.30

Western Australia
Rules of the Supreme Court
   Ord 18, r 4 ....15.10
   rr 12, 13 ....15.21
   Ord 83, r 1 ....15.19

Canada

British Columbia
Class Proceedings Act 1995, SBC 1995,
   c 21 ....1.04, 14.01,
         14.05, 14.17, 14.26, 14.30, 14.37
   s 1 ....14.14, **App 14/2 250**
   s 2 ....**App 14/2 250**
     (1) 14.11
   s 3 ....**App 14/2 250**
   s 4 ....14.07, **App 14/2 250**
     (1)(b) 14.09
     (2) 14.23
   s 5 ....**App 14/2 251**
   s 6 ....14.28, **App 14/2 251**
   s 7 ....14.25, **App 14/2 252**
     (d) 14.10
   ss 8–10 ....**App 14/2 252**
   s 11 ....14.35, **App 14/2 253**
   s 12 ....14.31, **App 14/2 253**
   s 13 ....**App 14/2 253**
   s 14 ....14.31, **App 14/2 253**
   s 15 ....14.34, **App 14/2 253**
   s 16 ....14.11, **App 14/2 253**
   ss 17–19 ....**App 14/2 254**
   s 20 ....**App 14/2 255**
   ss 21–26 ....**App 14/2 256**
   s 27 ....14.35, **App 14/2 256**
   s 28 ....**App 14/2 257**
   s 29 ....14.36, **App 14/2 257**
   s 30 ....**App 14/2 257**
   s 31 ....14.36, **App 14/2 258**
   s 32 ....**App 14/2 259**
   s 33 ....14.36, **App 14/2 259**
   s 34 ....**App 14/2 260**
   s 35 ....14.32, **App 14/2 260**
   s 36 ....**App 14/2 261**
   s 37 ....14.45, **App 14/2 261**
   s 38 ....**App 14/2 261**
   s 39 ....14.46, **App 14/2 262**
   ss 40–45 ....**App 14/2 263**
Court of Appeal Act
   s 14(1)(a) ....**App 14/2 261**
Court Order Interest Act
   s 7 ....**App 14/2 262**
Crown Proceeding Act, RSBC 1979, c 86
   s 4(1) ....**App 14/2 263**
Interpretation Act
   s 41 ....**App 14/2 263**
Offence Act
   s 5 ....**App 14/2 263**

Ontario
Act Respecting Champerty, RSO 1897,
   c 327 ....14.38, **App 14/1 246**
Class Proceedings Act 1992, SO 1992,

Table of National Legislation from Other Jurisdictions

c 6 ....1.04, 14.01,
    14.05, 14.11, 14.17, 14.23, 14.26, 14.30,
        14.37, 14.39, 14.41, 14.45
s 1 ....14.14, **App 14/1 237**
ss 2–4 ....**App 14/1 237**
s 5 ....14.07, **App 14/1 237**
    (1)(b) 14.09
    (2) 14.28
s 6 ....14.25, **App 14/1 238**
    (4) 14.10
ss 7, 8 ....**App 14/1 238**
ss 9, 10 ....**App 14/1 239**
s 11 ....14.35, **App 14/1 239**
s 12 ....14.31, **App 14/1 239**
s 13 ....**App 14/1 239**
s 14 ....14.34, **App 14/1 239**
s 15 ....**App 14/1 239**
ss 16, 17 ....**App 14/1 240**
ss 18–23 ....**App 14/1 241**
s 24 ....14.36, **App 14/1 242**
s 25 ....14.35, **App 14/1 243**
s 26 ....14.36, **App 14/1 243**
s 27 ....**App 14/1 244**
s 28 ....14.46, **App 14/1 244**
s 29 ....14.32, **App 14/1 245**
s 30 ....**App 14/1 245**
s 31 ....14.42, **App 14/1 246**
s 32 ....**App 14/1 246**
s 33 ....14.38, **App 14/1 246**
s 34 ....14.31, **App 14/1 247**
ss 35–39 ....**App 14/1 247**
Courts of Justice Act
   s 131(3) ....**App 14/1 246**

Law Society Act, RSO 1990, c L-8
   s 59(1) 14.41–2
     (5) 14.43

Regulation 771/92
   s 10 ....14.43

Solicitor's Act, RSO 1990,
   c S-15 ....**App 14/1 246**
   s 28 ....14.38

Quebec
Civil Code
   Arts 59, 67 ....**App 14/3 265**
   Arts 234, 235 ....**App 14/3 264**
   Book IX (1978) 1.04, 14.01
   Arts 999–1002 ....**App 14/3 264**

Art 1003 ....**App 14/3 264**
   (b) 3.26
Arts 1004–1010 ....**App 14/3 265**
Arts 1010.1, 1011–1018 ....**App 14/3 266**
Arts 1019–1026 ....**App 14/3 267**
Arts 1027–1030 ....**App 14/3 268**
Arts 1029–1040.....................**App 14/3 267**

Netherlands

Group Actions Act 1994 ....1.04

Portugal

Law 83/95 of 31 August 1995 ....1.04

South Africa

Contingency Fees Act No 66,
   1997 ....11.06, 11.83

Spain

Civil Procedure Act (Act 1/2000 of 10 January
   2000) 1.04
United States
Constitution...13.11
Comprehensive Environmental Response Compensation Liability Act 23.09
Federal Rule of Civil Procedure 1.03, 3.28
   r 23 ....3.25–6, 3.36, 13.01,
     13.09, 13.11, 13.13, 13.29, 13.32, 13.42,
     App 13 219–221,14.01, 14.19, 15.26
    (a) 5.36, 13.04–5,
                          13.07–8, 13.24
    (b) 3.25, 13.05, 13.08, 13.24
      (1) 13.04
      (2) 13.04, 13.14
      (3) 13.04, 13.08,
             13.10, 13.19, 13.25–6, 13.41
    (c)(2)..**13.10**
    (e) **13.13**
   r 42(a) 15.20

TABLE OF INTERNATIONAL TREATIES AND CONVENTIONS

Convention on Human Rights
    Art 6 ....2.31

TABLE OF EUROPEAN UNION LEGISLATION

Directives

Dir 65/65/EEC 16.17

Dir 75/318/EEC
    Annex 16.17
Dir 75/319/EEC 16.19

Council Dir 84/450/EEC [1984] OJ L250/17 (misleading advertising) 9.27

Dir 85/374/EEC (European Product Liability Directive) 3.38, 16.14, 16.16
    Art 6 ....31.12
    Art 7(e) 16.21
    Art 8(1)..31.12
Council Dir 85/577/EEC [1985] OJ L372/31 (contracts negotiated away from business premises)..9.27

Dir 87/34/EEC 10.03
Council Dir 87/102/EEC [1987] OJ L101/17 (consumer credit) 9.27

Council Dir 89/552/EEC [1989] OJ L298/23 (television broadcasting activities)
    Arts 10–12..9.27

Council Dir 90/314/EEC [1990] OJ L158/59 (package travel, holidays and tours) 9.27

Dir 91/356/EEC 16.19

Dir 92/27/EEC 16.17
Council Dir 92/28/EEC [1992] OJ L113/13 (advertising of medicinal products for human use) 9.27, 16.17
    Art 12 ....9.27
Dir 92/318/EEC 16.17

Council Dir 93/13/EEC [1993] OJ L95/29 (unfair terms in consumer contracts).............9.27
Dir 93/42/EEC 20.02

Dir 94/47/EC [1994] OJ L280/83 (timeshare)...9.27

Dir 97/7/EC [1997] OJ L144/19 (distance contracts)...9.27
Dir 97/36/EC..9.27
Dir 97/55/EC [1997] OJ L290/18................9.27

Dir 98/27/EC [1998] OJ L166/51 (Injunctions Directive)..1.10, 9.10–11, 9.17, 9.22, 9.27
    Recital (2) 9.25
    Art 2 ....9.19
        (2) 9.24
    Art 3 ....9.12
    Art 4 ....9.15
    Art 5 ....9.16
    Art 7 ....9.26

Dir 99/44/EC [1999] OJ L171/12 (sale of consumer goods and associated guarantees)...9.27

ABBREVIATIONS

ACCC	Australian Competition and Consumer Commission
ADR	Alternative Dispute Resolutions
AMC	Ashurst Morris Crisp
BC CPA	Class Proceeding Act 1995, SBC 1995, c 21
BES	Business Expansion Scheme
Bindmans	Bindman and Partners
BSE	Bovine spongiform encephalopathy
CABs	Citizens Advice Bureaux
CCBE	Council of Bars and Law Societies in Europe
CFA	Conditional fee agreement complying with section 58 of the Courts and Legal Services Act 1990 (as substituted by section 27 of the Access to Justice Act 1999)
CJD	Creutzfeldt-Jakob Disease
CLS	Community Legal Service
Commission (the)	Legal Services Commission
CPR	Civil Procedure Rules 1998, as amended
CSM	Committee on Safety of Medicines
CW	Canary Wharf Limited
DLR	Docklands Light Railway
FCA	Federal Court of Australia Act
FDA	Food and Drug Administration of the United States of America
Freeth Cartwright	Freeth Cartwright Hunt Dickens
FSA	Financial Services Authority
Fund (the)	Legal Services Fund
GLO	Group Litigation Order, as specified under CPR Rule 19
GM	Guinness Mahon
HCPs	Health care professionals
hGH	Human growth hormone
HSE	Health and Safety Executive
IBNR	Insured but not reported claims
ITC	Independent Television Commission
IUCD	Intrauterine contraceptive device

Abbreviations

LBTH	London Borough of Tower Hamlets
LDDC	London Docklands Development Corporation
Lead case(s)	A case selected from those within the GLO for some or all of its issues to be tried in advance of other cases. Sometimes called a test case, although it might be appropriate to distinguish between, on the one hand, a case or cases selected for trial from amongst a number of other cases which have also been issued, where the other cases are possibly stayed and, on the other hand, a situation where only one or a small number of cases are brought to test liability when proceedings are not issued in other similar cases, although they might follow if the first succeeds. It would be more appropriate to describe the former situation as lead cases and the latter as test cases
LEI	Legal expenses insurance
Leigh Day	Leigh Day & Co
LK	Leon Kaye, Collin and Gittens
LS Gaz	Law Society's Gazette
MCA	Medicines Control Agency
MMR	Measles–mumps–rubella
MPA	Multi-party action, a generic term
NAG	Norplant Action Group
NCES	National Childhood Encephalopathy Study
NHL	Non-Hodgkins Lymphoma
O&Y	Olympia & York Canary Wharf Limited
Ontario CPA	Class Proceeding Act 1992, SO 1992, c 6
PFR	Pneumoconiosis Field Research
PID	Pelvic inflammatory disease
RA	Radio Authority
RITC	Reinsurance To Close
Roussel	Roussel Laboratories Limited
RSC	Rules of the Supreme Court
S4C	Welsh Fourth Channel Authority
SAHSU	Small Area Health Statistics Unit
TPA	Trade Practices Act 1974 (Cth)
VWF	Vibration white finger

Part I

INTRODUCTORY

1

INTRODUCTION: THE PHENOMENON OF MULTI-PARTY ACTIONS IN ENGLAND AND WALES

The primary purpose of this book is to provide guidance to those involved in the management of a multi-party action on the procedural rules and techniques which may be used and the issues which may arise. **1.01**

A multi-party action has sometimes been known in the UK as a group action and elsewhere as a class action. Although the terms are sometimes used interchangeably, there are technical differences between these terms when applied in the context of a specific jurisdiction: a US class action, for instance, is a particular phenomenon and different from an Australian class action. The term used in the Civil Procedure Rules of England and Wales is Group Litigation Order (GLO), which is again a different mechanism. This situation is one in which a number of claims having some similarity, usually involving the same issue or product and/or same defendants, are formally co-ordinated and administered together by the same judge. The conduct of group actions in England and Wales has been described as now governed by a tried and established framework of rules, practice directions, and subordinate legislation, albeit recently developed.[1] Multi-party actions have only become a recognisable phenomenon in a small number of jurisdictions of the world—albeit influential jurisdictions—in the last quarter of the twentieth century. **1.02**

In the USA, class actions have been permitted since 1938 and have flourished particularly since the Federal Rule of Civil Procedure was significantly revised in 1966. However, as discussed in chapter 13, the class action procedure has tended to be used in US jurisdictions for some types of claim, such as investor protection or general consumer cases such as overcharging, but less so for others, such as product liability actions.[2] US judges tend not to like class actions of certain categories **1.03**

---

[1] *Lubbe v Cape plc* [2000] 1 WLR 1545 per Lord Bingham of Cornhill CJ, 1559.
[2] See DR Hensler, B Dombey-Moore, B Giddens, J Gross, EK Moller and NM Pace, *Class Action Dilemmas: Pursuing Public Goals for Private Gain* (RAND Institute for Civil Justice, 1999).

because they can be tied up in them for years. It has been said that insufficient empirical evidence exists to indicate whether mass tort claimants are better served by formal aggregation, through class certification, by information aggregation, or by some ambiguous middle ground such as the American multi-district litigation procedure.[3]

1.04 The US procedural approach was copied in Quebec in 1978.[4] Rules dealing with multi-party claims have been created in Australia[5] and Canada[6] in the 1990s, which are discussed in Part IV. Such rules are virtually unknown in third world countries and in many developed states, such as most jurisdictions of the European Union, Japan and New Zealand. A Group Actions Act came into force in the Netherlands on 1 May 1994. Some class action provisions (with limitations) are contained in the Portuguese Law 83/95 of 31 August 1995. The Scottish Law Commission has considered[7] but in 2000 rejected a need to introduce a multi-party rule. Proposals have languished in Sweden[8] and Finland[9] but might be revived. The Civil Procedure Act (Act 1/2000 of 10 January 2000) brings into force in Spain from January 2001 a procedure under which groups of consumers or users may sue. The European rules remain almost needed.

1.05 In Europe, multi-party litigation seems mostly unknown. In contrast, there has been a succession of major multi-party actions in the United Kingdom and the numbers involved have shown marked growth, particularly when compared with other European jurisdictions. The group action phenomenon in this country goes back to around 1980 and initially divided into the two categories of transport accidents (Lockerbie, Kegworth, Clapham Junction, Zeebrugge) and pharmaceutical or medical device products (vaccines, tranquillisers, various contraceptives). Since the mid-1990s, techniques of concerted management of claims have also been applied in other areas such as insurance or investor protection claims (Lloyd's, Guinness Mahon), environmental issues (Sellafield, Docklands), and housing issues.

1.06 The rise of multi-party actions has been influenced by a number of factors,[10] particularly including the availability of methods of funding the investigation and pursuit of legal claims such as through legal aid; claimants' exposure to the financial risk of losing (this risk has been suspended in England and Wales where

---

[3] See DR Hensler, B Dombey-Moore, B Giddens, J Gross, EK Moller and NM Pace, *Class Action Dilemmas: Pursuing Public Goals for Private Gain* (RAND Institute for Civil Justice, 1999).
[4] Quebec Civil Code, Book 1X (1978).
[5] Amendments in 1992 to the Federal Court Act.
[6] Ontario Class Proceedings Act 1992 and British Columbia Class Proceedings Act 1995.
[7] Scottish Law Commission, *Multi-Party Actions: Report by Working Party* (1993); Scottish Law Commission, *Multi-Party Actions: Court Proceedings and Funding* (1994).
[8] SOU 1994:151 but 1994 proposals have been revived in 2000.
[9] [1999] Consumer Law Journal 140.
[10] CJS Hodges, 'Factors influencing the incurrence of multiple claims' [2000] 289.

Chapter 1: Introduction

claimants have been funded by legal aid); as well as the availability of litigation procedural rules. It is an important feature of the development of multi-party litigation in this country during the 1990s that several of these aspects have been the subject of major reform. It is, therefore, important to note the history of the development and reform of these aspects in order fully to understand how multi-party actions developed, how they are heavily influenced by factors such as funding mechanisms, how reform of any of these factors will affect multi-party actions in future, and to unravel the various strands of these issues. A number of the strands are complex and interrelate to a considerable extent so that a complete understanding of how the relevant pressures will affect the development of an action can be difficult to achieve. Information on many of these aspects is included in this book, although this is not a book on legal history but for practitioners.

In England and Wales, there was no Rule of Court to assist the court or parties in managing group actions until the introduction of Part 19.III of the Civil Procedure Rules 1998 with effect from 1 April 2000. Until this Rule was introduced, the formal techniques which may be applied to achieve just and efficient determination of a plethora of individual claims evolved as a matter of necessity on an *ad hoc* basis as the courts and parties involved in a succession of major cases, particularly from the mid-1980s, have been faced with the challenge of coping with them. The protagonists were confronted with considerable uncertainty over what sometimes seemed like major and intractable problems in managing the sheer number of individual claims. The developing experience of these cases led to the conclusion that different cases can have different features, which require that they may need to be managed differently. It was found to be a mistake to assume that each case, even cases of the same legal type such as product liability claims, should be handled exactly according to an immutable blueprint. Lord Woolf, who reviewed the situation in 1995–6 as part of his general review of civil procedure, initially favoured a prescriptive approach to multi-party actions but came to the view that the court should be allowed wide discretion in selecting management techniques appropriate to the particular case. Similarly, the Supreme Court Rules Committee, which subsequently assumed responsibility for drafting the Civil Procedure Rules and Practice Directions, ended up with the Rule on multi-party procedure which was short and generalised, hence permitting maximum flexibility. **1.07**

Part 19.III is discussed in detail in Part I of this book. Its approach is to establish a *framework* for the management of multi-party situations, so that the court may deal *flexibly* with the particular problems of each case within a structure created by the Rule.[11] Accordingly, the Rule does not set out to prescribe the individual **1.08**

---

[11] Lord Chancellor's Department, *Multi-Party Situations: Draft rules and practice direction: A Lord Chancellor's Department Consultation Paper* (1999).

management techniques which may be adopted in any given circumstances, nor give guidance on what techniques may be appropriate in particular circumstances. Since Part 19.III is fairly limited in its scope, there remains a need for a wider examination and explanation of the techniques which may be deployed in managing a multi-party action and an analysis of the pros and cons of these techniques.

1.09 Accordingly, Part I also provides a critical commentary on the range of management techniques and relevant issues which have arisen out of the experience of the major cases to date, in order to assist the parties, their lawyers, and the court in selecting appropriate techniques to manage a future situation. This summary is based on the factual histories of the major cases for which the management histories and techniques are summarised in Part V. Each chapter in Part V was written by a senior lawyer who was involved in the particular case. These summaries concentrate on describing the procedural and managerial aspects of the cases: considerations of space require that these summaries cannot be full histories nor deal with all the substantive issues of fact or law which were in issue or resolved, although at least some of these aspects are mentioned so as to give background, since the facts of many of these cases are not widely available and some are of considerable interest.

1.10 Part II considers three alternative mechanisms in which multi-party litigation might be managed: Rule 19.II on representative actions where all parties have the same interest (which basically repeats previous procedural law in modernised form); a new mechanism for consumer organisations to bring injunctions in certain circumstances, implementing Directive 98/27/EC; and English proposals for a wider mechanism for claims brought by consumer organisations. The issue of a group action mechanism is increasingly being considered at European level. First, the European Commission's Directorate-General on Justice and Home Affairs is preparing working papers on recovery of legal costs and lawyers' fees and on the collective interests of consumers in civil litigation (group actions) as part of its objective of ensuring an area of legal security and equal access to justice.[12] Secondly, the Directorate-General on Internal Market has reproduced in its Green Paper on liability for defective products a question on whether there should be better arrangements for the common representation of similar interests.[13] Whilst these issues might be pursued slowly, if at all, at European level, it is relevant that they are now being considered at this level, having not been done so before.

---

[12] European Commission, *Scoreboard to review progress on the creation of an area of 'Freedom, Security and Justice' in the European Union*, COM (2000) 167 final/2, 13 Apr 2000.

[13] COM (1999) 396 final, 28 July 1999.

Chapter 1: Introduction

1.11 In Part III, the book considers the issues of how multi-party litigation is funded. This is of fundamental importance to litigants, lawyers, and judges and vital to an understanding of how multi-party actions have developed and may develop in future.[14] No civil litigation claim will normally be pursued or defended unless it is financially viable. This has two aspects. First, the potential benefit to the claimant in damages and costs recovered should exceed the risk in costs. The defendant faces a mirror image of this costs/risk trade-off. Secondly, the claimant and defendant must be able to fund any costs payable to their lawyers, experts, and in court fees as the case proceeds. In practice, funding is usually the key to the investigation, commencement, and continuation of a claim. This is particularly true of multiple claims, where economies of scale can assist claimants in spreading both the risk of the litigation and the funding burden. Mechanisms of funding and reducing risk are particularly important in multiple claims, in view of what is often either an immediate liability to pay one's own side's costs and (in those jurisdictions that have this rule, as in England and Wales) very significant risk of liability for the other side's costs. Part III therefore examines various funding methods current in England and Wales, notably public funding (and the particular fund for multi-party claims) and conditional fee arrangements (plus their associated insurance policies).

1.12 Part IV discusses the class actions rules in the USA, Ontario, British Columbia and Australia. It is important to recognise the different functions of the rules in different jurisdictions, so as to avoid making inappropriate comparisons. The US model of a class action rule exists generally to try a defined class of claims which all have common questions, under which those claims which are tried are by definition representative of the class and their resolution binds and is dispositive of all claims in the class: all succeed or all fail. Observance of the formal procedural rules is required, as is observance of constitutional requirements such as of due process. In contrast, the English and Welsh model takes a more flexible approach with fewer legal rules relating to definition of the group and affording the judge considerable discretion. Under this model, the purpose is merely to afford a mechanism under which a number of similar (not necessarily identical) claims can be managed effectively and efficiently. It is not necessarily expected that all claims will be resolved by the same mechanism(s) or reach the same substantive result.

1.13 The management of multi-party actions in England and Wales stands at a crossroads after major reforms have been undertaken which will transform the circumstances in which they arise and must be managed. This book aims to give

---

[14] It has been questioned whether the introduction of conditional fee agreements, insurance policies, and The Funding Code will put an end to the historical flourishing of multi-party claims in England and Wales: M Harvey, 'Funding Personal Injury Litigation in the New Millennium' [2000] JPIL 31.

Chapter 1: Introduction

assistance to judges and lawyers who are faced with the daunting task of deciding how best to achieve the fair and efficient handling of multi-claimant litigation by providing concise but reliable reports on those techniques which have been applied in a succession of major cases and some analysis of the advantages and disadvantages of certain approaches. Selection of the right approach in the circumstances of a new case is a challenge to good judgement. What is required in each case is a blend of experience, foresight, flexibility, common sense, and imagination. The law is stated as at 1 July 2000.

Part II

Managing Group Litigation

2

BASIC PRINCIPLES AND ISSUES

A.	Judicial Discretion and Flexibility	2.01	F.	Developments in Practice	2.23
B.	Fundamental Management Issues	2.06		CJD litigation	2.24
				Norplant litigation	2.25
C.	The Two Competing Approaches	2.08		Tobacco litigation	2.27
				MMR litigation	2.30
D.	Tactical Positions	2.14		Human rights considerations	2.31
E.	Lessons from the Case Histories	2.20	G.	The Contemporary Approach	2.32

A. Judicial Discretion and Flexibility

When from the mid-1980s the courts were faced with the Herculean task of managing multi-claimant actions, involving considerable technical problems,[1] there was no rule of court or body of experience on which to draw. A succession of judges was forced to innovate and adopt increasingly interventionist case management techniques. Decisions which departed from tradition were not uncriticised by those adversely affected. However, counsel for the plaintiffs in the benzodiazepine litigation accepted at the start that without 'ring-fencing' the litigation could not be controlled.[2] Overall, it can be seen that the courts achieved remarkable success in the orderly and efficient control of the cases[3] and none was ultimately allowed to become unmanageable.[4]

2.01

These factors were recognised in a series of candid judgments in which the Court of Appeal stressed the need for innovation and for the management court to exercise extensive discretion, largely unfettered by appellate control:

2.02

---

[1] C Harlow and R Rawlings, *Pressure Through Law* (1992) 136.
[2] *AB & Others v John Wyeth & Brother Limited* [1996] 7 Med LR 267, 271.
[3] The interests of claimants, manufacturers, and insurers that may need to be balanced are diverse: R Dingwall and T Durkin, 'Time, Management and Procedural Reform' in AAS Zuckerman and R Cranston, *Reform of Civil Procedure* (1995).
[4] A salutary historical precedent was that the legal process took practically two decades to conclude claims arising from phocomelia caused by thalidomide in the early 1960s: see C Harlow and R Rawlings, *Pressure Through Law* (1992) 184–186.

Inevitably, High Court judges assigned to the control of such litigation must depart from traditional procedures and adopt interventionist case management techniques. If the judges charged with the control of such actions did not undertake this innovative role, the system of justice in respect of such cases would break down entirely. That result could not be tolerated. Not surprisingly, the Court of Appeal has given its imprimatur to the creative role, in procedural terms, of judges to whom such litigation is assigned: see *Horrocks v Ford Motor Co Limited* unreported, 'The Times', February 15, 1990.

... A court of record has an inherent power to control its procedure so as to promote the achievement of justice and to avoid injustice insofar as it is reasonably practicable to do so. This proposition of law is not in doubt. See *Bremer Vulkan Schiffbau und Maschinenfabrik v South India Shipping Corporation Ltd* [1981] 2 WLR 141, at 147. But in the context of group actions it is relevant to consider the scope of the court's inherent jurisdiction. I know of no better summary of the extent of the inherent jurisdiction of the High Court than that given by Sir Jack Jacob in a seminal paper published in 1970: see, IH Jacob, 'The Inherent Jurisdiction of the Court', 1970 Current Legal Problems 23. Sir Jack said (at page 51):

> '... the inherent jurisdiction of the court may be defined as being the reserve of fund of powers, a residual source of powers, which the court may draw upon as necessary whenever it is just or equitable to do so, and in particular to ensure the observance of the due process of law, to prevent improper vexation or oppression, to do justice between the parties and to secure a fair trial between them'.

See also Halsbury, 'Laws of England', volume 37, paragraph 14. The procedural powers of a judge in control of a group action are not tied to transitional procedures. Subject to the duty to act fairly, the judge may and often must improvise: sometimes that will involve the adoption of entirely new procedures. The judge's procedural powers in group actions are untrammelled by the distinctive features of the adversarial system. The judge's powers are as wide as may be necessary to control the litigation fairly and efficiently.

...

... In my view the Court of Appeal ought to be particularly reluctant in group actions to interfere with a trial judge's procedural direction. A judge invariably has a much better perspective of the interests of all the parties and of the needs of efficient case management than the Court of Appeal can ever achieve. Moreover, interference by the Court of Appeal with the trial judge's directions on one aspect will often upset the coherence of the entire structure of the litigation. In my judgment such appeals ought to be discouraged.[5]

Group actions involve great advantage to plaintiffs, who are able to join together to bring actions which, on their own, would never be possible. But they must be conducted in such a way that they do not involve injustice to other parties. There are no rules of court specifically dealing with group actions. The judge to whom they are assigned can and should devise procedures to deal with the specific problems of the litigation before him. He will need to be inventive and firm if the trial and interlocutory proceedings are not to be unmanageable. In such litigation this court will

---

[5] *AB & Others v John Wyeth & Brother Limited* [1993] 4 Med LR 1, CA 6 per Steyn LJ.

A. Judicial Discretion and Flexibility

be especially reluctant to interfere with the judge's exercise of his discretion, since he knows far more about the litigation than we can do.[6]

2.03 As early as 1990, in other words some years before Lord Woolf's revolutionary proposals for the introduction of case management into civil procedure which resulted in the Civil Procedure Rules 1998, the courts had recognised the need for the case management principle not only to be introduced but to take precedence over the rights of individual litigants. In litigation arising out of the Hillsborough Stadium disaster, involving 900 claims for personal injury or death against the police and third party claims against the football club and a firm of engineers who had designed the stadium, Steyn J said:

> [This] is complex multiparty litigation. In such litigation the sporting theory of justice, or what Prof Wigmore called the 'instinct to give the game fair play', ought to have no place. In such litigation, in the public interest, the concept of a party being *dominus litis* ought, as far as possible, to be subordinated to case management techniques controlled by the court. Subject to preserving the protections offered by the adversarial system, the court ought to control the pace of the litigation.[7]

2.04 The courts have accepted that no two multi-party cases are necessarily the same.[8] On the contrary, individual circumstances differ widely and different procedural solutions have been adopted to suit the particular circumstances of each case.[9] Whilst it may well be sensible to provide the parties and the court with a general framework within which to operate, as Rule 19.III seeks to do, it is a mistake to fetter the court's discretion to adopt relevant and innovative solutions.[10] The Law Society's 1995 Report stated: 'We believe that considerable procedural flexibility is essential. . . . It is not practicable to lay down criteria that will be applicable to all cases, even if it were desirable to do so.'[11] Similarly, Lord Woolf reported that: 'The need for imagination and creativity in dealing with such litigation is attested to by every judge who has tried such a case.'[12]

---

[6] *AB and Others v John Wyeth and Another* [1994] 5 Med LR 149, CA 153 per Stuart-Smith LJ.
[7] *Chapman v The Chief Constable of South Yorkshire Police and others; Rimmer v The Chief Constable of South Yorkshire Police and others*, The Times, 20 Mar 1990.
[8] *B and Foster v Roussel Laboratories Limited* (May J, 30 June 1997).
[9] For example, trying preliminary issues on causation (Pertussis) or limitation (Opren and tobacco) may be more appropriate than trying lead cases (HIV). No cut-off date for claimants to join the group has been sought by any party or ordered in the Gravigard litigation. The Legal Aid Board was clearly against cut-off dates: Legal Aid Board, *Issues arising for the Lord Chancellor's Department and the Legal Aid Board from multi-party actions* (May 1994) para 2.27. It is suggested that cut-off dates are very important in some cases but not in others. Flexibility is the key.
[10] There is a fundamental difference of approach here between the English model of a multi-party action and the US Federal class action model. Since decisions under the latter bind all class members, flexibility is inappropriate and the certification criteria must be applied strictly. In contrast, the former is a management tool for efficient administration and the claims of individual group members may not be resolved in the same way, so flexibility and innovation are acceptable.
[11] Law Society, *Group actions made easier* (1995) paras 6.9.1 and 6.9.4. This approach was endorsed by Lord Woolf: see his *Final Report* (1996) ch 17. 21, 32.
[12] Lord Woolf, *Access to Justice: Final Report* (1996) ch 17 para 32.

2.05 The approach by the court towards management of a multi-party action should be spontaneous, as May J said in the Norplant litigation: 'Inventive case management requires the court to take the steps which it regards as appropriate whether the parties ask for them or not.'[13] The court should be careful, however, that the extent of its imagination and discretion remains proportionate to the case, as Ian Kennedy J said in the benzodiazepine litigation: 'the means of control should be proportionate to the object and the object to the resulting hardships'.[14] It is the function of this book to assist the selection of appropriate techniques by providing a compendium of the techniques which have been adopted in particular circumstances.

B. Fundamental Management Issues

2.06 Two fundamental issues over the management of a multi-party action are, first, what approach should be adopted to manage a particular multi-party action and, secondly, what part each of the actors should play in selecting and controlling the approach. These issues were hotly debated throughout the 1990s. They were not formally resolved by the end of the decade but the solutions adopted in cases and the developments in reforms of civil procedure and funding clearly indicated a way forward.

2.07 In some cases, as can be seen from the case histories set out in Part V of this book, particularly those cases which were speculative, these issues could be of major tactical importance, since they might have significant impact on both the costs which one or other party would have to incur and also the tactical position of the parties and even the ultimate outcome. Of course, the answer to the question about who controls the litigation is that the managing judge does so, but his power is only exercisable once he assumes the management of a case. In contrast, the position that tended to arise in cases up to the end of the 1990s was that parties might fight tactical battles before a co-ordinating judge was appointed. For example, in some cases, claimants might typically obtain public funding for investigation of generic issues, advertise for potential claimants to come forward, refrain from investigating individual cases, either at all or in detail and possibly only by soliciting unverified answers to questionnaires, draft Master Statements of Claim but not individual pleadings, select a small number of individual cases to be put forward as lead cases, and select certain issues to be put forward for trial as generic issues. All these matters might be substantially dealt with before a summons for directions was issued so that the matter could come before a judge and, possibly, before pleadings were issued. The aims would be to establish a sufficiently viable number

---

[13] *B and Foster v Roussell Laboratories Ltd* (May J, 30 June 1997).
[14] *Nur v John Wyeth & Brother Limited* [1996] 7 Med LR 300, 304.

of claimants, but reduce investigation costs to a minimum. Indeed, the attitude of the Legal Aid Board after the benzodiazepine case was that the vast majority of the money wasted in that case had been spent on investigating individual claims, so it would be more efficient to resolve multi-party actions by funding only investigation of generic issues rather than individual cases.[15] This approach and its drawbacks are discussed below.

C. The Two Competing Approaches

Two basic competing models have been put forward for managing a multi-party action. In the first model, which can be called the 'generic model', it is assumed that all individual cases are legally valid, financially viable, and similar. Accordingly, individual cases do not require to be verified, thus saving considerable expense. The claims can be progressed simply by selecting issues which are common to all of the cases (common or generic issues) and deciding those *in vacuo* before individual cases are considered. This, it is argued, would save considerable costs since, first, the cost of a trial of generic issues would be limited and, secondly, the outcome of a generic trial would subsequently be likely to be cost efficient, since either all cases would fail on the determination of the generic issues or they might be settleable. **2.08**

In response, it is pointed out that the generic model depends on various assumptions which cannot be taken for granted in certain types of case. Not only might the assumptions on validity, viability, and similarity be optimistic but, it is argued, history has shown them to be incorrect, at least in particular types of case. For example, many individual cases in product liability cases (and some environmental damage cases, as illustrated by the *X Co* case[16]) need to be scrutinised for legal viability since they can advance claims that are frequently either weak (benzodiazepine, Gravigard, Myodil[17]) and/or speculative (tobacco[18]) and, in any event, issues must be identified which are genuinely common. Accordingly, it is argued that the generic model proceeds on a premise, which may be wholly false in some cases, that most or all of the individual claims are valid, viable, and similar when initial screening would show that they are not. If that is so, the litigation could not and should not be seen to be viable at the start, thereby saving all subsequent costs. A detailed consideration of these manageability issues when deciding whether to make a Group Litigation Order (GLO), as occurs in the equivalent US certification **2.09**

---

[15] Legal Aid Board, *Issues Arising for the Legal Aid Board and the Lord Chancellor's Department from multi-party actions* (1994); Legal Aid Board, *When the price is high* (1997).
[16] See ch 25 below.
[17] See chs 22, 20, and 21 below.
[18] See ch 32 below.

hearing, would help to ensure that only cases which are properly suited to GLO treatment proceed in this way.

2.10 As a development of these thoughts, the second or 'individual case' model takes the approach of requiring all individual cases to be scrutinised and filtered at the outset. It is only thereafter that decisions on the appropriate management techniques should or, indeed, can be taken. It is only at that stage that the issues which actually arise in those cases which pass the filtering stage can be identified. These issues might turn out to be entirely different from what they were asserted to be at the outset, prior to proper scrutiny.[19] Accordingly, management techniques might have been applied which were inappropriate and a waste of costs. For example, it might be concluded that there are *no* genuine generic issues, so co-ordination of individual claims is inappropriate.

2.11 The major response to the individual case model has been by the Legal Aid Board, which argued, in the aftermath of the expensive collapse of the benzodiazepine litigation, that the expense of investigating individual claims was the largest element and should therefore be avoided.[20] The Board argued that a cheaper way of resolving group claims would be simply to select either a test case or a small number of claims (say ten) and try them. The selected claims would be subject to (some) scrutiny, validation, and verification. The Board adhered to this approach for some years, during which both theory and practice evolved. In its 1999 proposals for funding 'very expensive' cases and multi-party actions from the Community Legal Service Fund, the Board repeated its test case approach of funding 'only the minimum number of individual cases required to demonstrate the generic claim'. The Board supported this approach on the principle that: 'Care must be taken to ensure that an individual issue is not litigated in more than one case. Funding for a public interest case should be refused or delayed if other cases are already being brought to deal with the issue in question.'[21]

2.12 This approach can be criticised on the basis that it fails to confront the problem of the assumption that the cases selected are representative of the other claims. It is argued that, in certain types of case at least, the fact of representativeness simply cannot be established without initial scrutiny of all individual claims. Furthermore, there remains the objection that, as with the 'generic model', the non-selected cases, which might form a very large number, would remain unvalidated and therefore the entire group action would remain unassessed for financial

---

[19] Note the significant amendments to claimants' pleaded cases in the benzodiazepine and Sellafield litigation.
[20] Legal Aid Board, *Issues arising for the Legal Aid Board and the Lord Chancellor's Department from multi-party actions* (1994). The majority of the £40 million cost in the benzodiazepine litigation was spent on investigating individual claims: see also Legal Aid Board, *The Funding Code* (1999).
[21] Legal Aid Board, *The Funding Code* (1999) paras 4.17.6 and 7.12.

C. The Two Competing Approaches

viability. It may be, and a number of case histories in Part V support this, that if the individual claims were validated properly at the start, a significant number would be rejected, with the result that the approach to financial viability and management of the remainder would be entirely different.

Critics of the generic theory have portrayed it in the following way.[22] A multi-party action (particularly in product liability cases) would typically be generated or expanded by the activities of claimants' solicitors through encouraging claimants to come forward in response to advertising or concern expressed in the media. Media interest might initially cover a particular product or safety issue but could subsequently relate to the mere existence or development of the group litigation. There may be a 'bandwagon' effect. Public funding might have been sought and granted in order to investigate a generic case but any funding for investigation of individual claims would typically have been limited to a small number of individual cases selected at random as supposedly representative cases. Formal steps in the litigation would be commenced by claimants' legal teams drafting Master Statements of Claim in ignorance of proper information on the issues which arise in individual claims. No claims, or very few individual claims, would usually have been scrutinised at that stage. The analysis in the Master Statement of Claim would concentrate solely on an analysis of the supposed generic case against the defendants and typically cover a very wide range of possible allegations which might in theory be raised against a defendant, but which may be quite irrelevant when tested against the allegations which are actually raised by individual cases.[23] Master Statements of Claim would simply repeat standardised and extensive allegations of a company's supposed failure in design, research, marketing, advertising, information, and warning, whether or not these aspects are in fact relevant when tested against individual claims. This can be criticised as a 'kitchen sink' approach to pleading, comprising a 'production line' approach to standardised, wide-ranging pleadings and allegations which were repeated in successive cases which dealt with different subject matter. It is noteworthy here that the Master Statements of Claim in the pertussis, Opren, Gravigard, benzodiazepine, and Norplant cases were very similar in the generalised approach that they adopted. In many of those cases it had simply not been established that fundamental aspects of the initial allegations were anything other than hypothetical and it was inevitable that the initial allegations were subsequently subject to substantial amendment. It is suggested at paragraphs 4.42 *et seq* below that Master Statements of Claim are only useful if used in conjunction with, rather than in advance of, individual statements of claim at a point in time

2.13

---

[22] See GR Hickinbottom, 'The Defendant's Perspective' (Mar 1996) The Litigator.
[23] For example, the Master Statement of Claim in the Gravigard intrauterine contraceptive device litigation against GD Searle & Co Ltd made extensive allegations against a particular product which had not been used by any of the plaintiffs in the outstanding individual cases: see ch 20 below.

Chapter 2: Basic Principles and Issues

where the general nature of the allegations in individual claims has been verified and is well understood.

D. Tactical Positions

2.14 The arguments over the competing management models can also be analysed in terms of the tactical strategy and sometimes self-interest of the proponents. Proponents of the generic theory have almost entirely been claimants' lawyers, whereas the theory requiring scrutiny of individual cases has been supported on behalf of defendants.[24] The objectives of the typical generic model outlined above might be said to be as follows:

- maximising the number of individual claimants in the group. This would exert pressure in a number of ways.[25] First, the financial viability of the action would be increased, since it would be assumed that every member of the group would have a viable claim and would be entitled to average assumed damages, thereby increasing the total damages claimed, but also reducing the costs nominally attributable to each claimant. This prospect would assist in satisfying the cost-benefit viability tests, whether the case was publicly or privately funded. Secondly, the larger the number of claimants, the greater would be the public perception that the individual cases had legal merit and the greater would be the pressure on the defendants to settle.
- avoiding the cost of investigation of individual claims. This has obvious advantages for saving money under a conditional fee agreement or where public funding is limited.
- incurring the cost of investigating generic issues. This work would be restricted to a small number of firms (financially highly advantageous to them) usually with larger resources or leading reputations in multi-party action (MPA) work.
- succeeding at a generic trial on some general issues which might be relatively easy to establish. For example, the plaintiffs might press for determination of whether a product was capable of causing damage of the type alleged. This issue of general causation might not be too difficult to establish for some products, such as medicines,[26] but would leave unresolved issues of individual and proximate causation. It might be possible to say after a favourable decision on general causation (for example, is the product capable of causing damage?) that it had been established that the product was dangerous, thereby making continued defence of the

---

[24] See Lord Woolf, *Access to Justice: Final Report* (1996) ch 17 para 32.
[25] One view is that group litigation functions partly to make law accessible to individuals, partly as a counterbalance to corporate weight: C Harlow and R Rawlings, *Pressure Through Law* (1992) ch 3.
[26] See paras 16.15 *et seq* below.

D. Tactical Positions

product more difficult and possibly less commercially attractive since the market image of the defendant or product would have been seriously tarnished by a well-publicised 'loss' in the legal dispute.

2.15 One approach may be to seek to portray the MPA as a public inquiry,[27] under which generic issues (how did this happen?) would be of greater interest than individual issues (did it happen to this person and how?). The civil courts have always rejected that function. It is axiomatic that the nature of the judicial process in the context of liability claims in civil litigation is simply to adjudicate on questions of liability between citizens and, where liability is established, to award monetary compensation as damages.[28]

2.16 The generic approach was favoured by the Law Society in its 1995 Report but only by a majority.[29] The Report and its 'draft scenario' at Appendix A proposed:

- defendants should give early (ideally pre-action) discovery;[30]
- in contrast, discovery by claimants should only be given in lead cases;[31]
- only an appropriate sample of lead or test cases should be allowed to go forward and be investigated, the rest being stayed (no criteria are suggested as to how individual cases could be identified as worthy of being in the sample or of how anyone could be sure that individual issues, and hence any common issues, had been identified);[32]
- defendants should only be allowed to investigate an individual claim which had not been identified as a lead case if this were ordered by the court where the defendant had justified this 'by evidence'.[33]

2.17 The majority proposals in the Law Society Report were criticised as partisan, likely to produce injustice to defendants who are asked to produce all their evidence while most claimants produce nothing, and likely to impede the facilitation

---

[27] A strong motivation of some claimants to further an MPA may be to 'get at the truth' of what happened. See C Harlow and R Rawlings, *Pressure Through Law* (1992) 133. This motivation may be a response to the inadequacy of a regulatory system as an effective control, or ignorance of the existence of, or of the scientific complexities involved in, regulatory mechanisms.

[28] *AB v John Wyeth & Brother Limited* [1994] 5 Med LR 149, CA, 153 per Stuart-Smith LJ. See also *Davies v Eli Lilly & Co and Others (No 2)* The Times, 23 July 1987.

[29] The Law Society, *Group Actions Made Easier* (1999). This Report did not make clear that on those occasions on which it refers to a majority and a minority of views of members of the committee, the same majority (pro-plaintiff) and the same minority (pro-defendant) were involved in all these crucial issues. The debate was simply politicised and these issues cannot be regarded as being resolved by a particular show of hands.

[30] ibid, 6.15.1, 6.15.2.

[31] ibid, 6.15.4.

[32] ibid, 6.13.2 and 4.

[33] ibid, 6.13.5. It is unclear what is meant by 'evidence' here, nor what evidence could be relevant. There is circularity in requiring a defendant to obtain evidence of the individual claim that he is supposedly prevented from investigating. See C Gibson, 'Group Actions' in M Mildred (ed), *Product Liability: Law and Insurance* (Lloyd's of London Press, 1996).

of early settlement. They were also criticised as offending the principle of maximum flexibility by requiring too much formality of approach in each case.[34]

2.18 The assumption underlying these recommendations of the Working Party was repeated in Lord Woolf's 1996 Issues Paper, that namely 'the Group [deserves to be given] a better chance of success'. This is a striking assumption given that there was and remains no evidence that group actions had been failing when they deserved to succeed. It was said that the problem was not with the fact that the success rate was *too* low but with the reasons why it was *so* low.[35] The evidence from the major cases recorded in this book is that in certain types of MPA, notably product liability claims, when individual claims have been analysed the overwhelming majority have been shown to fail on legal or factual grounds. As Gibson has argued, it does not follow that there is a problem with the system because a substantial piece of litigation collapsed unless the quality of the system is measured solely by the number of claimants who obtain compensation.[36]

2.19 In contrast to the position of claimants, the tactical aims of defendants concerned to counter the generic model would be:

- to make representations to the Legal Services Commission or CFA insurers against the grant or continuation of funding of weak claims;[37]
- to have the case management agenda controlled by the court from an early stage rather than being set by plaintiff lawyers for some time before the litigation reached court;
- to object to uncontrolled advertising by plaintiff lawyers, since this could tend to encourage weak claims;[38]
- to investigate individual cases so as to verify the existence of common issues, to weed out weak claims, and be able to settle good claims, if so wished.

E. Lessons from the Case Histories

2.20 Comparison of the strategies analysed above shows that the pressures which the two factions might exert on the management of a MPA are largely of different types, exerted at different points in time and with different effects. The case histories in Part V show that in general, as may be anticipated, where judicial control

---

[34] Comments made at a seminar on multi-party litigation at The Law Society, Feb 1996.
[35] GR Hickinbottom, 'The Defendant's Perspective' (Mar 1996) The Litigator 62: GR Hickinbottom, 'Learning from the Benzodiazepine Litigation' (July 1997) The Litigator 207. See also the statistics on success rates discussed in ch 33.
[36] C Gibson, 'Group Actions' in M Mildred (ed), *Product Liability: Law and Insurance* (Lloyd's of London Press, 1996).
[37] See paras 12.64 *et seq* below.
[38] See the discussion on advertising in ch 6 below.

was not available or not strong the effects of pressures exerted by plaintiff lawyers proved greater than those of defendants. Not surprisingly, factionalist complaints were traded, particularly with defence lawyers complaining about the financial self-interest of claimant lawyers, and with the latter complaining about the larger financial resources of the defendants.

As discussed above, claimants and defendants fought hard in successive cases over whether the management model which each favoured should be that which governed the litigation. This was principally because the management method which prevailed might have a significant effect on the outcome of the litigation. **2.21**

The advantages and disadvantages of the two opposing management models were fought out in practice in the large cases of the 1990s—principally the benzodiazepine litigation of 1987–94 and the cases on Norplant, MMR, and tobacco at the end of the decade. In between these two series of practical events, there was extensive debate on the management models and issues, and the arguments set out above can be followed in a sequence of documents which principally comprise: **2.22**

- *Guide for Use in Group Actions* Working Party of the Supreme Court Rules Committee 1991
- *Report on Proposals to the Lord Chancellor relating to the Legal Aid aspects of Multi-Party Actions* Legal Aid Board 1991
- *Arrangements for Multi-Party Actions* Legal Aid Board 1992
- *Issues arising for the Legal Aid Board and the Lord Chancellor's Department from multi-party actions* Legal Aid Board 1994
- Report of the Law Society's Working Party on Multi-Party Actions of its Civil Litigation Committee *Group Actions Made Easier* 1995
- *Issues Paper: Multi-Party Actions* Lord Woolf 1996
- *When the price is high* Legal Aid Board 1997
- *Multi-Party Situations: Consultation Paper* Lord Chancellor's Department 1997
- *The Funding Code* Legal Aid Board 1999
- *Multi-Party Situations: Draft rule and practice directions. A Lord Chancellor's Draft Consultation Paper* Lord Chancellor's Department 1999

F. Developments in Practice

A resolution of the issue of managerial models emerged from decisions in the cases that had to be dealt with in the later 1990s, notably CJD, Norplant, tobacco, and MMR. These took place against the background of the development of the new approach to litigation procedure based on Lord Woolf's proposals.[39] **2.23**

---

[39] Lord Woolf, *Access to Justice: Interim Report* (1995) and *Final Report* (1996).

CJD litigation

2.24 The generic model was adopted in the growth hormone CJD litigation but led to serious confusion. As explained in chapter 28, there was a trial in 1996 of generic issues of liability with no evidence of individual cases and a concession by the defendants of medical causation (general causation, not individual or proximate causation). Enormous difficulty and expense ensued in applying the judgment, which included an unanticipated finding of fact, to the facts of the individual cases. Accordingly, it was accepted that the generic approach was inappropriate, at least in its pure form, without at least a sample of individual cases fully pleaded on the issue of (in a product liability case) breach or causation.[40]

Norplant litigation

2.25 The issue of whether the generic or individual case model should be adopted then arose squarely in the Norplant, Lariam, and tobacco cases. In June 1997, the parties to the Norplant litigation (see chapter 31) advanced classic arguments, with claimants favouring the generic approach and defendants arguing for the individual case approach. There was the normal background that the claimants had prepared a Master Statement of Claim and the defendants wished to see medical reports in 47 of the then 84 claims. The unhappy experience of the CJD litigation clearly influenced the decision of May J. He favoured a modified individual case approach, stressing the need for co-operation between the parties. He ordered the claimants to choose between five and ten individual cases after consultation with the defendants and to particularise those claims. He struck out part of the Master Statement of Claim and in effect laid it aside, without formally discarding it.

2.26 The reasoning outlined by May J is important in relation to the court's general approach to management of a multi-party action and should be considered in full:

> Although I agree with Mr Henderson that a group should not be constituted until it is evident that there is a proper group, it seems to me obvious that, if there is to be litigation by a number of plaintiffs about Norplant, it should be gathered together under one court umbrella.
>
> . . .
>
> Group actions, where a large number of individual plaintiffs seek to bring broadly similar claims usually against one or more large organisations are notoriously problematic. They are problematic for the parties: they are problematic for the court. They are the subject of Chapter 17 of Lord Woolf's Final Report. The court does not as yet have detailed Rules of Court describing how actions of this kind should be managed. The judge is encouraged

---

[40] M Mildred, 'The Human Growth Hormone (Creuzfeld-Jacob [*sic*] Disease) Litigation' [1998] JPIL 251.

F. Developments in Practice

'... to devise procedures to deal with the specific problems of the litigation before him. He will need to be inventive and firm if the trial and interlocutory proceedings are not to be unmanageable.'—see *AB and others v John Wyeth and Brother Ltd* (1994) PIQR 109 at 116.

It is obvious that the court's first aim is to be fair and in doing so to enable the parties to have issues which matter determined economically and in a way that will give all parties the opportunity of resolving what is in dispute expeditiously. It is also, I think, obvious that a procedure which suits one situation may not suit another. Claims by a number of individual plaintiffs against a single corporate defendant will be less difficult perhaps to manage than such claims against a number of defendants; third parties are almost certain to result in complications; and so forth. The court will aim to devise with the co-operation of the parties procedures where a judicial determination reached economically will have the best chance of resolving commercially all that is in dispute. I think that four of the principal considerations for which the court will have to find a balance are that:

(a) it will be very expensive and time-consuming if a large number of individual plaintiffs all have to progress their cases fully before there has been any decision whether any one of the cases is basically sound: but it is not easy to see how defendants can deal commercially with a large number of potential claims if only a few of them are to be progressed.

(b) if issues are not carefully confined, the danger of getting bogged down is palpable. Individual plaintiffs will not be well served if the devised procedure results in years of very expensive interlocutory litigation during which lawyers and others earn money but plaintiffs do not get any result. But issues which are so confined that they are not sufficiently determinative to be commercially helpful will also be unsatisfactory.

(c) arrangements must be made for costs and to deal with limitation periods for any plaintiff whose action is deferred.

(d) the court needs and will require the active co-operation of all parties. It has been said that group actions involve great advantages for plaintiffs and that they must be conducted in such a way that they do not involve injustice to other parties (see the *Wyeth* case at p.116). At the same time, defendants will not be allowed to frustrate by non-cooperation the expeditious and economic progress of the litigation.

I have already said that what is suitable for one situation may not suit another. There are precedents for conducting group actions by concentrating on generic issues and having documents called Master Pleadings. This is a procedure which Lord Woolf's Report seems to favour. Master Pleadings have not always proved to be satisfactory. In my view it should not be assumed that this is necessarily the best way to proceed and parties should not, in my view, embark on setting up a structure for a group action without seeking the court's directions as to what that structure should be. It seems to me that in principle [the defendant's counsel] is correct that generally speaking cases such as this should start with particular claims and then consider whether generic issues emerge from a selection of individual cases. It may then be agreed that there are generic issues suitable for determination as such. On the other hand it may be that the fair and economic way forward is to proceed with an individual test case or with a handful of selected individual cases on the basis that a determination of that or those cases will go a long way to determining all such cases, if not in law, at least commercially. Each group of cases will depend on its own individual circumstances. But I express a tentative general preference for the individual approach rather than the generic approach, since the individual approach is more likely to result in economic and manageable litigation and the generic approach more likely to lead to an unmanageable public inquiry. Upon this approach the parties would have orthodox individual pleadings and then probably a short document defining common issues which experts' reports would address.[41]

Tobacco litigation

2.27 The situation which faced the court in the tobacco litigation in 1997–8[42] again had some of the classic confrontational features of the two models. Wright J first refused formally to declare that the individual cases should be co-ordinated as a multi-party action, although this was unnecessary as all claims were proceeding in the same court and co-ordinating directions were given. He then discarded the Master Statement of Claim and ordered that the claimants and defendants should each select five cases, for which full individual Statements of Claim and Defences should be served. This modified individual case approach could only, of course, be adopted on the basis that all, or most, of the individual cases had been investigated. Absent such investigation, selection of lead cases illustrative of the majority, and certainly selection of those most favourable to the position of either party, could not be undertaken by either party.

2.28 The tobacco litigation was also significant in being the first multi-party action undertaken on a CFA—and without costs insurance for the plaintiffs—and the last major one concluded before the new approach under the Civil Procedure Rules 1998 (CPR). As had happened with a number of previous multi-party actions, the investigation by claimants' solicitors of their clients' cases was undertaken essentially by clients completing standard form questionnaires, without checking of details by the lawyers against other evidence, notably the medical records. It was agreed that the solicitors for one of the defendants should carry out the task of collecting all the claimants' medical records. This time-consuming task was therefore initially funded by the defendants, thus saving expenditure by the claimants and their solicitors under the CFA, although the costs would ultimately have been payable by the claimants if an order had been made to that effect. This situation has obvious advantages for claimants and their lawyers. However, it would not comply with their obligations under the approach required under the CPR and its protocols for claimants to investigate and fully disclose their cases before commencing proceedings.

---

[41] *B and Foster v Roussel Laboratories Ltd* (May J, 30 June 1997).
[42] See ch 32 below.

G. The Contemporary Approach

A further consequence of this arrangement was that, as might have been predicted, claimants' unchecked memories of their smoking histories and what warnings they received over several decades turned out in a number of cases to be unreliable. The strategy of pleading cases in advance of checking the facts of cases, particularly against medical records, led inevitably to a need to amend or discontinue certain claims, with normal orders to pay defendants' consequential costs. Thus, a strategy of pursuing a generic approach over an individual case approach in a CFA context led to costs orders against claimants where solicitors had not adequately investigated their cases. If such a situation were to recur, the court and affected claimants might well argue that responsibility for such costs under the CPR Parts 43–48 should rest with the lawyers rather than their clients.

2.29

MMR litigation

The MMR litigation[43] was possibly the first major multi-party case to fall under the CPR approach but it was before the publication of Part 19.III. As discussed at paragraphs 4.04 to 4.08 below, the court essentially adopted the protocol approach and required *all* claimants to serve relevant details of their cases when issuing writs (but not in earlier letters), after which defendants were to respond in accordance with the protocol. The claimants did not begin by seeking to proceed by way of Master Pleadings nor initial selection of test or lead cases.

2.30

Human rights considerations

A further factor which may influence the situation is that from October 2000 individuals have the right to have their cases determined within a reasonable time.[44] This would apply to both claimants and defendants. Indefinite or unreasonable postponement of the investigation or progress of cases might breach this principle. This may have consequences where no progress is made on individual cases which are not treated as test cases.

2.31

G. The Contemporary Approach

The current position is that the individual case model has largely predominated over the generic model in product liability cases, but with some modification. In some cases, a single test case approach may be entirely satisfactory, such as to resolve the single issue common to 90,000 policy holders in the same insurance company as to the legality of the company's policy on guaranteed annuity rates.[45]

2.32

---

[43] At the time of writing, this litigation is continuing: see para 4.04 below.
[44] Article 6 of the Convention on Human Rights, Sch 1 of the Human Rights Act 1998.
[45] *Equitable Life Assurance Society v Hyman* [2000] 3 WLR 529, HL.

In the product liability situation, the CJD[46] and Norplant[47] cases and American experience[48] show that a pure generic approach is essentially unworkable. In the Vibration White Finger occupational health case, a generic approach was used but it should be noted that problems were encountered at a late stage when alternative causation issues were identified in individual cases.[49] Selection of eight test cases in the respiratory disease litigation was also undertaken after all individual cases were pleaded and medical records disclosed.[50] The contemporary management of a group is somewhat uncertain, in the light of significant new influences emanating from the introduction of CFAs, and new funding arrangements under the Community Legal Service Fund for multi-party actions, and possible developments in interpretation of the new Civil Procedure Rules. Against this background, the following approach is suggested.

2.33 As discussed at chapter 4, each claimant has a *prima facie* obligation under the CPR to investigate his or her individual case and disclose it and relevant evidence to the prospective defendant in the pre-action phase. On joining a group, each claimant must normally serve particulars of claim.[51] Compliance with these requirements will involve investigation and verification of the facts of each claimant's case.[52] That is the normal situation. However, the court has power to order some other approach where it considers this to be appropriate. Nevertheless, the evidence and arguments for initial investigation and verification of individual cases are strong in cases involving mass torts and cases generated by publicity or lawyer-led. In achieving certainty of what management technique is to be adopted in a particular group, it may assist for the group to come under the managerial control of the court at an early stage, probably pre-action. It would be entirely in accordance with the overriding principle of the Rules[53] for the parties to save costs by collaborating in agreeing, first, those aspects of claimants' and defence cases on which evidence is to be proportionate and required and, secondly, a unified method of producing such evidence (such as defendants collecting medical records, if they are agreeable). If a limitation is to be placed on the verification of

---

[46] See ch 28 below.
[47] See ch 31 below.
[48] See ch 29 below.
[49] See ch 13 below.
[50] See ch 30 below.
[51] CPR, Rule 16.4.
[52] However, the Legal Aid Board stated in consultation documents prior to finalisation of The Funding Code 2000 that it favours a strong presumption in favour of funding a test case or a small number of sample claims, and against funding a large-scale group action. Legal Aid Board, *The Funding Code* (1999) para 7.12 (ii); Legal Aid Board, *A New Approach to Funding Civil Cases* (1999) para 12.4. On the basis of the case histories and above analysis, this approach may present difficulties if it is adopted in certain types of case. Further, if public funding is not to be available for the preliminary investigation of individual claims, claimants may have difficulty in complying with the CPR. The Funding Code itself is silent on this issue.
[53] CPR, Rule 1.

G. The Contemporary Approach

the facts of individual cases, the advantages and disadvantages should be well understood. It is not, of course, possible to prevent defendants from investigating available evidence of individual cases at their expense if they wish.

In conclusion, it must be noted that the case management techniques discussed below are not presented as a blueprint for adoption in every case, but as an armoury of possible options. Indeed, the case studies set out in Part V and discussed below can demonstrate quite wide variations of approach on some issues. Accordingly, the key approach must always be based on flexibility rather than blind precedent, albeit within the binding framework of the Rules. Before adopting a particular case management technique, it is important to consider the context in which it might be used and the consequences which it might have, in view of the particular importance in multi-party actions of avoiding inappropriate consequences. **2.34**

3

INITIATION

A. Overview: Group Litigation Order Issues	3.01	Information to be included in the application	3.14
B. How many Claimants Constitute a Co-ordinatable Group?	3.04	D. Certification: Jurisdiction and Court Discretion	3.16
C. Application for a Group Litigation Order (GLO)		E. Certification: Experience on Criteria and Discretion	3.24
Who can make an application?	3.07	F. Effect of the GLO	
Preliminary steps	3.10	The management court	3.39
To whom should the application be made?	3.11	Binding nature of orders and judgments	3.43
		G. Right to Challenge a GLO	3.54

A. Overview: Group Litigation Order Issues

3.01 Part 19.III of the Civil Procedure Rules 1998 (CPR) covers Group Litigation. It provides for the court to constitute a defined group of claims to be managed together pursuant to a Group Litigation Order (GLO), where there are common issues of fact or law[1] which are specified in the GLO ('the GLO issues'). Although this is not stated in the Rule or associated Practice Direction, the theory which underlies a GLO is that it will be more efficient for the courts and the parties if cases which arise out of the same or similar facts and give rise to common issues may be managed and resolved together rather than individually.[2] As Popplewell J said:

> Generic issues in the context of this case mean issues the resolution of which are likely to have a very substantial impact on the disposal of the action. It is not suggested that there is one issue which will necessarily be dispositive of the whole action, . . . they seek to prove that there are a number of issues which will undoubtedly

---

[1] Similarly, the definition of a Multi-Party Action in *The Funding Code* is 'any action or actions in which a number of clients have causes of action which involve common issues of fact or law arising out of the same cause or event': Legal Services Commission, *The Funding Code* (2000), Part 1 s 2.4.

[2] The co-ordination of individual actions which have sufficient similarities is in the public interest since it should lead to the efficient resolution of the claims at an overall cheaper cost than if each were pursued individually. The Law Society, *Group Actions Made Easier* (1995).

help materially to dispose of a number of actions but which will not of themselves be *wholly* dispositive. If therefore there are not generic issues or not generic issues of such materiality as to save costs in their determination it necessarily follows that each individual litigant will have to litigate the issues.[3]

3.02 There can be differences of view as to what issues cases raise and whether they are sufficiently similar to justify combined management. Whether multiple individual claims are to be managed together will be decided by the court, on the basis that it is possible to define the GLO issues. All claims within the GLO will be subject to the co-ordinated management of the management court. Great care must be taken in analysing the issues which in fact arise in a case, in defining them and in determining whether the GLO mechanism is appropriate.[4]

3.03 In approaching the management of a multi-party action, it is important to realise that:

> the effective and economic handling of group actions necessarily requires a diminution, compromise or adjustment of the rights of individual litigants for the greater good of the action as a whole. These rights include the parties' freedom of choice of solicitor and the defendant's right to investigate all the plaintiff's claims individually at the early stages in particular.[5]

B. How many Claimants Constitute a Co-ordinatable Group?

3.04 The Rules do not prescribe a minimum number of claims for which a GLO order will be made. The Practice Direction is also silent on the point, although a draft of it had stated that, in general, the court will not make an order unless there are at least ten separate claims raising common issues.[6] The number ten had been mentioned from 1992 to 1997 under the Legal Aid Board's Arrangements, which defined a multi-party action as:

> any action or actions in which 10 or more assisted persons have causes of action which involve common issues of fact or law arising out of the same cause or event.

3.05 However, the Board recognised by 1997 that the ten certificate rule was insufficiently flexible and that it is necessary to initiate control as soon as it is apparent that claims have the potential to form a multi-party action.[7]

---

[3] *R v The Number 8 Area Committee of the Legal Aid Board, ex p Megarry* (1 July 1994).
[4] These points are examined in detail at paras 2.08 *et seq* above and 4.17 *et seq* below.
[5] Lord Woolf, *Access to Justice: Issues Paper on Multi-Party Actions* (Lord Chancellor's Department, 1996). Specific matters quoted by Lord Woolf as examples, such as a diminution in the defendant's right to investigate all claims, may have since been affected by developing practice and now be permissible, but the general principle of subservience of individual rights to the interests of the enterprise as a whole stands good.
[6] CPR, draft Practice Direction para 1.2.
[7] Legal Aid Board, *When the Price is High* (June 1997) para 5.33.

The penultimate draft of Part 19.III included a requirement that one or more claimants have issued claims against one or more defendants or are likely to do so, but this was omitted from the final text. It is, however, relevant for the court to have a reliable estimate of the number of likely claimants. In *Group Action Afrika et al v Cape plc*[8] the court reversed a previous decision granting jurisdiction to a multi-party action on *forum non conveniens* grounds when it transpired that there would be 3,000 claimants rather than the five previously disclosed.

3.06

C. Application for a Group Litigation Order (GLO)

Who can make an application?

Rule 19.10 provides that the court may make a GLO to provide for the case management of claims where the criteria are satisfied (see next section). The Practice Direction specifies that an application for a GLO may be made either by a claimant or a defendant (or the court) and may be made at any time before or after any relevant claims have been issued.[9] This provision contains several innovations. First, before the Rule existed, the initiative for consideration of whether there should be co-ordination of cases within a group could only be made once at least some proceedings had formally been commenced and was generally only made by claimants' representatives. Both an application for a GLO and the Order itself can now be made either before or after the start of any claim.

3.07

Secondly, the initiative can be taken by any person who is or is likely to be a party, or by the court itself.[10] The court has power to make a GLO of its own initiative, subject to obtaining the consent of the Lord Chief Justice or Vice-Chancellor.[11]

3.08

The effect of this Rule is to permit potential multi-party actions to become subject to court control at a very early stage.[12] In many of the cases before the Rule was introduced, there was an extended period from the point at which it could have

3.09

---

[8] (Buckley J, 30 July 1999) affirmed by the Court of Appeal (29 November 1999), reported in [2000] 1 Lloyd's Rep 139. The decision on stay of proceedings was reversed on grounds not relating to the numbers issue: *Lubbe v Cape plc* [2000] 1 WLR 1545, HL.

[9] Practice Direction—Group Litigation, para 3.1.

[10] It had been recommended that defendants should be able to initiate a group action in The Law Society, *Group Actions Made Easier* (1995) draft Rule 1.2, and this proposal was made by Lord Woolf and carried into the Lord Chancellor's Department's Consultation Paper, *Access to Justice: Multi-Party Situations: Proposed New Procedures. A Consultation Paper* (Nov 1997).

[11] Practice Direction—Group Litigation, para 4.

[12] Lord Woolf concluded that: 'The earlier the court exercises control in a potential multi-party action the better chance of managing the case to a satisfactory resolution.' Lord Woolf, *Access to Justice: Final Report* (1996) ch 17, 14–16. The recommendation that an appointment of a co-ordinating judge may be made before issue of proceedings was made in Lord Chancellor's Department, *Access to Justice: Multi-Party Situations: Proposed New Procedures: A Consultation Paper* (Nov 1997) para 23.

been said that co-ordination of proceedings would result until the matter came before the court. It may be advantageous to claimants for matters to become subject to court control at an early stage so that they can seek appropriate directions, particularly on cost sharing. On the other hand, claimants may need time in order to investigate cases, arrange funding, and co-ordinate with other claimants, in which case they would not welcome pressure imposed by the court to make progress within set time limits. Equally, however, both claimants and defendants may come under time pressure where early co-ordination is sought or ordered by the court, and this may particularly affect activities such as investigation and liaison with others. The court will have an opportunity to exercise control of advertising and promotion of the cases within the GLO.[13]

Preliminary steps

3.10 The Practice Direction specifies three matters for the applicant and his solicitors to consider before applying for a GLO:

> 2.1 Before applying for a GLO the solicitor acting for the proposed applicant should consult the Law Society's Multi Party Action Information Service in order to obtain information about other cases giving rise to the proposed GLO issues.
> 2.2 It will often be convenient for the claimants' solicitors to form a Solicitors' Group and to choose one of their number to take the lead in applying for the GLO and in litigating the GLO issues. The lead solicitor's role and relationship with the other members of the Solicitors' Group should be carefully defined in writing and will be subject to any directions given by the court under CPR 19.13(c).[14]
> 2.3 In considering whether to apply for a GLO, the applicant should consider whether any other order would be more appropriate. In particular he should consider whether, in the circumstances of the case, it would be more appropriate for—
> (1) the claims to be consolidated; or
> (2) the rules in Section II of Part 19 (representative parties)[15] to be used.

To whom should the application be made?

3.11 The Practice Direction specifies[16] that an application should be made to the following:

— High Court in London: to the Senior Master in the Queen's Bench Division or the Chief Chancery Master in the Chancery Division. For claims that are proceeding or are likely to proceed in a specialist list, the application should be made to the senior judge of that list.

---

[13] See ch 6 below.
[14] This is discussed further in ch 5 below.
[15] See ch 9 below.
[16] Practice Direction—Group Litigation, paras 3.5–3.9.

D. Certification: Jurisdiction and Court Discretion

— High Court outside London: to a Presiding Judge or a Chancery Supervising Judge of the Circuit in which the District Registry which has issued the application notice is situated.
— County Courts: to the Designated Civil Judge for the area in which the county court which has issued the application notice is situated.

3.12 The Practice Direction also specifies that the applicant for a GLO should request the relevant court to refer the application notice to the judge by whom the application will be heard as soon as possible after the application notice has been issued. This is to enable the judge to consider whether to send the information specified in paragraph 3.4 of the Practice Direction to the Lord Chief Justice or Vice-Chancellor prior to the hearing of the application.[17]

3.13 The above directions do not prevent the judges referred to from making arrangements for other judges to hear applications for GLOs when they themselves are unavailable.

Information to be included in the application

3.14 There is no specified form or content for an application for a GLO. The Practice Direction specifies[18] that the following information should be included in the application notice or in written evidence filed in support of the application:

(1) a summary of the nature of the litigation;
(2) the number and nature of claims already issued;
(3) the number of parties likely to be involved;
(4) the common issues of fact or law (the 'GLO issues') that are likely to arise in the litigation; and
(5) whether there are any matters that distinguish smaller groups of claims within the wider group.

3.15 Neither the Rule nor the Practice Direction specifies that a hearing of the application for a GLO must occur, still less any procedural requirements for a hearing. However, the Practice Direction refers at one point to a hearing of the application (paragraph 3.4) but the context does not indicate that this is a requirement in every case.

D. Certification: Jurisdiction and Court Discretion

3.16 The court has discretion as to whether or not to make a GLO.[19] No criteria or guidance are stated in the Rule or the Practice Direction on how the court should exercise

---

[17] See para 3.17 below.
[18] Practice Direction—Group Litigation, para 3.2.
[19] Rule 19.11(1) uses the word 'may' not 'must'.

3.17 Before making a GLO, the judge is subject to requirements to inform his superiors, who may therefore be involved in the decision, but no criteria are specified in relation to the superiors' decision. The Practice Direction states:

> 3.3 A GLO may not be made in the Queen's Bench Division without the consent of the Lord Chief Justice or in the Chancery Division or a county court without the consent of the Vice-Chancellor.
>
> 3.4 The court to which the application for a GLO is made will, if minded to make the GLO, send to the Lord Chief Justice or the Vice-Chancellor (as the case may be) a copy of the application notice, a copy of any relevant written evidence and a written statement as to why a GLO is thought to be desirable. These steps may be taken either before or after a hearing of the application.

this discretion. No doubt the information required to be included in the application[20] will be relevant, but those matters of information do not constitute criteria.

3.18 The court remains bound by the 'overriding objective' of the CPR that cases must be dealt with justly, and that this includes, so far as practicable, saving expense and dealing with cases in ways that are proportionate to the amount of money involved, amongst other matters.[21] Accordingly, the criteria on which a GLO is or is not to be made are those set out in CPR, Rule 1, in which justice to the parties, saving expense, and proportionality for both claimants and defendants are seemingly the most important of the objectives listed there which would apply in a multi-party context.

3.19 The court's jurisdiction under Part 19.III arises where there are or are likely to be a number of claims which give rise to common or related issues of fact or law.[22] Thus, the jurisdictional requirement is that the individual claims which the court will have to manage give rise to common or related issues. This requirement is stronger than 'are likely to give rise' to such issues and requires a determination that the cases will in fact give rise to common or related issues. The requirement for the court to consider the issues before making a GLO is clear from the fact that the court must specify the GLO issues in the GLO so as to identify the claims to be managed as a group.[23]

3.20 The situation where there are *common or related* issues of fact or law, covered by Part 19.III, must be distinguished from where two or more people have *the same* interest in a claim, for which it is permissible under Part 19.II for one person to represent all other parties, since the outcome will by definition be the same in each of the claims.[24]

---

[20] See para 3.14 above.
[21] CPR, Rule 1.1.
[22] Combining CPR, Rules 19.11(1) and 19.10.
[23] Rule 19.11(2)(b).
[24] See ch 9 below.

D. Certification: Jurisdiction and Court Discretion

Two aspects of the wording of the Rule widen the jurisdictional criteria; the qualification that there are *likely to be* rather than just *are* qualifying claims, and the qualification of *related* issues to that of *common* issues of fact or law. One policy consideration is to provide the court with a potentially wide jurisdiction within which it may exercise its managerial discretion, so that the cases which it has to manage may be managed in an efficient, co-ordinated manner where this is appropriate. However, the court will wish to consider the circumstances in which it will be efficient, proportionate, and appropriate to co-ordinate the management of the claims in question and so exercise its discretion to order combined management of certain individual claims.

3.21

Accordingly, a court faced with considering whether to make a GLO must examine the following issues:

3.22

1. whether there are, or are likely to be, a sufficient number of claims;[25]
2. what issues of fact or law these claims give rise to;
3. whether such issues are common or related;[26]
4. whether the court can specify the GLO issues with sufficient particularity so as to identify those claims which are, and are not, to be managed within the group;
5. accordingly, whether the court has jurisdiction to make a GLO; and
6. whether the court should exercise its discretion to make the GLO in the particular circumstances of the case.

It follows that in many, if not all, cases the court should treat definition of the GLO issues with some care. This may often require consideration of the views of all affected parties and a certification hearing. There may be difficulty, at the initial certification stage, in analysing the issues which arise in the cases to be managed and, accordingly, in determining whether such issues are common or related. There may be insufficient understanding of the facts or legal issues even at an early stage by the parties. There may also be misunderstanding which later proves to be incorrect, or a temptation to overgeneralise about the issues or to jump to conclusions.[27] Chapter 2 has analysed the problems of putting the cart before the horse in investigating and analysing what claims are actually about. It may be tempting for the court simply to specify a wide GLO issue, such as 'all claims relating to x product/y company/z train crash'. In transport crash claims such an approach

3.23

---

[25] See paras 3.04 above and 4.17 *et seq* and 4.28 *et seq* below.
[26] The US criterion of predominance may also be relevant (see para 3.25 below). In the context of a decision to grant legal aid funding, Popplewell J said: 'It may well be that . . . the number of questions which are common are not sufficient to entitle the individual applicant to pursue their claim based on the cost/benefit question. . . . Anyone who has had experience of multi-party cases will appreciate that not every so-called common issue will be wholly dispositive of all the cases . . .' *R v The Number 8 Area Committee of the Legal Aid Board, ex p Megarry* (1 July 1994).
[27] See para 4.42 below.

may not give rise to difficulties since, assuming the correct defendants have been identified, issues of breach, damage, causation, and liability may be common. But in cases where individual issues predominate (such as product liability claims) or where there may be differing sub-groups of claims (such as the Lloyd's litigation) or where there may be a significant number of claims which have poor chances of success (such as having been generated by advertising), it must be recognised that far greater care will be needed in analysing the claims and issues and that if this analysis is not done at the initial certification stage, when the criteria for entry to the group are set,[28] there may be difficulties if it is not done promptly. The issues of specification of the entry criteria and verification of applications is discussed from paragraph 4.17 below.

E. Certification: Experience on Criteria and Discretion

3.24 Both as an exercise in comparative law but also in considering how an English or Welsh judge should exercise his discretion on the certification issue, it is instructive to consider the certification criteria and experience of multi-party certification in other jurisdictions. It must, of course, be recognised that a US and Canadian class action differs from a GLO in that, in the former, cases are tried which are representative of the class of claims and, if they succeed, all the cases of all members of the class also succeed, and vice versa. An English equivalent of that approach is under CPR Part 19.II, where one person may represent others who have the same interest in a claim. The GLO mechanism is not so restricted and more flexible. Nevertheless, the following discussion points to some relevant comparisons.

3.25 As discussed in chapter 13, the criteria in US Federal Rule 23[29] include:

(1) the class is so numerous that joinder of all class members is impracticable ('numerosity');
(2) common questions of law or fact exist ('commonality');
(3) the claims of the class representatives are typical of those of the unnamed class members ('typicality');
(4) the class representatives will adequately represent the interests of the class ('adequacy');
(5) individual actions would create a risk of inconsistent decisions establishing incompatible standards of conduct for the defendant; or
(6) individual actions would create a risk of individual decisions which would adversely affect the rights and interests of non-parties; or

---

[28] See paras 4.17 *et seq* below.
[29] This analysis focuses on Federal Rule 23: all individual states have class action rules, many of which mirror the Federal rule.

E. Certification: Experience

(7) the common questions predominate over the individual questions ('predominance'); and
(8) the class mechanism is superior to other methods of adjudication ('superiority', for Rule 23(b) cases).

3.26 It will be seen that Federal Rule 23 in effect requires the court to make a sufficient investigation into the merits of the case in the certification process. This is because the court must understand the claims, defences, relevant facts, and applicable substantive law in order to make a meaningful determination of the certification issues. In comparison, Quebec's legislation has a required condition that 'the facts alleged seem to justify the conclusions sought'.[30] This led to certification hearings of increased complexity and cost, although enabled the rejection of class actions which were not well founded or based on largely untested facts.[31] The different jurisdictions adopt slightly different approaches towards the criteria which limit legal issues.

3.27 The preliminary tests adopted, in descending order of ease of entry, are: existence or likelihood of common or related issues of fact or law[32] (England and Wales); (some) common issues of fact or law, with certification preferable for their resolution (Ontario and British Columbia, predominance being a factor but not a requirement, since the class procedure in those Provinces is viewed as a mechanism merely for resolving the common issues rather than the whole controversy);[33] identical, similar, or related questions of law or fact (Quebec); a substantial common issue of law or fact arising out of the same, similar, or related circumstances (Australia);[34] predominance of common questions of law or fact (USA).[35]

3.28 It can be seen that the English criterion of claims having common or related issues of fact or law is essentially similar to the US Federal criterion of 'commonality'. However, it is striking that the US Rule includes a number of criteria which are absent from the English Rule: namely, typicality; avoidance of inconsistent decisions and adversely affecting non-parties' rights; adequate representation; predominance; and superiority. It would seem that these extra criteria would be of assistance in determining the English issue of discretion: the extra criteria certainly seem similar to the overriding English criteria of just resolution, economy, and proportionality contained in CPR Rule 1.1 which certainly apply. It can also be asked whether the English and Welsh courts will encounter difficulties if some of the US criteria are not applied in this jurisdiction.

---

[30] Code of Civil Procedure, Art 1003(b).
[31] HP Glenn, 'The dilemma of class action reform' (1986) vol 6, No 2 OJLS 262–274.
[32] See the discussion in ch 9 on the mechanism of representative actions under CPR, Rule 19.II which operates on the test of the same interest for all parties represented.
[33] See ch 14 below.
[34] See ch 15 below.
[35] See ch 13 below.

3.29 The conclusion of chapter 13 on the US experience is that class actions are approved in various situations but appellate courts have relied particularly on the criteria of representation, typicality, predominance, and superiority (as it relates to manageability of the class action) in a sequence of decisions decertifying class certification in personal injury product liability cases. Their reasoning includes the realisation that many issues of fact that arise in such cases are not common to each class member, and that the number and size of mass tort class actions strain the court system,[36] particularly where publicity generates claims. Similarly, the Australian courts seem to be interpreting their commonality requirement as a requirement that the issues must tend to be dispositive of the litigation[37] and Canadian courts have recognised the need to define issues narrowly since resolution of common issues sometimes does not determine liability.[38]

3.30 It may, therefore, be relevant to identify cases in which individual issues predominate.[39] Analysis of this issue in the context of an English multi-party action is in its early stages but some types of case have been identified:

> It is no doubt the case that in product liability actions (especially in the pharmaceutical sector) individual issues pre-dominate over common issues, if only because of the different dates on which and different circumstances in which a patient is exposed to the drug in question with, no doubt, many possible outcomes.[40]

3.31 Similarly, the Law Society's 1995 Working Party concluded that:

> Usually, there will be no connection between the potential plaintiffs, save that they allege they have been injured by the same product. In drug or medical application[41] cases, in particular, liability (establishing, for example, whether the drug or the ailment for which it was prescribed was the primary cause of the unwanted side effect) may be difficult to determine; and common issues may be difficult to identify.[42] Quite frequently there will be a multiplicity of defendants who all manufactured similar products; and in drug cases there may also be claims against the prescribers.[43]

---

[36] An empirical study of US class actions indicates that the judicial economy which may be gained in class certification only occurs where the value of claims exceeds a financial threshold. R Bernstein, 'Judicial Economy and Class Actions' [1978] Journal of Legal Studies 7:349.

[37] See ch 15 below.

[38] See paras 14.16 and 14.34 below.

[39] Specific discovery may be ordered in US jurisdictions, particularly from claimants, in order to facilitate analysis of the issues and judge predominance.

[40] M Mildred, 'The Plaintiff's Perspective' (Mar 1996) The Litigator 70, 73; see also GR Hickinbottom, 'The Defendant's Perspective' (Mar 1996) The Litigator 26, 65.

[41] The term 'medical application' in this quotation is confusing. The standard definition of product sectors falls into medicinal products and medical devices. What seems to be meant here is any personal injury claim. Although product liability claims can involve damage to personal property, the vast majority of product liability claims involving *any* product (not just medicines or medical devices) involve personal injuries. Accordingly, the problem of defining common issues can arise for virtually *all* product claims.

[42] The Law Society, *Group Actions Made Easier* (1995) para 3.2(b). The point was repeated in the Lord Chancellor's 1997 Consultation Paper, para 2(b).

[43] The Law Society, *Group Actions Made Easier* (1995) para 3.2(b).

E. Certification: Experience

> . . . in the United States . . . it has been increasingly held that issues in individual cases are more important than common ones . . .[44]

3.32 As noted at paragraph 3.10 above, the Practice Direction states that in considering whether to apply for a GLO, the applicant should consider whether any other order would be more appropriate and, in particular, whether it would be more appropriate for the claims to be consolidated or for the rules in Part 19.II on representative parties to be used.[45] These requirements apply to an applicant but would seemingly equally apply to the court (as a draft of the Practice Direction provided).

3.33 Accordingly, consolidation or some form of combined or even individual management appear to be intended to take precedence over the GLO mechanism if any such alternative is practicable. This provision is similar to the US criteria of superiority of the chosen mechanism. The 1997 Consultation Paper on the Rule noted:

> It will be for the judge to decide, given the circumstances, whether to certify one [GLO] or whether another approach would be more suitable. The court will still be able to try an issue which affects a large number of claimants by means of one or more test cases, with the case proceeding as an individual claim outside [the Group].

3.34 These difficulties can be illustrated by the benzodiazepine litigation.[46] The benzodiazepine claims were brought by claimants who had taken one or more of three different benzodiazepine products made by three different manufacturers and prescribed by hundreds of doctors from the early 1960s to the late 1980s during which these different products were marketed for varying periods of time. There were many differences in the facts relating to each claimant: their underlying emotional or medical problems and histories; the advice or warnings given to each claimant from his or her physician; the extent to which each person followed their doctors' advice, and their reasons for doing so; whether each person took other medication and whether there may have been some interaction between medications; the extent to which each claimant relied on any information they may have received from the manufacturer; differences in prescribed dosages and whether these were recommended by the manufacturer; differences in duration of use; changes in the continually updated package literature and the extent to which each claimant read or followed it.

3.35 What each manufacturer of each of the different benzodiazepine products knew or should have known was different as to each condition claimed by the individual group member and needed to be considered as an evolving exercise over thirty

---

[44] The Law Society, *Group Actions Made Easier* (1995) para 5.2.2.
[45] Practice Direction, para 2.3.
[46] See ch 22 below.

years. Adequacy of warning and course of conduct were different as to each condition. As to each potential emotional or physical injury, different bodies of scientific literature had to be presented through expert evidence. The differences in injury altered the manner in which each plaintiff had to proceed to prove liability against the manufacturer of the product or products he or she took. Alternate causation would have been a key issue in the trial of the benzodiazepine claims, as all the symptoms that plaintiffs claimed were associated with their underlying medical conditions also appeared in the absence of use of that particular benzodiazepine product or any other drug. As Stuart-Smith LJ said:

> There are very considerable problems on causation; these involve distinguishing between the effects of the drug and the underlying condition for which it was prescribed, the problems caused by previous addiction to benzodiazepine drugs other than those prescribed by the Defendants, and distinguishing between symptoms due to the drugs or, in some cases, other drugs or excess alcohol, and the fact that many Plaintiffs may suffer at least some withdrawal symptoms in any event.[47]

3.36 The English approach to group treatment for benzodiazepine claims can be contrasted with the approach in the USA. In the USA, plaintiffs alleged various physical and psychological side effects from the benzodiazepine they took. In refusing to certify a class action under Rule 23, the court noted:

> In the appropriate case, class action litigation offers a sensible and workable vehicle for resolving significant disputes involving large numbers of litigants and potential litigants. The ill-advised deployment of the class action technique, however, inevitably occasions just the opposite. It imposes a relatively cumbersome format on largely personal disputes, while achieving very little, if any, gain in efficiency or economy.
> . . .even the most fundamental question—is the product dangerous—cannot with confidence be considered a common question, and thus the certification of a class or classes of individual users would not ensure the benefits that Rule 23 was intended to convey.[48]

3.37 The US court found that the purportedly common issue regarding the general safety of the drug inevitably launched into an enquiry that would be specific to each patient, including information such as each patient's dosage and use or misuse of the drug, alone or in conjunction with other medications; each class member's individual history of emotional and physical health; the circumstances under which the plaintiff ingested the drug; and the critical question of causation.

3.38 In analysing the issues in the case, it may initially appear that a common question might be whether the drug is capable of causing the injuries alleged. More detailed analysis, however, would reveal that causation in a medical product case is a highly individualised enquiry: there may be a plethora of issues, many of which would be

---

[47] *AB and Others v John Wyeth & Brothers Ltd and Roche Products* [1994] 5 Med LR 149, CA.
[48] *Pasternak v The Upjohn Company*, 95-CV-5987 (EDNY 19 Sept 1994).

particular to each case and require to be resolved in individual rather than generic trials.[49] Pharmaceutical product liability cases involving allegations of design defects or failure to warn are often complex.[50] Other types of case may involve much simpler issues where individual issues might not predominate, for example product liability cases involving manufacturing defects (where an individual product or batch is below specification, such as contaminated food)[51] or single event mass accident cases in which legal causation of each claimant's injury is identical and the major issues usually relate to defendants' conduct. Canadian courts have similarly tended to refuse certification in cases where there were many individual issues of reliance and causation which would not have satisfied their test of furthering resolution of common issues: in reality these supposedly common issues are individual issues.[52] The conclusion is that the court must have a sound grasp of the facts in issue, and hence of the issues which arise, in order to determine the optimal management strategy for resolving each issue.

F. Effect of the GLO

The management court

Rule 19.11(2)(a) provides that a GLO must specify the court (the 'management court') which will manage the claims on the group register. Rule 19.11(3) specifies that the GLO may

(a) In relation to claims which raise one or more of the GLO issues—
   (i) direct their transfer to a management court;[53]

3.39

---

[49] See *Alabama v Blue Bird Body Co.* 573 F 2d 309, 329 (5th Cir, 1978), holding class action unmanageable as resembling 'judicial fission' where it would bring in thousands of claimants whose claims would require a multitude of individual trials.

[50] See paras 16.15 *et seq* below.

[51] See details of product liability cases in C Hodges, *Report for the European Commission of the European Communities on the application of Directive 85/374/EEC on liability for defective products* (McKenna & Co, May 1994); C Hodges, 'Cases under the European Product Liability Directive' (1994) 5 APLR 97; and National Consumer Council, *Unsafe Products* (Nov 1995). Many examples involve small numbers of claimants: more well-known examples are contamination of the public water supply with aluminium sulphate (180 claims in 1992 settled after the regulatory proceedings); contaminated hazelnut yoghurt (some 28 claims in 1989 settled after resolution of a regulatory prosecution). It will be noted that both these instances settled before trial but after a regulatory investigation and disposal of regulatory proceedings, which will have saved substantial costs in the civil proceedings. This is typical of many manufacturing defect cases, which are usually investigated by public health, medicines, medical devices, vehicles, or trading standards agencies.

[52] See paras 14.18 *et seq* below.

[53] This had been recommended in The Law Society, *Group Actions Made Easier* (1995) 6.2.1. The Practice Direction—Group Litigation specifies that where the management court is a county court and a claim raising one or more of the GLO issues is proceeding in the High Court, an order transferring the case to the management court and directing the details of the case to be entered on the group register can only be made in the High Court.

        (ii)   order their stay until further order; and
        (iii)   direct their entry on the group register;
  (b) direct that from a specified date claims which raise one or more of the GLO issues should be started in the management court and entered on the group register;[54]
  (c) give directions for publicising the GLO.[55]

3.40   The management court may order that as from a specified date all claims that raise one or more of the GLO issues shall be started in the management court.[56] Failure to comply with such an order will not invalidate the commencement of the claim but the claim should be transferred to the management court and details entered on the Group Register as soon as possible. Any party to the claim may apply to the management court for an order under Rule 19.14 removing the case from the Register or, as the case may be, for an order that details of the case be not entered on the Register.[57]

3.41   The management court may give case management directions at the time the GLO is made or subsequently.[58] If the court decides not to make a GLO, each claim will proceed as normal on an individual basis in accordance with the normal rules.[59]

3.42   After a GLO has been made and unless the management court directs otherwise:[60]

(1) every claim in a case entered on the Group Register will be automatically allocated, or re-allocated (as the case may be), to the multi-track;
(2) any case management directions that have already been given in any such case otherwise than by the management court will be set aside; and
(3) any hearing date already fixed otherwise than for the purposes of the group litigation will be vacated.

Binding nature of orders and judgments

3.43   As a consequence of the making of a GLO, Rule 19.12 provides:

(1) Where a judgment or order is given or made in a claim on the group register in relation to one or more GLO issues—

  (a) that judgment or order is binding on the parties to all other claims that are on the group register at the time the judgment is given or the order is made unless the court orders otherwise; and

---

[54] For discussion of the group register see paras 4.12 *et seq* below.
[55] See ch 6 below.
[56] Practice Direction—Group Litigation, para 9.1.
[57] Practice Direction—Group Litigation, para 9.2.
[58] See paras 5.03 *et seq* below.
[59] Practice Direction—Group Litigation, para 4.1.
[60] Practice Direction—Group Litigation, para 7.

F. Effect of the GLO

    (b) the court may give directions as to the extent to which that judgment or order is binding on the parties to any claim which is subsequently entered on the group register.

(2) Unless paragraph (4) applies,[61] any party who is adversely affected by a judgment or order which is binding on him may seek permission to appeal the order.

(3) A party to a claim which was entered on the group register after a judgment or order which is binding on him was given or made may not—

    (a) apply for the judgment or order to be set aside, varied or stayed; or
    (b) appeal the judgment or order

but may apply to the court for an order that the judgment or order is not binding on him.

3.44 It is obvious that issues which are decided as preliminary issues or in the lead actions in multi-party litigation can have a profound effect on the remaining actions. Whilst it may be argued that it is contrary to the overriding principles of the CPR for the courts to permit relitigation of the same point between the same parties, the issue in a multi-party action is whether the points which have been decided and the parties are in fact the same as arise in subsequent cases. The answer to this question will determine whether and to what extent it is just to consider the issues which arise in later cases or in other cases in the cohort which is being managed together. Rule 19.12(1)(a) quoted above establishes that an order or judgment given in relation to one of the GLO issues is binding on all the parties then on the group register and, if the court so directs, also on later entrants. But certain issues decided may not be 'in relation to the GLO issues'. This is a further reason why definition of the GLO issues is of critical importance.

3.45 Certain authorities which pre-dated the CPR exist in relation to issue estoppel and abuse of process but these concepts have been developed in relation to unitary actions and their applicability in the multi-party context is as yet not fully clear. Issue estoppel was first introduced into English law as a species of *estoppel per rem judicatam* in 1964.[62] The concept had previously been recognised in the Australian courts and some US states. In the *Thoday* case Diplock LJ discussed 'cause of action estoppel' where determination of a cause of action between parties cannot be reopened between the same parties, and went on to define issue estoppel:

> There are many causes of action which can only be established by proving that two or more different conditions are fulfilled . . . If in litigation upon one such cause of action any of such separate issues as to whether a particular condition had been fulfilled is determined by a Court of competent jurisdiction, either upon evidence or upon admission by a party to the litigation, neither party can, in subsequent litigation between one another upon any cause of action which depends

---

[61] This relates to disclosure of documents, see paras 7.02 *et seq* below.
[62] *Thoday v Thoday* [1964] 1 All ER 341.

upon the fulfilment of the identical condition, assert that the condition was fulfilled if the Court has in the first litigation determined that it was not, or deny that it was fulfilled if the Court in the first litigation determined that it was.

3.46 This statement was later approved by the House of Lords.[63] However, Diplock LJ had before then qualified his statement in a subsequent case[64] and held that the issue estoppel which would normally arise would not apply between the same parties if there were special circumstances such that:

> further material which is relevant to the correctness or incorrectness of the assertion and could not by reasonable diligence have been adduced by a party in the previous proceedings has since become available to him.

3.47 In 1991[65] the House of Lords upheld previous decisions that an issue estoppel does not arise in relation to litigation between the same parties on a previously decided point. There is a complete bar unless, on the basis of Lord Diplock's qualification in *Mills v Cooper*, which was approved, a specific exception exists where further material becomes available relevant to the correct determination of a point involved in the earlier proceedings which could not by reasonable diligence have been brought forward in those proceedings. Such further material might include matters of law as well as matters of fact. In *Arnold* the same issue was therefore allowed to be relitigated between the same parties, albeit in respect of a different period of rent (the case concerned the validity and construction of a rent review clause in a lease), on the ground that subsequent decisions of higher courts showed that the earlier first instance decision between the parties was wrong.

3.48 The traditional issue estoppel rule has also been extended in other cases. Previous decisions had held an issue estoppel to apply only in respect of issues already litigated as between identical parties. Two decisions at first instance have held that an issue of negligence determined in a particular way against and between co-defendants in one case is binding in subsequent proceedings between those defendants. In *North West Water Authority v Binne & Partners*[66] victims of an explosion sued defendants A, B, and C for negligence. Defendant A was held wholly to blame. In subsequent proceedings defendant B sued defendant A for damages founded upon the same negligence. The court struck out defendant A's defence. Drake J decided that the issue estoppel applied since the issue of negligence had been determined 'for all practical purposes' as between both defendants in the earlier proceedings. Similarly, in *Wall v Radford*[67] a determination in earlier proceedings that defendants A and B were equally liable to the plaintiff in negligence for a road

---

[63] *Thrasyvoulou v Secretary of State for the Environment* [1990] 2 WLR 1.
[64] *Mills v Cooper* [1967] 2 QB 459.
[65] *Arnold v National Westminster Bank PLC* [1991] 2 WLR 1177.
[66] [1990] 3 All ER 547.
[67] [1991] 2 All ER 741: see also *Talbot v Berkshire County Council* [1994] QB 290.

F. Effect of the GLO

traffic accident was held to give rise to an estoppel when A tried to sue B. Popplewell J held that:

> Although a *separate* duty is owed to another driver from that owed to a passenger that does not mean in the instant case that the duty is in any way *different*. The facts giving rise to a breach of that duty are identical and liability for that breach of duty is identical . . . It is not a different duty. It is the same duty owed to a different person . . . The object of the courts must be to do justice between the parties with expedition and without undue technicality. I ask myself what justice is there in allowing one party to have a second bite at a cherry? What expedition is there allowing the relitigation of identical facts which have already been decided? The answer to both those questions is plain.

3.49 On the facts of these cases, it is difficult to see how the two defendants could seek to argue that the issue of their negligence remained undecided: all the issues had been decided in the earlier action. An example of a common situation in which these cases might be applied would be a personal injury claim by a single claimant against a manufacturing company and prescribing doctor or regulatory authority as co-defendants.

3.50 However, Drake J expressed his judgment in the *North West Water* case in terms which seem to extend the doctrine of issue estoppel beyond the situation of two decisions involving the same parties to two decisions in which only one party is common:

> It was unreal to hold that the issues related in two actions arising from identical facts were different *solely* because the parties were different or because the duty of care owed to different persons was in law different . . . there was no real or practical difference between the issues to be litigated in the new action and that already decided.

3.51 This situation has arisen in two cases (one in 1990 which was not cited in the *Arnold* case nor *Wall v Radford* and the other in chambers in 1988 and therefore unreported at the time) which specifically involved multi-party actions. The earlier case concerned the pertussis whooping cough vaccine litigation in which one action was selected as a test case for the trial of causation as a preliminary issue and the remaining actions were stayed. It was held in the test case that causation was not proved. One of the plaintiffs whose action had been stayed subsequently sought to bring a similar action but against a different defendant, arguing that the injection was given at a time when the concentration of the pertussis vaccine was greater than that considered in the test case and therefore a more potent source of damage. Stuart Smith J held that this was not a material distinction and struck out the action as an abuse of process of the court to relitigate the same issue in the absence of fresh evidence that bore materially on the issue of causation.[68]

---

[68] *Godfrey v Department of Health and Social Security* (25 July 1988), referred to in *Ashmore v British Coal Corporation* [1990] 2 All ER 981, 986.

3.52 The same judge, this time sitting in the Court of Appeal, applied the same reasoning in striking out a claim by one of 1,500 plaintiffs where the issues had already been determined in fourteen lead cases.[69] The claims were for equal pay and were heard by a tribunal, rather than a court, which had gone to 'great pains to devise a method which enabled *all* issues of fact to be investigated at length' (emphasis added) and had expressly stated that a decision in any of the lead cases would not be binding in any of the other cases but 'might well assist' in their resolution. Nevertheless, it was held that it was an abuse of process for the tribunal subsequently to be invited to reach different findings of fact on the same evidence. Stuart Smith LJ said, albeit obiter, that the test for determining whether fresh evidence is of such a kind that the court should permit a claim which would otherwise be an abuse of process of the court is that it 'should entirely change the aspect of the case'.

3.53 It may be argued that the extension of the doctrine of issue estoppel in the first instance decisions in the *North West Water* case and in *Wall v Radford* could not be justified on the previous authorities. Arguments could be made on public policy grounds both for and against this approach. In multi-party litigation, it might be relevant to consider factors such as the selection of the lead cases and whether they were truly both representative and inclusive of the range of facts which arose in other cases in the scheme, such that decisions made in the lead cases could with justice be applied in other cases. Where these factors are unfavourable, issues which are unresolved between the parties must be given proper consideration.

G. Right to Challenge a GLO

3.54 It may not be possible to give notice directly to all persons potentially affected by the making of a GLO. Where the court makes an order of its own initiative, without hearing the parties or giving them an opportunity to make representations, a party affected by the order may presumably apply to have the order set aside, varied, or stayed. Similarly, where a hearing has been held or certain parties were given the opportunity to make representations, and a particular party was not given notice or the opportunity to make representations, the position is not covered by Rule 19.III. A draft of the Rule provided that such a party would have a right to challenge the making of the order, so as to have the order set aside, varied, or stayed.[70] It was to have been specified that such an application was to have been made within such period as may be specified by the court or not more than seven days after the date on which the party making the application became aware of the order.[71]

---

[69] *Ashmore v British Coal Corporation* [1990] 2 All ER 981.
[70] See Lord Chancellor's Department, *Multi-Party Situations: Draft rules and practice directions. A Lord Chancellor's Department Consultation Paper* (1999) paras 17–19.
[71] Note, however, the restrictions imposed by Rule 19.12(3).

4

INVESTIGATING, COMMENCING, AND PLEADING CLAIMS

A.	Pre-Action Protocols	4.01	Financial viability		4.28
B.	Pre-Action Discovery	4.09	Joining the register		4.32
C.	The Group Register: Claimants' Membership of the Group	4.12	D. Particulars of Claim		4.36
	Criteria and verification	4.17	Group Particulars of Claim		4.40

A. Pre-Action Protocols

Claimants should conform with pre-action protocols before issuing their claims. A major feature of the approach under the Civil Procedure Rules 1998 (CPR) is that a significant amount of work which used to be done *during* the litigation process (for example, exchange of information on the nature of the case or defence, search for and disclosure of documentary evidence, obtaining evidence from witnesses and experts), which may have considerable relevance to the initial risk assessment by claimant and solicitor in deciding whether to take on a case, has now been moved forward into the *pre-action* stage. What is expected of parties during the pre-action stage is or will be governed by approved pre-action protocols.[1] Non-compliance with a protocol can lead to adverse costs sanctions for a party if court proceedings are issued later. **4.01**

The position can be illustrated by reference to the personal injury protocol. In accordance with the principle that the parties are to be open about revealing the nature of their cases, the main features of the personal injury protocol are: **4.02**

- the claimant must write a letter of claim to the defendant with a clear summary of the facts, and specifying the nature of injuries suffered and of any financial loss. In order to do this, the claimant will have to research the case and provide

---

[1] CPR, Practice Direction—Protocols.

sufficient information to enable the defendant to commence investigations and to put at least a broad valuation on the claim. There is a standard format.
- The defendant should reply within twenty-one calendar days of the date of posting of the letter identifying the insurer (if any). If there has been no reply by the defendant or insurer within twenty-one days, the claimant will be entitled to issue proceedings.

  The defendant('s insurers) will have a maximum of three months from the date of acknowledgement of the claim to investigate. No later than the end of that period the defendant (insurer) shall reply, stating whether liability is denied and, if so, giving reasons for their denial of liability.
- If the defendant denies liability, he should enclose, with the letter of reply, documents in his possession which are material to the issues between the parties, and which would be likely to be ordered to be disclosed by the court, either on an application for pre-action disclosure, or on disclosure during proceedings.
- Before any prospective party to the action instructs an expert he should give the other party a list of the names of one or more experts in the relevant speciality which he considers are suitable to instruct.

  If all the experts are objected to, then the parties may instruct experts of their own. It would be for the court to decide subsequently, if proceedings are issued, whether either party had acted unreasonably.

  If the second party does not object to a nominated expert, then he shall not be entitled to rely on his own expert within that particular speciality unless:

  a. the first party agrees.
  b. the court directs.
  c. the first party's report has been amended and the first party is not prepared to disclose the original report.

  Either party may send to the expert written questions on the report, relevant to the issues, via the first party's solicitors. The expert should send answers to the questions separately and directly to each party.

4.03 Thus, the process of gathering and disclosing evidence is largely to occur right at the start of a claim, rather than occur in a sequence of events during the litigation process: both the activities and the costs are 'front loaded'. This initial investigation and risk assessment accords precisely with the risk assessment which is required in order to decide whether the risk is acceptable for a conditional fee agreement (CFA) to be agreed, and what the level of risk is so that the appropriate uplift (success fee) can be agreed.[2] It is a pre-action process which is particularly important to undertake in a type of claim which may generate weak or spurious individual claims, in order to identify weak claims and weed them out.

---

[2] See ch 11 below.

A. Pre-Action Protocols

4.04 The court applied the protocol approach, with some modifications, in the first major multi-party action which was brought under the CPR but before the introduction of Part 19.III. In the MMR litigation, there were thought to be some 1,900 claimants, of which 106 had issued (but not necessarily served) writs involving some five vaccine manufacturers and four doctors. The claimants had not served particulars of claim and did not wish to do so but wished to seek pre-action discovery. At a preliminary hearing, Master Turner had indicated: 'The difficulty I see is if you do not have some form of Statement of Claim you do not know what the issues are before you get the pre-action disclosure, which actually seems to be the cart before the horse situation.'[3]

4.05 At the subsequent substantive case management conference, Master Ungley[4] approached the case 'in the spirit of the new Civil Procedure Rules and bearing in mind the various dicta . . . in some of the earlier group litigation cases'. He applied the protocol approach, with its built-in disclosure requirements, instead of under CPR Part 8. He said:

> One thing that seems to me essential in any group litigation case is that the cards which each side are entitled to see should be on the table at as early a moment as is realistically and fairly possible. Were the actions to all be in the same condition, in other words, were all claims to have been issued or were none of the claims to have been issued, it would be easy to make common ground for both types of case, but that is not this situation. It seems to me that the proper way to go forward in this case is to approach the question of discovery on the basis of the pre-action discovery which is given under the protocols established under the Civil Procedure Rules.
>
> Accordingly, it seems to me that the Claimants should give to the Defendants as each claim is started the information as to the facts upon which the claim is based, together with the nature of the injuries suffered, but, having regard to a concession that has already been made, no requirement should be made to outline the financial loss currently incurred.
>
> In response to that, it seems to me that the Defendants must comply with the spirit of paragraph 3.10 of the protocol . . . and provide documents in their possession material to the issues as identified by the Claimants in their letters of notification.
> . . .
> So far as the disclosure which the Defendants must give, it is disclosure on the standard basis. They have the power to control the amount that they disclose and to explain why they have so controlled it. So far as the issues are concerned, it is up to the Claimants to make clear in their letters of claim, and indeed in their claim forms, what the issues between the parties are.
>
> As I have indicated, I do not think that at this stage it is appropriate to go beyond making sure that the identification of the Claimants is got under way, the nature of the claims is made sufficiently clear to the Defendants, and the Defendants are put in the position which they would be under the protocols were all these cases commenced.

---

[3] *In the Matter of MMR/MR Vaccine Litigation* (Master Turner, 14 Apr 1999).
[4] *Paul Sayers (and others) v SmithKline Beecham PLC and others* (Master Ungley, 3 Sept 1999).

Then the matter will start to move forward with the creation of the register and the number of claims and their nature. I do not propose to make orders further than that.

4.06 Each claimant was, therefore, ordered when issuing proceedings (but not before) to produce in letter form an individual claim notification setting out the nature of his or her case, a summary of the facts upon which the claim was based and the nature of the injuries suffered, identifying the issues raised against each defendant so as to enable them to address such issues in response, together with such medical records as were in his or her (or the lawyers') possession and a mandate for the defendants to inspect the original medical records.

4.07 It will be noted that this approach applied the CPR principles that claimants must initially investigate and state their cases (a change from practice prior to the CPR) and defendants must then respond and disclose relevant documents. The Master accepted in this case the concession agreed by the parties that information to verify financial loss need not be served at this point (the claims were by children, many involving issues of long-term care which would have been difficult to quantify at this stage). Significantly, the Master adopted a sequential approach to handling the litigation: he required the parties to serve their cases and documents so that the issues in the case could be identified but provided that subsequent consideration of how the case should be taken forward should await consideration of those issues and knowledge of what was or was not disputed.

4.08 Importantly, Master Ungley noted that it was possible, if not probable, that the nature of the claims would change, from a horizontal attack on the safety (in alleged 'design' or failure to warn) of MMR vaccines as a whole to more limited allegations that particular batches were sub-standard (a manufacturing defect claim). It would follow that since the nature of the case might be different, the nature and extent of discovery would likewise significantly alter. Under the former approach, all research, development, regulatory, and labelling documentation would be potentially relevant, which could be very extensive, whereas under claims alleging manufacturing defects the essential documentation would be more restricted, essentially involving specifications, batch records, and some post-marketing safety records. It was, therefore, crucial for the claimants to state first the nature of their case so that the defendants could respond to it appropriately. Thus, in rejecting an application for research to be undertaken, Master Ungley commented: 'it is the Claimants who bring the claim and it is the Claimants who must prove their case. They are not entitled to require the other party to indulge in enormously expensive original research in order to see whether or not they have a case.'

B. Pre-Action Discovery

Although there is a general power under CPR Part 8 for the court to order pre-action discovery,[5] this may have limited relevance in multi-party actions in view of the requirements to observe pre-action protocols and early case management for a Group Litigation Order (GLO) under the CPR: it is not provided for in Part 19.III. As discussed at paragraphs 4.04 to 4.08 above, orders made in the MMR litigation in 1999 essentially required compliance with the protocol approach, which includes some discovery obligations on both sides, and rejected a pre-action discovery request that would have involved extensive disclosure solely by defendants in circumstances where they would not have known the nature of the claimants' case and so been unable to make relevant or proportionate disclosure. 4.09

The Law Society's 1995 Report (before the Woolf reforms which led to the CPR) suggested that pre-action discovery by defendants should be regarded as the norm.[6] However, the proposal in the Report was made, as it acknowledged, against the background that previous applications for pre-action discovery by claimants in group actions had generally been unsuccessful. There were two reasons for this, which are still relevant. First, pre-action discovery can be used as a simple fishing expedition seeking to view the entirety of a defendant's documentation before any coherent case has been made out. Secondly, if a claim cannot be formulated and verified there is no justification for pre-action discovery. Conversely, there is clearly no such justification if a claim can be formulated.[7] 4.10

It used to be said that it was sometimes difficult to plead a product liability case because all the potential evidence of whether or not the manufacturer was negligent was in the possession of the prospective defendant. The point has less force since the addition of a new cause of action in strict liability under Part I of the Consumer Protection Act 1987, which makes it very much easier—as was intended—for a product liability case to be advanced, since liability turns not on the conduct of the manufacturer but on whether the product was defective under an objective test of the expectation of safety. Thus, the extent of documentation relevant to a claimant's allegation that a product is defective, under the new law, should be very much less than might theoretically be relevant to whether the defendant's conduct constituted negligence. Any rationale for pre-action or early discovery by defendants under the new law is, therefore, substantially reduced. 4.11

---

[5] Continuing the previous provisions of RSC Ord 24 r 14.
[6] The Law Society, *Group Actions Made Easier* (1995) para 6.15.1.
[7] This was the basic rationale for the Court's rejection of the pre-action discovery application by the Gravigard plaintiffs in 1990: see ch 20 below. *R v GD Searle & Co Ltd* (Anthony Diamond QC, 9 Mar 1990).

C. The Group Register: Claimants' Membership of the Group

4.12 A register is the mechanism for efficient confirmation of the membership of the group of claimants. If properly applied, it can also act as a filter in assisting to remove those claims that are not genuinely within the scope of the group constituted by the GLO.[8] This mechanism evolved from practice as it developed in certain cases.[9] It provides for certainty as to who is a member and who is not, or has left, at any particular time, which is essential for various reasons, not least costs accounting. The fact of membership during a particular accounting period will have cost consequences for members, as discussed in chapter 8. It will also be the basis for an assessment of whether or not the multi-party action is economically viable and should be permitted to continue or be stopped. The basic theory is that an individual claim must be issued in the normal way and may then either proceed under normal court management rules or become subject to management within the GLO.

4.13 Rule 19.11(2)a specifies that where the court makes a GLO, the GLO must contain directions about the establishment of a Group Register on which the claims managed under the GLO will be entered. The Practice Direction specifies that once a GLO has been made a Group Register will be established on which will be entered such details as the management court may direct of the cases which are to be subject to the GLO.[10]

4.14 Neither the Rule nor Practice Direction gives further specification or guidance as to the details of directions that should be given. In some cases, it will be appropriate for directions to include any actions necessary to verify that existing claims comply with the criteria established, so that they may either be confirmed on the register or leave the group. If a claim leaves the group, it still exists as a unitary claim unless further action is taken to discontinue, strike out, stay, or settle it.

4.15 The Practice Direction further provides:

> 6.2 An application for details of a case to be entered on a Group Register may be made by any party to the case.
> 6.3 An order for details of the case to be entered on the Group Register will not be made unless the case gives rise to at least one of the GLO issues. (CPR 19.10 defines GLO issues).
> 6.4 The [management] court, if it is not satisfied that a case can be conveniently

---

[8] Lord Chancellor's Department, *Multi-Party Situations: Draft rules and practice direction. A Lord Chancellor's Draft Consultation Paper* (1999) para 21.

[9] Lord Chancellor's Department, *Access to Justice: Multi-Party Situations: Proposed New Procedures: A Consultation Paper* (1997) para 32(b) and (d). It was ordered in the MMR litigation in 1999, before Part 19.III was introduced but under the Civil Procedure Rules. See Specimen Order at Appendix G.

[10] Practice Direction—Group Litigation, para 6.1.

C. The Group Register

case managed with the other cases on the Group Register, or if it is satisfied that the entry of the case on the Group Register would adversely affect the case management of the other cases, may refuse to allow details of the case to be entered on the Group Register, or order their removal from the Register if already entered, although the case gives rise to one or more of the Group issues.

6.5 The Group Register will normally be maintained by and kept at the [management] court but the court may direct this to be done by the solicitor for one of the parties to a case entered on the Register.

6.6 (1) Rule 5.4 (supply of documents from the court records) applies where the Register is maintained by the [management] court. A party to a claim on the Group Register may request documents relating to any other claim on the Group Register in accordance with rule 5.4(1) as if he were a party to those proceedings.

(2) Where the Register is maintained by a solicitor, any person may inspect the Group Register during normal business hours and upon giving reasonable notice to the solicitor; the solicitor may charge a fee not exceeding the fee prescribed for a search at the court office.

4.16 The manager of the register may wish to allocate an individual identifying number to each member and promptly or periodically notify the other parties.[11] There is no provision for whether a fee is payable for registration, but where the lead solicitor is the manager of the register he will include this in his costs.

Criteria and verification

4.17 Setting criteria for membership of the register is the mechanism by which the court controls membership of the group. The importance of establishing accurate criteria cannot be overemphasised. The absence of proper controls at the point of entry can lead to inordinate and inexcusable delay[12] and otherwise threaten the ongoing efficient management of the group. The Law Society's Working Party endorsed the principle that criteria need to be set for the entry and continued participation of individual claims in any group.[13] The court may establish criteria through its definition of the GLO issues in the GLO and/or through specific criteria relating to the claims on the group register.

4.18 As mentioned above, the management court has power to direct those details of cases which are required to be entered on the group register.[14] An earlier draft of the Rule referred specifically to giving directions about the *criteria* which a claim

---

[11] The Law Society Working Party recommended the mechanism of joining a GLO by registration (with a token fee of £25) as simpler than requiring individual writs to be issued. In the event, Part 19.III requires that claimants both issue proceedings and join the register. From Apr 1999, the fee to issue an individual writ is £300 for a claim not exceeding £50,000, £400 for a claim exceeding that amount.
[12] *AB and Others v John Wyeth & Brother Ltd* [1996] 7 Med LR 267, 292.
[13] Law Society, *Group Actions Made Easier* (1995) para 6.9.
[14] Practice Direction—Group Litigation, para 6.1.

must meet in order to be entered on the register, and the associated draft of the Practice Direction stated:

> The court will usually define the criteria for entry on the register at the case management hearing. Criteria will often be based on verifiable factual requirements— eg that the claimant was taking a certain drug during a certain timeframe and that the claimant suffered a particular type of illness.

4.19 The management court also has power to direct that:

> The specific facts relating to each claimant on the Group Register may be obtained by the use of a questionnaire. Where this is proposed, the management court should be asked to approve the questionnaire. The management court may direct that the questionnaire completed by individual claimants take the place of the schedule referred to in paragraph 14.1(2).[15]

4.20 This mechanism may give rise to problems. Difficulties can arise over filtering and verification of claims. The objective, consistent with the overriding objective of the CPR,[16] should be to facilitate cost-efficient ease of access by claimants to the administrative arrangements of the group. On the other hand, objectives of good administration of the group require fairness between litigants and also verification of claims so that claims are only included in the group if they satisfy the criteria set by the court. The problems which can be caused by inadequate verification are discussed in chapter 2. Various approaches might be adopted towards verification. The manager of the register clearly has a duty to ensure that the applicant has provided acceptable evidence that the criteria are satisfied. The duty to provide that evidence lies with the claimant and his or her solicitor. The 1999 Consultation Paper stated that: 'The criteria will naturally vary from case to case, and may be fairly loose or quite strict depending on individual circumstances. It may be necessary for several generic issues to be resolved or claims to be decided before the criteria can be established.'[17] Particulars of claim must be verified by a statement of truth[18] and this may be an appropriate mechanism in relation to questionnaires, applications to join the register, or other written assertions of fact.

4.21 Consideration of the case histories in Part V of this book in fact shows that it may be that setting entrance criteria or subsequent screening and verification of individual facts may not be so crucial or extensive an exercise in certain types of case,

---

[15] Practice Direction—Group Litigation, para 14.3.
[16] CPR, Rule 1.
[17] Lord Chancellor's Department, *Multi-Party Situations: Draft rules and practice direction. A Lord Chancellor's Draft Consultation Paper* (1999) para 22. The Consultation Paper defined a generic issue as an issue capable of being posed and answered as a single question—eg is this particular drug capable of causing this particular illness?
[18] CPR, Part 22.

C. The Group Register

such as actions by investors[19] or some transport cases[20] or where telephone bills have been continuously overcharged. For example, verification of the facts that claimants were investors in the defendant may be uncontroversial, although verification of losses, which would be necessary to establish viability, may be more difficult. In these circumstances, it may be justifiable to set a list of factual criteria, or use a questionnaire, and permit self-certification without much verification of the truth of the answers at an early stage.

On the other hand, there are clearly cases where not only the precise definition of the entry criteria but also verification that applicants in fact satisfy the criteria may be important.[21] The case histories show that this is likely to be relevant in the more complex personal injury cases and in any case which is lawyer led, rather than claimant led, ie where claimants have been attracted to join the litigation by advertising,[22] such that there is a significant risk that their claims may not fall within appropriate criteria, or not be viable, and may need to be weeded out.[23] In these cases, it is difficult to see how unverified answers to a questionnaire could be relied on for crucial issues where personal recollection may be mistaken or inaccurate, such as limitation and what information or warnings a patient was given by his or her doctor. The questionnaire mechanism provides no direct interview between claimant and lawyer which would afford an opportunity for the full facts to be ascertained, documents reviewed, and the claimant and his evidence assessed.[24] Further, where the relevant questions have been set by the lawyer without approval by the defence or the court, there is a danger that the questions selected will not be complete or relevant. As the draft Practice Direction stated, it will often be appropriate to base criteria on verifiable factual requirements. If not otherwise required by the Rules, it may be appropriate to require that medical records or a

4.22

---

[19] For example, where it is possible to identify the right of those coming forward by other means, as in the Lloyd's litigation where names were published in a list: see ch 23 below.

[20] Although a colloquial saying in the USA is: 'It's amazing how many people you can fit into a bus/plane/train!'

[21] There is evidence from the USA that up to a third of claimants claiming long-term disability exaggerate their symptoms, and one UK medical assessor considers that up to 75% of claims which he forensically reviews have significant omissions within the history disclosed to the assessing physician, about 10% of which fall into the fraudulent category: J Slesinger, Solicitors Journal (28 Nov 1997) 1124.

[22] For further discussion see ch 6 below and for considerations relating to cut-off date see paras 5.54 *et seq* below.

[23] The Legal Aid Board pointed out its frustration in the efficiency of the screening process, where it had to rely on lawyers who have a financial interest in the outcome. Legal Aid Board, *Issues for the Lord Chancellor's Department and the Legal Aid Board in multi-party actions* (1994). Lord Nicholls of Birkenhead has stated that 'the court, with their enhanced powers of case-management, must seek to evolve means of weeding out obviously hopeless claims as expeditiously as is consistent with the court having a sufficiently full factual picture of the circumstances of the case'. *Phelps v Hillingdon LBC* [2000] 3 WLR 776, 804, HL.

[24] See the problems of the use of questionnaires without verification of answers in the tobacco litigation: ch 32 below.

Chapter 4: Claims

doctor's certificate be produced at this stage which verify that the claimant was, for example, using a certain product,[25] or exposed to a particular environmental hazard,[26] during a certain time frame, that the claimant suffered a particular illness, and that the product or exposure caused the illness.

4.23 In cases where understanding had not evolved so as to provide for entrance criteria, their crucial importance was recognised retrospectively. Pre-echoing the requirements of Part 19.III in requiring criteria to be set by the judge at the outset, Ian Kennedy J said in the benzodiazepine litigation: 'The question of the entrance criteria is a critical one, though . . . if similar litigation were to be proposed in the future it might be that the court itself should be involved in the setting of those criteria.'[27]

4.24 In that litigation, the absence of entry criteria necessitated a subsequent review of cases, which delayed proceedings significantly. The review was not, however, carried out against criteria set by the court or involving all the parties. In the Myodil litigation, screening of the initial cohort of some 4,000 led to 426 claims being identified which could then be settled. In that case, the criteria were arrived at by consensus between the parties, in an unusual example of effective collaboration. Lord Woolf concluded:

> In many cases, testing the likely viability of a sufficient number of individual cases cannot fairly be postponed until resolution of the generic issues is contemplated. This is because of the interdependence of the generic and individual issues. The latter shape the former. The cost-benefit justification of the proceedings depends on an adequate number of sufficiently promising cases. And, bearing in mind the adverse effects of a group action on defendants, it is necessary as a matter of basic justice to which they too are entitled.
>
> This does not of course mean that examination of each case is required initially. More selective methods can be used. Although defendants traditionally oppose any selection of lead cases, there is a growing recognition that statistically valid samples of the wider group may be helpful in establishing criteria which individuals must meet to join the action. But above all, consideration of individual cases must not be allowed to paralyse overall progress of the group action.
>
> . . .
>
> The court should usually aim to treat as a priority the determination of the generic issues while establishing economic methods of handling the individual cases.[28]

4.25 Lord Woolf, whose comments were made in the climate of developing understanding some four years before the Rule was finalised, therefore accepted that the likely viability of a sufficient number of individual cases had to be assessed at an

---

[25] See case histories relating to benzodiazepines, Myodil, and tobacco at chs 22, 21, and 32 below.
[26] See the emergence at a later stage in the *X Co* case that some claimants were not exposed as initially alleged: ch 25 below.
[27] *AB and Others v John Wyeth and Brother Ltd* [1996] 7 Med LR 267, 291.
[28] Lord Woolf, *Access to Justice: Final Report* (1996) ch 17, paras 34, 35 and recommendation (8).

C. The Group Register

initial stage. He went on to accept that the court should establish a filter mechanism in order to exclude weak or hopeless cases, either by preventing them entering the action in the first place (if the court were involved at a sufficiently early stage), or by weeding them out from the ongoing group, by means of some sort of audit.[29] He suggested that the parties, the Legal Aid Board (now the Legal Services Commission), and the court should agree criteria for drawing up standard questionnaires, which would be answered by each plaintiff.

One consequence of failure to verify claims may be that it later emerges that substantial amendment is required to the nature of the allegations, pleadings, or to the shape of the multi-party action:[30] it may be that management decisions have been taken that would have been different if the true nature of the claims, or a group of them, had been understood. The courts have commented on some of these aspects in successive hearings in the benzodiazepine litigation: **4.26**

> It is essential that all pleaders should avoid the mistake of allowing an unsustainable claim to remain as a 'passenger' to what may be a substantial claim against another defendant. This litigation is unwieldy enough when care is taken to confine it to viable cases. It can scarcely sustain even a handful of straws.[31]

And:

> I do not accept the argument that it is not necessary that cases other than lead cases should commit themselves to any definite case on injury until a much later stage. Naturally only a very small number, perhaps 1 or 2% of the whole, will be chosen as lead cases, but whichever cases are chosen must exemplify, and be supported by, a sufficient cohort to justify a trial of the issue they raise. Secondly it would be asking too much of human nature to leave the identification of a claimant's injuries until it had been demonstrated which of these many injuries were capable of being caused by the ingestion of Ativan.
>
> In my judgment it is essential that plaintiffs should take and maintain a position on what injuries they have suffered now. Wyeth are already sifting cases to begin identifying triable issues and potential lead cases. If I were to allow a further period within which plaintiffs might serve further and better medical reports still more delay would be caused.
>
> In my judgment it is necessary for the orderly progress of this litigation that there should be no substantial amendments after the final extended cut-off date. I would allow minor tidying amendments, or amendments to introduce new symptoms which have first made their appearance after the original pleading. But I would not allow amendments to introduce new matters of complaint or to allow further substantiation of complaints pleaded but not hitherto substantiated.[32]

---

[29] Lord Woolf, *Access to Justice: Final Report* (1996) ch 17, paras 39, 51–55.
[30] See the *X Co* case at ch 25 below.
[31] *L & W v John Wyeth & Brother Limited* (Ian Kennedy J, 6 May 1992).
[32] *Nur v John Wyeth & Brother Limited* [1996] 7 Med LR 300, 304; leave to appeal to the Court of Appeal was refused (Rose LJ, 28 July 1993).

4.27 Similarly, it has been noted in the USA that weak cases are drawn into multi-party claims by stronger claims (the 'vacuum cleaner' effect) and that this adverse selection of weaker claims represents a transactional cost that must be borne by stronger claims and which may dilute both the chances of settlement or success and any money available in settlement ('wealth redistribution') such that those with stronger claims may be better off pursuing individual claims outside a group.[33] In England and Wales, where grouping of cases is mandatory, the application of appropriate entry criteria will benefit claimants with strong cases, whose prospects would otherwise be diluted by the admission of weaker claims. The ultimate risk is that if unsubstantiated claims are allowed into the group which later turn out not to be valid, the consequences will be that the group itself may be halted or may be allowed to continue when it is not viable.[34] This leads to consideration of financial viability.

Financial viability

4.28 The requirement for proportionality in both an individual case and the group as a whole cannot be assessed in the absence of an assessment of the costs, likely damages, and chances of success at the levels of each individual case and the group. The assessment requires that individual cases are understood to be viable, as was made clear in the benzodiazepine litigation:

> In group litigation . . . no individual action can lend weight to the generic balance unless it first has a favourable inherent balance, and then only to the extent that it has such a balance.[35]

And:

> The question is not simply whether there are enough plaintiffs, the question is whether there are enough plaintiffs with clear and substantial enough cases on these issues that they can contribute to the body of claims which must underwrite the costs of the generic issues.[36]

4.29 An accurate evaluation of the number of viable individual cases was required under the legal aid system in order for the Board to be able to satisfy itself whether the 'reasonableness' test was satisfied:[37]

---

[33] MD Green, *Bendectin and Birth Defects* (University of Pennsylvania Press, 1996) 249–250; I Ayres, 'Optimal Pooling in Claims Resolution Facilities' (Autumn 1990) 53 Law and Contemp Probs at 159, 160, 169.

[34] In the USA, applications can be made to decertify a class. This is not specifically provided for under Rule 19.III but there is no reason in principle why such an application or order could not be made in an appropriate case. The same result might be achieved by adopting directions in individual cases, rather than by collective treatment, where that is appropriate.

[35] *AB and Others v John Wyeth & Brother Ltd* [1996] 7 Med LR 267, 278.

[36] *AB and Others v John Wyeth & Brother Limited* (20 Oct 1993).

[37] Legal Aid Act 1988, s 15(3). In its Guidance, the Board made clear that any person applying for civil legal aid in a multi-party action must still satisfy the usual means and merits tests on an in-

C. The Group Register

The cost/benefit analysis cannot be carried out by the legal aid authorities until they know at least (a) whether there will in fact be a multi-party action, (b) what generic issues are likely to arise, (c) what is the approximate cost of the likely generic issues, (d) approximately how many plaintiffs' cases are likely to raise each generic issue . . .[38]

The same approach should apply irrespective of the funding mechanism, since legal aid was merely a conditional loan, similar in effect and interest to private loans or cover under CFAs. In fact, these considerations are particularly important where cases are being financed on CFAs. The fact that claimants' lawyers assume financial risk encourages but does not guarantee either the fact or accuracy of evaluation of the evidence in individual cases before putting them forward, since the pressures on solicitors acting on CFAs to cut costs may mean that cases are inadequately investigated.[39] It remains to be seen whether insurers will fulfil the strong managerial role which the Legal Aid Board found necessary to develop in controlling its cases, as discussed in chapter 12. 4.30

American lawyers have stressed the fundamental importance under a contingency fee system of adequate investigation and screening of potential cases. In the 19 months to June 1997, one New Jersey law firm received 323 calls from potential clients wishing to institute medical negligence claims. Only one claim was commenced although 11 others were being evaluated further. Of the 96 per cent rejected, 23 per cent of potential claimants might have been injured through negligence but were insufficiently seriously injured to warrant the expense of litigation, 22 per cent had pre-existing conditions that made proof of causation difficult, the limitation period had expired in 12 per cent, 11 per cent involved bizarre or incoherent stories, 9 per cent involved people with transitory injury not worth claiming, 9 per cent concerned patients who had had a poor result of orthopaedic or neurosurgery not due to negligence, 6 per cent did not comply with recommended medical treatment, and 4 per cent lied to their lawyers on important facts.[40] 4.31

Joining the register

The Rule and Practice Direction are silent on the procedure to be followed by a party who wishes to join the group. Earlier drafts specified that the applicant must send a copy of his or her claim form to the manager of the register together with a request for entry on the register. The claim form would generally need to contain 4.32

---

dividual basis. Thus, it must be established that each individual claim must be reasonable and viable on its own merits. *Legal Aid 1996/97 Handbook*, para 17-02. *R v Legal Aid Board, ex p Belcher* (15 July 1994).

[38] *R v Legal Aid Board, ex p Belcher* (Dyson J, 15 July 1995).
[39] This view is supported by the tobacco case history in ch 32 below.
[40] E Grove and M Ferrara, *New England Journal of Medicine* (5 June 1997) 1680.

Chapter 4: Claims

sufficient information to show that the criteria set by the court for entry on the register have been met. If the claim form does not show that the criteria have been met (for example, because it was issued before the criteria were determined), a document showing that the criteria have been met should also be sent.[41]

4.33 The manager of the register may be faced with applications for which it is uncertain whether or not the criteria for entry are satisfied. An earlier draft of the Rule specified that where he considers that the criteria for entry on the register may not have been met, the manager may refer the claim to the court for the court to decide whether the criteria have been met. The management court retains a discretion to order the removal of a case from the register where it is not satisfied that the case can be conveniently case managed with the other cases on the register, or that the case management of the other cases would be adversely affected.[42]

4.34 Claimants may wish to join the Group at different times. As mentioned above,[43] the Practice Direction (at paragraph 9.1) provides that, after the GLO has been made, any new claim must be started at the management court. The claim must be started in the normal way. Particulars of claim must be served in accordance with other provisions of the CPR.

4.35 Recognising that difficult limitation issues can arise, the 1997 Consultation Paper proposed that the act of joining the register should mean the same as 'bringing an action' for the purposes of the Limitation Act. The Rule is silent on this point, but the 1999 Consultation Paper noted that concern was expressed at removing the court's supervision of this fundamentally important issue. The Lord Chancellor's Department concluded that where a person wishes to bring a claim within the scope of the group, a claim form should be issued in the normal way, followed by registration, and that after the particulars of claim had been served, the claim would normally be stayed in accordance with directions of the court.[44]

D. Particulars of Claim

4.36 The normal position under the CPR is that each claimant must serve particulars of claim, in accordance with Rule 16.4.[45] The court will expect claimants to have

---

[41] Lord Chancellor's Department, *Multi-Party Situations: Draft rules and practice direction: A Lord Chancellor's Department Consultation Paper* (1999) para 30.
[42] Practice Direction—Group Litigation, para 6.4.
[43] para 3.40 above.
[44] Lord Chancellor's Department, *Multi-Party Situations: Draft rules and practice direction: A Lord Chancellor's Draft Consultation Paper* (1999) 31; this was provided for in the draft Rule at 2(2)(b)(iii) but omitted from the finalised Rule.
[45] This was specified in a draft of the Group Litigation Rule, para 2(2)(b)(iii), but omitted from the final draft, presumably because it is unnecessary to repeat Rule 16.4.

D. Particulars of Claim

complied in substance with the terms of an approved pre-action protocol:[46] non-compliance leading to the commencement of proceedings or costs which are unnecessary may lead to the imposition of costs sanctions, subject to any order by the court varying this. Particulars of claim must include:[47]

(1) a concise statement of the facts on which the claimant relies;
(2) details of interest claimed;
(3) aggravated or exemplary damages claimed and grounds for claiming them;
(4) provisional damages and grounds for claiming.

Particulars of claim may include:[48] 4.37

— any point of law on which the claim is based,
— the name of any witness the party proposes to call, and
— may attach a copy of any document necessary to the claim, including any expert report.

In a personal injury claim, the particulars of claim must:[49] 4.38

— state the claimant's date of birth,
— state brief details of the claimant's personal injuries,
— attach a schedule of details of any past and future expenses and losses which he claims, and
— attach a report from any medical practitioner relied on.

Particulars of claim must be verified by a statement of truth.[50]

Under a GLO, the management court has power to give directions about the form that particulars of claim relating to claims which are to be entered on the group register should take. This power needs to be understood in the context of the next section. 4.39

Group Particulars of Claim

The Practice Direction includes powers for the management court to direct that the GLO claimants serve 'Group Particulars of Claim', which are intended to form a convenient summary of all the individual claims. The assumption underlying this mechanism is that it is possible, first, to summarise general allegations which arise which relate to all claims and, secondly, to summarise in a schedule[51] 4.40

---

[46] Practice Direction—Protocols, para 2.2.
[47] CPR, Rule 16.4.
[48] Practice Direction 16:11.3.
[49] Practice Direction 16:4.1.
[50] CPR, Part 22.
[51] It may also be directed that questionnaires completed by each claimant may take the place of a schedule: Practice Direction—Group Litigation, para 14.3. For problems with questionnaires, see para 4.22 above.

which of the general allegations are relied on in each case and any specific facts arising in individual cases which are relevant.[52] This mechanism might be of considerable assistance in some types of case. Yet the court should exercise some care that the assumptions just mentioned are satisfied before adopting this mechanism, since experience has shown that it is not the preferred approach in some types of case, as discussed below.

4.41 A practice developed in the major product liability cases from the mid-1980s until the mid-1990s for pleadings to be in the form of a Master Statement of Claim, which could be adapted by incorporation (in whole or part) into individual statements of claim.[53] This solution first arose in the Opren litigation[54] when the plaintiffs' counsel drafted a statement of claim in the first individual action[55] which turned out to be a long document and included extensive allegations of general and individual causation. Rather than repeat the general allegations *verbatim* in all subsequent statements of claim, cross-references were made and allowed. In general terms, therefore, the Master Statement of Claim contained the allegations of negligence and general causation. It outlined the types of injury that the agent is allegedly capable of causing. Each individual statement of claim adopted those parts of the Master pleading that were appropriate and also gave particulars pertaining to the individual history of the claimant (for example, details of use such as dosage, duration, etc, alleged injuries, and specific loss claimed). There would, similarly, be Master and individual Defences. This mechanism preserved the individual identity of each claim but was thought to be efficient in avoiding repetition.[56]

4.42 However, the adoption of Master pleadings was later questioned and, in certain cases, rejected. In some cases, claimants' advisers attempted to proceed by producing a Master Statement of Claim *in vacuo* without individual statements of claim.[57] As discussed in chapter 2 above, this approach was controversial and led to difficulties. It can be argued that a Master Statement of Claim is only an efficient and appropriate mechanism where it forms an intentional adjunct to individual statements of claim where the general nature of the issues which arise in the

---

[52] Practice Direction—Group Litigation, para 14.1. Such directions should include directions as to whether the Group Particulars should be verified by a statement or statements of truth and, if so, by whom: ibid, para 14.2.

[53] Supreme Court Procedure Committee, *Guide for use in Group Actions* (1991) ch 5.4.

[54] See ch 18 below.

[55] See ch 18 below.

[56] Another technique, which was used in the benzodiazepine (see ch 22) and Gravigard (see ch 20) cases where there was a delay before Master pleadings were produced, was for the parties to produce non-binding draft pleadings and commentaries describing the essential nature of the case. This enabled the parties and the court to continue to make progress in analysing the issues.

[57] See, for example, the benzodiazepine (ch 22), Gravigard (ch 20), and tobacco (ch 32) cases.

D. Particulars of Claim

individual cases is absolutely clear at the start and not subject to verification or change.[58]

4.43 At Lord Woolf's Inquiry Seminar on Multi-Party Actions on 9 February 1996 Mr Justice May stated a view that it may be more efficient to proceed on the basis of individual pleadings where cases raise differing issues, even if there are some common issues. He subsequently ordered this approach in the Norplant litigation, striking out references in individual statements of claim to a Master Statement of Claim and ordering that a specimen number of individual claims be pleaded by claimants and short defences served, so that the Court could then identify the range of issues which arose in the litigation.[59] In that case, he said:

> . . . generally speaking cases such as this should start with particular claims and then consider whether generic issues emerge from a selection of individual cases. . . . upon this approach the parties would have orthodox individual pleadings and then probably a short document defining common issues which expert reports would address.
>
> . . .
>
> The trouble with a long and discursive document such as has been produced, without encouragement from the court, for the plaintiffs in this case is that, whereas it may set out a general thesis, it is not, in my view, a suitable vehicle for defining issues succinctly. It is more in the nature of an experts' report than a pleading. If the defendants were required to deal with it as a pleading, which is what the plaintiffs ask me to order, they would require a substantial time to do so at the end of which the case would, I think, be bogged down and Mrs B and Mrs Foster (and the other potential plaintiffs) would be little closer to a determination of their claims. The parties would or might be required to deal with matters which turn out to be of no relevance to any issue which matters to individual cases. I am not persuaded by Mr Goldsmith's submission that the court should take what it has, for better or for worse, and move forward. That seems to me to be inviting trouble, if, as I think, that is not the fair and economic way to proceed. Better to take a step back perhaps and then proceed on a less boggy path. I am not dissuaded from doing so by the suggestion that the plaintiffs would nevertheless wish to retain the entire contents of the Master Particulars of Claim.[60]

---

[58] The use of a Master Statement of Claim as avoiding duplication in individual statements of claim can be seen in the Myodil case (ch 21 below). The adoption of a Master Statement of Claim was commented on with approval by Lord Bingham of Cornhill CJ in the Vibration White Finger litigation (quoted at para 29.18 below) on the basis that it should lead to savings by avoiding contesting multiple individual actions, but for the reasons discussed in ch 2 and below it is suggested that this is erroneous and a *non sequitur*: other mechanisms, such as selection of lead actions, can achieve that result.

[59] *B and Foster v Roussel Laboratories Limited* (May J, 30 June 1997). This approach has some similarities with the US practice which occurs, prior to certification, of submitting written briefs, so that the issues which are important, such as whether or not there are common issues and whether individual issues predominate, can be established by the court before it makes its decision.

[60] *B and Foster v Roussel*, ibid.

4.44 The draft Master Statement of Claim in the tobacco litigation was similarly dispensed with by Wright J, who ordered individual pleadings of ten lead cases. This change in approach was influenced, as discussed in chapters 2 above and 32 below, primarily by the realisation that an individual case approach was preferable to a generic issue approach in the particular litigation, in circumstances where there was uncertainty as to whether the Master allegations had been fully investigated and so represented an accurate or complete summary of the issues which arose in the individual cases, rather than an unverified statement of a hypothetical case.

4.45 Accordingly, the optional procedure mentioned in the Practice Direction as to adoption of Group Particulars accompanied by a schedule of details of individual claims appears not to be intended, as a general rule, to revert to the historical practice referred to above of some cases dispensing altogether with individual particulars of claim.[61] It is true that the management court has power to give directions about the form of individual particulars of claim,[62] but this is not expressed as a power to dispose with the requirement for individual particulars of claim.

4.46 The conclusion of the cases discussed above is that Group Particulars must be a genuine summary of the issues which arise in individual cases and should only be used where the individual issues are also stated.

---

[61] In this connection, it has been held that individual facts and not a common form of pleading should be stated in relation to a request for extension of the limitation period. *AB v John Wyeth & Brother Ltd and another* [1991] 2 Med LR 344.

[62] Practice Direction—Group Litigation, para 14.4.

5

INITIAL MANAGEMENT OF THE GROUP

A. Managing Judge	5.01	D. Representation Issues	
		Lead solicitor	5.24
B. Directions	5.03	Protection of claimants: the independent trustee	5.33
C. Preliminary Issues, Lead Cases, and Test Cases	5.09	E. Cut-off Dates	5.39
		Cut-off dates and limitation	5.54

A. Managing Judge

From the start of the modern history of multi-party actions in this jurisdiction, it has consistently been recognised that they should be managed by a single judge.[1] The Law Society's Working Party and Lord Woolf advocated the involvement of a single judge as early as possible in the process and the establishment of a panel of judges who have training and experience in managing group actions. Cases in which a succession of judges are appointed run the risk of suffering from inconsistency or lack of forward momentum.[2]

5.01

The Practice Direction provides that:[3]

5.02

> A judge ('the managing judge') will be appointed for the purpose of the GLO as soon as possible. He will assume overall responsibility for the management of the claims and will generally hear the GLO issues. A Master or a District Judge may be appointed to deal with procedural matters, which he will do in accordance with any directions given by the managing judge. A costs judge may be appointed and may be invited to attend case management hearings.

---

[1] Supreme Court Procedure Committee, *Guide for use in Group Actions* (1991); Law Society, *Group Actions Made Easier* (1995); Lord Woolf, *Interim Report* (1995) and *Final Report* (1996).

[2] See chs 20 and 32 below.

[3] Practice Direction—Group Litigation, para 8. Before this rule, the traditional approach was for the plaintiffs' solicitors to write to the Lord Chief Justice or latterly the Senior Master of the Queen's Bench Division, requesting the appointment of a judge and the issue of a Practice Direction that all claims should come under his jurisdiction.

B. Directions

5.03 The managing judge will control the management of the Group Litigation Order (GLO). He may give case management directions at the time the GLO is made or subsequently.[4] Specific management powers are set out in Rule 19.13, which provides:

> Directions given by the management court may include directions—
> (a) varying the GLO issues[5];
> (b) providing for one or more claims on the group register to proceed as test claims[6];
> (c) appointing the solicitor of one or more parties to be the lead solicitor for the claimants or defendants;
> (d) specifying the details to be included in a statement of case in order to show that the criteria for entry of the claim on the group register have been met;
> (e) specifying a date after which no claim may be added to the group register[7] unless the court gives permission; and
> (f) for the entry of any particular claim which meets one or more of the GLO issues on the group register.

5.04 As discussed in chapter 2, the power of the co-ordinating judge in a GLO to exercise a wide, innovative managerial discretion was established at least fifteen years before the Woolf revolution based on this principle. Successive imaginative decisions have been upheld by the Court of Appeal. One consequence of this is that it affords the parties' lawyers opportunities to make innovative management proposals. A further consequence is that parties can find themselves suddenly under very great and unexpected pressure. The Court of Appeal has said:

> Group actions involve great advantage to plaintiffs, who are able to join together to bring actions which, on their own, would never be possible. But they must be conducted in such a way that they do not involve injustice to other parties. There are no rules of court specifically dealing with group actions. The judge to whom they are assigned can and should devise procedures to deal with the specific problems of the litigation before him. He will need to be inventive and firm if the trial and interlocutory proceedings are not to be unmanageable. In such litigation this court will be especially reluctant to interfere with the judge's exercise of his discretion, since he knows far more about the litigation than we can do.[8]

5.05 The essence of judicial case management is that the co-ordinating judge will wish to give regular management directions, often at hearings which he may initiate

---

[4] Practice Direction—Group Litigation, para 12.1.
[5] The Practice Direction—Group Litigation, para 12.2 specifies that any application to vary the terms of the GLO must be made to the management court.
[6] See Abbreviations.
[7] See paras 4.12 *et seq* above.
[8] *AB & Others v John Wyeth and Another* [1994] 5 Med LR 149 per Stuart-Smith LJ.

B. Directions

himself. In addition to giving orders on the time and format of pleadings, exchange of evidence, and mode of trial, one technique open to him is to give non-binding 'Indications' of orders which he is provisionally minded to give in future unless persuaded to the contrary. A further technique is to call less formal meetings of representatives—as occurred in the Lloyd's litigation[9]—in order to encourage information sharing and discussion of possible management options. In the HIV litigation, the judge made comments during a hearing in chambers with the specific intention of encouraging settlement.[10]

The issues which the court will need to consider include: **5.06**

(1) the number of claimants in, or likely to be in, the group;
(2) a cut-off date for joining or leaving the group;
(3) what publicity, if any, should be given to the group and to individual hearings and by whom;
(4) relevant aspects of funding and the implications;
(5) the extent to which there is sufficient commonality between plaintiffs;
(6) appointment of a lead solicitor;
(7) who will hold the register;
(8) how often the register will be updated;
(9) manner and timing of communicating updates of the register to the court and other parties;
(10) definition of the issues in the GLO;
(11) issues requiring further pleading;
(12) criteria for admission to the register;
(13) what verification should be produced or undertaken of satisfaction of the criteria for admission to the register;
(14) costs-sharing arrangements;
(15) aspects of pre-action protocols already complied with or outstanding;
(16) method of selection of test cases, if appropriate;
(17) extent, proportionality, and timing of disclosure of documentary evidence by all parties;
(18) expert evidence;
(19) issues to be delegated by the judge to a more junior judge (normally a Master).

In personal injury actions, the following matters should also be considered:[11] **5.07**

---

[9] See ch 23 below.
[10] See para 19.20 below.
[11] A plaintiff who alleges personal injuries waives his normal right to confidentiality in his medical history and his manner of life: *Hay v University of Alberta Hospital* [1991] 2 Med LR 204, 207 per Picard J, adopted in *Nur v John Wyeth & Brother Ltd* [1996] 7 Med LR 300, 306.

- orders intended to ensure that claimants secure the production by hospital authorities and general practitioners of all relevant medical records so that they may be disclosed to the defendants' solicitors. An Indication may be given that such disclosure should be given readily in response to appropriate letters of authority without further order and the court might order costs of any unnecessary application against any person whose conduct merits it;
- an order imposing a condition that the plaintiffs attend a medical examination by the defendants' medical advisers.

5.08 A specimen order of preliminary directions is at Appendix G. However, it should be emphasised that both the content and timing of any directions made should be carefully considered in the light of the particular circumstances.

C. Preliminary Issues, Lead Cases, and Test Cases

5.09 A principal reason for co-ordinating similar actions is to avoid the trial of every individual claim on all issues. As Lord Donaldson MR said:

> Trying 1500 cases together is much cheaper than trying 1500 cases separately, so the plaintiffs as a group can spend more before they reach the economic limit. But however you arrange things, and whether there are 1500 plaintiffs or only one, there is always some economic limit. That is the long and the short of the problem.[12]

5.10 The approach which the English courts have developed to take forward resolution of all the cases in the group is to select a small number of lead or test claims.[13] Accordingly, Rule 19.13(b) specifies that the court may manage one or more claims as test claims.[14] However, it was stated in the Consultation Paper that the test claim mechanism 'will not be appropriate in all cases. It may also be necessary to deal with individual issues in individual claims. The rules are not intended to lay down a rigid formula for every possible permutation.'[15] It has to be recognised that the test case approach is a compromise.[16]

5.11 The claims which are managed in a co-ordinated fashion under a GLO remain no more than a collection of *individual* claims,[17] each of which must ultimately be

---

[12] *Davies (Joseph Owen) v Eli Lilly & Co* [1987] 1 WLR 1136, CA at 1143 per Lord Donaldson MR. The development in judicial attitudes towards case management is illustrated by the fact that a change in policy to be more ready to grant separate trials on liability and damages, which had previously only been in 'extraordinary and exceptional cases', occurred in 1974: *Coenen v Payne* [1974] 1 WLR 984.

[13] These words are often used interchangeably, but see suggested differentiation in the Abbreviations.

[14] Practice Direction—Group Litigation, para 12.3 states that the management court has this power and para 15.1 states that it may give directions for the trial of common issues and for the trial of individual issues.

[15] Lord Chancellor's Department, *Multi-Party Situations: Draft rules and practice direction. A Lord Chancellor's Department Consultation Paper* (1999) para 23.

[16] C Harlow and R Rawlings, *Pressure Through Law* (1992) 129.

[17] Lord Irvine of Lairg LC, *Hansard*, HL (Series 5) vol 596, col 521(19 Jan 1999).

resolved. The objective is to dispose of all the claims as efficiently and swiftly as possible. In deciding on the managerial mechanism to move forward resolution of all the individual claims, the paramount consideration is that the court must be satisfied that the selected approach will be *dispositive* of as many cases or issues as possible in as efficient and proportionate a manner as possible. This may involve achieving a degree of confidence that all cases likely to be involved have come forward, perhaps by imposition of a cut-off date, and are valid and viable: these aspects are discussed below. The optimal approach depends entirely on the nature of the particular case and the issues which arise. Selecting the right approach is perhaps the single most important management decision in a GLO and can require great skill, experience, and thought. Furthermore, you will only know if you are right in retrospect.

In the Vibration White Finger litigation,[18] Lord Bingham of Cornhill CJ favoured selection of lead cases on the basis of diversity of issues and also of chances of success, although this may be wishful thinking in practice unless care is taken to select cases which are poor, such as including selection of some cases by opponents after they are apprised of sufficient details of individual facts in a sufficient number of cases: 5.12

> It is of obvious importance that they should represent a genuine cross-section, in particular so far as the strengths and weaknesses of different cases are concerned. The reason for this is obvious. If the strongest case were to fail, then it would necessarily follow that the plaintiffs would have a very poor chance of success in weaker cases. If, on the other hand, the weakest case were to succeed, the Defendants would recognise that they had little chance of successfully defeating the stronger cases.[19]

It may be possible to identify issues which arise in all or a majority of individual claims and to try some or all of these common or generic issues before proceeding with any further procedural steps in the majority of individual cases, which would remain stayed. The objective of this approach would be either that one of the issues determined would itself be dispositive of the litigation as a whole (for example, the claims fail on liability)[20] or would be dispositive of issues which arise in many claims (for example, the defendants were in breach of duty and/or that breach caused the type of loss of which many claimants complain), or that the court could set out guidelines which would indicate the likely outcome in as many individual cases as possible.[21]   5.13

Lord Woolf said in his 1995 Report: 5.14

> There are three basic matters which a judge is almost invariably going to have to start to tackle at the certification stage and immediately after in an MPA:

---

[18] See ch 29 below.
[19] See para 29.17 below.
[20] In *Equitable Life Assurance Society v Hyman* [2000] 3 WLR 529, HL resolution of the single issue of the Society's policy on payment of final bonuses applied to 90,000 policyholders.
[21] *Hyman and Williams v Schering Chemicals Ltd*, The Times, 10 June 1980, CA.

(a) Deciding whether there are generic issues present and whether they can be effectively decided within the [MPA] (this bears particularly on the composition and identity of the proposed beneficiaries of the proceedings).
(b) Deciding whether there are issues applicable to certain individuals which need to be determined separately as to those individual claims; and if so establish machinery for that purpose.
(c) Deciding the order in which the issues identified at (a) and (b) are to be determined.[22]

5.15 Various examples are available of possible approaches. Approaches that were adopted in the earlier cases were later seen to have drawbacks and practice has evolved. In the first major case, involving pertussis vaccine, Stuart-Smith LJ decided to take the case forward on the basis of a single test case. When it was decided in that case that the vaccine was not capable of causing permanent brain damage or death in young children to whom it is administered, all other cases in the group were not proceeded with.[23] Similarly, the Sellafield leukaemia claims were also resolved after the allegations on general causation failed, having been tried in two test cases.[24] In that litigation, the defendant as well as the claimants had a paramount commercial need to establish as early as possible whether there was any generic case: accordingly, only two out of a larger cohort of claimants were selected as test cases in order that the first decision to be given would include a determination of general causation. Further, there was not a 'claimant bandwagon' issue in the case: although individual claimants might have failed because of alternative causation (for example, their cancers were of the 'wrong' type, not caused by radiation), there were unlikely to be many claimants whose cases were totally speculative, in the sense of having been attracted by publicity, since the cohort of claimants was limited by particular disease states and geographical proximity to the defendants' site.

5.16 In the pertussis[25] and Opren[26] cases, only one or two test cases were taken forward. One problem with this is that where there is a small number of test cases, the strategy is vulnerable if the case collapses. The first test case put forward in the pertussis litigation had to be withdrawn at a late stage when it became clear that the evidence which emerged in that individual case was inconsistent, so a second test case had to be developed, with some loss of time and cost. The same frustration would have occurred if the test case(s) had failed on their individual facts, which were not representative of the other stayed cases. The answer to this problem is to ensure that the facts of the individual cases are properly screened, and to select a

---

[22] Lord Woolf, *Access to Justice: Final Report* (1996) ch 17, paras 34 and 35 and recommendation (8).
[23] *Loveday v Renton and the Wellcome Foundation Limited* [1990] 1 Med LR 117: see ch 17 below.
[24] *Reay v British Nuclear Fuels plc* [1994] 5 Med LR 1: see ch 24 below.
[25] See ch 17 below.
[26] See ch 18 below.

C. Preliminary Issues

sufficient number of test cases and/or hold some in reserve. Ian Kennedy J said in the benzodiazepine litigation:

> It was also common ground that the issues to be tried would be identified from a review of the available individual statements of claim. Generic counsel feared that, if one proceeded by lead cases, some or all of those cases might fail on their own facts and thus provide no lead. To my mind that was always an unreal fear, for there was no advantage to either defendant in such a result, and that was confirmed by their counsel. Cases would be chosen which were sound on their own facts, and which could not be defeated on limitation points: if necessary, other cases could be held in reserve.[27]

5.17 The problem of a test claim dropping out is now addressed by Rule 19.15, which provides:

> (1) Where a direction has been given for a claim on the group register to proceed as a test claim and that claim is settled, the management court may order that another claim on the group register be substituted as the test claim.
> (2) Where an order is made under paragraph (1), any order made in the test claim before the date of substitution is binding on the substituted claim unless the court orders otherwise.

5.18 The Court of Appeal has held that the costs consequences where a lead claimant either does or does not accept a payment into court are matters for the judge's discretion in the context of the group litigation and that the normal consequences in unitary actions may not necessarily follow in the group context.[28]

5.19 In the Myodil litigation, the lawyers for both sides agreed to proceed by way of scrutinising all individual claims which came forward and explicitly rejected a test or lead case approach. This was seen as weeding out claims which did not fit the criteria for the case and facilitating settlement of those claims which appeared to fall within the criteria.[29]

5.20 The experience of the human growth hormone litigation[30] clearly established the dangers if generic issues are tried when divorced from the facts of individual cases, particularly in relation to issues of negligence or causation. As Mildred commented on the growth hormone case:

> In this case the question whether the trial judge did elide questions of breach and causation is unresolved as is the consequence of failure on the part of plaintiffs in a 'generic issue' trial to lead evidence on the causative outcome of an (unanticipated) finding of fact. The latter may provide cogent support for the addition to generic issues of at least a sample of individual cases fully pleaded on the issue of breach causation. The advantage of such an approach appears to have been accepted by the

---

[27] *AB and Others v John Wyeth & Brother Ltd* [1996] 7 Med LR 267, 276.
[28] See para 29.19 below.
[29] See ch 21 below.
[30] See ch 28 below.

judges presently supervising the interlocutory stages of Norplant, Lariam and tobacco litigation.[31]

5.21 Where limitation is an issue this can be an efficient dispositive approach to adopt, as in certain groups in the Opren litigation and the tobacco cases. A preliminary hurdle is only likely to save time and costs if it is assumed that the plaintiffs' case will fall at this hurdle. Few preliminary issues concerning breach of duty or defect will be determinative of liability, particularly in cases involving prescription/administration by a learned intermediary. Where duty of care, warnings, and proximate causation were overlapping and required a careful examination of the whole background to the litigation, Mr Justice Ian Kennedy refused the plaintiffs' applications for trial of preliminary issues in the benzodiazepine litigation.[32] Where progressing the litigation speedily was of importance, as in the HIV/haemophilia blood product litigation, and there would be no saving if just a duty question were to be tried since causation was relatively straightforward, Ognall J decided it was impracticable to select effective issues for preliminary trial.[33]

5.22 It is, of course, necessary to end up with a determination on all issues which arise in each individual case. For the dangers of trying to select test cases before individual cases have been investigated and pleaded, see chapter 2 above. There may be situations in which it will be appropriate to set out to try each individual case and not to attempt to aggregate issues. For example, the US experience shows that where individual issues predominate over common issues, there may well be no advantage in selecting issues which are supposedly common, since this will not avoid further litigation on the unresolved issues in individual cases, nor argument that cases are dissimilar from the cases which have been determined.[34] This reinforces the importance of identifying the issues which arise in the general body of cases at an early stage:

> Where the determinative issues are largely of an individual nature they must be addressed and dealt with head-on. They cannot be avoided by dealing with other issues that are not determinative, in the vague hope that one way or another the litigation will be resolved before the determinative issues are addressed.[35]

And:

> The proposition that all individual cases will need investigation is thus not controversial: the real question is in what order steps ought to be taken.[36]

---

[31] M Mildred, 'The Human Growth Hormone (Creuzfeld-Jacob [*sic*] Disease) Litigation' [1998] JPIL 251, 260.
[32] See ch 22 below.
[33] See ch 19 below.
[34] See ch 13 below.
[35] GR Hickinbottom, 'The Defendant's Perspective' (Mar 1996) The Litigator 62, 65.
[36] M Mildred, 'The Plaintiff's Perspective' (Mar 1996) The Litigator 70, 73.

D. Representation Issues

Various schemes of case selection have been considered. The selection of cases will depend upon the parameters of the particular litigation involved. In recent product liability cases, judges have requested the selection of ten cases which will give a sufficient range of individual facts to be generally illustrative of the facts of the complete cohort. The solicitors for the parties have been permitted to choose five cases each or, perhaps optimistically, to collaborate over the selection of the ten. 5.23

D. Representation Issues

Lead solicitor

The role of lead solicitor, or a co-ordinating committee, has evolved as a practical necessity. The incumbent(s) may be charged with (a) co-ordinating the administration of the proceedings on behalf of the claimants, (b) having the conduct of the proceedings on their behalf, and (c) managing the group register. An advantage of specifying that a specific representative is to have conduct of the proceedings on behalf of *all* the claimants is to help overcome differences of view between claimants or their legal advisers. 5.24

The need for proper management and control of a large number of claimants is well recognised.[37] It is not realistic for informal representation arrangements to apply in group litigation. The court has said that it has to know who is speaking for a particular claimant and it 'is not equipped to debate in correspondence with every claimant in person what they would or would not like and whether they are or are not shoulder to shoulder with' everyone else.[38] Such litigation could not continue other than with one voice speaking definitively for all claimants or, at any rate, groups of claimants.[39] Given the complex nature of multi-party litigation, that voice must have experience in running such a case: 'The reality is this: this litigation could not possibly be conducted without the assistance of experienced counsel and solicitors.'[40] 5.25

At the commencement of the early group actions, a number of solicitors' firms realised that each had clients with ostensibly similar claims and that they should all co-ordinate. Since the late 1980s, the Law Society has offered the services of its Disaster Co-ordination Service, later renamed Multi-Party Action Co-ordination Service, which can facilitate co-ordination amongst claimants' lawyers and channel potential claimants who contact the Law Society to those solicitors involved. 5.26

---

[37] Adequate representation is, similarly, a class action certification requirement under the rules for US Federal courts and in Canada (see chs 13 and 14 below). Some of the logistical difficulties are referred to at paras 23.33 *et seq* below.
[38] *Re Benzodiazepine Litigation* (Ian Kennedy J, 25 May 1995).
[39] *AB & Others v John Wyeth & Brother Limited* [1996] 7 Med LR 267, 288, and 289.
[40] *AB and Others v John Wyeth & Brother Ltd* [1997] 8 Med LR 57, CA 66 per Stuart-Smith LJ.

The Practice Direction now specifies that a copy of the GLO should be sent to the Law Society.[41]

5.27 The problem of how the plaintiffs' legal team should be organised was solved in the late 1980s by creating a two-tier system, with a central firm or firms co-ordinating the others. The co-ordinating firm would handle issues which were common or generic to the litigation and each 'satellite' firm would be responsible merely for issues which were specific to its particular clients. The co-ordinating committee of perhaps half a dozen firms, together with a lead solicitor, would be elected by all firms who had clients.[42] Members of the co-ordinating committee would each be assigned a particular task, such as liaising with the defendants or experts or the other plaintiffs' firms, or dealing with documentary evidence or with the media. In 1991, the *Guide for use in Group Actions* recorded the practice that the 'generic' costs of the co-ordinating committee should normally be paid for by all involved in the group on an equal basis. The function of a lay interest group for victims of disasters was also referred to.

5.28 Although the *Guide* was written on the basis that claimants' interests would be best served by combining together in the manner described, it also suggested that consideration should be given to whether an individual client's interests would be better served by pursuing an individual approach, which may have the advantage of speed. Another issue for consideration mentioned was in what country and in what court the claim should best be brought.

5.29 In 1994, the Legal Aid Board imposed greater discipline on the management of cases which it funded by introducing tendering for contracts, restricting the number of firms appointed at both central and satellite level, and in some cases imposing all-work contracts granting exclusivity to a single firm. Judicial reviews of such exclusive arrangements failed.[43] Central control of multi-party actions (MPAs) by the Community Legal Service is continued under the Funding Code 2000.[44] The trend under the Rule is perhaps for a single solicitors' firm to handle a GLO, reflecting increased specialisation and consolidation by firms.

5.30 The two-tier system may remain a useful mechanism for a group which includes claimants who are not publicly funded or where there are large numbers of

---

[41] Practice Direction—Group Litigation, para 11(1).
[42] W McBryde and C Barker, 'Solicitors' Groups in Mass Disaster Claims' (1991) 141 NLJ 484. Supreme Court Procedure Committee, *Guide for use in Group Actions* (1991) ch 1. The arrangement was approved in *East Coast Aggregates v Parra-Pagan and Others; Ross v Owners of the ship 'Bowbelle' and the Owners of the ship 'Marchioness'*, Queen's Bench Division (Admiralty Court), [1977] 1 Lloyd's Rep 196: see ch 18 below.
[43] *R v Legal Aid Board, ex p Donne & Co* [1996] 3 All ER 1.
[44] See ch 12 below.

D. Representation Issues

claimants.[45] This system, although democratic, inevitably encourages competition. Historically, such competition encouraged early advertising for claimants and vying for position. There might be inefficiencies and duplication in co-ordinating several hundred or more individual firms, perhaps with each having a few clients. Deadlines might be missed. In some instances there was dissension as to strategy.

5.31 The Rule and Practice Direction are silent on the role or office of a lead solicitor, although a draft of the Practice Direction provided:

> 6.3 The court will usually direct there to be a lead solicitor who will co-ordinate the administration and have the conduct of the proceedings on behalf of the claimants. The lead solicitor will usually manage the [MPA] register. The parties should try to agree who should be the lead solicitor. However, in the absence of agreement, the court may make the appointment. If required to do this it may consult with the Law Society or the Legal Aid Board.
> 6.4 The court may also decide that a co-ordinating committee should be established.

5.32 The problem for the future is that of imposing order on claimants' firms not funded publicly but by conditional fee arrangements. It was recognised that the court could ultimately impose a solution limiting representation[46] and this is formalised in the power to appoint a lead solicitor under Rule 19.13(c). It is rare for there to be a multiplicity of defendants but it can occur, such as in the Lloyd's litigation, which involved some 12,000 plaintiffs and 300 defendants.[47]

Protection of claimants: the independent trustee

5.33 Lord Woolf noted that group actions can attract weak, hopeless, and speculative claims and are an area of litigation which is even more lawyer driven than any other, with potential conflicts of interest between lawyers and group members.[48] He also remarked on the opportunities for self-interested behaviour by lawyers:[49]

> Particular forms which this has taken include bringing claims known to be unfounded for harassing purposes and genuine but limited value claims, knowing in both cases that defendants will feel impelled to settle on terms advantageous to the lawyer though possibly of little benefit to the group members.[50]

---

[45] Two firms were appointed by the Legal Aid Board to handle generic issues in the MMR litigation which reached the courts in the later 1990s, involving some 1,900 claimants who instructed around 90 firms.

[46] Law Society, *Group Actions Made Easier* (1995) 6.32; Lord Woolf, *Access to Justice: Final Report* (1996) 17.31.

[47] See ch 23 below.

[48] Lord Woolf, *Access to Justice: Final Report* (1996) 17.71. Note also the scope for clashes of interest amongst claimant members of the coalition: C Harlow and R Rawlings, *Pressure Through Law* (1992) 115 and 132–135.

[49] See the discussion on conflicts of interest at paras 11.63 *et seq* below.

[50] Lord Woolf, *Access to Justice: Final Report* (1996) 17.70–79.

5.34 He concluded that such problems arise because of the relative absence of client control. To remedy this, he suggested, first, that the courts should promptly dismiss meritless or frivolous multi-party claims and impose sanctions on lawyers who do not observe expected standards of professional behaviour. Secondly, he proposed that the court should ensure that the interests of members of the group are represented and protected. This might be achieved by a formally constituted action group. Alternatively, the court should appoint a trustee, funded publicly. Given the complexities of multi-party litigation and the potential for conflicts, it is perhaps curious that there has been little pressure in subsequent cases for the appointment of a trustee, particularly since this mechanism would afford considerable protection to claimants' lawyers in the event of difficulties.

5.35 An alternative approach was called for in 2000 after the Breast Radiation Injury actions in which a single firm was awarded an exclusive legal aid contract to represent all of the 125-odd claimants. At the end of the litigation, objections were taken on behalf of three privately paying claimants to the work done by the firm and thus its costs. It was argued that too much power was concentrated in a single firm and that supervision by a steering committee or an independent lawyer would have been preferable.[51]

5.36 There is similarity here with the requirement of US Federal Rule 23(a) that the parties seeking to represent the class will fairly and adequately protect the interests of the class. As noted at chapter 13, the US Federal courts require not just that there will be no conflicts of interest between the class representatives but also that the lawyers representing the proposed representatives of the class should be viewed as competent to handle the case. Professor Green has commented that the distortion in roles of lawyer and client and the conflict created by the fact that the lawyers' financial stake is often greater than that of any single plaintiff is perhaps the most problematic aspect of aggregation of claims in the USA.[52]

5.37 The suggestion mooted by Lord Woolf that a lead solicitor should have autonomy, whether in pressing negotiations or in taking any steps in the action, without referring back to individual clients is fraught with difficulty. When this point was discussed at the International Bar Association meeting in October 1994, Mr Justice Vincent, an Australian High Court judge, summed up with a clear warning of the dangers of claimant lawyers acting autonomously from their clients, on the dangerous assumptions that the issues are too complex for clients to understand and there are too many of them to contact. Whilst the practical and logistic problems must be recognised, there are issues of who is controlling the litigation and in whose best interests it is run. The point is important where there

---

[51] R Stockdale, 'High cost of class actions re-visited' (Jan 2000) Medical Litigation 11.
[52] MD Green, *Bendectin and Birth Defects: The Challenge of Mass Toxic Substances Litigation* (University of Pennsylvania Press, 1996) 252.

E. Cut-off Dates

are genuine differences between groups of claimants, for example over whether to accept a settlement or continue the litigation, perhaps for non-financial reasons.[53]

5.38 The 1997 Consultation Paper noted that the court should approve settlements because, *inter alia*, it is important to ensure that lawyers do not benefit themselves while obtaining minimal benefit for their clients or, alternatively, profiting from the vulnerability of commercially sensitive defendants.[54] A draft of the Rule (paragraph 9) included this power but it was omitted from the final text.

E. Cut-off Dates

5.39 As noted above,[55] Rule 19.13(c) provides that the management court may give directions specifying a date after which no claim may be added to the register unless the court gives permission.

5.40 The Practice Direction provides:[56]

> The management court may specify a date after which no claim may be added to the Group Register unless the court gives permission. An early cut-off date may be appropriate in the case of 'instant disasters' (such as transport accidents). In the case of consumer claims, and particularly pharmaceutical claims, it may be necessary to delay the ordering of a cut-off date.

5.41 An earlier draft of the Practice Direction specified:

> 6.5 A date after which no more claims may be entered on the register is most likely to be considered where there are an unascertainable number of potential claimants. In such situations it is desirable that the defendant's potential liability is established as soon as possible.
>
> 6.6 Parties wishing to join after the cut-off date must apply for the court's permission to be allowed to join the [Group]. They will need to provide reasons why they did not meet the cut-off date. As a condition of joining the [Group] in these circumstances, the court may require a late party to accept an equal share in the liability for the costs of the [Group] from a date before the date he joins the [Group].

5.42 An important feature of management of multiple claims is that the court will be concerned to see their orderly progress without undue delay. Claimants may come forward at different times. The court will wish to establish whether there is a group which contains a sufficient number of cases which justify and permit

---

[53] As occurred in the Opren litigation: see C Harlow and R Rawlings, *Pressure Through Law* (1992) 133.
[54] Lord Chancellor's Department, *Access to Justice. Multi-Party Situations Proposed New Procedures. A Consultation Paper* (Nov 1997) para 40.
[55] para 5.03 above.
[56] Practice Direction—Group Litigation, para 13.

co-ordination, to permit those plaintiffs who come forward to have their cases progressed expeditiously and to permit the defendants to know the number and nature of the claims against them. The number of litigants and the issues raised must be defined, if proper progress is to be maintained. The alternative may be a continuous stop-start situation with progressive redefinition of the fundamental parameters of the numbers, issues, and economic viability.

5.43 Thus, the purpose and effect of the imposition of a cut-off date were explained by Ian Kennedy J in the benzodiazepine litigation:

> My duty, as the judge nominated to monitor the progress of these actions and to hear the interlocutory summons which arise, is to secure the orderly progress of this litigation.
>
> . . . It is only by a substantial number of plaintiffs banding together that their claims have reasonable prospects of success which are a prerequisite to the grant of legal aid.
>
> . . .
>
> A time must come when doing justice between the parties requires that the doors of the scheme be closed so that an ascertained body of claimants becomes defined, lead cases are chosen to illustrate particular points, and that body of cases goes forward towards trial.[57]

5.44 The judge confirmed his approach five years later:

> Any decision about a cut-off date involves a compromise. One seeks to include as many claimants as possible, but on the other hand those who come forward in timely fashion have a right not to have their cases unduly delayed. Defendants are entitled to have the litigation against them conducted with reasonable expedition so that they know their position.[58]

And:

> . . . the proposal that the Scheme can remain open-ended is impractical. Lead cases must be chosen. They must be drawn from a distinct group of claims and reflect all the reasonable permutations within the group . . .[59]

5.45 This approach was approved by the Court of Appeal:

> The judge had been greatly concerned to apply cut-off dates for claimants to be included in the group litigation. Essentially there were two such dates: first, a date by which the claimant was to apply for legal aid and secondly, assuming that legal aid was granted, the date by which the writ in the action was to be served. This was essential to the proper control of the litigation for a number of reasons: first, it was important that there would be enough claims to justify proceeding with the group litigation. Litigation of this kind is extremely expensive and frequently the damages recoverable are only modest. But if there are a large number of such claims, it makes economic sense for all plaintiffs to join together to prosecute, with the assistance as

---

[57] *AB v Wyeth & Brother Limited and Another* [1991] 2 Med LR 341: see ch 22 below.
[58] *AB and Others v John Wyeth & Brother Ltd* [1996] 7 Med LR 267, 273.
[59] *AB and Others v John Wyeth & Brother Ltd* [1996] 7 Med LR 267, 274.

E. Cut-off Dates

a rule of legal aid, an action which individually or in small numbers they could not possibly do. Secondly, it is important to have a sufficient pool of cases from which lead actions can be drawn so that the relevant issues can be determined and the decision in those cases will bind other cases. Thirdly, it is important for the defendants to know the extent of the claims against them. In the course of a number of directions hearings the judge imposed cut-off dates; but on several occasions he was obliged to extend them.[60]

A cut-off date might be set by which time all applications should be made to join the scheme which the judge will administer, or legal aid applications made for claims to be included in existing co-ordinated proceedings.[61] The court might sanction publicity of the group proceedings and of a cut-off date, where there is reason to believe that a significant number of claimants have not yet come forward and that this approach would be the most appropriate method of informing them of the opportunity. Other methods of communication, perhaps more targeted, might be more appropriate in some circumstances.

5.46

In the advanced stages of the Lloyd's litigation, there remained 1,568 Lloyd's names who had not reached settlements with Lloyd's, 148 of whom were claimants in a particular group action in which it had been ordered that there should be trial, in relation to three sample names, of the threshold issue of whether the names had been fraudulently induced to become or remain underwriting members of the Lloyd's market by reason of Lloyd's failure to disclose the nature and extent of the market's liability for asbestos related claims. Cresswell J ordered that individuals who wished to reserve the right to advance such allegations against Lloyd's must provide written notice to Lloyd's solicitors by a particular date (extended for those resident outside Europe). The judge stated that it would then be necessary for each such individual to instruct one of two named legal representatives or apply to the court for directions before a fixed date. The order usefully stated the consequence of failure to comply, namely that the individual would be precluded from advancing such allegations without the court's permission.[62]

5.47

There may, however, be good reasons for *not* imposing a cut-off date, as Mildred has observed:

5.48

> There is no point in having a cut-off date unless it is well publicised; that very publicity will bring forth a cascade of claims including claims by those not in reality certain whether the basic criteria are fulfilled (for example exposure to the product in question), let alone whether they have any prospect of getting home on either liability or causation. The greater the pressure of time on constant resources, the less each claim can be evaluated before the cut-off date passes.
> . . .

---

[60] *AB & Others v John Wyeth & Brother Ltd* [1997] 8 Med LR 57, 61 per Stuart-Smith LJ.
[61] eg *In Re Benzodiazepine Litigation* (Ian Kennedy J, 4 July 1991).
[62] *Jaffray v Society of Lloyd's*, The Times, 4 Nov 1999: see ch 23 below.

Thus, the definitional purpose of the date is likely to have the paradoxical effect of increasing the proportion of the group with weak claims rather than strong claims or indeed with no claims at all.[63]

5.49 Further, the circumstances of a case may not require that a cut-off date need be imposed. For example, no cut-off date was requested by the parties or ordered in the Gravigard,[64] hGH,[65] or respiratory disease[66] litigation. In the former, it did not appear from the circumstances that, given general knowledge of the litigation amongst the potential claimants and given the passage of several years, significant or any further claimants would come forward. In the latter case, there were two problems. The group had not crystallised and might not do so for many years. Further, there was concern to avoid adverse health consequences for those who were not claimants.

5.50 Consideration must be given to the timing of the date selected. Obvious factors will include the nature of the injury or damage, the time when they occurred or when they would be expected to manifest themselves, the extent of media publicity, the potential numbers involved, and the numbers who have so far come forward. Where it is clear that there is sufficient similarity between individual cases, and there is 'a sufficiently representative sample of the whole body of potential claimants that one may be reasonably confident that lead cases can be selected which will effectively dispose of the entirety of [the] litigation', it may well be appropriate to impose an early cut-off date and proceed with an identified group of actions.[67]

5.51 The problem with declaring an early date is what to do with latecomers. Should the case in a second group be stayed or allowed to join the first group, thus delaying the first group? In the benzodiazepine case the judge said:

> The Board argued that if the Scheme were to be closed too soon a second scheme would be inevitable, and that they would be faced again with the great costs of the scientific enquiry. I disagree . . .[68]

5.52 The imposition of an early cut-off date may provoke a rush of poorly investigated claims or, where plaintiffs are funded by legal aid or insured, provoke seizure in the

---

[63] M Mildred, 'Group Actions Present and Future' [1994] JPIL 276. This point was echoed by Lord Woolf in his *Final Report* (1996) 17: IV. II: '. . . the setting of cut-off dates . . . can cause the swamping of valid claims with weak or hopeless claims. Defendants may suffer from the adverse publicity resulting from the number of potential claimants and may have to bear the expenses of the individual investigation of such cases.' A rush of cases was precipitated in the Norplant litigation—see ch 31 below.
[64] See ch 20 below.
[65] See ch 28 below.
[66] See ch 30 below.
[67] *AB v Wyeth & Brother Ltd and Another* [1991] 2 Med LR 341, 344.
[68] *AB v Wyeth & Brother Ltd and Another* [1991] 2 Med LR 341 per Ian Kennedy J: see ch 22 below.

E. Cut-off Dates

administration by those who fund litigation (the Legal Aid Board or insurers). Events other than the issue of a writ may be appropriate triggers:

> An important constraint is that I should not impose a cut-off date which would force the Legal Aid Board to expend public money on a host of protective Writs or face the risk of doing injustice to individual applicants. The debate has revealed this: that it will be best to impose an initial cut-off date by reference to the making of an application for legal aid, not to its granting . . .
>
> But there must be a second date by which successful applications for legal aid must either have fruited as served proceedings or have been abandoned (and private funded cases must also have their proceedings served by that date).[69]

5.53 There is little point in selecting an early date where it is clear that a large rump of latecomers may appear. This promotes neither certainty as to the number of claimants who are within the co-ordinated arrangements, nor the possibility of settlement. Further, significant financial consequences flow from the numbers involved. It is conceivable that groups or sub-groups might not be viable if there are insufficient numbers.

Cut-off dates and limitation

5.54 The interrelation between a cut-off date and the limitation period must be considered. Failure to observe the set date (or dates) will place an individual case outside the managed scheme of litigation. The courts found in the Opren litigation[70] in the late 1980s that it was a mistake to allow too much leniency in permitting claimants to join successive groups by allowing further cut-off dates. In the Opren litigation, claimants came forward over some six years, during which the court imposed cut-off dates which resulted in the creation of four groups. However, the accommodating approach by the court in allowing claimants notionally to join successive groups was in retrospect shown to be flawed and costly. The decision resulted in expensive limitation hearings which showed that the claims of most of those who had been allowed to join the later groups were barred by limitation and it was not appropriate for the court to exercise its discretion in the claimants' favour.[71] Inevitably, the expectations of latecomers who had been allowed into the sub-groups were raised and then dashed. The efficient solution would simply be not to permit latecomers to join co-ordinated arrangements.

5.55 The advantages of plaintiffs joining in a scheme are obvious: they include cost sharing and a reduction in the level of exposure to payment of plaintiffs' or defendants' costs in the event of failure, the availability of increased facilities and

---

[69] *AB and Others v John Wyeth & Brother Ltd* [1996] 7 Med LR 267, 274 per Ian Kennedy J.
[70] See ch 18 below.
[71] *Nash and Others v Eli Lilly & Co and Others* [1991] 2 Med LR 169; *Berger and Others v Eli Lilly & Co and Others* [1992] 3 Med LR 233, reversed in part [1993] 1 WLR 782, CA.

expertise, and the advantages of greater media and negotiating pressure. Failure by a putative plaintiff to meet a date which would permit joining a scheme does not in theory mean that he is prohibited from pursuing his action on an individual basis. However, latecomers might not be granted public funding or insurance and the contemporary approach of the courts increasingly supports striking out such claims and post-cut-off date actions will be looked at even more critically on the question of limitation.[72]

5.56 The imposition of a cut-off date should not be confused with its effects, both in relation to any public funding and in relation to subsequent stays of proceedings by latecomers:

> The effect of my imposing a cut-off date is not to bar a claimant's right: I have no power to do that. The effect of a cut-off date is only that a claimant may be too late to join the group of claimants to which the scheme applies. It may be that there will be a second group to which late claimants may gain admittance, but of necessity the cases within the present group will be heard and determined first, and so at the very lowest a claimant who does not join the present Scheme before the cut-off greatly delays the resolution of this complaint.
>
> But, and this is the danger that I must stress, the Limitation Act can extinguish a claimant's right and bar him altogether . . . time is passing, and it is imperative that potential claimants who would wish to be considered as serious claimants should consult solicitors forthwith. It is impossible, as well as inappropriate, for me in the course of this judgment to give any better guidance than to say that time is not on their side . . . What is absolutely certain is this: it is not possible for potential claimants to wait to see the outcome of the Scheme litigation, and only then, if the Scheme plaintiffs succeed, to advance their own claims. Such inaction would effectively be fatal.[73]

5.57 This approach was approved by the Court of Appeal:

> What the judge did was no more nor less than this. He decided that those Halcion claimants who had not made their applications for legal aid by September 24, 1991, should not be entitled to join the existing group litigation. He did not—indeed he could not—say that they would forever be precluded from presenting their claims . . .
>
> . . .
>
> [However] . . . there is no such principle [that claimants who fall within a Practice Note declaring that a group of claims should be co-ordinated should be permitted to advance their claims without further judicial management] . . .
> The nature of the orders was simply to impose and thereafter maintain time limits for those who wished to participate in the existing group litigation and it is clear that this was well within the judge's powers.[74]

---

[72] *Nash and Others v. Eli Lilly & Co and others*, The Times, 13 Feb 1991; *AB and others v John Wyeth & Brother Limited and others* (Ian Kennedy J, 4 July 1991).
[73] *AB v Wyeth & Brother Limited and Another* [1991] 2 Med LR 341.
[74] *AB & Others v John Wyeth & Brother Limited* [1993] 4 Med LR 1, 6 per Steyn LJ.

6

ADVERTISING

A.	The Issue	6.01
B.	Regulatory Controls	6.05
C.	Judicial Comments	6.10
D.	Advertising under Part 19.III	6.29

A. The Issue

6.01 The history of multi-party actions strongly suggests that some of them have been essentially lawyer led.[1] There should be no objection to solicitors advertising their services to consumers in general terms, for example as specialists in personal injury litigation, although this is prohibited in most other European states. Consumers need information on the availability of legal services and specialisations.[2] The financial risks and cost-benefit balance of risk of some claims, particularly where costs are high or damages or chances of success are low, may mean that the number of claimants involved in a group is crucial to its financial viability. However, product liability multi-party actions have been fuelled by advertisements stating the name of a particular product and implying that compensation would be available. There have been persistent calls for this practice to be prohibited, on the following basis.

6.02 It is argued that the impression can be created in the mind of the public that liability and compensation are foregone conclusions.[3] Advertisements and articles of

---

[1] It has been said that multi-party cases are more prone to being 'constructed by lawyers'. R Smith, *Justice: redressing the balance* (Legal Action Group, 1997) 55. See references to the development and 'exceptionally creative role' of 'disaster lawyers' in C Harlow and R Rawlings, *Pressure Through Law* (1992) ch 3, also cited in C Wells, *Negotiating Tragedy: Law and Disasters* (Sweet & Maxwell, 1995).

[2] Consumers' Association, *Which?* (Apr 1997).

[3] '... dissatisfaction, coupled with ignorance of how to release it, is wide open to shaping by legal advisers and by press reports of how others have acted'. S Hedley, 'Group personal injury litigation and public opinion' (1994) 14 Legal Studies 70.

Chapter 6: Advertising

this type themselves attract further media attention and what the Legal Aid Board, the Law Society, and lawyers[4] have described as a 'bandwagon' can easily be created. Potential claimants and further solicitors can attempt to scramble on board. Reports of increased numbers and the resultant further media interest, presented as 'public concern',[5] have historically increased pressure on the Legal Aid Board and created an impression that even the 'merits' test need not be applied so rigorously at the initial stage, on the basis that there must be something in the cases if there are so many of them. The case histories include a number of cases in which advertising and media attention were instrumental in creating a group of claimants.[6] They also show that many individual cases put forward in group actions after advertising are weak and fail. Accordingly, not only can false expectations be aroused in consumers by this advertising but individuals can be encouraged to externalise blame for problems which are an inevitable part of life and to demand that 'someone should pay'—the compensation culture.[7] The activities of some solicitors have led to complaints of 'ambulance chasing'.[8] No proper mechanism has yet been proposed to curb this phenomenon. The Law Society prefers not to regulate explicitly in this area. It will be obvious that major financial gains stand to be made by those lawyers who carry out generic or co-ordination work on cases which they do not fund personally. Early publicity may clearly assist in achieving a central position on a steering committee or an all-work Community Legal Service contract or a large number of clients.

6.03 Publicity of litigation over safety issues may also lead to a loss of public confidence in public health programmes, with potentially serious health consequences. For example, concern over the safety of vaccines has led to a fall in the number of children being immunised and a rise in the incidence of the disease, with morbidity and death.[9]

---

[4] L Kaye, 'Prepare for group action' (1997) 3 *The Eagle* 21: M Day, The *Independent*, 22 Mar 1997.

[5] For comments on use of MPAs as campaigning devices, possibly as only one facet of a group's activities, see C Harlow and R Rawlings, *Pressure Through Law* (1992) and S Hedley, 'Group personal injury litigation and public opinion' (1994) 14 Legal Studies 70.

[6] See chs 24 and 25.

[7] See F Furedi, *Courting Mistrust: The hidden growth of a culture of litigation in Britain* (Centre for Policy Studies, 1999). See also M Day, 'The Americanisers' (May 1997) Journal of British Insurance Law Association. See further the response to that article, which criticised US plaintiffs' bar lawyers thriving on contingency fees 'by ramping-up the expectations of frequently unmeritorious parties': JRA Wylde (1997) Journal of British Insurance Law Association.

[8] *The Times*, 22 Jan 1996; LS Gaz, 3 Apr 1997. *Legal Business*, Feb 1999, 44. In the USA, it has been said that the modern entrepreneurial lawyer enlists plaintiffs as inventory. MD Green, *Bendectin and Birth Defects* (University of Pennsylvania Press, 1996).

[9] European Federation of Pharmaceutical Industries and Associations, *Response to Green Paper on Liability for Defective Products* (1999) 9.10. For an analysis of the US position, see RL Manning, 'Changing Rules in Tort Law and the Market for Childhood Vaccines' (Apr 1994) Vol XXXVII (1) *The Journal of Law and Economics* 247. It has been commented that English litigation on MMR

B. Regulatory Controls

The larger the number of individual claims which appear to be included in the cohort, the stronger appears the argument that a multi-party action is viable, on the basis that it satisfies the test for public funding. This is an inherent weakness in such a system and it clearly encourages the sort of advertising by solicitors criticised above. It has been said that 'disaster cases require exceptionally sensitive handling; too high expectations may result from campaign statements designed to drum up support or generate pressure for a settlement'.[10] **6.04**

B. Regulatory Controls

Barristers' rules of professional conduct prohibit advertising or discussing ongoing cases. The Solicitors' Practice Rules are drafted in non-specific terms: **6.05**

> Solicitors may at their discretion publicise their practices, or permit other persons to do so . . . provided there is no breach of these Rules and provided there is compliance with a Solicitors' Publicity Code promulgated from time to time by the Council of the Law Society with the concurrence of the Master of the Rolls.[11]

More generally, the Rules require solicitors not to do anything which compromises the good repute of the solicitor or of the solicitors' profession. The Solicitors' Publicity Code states that publicity must not be inaccurate or misleading in any way, or in bad taste. It requires compliance with the British Code of Advertising Practice and the ITC Code of Advertising Standards and Practice. No specific advice is, however, given on advertising for present or past patients wishing to bring personal injury claims.[12] In contrast, the Bar Code of Conduct is interpreted more strictly. It includes a prohibition on any advertising or promotion which indicates or implies any willingness to accept a brief or instructions otherwise than in accordance with the Code. **6.06**

The reference to the British Code of Advertising Practice is instructive. People under treatment for illness or who, for other reasons, take medicines long term have long been recognised as being a vulnerable section of society meriting special attention in relation to advertising. Care must be taken to avoid such people being **6.07**

(measles-mumps-rubella) vaccine is based on a speculative but unproven link and may give rise to serious health issues as publicity gives rise to a fall in confidence in immunisation: AGM Campbell, 'The paediatrician and clinical negligence' in M Powers and N Harris, *Medical Negligence* (3rd edn, 2000).

[10] C Harlow and R Rawlings, *Pressure Through Law* (1992) 135.
[11] Solicitors' Practice Rules 1990 (as amended), made under s 31 of the Solicitors Act 1974 and s 9 of the Administration of Justice Act 1985.
[12] The Advertising Standards Authority ruled in 1996 that advertisements by solicitors of a 'no win no fee' arrangement without further qualification or mention of the cost of insurance was a breach of the British Code of Advertising Practice and hence of the Law Society rules: LS Gaz, 10 July 1996.

misled by advertising activities relating to products or services relevant to their medical condition. Advertising may mislead either by creating unjustified prospects of benefit or underestimating the potential for side effects. All advertising for medicinal products is therefore controlled under European law. Prescription-only medicines may not be advertised to the public at all. There are specific rules relating to advertising of products whose status allows them to be available to the general public without the intervention of a doctor.

6.08 Non-broadcast advertising in the UK is controlled by the British Code of Advertising Practice drawn up by the Committee of Advertising Practice (CAP). There are special rules for health products and therapies. The guiding principle of the Code is that advertising should be responsible and should not mislead by inaccuracy or omission. It must avoid unnecessary disappointment. The Advertising Standards Authority (ASA) is an independent body set up to scrutinise the operation of the Committee of Advertising Practice. The Independent Television Commission (ITC) Code governs advertising on television. It is drawn up under the Broadcasting Act 1990. The ITC Code contains provisions for medicinal advertising which are consistent with the Code of the Proprietary Association of Great Britain (PAGB).

6.09 There is no requirement in this country such as that of the American Bar Association Model Rules of Professional Conduct to keep a copy or recording of every advertisement issued for two years after its last dissemination.

C. Judicial Comments

6.10 There has been widespread condemnation of inappropriate proactive advertising by lawyers of multi-party litigation. The point was raised by the judge in the benzodiazepine litigation at a relatively early stage of the co-ordinated proceedings in 1992:

> I would refer to a fourth factor, an advertisement inserted in a local newspaper by a firm of Liverpool solicitors inviting approaches by persons who had been prescribed Halcion. I am told that the advertisement was within the guidelines issued by the Law Society, and I am content to accept that it was. It stated in prominent type COMPENSATION and HALCION, and in smaller type explained that there was a possibility of an entitlement. I am anxious about the wisdom of such an advertisement in such terms for it is likely to draw in a number of complaints with no case or no substantial case. I have already adverted to the high drop-out rate throughout this litigation.[13]

---

[13] *AB and Others v John Wyeth & Brother Ltd* (Ian Kennedy J, 6 May 1992), quoted in [1993] 4 Med LR 1.

C. Judicial Comments

The Court of Appeal shared the judge's anxiety both in respect of this advertisement[14] and over the effect of poor claims encouraged by media publicity generally: **6.11**

> It is understandable that, with the general tone of the media attention which these drugs had received and the advertisements put out by some solicitors, many people who in reality had no claim were persuaded that they had a chance of receiving an award. On the other hand, no one doubted that there were sets of proceedings in being about which no criticism of apparent triviality or lack of substance could be made: they were not the problem. The insubstantial cases made the assembly of a critical mass the more difficult . . . .[15]

The Law Society's 1995 Working Party accepted that even a group of essentially meritorious claimants will 'inevitably attract "hangers on" whose cases would not stand up to any sort of close examination—individual inquiry is the defendant's best weapon in trying to dispose of them'.[16] Further, the Law Society itself recognised that many multi-party cases, such as those involving some pharmaceutical products and tobacco claims and the Sellafield radiation cases, were 'novel' and it is 'at best doubtful whether [they] should qualify for legal aid on the normal merits test'.[17]   **6.12**

Similarly, the Legal Aid Board has said: 'it may be no coincidence that an action where significant numbers of cases may have been generated by publicity is also an action where a very significant proportion of the plaintiffs were found to have little or no prospect of success . . .' and 'the most common comment from defendants . . . is to say that the main reason for such problems is that neither the Board nor the plaintiffs' solicitors exercise sufficient care in weeding out weak or hopeless cases'.[18]   **6.13**

The Working Party Report expressed grave disquiet about advertising for clients and publicity for group litigation: **6.14**

> Advertisements for clients for pending or anticipated court actions are in reality a mechanism for building up a client list. The existence of a large number of clients may be necessary to demonstrate the cost-effectiveness of any proposed litigation as required by (for example) the Legal Aid Test (15(3)). Advertisements alone are however unlikely adequately to convey the difference between participating in a prospective claim and participating in a settlement action (as seen for example in the Dalkon Shield or breast implant cases).

---

[14] *AB and Others v John Wyeth & Brother Ltd* [1993] 4 Med LR 1, 4 per Balcombe LJ.
[15] *AB and Others v John Wyeth & Brother Ltd* [1996] 7 Med LR 267, 278; see also *AB and Others v John Wyeth & Brother Ltd* [1997] 8 Med LR 57, 73 per Brooke LJ.
[16] Law Society, *Group Actions Made Easier* (1995) para 2.2.2.
[17] Law Society, *A Better Way Forward* (1995) paras 12.12–12.14.
[18] Legal Aid Board, *Issues arising for the Legal Aid Board and the Lord Chancellor's Department from multi-party actions* (1994) paras 2.9 and 2.21.

Chapter 6: Advertising

The judiciary are clearly concerned about advertising. A number of adverse comments have been made by judges about firms of solicitors advertising for victim clients. The fact that those advertisements were arguably within the Law Society's rules suggests that further guidance is needed as to the application and interpretation of the latter.

The Working Party recognised that an advertisement may be the wrong vehicle for conveying to the public the complexities of the litigation process and concluded that there were grounds for distinguishing between 'advertising' during the initial stages of an investigation, and 'publicity' needed for court orders concerning eg cut-off dates once a case has commenced.

The Working Party's view was that advertisements prior to the inception of a group action can only be controlled by the Law Society. However, once a multi-party action has been declared by the court, there is a strong argument that at least the timing and placement of subsequent advertisements should be approved by the Court.[19]

6.15 This recommendation that a court should have power to approve all advertisements after a multi-party action comes before it was not, however, carried through to the draft Rule which the Law Society suggested[20] and has not been explicitly included in Rule 19.III. Instead, what remained in the Law Society's Report was a caution against inappropriate advertising:

Practitioners should bear in mind that the victims of accidents and their relatives, consumers of a product who have been recently advised that it is dangerous, and patients recently alerted to a potential problem with their medical treatment are frequently in an emotional and vulnerable state, especially immediately after the accident or the announcement.

If practitioners become aware (either from instructions already received from one or more clients, or from media coverage of a particular event or announcement) that there may be a large number of potential claimants in a particular context, they may decide it is appropriate to publicise their services generally or to advertise specifically for clients. However, as particular skills and expertise (including organisational skills) are required to take a leading role in group actions which sometimes involve claims that are novel or enter into new and untested areas of law, practitioners should not

- (i) make representations of expertise which are in any way false or misleading (which in any event would be a breach of the Practice Rules)
- (ii) generate a demand for legal services which they may not be able to satisfy either in terms of the volume of work involved or the type of expertise required
- (iii) overstate the potential for success.

---

[19] Law Society, *Group Actions Made Easier* (1995) paras 6.6.7–6.6.10.

[20] ibid, para 6.6.10. However, the Law Society did propose amendment of the Green Form Regulations to require practitioners to seek prior Board authority before undertaking 'pro-active campaigns' involving 'marketing methods which amount to drumming up green form business where there is no evident demand for advice'. Law Society, *A Better Way Forward* (1995) paras 12.32, 12.33.

C. Judicial Comments

6.16 The Working Party's proposals in relation to advertising the potential for a group action invite solicitors contemplating direct advertising for claimants 'to consider carefully the most appropriate timing, form and medium' for such publicity and the need to be 'satisfied that those claims have a reasonable potential for success'.

6.17 The Law Society has not, however, amended its Code nor introduced guidance. It has been slow to criticise advertisements condemned by judges and others and it has been criticised itself for looking primarily to the interests of its members rather than of its members' customers, the public.[21] Yet the Lord Chancellor's Advisory Committee on Legal Education and Conduct concluded that the Law Society's rules fail to give solicitors the clear and principled guidance needed. The Committee believed that the public interest requires an explicit rule prohibiting solicitors from expressing personal opinions during proceedings in which they are involved.[22]

6.18 In contrast, the Law Society did propose amendment of the Green Form Regulations to require practitioners to seek prior Board authority before undertaking 'pro-active campaigns' involving 'marketing methods which amount to drumming up green form business where there is no evident demand for advice'.[23] A pre-approval mechanism such as this operates for over-the-counter medicines under the PAGB Code. Such a scheme would seem entirely appropriate for solicitors' advertising of group actions, certainly where they may involve personal injury or safety issues.

6.19 In litigation in 1996 following the sinking of the *Marchioness* pleasure boat, Clarke J distinguished between functions of a steering committee of solicitors which would be permitted costs reimbursement on taxation and those which would not:

> In my judgment care has to be taken before the costs of publicity are permitted on an inter partes basis. It appears to me that it is one of the natural functions of a steering committee of claimants' solicitors after a disaster of this kind to deal with the media. That function in essence involves the work of protecting claimants from what may be unwelcome pressure from different parts of the media after a catastrophe. Such assistance may well give real comfort to those in distress and can fairly be regarded as satisfying Sir Robert Megarry's tests [in *Re Gibson's Settlement Trusts* [1981] Ch 179, [1981] 1 All ER 233 of 'costs of and incidental to' the proceedings under RSC Order 62 rule 1(4)].

---

[21] GR Hickinbottom, 'Learning from the Benzodiazepine Litigation' (1997) The Litigator 207. The adequacy of the Law Society's guidance and regulation of such advertisements was questioned as being unable to deal with the effects of opening Pandora's box on advertising. *Daily Telegraph*, 3 Sept 1993; LS Gaz, 8 Sept 1993.
[22] New Law Journal (9 May 1997).
[23] Law Society, *A Better Way Forward* (1995) paras 12.32, 12.33.

However, there are other types of publicity which do not, in my judgment, satisfy those tests. Examples of such conduct would be conducting a media campaign in order to put pressure upon the defendants to admit liability or in order to put pressure upon the authorities to commence criminal proceedings. Civil claims should be pursued in the civil courts and not through the media and pressure with a view to criminal proceedings cannot be said to give rise to costs of or incidental to civil proceedings.[24]

6.20 The Association of Personal Injury Lawyers recognised the problem in the mid-1990s and in December 1996, after much discussion, adopted a Code of Conduct which prohibited knowingly making a statement which may give an actual or prospective client false expectations. The Code also prohibited directly contacting a potential client except through advertising which complies with the Code of Practice of the Advertising Standards Authority and with professional rules. This would prohibit cold calling accident victims and sending unsolicited mail but not apparently untargeted media exposure.

6.21 In his Access to Justice Review, Lord Woolf also referred in 1995 to the disadvantages of advertising, which were stated to include 'building up false hopes/expectations, encouraging litigation in weak cases and those cases then weakening stronger ones, and advertising by solicitors who do not have the appropriate experience or expertise'.[25] Lord Woolf asked whether the Law Society's proposals went far enough to overcome these disadvantages. He also asked whether there is sufficient screening at the outset. 'How can screening by the Legal Aid Board or others be made more effective in order to reduce the risk of including large numbers of weak/hopeless claims within the overall group?' In 1996, Lord Woolf spoke publicly of his unease at hearing law firm advertisements breaking into the programming on the radio station Classic FM: 'I can't help thinking there is something wrong with a society where we have to encourage people to sue each other.'[26]

6.22 A 1996 survey of 200 law firms found that 58 per cent held the view that their advertising might create unjustified expectations and that 67 per cent agreed that there was a need for clear and acceptable marketing guidelines so as to prevent undue pressure on potential clients.[27] The Lord Chancellor's 1997 Consultation Paper did not address the advertising issue but merely noted that the judge would discuss with the parties at the certification hearing a preliminary strategy for any publicity which might be necessary, such as to alert existing and potential claimants to the existence of the Group Litigation Order (GLO).

---

[24] *East Coast Aggregates v Parra Pagan and Others; Ross v Owners of the ship 'Bowbelle' and the Owners of the ship 'Marchioness'*, Queen's Bench Division (Admiralty Court), [1997] 1 Lloyd's Rep 196.
[25] Lord Woolf, *Access to Justice: Issues Paper on multi-party actions* (1995). See comments on dashed expectations in the case of 100 women whose claims failed when only twelve were settled: J Millington, 'Breast Cancer Radiation Claims' (Sept 1999) Medical Litigation 7.
[26] LS Gaz, 16 Oct 1996.
[27] Litigation (May 1997) Vol 16, No 6.

C. Judicial Comments

6.23 It has been suggested that the advertisement of cut-off dates should be issued by some independent person, such as the Official Solicitor. As soon as a GLO is made, the co-ordinating judge has an opportunity to control matters. Thus, the first orders made in the tobacco litigation in July 1997 included a ban on any of the parties or their lawyers commenting on the matter to the media, save that a copy of the order could be given out. This order was then overturned by the Court of Appeal.[28] In his judgment, Lord Woolf MR did not consider the detailed history of lawyer-led multi-party litigation and its consequences, nor did he refer to the comments referred to above which he had himself made in his Issues Paper on the problems of advertising in the context of a GLO.

6.24 Lord Woolf MR said:

> The situation is one in which it is easy to fan emotions which will make the task of the courts to resolve the complex issues involved and do justice between the parties more difficult. As Chief Justice Rehnquist pointed out in *Gentile v State Bar of Nevada* [1991] 500 1 US 1030; 111 SCR 2720, extra-judicial statements by legal representatives can be especially unhelpful since they are likely to be received by the media as specially authoritative even if they are inaccurate. The professionalism and the sense of duty of legal advisers who conduct litigation of this nature should mean that the courts are able to rely on the legal advisers to exercise great self-restraint when making comments to the press, while at the same time recognising the need for the media to be properly informed of what is happening in the proceedings. Sensible co-operation and an absence of excessive adversarial behaviour on the part of the legal advisers of all parties is essential if multi-party litigation such as this is to be conducted in the proportionate manner which the interests of their clients and justice require.[29]

6.25 The Court went on to hold that access by the public or media could be given to proceedings in chambers at the discretion of the judge but continued:

> For the majority of lawyers to treat what happens in chambers in any other way [than a confidential manner] would not be in accord with proper professional behaviour . . .
>
> . . . while lawyers will be expected to continue to exercise self restraint as to what is said, any order, judgment or account of the proceedings in chambers can, except in the special cases, be communicated to those who did not attend without any concern that such a communication will create any risk of the imposition of a penalty. If the court wishes to restrain such communication, then it will have to make an appropriate order, when it has the power to do so . . .
>
> [In summary:]
>
> 2. What happens during the proceedings in chambers is not confidential or secret and information about what occurs in chambers and the judgment or order pronounced can, and in the case of any judgment or order should, be made available to the public when requested.
>
> . . .

---

[28] *Hodgson v Imperial Tobacco* Ltd [1998] 41 BMLR 1.
[29] ibid.

4. To disclose what occurs in chambers does not constitute a breach of confidence or amount to contempt as long as any comment which is made does not substantially prejudice the administration of justice.

6.26 However, Wright J subsequently gave his views on both the facts and consequences of lawyer-led litigation in the dispositive judgment on the tobacco litigation. He concluded:

> . . . it is plain that the entirety of the Plaintiffs' cases are contentious to a degree . . . it must be acknowledged that the Plaintiffs' chances of establishing their primary case is to a degree speculative . . . Taking a broad view, it seems to me to be plainly legitimate to say that the prospects of success in this litigation on behalf of any Plaintiff is by no means self-evident . . .
>
> No plaintiff suggests that his delay until 1996 was because he was waiting for some firm of Solicitors to undertake to conduct the action on the basis of a CFA. The reality, it is plain, in my judgment, is that the advertised willingness of those solicitors to conduct the litigation upon that basis was the stimulus that ultimately led all these eight Plaintiffs to instruct Messrs Leigh Day to bring proceedings on their behalf.
>
> . . . It is a matter of some concern to me that I have been driven to the conclusion that the reasons pleaded in the various Statements of Claim are the product of the ingenuity of the Plaintiffs' legal advisers, and do not represent either the reality, or the instructions given by each individual Plaintiff. I can only say that this is to be deprecated.
>
> . . .
>
> [in relation to a particular case, the claimant] himself simply left everything in the hands of the lawyers, and the impression that I have in his case is similar to that which I have in all the others, namely that in each case the litigation is lawyer-driven.[30]

6.27 In the MMR litigation, the parties agreed and the court approved a press statement after the first management conference which merely stated that preliminary directions had been ordered but that the hearing was held in private and the parties were therefore unable to comment on the proceedings, although the court had given permission for release of copies of the directions order once the original had been sealed.[31]

6.28 Publicity of litigation involving a product may affect the ultimate availability of that product. After the collapse of the Norplant litigation in February 1999, the manufacturer issued a press statement quoting its 'angry reaction' that 'nearly 4 years of adverse publicity associated with the action had significantly damaged the reputation of Norplant as a viable contraceptive option, and that the proceedings

---

[30] *Hodgson & Others v Imperial Tobacco Ltd & Others*, Queen's Bench Division (Transcript), 9 Feb 1999.
[31] *Paul Sayers (and Others) v SmithKline Beecham PLC and others* (Master Ungley, 3 Sept 1999).

had wasted taxpayers' money in the form of legal aid'.[32] Two months later, the company withdrew the product from the market and 'angrily denounced' the long-running 'trial by media', saying: 'In effect, a major therapeutic advance, fully approved by the UK Medicines Control Agency, and widely welcomed by doctors and users has been killed off for non-medical reasons by an "unholy alliance" of bureaucrats, lawyers and the media.'[33]

D. Advertising under Part 19.III

6.29 Rule 19.11(3)(c) empowers the court that makes a GLO to include in it directions for publicising the GLO.[34] Under the heading of 'publicising the GLO', the Practice Direction specifies[35] that a copy of the GLO should be supplied:

(1) to the Law Society, 113 Chancery Lane, London WC2A 1PL; and
(2) to the Senior Master, Queen's Bench Division, Royal Courts of Justice, Strand, London WC2A 2LL.

6.30 It is clear that the court has power to give general directions applicable to all the claims within the scope of the GLO, which are wide enough to control publicity about such cases and, in an appropriate case, restrict those comments by parties or lawyers which are strongly promotional in character. The difficulties which have been highlighted above have generally arisen in cases where there has been a lengthy 'phoney war' between the parties before the court became involved in managing the case. The court's power under the Civil Procedure Rules 1998 to make a GLO at an early stage may provide a mechanism to influence the issue of lawyer-led cases in the crucial early stages.

---

[32] Hoechst Marion Roussel press release (8 Feb 1999).
[33] Hoechst Marion Roussel press release (30 Apr 1999). See further VA Entwistle, IS Watt and F Johnson, 'The case of Norplant as an example of health technology' (6 May 2000) *The Lancet* 1633.
[34] After judicial criticism of tobacco litigation as lawyer driven in 1999, it was argued that it was acceptable to inform individuals about their rights to claim: M Mullally, 'Action goes up in smoke' (4 Mar 1999) Legal Week. Yet the judge's fundamental objection had been that the particular claims involved were in fact highly speculative: *Hodgson & Others v Imperial Tobacco & Others*, Queen's Bench Division (Transcript) 9 Feb 1999. Whilst the loss of costs (reportedly £2.5 million) was to the claimants' solicitors and not public funds in this case, there was a potential exposure of the clients to the risk of bankruptcy and a loss to defendants of unrecovered costs, in this case reportedly amounting to some £14 million.
[35] Practice Direction—Group Litigation, para 11.

7

FURTHER MANAGEMENT ISSUES

A. Leaving the Group	7.01
B. Documentary Evidence	7.02
C. Expert Evidence	7.08
D. Expert Evidence in Personal Injury Claims: Medical Report Attributing Individual Injury to the Product or Negligent Act	7.11
E. Settlement of Proceedings	7.20
F. Court may Make Aggregate Award	7.22
G. Striking Out	7.23

A. Leaving the Group

7.01 Rule 19.14 provides that a party to a claim entered on the group register may apply to the management court to be removed from the register. If the management court orders the claim to be removed from the register it may give directions about the future management of the claim. Additionally, where the court has decided that the criteria for entry on the register have not been met in a particular claim (generally on referral from the manager of the register), it may order that the claim leave the Group Litigation Order (GLO) arrangements. Where the court orders a claim to leave the Group, it may give further directions in that claim which may involve a continuing liability for the costs of the Group.

B. Documentary Evidence

7.02 The Civil Procedure Rules 1998 (CPR) have introduced a new approach to disclosure of documentary evidence. CPR Part 31 has introduced a more limited and proportionate approach than the previous comprehensive approach. The new approach involves a reasonable search for documents and the giving of standard disclosure (as defined in the Rules).[1] Disclosure during the action may also be influenced by the new pre-action disclosure obligations arising under the protocol approach.

7.03 There had been a trend towards limiting the extent of disclosure in all multi-party actions for some years before the CPR. This was because the extent of documentation which would be relevant under the old rules was frequently enormous and only a limited quantity of documentation was usually in fact relevant to the issues.[2] In the succession of pharmaceutical product liability actions, for example, allegations typically related to the entirety of the design, research, regulatory, manufacturing, marketing, and post-marketing documentation on a product over several decades. The extent of the discoverable documentation usually covered tens of millions of documents and it cost millions of pounds to produce it. The same applied to multiple actions in the Lloyd's litigation, where the parties sensibly agreed disclosure in specimen cases.[3] The *Guide for use in Group Actions* recognised that: 'Discovery by defendants will often have to be limited to prevent its sheer volume being oppressive to plaintiffs and defendants alike.'[4] Not surprisingly, the courts did increasingly accept the need to limit discovery in multi-party actions to certain categories of documents. An order limiting discovery could be made where the court was satisfied that discovery was not necessary, or not necessary at that stage of the action, either for disposing fairly of the action or for saving costs.[5] The *Guide* accepted that, in some situations:

> it may be appropriate to order that a very general listing of categories be made in the first instance, leaving it to the inspecting party to call for supporting documents in sample sub-areas in the manner of an auditor calling for supporting invoices until satisfied either that no further investigation is required or that an order for much wider detailed investigation should be applied for.

7.04 Whilst this approach may be sensible in theory, it might not significantly have reduced the amount of preparatory work by defendants since the underlying documentation may have had to be assembled and considered by the defendants' solicitors before disclosure of the outline category is made so as to avoid embarrassment either over the subject matter or over the speed with which disclosure might be ordered.

7.05 The approach under the CPR is for the parties to discuss the issues in the case and the documents which will be relevant for the court to see in order to determine the issues in dispute. Documentation on undisputed issues may well not be necessary.

---

[1] CPR, Rule 31.5, 31.7.
[2] See D Mackie, 'Discovery in Commercial Litigation' in AAS Zuckerman and R Cranston (eds), *Reform of Civil Procedure* (1995). See also *Dolling-Baker v Merritt* [1990] 1 WLR 1205.
[3] See ch 23.
[4] Supreme Court Procedure Committee, *Guide for use in Group Actions* (1991) ch 6.
[5] RSC Ord 24, r 2(5) and (6); *Dolling-Baker v Merritt* [1990] 1 WLR 1205.

B: *Documentary Evidence*

The problem in a multi-party action is that it may not be clear for some time what the allegations are, what issues are disputed, what evidence might be relevant, and what issues (and therefore evidence) may be required at what stage in the proceedings. A preliminary issue may be heard first (perhaps two years after a multi-party action starts) and it may subsequently not be necessary to have any further evidence, or to have only evidence on particular issues. Should the parties meanwhile carry out exhaustive and expensive disclosure exercises on the basis that this might be needed and, if it is, that it would delay the proceedings for it to be carried out subsequently? In the Myodil litigation, discovery was ordered to be dealt with in one stage after all the issues were identified in the pleadings and not on any rolling basis.[6] In many of the other multi-party actions, an extensive exercise was put in train at an early stage and disclosure took place on a rolling basis, perhaps while other issues were dealt with, so that there would be no overall delay. The conclusion is that the parties and the court should address both the extent and timing of disclosure at an early stage, in the light of the particular circumstances of the case. The Law Society's 1995 Report concluded that the court should have power to give specific directions for early discovery against any party at any stage on any specific question or issue, where this will assist in the fair disposal of the action.[7]

The Law Society's 1995 Report suggested that discovery should be provided at an early stage only by defendants. This arguably rather illogical and biased approach has been overtaken by the CPR. Both claimants and defendants typically hold information relevant to liability. Documents from both parties are required, both as evidence in the action and for furthering the possibility of settlement. The Law Society also suggested that discovery by plaintiffs in individual cases should only be given in those cases put forward or selected as lead cases.[8] For the reasons discussed above in chapter 2 and relating to verification,[9] this may not assist in settling or disposing of cases. Furthermore, the history of the succession of leading cases is that they contain large numbers of claims which need to be weeded out. This process should obviously take place as early as possible.

7.06

Rule 19.12(4) provides that, unless the court orders otherwise, disclosure of any document relating to the GLO issues by a party to a claim on the group register is disclosure of that document to all parties to claims:

7.07

(a) on the group register; and
(b) which are subsequently entered on the group register.

---

[6] See *Chrzanowska v Glaxo Laboratories Limited* (Transcript: Sellers) Queen's Bench Division, The Times, 16 Mar 1990 (Steyn J, 2 Mar 1990) and ch 21 below.
[7] The Law Society, *Group Actions Made Easier* (1995) para 6.15.2.
[8] ibid, para 6.15.4.
[9] paras 4.17 *et seq* above.

C. Expert Evidence

7.08 The CPR provides that expert evidence shall be restricted to that which is reasonably required to resolve the proceedings.[10] The court has power to direct that evidence on a particular issue is to be given by one expert only.[11] This may not, however, be appropriate in cases as complex as multi-party litigation usually is.

7.09 In the MMR & MR Vaccines litigation, the claimants accepted that there was no epidemiological evidence to support the alleged association between use of the vaccines and a number of identified conditions, notably autism and inflammatory bowel disorder. They sought an order that an epidemiologist be appointed to conduct new research which, they hoped, would support the allegation. The application was that the Court should appoint the epidemiologist as a 'joint expert', but that, in fact, the research be funded by the defendants alone. The Court rejected the application, commenting that it was not the function of the Court to order new research, even if that research might assist one party in proving or disproving their case: '[The claimants] are not entitled to require the other party to indulge in enormously expensive original research in order to see whether or not they have a case.'[12]

7.10 The importance of efficient organisation by all parties right from the outset was stressed in the *Guide*. It recommended consideration be given to computerised litigation support systems and keeping at least 'core documents' on computer storage systems, while recognising that loading documents onto a computer is expensive and time-consuming.

D. Expert Evidence in Personal Injury Claims: Medical Report Attributing Individual Injury to the Product or Negligent Act

7.11 In a personal injury claim where the claimant is relying on the evidence of a medical practitioner, the claimant must attach to or serve with his particulars of claim a report from a medical practitioner about the personal injuries which he alleges in this claim.[13]

7.12 Prior to the introduction of the CPR on 26 April 1999, a statement of claim in a personal injury action in the High Court had to be accompanied by a medical ex-

---

[10] CPR, Part 35.1.
[11] CPR, Part 35.7.
[12] *Paul Sayers (and Others) v SmithKline Beecham Plc and Others* (Master Ungley, 3 Sept 1999).
[13] Practice Direction—Statements of Case, para 4.3. For similar reasons, a schedule of details of any past and future expenses and losses claimed must also be served. See now Practice Direction—Statements of Case, para 4.2.

D. Expert Evidence: Personal Injury Claims

pert's report 'substantiating all the personal injuries alleged in the statement of claim which the plaintiff proposes to adduce in evidence as part of his case at the trial'.[14] It has been standard practice for copies of medical records in the possession of the plaintiff and a consent to inspect the originals of medical records to be made available as early as possible.[15]

It has been good practice for medical reports to state the full medical history upon which the opinion is given. The situation arose in the benzodiazepine litigation that medical reports were written by doctors who relied upon a statement of the plaintiff's medical history written by the plaintiff or his solicitors and such document may have contained other privileged material:

7.13

> What is apparently needed in this situation is a test which, first of all, is clear; which, secondly, can be complied with economically and expeditiously; and, above all, which will assist in achieving justice in this scale of litigation... What is needed, in my judgment, is an approach which reconciles the requirements of the defendant to know the medical history relied upon by the plaintiff's doctor and the source of that history so that the defendants are able to make an assessment of its validity, and the legitimate interests of the plaintiff to preserve his legal professional privilege. It is also necessary to take into account the fact that in due course the defendants' doctors will have the opportunity to examine the plaintiffs, and they can take an independent history and explore matters which the plaintiffs' doctors may not have considered... In my judgment, the principle which should apply and should be followed in cases of this sort is as follows. On a request made by the defendants on legal and medical advice each plaintiff should, in so far as this has not already been done, provide the details of the full relevant medical history of the plaintiff relied on by the plaintiff's doctor for the purpose of preparing the report served with the statement of claim, in so far as that history is derived from a written document supplied to that doctor which has not already been disclosed. In addition, the identity and the author of that written document and its date should be disclosed. The identification of the document should not be treated as a waiver of any privilege that the plaintiff has in respect of that document.[16]

Also:

> The purpose of rule 12(1A) is to ensure that a plaintiff has proper medical evidence before beginning an action for personal injuries. A defendant can at once decide whether or not he needs to obtain medical evidence of his own, so contributing to the early settlement or speedy trial of the claim.[17]

It was held that a medical report must *verify* the plaintiff's complaints and *attribute* them to the defendant:

7.14

---

[14] RSC Ord 18, r 12(1A).
[15] These aspects could be requested under the spirit of the Pre-Action Protocol for Personal Injury Claims.
[16] *B v John Wyeth & Brother Ltd* [1992] 1 WLR 168, 172, 173 per Woolf LJ.
[17] *L & W v John Wyeth & Brother Limited* (Ian Kennedy J, 6 May 1992).

> By definition a condition is not an injury unless its presence is attributable[18] to the accident. ... The onus is on the plaintiff.
>
> All the personal injuries alleged are required to be substantiated. ...What is required is a report which substantiates all the injuries with sufficient particularity that one is not left in any doubt what is and what is not attributed to the accident or other event.[19]

7.15 A report does not substantiate an injury:

> unless it both verified it and attributed it to the matters of which complaint was being made. In the case of complaints which are not organic, and so not observable by the reporting doctor, verification and attribution for practical purposes elide. While it is not for the doctor to make the final decision whether the plaintiff's complaints are accurate, he must decide whether that account, if accepted, is consistent with taking the drug and can, in the circumstances of the case, fairly be attributed to the drug.
>
> ... the supporting doctor must identify those complaints which he will support as being caused by the breaches of duty, thus as *injuries*.[20]

7.16 In particular circumstances, there may be unavoidable limitations on the extent of a medical report. For example, in a claim involving allegations of contamination of the public water supply in the Oxford and Swindon area with the organism cryptosporidium, the Court of Appeal recognised that:

> ... in the absence of pathological tests identifying the specific organism responsible for the symptoms, the most any medical report could say is that, firstly, the plaintiff complained to the doctor of symptoms on the relevant date which were compatible with gastro-enteritis from a cause not pathologically determined. Secondly, that the symptoms could be caused by cryptosporidium and many other organisms. Thirdly, that a definitive diagnosis could only be circumstantial taking into account a possible source, the timing of the infection, and, I would add, presumably the number of patients complaining of similar symptoms. If the number of patients exceeded those who might in normal circumstances be expected to present to their general practitioners with symptoms it would suggest the possibility of a more widespread cause than contaminated food in a particular household. It would not of course mean that it was due to cryptosporidium, for it might be due to another organism in the water which was incapable of detection. Nevertheless [the medical expert's] opinion is important, for it indicates what it is reasonable to expect to be contained in a medical report to substantiate or support the plaintiffs' claims in this case.[21]

7.17 In this context, the Court of Appeal accepted that the meaning of the requirement in the then Order 18, rule 12(1C) for the medical report to substantiate the injuries was:

---

[18] It is suggested that this should in practice mean 'attributed' not 'attributable'.
[19] *L & W v John Wyeth & Brother Limited* (Ian Kennedy J, 6 May 1992).
[20] *Nur v John Wyeth & Brother Limited* [1996] 7 Med LR 300, 302 per Ian Kennedy J.
[21] *Lort v Thames Water Utilities Limited* (CA, 29 Jan 1993), per Beldam LJ. See also *Prince v Palmer and others* (District Judge Diamond, 22 June 1993).

E. Settlement of Proceedings

In this context . . . used simply in the sense of a report from a medical practitioner confirming that the plaintiff was at the material time suffering from the injury or symptoms complained of in the statement of claim. On occasions the report may contain an opinion of the medical cause. In the case of injury presenting with physical signs a doctor can confirm the presence of such signs. Often a doctor can only corroborate the plaintiff to the extent that he saw him on the relevant occasion, that he was complaining of symptoms and that the symptoms of which he was told, or the signs which he observed, were, in the opinion of the doctor, compatible with a condition with a medical description, for example, of dermatitis. Merely because a particular label is put upon the condition and because the doctor is unable to relate it to a particular organism cannot mean that the medical report does not comply with the rules, particularly where, as here, there is expert evidence that a medical report could not be expected to go further in the absence of pathological tests. It may be, and it often is, necessary for evidence from experts in other disciplines—for example, epidemiology, bacteriology, embryology—to explain to the court, on the balance of probabilities, the medical causation for the symptoms of which the plaintiff complains. In the present case there will no doubt be evidence which either does or does not confirm the presence in the water supply, at the relevant time, of cryptosporidium. Given that evidence, the prevalence of complaints in the area of similar symptoms and the other circumstantial evidence, it will be for the judge at trial to say whether in the case of any given plaintiff he is satisfied that on the balance of probability the symptoms of which he complains, though compatible with an origin from other organisms, was in fact caused by cryptosporidium. It is to be noted that the parties at the hearing of the generic issue wish to call some five experts each in various disciplines and they are required to give each other notice of the disciplines concerned. This is a case in which the origin of the condition from which the plaintiffs allege they have suffered does not depend solely on medical opinion.[22]

7.18 The court may, in the exercise of its discretion, strike out a claim in which the medical report does not substantiate the injury. It may also strike out a claim in which a medical report substantiating the injury has not been served by a cut-off date.[23]

7.19 In a multi-party action, it would be good practice for the issues on which medical opinion is required to be established before inadequate reports have been served. It may be necessary for the legal, medical, and technical experts to discuss this and agree criteria in advance. It may also be wise for the court to be involved.

E. Settlement of Proceedings

7.20 There is obviously no general impediment to a claimant and defendant agreeing to settle a case: this is an overriding objective of the CPR. As the 1999 Consultation

---

[22] ibid.
[23] *Nur v John Wyeth & Brother Limited* [1996] 7 Med LR 300, 302 per Ian Kennedy J; leave for the plaintiff to appeal to the Court of Appeal was refused (Rose LJ, 28 July 1993).

Paper noted, there are many circumstances where settlement of claims that are not involved as test claims may not only be appropriate, but also beneficial to efficient management and in keeping with the spirit of the Civil Procedure Rules 1998. However, in the context of a multi-party action, the concern was expressed that the court should control the ability of plaintiffs to leave the group where they are lead or test cases, in order not to delay the resolution of issues important for those remaining. One fear was that defendants might 'pick off' lead cases so as to destabilise the litigation.[24]

7.21 A draft of Rule 19.III adopted the approach that, where the court directs that a claim or claims are to stand as test claims, it will normally be appropriate for the court to direct that those claims may not be settled or compromised without the court's permission. The justification given for this in the 1999 Consultation Paper was that test claims are conducted for the benefit of all the parties in the same class within the group. The Lord Chancellor's Department changed its mind on the proposal that any settlement in a GLO should be approved by the court, since it was concerned that such a rule may be counter-productive to the efficient management of a particular GLO. Rule 19.15 clearly envisages that a test claim may be settled, since it provides that where a test claim is settled the management court may order that another claim on the group register be substituted as the test claim.

F. Court may Make Aggregate Award

7.22 In some GLOs, defendants have made global offers of settlement, of a total sum which they and/or insurers are prepared to offer, but without specifying how much is offered to each individual claimant.[25] If claimants wish to accept the offer, it is up to them to devise a mechanism to agree how the aggregate sum is to be distributed amongst them. This approach was provided for in a draft of the Practice Direction and was expressed to apply, provided that the parties agree, where the court makes a finding of liability but it is still possible for the court to conclude quantum. In these circumstances, it may be advisable for the court to give directions on a mechanism or scheme to decide on distribution.

G. Striking Out

7.23 In the context of a GLO, the court may consider the extent to which the proceedings are oppressive, vexatious, and unjust as far as defendants and the court are concerned. It may consider the question of the viability of the entire action or certain claims within it on a cost-benefit basis.

---

[24] The Law Society, *Group Actions Made Easier* (1995) para 6.11.3.
[25] An example was the *X Co* case: see ch 25 below.

G. Striking Out

In the benzodiazepine litigation, a succession of claims were struck out as being an abuse of the process of the court, frivolous, vexatious, and otherwise bound to fail, and for inordinate and inexcusable delay: **7.24**

(a) Claims against GP prescribers, which constituted 2.8 per cent of the total claims in the group claims;[26]
(b) Each case which remained unaudited unless the fact of positive audit had been notified to the defendants by a certain date;[27]
(c) Cases that failed to comply with the extended 'window' period for serving proceedings;[28]
(d) Failure to serve any or all of the documents required;[29]
(e) Stayed cases where plaintiffs had not given authority to approach their general practitioners;[30]

> group litigation does not involve plaintiffs having advantages but no disadvantages ... It is an inevitable concomitant of proceeding by group action that those cases which fail to meet the controls are struck out. It is not relevant to say that less stringent standards apply in unitary actions, and that the failing group litigant is being harshly treated.
>
> ...
>
> Group actions provide advantages for plaintiffs who are by that means enabled to pursue claims which otherwise they could not. But a course which the court permits the better to do justice between the primary parties must not be allowed to do injustice to others. There are few advantages which do not bring concomitant restrictions on one's actions. The restriction in this instance has to be that claims against secondary parties may have to be abandoned where they can only be pursued at the cost of an injustice.[31]

(f) Finally, the remaining non-legally aided plaintiffs, thereby disposing of the entire action.[32]

The grounds on which the court might exercise its power to strike out claims within a group action were extensively explored in judgments at first instance and confirmed by the Court of Appeal. These deserve to be set out verbatim. In approving the striking out of the claims against the general practitioners in the benzodiazepine litigation, the Court of Appeal approved the following considerations taken into account by the Judge: **7.25**

---

[26] *Nur v John Wyeth & Brother Limited* [1996] 7 Med LR 300; affirmed *AB & Others v John Wyeth & Brother Limited* [1994] 5 Med LR 149, CA.
[27] *A B & Others v John Wyeth & Brother Limited* (Ian Kennedy J, 20 Oct 1993).
[28] *A B & Others v John Wyeth & Brother Limited* (Ian Kennedy J, 20 Oct 1993).
[29] *A B & Others v John Wyeth & Brother Limited* (Ian Kennedy J, 20 Oct 1993).
[30] ibid.
[31] *Nur v John Wyeth & Brother Limited* [1996] 7 Med LR 300, 305 and 308.
[32] *AB and Others v John Wyeth & Brother Limited* [1996] 7 Med LR 267; affirmed in *AB and Others v John Wyeth and Brother Limited* [1997] 8 Med LR 57, CA.

Chapter 7: Further Management Issues

1. they cannot properly defend the claims against them without being present at the generic trial;
2. the claims made against them could not reasonably have been brought if the primary claims were not being advanced;
3. the cost to the Health Authorities of taking as limited a part in the generic trial as they can fairly take would bear no sensible relationship to any benefit that the plaintiffs might hope to obtain from their inclusion;
4. the proposal that these claims should stand over for perhaps another four years would involve a delay which is bound to cause injustice in that it will then be necessary to examine the details of presentations, impressions, diagnosis and treatments 15 or more years in the past, and when the passage of time will involve that more prescribers are dead and more still disabled in their recollection.

    This conclusion was based upon evidence from the solicitors for the general practitioners, which the judge broadly accepted, to this effect: A large number of the prescribers were either dead or retired; in about half the cases the treatment criticised was given before 1980; about a quarter between 1980 and 1985 and the remaining quarter after 1985. In these circumstances, any recollection of why the drug was prescribed, in the particular dose, or for the period in question, why the drug may have been changed and what advice was given to the patient, is likely to be dim or non-existent; there are also problems with lost, incomplete or indecipherable notes;

5. [In the context that the vast majority of the plaintiffs were legally aided, a cost-benefit analysis was clearly unfavourable.] Since the hypothesis upon which the claims against the prescribers [were] to be pursued [was] that the actions will have failed against the manufacturers any damages that legally aided plaintiffs might recover against the prescribers and health authorities would be consumed by the legal aid charges for the costs of the unsuccessful claims against the manufacturers. We would moreover add, although the judge did not advert to this, that the successful manufacturers, who will presumably have been granted an order for costs against the plaintiffs not to be enforced without leave of the court, might well apply to the court for such leave, if a sum of money was available in their hands as a result of actions against the prescribers. The judge therefore concluded that there would be no benefit to the plaintiffs in pursuing the litigation against the prescribers.

    As against this the costs already incurred and likely to be incurred in the future by the prescribers, which will be irrecoverable win or lose, the judge described as astronomical;

6. [It was proposed that generic trials against the manufacturers should continue whilst the claims against the practitioners were stayed. It was accepted that those trials would include issues which affected the prescribers. If the prescribers took no part in the generic trials, they could have no input on important questions. They would also not be bound by the findings of the judge in relation to them, thereby defeating the whole object of the generic trials, which was to decide such issues in a manner that would be binding on interested parties.]

...

The classic statement of the law in relation to striking out for abuse of process is to be found in the speech of Lord Diplock in *Hunter v Chief Constable of West Midlands Police* [1982] AC 529. At p 536 he said:

G. Striking Out

'My Lords, this is a case about abuse of the process of the High Court. It concerns the inherent power which any court of justice must possess to prevent misuse of its procedure in a way which, although not inconsistent with the literal application of its procedural rules, would nevertheless be manifestly unfair to a party to litigation before it, or would otherwise bring the administration of justice into disrepute amongst right-thinking people. The circumstances in which abuse of process can arise are very varied; those which give rise to the instant appeal must surely be unique. It would, in my view, be most unwise if this House were to use this occasion to say anything that might be taken as limiting to fixed categories the kinds of circumstances in which the court has a duty (I disavow the word discretion) to exercise this salutary power.'

In *Ashmore v British Coal Corporation* [1990] 2 QB 338 the appellant's counsel argued that, because she was not estopped under the principle of *res judicata*, her claim could not be struck out as an abuse of the process, a somewhat similar submission to that advanced by Mr Scrivener that because the plaintiffs' claims are viable, they cannot be prevented from bringing them. This court rejected the submission. At p 348B Stuart-Smith LJ said:

'... A litigant has a right to have his claim litigated, provided it is not frivolous, vexatious or an abuse of the process. What may constitute such conduct must depend on all the circumstances of the case; the categories are not closed and considerations of public policy and the interests of justice may be very material ...'

The court is concerned to see that its proceedings are not used in a way that is oppressive and vexatious to the other party or which involves serious injustice to him. If the court is satisfied that the proceedings do have that effect, it has power to strike out on the grounds that they are vexatious and an abuse of process.

Nor do we accept Mr Scrivener's analysis that the plaintiff must be guilty of unreasonable or blameworthy conduct before his action is struck out. In none of the cases is this the test. Quite plainly, unreasonable or blameworthy conduct in the course of litigation is not by itself sufficient to constitute an action as an abuse of process ... It is the effect on the courts themselves and the defendant that is important.

...

In most cases it will be quite inappropriate for the court to enter upon the sort of cost benefit analysis which the judge undertook here. The court cannot weigh the plaintiff's prospect of receiving £1,000 against the defendants' costs of £10,000 which may be irrecoverable; that can only be done at the trial; alternatively it is a matter for the commercial judgment of the defendant whether he attempts to reach a settlement with the plaintiff: and in so doing he has to take into account as part of the equation that the plaintiff is legally aided or impecunious. But this case is quite different. One can see at a glance that the prescriber defendants will be put to astronomical expense in defending these contingent claims. And to what end? If the plaintiffs stood to obtain a substantial benefit, the position might well be different. But here the benefit is at best extremely modest, and in all probability nothing. That involves great injustice to the defendants. It is no answer that there are public authorities or insurance associations that are footing the bill. The National Health Service has better things to spend its money on than lawyers' fees and the cost of medical insurance is a matter of public concern.[33]

---

[33] *AB & Others v John Wyeth and Another* [1994] 5 Med LR 149 per Stuart-Smith LJ.

7.26 The Court of Appeal also held that the Judge would have been entitled to take into account the following issues:

(a) A limitation defence existed in over 90% of the cases;
(b) Very considerable problems on causation. These involved distinguishing between the effects of the drug and the underlying condition for which it was prescribed and other issues, including the difficult question of balancing the benefit of the drug against the undesirable consequences of taking it.[34]

7.27 The court has power to strike out a case as an abuse of process in the context of the fate of the group to which it belongs:

> It is capable of amounting to an abuse of process that a case only began as part of co-ordinated litigation which has since broken down. Furthermore, delay, whether during the period of co-ordination or since it was lost, is a factor in assessing abuse of process.[35]

7.28 In exercising this power, it is relevant to consider the impact on the defendants of prolonging litigation:

> I am not satisfied that Wyeth can show that they have suffered direct economic loss as a result of the continuance of this litigation . . . But I am satisfied that the defendants do suffer prejudice by its continuance in the sense spoken of by Lord Denning MR in *Biss v Lambeth Health Authority* [1978] 1 WLR 382 at p 389G:
>
>> 'There comes a time when it is entitled to have some peace of mind and to regard the incident as closed.'

7.29 In considering whether to strike out for abuse of process, the court is entitled to take into account the fact that legal aid has been withdrawn and that there is no effective means of progressing the actions:

> The plain fact is . . . that without funding there was no prospect whatever of this case even being brought to trial, let alone to a successful outcome for the plaintiffs . . . once the judge has reached this conclusion, coupled with the conclusion that there was no prospect of funding, he had no alternative but to strike the action out.
> . . .
> Once it is apparent to the judge that the case cannot be brought to trial, it is his duty not to prolong the agony any longer. He must put a stop to further needless expense and strike the action out . . . in substance this is what the judge did when he adjourned the hearing on several occasions to enable the plaintiffs to put their house in order. It was implicit in his action that if they did not, the proceedings would be struck out.[36]

7.30 The Judge's reasons for striking out the non-legally aided plaintiffs, bringing to an end the benzodiazepine litigation, were:

---

[34] *AB & Others v John Wyeth and Another* [1994] 5 Med LR 149 per Stuart-Smith LJ.
[35] *AB and Others v John Wyeth & Brother Ltd* [1996] 7 Med LR 267, 290.
[36] *AB and Others v John Wyeth & Brother Ltd* [1997] 8 Med LR 57, 66, 67 per Stuart-Smith LJ.

G. Striking Out

Firstly, I take account of the conclusion of the Legal Aid Board upon the advice of experienced counsel that neither the claims against Wyeth nor those against Roche met the reasonableness test to justify the Board's further support. Nothing has been put before me to persuade me that there was any error of substance on the part of counsel advising the Board that would have invalidated the conclusion. Counsel had to advise in the light of the decisions and rulings in that action. Counsel's advice is no more than one factor that I have to consider.

Secondly, since this is group litigation I am to make my own assessment of its viability, as decided by the Court of Appeal in *AB v John Wyeth* (1994) *supra*. The costs to the defendants of defending these claims will be enormous, and the costs of the generic work will become increasingly disproportionate as numbers fall. The amounts that individuals can hope to recover are in litigation terms modest indeed, and are certain to be further reduced by irrecoverable costs, in the case of those that have entered conditional fee arrangements by the success fee, and where the person was legally aided any recovery will be subject to the Legal Aid Board's charge. There is a serious issue on primary liability, and even with that decided in the plaintiffs' favour there will in many cases be limitation problems, and the other difficulties which I have already discussed in terms of state before ingestion, state under treatment, and the attribution of demonstrated complaints between the benzodiazepines and intercurrent causes and ingestions.

Thirdly, there remain the defects in the amended master statements of claim, reflecting as they do that three years after the master statements of claim were first served the plaintiffs' side had not taken a final position on the nature of the adverse effects of ingestion. I refer here to the broad nature of the effects, and not to that of which particular symptoms pleaded individually are attributable to either drug. The amendments now proposed to the amended master statement of claim, if they were to be allowed, and I have not been asked to rule on that, would extend the enquiry. Most significantly by going back towards 1960 it will be more difficult to show what the state of responsible opinion then was.

Fourthly, no structure is proposed effectively to re-unite the remaining plaintiffs. Only a minority are proposed to be represented by solicitors, and no plans are made for, let alone agreed with, the balance.

Fifthly, if I consider the practicalities facing the conditional fee plaintiffs, they are considerable, as I have shown. I do not have confidence that effective progress can be made. I have earlier said that it would be no kindness to these plaintiffs to allow the litigation to continue only to have it run into the sand.

Sixthly, I have said that it is a relevant factor that these actions would not have begun but for the support of the Legal Aid Board, and now it has been withdrawn. It is apparent that part of the motivation to continue with the claims is a perception that the plaintiffs have been badly treated by the Board.

Seventhly, the delay of which I have spoken brings its own prejudice, not merely fading memories as witnesses age, but entails that the defendants have been under the threat of this litigation for much longer than was necessary.

Finally, where defendants have been faced with some 5,000 sets of proceedings, and certainly in the case of Wyeth have examined the majority of them, and thereafter that total has reduced to seventy, whether by striking out, discontinuance, the product of the audit or a decision not to continue with legal aid withdrawn, those defendants are justified in pointing to the pursuit of that small remainder as an abuse of process, certainly where they demonstrate no greater overall viability than these cases do.[37]

Further on appeal:

In the circumstances of this case delay and prejudice to the defendants were really properly to be regarded as one of the circumstances to be taken into account in considering whether the proceedings were an abuse of process and were to be struck out under the court's inherent jurisdiction.[38]

7.31 Having reviewed authorities on the court's inherent jurisdiction, Brooke LJ said:

Three themes emerge . . . The first is that the court has an inherent jurisdiction to step in and prevent its process being abused for the purpose of injustice, or in order to maintain its character as a court of justice. The second is that the court should be very slow to exercise this summary power (see also *Metropolitan Bank Ltd v Pooley* (1885) 10 App Cas 210, per Lord Blackburn at p 221: 'it should not be lightly done'). The third is that the category of case in which the court should be willing to exercise this power is, almost by definition, never to be closed.

. . .

. . . In very large-scale group litigation the exercise of the inherent jurisdiction of the court should not necessarily be fettered by rules that were designed for individual litigation.

. . .

It is a central feature of the judgment complained of that the judge found, on what appeared to me to be overwhelming grounds, that a fair trial was now no longer possible.[39]

7.32 Following the discontinuation, on the advice of counsel, of forty-one claims for work related upper limb disorders arising out of the use of VDUs, the Court of Appeal followed the *Wyeth* decision and upheld a decision to strike out a single remaining claim within the group as oppressive and an abuse of process on the basis of an inescapable inference that this claim should likewise be regarded as unarguable unless the claimant were able to point to some circumstance indicating that it was worthy of further legal process on its own account.[40]

---

[37] *AB and Others v John Wyeth & Brother Ltd* [1996] 7 Med LR 267, 292.
[38] *AB and Others v John Wyeth & Brother Ltd* [1997] 8 Med LR 57, 68 per Stuart-Smith LJ.
[39] *AB and Others v John Wyeth & Brother Ltd* [1997] 8 Med LR 57, 70–72 per Brooke LJ.
[40] *Longworth v Prescription Pricing Authority* (13 Feb 1998, CA).

8
COSTS

A.	Individual and Common Costs	8.01	E. Costs on Joining or Leaving a Group	8.20
B.	Liability of Individuals for Common Costs: Several, not Joint	8.09	F. Cost-Sharing Arrangements	8.22
C.	Lead Solicitors	8.12	G. Decisions on Costs	8.24
D.	The Issue of Mixed Winning and Losing	8.16	The *BCCI* case	8.25
			The *Watson Burton* case	8.27
			The *Nationwide* case	8.31

A. Individual and Common Costs

The general rules on costs are in Part 44 of the Civil Procedure Rules 1998 (CPR). Detailed consideration of Part 44 is outside the scope of this book but the key aspects should be remembered. The court has a discretion as to the award, amount, and timing of payment of costs. The general rule is that the unsuccessful party will be ordered to pay the costs of the successful party, but the court may make a different order. In deciding what order to make about costs, the court must have regard to all the circumstances, including: 8.01

(1) the conduct of all the parties;
(2) whether a party has succeeded on part of his case, even if he has not been wholly successful; and
(3) any payment into court or admissible offer to settle drawn to the court's attention.

Special rules apply where the court has made a Group Litigation Order (GLO). By their nature, costs in group litigation are likely to be potentially high. In accordance with the principle of transparent and continuous management, there is an explicit provision that the court may require the parties to provide information about costs that have already been incurred.[1] 8.02

---
[1] Practice Direction: Parts 43–48, para 52.1(2).

8.03 Two distinct types of costs are recognised by Rule 48.6A, common costs and individual costs, recognising practice which had developed before the rule was written. These are defined as follows:

> (2) In this rule—
>> (a) 'individual costs' means costs incurred in relation to an individual claim on the group register;
>> (b) 'common costs' means—
>>> (i) costs incurred in relation to the GLO issues;
>>> (ii) individual costs incurred in a claim while it is proceeding as a test claim; and
>>> (iii) costs incurred by the lead solicitor in administering the group litigation; and
>> (c) 'group litigant' means a claimant or defendant, as the case may be, whose claim is entered on the group register.

8.04 As to individual costs, the starting point is that the rules applicable in unitary claims will apply. Thus, subject to the court's discretion, a claimant who does not succeed on liability (for example, where his claim fails on limitation or because of a fundamental defence such as failure to establish personal reliance on a failure to warn) can expect to be liable to the defendant for the costs attributable to defence of that individual claim, even if other claimants succeed on liability. Conversely, if the claimant wins, the defendant will normally be liable for the costs attributable to that case. These basic propositions are, however, modified in group litigation, as discussed below.

8.05 An individual claimant who is less successful on his individual claim than the majority of claimants may escape the rigours of the normal approach to awarding individual costs against him in the situation mentioned in the Practice Direction on Parts 43–49:

> 52.2 Rule 44.3(4)(b) provides that, in deciding what (if any) order to make about costs, the court must have regard to whether a party has succeeded on part of his claim. This will be especially relevant in a group litigation claim. The court may decide, for example, that because the claimants have succeeded on the issue of liability, it would be inappropriate to make a costs order against a particular claimant who happens to have been unsuccessful on issues regarding the amount of damages (eg because the amount of damages awarded to him was substantially reduced by a successful plea of contributory negligence).

8.06 The position on common costs can be complicated. The 1999 Consultation Paper pointed out that the rule does not specify that in general common costs should be ordered to follow success or failure on the common issues, without regard to the success of individual claims on their own facts. The Consultation Paper stated that it is sufficient in this respect to rely on the court's general

B. Liability for Common Costs

discretion as to costs.[2] The GLO Practice Direction states that the management court may give directions about how the costs of resolving common issues or the costs of claims proceeding as test claims are to be borne or shared as between the claimants on the group register.[3]

8.07 Membership of group litigation normally automatically incurs a several share of liability for a proportion of the costs of the common enterprise. The percentage proportion and thus the extent of the financial risk are, of course, dependent on the number of other people in the group. But there is considerable advantage for individuals that the liability of each is only for his percentage share (several) and not for the whole (joint and several).

8.08 Rule 48.6A provides that:

(3) Unless the court orders otherwise, any order for common costs against group litigants imposes on each group litigant several liability for an equal proportion of those common costs.
(4) The general rule is that where a group litigant is the paying party, he will, in addition to any costs he is liable to pay to the receiving party, be liable for—
 (a) the individual costs of his claim; and
 (b) an equal proportion, together with all other group litigants, of the common costs.

B. Liability of Individuals for Common Costs: Several, not Joint

8.09 The Opren litigation established the precedent that costs in any lead action within co-ordinated arrangements (which may include some individual costs but are likely to involve large common costs) which are ordered to be borne by the individual lead claimant should be borne proportionately by all the claimants within the group and that such liability be several and not joint.[4] It had previously been sought to avoid every group member having a liability by selecting a lead action in which the claimant was legally aided with a nil contribution, thereby shielding

---

[2] Lord Chancellor's Department, *Multi-Party Situations: Draft rules and practice direction. A Lord Chancellor's Department Consultation Paper* (1999) para 37. In *Bairstow v Queens Moat House plc and others*, unreported judgment of Mr Justice Nelson, Queen's Bench Division, 14 Apr 2000, three former directors who were found to have jointly put forward a false case in separate actions and in defending claims against them, all of which they lost, were held to be jointly and severally liable for the common costs of the actions, which were unconsolidated but heard together. A fourth director, who was not involved in the falsity, was liable for up to 25% of such common costs.
[3] Practice Direction—Part 19B1, para 12.4.
[4] *Davies v Eli Lilly & Co Ltd* [1987] 1 WLR 1136. *Ward v Guinness Mahon plc* [1996] 1 WLR 894, CA. See also *Chrzanowska v Glaxo Laboratories Ltd*, Queen's Bench Division, The Times, 16 Mar 1990 (Transcript: DL Sellers) (Steyn J, 2 Mar 1990). This result was supported in Lord Woolf, *Access to Justice: Final Report* (1996) 17.60, save in relation to an opt-out scheme.

non-legally aided claimants,[5] but courts did not support that view. Instead, the courts adhered to the normal policy that recognised the sense in enabling claimants to make an assessment of their potential liability for costs. This rule was adopted in subsequent group actions and the standard order usually provides for liberty to apply to the court in order to provide for changed circumstances.

8.10 The Law Society's 1995 Working Party concluded that whilst it might be unusual that, if the defendant wins on a trial of common issues, the liability of the claimants for the defendants' common costs should be several rather than joint, they saw no real alternative if the costs risk to individual claimants were not to be wholly disproportionate and such that no claimant could ever satisfy the then private client test for legal aid.[6] It is suggested, however, that in differing circumstances, where the cost-risk ratio is not as it was under the legal aid rules, such as in a conditional fee case, a different approach might be justified.

8.11 The result that the liability of individual claimants be limited to the proportionate share of the overall costs, whether incurred by the claimants or payable by the claimants to the defendant, and that such liability be several and not joint, was subsequently upheld by the Court of Appeal in *Ward v Guinness Mahon Plc*.[7] The court recognised that it would have been possible for the claimants to arrange their affairs so that a lead claimant be indemnified by the others, perhaps through a fund or guarantee. However, the court was persuaded, following the Law Society Report's conclusions discussed above, first, that the role of lead claimant would, if the contrary had been ordered, be one that no well-advised claimant would be wise to accept and, secondly, that 'the purpose of selecting lead cases would be vitiated if regard had to be paid not to the issues in particular actions but to the willingness of the particular [claimants] to accept a high degree of risk'.[8] As the court recognised, this approach means that successful defendants may have to enforce costs orders against each individual claimant and may be unable in practice to do so. It may be argued that this approach should be revised given the subsequent fundamental change towards litigation funding being based on conditional fee agreements (CFAs) backed by insurance policies, under which policies could be arranged to cover exposure to lead claimants' costs and joint liability.

---

[5] Supreme Court Procedure Committee, *Guide for use in Group Actions* (May 1991) ch 4.
[6] The Law Society, *Group Actions Made Easier* (1995) para 7.4.
[7] [1996] 1 WLR 894; see ch 27 below.
[8] ibid, 901.

C. Lead Solicitors

The Practice Direction provides: 8.12

> Where the court appoints a lead solicitor in accordance with rule 19.13 the court may direct that recoverable costs may include the costs incurred by the lead solicitor in administering the group litigation. This may include costs that are unique to the Group Litigation such as convening meetings of litigants or producing a new[s] sheet for the parties.[9]

Although not included in Rule 48.6A, a draft of the Rule (at 12e) provided that, where a lead solicitor has been appointed, the costs of work done by any other solicitor after the date of the appointment of the lead solicitor will generally be disallowed unless the court has directed otherwise. This principle would still apply, so approval would therefore be needed in order to recover the costs of work by any other solicitor: presumably this wording requires the approval to precede the work. 8.13

It should normally be a straightforward matter, particularly if appropriate computerised time recording files are established at the start and accurately kept, for lawyers to record what work relates to common issues and what to each individual claim. The position may be less clear in relation to work done in preparation for and at hearings. In order to clarify this matter, Rule 48.6A(5) provides: 8.14

> Where the court makes an order about costs in relation to any application or hearing which involved—
> (a) one or more GLO issues; and
> (b) issues relevant only to individual claims,
> the court will direct the proportion of the costs that is to relate to common costs and the proportion that is to relate to individual costs.

The Practice Direction supplements this by providing that it is the duty of the legal representatives to raise this matter with the court and if the court does not deal with the point the costs officer will make a decision as to the relevant proportions at or before the commencement of the detailed assessment of the costs.[10] In the '*Marchioness*' case, the court emphasised the importance of making orders at the outset, which deal with how costs are in principle to be dealt with.[11] 8.15

---

[9] Practice Direction, para 52.1 (3).
[10] Practice Direction: Parts 43–48, para 52.3.
[11] *East Coast Aggregates v Parra-Pagan and Others; Ross v Owners of the ship 'Bowbelle' and the Owners of the ship 'Marchioness'*, Queen's Bench Division (Admiralty Court), [1997] 1 Lloyd's Rep 196.

D. The Issue of Mixed Winning and Losing

8.16 Where the claimants win on the common issues but some individual claimants fail on their individual facts, the Law Society's Working Party identified three possible approaches:

(a) *the common issues approach*. Common costs should follow the common issues event. Claimants should recover common costs in full. The outcome of individual claims would be disregarded save in relation to individual costs.

(b) *the individual costs approach*. Successful claimants should recover that percentage of common costs which is the percentage of individual claims which ultimately succeed. The shortfall could be shared amongst all claimants.

(c) *individual costs with set-off*. This is the same as (b) but, in addition, the defendants should recover the percentage of their common costs which is the percentage of individual claims which fail. There would then be a set-off between the two liabilities.

8.17 The Law Society Working Party Report commented that there are persuasive arguments each way. Votes on the Working Party on this issue divided essentially on partisan lines, with the pro-claimant majority favouring the common costs approach. Solutions (b) and (c) would, those with pro-claimant views argued, penalise successful claimants for having joined forces with unsuccessful claimants. On the other hand, these approaches would impose an incentive on claimants to ensure that proper initial scrutiny of claims is undertaken and that only genuine claims are permitted to remain within the group. Individual claims benefit from being brought as a cohort and should accept risks as well as benefits of this concerted exercise. The trial of common issues will only be economically justifiable if there is a sufficient number of individual claims which will be materially advanced by the determination of that issue. The normal rule in unitary actions is that a defendant is entitled to set off any award of costs in his favour against any costs or damages awarded to his legally aided opponent.[12] A draft of Rule 48.6A (at 12d) adopted the 'no set-off' rule but the final Rule and Practice Direction are silent on the issue.

8.18 In each of the most recent major cases,[13] the courts have rejected the 'common issues' approach and made costs-sharing orders broadly adopting the 'individual costs' approach. In both the tobacco and Norplant cases, the claimants obtained leave to appeal but both group actions collapsed before the matter was heard by the Court of Appeal.

---

[12] *Lockley v The National Blood Transfusion Service* [1992] 2 All ER 589.
[13] The tobacco litigation, see para 32.50 below; the Norplant litigation, see para 31.25 below; and the MMR litigation.

8.19 A specimen costs-sharing order, based on that made by Wright J in the tobacco litigation, is attached to the draft GLO at Appendix G. The practical effect of this order is that:

(a) a claimant who (succeeds or) settles his claim on terms that his costs are paid by the defendant will recover his individual costs and his share of the group's common costs, as calculated at the time of the settlement if other cases continue; this will reduce the overall liability of the remaining members of the group for common costs;

(b) a claimant who is ordered to pay the defendant's costs on discontinuance or dismissal will be liable:
  (i) to the defendant in respect of the individual costs incurred by that defendant in relation to that claimant, plus a proportionate share of the defendant's common costs at that time; and
  (ii) to his own lawyers in respect of his individual costs plus his proportionate share of the common costs at that time.

An order on this basis has the advantage of protecting the individual claimant by limiting his liability to a several share of the common costs. An independent funder of claimants, such as the Community Legal Service or solicitors acting under a CFA, would, however, be at risk of not obtaining the complete recovery against their outlay on the group litigation in the event that not all the claimants that they support are successful. The principal response to that point is that an alternative result would be unfair to the defendants (by reference to the principle expressed in CPR Rule 1.1(2)(a) that the parties must be on an equal footing) and that the courts' policy should be to encourage solicitors and funders to undertake proper scrutiny of the cases that they support and to discourage the bringing of weak claims. The issue of recovery of common costs becomes more significant for claimants' solicitors who act on a CFA basis, since it is not only the total amount of their common costs that might be reduced but also the associated proportionate success fee.

E. Costs on Joining or Leaving a Group

8.20 Rule 48.6A provides:

(6) Where common costs have been incurred before a claim is entered on the group register, the court may order the group litigant to be liable for a proportion of those costs.

(7) Where a claim is removed from the group register, the court may make an order for costs in that claim which includes a proportion of the common costs incurred up to the date on which the claim is removed from the group register.

8.21 Where a claim is discontinued or withdrawn the 1999 Consultation Paper stated

F. Cost-Sharing Arrangements

8.22 It has been common practice for the parties to seek to establish, at an early stage, certain aspects of the rules which will apply to costs. This may be by means of contractual arrangements for liabilities as between claimants. Alternatively, it may involve requesting the court to give directions. Certain aspects are uncontentious but some of the more complex aspects have been hotly debated. Achieving certainty on costs aspects has obvious advantages to the parties and their funders or insurers[14] but the courts may be reluctant to give up at too early a stage their discretion over awarding costs, because of being unable to reach a just decision in the light of circumstances which may not be foreseen and in order to retain a sanction to encourage control and orderly behaviour.

8.23 It is accepted[15] that all claimants within the co-ordinated arrangements, whether publicly funded or not, should share equally in being responsible for the costs of both the lead actions and all 'generic' work, such as the work of any co-ordinating committee, irrespective of when they join or leave the group. There is no reason for any other arrangement to apply under CFAs. Accounting is normally carried out by claimants co-ordinating the solicitors on a quarterly basis.

G. Decisions on Costs

8.24 The principles discussed above may lead to seemingly different decisions when applied in the particular circumstances of complex cases. The change in approach to costs from 1999 under the CPR has also had an impact on the analysis of winning and losing a multi-party lead case. Various recent decisions are set out below.

The *BCCI* case

8.25 In the BCCI litigation, the court tried test cases by five employees representing some 300 ex-employees who were claiming that the bank's illegal activities amounted to a breach of the implied term of trust and confidence in their contracts of employment and that the breach had caused them damage by way of stigma preventing or impeding them obtaining further employment. Lightman J held that the bank was in breach of contract but that each of the five employees

---

[14] See *Ward v Guinness Mahon plc* [1996] 1 WLR 894, 900 per Sir Thomas Bingham MR: see para 27.19 *et seq* below.

[15] The Law Society, *Group Actions Made Easier* (1995) para 6.11.4.

G. Decisions on Costs

failed on proof of loss and causation and the bank succeeded on most of the issues of remoteness and contributory negligence.[16] In considering costs,[17] the court took into account the many issues raised, their importance, the time taken on them, and the time wasted or lost by reason of fault on one side or the other. The Judge considered that he should take an overview of the case as a whole and reach a considered conclusion on two questions: first, who succeeded in the action and, second, what order for costs justice required. In relation to the first question he held that honours were even. He commented that:

> Before the CPR, a party who established a breach of contract but could prove no loss would be held to have lost and (almost as of course) be subject to an adverse order for costs. In case of group actions, such an order might have been modified to a limited degree to reflect that party's success on generic issues. But that approach no longer holds sway. I can and should take a realistic view of the outcome of the litigation in deciding who in the particular context of this test action is successful. This context is critical. It has guided and shaped the litigation throughout for the benefit of all parties, and not least in the choice of claimants. It is not possible or just to have regard only to the lack of success of the Test Case Employees in establishing their personal loss. That failure is only one half of the picture. The full picture is that, whilst the Bank has successfully warded off all claims by the Test Case Employees, the judgment (as I have already said) opened the door to possible successful claims by the Other Employees, and beyond this (for the benefit of all concerned and in fulfilment of the essential purpose behind the action) has cleared the way for a more expedited resolution of such claims.

The Judge concluded that the proper order was to make no order as to costs, both on the basis of who had been successful and on what justice required. **8.26**

> This outcome as to costs gives due weight to the purpose underlying the trial of this test action, the conduct of the trial and the outcome of the various issues. Indeed, as I see it, any other outcome would be unjust. It would be quite wrong that the Bank should pay any part of the costs of the Test Case Employees having regard in particular to the false evidence they gave. It would be quite wrong for the Test Case Employees to pay any part of the costs of the Bank whose dishonesty (as I have held rejecting the sustained arguments of its Counsel) constituted such a serious breach of contract and brought about these proceedings. I may add that I would be troubled, if I did make any order in favour of the Bank, that I might thereby defeat one of the purposes of these proceedings. For if I were to make an order for costs against the Test Case Employees, it would be necessary likewise to make orders for payment against the Other Employees on whose behalf (in effect) this test action has been fought. Such an order could well preclude further pursuit of their claims or cancel out any likely recovery against the Bank and in effect render the successful establishment in this action of the breach of contract of nugatory effect. But I emphasise that, even [if] I disregard this consequence of an adverse order against the Test Case

---

[16] *Bank of Credit and Commerce International SA v Ali and others (No 4)*, Chancery Division, The Times, 2 Mar 2000, 149 NLJ 1222, 4 Nov 1999.
[17] *Bank of Credit and Commerce International SA v Ali and Others* [1999] 2 All ER 83.

Employees, the balance of justice clearly requires that I make no order as to costs, and I so decide.

The *Watson Burton* case

8.27 The rule that all claimants have a proportionate liability for the costs of lead actions has been further upheld in the CFA era by the Court of Appeal in *Ochwat and Parylo v Watson Burton (a firm)*.[18] In that case, two lead actions were tried out of a group of over 100 claimants who claimed that they had suffered hearing loss as a result of being subjected to excessive noise in the course of their employment. The claimants subsequently brought actions against their solicitors for negligence in advising or permitting them to settle their claims under a compensation scheme which had been set up.

8.28 Two of these claims were heard as lead actions. The Judge held that the defendants owed them a duty of care and were in breach of that duty but that the claimants had failed to show that they had suffered any loss as a result of the breach. The Judge adopted a broad-brush approach to costs, which was not criticised. She ordered that the defendants should have their costs excluding the issues of duty and breach of duty, which she assessed at 25 per cent of the total. Accordingly, she ordered that the claimants should recover 75 per cent of their costs from the two lead claimants (who were both legally aided). The Court of Appeal dismissed an appeal against this order.

8.29 In relation to the other group claimants, the Judge said:

> It seems that if common issues are tried on a preliminary basis, a costs sharing scheme might sensibly be limited to those issues, but if the litigation proceeds by lead actions, it must in my view be contemplated that the group will stand behind the lead plaintiffs for the whole of their costs, not just the costs of the generic issues.

8.30 It followed that each of the common claimants would have to pay 75 per cent of the defendants' costs, but the Judge reduced the figure to 25 per cent, having been told that the plaintiffs were not advised that they might be liable for a share of the whole of the defendants' costs of the lead actions. The Court of Appeal overturned that award and held each of the common claimants liable for the prima facie figure of 75 per cent of the defendants' costs. The Court of Appeal said that if the claimants were not advised that the costs of the lead actions should be borne proportionately between them, then they should have been and there was no reason why the defendants should suffer a disadvantage if they were not. The Court saw no proper basis for making a distinction between the lead claimants and the other common claimants: to do so would be unjust to the defendants and also, at least theoretically, to the lead claimants.

---

[18] Court of Appeal (Civil Division) (Transcript: Smith Bernol), 10 Dec 1999.

G. Decisions on Costs

The *Nationwide* case

In *Nationwide Building Society v Various Solicitors*[19] a single plaintiff brought claims against nearly 500 solicitors who were all indemnified by the Solicitors' Indemnity Fund. A High Court judge called an informal meeting of the parties, which was followed by formal directions creating a managed list in a particular county court and directions for the management of cases within that list. From a pool of around 248 cases, there was created an active list of 100 cases and a standby list of a further 50 cases. All cases in the managed list which were not on the active or standby lists were placed under a moratorium for further steps after close of pleadings. Twenty-five claims were then tried at a single hearing, following which a separate hearing to assess damages was held in 20 of those claims. Up to the date of judgment on damages, 215 claims subject to the process were disposed of: 25 by judgment after trial (in which the claimant succeeded on issues of liability in 22 but failed in 3); 38 on discontinuance by the claimant; 50 by the claimant's acceptance of a payment into court; and 102 by negotiated settlement.

8.31

Some costs orders had been made at individual previous stages of the process, but the general issue remained of who should be liable for the 'generic costs', on what basis, and in what proportion. Blackburne J first rejected an argument that there should be no order for generic costs but that each side should bear their own generic costs. It had been argued that the management process and trial had enabled wide-ranging issues of lender fault to be tested and enabled many parties who were not involved in the trial to gauge the level at which to pitch or accept an offer of settlement, taking into account where appropriate the claimant's contributory negligence. The Judge held that many cases serve some wider purpose in deciding an issue which has importance beyond the interests of the parties to the particular dispute and that has never been a reason for leaving each side to bear its own costs attributable to that issue.

8.32

Turning to the generic costs, the Judge saw no good reason why the costs of discrete generic issues which were decided wholly or substantially in the claimant's favour should not follow the event as in the normal case of the case-specific costs. He noted that this case was not conventional group litigation where one or more test cases were brought to trial, but that the purpose of the managed process had been to bring to trial a representative cross-section of claims with a view to obtaining a judgment which would facilitate the disposal of as many as possible of the claimant's other claims. He accepted that it would be detrimental to the cause of managed litigation of this kind if the whole burden of the generic costs were to fall on the particular group of claimants or, in this case, defendants, who were

8.33

---

[19] Chancery Division, 148 NW 241, 142 SJ LB 78, The Times, 5 Feb 1998 (Transcript: Beverley F Nunnery).

selected for trial. In contrast, he followed the principle that the costs burden should be apportioned between as many of the defendants as could fairly be said to have benefited from the process. The Judge noted practical difficulties of calculation and apportionment. He said that the temptation was to allocate generic costs rateably between all of the actions as were live from time to time, but noted that the number of claims reduced as time went on and that the costs were incurred at different rates over the period depending on the stage of the managed process that was reached.

8.34 Taking a broad approach that the claimant had become entitled to its costs in roughly 78 per cent of the 215 claims (and defendants had been entitled to their costs in just over 11 per cent of the claims, with the remainder being disposed of on terms that each side should bear their own costs or that the sum paid by a defendant was inclusive of costs) the Judge ordered that the defendants should pay 60 per cent of the claimant's generic costs up to the date of the second judgment on quantum. The defendants' liability would be several, rather than joint and several, and would be time-apportioned (ie the total would be spread equally over the total number of weeks involved, rather than calculated on the basis of which costs were historically incurred during each particular week). The Judge did not think it appropriate to place a greater costs burden on a defendant because a claim against him involved a greater number of generic issues or a greater amount of overall case management.

9

OTHER PROCEDURAL MECHANISMS

A. Various Alternatives	9.01	Powers of qualified entities	9.15
B. Part 19.II—Representative Parties	9.03	Courts	9.17
		Remedies	9.19
C. Actions for an Injunction to Protect the Collective Interests of Consumers		The collective interests of consumers	9.25
Overview	9.09	D. Proposals on Representative Actions by Organisations	9.27
Qualified entities	9.10		

A. Various Alternatives

Part 19.III on Group Litigation, discussed above, may be the preferred mechanism for making or handling multiple claims, at least on historical precedent, but it is not the only mechanism which might be available. The trigger for Part 19.III is the wide test of where there are common issues of fact or law in a number of claims, all of which have been commenced. In contrast, a more restrictive trigger, where more than one person has the same interest in a claim, is specified in Part 19.II on representative actions, discussed in the first part of this chapter. Here, one or more claimants may bring an action to represent all members of the same class. The latter rule effectively reproduces a previous rule which was not thought to be applicable in most multi-party situations. 9.01

Further alternatives may be available under new procedural mechanisms which are either being introduced or considered for single actions brought by representative organisations, such as consumer organisations, trade unions, or trade associations. These options, discussed later in this chapter, represent novel and untested approaches to government policy on increasing access to justice,[1] and the nature and extent of their possible effects are unclear. 9.02

---

[1] Department of Trade and Industry, *White Paper: Modern markets, confident consumers* (1999); European Commission, *Consumer Policy Action Plan 1999–2001* (1999).

B. Part 19.II—Representative Parties

9.03 The Civil Procedure Rules 1998 (CPR), Part 19.II specifies rules on representative parties in certain instances:

- representative parties with the same interest (Rule 19.6);
- representation of persons who cannot be ascertained in relation to the estate of a deceased person, properly subject to a trust, or the meaning of a document or statute (Rule 19.7);
- representation of a person who has died (Rule 19.8);
- a claim by one or more members of a company, body, or trade union for the company, body, or trade union to be given a remedy open to it (a 'derivative claim': Rule 19.9).

The above Rules are set out in Appendix C. Detailed consideration of these Rules is outside the scope of this book save to note the similarities and differences of the rules on representative actions and GLOs.

9.04 Rule 19.6 permits representative actions by or against one or more individuals who stand as representatives of a larger group of individuals who all have the same interest in the claim. This rule merely repeats the previous rule without alteration[2] so, in principle, the previous authorities should continue to apply. An important function of the rule is to achieve economy in avoiding the complexity and cost of requiring unnecessary duplication of claimants or defendants. Thus, for example, an action could be commenced against all members of an unincorporated association, such as a club or society, by suing two or more members 'sued on their own behalf and on behalf of all other members of the [association]'.[3]

9.05 The crucial words of the rule are that the representative(s) and all the other members of the group who are being represented must have *the same interest* in the claim. In the leading case, the House of Lords prefigured precisely the difference between what is now analysed as a common interest under Part 19.III and the same interest under Part 19.II:

> considering whether a representative action is maintained you have to consider what is common to the class and what differentiates the cases of individual members. Given a common interest and common grievance, a representative suit was in order, if the relief sought was in its nature benefit to all whom the plaintiff proposed to represent.[4]

---

[2] RSC Ord 15, r 12; for a summary of relevant case law prior to 1999 see *The Supreme Court Practice* (1999) 15/12.
[3] *London Association for Protection of Trade v Greenlands Ltd* [1916] 2 AC 15, 30 per Lord Atkinson.
[4] *Duke of Bedford v Ellis* [1901] AC 1, HL.

B. Part 19.II—Representative Parties

The courts have generally[5] applied the 'same interest' requirement strictly, with the result that the mechanism would not be permitted where there are several interests in the same proceedings.[6] Thus, several claims for damages for breach of individual contracts would not be pursued by a representative action where none of the persons represented have any interest in the damages recoverable by the particular claimant seeking to represent them: in such a claim, there must be both a common 'wrong' and a common 'right' or common purpose. This restrictive interpretation has led to the result that:

9.06

> Where the claim is for damages the machinery of a representative suit is absolutely inapplicable. The relief which he is seeking is a personal relief applicable to him alone, and does not benefit in any way the class with whom he purports to be bringing action.[7]

Accordingly, a representative claim will only be permitted in tort where every person represented against whom a judgment may be given is under the same liability and has the same defences and no others in respect of the claim for which the action is brought.[8]

In order to ameliorate this restrictive approach, an alternative formulation of the test has been developed, that there must be 'a common interest, a common grievance and relief in its nature beneficial to all'.[9] In *Prudential Assurance Co Ltd v Newman Industries Ltd*[10] Vinelott J held that the representative action could be utilised in a damages claim provided two conditions apply. First, an order could not be made in favour of a representative plaintiff if that order could potentially confer upon a member of the represented class a right which he or she would not have been able to exercise in a separate action, or deprived the defendant of a defence upon which that defendant could otherwise successfully rely (for example, a limitation defence) in a separate action. Secondly, no order would be made in favour of their representative plaintiff without there being an element common to the claim of all members of the class which the representative plaintiff holds himself out as representing. This approach was followed in *EMI Records v Riley*[11] and

9.07

---

[5] See J Seymour, 'Representative Procedures and the Future of Multi-Party Actions' [1999] MLR 564.
[6] *Markt & Co Ltd v Knight Steamship Co Ltd* [1910] 2 KB 1021, CA per Fletcher Moulton LJ.
[7] ibid.
[8] *Hardie & Lane Ltd v Chiltern* [1928] 1 KB 663, CA.
[9] *Duke of Bedford v Ellis* [1901] 1, 8, HL per Lord Macnaughten; *Janson v Property Insurance Co Ltd* (1913) 19 Com Cas 36, 42; *Hardie & Lane Ltd v Chiltern* [1928] 1 KB 663, 677; *Smith v Cardiff Corporation* [1954] 1 QB 210, 220–221; *J Bollinger SA v Goldwell Ltd* [1971] RPC 412, 418; *Pan Atlantic Insurance Co Ltd and Republic Insurance Co v Pine Top Insurance Co Ltd* [1989] 1 Lloyd's Rep 568, 571.
[10] [1981] Ch 229, [1979] 3 All ER 507.
[11] [1981] 2 All ER 838, [1981] 1 WLR 923.

M Michael Furriers Ltd v Askew[12] but not in *News Group Newspapers Ltd v Society of Graphical and Allied Trades '82 (No 2)*.[13] In view of the introduction of Part 19.III permitting group litigation on the basis of the less stringent common interest test, these previous judicial disagreements over attempts to relax the test may now have much less relevance. It would seem that the same interest test, re-enacted in Part 19.II, may continue to be interpreted strictly without causing major difficulty.

9.08 The group of persons sought to be represented must be defined in the writ with sufficient clearness and precision.[14] A representative claimant has sole control over the action (*dominus litis*) and can direct, discontinue, compromise, etc the claim as he pleases, without reference to the represented parties. Any judgment or order in the action will bind all persons represented in the claim unless the court otherwise directs, but may only be enforced by or against a person who is not a party to the claim with the permission of the court.[15] Accordingly, there are many similarities between this representative action and the American class action mechanism.[16] The English 'same interest' requirement prevents the representative action mechanism from applying in many multi-party situations[17] and this has contributed to the introduction of the Group Litigation Order rule.

C. Actions for an Injunction to Protect the Collective Interests of Consumers

Overview

9.09 Under a mechanism to be introduced in January 2001, an approved consumer organisation based in other European Community Member States is in certain circumstances empowered to apply for an injunction in the United Kingdom (and vice versa) to restrain breach of specified consumer protection and trading legislation committed by entities based in the United Kingdom, the effects of which breach adversely affect consumers in the organisation's state. The organisation is therefore acting as a quasi-regulator, where a regulatory authority either does not exist or chooses not to act. This European approach contrasts with the US development of the damages compensation claim class action as a mechanism for regulating industry, facilitated by the incentive of substantial conditional fees

---

[12] (1983) 127 SJ 597, CA.
[13] [1987] ICR 181.
[14] *Markt & Co Ltd*, n 6 above, 1033, 1034.
[15] CPR, Rule 19.6(4).
[16] See ch 13 and paras 3.24 *et seq*.
[17] Supreme Court Rules Committee, *Guide to Group Actions* (1991).

C. Actions for an Injunction

payable in successful cases to plaintiffs' class counsel.[18] Damages claims may not be brought under this European mechanism.

Qualified entities

A qualified entity[19] may bring an action for an injunction in respect of any act contrary to the national laws of Member States of the European Community which transpose the Directives listed at Table 9.1 which harms the collective interests of consumers. These rights arise under Directive 98/27/EC on injunctions for the protection of consumers' interests ('the Injunctions Directive').[20] **9.10**

The United Kingdom legislation implementing the Injunctions Directive was not available at the time that this book went to press: the following analysis is based on the Directive and on implementing proposals published by the Department of Trade and Industry.[21] **9.11**

A 'qualified entity' is defined as[22] any body or organisation which, being properly constituted according to the law of a Member State, has a legitimate interest in ensuring that the purpose of protection of the collective interests of consumers in relation to the specified Directives is complied with, in particular: **9.12**

(a) one or more independent public bodies, specifically responsible for protecting the interests of consumers in Member States, such as the Office of Fair Trading in the United Kingdom, and/or
(b) organisations whose purpose is to protect consumers' interests in accordance with the criteria laid down by their national law.

Subject to their meeting certain objective criteria, it is proposed that the UK legislation will provide that qualified entities (bodies with legal capacity and standing to bring actions before both the UK courts and the competent authorities of other Member States where an infringement exists which affects the interests protected by that entity) will be designated Named Bodies by the Secretary of State and will be able both to investigate alleged infringements and take legal action to eliminate the effects of infringements within those Directive areas where they have a legitimate interest in compliance. Failure by a Named Body to exercise its powers independently and/or impartially will lead to the power to act being revoked. **9.13**

---

[18] This US approach was criticised by some European speakers at the conference on class actions organised by Duke University and the University of Geneva at Geneva on 21 and 22 July 2000 as distorting and undermining the role of regulators and by providing exaggerated compensation to private operators to act as quasi-regulators.
[19] Defined below.
[20] [1998] OJ L166/51.
[21] Department of Trade and Industry, *Injunctions Directive: Implementation of Directive 98/27/EC on Injunctions for the Protection of Consumers' Interests: A Consultation Paper* (Feb 2000).
[22] Directive 98/27/EC, Art 3.

9.14 Not only independent public bodies but also public consumer protection bodies and private consumer organisations are to be eligible to be designated under the implementing regulations. The categories of Named Bodies contemplated include the trading standards departments, the statutory utilities regulatory authorities, self-regulatory bodies, and trade associations as well as consumer organisations.

Powers of qualified entities

9.15 A qualified entity may request the authorities of the Member State in which it is located to communicate to the European Commission that it is qualified to bring an action under this Directive, and the Member State concerned shall inform the Commission, which is required to draw up a list of qualified entities and publish it in the *Official Journal* of the European Communities, updated every six months.[23]

9.16 Member States have a discretionary power to specify that the party that intends to seek an injunction can only start this procedure after it has tried to achieve the cessation of the infringement in consultation with either the defendant or with the defendant and a qualified entity. If a Member State requires such prior consultation, it must adopt appropriate rules which must be notified to the Commission and published in the *Official Journal* of the European Communities. It is for each Member State to decide whether the party seeking the injunction must consult the qualified entity. If the cessation of the infringement is not achieved within two weeks after the request for consultation is received, the party concerned may bring an action for an injunction without any further delay.[24]

Courts

9.17 Member States must designate the courts or administrative authorities which are competent to rule on proceedings of this type commenced by qualified entities. The UK proposes designating the courts (High Court and county court) as the competent authority to rule on proceedings commenced under the Injunctions Directive, save in relation to radio and television advertisements and television sponsorship, which will continue to be dealt with by existing bodies: the Independent Television Commission (ITC), the Radio Authority (RA), and the Welsh Fourth Channel Authority (S4C). Medicines and financial investment services advertising will be largely dealt with by the Medicines Control Agency (MCA) and the Financial Services Authority (FSA) respectively.

9.18 Applications for summary injunctions will be possible and breaches of court orders will be enforceable through the courts as contempt. Normal costs rules will apply in all court proceedings.

---

[23] Directive 98/27/EC, Art 4.
[24] Directive 98/27/EC, Art 5.

C. Actions for an Injunction

Remedies

Appropriate remedies must include:[25] 9.19

(a) an order with all due expediency, where appropriate by way of summary procedure, requiring the cessation or prohibition of any infringement;
(b) where appropriate, measures such as the publication of the decision, in full or in part, in such form as deemed adequate and/or the publication of a corrective statement with a view to eliminating the continuing effects of the infringement;
(c) in so far as the legal system of the Member State concerned so permits, an order against the losing defendant for payments into the public purse or to any beneficiary designated in or under national legislation, in the event of failure to comply with the decision within a time limit specified by the courts or administrative authorities, of a fixed amount for each day's delay or any other amount provided for in national legislation, with a view to ensuring compliance with the decisions.

Named Bodies will have the power to accept undertakings from traders that they will stop an infringement. Public Named Bodies will also have the power to obtain documents and information to facilitate the investigation of complaints and ensure compliance with undertakings or court orders. Named Bodies will only have the power to apply for an injunction provided they have notified the defendant trader and the Lead Body and the latter has been unable to stop the infringement within two weeks of notification. 9.20

To achieve co-ordination of investigations into complaints and eventual legal action thereafter, the UK proposes designating a Lead Body (the Director General of Fair Trading (DGFT)) save in relation to radio and television advertisements and television sponsorship where the existing bodies (ITC, RA, S4C, FSA, and the MCA as aforesaid) will assume this role. 9.21

The DGFT will: 9.22

- be under a duty to consider complaints referred to it unless these are being considered by another Named Body;
- have the right to refer consideration of complaints about breaches to trading standards departments under a duty to enforce (applying the Home Authority principle);
- co-ordinate arrangements with other Named Bodies in a particular Directive area;

---

[25] Directive 98/27/EC, Art 2.

- be the body which qualified entities (including those from other Member States) will be required to consult (together with the defendant trader) at least two weeks before seeking an injunction;
- maintain a central record of undertakings given to Named Bodies;
- provide advice to other Named Bodies; and
- publish reports on action taken.

9.23 The DGFT will also liaise closely with equivalent bodies in other Member States.

9.24 The provisions of Directive 98/27/EC and the remedies available under it are without prejudice to the rules of private international law;[26] thus private actions for damages or other relief are not affected.

The collective interests of consumers

9.25 The collective interests of consumers is defined in Recital 2 of the Directive to mean interests which do not include the accumulation of interests of individuals who have been harmed by an infringement. Interpretation of this concept is a matter for the courts. However, guidance from the Department of Trade and Industry is proposed and also an objective test in the regulations as to when there is a reasonable likelihood that an infringement will continue or be repeated so as to put the general body of consumers at risk.

9.26 Individuals who have been harmed by an infringement may, therefore, bring individual claims as permitted by the domestic law of the Member State. Both this definition of collective interests and the remedies under the Directive would need to be amended in order to permit, for example, a cumulation of individual claims for damages or some form of collective claim for damages. However, the Directive expressly does not prevent Member States from adopting or maintaining in force provisions designed to grant qualified entities and any other person concerned more extensive rights to bring action at national level.[27]

D. Proposals on Representative Actions by Organisations

9.27 In July 2000 the Lord Chancellor issued a Consultation Paper on possible new legislation which would permit certain proceedings to be brought by organisations on behalf of persons whose collective interests they support and represent.[28] It would not be necessary for the organisation itself to have a direct interest in the proceedings in order to act in a representative capacity. The Consultation Paper

---

[26] Directive 98/27/EC, Art 2.2.
[27] Directive 98/27/EC, Art 7.
[28] Lord Chancellor's Department, *Representative Actions: Proposed New Procedures* (2000).

D. *Representative Actions*

Table 9.1: List of Directives for which action is permitted under Directive 98/27/EC

Directive	UK Implementation
Council Directive 84/450/EEC on misleading advertising, 10 September 1984[a]	The Control of Misleading Advertisements Regulations 1988, SI 1988/915, amended by SI 2000/914
Council Directive 85/577/EEC to protect the consumer in respect of contracts negotiated away from business premises, 20 December 1985[b]	The Consumer Protection (Cancellation of Contracts Concluded away from Business Premises) Regulations 1987, SI 1987/2117
Council Directive 87/102/EEC on consumer credit, 22 December 1986[c]	The Consumer Credit (Exempt Agreements) Order 1989, SI 1989/869; The Consumer Credit (Total Charge for Credit, Agreements and Advertisements) (Amendment) Regulations 1999, SI 1999/3177
Council Directive 89/552/EEC on the pursuit of television broadcasting activities, 3 October 1989 (Articles 10 to 12)[d]	The Broadcasting (Prescribed Countries) (Amendment) Order 1993, SI 1993/3046; The Broadcasting (Foreign Satellite Programmes) (Specified Countries) (Amendment) Order 1993, SI 1993/3047; The Broadcasting (Foreign Satellite Programmes) (Specified Countries) Order 1994, SI 1994/453; The Broadcasting (Prescribed Countries) Order 1994, SI 1994/454; The Satellite Television Service Regulations 1997, SI 1997/1682; The Television Broadcasting Regulations 1998, SI 1998/3196; The Television Broadcasting Regulations 2000, SI 2000/54
Council Directive 90/314/EEC on package travel, package holidays and package tours, 13 June 1990[e]	The Package Travel, Package Holidays and Package Tours (Amendment) Regulations 1992, SI 1992/3288; The Package Travel, Package Holidays and Package Tours (Amendment) Regulations 1998, SI 1998/1208
Council Directive 92/28/EEC on the advertising of medicinal products for human use, 31 March 1992[f]	The Medicines (Advertising) Regulations 1994, SI 1994/1932, and the Medicines (Monitoring of Advertising) Regulations 1994 (implementing Article 12 of 92/28/EEC), SI 1994/1933; The Medicines Act 1968 (Amendment) Regulations 1995, SI 1995/2321; The Medicines (Advertising and Monitoring of Advertising) Amendment Regulations 1999, SI 1999/267
Council Directive 93/13/EEC on unfair terms in consumer contracts, 5 April 1993[g]	The Unfair Terms in Consumer Contracts Regulations 1994, SI 1994/3159; The Unfair Arbitration Agreements (Specified Amount) Order 1996, SI 1996/3211; The Unfair Terms in Consumer Contracts Regulations 1999, SI 1999/2083

Table 9.1 (*continued*)

Directive	UK Implementation
Directive 94/47/EC on the protection of purchasers in respect of certain aspects of contracts relating to the purchase of the right to use immovable properties on a timeshare basis, 26 October 1994[h]	The Timeshare Regulations 1997, SI 1997/1081
Directive 97/7/EC on the protection of consumers in respect of distance contracts, 20 May 1997[i]	The Consumer Protection (Distance Selling) Regulations 2000, SI 2000/2334
Directive 99/44/EC on certain aspects of the sale of consumer goods and associated guarantees[j], 25 May 1999	Not yet implemented
Draft Directive on e-commerce	Not yet implemented

[a] [1984] OJ L250/17, as amended by Directive 97/55/EC, [1997] OJ L290/18.
[b] [1985] OJ L372/31.
[c] [1998] OJ L101/17.
[d] [1989] OJ L298/23, as amended by Directive 97/36/EC.
[e] [1990] OJ L158/59.
[f] [1992] OJ L113/13.
[g] [1993] OJ L95/29.
[h] [1994] OJ L280/83.
[i] [1997] OJ L144/19.
[j] [1999] OJ L171/12.

accepted that such a change would require primary legislation. The Lord Chancellor's decision to facilitate representative actions was presented as part of his ongoing civil justice reforms in order to provide a legal framework enabling greater and more effective access to justice for individuals by allowing them to be supported by organisations with their interests at heart. However, it was accepted that any such change in the law must achieve a balance between increasing access to justice and avoiding inappropriate and burdensome litigation.

9.28 It is proposed that representative actions could be made on behalf of individuals who can be clearly identified or named, or a group of unnamed individuals who cannot be named but belong to a clearly identifiable group. The range of claims and remedies available for representative actions on behalf of named individuals should be the same as if they had brought the claims themselves but damages should not be available in a claim which includes unnamed individuals. Organisations seeking to bring a representative action should satisfy the court that they are an appropriate body to represent the interests of the claimant(s) and that the claim is an appropriate way to proceed. The representative action would be defined as claims made by, or defended by, a representative organisation on behalf of all, or all except one or more, of a group of individuals who may or may not be individually named but are clearly identifiable.

D. *Representative Actions*

9.29 The body or organisation wishing to act in a representative capacity would require permission from the court to issue proceedings. Compliance with a pre-action protocol should be expected. Where possible, the application should provide the court with the names of those it represents and demonstrate that they consent to being represented by the applicant. Where it is not possible to name the claimants, they should be identified as clearly as possible.

9.30 The applicant should satisfy the court of its genuine interest in the matter by demonstrating an awareness of the issues or support for the groups involved. An applicant should be expected to assist the court to determine whether it is the best party to represent the interests of the group by identifying other interested parties. In the interests of justice to both parties the applicant would have a particular duty to establish that the representative action is the most appropriate way to proceed.

9.31 The issue of how the representative organisation and the claimant(s) determine their responsibility for costs should be a matter between themselves. Certain costs are insurable and some associations might have an agreement to pay legal costs on behalf of their members. Those parts of the Funding Code relevant for funding public interest cases might be relevant. In a situation where a number of people who could bring an action decide to form a representative body to take action instead, provision should be made for the court to look at the finances of the representative body and the court should be satisfied that the body is truly representative. Whatever criteria the applicant might be required to meet, the court would have discretion to override this if appropriate.

Part III

FUNDING MULTI-PARTY ACTIONS

This Part considers the mechanisms for funding claimants in multi-party actions. There are various distinct systems:

1. private resources,
2. personal legal expenses insurance,
3. trade union scheme,
4. conditional fee arrangement (CFA),
5. public funding by the Community Legal Service.

The above five systems of funding are not mutually exclusive and it may increasingly be possible to combine aspects of them. Systems 2, 4, and 5 are now considered in detail. Funding is a complex subject. It has been said: 'Without some external source of finance, there is no way to fund legal advice for a group of claimants.'[1] Trade union and mutual benefit funding is a form of legal expenses insurance and will not be considered separately. They have traditionally been the principal funding source for workplace accident claims.[2] The financial risk to a party in litigation must be acceptable. The financial considerations which arise in multi-party actions can be particularly complex. A sequence of difficult and contentious issues can arise, involving access to justice, conflicts of financial interest between lawyers and clients, complex costs arrangements in a GLO, and case management decisions which can have a major impact on the financial aspects of the litigation and hence on its outcome.

The funding requirement and/or financial risk of a case may be unacceptable to an individual claimant. The advantage of a multi-party action arrangement is that if the requirements for funding costs and risk can be shared between several claimants, then one or both requirements may become sufficiently acceptable to make the action financially viable.

However, a multi-party action will involve increased costs to claimants because of the cost of communicating with and representing the number of individual claimants involved. The costs which a corporate defendant may be prepared to pay may be considerably greater than for a single or small number of actions because of the increased risk that may be posed to its brand or product. In any event, multi-party claims also typically involve extensive and complex issues, requiring intensive resources of solicitors, barristers, experts, and witnesses of fact, all of which make high costs inevitable.[3]

---

[1] T Weekes, LS Gaz 94/47 (10 Dec 1997).
[2] P Pleasance, S Maclean and A Morley, *Profiling Civil Litigation: The Case for Research* (Legal Aid Board Research Unit, 1996).
[3] Legal Aid Board, *Legal Aid—Targetting Need* (1995).

10

LEGAL EXPENSES INSURANCE

Solicitors have a duty to advise clients on whether their liability for costs may be covered by insurance.[1] Legal expenses insurance (LEI) policies are typically sold as 'add-ons' to other policies, particularly motor vehicle, household, and building policies. The existence of LEI cover may not only affect a person's decisions in litigation but also interrelate with the availability of public funding or after-the-event insurance, which are topics discussed in the two succeeding chapters. The existence of a sufficient number of individual claimants with adequate LEI cover may, on the assumption that such cover can be aggregated, provide significant funding for a multi-party action. **10.01**

It is estimated that in 1998 there were 15 million policies in force, representing gross written premium of £110–20 million. About half of the gross premium was derived from policies covering uninsured loss recovery of motoring risks, and roughly a quarter each for other personal accounts (especially sold with household and building cover) and commercial cover.[2] In 1997 there were approximately 12.6 million LEI policy units in force, generating 337,000 claims with aggregate value of £39.5 million.[3] The level of market penetration has grown only moderately during the 1990s[4] whereas LEI is much more widespread in Germany, Sweden, and France.[5] Although 17 per cent of adults may have LEI cover, many **10.02**

---

[1] Solicitors' Costs Information and Client Care Code 1999, para 4(j). There has been evidence that some solicitors are not observing this duty (17 Sept 1999) New Law Journal 1372.

[2] N Stanbury, *Legal Expenses Insurance and Assistance Insurance* (Monitor Press, 1999).

[3] Association of British Insurers, *Factsheet: Legal Expenses Insurance* (1999).

[4] The Law Society, *Legal Expenses Insurance In The UK: A Report By Consumers' Association and The Law Society* (1991); Sir Peter Middleton, *Review of Civil Justice and Legal Aid* (Lord Chancellor's Department, 1997) 80; N Rickman and A Gray, 'The Role of Legal Expenses Insurance in Securing Access to the Market for Legal Services' in AAS Zuckerman and R Cranston (eds), *Reform of Civil Procedure* (OUP, 1995).

[5] Lord Chancellor's Department, *Consultation Paper: Eligibility for Civil Legal Aid* (1991). In Sweden, 80% of the population is covered by a compulsory legal expenses insurance system primarily covering opponents' costs, which from 1973 to 1997 was an adjunct to the comprehensive legal aid system covering own costs. From 1997, the Legal Aid Act 1996 introduced radical reforms with the principal aim of achieving cost savings, under which access to legal aid is only available once LEI cover is exhausted: see F Regan, 'Retreat from Equal Justice? Assessing the Recent Swedish Legal

Chapter 10: Legal Expenses Insurance

people who have this have low awareness of the fact[6] and solicitors' practice in ascertaining whether clients have LEI cover has been criticised.[7]

10.03 LEI policies are provided by a small number of specialist providers.[8] Although there are general similarities between the policies of different providers, the terms of each contract must be considered. One important issue, as with all prospective insurance policies, is whether cover is 'occurrence based' (loss arising out of an event occurring within the period of insurance) or on a 'claims made' basis (loss for which the claim occurs within the period of insurance). Cover only arises under some policies three or six months after acceptance, in order to limit insurers' exposure to adverse selection (insureds buying cover when they know or suspect that a claim might arise). The level of any excess, or term requiring the insured to contribute a fixed proportion of the loss, perhaps 10 per cent, must be considered. As with all insurance, the insured must comply with the requirement to notify the insured promptly of the loss, failing which the insurer may deny cover.

10.04 The main advantage of LEI is its low cost. The average premium in 1998 was about £8, with most in the range of £5–15. The insurance premium is recoverable, subject to the court's discretion on costs, from the losing party.[9] Another advantage is the availability of legal advice lines for very low additional cost (20p–£1).[10]

10.05 There are various disadvantages and pitfalls with LEI policies, of which the following are particularly relevant. First, the limit of indemnity is usually £25,000 or £50,000 on personal policies: few would go as high as £100,000 and then only for

---

Aid and Family Law Reforms' [2000] CJQ 168. LEI is facilitated where costs are fixed, proportionate, and modest, as in Germany, where in 1997 annual premium income was £1.6 bn, there were 3 million claims, giving rise to £800m income in legal fees to the country's 90,000 lawyers: V Prais (17 Sept 1999) NLJ 1372.

[6] Consumers' Association, *Policy Report: Legal expenses insurance: realising its potential* (1998). A survey carried out for the Consumers' Association in 1997 found that those most likely to have LEI cover were male, aged 35 to 54, social classes ABC, and more affluent.

[7] Consumers' Association, 'Solicitors on Trial' *Which?* (Oct 1995) 8.

[8] Notably DAS Legal Expenses Insurance Co Ltd, FirstAssist (an insurance management organisation wholly owned by Royal and Sun Alliance), Eastgate Assistance (an insurance management organisation providing LEI underwritten on behalf of Lloyd's syndicates). An insurer wishing to provide LEI after 1 July 1990 is required by The Insurance Companies (Legal Expenses Insurance) (Application for Authorisation) Regulations 1990, SI 1990/1160 to obtain authorisation from the Department of Trade and Industry, unless exempted. Insurers authorised to carry on any class of general business before that date were deemed under the Insurance Companies Act 1982 to be authorised to provide LEI under a separate section of such a general policy. LEI business must comply with The Insurance Companies (Legal Expenses Insurance) Regulations 1990, SI 1990/1159, implementing Directive 87/34/EEC.

[9] Access to Justice Act 1999, s 29.

[10] There were 640,000 calls to advice lines in 1997, an increase of 170% since 1990. Association of British Insurers, *Factsheet: Legal Expenses Insurance* (1999).

commercial entities on a 'stand alone basis'. Whilst these levels would cover small claims and most fast track claims, cover could easily be exhausted for other claims. The litigant needs to consider exposure if the case is lost: if half of £25,000 cover is notionally allocated against the risk of opponents' costs and VAT is included, that only leaves some £10,600 for his own costs.[11]

10.06 Secondly, policies typically impose a merits test and/or reasonable cost-benefit requirement, such as that the insured's case must have reasonable prospects of success, having regard to overall cost, and will probably achieve a worthwhile result, such that the strength of the legal position and the cost-benefit risk justify taking the proceedings. Difficulties can arise over a number of aspects: whether such tests are satisfied, and hence whether this condition precedent for indemnity under the policy is satisfied; what evidence is required from whom in order to establish that the tests are satisfied (independent expert or legal opinions may be called for); and whether the cost of such preliminary investigation is covered under the policy. Some insurers make an assessment charge for the cost of assessing whether to provide cover.

10.07 Thirdly, there may be differences of view over choice of solicitor. The insured must be free to choose a lawyer to defend, represent, or serve his interests in any inquiry or proceedings.[12] The wording of some LEI policies has been criticised as breaching this provision:[13] non-compliance would lead to unenforceability and may be a criminal offence.[14] However, it has been said that the insurer retains choice of representation in various circumstances. First, the insurer is free to deal with the matter itself through its own lawyer before the insured issues proceedings. Secondly, although the insurer is prevented from imposing its choice on an unwilling insured, or of restricting the insured's choice, the insurer may advise or in practice select a lawyer unless the insured objects. There are clear advantages for the insurer of speed, trust, and cost (negotiation of low rates for volume business) if it is enabled to use one of its panel lawyers. Thirdly, the insurer may be able to demonstrate that the insured's choice of lawyer is inappropriate, given the nature or location of the dispute, the nominated lawyer's expertise, or the forum of proceedings.[15]

10.08 Fourthly, there may be a difference of view in relation to how the proceedings should be conducted. For example, the insurer may conclude that the proceedings should be discontinued or that cover should be withdrawn, perhaps if it appears

---

[11] D Greer, 'Legal expenses insurance—have they *really* got you covered' (21 May 1999) NLJ 781.
[12] The Insurance Companies (Legal Expenses Insurance) Regulations 1990, r 6.
[13] D Greer, 'Legal Expenses insurance—have they *really* got you covered' (21 May 1999) NLJ 781.
[14] Insurance Companies Act 1982, ss 71 and 81.
[15] N Stanbury, *Legal Expenses Insurance and Assistance Insurance* (Monitor Press, 1999).

that a reasonable settlement is unlikely to be achieved or if the insured does not accept a reasonable offer. There is considerable scope for differences of view as to conduct of proceedings in a multi-party situation. Whilst LEI policies include dispute resolution clauses, they may be cumbersome, expensive, and cause delays in practice.[16] The formal position is that the solicitor is instructed by the insured but must report to both insured and insurer. A solicitor who conceals relevant information from the LEI insurer, such as the fact that relevant action has been taken, or the existence or nature of counsel's adverse opinion, may be liable to the insurer for negligence, negligent misstatement, or fraudulent misrepresentation.[17]

10.09 An LEI insurer will not ordinarily be liable above the limit of indemnity for opponents' costs.[18] However, a liability insurer may be liable, under the court's discretion to award costs against a non-party, in exceptional circumstances, if he intermeddles in the conduct of the case in a wanton and officious manner, such that control of the litigation does not remain with the insured and solicitor. The court has held that a liability (not LEI) insurer who took control of the defence of an impecunious defendant in order to limit his exposure may be liable in excess of the limit of indemnity.[19]

---

[16] The Insurance Companies (Legal Expenses Insurance) Regulations 1990, reg 8, requires the contract to include an arbitration clause and reg 9 requires that in the event of a conflict of interest arising the insurer must notify the insured in writing that the insured has a right to independent legal advice and may refer the matter to arbitration.
[17] *DAS Legal Expenses Insurance Co Ltd v Hughes Hooker & Co* (6 Nov 1995).
[18] *Murphy and Another v Young & Co's Brewery and Sun Alliance* [1997] 1 WLR 1591, CA.
[19] *TGA Chapman Ltd and Another v Christopher and Sun Alliance* [1997] 1 WLR 12, CA; *Citibank NA and Others v Excess Insurance Co Ltd*, Queen's Bench Division (Transcript), 7 Aug 1998.

11

CONDITIONAL FEE ARRANGEMENTS

A.	Background	11.01	H.	The Need for Risk Assessment	11.49
B.	Permitted Conditional Fees	11.07	I.	Risks of Different Types of Case	11.53
C.	Setting the Uplift	11.13	J.	Financial Implications of Different Types of Case	11.55
D.	The Costs Risk and the Insurance Solution	11.18	K.	The Bar and CFAs	11.62
E.	Risk Assessment under CFAs	11.23	L.	Conflicts between Lawyer and Client with CFAs	11.63
	Risk for the client	11.24			
	Risk for the lawyers	11.25			
	Risk for insurers	11.27	M.	Risk Assessments and CFAs in Multi-Party Actions: The Future	11.73
	Funding of investigation costs	11.29			
	Payment of insurance premiums	11.30			
F.	Recoverability of Success Fees and Insurance Premiums	11.35	N.	Economic Impact on Defendants	11.82
G.	Notification and Challenge	11.43	O.	The International Context	11.83

A. Background

A conditional fee arrangement (CFA) allows the client to transfer some risk to his lawyer, whose level of remuneration is contingent on the outcome of the case. Where such arrangements are coupled with insurance policies, the client may reduce his risk almost to zero. Until the later 1990s, CFAs between lawyer and client were not enforceable in English law (and were both torts and crimes[1] until abolition of the medieval offences of 'maintenance' and 'champerty' by the Criminal Law Act 1967), although speculative fees have long been known in Scotland but not extensively used. Maintenance is the giving of assistance or encouragement to one of the parties to litigation by a person who has neither interest in the litigation

11.01

---

[1] *British Waterways Board v Norman* [1993] 22 HLR 232; *Aratra Potato Co Ltd v Taylor Joynson Garrett (a Firm)* [1995] 4 All ER 695; Solicitors Rules of Professional Conduct, rule 8; Solicitors Journal, 1 May 1998; Bar Code of Conduct, para 308; see also the Scottish decision *Quantum Claims Compensation Specialists Ltd v Powell*, The Times, 26 Feb 1998.

nor any other motive recognised by law as justifying the interference. Champerty is a form of maintenance whereby the maintainer has an interest in the proceeds of the litigation.[2]

11.02 In 1979 the Royal Commission on Legal Services rejected contingency fees in this country, on the basis that to give lawyers a direct financial interest in their cases endangers the profession's independence and objective disinterest. Law Society rules were changed in 1987 to permit solicitors in England and Wales to act on a contingency basis when representing clients making claims in foreign jurisdictions where such arrangements were allowed and also in non-contentious business. This facilitated claims being brought by English and Welsh plaintiffs in the USA.

11.03 In 1988 both the Civil Justice Review and the joint Law Society and Bar Council committee on the future of the legal profession (the Marre Committee) recommended that CFAs should be considered. Some proposals were put forward the following year in the Lord Chancellor's Department's Green Paper on Contingency Fees, in line with government policy of deregulation and encouraging competition and consumer choice. Given the absence of widely purchased legal expenses insurance, the financial limitation of legal aid to the poorest, and the comparatively high cost of legal services for litigation, both in absolute terms and in relation to prevailing levels of damages awarded, there was an argument that there was a sector of the public which was 'too rich' for legal aid but 'too poor' to meet the costs of legal action and that this sector was substantial and growing. The group is described by the acronym 'MINELAS'—middle income not eligible for legal aid sector. One of the counter-arguments was that if members of this sector had considered the ability to litigate to be sufficiently important they would have purchased more legal expenses insurance. The change in the law may have owed something to the Scottish background of the then Lord Chancellor, Lord Mackay of Clashfern, since a form of conditional fees has been permitted, although not widely used, in Scotland for some time. However, as a result of the legal aid crisis in the early 1990s, it became a fiscal, practical, and political necessity for a viable CFA to be available by 1995, both as an alternative to and ultimately replacing legal aid for the poor and to extend access to justice to those with middle incomes.

11.04 The Courts and Legal Services Act 1990, section 58, was the enabling legislation which permitted CFAs to be introduced in England and Wales in 1995 for personal injury, human rights, and insolvency cases.[3] They were extended in 1998 to all civil cases except family cases.[4] Conditional fees must be specified in a written

---

[2] *Giles v Thompson* [1993] All ER 321, HL.
[3] The Conditional Fee Agreements Order 1995, SI 1995/1674 and The Conditional Fee Agreements Regulations 1995, SI 1995/1675.
[4] Conditional Fee Agreements Order 1998, SI 1998/1860.

agreement between the person providing advocacy or litigation services and the client, under which normal fees, or normal fees plus an uplift calculated as a percentage of the recovery, are to be paid in the event of success.[5] Any percentage uplift must be stated in the agreement. Contingency arrangements are not allowable in criminal proceedings.

There were two main reasons for the five-year delay between the enabling legislation and its implementation in 1995. One was the negotiation of appropriate insurance policies at acceptable premiums to cover the risk of liability for opponents' costs in the event of failure. This is discussed below. The second issue was difficulty in deciding on the maximum percentage uplift which should be allowed.[6] The two issues are linked, since both affect the litigant's risk, cost, and potential recovery. In a consultation paper in 1991[7] the Lord Chancellor said:

11.05

> The uplift must be sufficient to allow lawyers to absorb losses sustained in unsuccessful cases, but there must be no risk of very high payments in successful ones, which are substantially above in cash terms what the lawyer would ordinarily have received for his work. To allow this might generate a risk of the lawyer developing an improper personal interest in a particular case. It is difficult to be sure at what level to pitch the uplift to balance these competing considerations, but an uplift of 10% on the costs otherwise payable might be about right.

The maximum uplift currently allowed is 100 per cent.[8] As to present government thinking regarding the limit on a success fee, see below.[9]

11.06

B. Permitted Conditional Fees

From 30 July 1998, CFAs for advocacy on litigation services, in which all or part of the fees and expenses are to be payable only in specified circumstances, are available

11.07

---

[5] Economic analysis indicates that a system where lawyers' fees are based on a controlled percentage of timed work is preferable to one based on a percentage of the total damage award in ability not to encourage claims with low probability of success. DN Dewees, JRS Prichard and MJ Trebilcock, 'An Economic Analysis of Cost and Fee Rules for Class Actions' [1981] 10 Journal of Legal Studies 155–185.

[6] In 1992, the Master of the Rolls, Lord Donaldson, was reported as describing an uplift of 10% as 'a damn silly arrangement'! The Law Society was in favour of a 20% uplift but also said that it could make an argument for an uplift of 100% on the basis that it would allow a lawyer to break even if only half the cases taken on a conditional fee basis were successful. In mid-Jan 1993 the Lord Chancellor published a draft Statutory Instrument under which the permitted uplift was 20%. No assessment was undertaken of the likely increased costs of litigation which would result from different uplifts. *Hansard*, HC (Series 6) vol 323, col 324W (18 Jan 1999).

[7] Lord Chancellor's Department, *Commencement of s 58 of the Courts and Legal Services Act 1990—Conditional Fee Agreements* (12 Apr 1995).

[8] The Conditional Fee Agreements Order 2000, SI 2000/823. The English scheme of a 100% uplift and 25% cap was copied in South Africa by the Contingency Fees Act, No 66, 1997 which came into force on 23 Apr 1999.

[9] See para 11.13.

Chapter 11: Conditional Fee Arrangements

for all civil cases except family cases.[10] There is a distinction between agreements which do, and do not, provide for an additional success fee to be paid.[11] It must be remembered that although CFAs are colloquially known as 'no win no fee' arrangements, there is no legal requirement for the agreement to be that there will be no payment in the event that there is not success, even though this may be what is often agreed. Instead, the basic legal control relates to regulation of the success fee. Legal aid was withdrawn for personal injury claims from April 2000.[12] The legislation also permits recovery of the insurance premium (against future risk of paying an opponent's legal costs) and the success fee.[13]

11.08 The agreement between legal representative and consumer must be in writing and signed by both parties.[14] It must state that, immediately before it was entered into, the legal representative drew the client's attention to the following matters:[15]

(a) the circumstances in which the client may be liable to pay the costs of the legal representative in accordance with the agreement,
(b) the circumstances in which the client may seek assessment of the fees and expenses of the legal representative and the procedure for doing so,
(c) whether the legal representative considers that the client's risk of incurring liability for costs in respect of the proceedings to which agreement relates is insured against under an existing contract of insurance,
(d) whether other methods of financing those costs are available, and, if so, how they apply to the client and the proceedings in question,
(e) whether the legal representative considers that any particular method or methods of financing any or all of those costs is appropriate and, if he considers that a contract of insurance is appropriate or recommends a particular such contract—

---

[10] Courts and Legal Services Act 1990, s 58 as substituted by Access to Justice Act 1999, s 27; The Conditional Fee Agreements Order 1995, SI 1995/1674; The Conditional Fee Agreements Order 1998, SI 1998/1860. From July 1995 until 30 July 1998 conditional fees were permitted only in relation to three categories of proceedings: proceedings for personal injuries or death; proceedings involving company winding up, insolvency administration, and similar situations; or proceedings before the European Commission of Human Rights or European Court of Human Rights. It was reported that, after July 1998, there was a surge in defamation cases and the first successful trial (without claimant insurance) was reported within six months: *Morelli and Coyle v Sunday Times*. See SJ, 8 Jan 1999.

[11] This took into statute law the decisions of the courts that there were no longer public policy grounds to prevent lawyers working for less than their normal fees if they were unsuccessful (*Thai Trading Co (A Firm) v Taylor* [1998] 3 All ER 65, CA) and that it was lawful for a CFA to apply in an arbitration (*Bevan Ashford v Geoff Yeandle (Contractors) Ltd* [1993] 3 All ER 238, ChD), which s 58A(4) of the 1999 Act permitted explicitly; but see *Geraghty & Co v Awad Awwad* (CA, Schiemann LJ, 25 Nov 1999).

[12] The Access to Justice Act 1999, Sch 15 brought into force by The Access to Justice 1999 (Commencement No 3, Transitional Provisions and Savings) Order 2000, SI 2000/774.

[13] See para 11.35 below.

[14] The Conditional Fee Agreements Regulations 2000, SI 2000/692, reg 6.

[15] The Conditional Fee Agreements Regulations 2000, SI 2000/692, reg 4.

B. Permitted Conditional Fees

(i) his reasons for doing so, and
(ii) whether he has an interest in doing so.

The agreement must also state:[16]

(a) the particular proceedings or parts of them to which it relates (including whether it relates to any counterclaim, appeal, or proceedings to enforce a judgment or order);
(b) the circumstances in which the legal representative's fees and expenses or part of them are payable;
(c) what, if any, payment is due—
   (i) if those circumstances only partly occur;
   (ii) irrespective of whether those circumstances occur; and
   (iii) on the termination of the agreement for any reason; and
(d) the amounts which are payable in all the circumstances and cases specified or the method to be used to calculate them and, in particular, whether the amounts are limited by reference to the damages which may be recovered on behalf of the client.

11.09 A CFA which does not comply with the statutory parameters remains prohibited by rule 8 of the Solicitors Practice Rules, unenforceable under section 58(1) of the Courts and Legal Services Act 1990,[17] and is unenforceable under the common law doctrines of maintenance and champerty.[18]

11.10 The prohibition against contingency fees should be distinguished from the indemnity principle.[19] If a person enters into an agreement with his lawyer that the

---

[16] The Conditional Fee Agreements Regulations 2000, SI 2000/692, reg 2.

[17] As substituted by the Access to Justice Act 1999, s 27. Contingency fees were not intended to be legitimated by the 1999 Act: *Hansard,* HC Standing Committee E Access to Justice Bill [Lords], col 254 (11 May 1999).

[18] See para 11.01 above. The common law rule was based on public policy considerations directed against wanton and officious meddling in the disputes of others in which the maintainer has no interest at all. Public policy, however, changes with time. Legal aid and trade union funding of litigation are well-established exceptions to the rule against maintenance and are supported by public policy considerations. A term that 'Apart from disbursements our bills will be delivered when each matter is finalised in all respects with a 20 per cent reduction from solicitor/client costs for any lost cases' was held to be unenforceable in *Aratra Potato Company Ltd v Taylor Joynson Garrett* [1995] 4 All ER 695 but this was stated to be wrongly decided in *Thai Trading Co (a Firm) v Taylor* [1998] 3 All ER 65, CA per Millett LJ.

[19] See *Thai Trading Co (a Firm) v Taylor* [1998] 3 All ER 65, CA per Millett LJ and the Scottish decision *Quantum Claims Compensation Specialists Ltd v Powell,* The Times, 26 Feb 1998. Although it was later shown in *Hughes v Kingston upon Hull City Council* [1998] All ER (D) 563 that *Thai Trading* was strictly questionable, in that the earlier decision of *Swain v The Law Society* [1983] AC 598, HL had not been cited to the court and was binding. There was general acceptance that contemporary policy was in favour of contingency fees and the professional rules could permit them. Amendments were quickly made to professional rules: Solicitors Rules of Professional Conduct, rule 8; SJ, 1 May 1998; Bar Code of Conduct, para 308. However, *Geraghty & Co v Awad Awwad,* n 11 above, held that only contingency fees permitted by statute were lawful.

lawyer will not charge for work done on the litigation and wins the claim, under the indemnity principle the opponent has no liability to pay any costs because the client cannot recover from the defendant a sum greater than the costs for which he was liable to his solicitor.[20] As a separate rule, if he enters into a CFA outside the permitted statutory parameters and wins, his costs are irrecoverable from his opponent.[21] The law has now been clarified that the legality and enforceability of a CFA which complies with statutory conditions exists as an exception to a general prohibition against all forms of contingent fee arrangements. Thus, from 1999 valid CFAs can encompass arrangements involving success fees (an uplift on the basic fee), speculative fee arrangements (*Thai Trading*), and discounts on normal rules, payable in specified circumstances.[22]

11.11 The Judicial Committee of The Academy of Experts issued a guidance note in 1995 that any form of CFA for expert witnesses is incompatible with the experts' duty of independence and impartiality. Such an agreement would also not satisfy the conditions for a permitted CFA.[23] The proposed *Code of Guidance for Experts* requires payment on a daily or hourly rate basis and prohibits payment contingent on the nature of the evidence given or on the outcome of a case. As a matter of professional conduct, solicitors must not make or offer to make payments to a witness contingent upon the nature of the evidence given or upon the outcome of a case. It is possible, subject to prior agreement, to delay paying an expert until the case has concluded, but the fee must not be calculated dependent upon the outcome.[24]

11.12 Litigation funding agreements with a third party funder, rather than a lawyer, are also permitted, where they satisfy the criteria, where the Lord Chancellor prescribes. This mechanism is intended to permit what is referred to as a Contingency Legal Aid Fund. The government did not favour such a mechanism as a publicly funded scheme because of the danger of adverse selection (good cases being run on private CFAs outside the scheme and the scheme being left with poor cases) but took enabling powers in case of need: no implementing regulations have been made. In these cases, the funder pays the lawyer in the normal way and, in successful cases, is able to recover those costs and a success fee from the other side. The success fee would be paid into the fund to help meet the cost of lawyers' fees if unsuccessful.

---

[20] *Gundry v Sainsbury* [1910] 1 KB 645; *British Waterways Board v Norman*, The Times, 11 Nov 1993; overruled by *Thai Trading*, above; J Levin, 'Solicitors Acting Speculatively and Pro Bono' [1996] CJQ 44.

[21] *Wells and Coles v Barnsley Metropolitan Borough Council; Leeds City Council v Carr*, unreported judgment of Divisional Court (Kennedy LJ, Jowitt J, 15 Oct 1999).

[22] ibid; see Courts and Legal Services Act 1990, s 58(1) as substituted by Access to Justice Act 1999, s 27.

[23] Courts and Legal Services Act 1990, s 58(1).

[24] The Law Society, *The Guide to the Professional Conduct of Solicitors* (8 edn, 1999) para 21.11; Coleman J has said that his practice is always to ask experts if they are remunerated on a contingency or conditional fee basis: *SESA GOA & A/S Bulk & Silimna* (3 Dec 1997).

C. Setting the Uplift

11.13 The Lord Chancellor has the power to specify the maximum permitted percentage uplift that shall apply from time to time.[25] The maximum uplift currently permitted is 100 per cent.[26] It is proposed that there should be no limit for cases in the Commercial Court, the Admiralty Court, or the Technology and Construction Court.[27] Various provisions of the code of solicitors' professional ethics underlie the proposition that the specific percentage uplift agreed in a particular case must reflect the actual risk which that case represents. A solicitor must, for example, act in his client's best interests, do nothing to bring himself or his profession into disrepute, not take unfair advantage of a client nor overcharge for work done.[28] Thus, the Law Society's Handbook states that the success fee should be calculated to reflect the degree of risk, based on the prospects that the case will succeed on liability, and the degree of financial subsidy which the firm will be providing in funding the case.[29]

11.14 The solicitor is required to provide to the client, at the time of agreeing to take the case on a CFA, written reasons for setting the success fee at a specific level.[30] This in effect requires preparation of a written risk assessment of the case[31] on the basis of the available contemporary information. The document may subsequently be disclosable to a paying party and considered by the court if a challenge is made to the level of the success fee at final assessment. Counsel are not required to produce written reasons for the client. The agreement must distinguish elements of the success fee relating to the risk of the solicitor not being paid all or any of his costs and the risk of having himself to meet other costs if the case is lost. The court must be informed, in the particulars of claim or defence filed with the court, that the case is being funded with a CFA which affects a success fee and that insurance has

---

[25] Courts and Legal Services Act 1990, s 58(8).
[26] The Conditional Fees Agreements Order 2000, SI 2000/823.
[27] Lord Chancellor's Department, Consultation Paper, *Conditional Fees: Sharing the Risks of Litigation, The Government's conclusions following consultation on the above paper* (2000).
[28] Solicitors' Practice Rules 1990, rules 1, 12.14, and 14.10. See The Law Society, *The Guide to the Professional Conduct of Solicitors* (1999).
[29] M Napier and F Bawdon, *Conditional Fees: A Survival Guide* (The Law Society, 1995). Some firms have not followed this approach but have adopted practices which appear to be contrary to professional ethics and subject to revision on court assessment; one has contracted only at either 0% or 100% uplift, and another at a standard 75%: K Underwood, SJ, 6 Sept 1996; K Underwood, *No Win No Fee No Worries Conditional and Contingency Fees Explained* (CLT Professional Publishing Ltd, 1998); RCA White and R Atkinson, 'Personal Injury Litigation, Conditional Fees and After-the-Event Insurance' [2000] CJQ 118, 128.
[30] Lord Chancellor's Department, *A Lord Chancellor's Department Consultation Paper, Conditional Fees: Sharing the Risks of Litigation, The Government's conclusions following consultation on the above paper* (2000) para 25.
[31] The Law Society, *Guide to the Professional Conduct of Solicitors* (1999) para 13.04.

been taken out to cover a risk in costs. However, the court should not receive any other details unless the success fee or premium is challenged on final assessment.[32]

11.15 The Law Society has calculated a probability table which specifies the percentage success fee appropriate to the percentage prospect of success, based on the formula:[33]

$$\frac{\text{prospects of failure}}{\text{prospects of success}} \times 100 = \text{success fee}$$

This leads to the conclusion that it is not financially advisable for a solicitor to accept a case on a conditional fee basis with less than a 50 per cent chance of success. The Handbook gives the illustration that a solicitor who insists on a 100 per cent success fee for a case which is 99 per cent certain to succeed 'may' (in nearly every case this must mean 'will') be taking unfair advantage. The sanction which is available to the client is that the client may require the solicitor's bill, including barrister's fees, to be reviewed by the court and, if appropriate, reduced ('assessed'). The court may reduce the percentage uplift of a success fee having regard to all relevant factors including:

(1) the risk that the circumstances in which the fees or expenses would be payable might not occur (ie the risk of losing) and
(2) the disadvantages relating to the absence of payments on account (ie the level and duration of financial subsidy of the litigation provided by the firm) and
(3) whether the amount which might be payable under the CFA is limited to a certain proportion of any damages recovered by the client.[34]

11.16 The third factor listed reflects a major concern which was raised in objection to the introduction of conditional fees. It was pointed out that the lower the value of a claim, the higher the costs would be in proportion to the claim. Costs might swallow up small value claims.[35] The Law Society's response was to include in its model agreement a cap on a solicitor's success fee of 25 per cent of a client's damages. Similarly, the Bar's recommended terms of engagement cap a barrister's success fee at 10 per cent of damages, although under the Law Society's model agreement the 10 per cent must be included in the solicitor's 25 per cent. Neither the 25 per cent cap nor the Law Society's model agreement are binding. It remains

---

[32] Lord Chancellor's Department, *Consultation Paper, Conditional Fees: Sharing the Risks of Litigation, The Government's conclusions following consultation on the above paper* (2000) paras 28, 62.
[33] See also D O'Mahony, S Ellson, D Marshall and P Bennett, *Conditional Fees: Law and Practice* (Sweet & Maxwell, 1999).
[34] Courts and Legal Services Act 1990, s 58 as substituted under the Access to Justice Act 1999, s 27; Civil Procedure Rules, Part 44.
[35] The Lord Chancellor established an inquiry into unregulated claims assessors after a complaint by the Law Society that consumers' damages were being eroded by over-large success fee percentages and proper advice was not being given on costs insurance.

D. The Insurance Solution

to be seen whether non-binding self-regulation will prove to provide sufficient consumer protection.

11.17 It is also relevant that a solicitor has a duty to advise his client of the availability of other methods of funding and to keep him advised as his circumstances change. A client is not bound to apply for, nor accept an offer of, public funding, neither is the client bound to enter into a CFA. Where a client qualifies for public funding with no contribution, the Law Society's Handbook on conditional fees considers that it is almost impossible to see that a CFA could be the preferred option.[36] However, where a client qualifies for public funding but has to pay a contribution, the Handbook considers that a CFA may be his best option—although this is a judgement that needs to be carefully weighed.

D. The Costs Risk and the Insurance Solution

11.18 Critical to the operation of conditional fees is a mechanism to minimise the risk to a claimant of being ordered to pay his opponent's costs if the claimant should lose.[37] The search for a solution was a major factor in the five-year delay between the theoretical enablement of conditional fees in the 1990 Act and their practical introduction in 1995. Leading claimant lawyers acting through the Law Society negotiated extensively with insurance interests to devise an insurance mechanism to cover the costs risk. There was, of course, an element of self-interest for claimant lawyers here: they would not attract much business unless members of the public with average means could be persuaded that the risk of embarking upon litigation would not in future imperil their existing assets. Not altogether surprisingly, however, few insurers regarded the risk as a commercial proposition.

11.19 Progress was possible because of the ability of claimants' solicitors to persuade insurers that the risks of a scheme would be acceptable because a scheme could be devised which would include adequate quality control, the avoidance of adverse selection, and a convergence of solicitors' and insurers' interests.[38] An objective standard for the competence of personal injury solicitors was established by the Law Society's Personal Injury Panel. This was set in motion in August 1993, partly in response to concern and adverse publicity regarding 'a number of notorious PI

---

[36] M Napier and F Bawdon, *Conditional Fees: A Survival Guide* (The Law Society, 1995).
[37] On balance, the English cost allocation rule is supported on economic principles: N Rickman, 'The Economics of Cost Shifting Rules' in AAS Zuckerman and R Cranston (eds), *Reform of Civil Procedure* (OUP, 1995). The rule aims to discourage weak cases, to encourage early settlements that reflect the strength of each party's case, and to enable the winner to have the remedy, if plaintiff, or to fend off the claim, if defendant, without having to meet the costs generated by the losing party opposing or pressing the claim unsuccessfully: Lord Chancellor's Department, *Regulatory impact assessment: Improvement in the availability and use of conditional fees* (1998).
[38] M Napier and F Bawdon, *Conditional Fees: A Survival Guide* (The Law Society, 1995).

cases which had been badly handled by inexperienced solicitors'.[39] The panel had 1,884 members by 1995 but 3,000 by 1997.[40]

11.20 Members of the Personal Injury Panel must have been qualified for at least three years and to have had certain relevant experience, such as to have carried out or supervised at least sixty personal injury instructions in the five years prior to the application, or at least thirty-six such instructions in the prior three years. At least ten of the cases should have been set down for trial, two of which involving a dispute over liability. Lists of required knowledge cover areas of law, procedure, ethics, and professional skills. Members are assessed and reselected every five years.

11.21 Some 1,300 firms have members of the Personal Injury Panel. About 75 per cent of the Personal Injury Panel membership (10 per cent of the profession) are registered as members of the Accident Line scheme, which was launched on 30 June 1994, replacing the Accident Legal Advice Services (ALAS!) which had existed since June 1987. This scheme offers collective marketing through a freephone number and leaflet which are nationally promoted and a free initial half-hour interview for anyone who has been involved in an accident. The scheme achieved instant success: in its first year, 30,000 referrals were made against a forecast that the previous 3,000 per year would increase to 10,000. Since October 1995, members of Accident Line have been able to participate in a Law Society after-the-event insurance scheme for use with CFAs, called Accident Line Protect.

11.22 In the first four years to mid-1999, a total of over 55,000 CFA insurance policies were issued,[41] but this was considerably below the number of personal injury cases funded by legal aid[42] (in 1996–7 some 72,000 general cases plus some 12,000 clinical negligence cases[43]).

E. Risk Assessment under CFAs

11.23 It is necessary to assess the financial risk of any case at the outset. This is particularly so of a case funded by a CFA. Several different risks can be identified: those to the client, the lawyers, and the insurers.

Risk for the client

11.24 The financial risk should normally be negligible under a CFA system where the

---

[39] M Napier and F Bawdon, *Conditional Fees: A Survival Guide* (The Law Society, 1995).
[40] SJ, 14 Feb 1997.
[41] *Hansard*, HC (Series 6) vol 330, col 132W (27 Apr 1999).
[42] *Hansard*, HC Standing Committee E Access to Justice Bill [Lords], cols 144–145 (4 May 1999).
[43] *Hansard*, HC Standing Committee E Access to Justice Bill [Lords], col 164 (4 May 1999).

E. Risk Assessment

client is protected by an insurance policy with an appropriate level of cover. Appropriate protection may be available for (i) payment of the client's own lawyers and experts during the case, (ii) the risk of having to pay the opponents' costs if he loses, and (iii) payment of initial investigation necessary to determine what the chances of success of the case are, whether it can be taken on under a CFA, and what the appropriate level of uplift (success fee) should be, involving legal and possibly expert fees. As the market for CFA insurance develops, a number of policies have become available, offering a range of options on different financial and other terms, some of which include cover for own lawyers' as well as opponents' costs, or which include disbursement funding. These generally exclude cover for multi-party actions but insurers may be persuaded to cover some cases or aspects, perhaps on a risk-sharing basis with public support funding.[44]

Risk for the lawyers

The lawyer is normally risking his profit costs and under-recovery of overheads in taking on a CFA case (aspect (i) for the client) and in undertaking initial assessment (aspect (iii)) if he funds that aspect. The solicitor who enters into a CFA with a client will have to consider not only the financial position of the firm but also exposure to costs of those subcontractors whom he may wish to employ, notably counsel and experts. It may be possible to arrange a CFA with counsel but this is an unethical arrangement with experts. **11.25**

In undertaking a risk assessment, the lawyers will need to consider the inherent chances of success of the particular case, the likely costs of the case, its likely duration, and whether their firm can afford to take it on. A sequence of relevant aspects are considered in this chapter. **11.26**

Risk for insurers

While the risk of success in a particular case should be—and be assessed as being—the same for client, lawyers, and insurers, the financial consequences differ. In particular, the risk to the businesses of solicitors and insurers differs, since each business will have a particular structure and sensitivity to risk. In simple terms, a solicitor might afford to lose more CFA cases than an insurer, before making a loss. **11.27**

The next issue is the need to examine the specific aspects of funding of investigation costs and insurance premiums and their recoverability. This can be a complex issue to understand and, therefore, to explain to a client.[45] **11.28**

---

[44] See para 12.30 below.
[45] RCA White and R Atkinson, 'Personal Injury Litigation, Conditional Fees and After-the-Event Insurance' [2000] CJQ 118.

Funding of investigation costs

11.29 In complex cases, the solicitor may not be able to conclude an acceptable risk assessment without undertaking significant investigation into the facts and merits of the case. A good example of this might be medical negligence cases, which can involve extensive expert evidence. Who is to pay for this? Some public funding may be available, particularly in relation to the costs of initial investigation or to support expensive litigation.[46]

Payment of insurance premiums

11.30 A claimant who enters a CFA should in nearly all cases obtain insurance cover against the risk of being ordered to pay the opponents' costs if he loses. There is no stipulation or restriction of substantive or professional law on who has to pay the premium, nor on how much cover should be obtained. Premiums may be paid by clients, solicitors,[47] or others. (Research showed that in 1996 clients paid the premiums in as many as 96 per cent of cases.[48]) There is a duty on the solicitor to explain to clients the availability and advantages of insurance cover. Clients might be attracted to dispense with cover, particularly if they have difficulty funding the premium. Solicitors should be able to demonstrate that they have exercised considerable care in advising clients in such a situation in view of the considerable risks to clients. The situation in which it can genuinely be in a client's interests not to have such cover will be very rare.[49]

11.31 Where insurance has become an integral part of the system, there is a convincing argument that defendants will be unjustifiably prejudiced if claimants do not have insurance where this could otherwise have been available, particularly where the claimants have insufficient realisable assets. When CFAs were introduced, there was much discussion that the poor would be denied access to justice if they could not afford the premiums, particularly the higher insurance premiums which would be necessary for the more complex cases such as medical negligence.[50] At that stage, there was little reliable information on the likely level of insurance premiums but the lowest figure then quoted for a medical negligence case was £3,000.

---

[46] See ch 12 below.
[47] Thompsons fund insurance premiums, investigation costs, and any disbursements. The Lawyer, 15 Feb 1999.
[48] S Yarrow, *The price of success* (Policy Studies Institute, 1997) 78.
[49] The tobacco litigation 1996–9 was the first multi-party action in which clients did not have costs insurance and this was a factor in the decisions of remaining claimants to discontinue when the defendants offered such an arrangement which included a term that defendants would not seek to enforce their costs against claimants, after the lead cases had all failed on limitation issues.
[50] See various parliamentary debates.

F. Recoverability

When the new system was being debated Ministers asked why solicitors should not pay premiums themselves.[51] The managing partner at leading personal injury firm Irwin Mitchell retorted that even if premiums were at a fairly nominal rate of £100, firms would find the burden prohibitive: his own firm was then working on 400 conditional fee cases.[52] The proposition that lawyers could fund both the premiums and initial investigation was described by a Law Society spokesman as 'absurd to think that [it] is realistic. It would simply be unaffordable in most cases.'[53]

11.32

The Lord Chancellor's basic response on this issue was that every business other than solicitors incurs investigation costs in assessments of the potential for profitable investment in order to decide whether to enter into a contract on the basis that it is likely to prove profitable. It is only lawyers, reared in a legal aid culture, who were paid, win, lose, or draw and who wanted to be exempt from what every other business in the country would regard as an ordinary business cost. Nevertheless, the Lord Chancellor said that he would not rule out legal aid funding where the costs were too high. The Lord Chancellor referred to a number of other possibilities which he was considering. First, he noted that the cost of before-the-event insurance policies was very low (typically £4–20): he seemed to wish to encourage the middle classes to adopt this option as much as possible. Secondly, stop-loss insurance might be available for those lawyers who found that they had a succession of losing cases. Thirdly, the cost of after-the-event insurance might be quite modest in view of an extension of CFAs: he had heard of a premium of £362 covering both sides' costs to a limit of £6,000.

11.33

There may be an issue of insurance coverage on multi-party actions. Does the policy cover a case in a multi-party situation? None of the off-the-peg policies cover group claims but such cover may be negotiated.[54] Consideration needs to be given to various contingencies of costs liability covering individual and common costs, as discussed in chapter 8.

11.34

F. Recoverability of Success Fees and Insurance Premiums

The court has power to include, as part of any costs it may award against the losing party, first, any premium paid for an insurance policy taken out specifically against the need to meet the other side's costs in those proceedings and, secondly,

11.35

---

[51] See The Lawyer, 28 Oct 1997; the *Daily Telegraph*, 7 Nov 1997. As noted above, some solicitors fund premiums, investigation costs, and disbursements.
[52] NLJ, 24 Oct 1997.
[53] The *Guardian*, 7 Nov 1997.
[54] As it was for the Gulf War syndrome claimants in 1997; LS Gaz, 3 Sept 1997; SJ, 5 and 12 Sept 1997.

the successful lawyer's success fee.[55] A success fee and insurance premium are recoverable only for causes of action in respect of which the first CFA is signed or insurance policy taken out after 1 April 2000.[56] There is currently a dispute over whether a success fee is recoverable if the CFA is entered into before the issue of proceedings, without giving the defendant an opportunity to settle a notified claim.

11.36 A parallel provision applies to bodies, such as trade unions, which fund litigation on behalf of their members from the body's own resources and may not have separate insurance to meet the other side's costs. When such a body supports a successful case, costs awarded may include an amount equivalent to the insurance premiums that would have been recoverable. The bodies which may benefit from this provision, and on what terms, are subject to specification by the Lord Chancellor.[57] The additional amount which the prescribed body can recover towards the self-insurance element shall not exceed the likely cost to the member or other person of the premium of an insurance policy against the risk of incurring a liability to pay the costs of other parties to the proceedings.[58]

11.37 Only that element of the success fee which represents the risk the lawyer is taking of not being paid and/or having to pay disbursements if the case is lost is recoverable. Other elements, such as the cost of postponement of payment of fees or expenses or of foregoing payments on account, are not recoverable.[59]

11.38 Rules of court may provide that the amount awarded as costs need not be limited to the amount that the litigant would have been liable to pay his or her own lawyers if costs had not been awarded.[60] This breached the common law indemnity principle, under which a successful party in an action has a right to be wholly or partly indemnified against a liability for costs actually incurred in bringing or defending the proceedings, but no more. If no actual costs are agreed for payment by the client,

---

[55] Access to Justice Act 1999, s 29. The government considered that recoverability should be subject to the court's discretion in awarding costs, since automatic recoverability would be an inequitable balance of power between claimants and defendants: *Hansard,* HC Standing Committee E Access to Justice Bill [Lords], col 261 (11 May 1999).

[56] The Access to Justice Act 1999 (Transitional Provisions) Order 2000, SI 2000/900; see Lord Chancellor's Department, *A Lord Chancellor's Department Consultation Paper, Conditional Fees: Sharing the Risks of Litigation, The Government's conclusions following consultation on the above paper* (2000) para 46.

[57] Access to Justice Act 1999, s 30; The Access to Justice (Membership Organisations) Regulations 2000, SI 2000/693. Matters which the Lord Chancellor will take into account were stated at *Hansard,* HL (Series 5) vol 611, col WA 85 (30 Mar 2000).

[58] CPR Rule 44.3B(1)(b). See Lord Chancellor's Department, *A Lord Chancellor's Department Consultation Paper, Conditional Fees: Sharing the Risks of Litigation, The Government's conclusions following consultation on the above paper* (2000) para 102.

[59] CPR Rule 44.3B(1)(a). See Lord Chancellor's Department, *A Lord Chancellor's Department Consultation Paper, Conditional Fees: Sharing the Risks of Litigation, The Government's conclusions following consultation on the above paper* (2000) para 17.

[60] Access to Justice Act 1999, s 31.

F. Recoverability

then no costs should be paid by the losing party.[61] This change allows the development of insurance premiums which are inflated above the level required to cover the risk of the actual case, so as to cover insurers' costs of cases lost and investigation costs. There was concern that, without such a provision, the level of premiums could be challenged by losing parties as being champertous and this would threaten the financial viability of insurers of CFAs and, hence, the CFA system itself.

This issue is related to the appropriate level of lawyers' rates. Chief Taxing Master Hurst has pointed out that if solicitors are not permitted to recover success fees above their normal rates under a contingency contract, they could merely spread their risk by charging higher *basic* fees, thereby effectively building the success fee into the basic fee.[62] Chief Taxing Master Hurst thought that conditional fees would gradually become redundant and give way almost entirely to contingency fees. 'Ordinary' charging rates might vary between different types of case and become more finely tuned as more accurate data accumulated. He did not speculate as to what the courts' attitude would be on taxation. The analysis might run like this. Under a CFA, the basic fee would be subject to reduction on taxation but at that time it was proposed that the success fee would be recoverable from the unsuccessful defendant and presumably 100% of this would be recoverable. Under a contingency fee system, which would be simpler for clients and opponents to understand and operate, the single fee involved would be subject to taxation—but it is not clear how far the courts would reduce this on taxation: would the reduction on taxation apply to the entire fee (including notional success fee) or only to some smaller fraction equating to the historical basic fee but ignoring the success fee? Would it even be possible to distinguish a basic fee from a success fee within a new style higher rated contingency fee? The aim of enabling solicitors to profit from their success would be at the cost of a significantly increased overall cost to defendants and their insurers. 11.39

Recoverability benefits both claimants (who can recover damages in full, with no deduction other than the cost of any initial investigation and screening, such cost being either in full or the interest of any loan to fund it) and solicitors (who can recover their full basic and success fees, subject to taxation but not subject to any cap).[63] The Lord Chancellor stated that he regarded recovery of the success fee as the answer to the point that uplifts are bad because they are at the expense of 11.40

---

[61] The Stationery Office Limited, *Explanatory Notes: Access to Justice Act 1999* (1999) para 141; Lord Chancellor's Department, *Controlling Costs: A Consultation Paper* (1999) CP 4/99.

[62] NLJ, 20 Mar 1998. Hourly rates claimed in a multi-party case involving NHS radiotherapy treatment were reportedly in some cases almost four times the prevailing prescribed rates for legal aid work and very substantially higher than rates paid by the NHS to its own solicitors. Medical Litigation (May 1999) 14.

[63] Lord Chancellor's Department, *Regulatory impact assessment: Improvement in the availability and use of conditional fees* (1998).

claimants whose damages would otherwise be diminished.[64] Recoverability was also supported as tending to dispose of claims more rapidly, sensibly, and appropriately than previously.[65]

11.41 It is recognised that recoverability of success fees from defendants is not without its problems.[66] The Law Society accepted that the case for recoverability was 'far less clear' in commercial or contract litigation, when use of CFAs would be driven by the exercise of choice rather than economic necessity, as would be more likely in personal injury cases. It was objected that claimants have no incentive to withdraw an unmeritorious claim or to reach a sensible compromise.[67] The Legal Aid Board noted the danger of lawyer-driven litigation as lawyers would have an incentive to pursue claims regardless of whether the damages claimed were small or trivial.[68] Recoverability removes virtually all risk from claimants, who are enabled largely to escape the intended effect of the 'loser pays costs' rule, since claimants can retain damages largely undiminished by the deduction of the expense of achieving them, whereas the historical phenomenon of 'legal aid blackmail' on defendants to settle irrespective of merits is replaced by a comparable 'CFA blackmail'. Recoverability of substantial sums has an inflationary effect on insurance premiums.[69] Some commentators predicted that the government's decision to permit recoverability would alone increase damages awards by up to 40 per cent.[70] Lord Hunt of Wirrall summarised the issue as being that defendants would have to pay for cases won through a levy on cases lost: he asked whether access to justice did not require fairness between claimants and defendants.[71] On the other hand, the position of defendants and insurers was to be improved when they won cases, in that under a CFA-plus-insurance system their (taxed) costs would become recoverable in all cases, unlike previously when plaintiffs were legally aided. Further, the court retains a discretion on costs not to award the success fee or insurance premium in full.[72]

---

[64] *Hansard*, HL (Series 5) vol 591, col 1116 (23 July 1998).
[65] Per Lord Woolf, *Hansard,* HL (Series 5) vol 595, col 1154 (14 Dec 1998).
[66] Lord Goodhart and Lord Phillips of Sudbury described this as unfair to the losing party who has to pay three sets of costs (his own, his opponent's basic and success fees) plus the insurance premium where the opponent has chosen to protect himself against the risk of losing. *Hansard,* HL (Series 5) vol 597, col 603 (16 Feb 1999). K Underwood, an exponent of CFAs, stated that it is wrong for the success fee to follow the event and it would be better to have a one-off 25% to 30% increase in damages—Litigation Funding (Mar 1999).
[67] Letter to members from the Medical Protection Society, Dec 1998.
[68] Legal Aid Board, *The Legal Aid Board's response to the Lord Chancellor's consultation paper* (May 1988).
[69] Which were in any event subject at the same time to significant upward pressure as a result of a House of Lords decision that multipliers for personal injury awards should be calculated by reference to the returns available from risk-free index-linked government bonds, approximately 3% per annum: *Wells v Wells, Page v Sheerness Steel Co, Thomas v Brighton Health Authority* [1999] 1 AC 345.
[70] LS Gaz (22 July 1998).
[71] *Hansard,* HL (Series 5) vol 591, col 1108 (23 July 1998).
[72] 'I cannot think that it would be right that the courts should be obliged to award the success fee

As the Legal Aid Board recognised, a perverse incentive might operate in that defendants in cases with meritorious defences which were either unsuccessful at trial or settled on a commercial basis would end up paying more than defendants who had poor defences which only justified low success fees because of the increased costs. This situation is exacerbated where the defence also has to pay a success fee. Is it good public policy to impose a lesser penalty on the negligent or reckless, without incentive?

A conceptual difficulty is that the uplift percentage is agreed between solicitor and client as a matter of contract. But the agreement is that the financial obligation may be settled by a third party who has no ability to influence the terms—he is not involved at that stage but is expected to pick up a tab over the size of which he has no direct control. It is intended that defence lawyers would 'provide a proper check on the temptation for unscrupulous claimants' lawyers to set the success fee too high'.[73]

G. Notification and Challenge

Opponents must receive notification of the existence of a CFA and of an insurance policy, but not of the level of the fee nor price of the policy: failure to provide information about a funding arrangement in accordance with a rule, practice direction, or court order renders the percentage increase fee or insurance premium irrecoverable.[74] Notification should take place upon intimation to the opponent that a claim is being pursued or within seven days of entering into the CFA (if later). There is no requirement to inform the opponent where the CFA attracts no success fee.[75] Where the opponent has not been notified and he has been prejudiced by the failure to notify, the court has discretion on final assessment to disallow all or part of the success fee. In exercising this discretion the court should consider whether the disallowed element should be borne by the client, for instance where the omission was as a result of the client's instructions, or by the solicitor if failure to notify was his or her fault.[76]

The losing opponent may challenge the level of the success fee on final assessment

11.42

11.43

11.44

---

and insurance premium in full where it was otherwise exercising its discretion not to award costs or to award only part of the costs' per Lord Irvine of Lairg QC, *Hansard*, HL (Series 5) vol 596, col 975 (26 Jan 1999).

[73] *Hansard*, HC Standing Committee E Access to Justice Bill [Lords], col 259 (11 May 1999).
[74] CPR Rule 44.3B(1)(c).
[75] Lord Chancellor's Department, *A Lord Chancellor's Department Consultation Paper, Conditional Fees: Sharing the Risks of Litigation, The Government's conclusions following consultation on the above paper* (2000) paras 18, 55.
[76] Lord Chancellor's Department, *A Lord Chancellor's Department Consultation Paper, Conditional Fees: Sharing the Risks of Litigation, The Government's conclusions following consultation on the above paper* (2000) paras 22, 59.

on the basis that it was unreasonable given what the solicitor knew or ought reasonably to have known at the time the CFA was entered into. The government recognised that a significant proportion of clients have little or no experience to enable them to judge whether a success fee is reasonable and decided that protection from unreasonable success fees was required.[77] The losing opponent may also challenge on final assessment the choice of insurance cover and the cost of the insurance premium by demonstrating to the court that the choice was wholly unreasonable and generated excessive costs.[78]

11.45 The Law Society[79] had argued that the percentage should not be disclosed prior to conclusion or settlement of the case, since that would effectively disclose the privileged advice of plaintiffs' lawyers to their clients on the chances of success. However, various contrary views were put forward.[80] First, it is a fundamental principle of the new Woolf approach to litigation that all parties' costs should be transparent so as to encourage settlement, ie costs at each stage of the litigation should be disclosed so that opponents could evaluate their risk and consider settling when the comparative risks of exposure to recovery became adverse. This would not be achieved if a significant element of opponents' costs remained undisclosed. Unless a defendant knows whether a case against him is being run on a CFA or funded by the claimant personally, or whether insurance cover is or is not in existence for the defendant's costs, he is not in a position to assess his risk with a view to settlement or otherwise. If no insurance cover is available and the claimant has no assets, the assessment of risk by the successful defendant will have been entirely erroneous. Surely, it was argued, the transparency principle inherent in Woolf requires early disclosure of the existence of both a CFA and an insurance policy, as well as the percentage uplift.

11.46 Secondly, the research had shown that percentages should bear far greater affinity to the (disclosed) type of case than to the (undisclosed) advice on merits. All road traffic cases which passed the screening stage should, therefore, merit roughly the same (low) level of percentage. Whilst there might historically have been a greater range of risk in medical negligence cases than on legal aid,[81] those which passed

---

[77] Lord Chancellor's Department, *A Lord Chancellor's Department Consultation Paper, Conditional Fees: Sharing the Risks of Litigation, The Government's conclusions following consultation on the above paper* (2000) paras 35, 37.

[78] Lord Chancellor's Department, *A Lord Chancellor's Department Consultation Paper, Conditional Fees: Sharing the Risks of Litigation, The Government's conclusions following consultation on the above paper* (2000) para 68.

[79] The Law Society, *Ensuring Justice?* (1998).

[80] C Hodges, 'Access to Justice with Conditional Fees' (19 June 1998) New Law Journal; Lord Chancellor's Department, *Conditional Fees: Sharing the Risks of Litigation: A Consultation Paper* (1999), CP 7/99.

[81] The Legal Aid Board's May 1998 paper stated that 47% of its medical negligence cases closed in 1996–7 went no further than the investigative stage. Of those which proceeded further, 41% resulted in an agreement to pay or an award of damages. The net cost of the initial 47% was £14 million, compared with total net cost of £27 million—'a cause for real concern'.

the screening stage on CFAs should, as Litigation Protection's experience showed, have a more consistent success rate, and therefore justify success fees which would be more predictable—and also lower than might otherwise have been thought on risk grounds.

Thirdly, all the evidence on a case should be disclosed at an early stage under the new procedural rules, so all parties should have a full understanding of the chance of success. Revealing the percentage uplift in reality may not reveal a great deal of information to the opponent. On the one hand, it might mean that the first party has either a lower or, indeed, higher chance of success than normal. This may well be useful information in promoting early settlement. On the other hand, it may simply mean that the party and his lawyer have not assessed the risk correctly or are acting unethically: in either case, an entirely incorrect conclusion might be drawn by the opponent. The position can be camouflaged by the claimant's lawyer in effect building a significant element of success fee into his basic fee by agreeing with his client higher basic rates but a moderate success fee percentage, although this would be subject to assessment by the court.[82] Both the client and the losing opponent are able to challenge the level of both success fee and the insurance premium through an assessment by the courts.[83]

11.47

The Law Society agreed that the percentage uplift would have to be judged to some extent on the evidence available to the claimant's lawyer at the time he entered into the case and excluding unforeseeable evidence which emerged later (ie excluding hindsight). However, other factors would also be relevant, including the type of case, and whether the solicitor had carried out reasonable enquiries and screening or ignored sensible investigation. It would be advisable for solicitors seeking to defend percentages which were higher than normal for certain types of case to be able to produce written risk assessments recording exactly what investigation had been done, what evidence was available, and what justification there was for the level of risk decided on. There was thought to be no reason why judges would be inappropriate to carry out this task but costs judges would be appropriate.

11.48

H. The Need for Risk Assessment

Under a CFA, responsibility for initial scrutiny of the merits of a prospective client's case rests on that client's lawyer who, since he is to share the risk[84] and will

11.49

---

[82] CPR, Part 44.
[83] The Law Society had argued against this: The Law Society, *Ensuring Justice?* (1998).
[84] It is inherent in the CFA system that: 'Those with good claims are obliged to forgo part of their entitlement to finance the aspirations of the hopeless, the reckless and occasionally the fraudster'— T Aldridge, SJ, 31 Oct 1997. This tendency is reduced as the accuracy of the lawyer's risk assessment rises. Consumers may seek prior information on their lawyers' expertise and record of success.

not be paid if he backs a claim which fails, has an incentive to carry out a thorough and objective risk assessment and weed out poor cases. The Law Society's Handbook on conditional fees[85] stresses that before embarking on individual cases it is imperative for solicitors' firms as well as clients to undertake both general policy decisions on accepting such arrangements and accurate, objective risk assessments. The Handbook notes the financial risk to the firm of supporting frivolous, complex, or lengthy cases on a conditional fee basis. It notes actuarial calculations which indicate that a case with risk greater than 50 per cent (ie less than a 50 per cent chance of success) would not be reflected in the success fee. This system puts considerable power and responsibility in the hands of claimants' solicitors at the initial stage of deciding whether to pursue cases, particularly where, as under some insurance policies, there is no initial scrutiny of those decisions by the insurer or his agent.[86] Further, the risk assessment must be reviewed and remain accurate and favourable for the lifetime of the case if the solicitor is not to lose money. This involves developing new skills and systems.[87]

11.50 To the extent to which it was carried out before conditional fees were introduced, risk assessment was essentially the function of any counsel involved and of the Legal Aid authorities, rather than solicitors, whose function was essentially and necessarily partisan in arguing the applicant's case to the Board. Previously, the solicitor's function was merely to try and persuade the Legal Aid Board that the case was reasonable: the amount of preparatory work and serious assessment that was done at that stage could be limited since it was not essential in order for the legal aid tests to be applied and so the Board would not fund it. Significant relevant research could be deferred until much later in the action.

11.51 The need for early, informed, and accurate risk assessments under CFAs is consistent with the policy obligations of the Civil Procedure Rules 1998 (CPR), implementing the Woolf reforms. The effect of the Rules is to require all of the essential investigation into a case to be undertaken right at the start, even before proceedings are issued. This front loading of investigation and costs is specifically intended to enable the parties to carry out informed risk assessments at an early stage, so that they can either reach appropriate and early settlement of their dispute or be in a position to proceed through the litigation process swiftly. Indeed, the CPR are specifically designed to cut costs during the litigation process.[88] This would lower the previous cost-risk balance so as to make it easier to run higher risk cases.

---

[85] M Napier and F Bawdon, *Conditional Fees: A Survival Guide* (Law Society, 1997).
[86] Litigation Protection Limited's scrutiny of medical negligence claims being a notable exception—they reject at least 10% of cases accepted by solicitors. LS Gaz 95/12 (25 Mar 1998).
[87] The European Social Fund has donated £125,000 to develop the Risk Assessment In Litigation (RAIL) project, to research the needs of litigation solicitors and develop a training system: SJ, 20 Aug 1999.
[88] CPR, Rule 1.1.

Solicitors acting in a multi-party action who enter into a CFA which conforms to the statutory parameters have no general liability, such as for maintaining the action.[89] This was established earlier in the tobacco litigation, where there had been some interesting misrepresentation of issues related to the funding of CFAs. It was said that defendants in a multi-party action had argued (when in fact they had made no such application) that lawyers acting on a CFA were intimately involved in the action and therefore liable for costs.[90] Furthermore, it was claimed that CFAs would not be viable unless it was established that claimants' lawyers were not liable for costs if the claimant lost:[91] there had in fact been no serious suggestion that there would be any such liability, outside the existing scope of a wasted costs order.[92]

11.52

I. Risks of Different Types of Case

Certain types of case are more attractive risks under a CFA than others. There are two aspects to this. First, certain types of case are recognised as having generally higher chances of success than others. Secondly, there is the financial impact on the lawyers who are acting on the CFA, both in terms of cash flow and of ultimate fees received. These aspects will be examined in turn.

11.53

Table 11.1 shows the success rates from data reported by four surveys. The situation revealed by this data is generally consistent and points to the following conclusions. First, different types of case have intrinsically different chances of success. Road accident claims consistently have a high chance of success, with accidents at work generally good but some way behind. These cases generally involve simple issues of fact and law, with limited evidence and low costs. The outcome of medical negligence cases is much less certain and this is attributable to the fact that they often involve difficult issues of fact and expert opinion which are difficult to predict in the early stages of a case.[93] However, there is some indication that there may have been an increase in success rates over time and this might be connected with the moves towards increased specialisation.[94] The Legal Aid

11.54

---

[89] *Hodgson v Imperial Tobacco Limited* [1998] 2 All ER 673.
[90] *The Times*, 13 Feb 1998.
[91] The *Independent*, 27 Jan 1998.
[92] Supreme Court Act 1981, s 51(b) and RSC Ord 62, r 11.
[93] This was also found in a study of legal aid cases, where clinical negligence cases had a 30.6% success rate compared with 71.2% for all other types of personal injury. Legal Aid Board, *Testing the Code* (1999).
[94] The Legal Aid Board introduced a voluntary quality assurance scheme (franchising) in 1994. The Law Society's Medical Negligence Panel was created in 1993 and the Legal Aid Board later moved to instructing only franchised firms. See also Legal Aid (Prescribed Panels) Regulations 1998, establishing the Clinical Negligence Franchise Panel. From 1 Aug 1999, clinical negligence became the first area of law to be supplied solely through suppliers with quality assured accreditation. Some

Chapter 11: Conditional Fee Arrangements

Table 11.1: Success rates

	Pearson Commission 1974 survey of injuries where tort compensation was obtained (estimates)[a]	Lord Chancellor's Department 1991 review of all legal aid litigation[b]	Fennell 1993 survey of claims handled by APIL solicitors[c]	Shapland 1998 interviews on projections of typical cases[d]
road accidents	25%	84%	98%	90%+
accidents at work	10%	79%	94%	60–98%
medical negligence	—	42%	66%	21–75% 80% if issued
other negligence	3%[e]	61%	0% (single product case)	

[a] Cmnd 7054-II, Table 87.
[b] Lord Chancellor's Department, *Review of Financial Conditions for Legal Aid: A Consultation Paper* (June 1991).
[c] S Fennell, 'Access to Justice for Personal Injury Litigants' [1994] JPIL 30.
[d] J Shapland, A Otterburn, N Cantwell, C Corré, L Hagger, *Affording Civil Justice* (The Law Society, 1998).
[e] This figure was for other injuries possibly due to the act or omission of another, rather than other negligence.

figures show that a very high percentage of medical negligence cases failed sooner or later (80 per cent in 1996–7).[95] A very high percentage fell out after initial investigation and a third of cases which got beyond that stage failed. Lastly, the size of the sample figures specifically for 'other negligence' (which includes product liability) cases is sometimes too small to be meaningful but even so indicates that pharmaceutical cases had a very low success rate.

J. Financial Implications of Different Types of Case

11.55 In addition to the intrinsic success rate of particular types of case, different cases will have differing implications in relation to the financial ability of lawyers to take them on. A larger firm may be able to fund the delayed cash flow caused by taking

---

200 firms were accredited, whereas some 3,200 legal aid firms had previously been able to offer publicly funded advice: *Hansard*, Fourth Standing Committee on Delegated Legislation: Draft Legal Aid (Prescribed Panels) Regulations 1998, col 11 (27 Jan 1999).

[95] (Dec 1998) Medical Litigation 14; this showed only a 52% success rate of cases which passed investigation stage run by specialist panel solicitors compared with 35% by non-specialists; in 1993–4 the failure rate was 88%, per Legal Aid Board, *Annual Report* (1994).

J. Financial Implications

on a case which may not be resolved for an uncertain period, perhaps some years, and also be able to absorb the loss in turnover and profits if the case is ultimately lost.[96]

As with all cases, however funded, it should be remembered that CFAs are unsuitable in the following situations: **11.56**

- cases where the successful claimant's damages and costs are unlikely to be paid by the defendant, because the latter has insufficient available assets;
- cases where the damages and costs recovered are insufficient to cover the claimant's lawyer's basic costs and success fee and leave enough in damages.

Research indicates that CFAs present less risk in cases that do not involve the solicitors in much work, are of a type susceptible to standard procedures, are recognised as being good risks, and are concluded quickly. It has been said that only 'certainty' cases could be pursued.[97] Shapland's research[98] indicated the different consequences of running different types of cases and calculated the success fees which firms should be charging in their typical cases in order to meet the costs they incur in those cases, and compared them with those calculated under the formula recommended by the Law Society.[99] The former represented firms' maximum liability under a CFA in the particular case, not the average success fee which they should charge. The conclusions were: **11.57**

- *Road traffic accident* cases presented few problems under a CFA. Overall success rates were over 90 per cent. Early assessment of liability was straightforward, often based on the comprehensive evidence in a police report. Even cases which go to trial are unlikely very often to exceed the 25 per cent cap and the success fees charged by survey firms were at the right level.
- *Accident at work* cases differed in that they often proceed to issue and exchange of evidence before settling. The evidence is often more extensive than a road traffic case (for example, a complex machine or work practice) and less accessible (not always conveniently summarised in a report by the Health and Safety Executive). Costs and duration are therefore increased. Overall success rates were estimated at 60–98 per cent. Cases which go to trial are highly likely to breach the cap. The trial calculated that the actual success fee required was significantly higher than the official formula. Firms' calculated success fees seemed slightly lower than they should be.

---

[96] For research on the financial viability of firms operating on CFAs, see KPMG, *Conditional Fees: Business Case* (Lord Chancellor's Department, 8 Apr 1998), criticised in D Marshall, 'PI practice under the microscope' (12 June 1998) SJ; LS Gaz 95/15 (16 Apr 1998); and J Shapland, A Otterburn, N Cantwell, C Corré, L Hagger, *Affording Civil Justice* (The Law Society, 1998).
[97] T Lee (20 Jan 1998) The Lawyer.
[98] J Shapland, A Otterburn, N Cantwell, C Corré, L Hagger, *Affording Civil Justice* (The Law Society, 1998).
[99] M Napier and F Bawden, *Conditional Fees: A Survival Guide* (The Law Society, 1995).

- *Industrial disease* cases tend to be more costly and longer than workplace accident cases, involving complex technical and medical evidence. They are likely to go to exchange of evidence and trial. It was very unclear how such cases could be run on CFAs. Only a few specialist firms handled such cases and they can be strongly defended. Cases which go to trial would clearly breach the cap, as would many going to exchange of evidence. Firms in this area, who tended to have considerable experience, were calculating success fees accurately. But a 25 per cent cap was unrealistic for all cases and success fees were vulnerable if the defence forced more cases to go to trial.
- *Medical negligence* cases typically involve complex and extensive medical evidence, are costly, lengthy, require specialist lawyers, and are robustly defended. About half drop out after the first medical report. Success rates ranged from 21–75 per cent but those for issued cases were over 80 per cent. Funding medical negligence cases was problematic. It was predicted that many firms would stop doing this work.

11.58 The CFA mechanism should encourage lawyers to do a level of work which is optimal (ie lower than it was under legal aid) and proportionate to the sum in dispute. Although academic analysis of the effects of a CFA system is confused and far from complete,[100] it has been argued that a CFA is the most appropriate and efficient mechanism of achieving minimum delay and cost within the notoriously costly and lengthy tort compensation process.[101] Without such a mechanism, the theoretical reasoning is that a claimant is susceptible to opportunistic inflation of costs by his lawyer and the obvious answer is to remove the conflict of interest by instilling the lawyer with the same objective as the claimant. (This is also the motivation behind the adoption of lump sum bidding contests to provide legal services at a flat fee which has been pursued by the Legal Aid Board.[102] An alternative suggestion was for lump sum bidding contests for the transfer of the entire claim. This implied a joint venture agreement to share both profits and losses—a contingency fee agreement which, in its pure form, would involve the sharing of the recovered compensation in specified proportions, with the lawyer bearing some disproportionate share (perhaps 100 per cent) of the costs.[103]) The conclusion is that it will be cheaper to run cases—and hence multi-party cases—on a CFA system than under a legal aid system. This will lower the damages-cost risk and make it easier to pursue lower risk cases.

---

[100] N Rickman, 'The Economics of Contingency Fees in Personal Injury Litigation' [1994] *Oxford Review of Economic Policy*, 10:34.
[101] TM Swanson, 'The Importance of Contingency Fee Agreements' (1991) 11 (2) OJLS 193.
[102] *The Times*, 4 Feb 1997.
[103] TM Swanson, 'The Importance of Contingency Fee Agreements' (1991) 11 (2) OJLS 193.

J. Financial Implications

It would be surprising if the well-established historical phenomenon of low value 'try on' claims[104] were eradicated under CFAs and Woolf, particularly in view of the 'blackmail' element of recoverability of success fees and insurance premiums from defendants who lose or settle, coupled with insurance protection for claimants who lose and, under some policies, for lawyers who lose. There may also be an attraction for impecunious plaintiffs, especially those who do not own a home, to litigate without obtaining insurance cover.

11.59

Small value cases are not particularly attractive for either the claimant or his lawyer under a CFA system. The smaller the plaintiff's damages, the larger the percentage of them payable to his lawyer. In low damages cases, Alan Tunkel[105] has estimated that often a third of the damages—even in good risk cases with minimal work—would be swallowed by the legal fees. The Law Society cap of 25 per cent was intended to deal with this issue and appears to have been widely observed. Had the situation remained as it was between 1995 and 1998, it would have been prudent for regulations to make the cap mandatory. However, the fact that insurance premiums and success fees are recoverable from defendants made any cap irrelevant. Plaintiffs may still argue that defendants might deliberately attempt to increase the amount of work to be done on claims, particularly small claims, so as to make them uneconomic for plaintiffs and their lawyers to continue beyond a certain point and so settle. The Woolf reforms, including observance of pre-action protocols, judicial management, and use of costs penalties, would control this issue, by setting down clear parameters on what does or does not need to be done on a case. Further, the recoverability of success fees from defendants constitutes a powerful incentive for defendants to seek to minimise plaintiffs' lawyers' work. In this situation it is the defendant who will want to use the parameters of the protocols and the court's powers to limit work done by plaintiffs.

11.60

A study by KPMG has indicated that although there are some economic attractions for solicitors in pursuing high volume low margin cases, CFA firms would find it more financially rewarding to specialise in higher value cases. Such cases usually involve more work and, therefore, the lawyer benefits from the additional uplift if he wins. This would make multi-party actions attractive to some specialist firms.[106]

11.61

---

[104] P Pleasance, S Maclean and A Morley, *Profiling Civil Litigation: The Case for Research* (Legal Aid Board Research Unit, 1996) para 1.1.12.
[105] A Tunkel, 'Improving access to justice' (5 Dec 1997) NLJ.
[106] KPMG, *Conditional Fees: Business Case* (Lord Chancellor's Department, 8 Apr 1998).

K. The Bar and CFAs

11.62 The initial involvement of barristers in CFAs was low, leading to some criticism.[107] In fact there are good reasons why barristers approach conditional fees with caution. As sole practitioners, barristers are less able than solicitors' partnerships to absorb delays in cash flow and the risk of falls in income. The innate conservatism of many counsel, provided they can attract a reasonable income, means that they can in practice simply refuse conditional fee cases, although this conflicts with the duty to accept any case offered if they are available and the solicitor agrees to pay the barrister's rate (the 'cab rank' principle). Counsel who are enthusiastic or politically motivated, or junior and impecunious, might be more attracted to accepting conditional fee work. This may lead to a clear division of those who do and do not accept this type of work.[108] There are, however, difficulties for counsel in making risk assessments on cases which, unlike solicitors, they do not manage, control, or interface to the same extent with clients. Counsel are typically only involved intermittently in cases, for example in giving initial advice, settling pleadings, giving advice on evidence, advocacy at hearings. In recent years, solicitors have increasingly taken on some of these functions. In these circumstances, counsel are concerned about the accuracy of their initial risk assessments and whether they are kept informed of relevant information. Potential conflict has also been identified between the barrister's duties to the court, the client, and his insurer and the commercial pressures of CFAs, such as in respect of citing adverse authorities, advising on settlement, or the ability to withdraw from a case where the client or solicitor has not disclosed information relevant to the initial risk assessment and success fee. These factors may tend to encourage the development of risk-sharing arrangements amongst barristers and of one-stop solicitor-advocates.[109]

L. Conflicts between Lawyer and Client with CFAs

11.63 Conflicts between the interests of a lawyer and his client can arise under any system of litigation and litigation funding. For example, it might have been in the lawyer's interests to continue a claim, particularly a multi-party action, as long as possible so as to continue to be paid by the legal aid fund.[110] Separation of the functions of giving advice on funding (ie risk assessment) and representation amongst different counsel was specifically suggested by fifteen senior judges who

---

[107] Speech by J Foy at the College of Law Conditional Fees Conference (3 July 1996).
[108] Cases may be taken on by junior barristers to obtain experience: Legal Week, 4 Feb 1999.
[109] P Kunzlik, 'Conditional Fees: The Ethical and Organisational Impact on the Bar' [1999] MLR 850.
[110] The *Sunday Times* criticised lawyers who 'milked the system' by supporting speculative applications for legal aid. *Sunday Times*, 6 July 1997.

L. Conflicts between Lawyer and Client

wrote to the Lord Chancellor protesting at the award of legal aid in cases which it was apparent at an early stage had no reasonable prospect of success and were doomed to failure, based on advice of barristers who had an interest in the outcome.[111] The judges called for doubtful cases to be scrutinised by independent senior barristers.

11.64 A particular problem with a CFA system is that it gives rise to a number of conflicts of interest which are potentially acute and difficult to regulate. It is argued that there has, as yet, been no convincing answer to the charge, clearly established from American experience[112] and fully supported by common sense, that where lawyers have a financial stake in the outcome of litigation there is a clear conflict of interest and unethical behaviour can result.[113] The problems of conflict are even greater in a multi-party action.

11.65 A particularly strong warning on conflicts was issued by Lord Ackner during parliamentary debates on the Access to Justice Bill,[114] who repeated the dangers previously expressed in the Royal Commission on Legal Services (Benson Commission):[115]

> The fact that the lawyer has a direct personal interest in the outcome of the case may lead to undesirable practices including the construction of evidence, the improper coaching of witnesses, the use of professionally partisan expert witnesses (especially

---

[111] *The Times*, 28 July 1997; *Guardian*, 29 Jan 1999.

[112] 'The $4.3 billion mistake. Review and Outlook', *Wall Street Journal*, 17 June 1994 A14; (1997) 20 Commercial Lawyer 17. During debate on the extension of CFAs in 1997, an American lawyer working in London, DP Marchessini, warned strongly about the dangers of contingency or conditional fee systems, referring to the encouragement for lawyers to act unethically, as had occurred in 'countless' US cases: *The Times*, 11 Nov 1997.

[113] District Judge Osborne referred to this as a crucial weakness of a CFA system (Apr 1999) 18 CJQ 184. Lord Hunt of Wirrall, a solicitor, referred to vastly increased financial pressures under the CFA system and Lord Kingsland thought that a CFA system tests the ethics of members of the profession to the limit. *Hansard*, HL (Series 5) vol 595, cols 1172 and 1194 (14 Dec 1998).

[114] *Hansard*, HL (Series 5) vol 584, col 57 (9 Dec 1997). Lord Ackner pointed to the fact that very limited research was then available on CFAs and that the recently published report of the Policy Studies Institute was based on a very small sample and had concluded that 'on the basis of the evidence so far available, there is potentially cause for serious concern about the way risk is being assessed and uplift calculated'. S Yarrow, *The Price of Success* (Policy Studies Institute, 1997). Criticism was also expressed in the debates by Baroness Wilcox, a former Chair of the National Consumer Council, that the wording of CFAs was fiendishly complicated and confusing: this prompted a comment that contingency fees were a much simpler arrangement! The Bar Council also objected that a lawyer should not in any circumstances be permitted to have a direct financial stake in the outcome of his client's case, that a conflict of interest was inevitable, and that this could not be controlled by rules of professional conduct. General Council of the Bar, *Quality of Justice: The Bar's Response* (1989); see also F Burton, 'Conditional Fees: Is there still an ethical dimension?' [1998] JPIL 6. Concern was expressed by Dan Brennan QC, then Chair of the Association of Personal Injury Barristers, and by academics that too little was known about conditional fees and cases could be 'cherry picked': The Lawyer (30 Sept 1997). Robert Owen QC, Chairman of the Bar Council, was concerned that there would be too great a financial conflict of interest NLJ (3 Oct 1997) and that the public would be ripped off and pay more to lawyers. *The Times* (16 Oct 1997).

[115] Royal Commission on Legal Services in England and Wales, Final Report [1979] Cmnd 7648.

medical witnesses), improper examination and cross-examination, groundless legal arguments designed to lead the courts into error and competitive touting.

11.66 Various possible undesirable practices have been identified:

- A solicitor's subjective assessment of a client's case—initially or as the case progresses—may be at variance with the client's own view. There may be pressure on solicitors to be unduly pessimistic about chances of success, thereby justifying a higher success fee.[116]
- There is an incentive for the claimant's lawyer to delay disclosing the strength of what he believes to be a strong case so as to increase the work done and maximise fees (fee leverage).
- In the opposite direction, the Sheffield study noted the vulnerability, at least in the early years, of CFA solicitors to a change in defence tactics of delaying settlement of cases so as to increase the work needed or the funding period to an extent which financially destabilised the practice.[117]
- Similarly, a lawyer carrying large overheads may be compelled to settle early or below the appropriate amount in order to secure payment.[118]

11.67 A response to the last three problems lies in the ability of procedural judges to manage litigation and control non-observance of the 'cards on the table' approach. However, it would not be so easy to control the CFA lawyer who advises settlement at a substantial discount or prematurely so as to safeguard the payment of fees.

11.68 A further problem is that the CFA system tends to encourage the lawyers who are working on a CFA to restrict their costs by doing less preparation, particularly where their financial circumstances give rise to pressure on their cash flow. In the tobacco litigation, the claimant's lawyers firstly restricted their initial investigation of the facts of individual cases to requesting their clients to fill in questionnaires on details such as their smoking history and, secondly, agreed that the defendants' solicitors would carry out the task of obtaining all the medical records. Accordingly, clients were not interviewed so as to obtain witness statements or test the accuracy of clients' initial recollections. This led to later amendments or discontinuations, with adverse costs orders being made against those clients. Similarly, some of the medical records might have contained evidence that would have led to later amendment or discontinuation of a case. As Martyn Day, who was handling that litigation, has written: 'It is easy for a lawyer to stand up and say there are grounds for a legal action, having done next to no research on

---

[116] The *Economist*, 27 Sept 1997. It supported a move to out and out contingency fees with a 25% cap on costs.
[117] J Shapland, A Otterburn, N Cantwell, C Corré, L Hagger, *Affording Civil Justice* (The Law Society, 1998).
[118] Lord Clinton-Davis, *Hansard*, HL (Series 5) vol 596, col 789 (21 Jan 1999).

L. Conflicts between Lawyer and Client

either the science or the law . . . that seems wrong.'[119] The courts have always had power to award such costs against lawyers whose conduct is unreasonable or improper, and this may well be held to cover where inadequate investigation of a client's case led to the costs being incurred.[120]

11.69 These difficulties have been declared by Millett LJ in *Thai Trading Co (a firm) v Taylor* as being withstandable by lawyers. He defined three propositions relevant to modern conditions:

> First, if it is contrary to public policy for a lawyer to have a financial interest in the outcome of a suit that is because (and only because) of the temptations to which it exposes him. At best he might lose his professional objectivity; at worst he might be persuaded to attempt to pervert the course of justice. Secondly, there is nothing improper in a lawyer acting in a case for a meritorious client who to his knowledge cannot afford to pay his costs if the case is lost.[121] Not only is this not improper, it is in accordance with current notions of the public interest that he should do so. Thirdly, if the temptation to win at all costs is present at all, it is present whether or not the lawyer has formally waived his fees if he loses. It arises from his knowledge that in practice he will not be paid unless he wins. In my judgment the reasoning in *British Waterways Board v Norman* is unsound.
>
> Accordingly, either it is improper for a solicitor to act in litigation for a meritorious client who cannot afford to pay him if he loses, or it is not improper for a solicitor to agree to act on the basis that he is to be paid his ordinary costs if he wins but not if he loses. I have no hesitation in concluding that the second of those propositions represents the current state of the law.
>
> I reach this conclusion for several reasons. In the first place, I do not understand why it is assumed that the effect of the arrangement being unlawful is that the solicitor is unable to recover his proper costs in any circumstances. . . .
>
> In the second place, it is in my judgment fanciful to suppose that a solicitor will be tempted to compromise his professional integrity because he will be unable to recover his ordinary profit costs in a small case if the case is lost. Solicitors are accustomed to withstand far greater incentives to impropriety than this. The solicitor who acts for a multinational company in a heavy commercial action knows that if he loses the case his client may take his business elsewhere. In the present case, Mr Taylor had more at stake than his profit costs if he lost. His client was his wife; desire for domestic harmony alone must have provided a powerful incentive to win. Current attitudes to these questions are exemplified by the passage into law of the Courts and Legal Services Act 1990. This shows that the fear that lawyers may be tempted by having a financial incentive in the outcome of litigation to act improperly is exaggerated, and that there is a countervailing public policy in making justice readily accessible to persons of modest means. Legislation was needed to authorise the increase in the lawyer's reward over and above his ordinary profit costs. It by no means follows that it was needed to legitimise the long-standing practice of solicitors to act for meritorious clients without means, and it is in the public interest that they should continue to do so. . . .

---

[119] The Times, 14 Feb 1995.
[120] CPR, Rule 44.14(1)(b).
[121] See *Singh v Observer Ltd* [1989] 3 All ER 777; *A Ltd v B Ltd* [1996] 1 WLR 665.

> In my judgment, there is nothing unlawful in a solicitor acting for a party to litigation to agree to forgo all or part of his fee if he loses, provided that he does not seek to recover more than his ordinary profit costs and disbursements if he wins.[122]

11.70 Although Millett LJ said that his assessment was that contemporary risks of abuse by lawyers in contingency fees are minimal, he expressly limited this to cases where the basic fee, rather than the success fee, is in issue and to *small* cases.[123] These dangers are clearly increased where the costs and/or damages at risk are high, for example in expensive and complex litigation—notably multi-party claims. The position is made more critical where punitive damages are claimable.[124]

11.71 The government has asserted that fears of abuse of consumers by lawyers acting on CFAs has not materialised (but the only hard evidence for this was the limited Policy Studies Institute report) and that lawyers work within a strong code of ethics that is rigorously enforced by the self-regulating professional bodies. Nevertheless, the government is monitoring the use of CFAs[125] and preliminary results of independent research indicate that clients do not understand the information on CFAs even though they are provided with it.[126] Reliance on existing self-regulatory mechanisms may be inadequate given predictable opportunities for abuse. The issue is whether abuse will be widespread or insignificant and whether the existing mechanisms will provide adequate control.[127] The risk is a matter of concern given the strong evidence that many personal injury clients rely, often totally, on the advice and actions of their lawyers.[128] Mechanisms are needed for auditing the situation and for swift investigation and resolution of practical problems as and when they arise, since it would be a relatively simple matter for media reports of a few alleged horror stories to undermine public confidence in lawyers in the new world of CFAs. Lawyers should, therefore, take care and steps to avoid this issue. Review of percentage uplifts by procedural judges and recording this in each case, together with the type of case, would provide valuable statistical data for the monitoring of the system and enable lawyers to set percentages more accurately in future cases—normal ranges for particular types of cases could be established. In order to monitor how conflicts are dealt with, auditing of cases,

---

[122] *Thai Trading Co (a Firm) v Taylor* [1998] 3 All ER 65, CA.
[123] ibid.
[124] HSE Gravelle and M Waterson, 'No Win, No Fee: Some Economics of Contingent Legal Fees' (1992) 103 *Economic Journal* 1205.
[125] Lord Chancellor's Department, *Access to Justice with Conditional Fees* (Mar 1998).
[126] Lord Chancellor's Department, *Conditional Fees: Sharing the Risks of Litigation: A Consultation Paper* (1999) CP 7/99.
[127] The Master of the City of London Law Society, Anthony Pugh-Thomas, questioned whether the profession could still claim the right to regulate itself: LS Gaz 94/48 (17 Dec 1997). See also P Kunzlik, 'Conditional Fees: The Ethical and Organisational Impact on the Bar' [1999] MLR 850.
[128] D Harris et al, *Compensation and Support for Illness and Injury* (OUP, 1984); H Genn, *Hard Bargaining: Out of Court Settlement in Personal Injury Actions* (OUP, 1988).

including interviews with clients and lawyers, will be advisable for the foreseeable future.

The potential for abuse is increased in multi-party cases because of the larger sums at stake and the difficulties of comprehension by lay clients posed by more complex cases. It has been recognised that in these situations it may be necessary for the protection of individual clients' interests, as has been recognised in multi-party cases, for independent trustee(s) to be established who could give speedy views without disrupting the progress of litigation on, for example, whether settlements were in the interests of clients or merely recommended by their lawyers because of their desire to be paid some funds.

11.72

M. Risk Assessments and CFAs in Multi-Party Actions: The Future

The government view is that nothing about multi-party actions makes them unsuitable for CFAs despite the often exceptionally high costs.[129] As appears from the policies in Appendix 1, as at 1999, solicitors and insurers are wary of supporting claimants in multi-party actions. However, circumstances may well evolve and cases supported by CFAs or personal resources are not unknown. Insurance cover was agreed by Abbey Legal Protection in September 1997 for Gulf War Syndrome litigants.[130] It was said that if 700 of the 1,300 claimants each paid a premium of £600, thereby yielding a fund of £420,000 to cover the risk of costs and administration expenses, the insurer would cover twenty test cases. KPMG predicted that solicitors would become more self-confident, seeking to spread risk by seeking a volume of claims or by increasing specialisation.[131]

11.73

Only three serious policies emerged before 1997 but the market began to expand after the government encouraged this in late 1997. The insurer with the biggest volume in this field, Accident Line Protect, positively excludes clinical negligence, pharmaceutical, and tobacco cases, whether multi-party or not, in any event. It excludes multi-party cases larger than ten cases. Litigation Protection Limited will in theory consider multi-party cases but is known to be aware of the significant risks here and can be expected to take a very cautious attitude. The attitude of LawAssist is unclear.[132]

11.74

---

[129] *Hansard,* HC Standing Committee E Access to Justice Bill [Lords], col 168 (4 May 1999).
[130] LS Gaz, 3 Sept 1997; SJ, 5 and 12 Sept 1997.
[131] KPMG, *Conditional Fees: Business Case* (Lord Chancellor's Department, 1998).
[132] LawAssist was reported to be funding claims by the remaining handful of women over the Gravigard intrauterine contraceptive device. This was curious given the withdrawal of legal aid after some 8 years on the basis that further funding was unreasonable. The *Observer,* 9 Mar 1997. However, most of the women discontinued shortly afterwards. See ch 20.

11.75 Given the enormous difficulties which the Legal Aid Board had in accurately predicting the chances of success of multi-party cases and in controlling expenditure by lawyers funded by it,[133] a central issue is whether insurers will be able to exercise the necessary informed level of control over lawyers who work on conditional fees, particularly in expensive and multi-party cases. Insurers will need to be mindful of relevant lessons which the Legal Aid Board learnt at great cost in the 1980s on quality, scrutiny, quality control, supplier-induced demand, and so on.[134]

11.76 The involvement of insurers performing the previous function of the Legal Aid Board is an opportunity to apply increased discipline to claims selection and the requirement for reliable initial risk assessment, based on full and objective scrutiny of cases.[135] The economics of CFA insurance dictate that the insurer can afford to lose fewer cases than the solicitor. Such figures as have been released indicate that whilst the break even point of solicitors might be a 50 per cent success rate,[136] assuming that the costs of cases won and lost are roughly comparable, insurers need a much higher rate[137] in order to cover the cost of liability for opponents' costs. Naturally, the commercial balance depends on the level at which premiums are set.[138] Insurers may, therefore, insist on covering only cases which

---

[133] The Bar Council concluded that: 'A high proportion of the [multi-party] cases had been unsuccessful and large sums of public money have been wasted.' They drew a distinction between disaster cases and 'pioneering' cases, the latter including most pharmaceutical litigation. The pioneering cases had encountered a very high failure rate: 'In our view, this is because legal aid is being granted where it should have been refused . . .'. General Council of the Bar, *Response to the Government's Green Paper 'Legal Aid—Targeting Need'* (16 Oct 1995) 11.1 and 11.4.

[134] See ch 16 below.

[135] Compare the restriction in issues alleged, and parameters for claimants to join, in the tobacco litigation from when legal aid funding was envisaged to when the cases were funded on CFAs in SJ, 10 July 1992 and *The Times*, 28 Sept 1996.

[136] Lord Thomas of Gresham quoted a need for 92% success in order to break even: *Hansard*, HL (Series 5) vol 587, col 83 (9 Mar 1998).

[137] A 90% figure was quoted by the Bar Council: The Lawyer, 15 Feb 1999. DAS Legal Expenses Insurance quoted a 75% rate: *Post Magazine* (18 Feb 1999), but see research undertaken in April and May 1999 in which unidentified insurers quoted a requirement for only a 50% chance of success: RCA White and R Atkinson, 'Personal Injury Litigation, Conditional Fees and After-the-Event Insurance' [2000] CJQ 118.

[138] At 1 Oct 1997 Accident Line Protect had underwritten 28,000 policies since July 1995, of which 4,000 claims had been resolved. Success rates were not disclosed but premiums were increased at that date from £85 to £95.68 for road traffic accidents and to £161.20 for other cases (a 90% rise). Irwin Mitchell reported that 51 of their first 54 CFA cases resolved were successful: LS Gaz 95/13 (1 Apr 1998). Premiums would have totalled £4,950 as against insurers' liability for the three lost claims of perhaps three times that sum. Accident Line Protect again increased premiums from 1 Nov 1999 to £148 for road traffic cases (54% rise) and to £315 for other fast track cases (95% rise). Significantly, they also withdrew delegated authority from member firms for risk assessment of cases with estimated damages over £15,000 (multi-track), for which insurers' prior approval would be required and premiums set on a case-by-case basis. At that stage, Accident Line Protect had covered over 67,000 cases of which a third had been completed. LS Gaz 96/39 (13 Oct 1999) and 96/41 (27 Oct 1999). In September 2000, Accident Line Protect increased its premiums again: fast-track cases— road traffic accidents £300, other cases £650 apart from occupational disease cases £850; multi-track cases—a flat rate scheme replacing previous individual assessment, with road traffic

M. The Future

have been fully investigated,[139] and which have a strong chance of success. The chance of success demanded may well be higher than that which prevailed under the legal aid system.[140] This trend is for insurers to fund good cases but not cases with unclear or even average risk, which would have been funded by legal aid.

11.77 The early statistics on success rates of CFA cases first, confirm that success rates achieved have been critically close to break even point for both solicitors and insurers,[141] secondly, indicate that insurance premiums have been unsustainably low in relation to the size of the market (ie total premium income), and, thirdly, have led to solicitors' ability to assess risk being strongly criticised by insurers. Will the market grow sufficiently to keep premiums from rising considerably, or will they rise inexorably, assisted by loan arrangements and recoverability from defendants? Will some insurers incur losses such as to drive them out of the market or raise premiums to levels which tend to restrict access to justice?

11.78 It remains to be seen to what extent individual solicitors' risk assessments will turn out to be accurate,[142] what attitude they will take towards risk, and how this will change. Some might be prepared to take on more speculative actions, particularly if they have a high volume of CFA cases. However, firms which lose too often stand to lose their access to insurers.[143] In any event, the process would be

---

accidents £660, occupational diseases £2,900, all others £2,400 apart from clinical negligence which would not be covered. SJ, 25 Aug 2000. In November 2000 Accident Line Protect cut its panel of solicitors from 2,300 to 500 and Abbey Legal Protection took over administration of the scheme from the Law Society in order to impose greater commercial discipline: Post Magazine, 9 November 2000.

[139] Litigation Protection Ltd also have cases scrutinised by independent solicitors. Information from a conference as at Feb 1999 was that this leads to a rejection of a further 25%. Greystoke Ltd rely on covering only solicitors with a recognised track record and had a rejection rate of 30%.

[140] A 90% success rate was quoted by Litigation Protection Ltd on 500 policies written as at Feb 1999 at an average premium of £2,500. By contrast, the success rates of closed legal aid personal injury and medical negligence cases in 1996–7 were 17% for non-specialist firms and 28% for specialists (with 35% and 52% respectively for cases that went beyond initial investigation).

[141] It seems that the initial screening of claims taken on under CFAs under Accident Line Protect from 1995 to date was inadequate since costs claimed on unsuccessful claims substantially exceeded premium income for the insurer. Significantly, no figures were published. In contrast, the screening requirement imposed by Litigation Protection was weeding out many unsuitable medical negligence cases and was financially successful. The importance of screening was precisely one of the main lessons which the Legal Aid Board had had to learn at great cost in relation to multi-party actions.

[142] When CFAs were first introduced, it appeared that most solicitors initially adopted a prudent approach to risk. A survey by BDO Stoy Hayward 'exposed a worrying level of fear and negativity among small firms' to CFAs, that only a half of firms surveyed with under six fee earners had written procedures for risk management, and less than 4% of practices monitored their overall exposure to CFAs. SJ, 5 Mar 1999. One underwriter commented in 1988 that the ability of solicitors to assess risks was 'pretty appalling'. LS Gaz 95/12 (25 Mar 1998). A 1999 study reported insurers considering solicitors as poor at risk assessment. RCA White and R Atkinson, 'Personal Injury Litigation, Conditional Fees and After-the-Event Insurance' [2000] CJQ 118.

[143] In 1999 Accident Line Protect suspended cover from 30 firms and later withdrew cover from 11 of its 1,600 solicitors' firms for poor claims experience (practising adverse selection by only including claims in the scheme with lower chances of success) and poor administration although later reinstated some. LS Gaz (17 Feb 1999); SJ, 5 Mar 1999; *The Times*, 20 Apr 1999.

facilitated by the dissemination of reliable research on the actual success rates and costs of particular categories of cases and, hence, the level of basic costs, disbursements, risk, and percentage uplift which are applicable to each category. Insurers will monitor their own information on these matters but may be reticent about publishing it. Systematic and comprehensive research would be welcome.

11.79 An example of successful risk assessment can be seen in trade union funding of personal injury claims, which has been more successful than legal aid. A TUC report[144] showed that trade unions backed five times more personal injury cases[145] than the Legal Aid Board (150,000 and 30,000 cases respectively in 1996–7). Trade unions had a 96 per cent success rate and recovered £330 million in damages at no cost to the taxpayer, also allowing £179 million to be recouped by the Department of Social Security. This worked out at an average compensation award of £50.23 per union member. Eighty-five per cent of cases settled for less than £10,000 and the mean average settlement was just over £2,000. In commenting on this system, Baroness Dean of Thornton-le-Fylde, a former General Secretary of a trade union, stressed that this system could only work as long as the 'loser pays' rule was retained. The trade unions effectively act as insurers, had the resources to investigate those claims which they thought appropriate but were not afraid to tell members either that they did or did not have a case worth pursuing.[146]

11.80 Will claimants be prepared to take the risk of multi-party actions without insurance cover? Fifty people did so in the tobacco litigation, claiming that the issue was important and they had no significant assets to protect.[147] Costs orders were made against them on amendments, discontinuance, and dismissal although, in the event, the defendants did not enforce them. It may be argued that such claims should not be permitted as being prejudicial to defendants and that the claimants' lawyers have not acted ethically in giving completely disinterested advice. In such a situation, the arguments for particular scrutiny and control by the court and professional bodies and for the appointment of an experienced independent trustee to represent the overall and possibly disparate interests of lay clients are strong.

11.81 It was claimed following the collapse of the tobacco litigation in 1999 that a multi-party action could not be run on a CFA.[148] This statement needs to be examined further. First, it was made principally by the solicitors who had just been

---

[144] R Oliver, *Fairness for Victims 1997 survey of union legal services* (TUC, 1997).
[145] The Fennell study indicates that cases funded by trade unions are almost exclusively, as may be expected, for accidents at work with a small number of motor accidents, both of which have high anticipated success rates.
[146] *Hansard*, HL (Series 5) vol 584, col 99 (9 Dec 1997).
[147] LS Gaz, 2 Oct 1996.
[148] See Legal Week, 4 Mar 1999.

criticised by the judge for originating these lawyer-led claims which were speculative and bore insufficient relation to the reality of the clients' factual situations on which they were purportedly based (see chapter 32). Secondly, these remarks might be seen as a political statement in the context of the extended history of reform of the legal aid and CFA systems, designed to lobby the government to continue public funding for multi-party actions and high cost cases.[149] The economic reality of the situation was that although it was widely reported that Leigh Day & Co, the firm that had been pursuing this litigation the longest, had lost its investment worth some £2.5 million, the firm also said that the risk of losing this amount had been budgeted for: the sum was absorbable given the size of the firm's total turnover and profitability.[150] The ability of a firm to absorb a loss is clearly dependent on the size of the loss relative to its overall resources. Thus, American plaintiff law firms that benefit from huge contingency fees in successful cases are enabled to reinvest in funding further cases themselves. In response to the statements quoted above that no multi-party case could be run on a CFA, it was pointed out that there was no reason why cases with merit (ie cases with low risk, which the tobacco cases clearly were not) could not be undertaken on a CFA.[151] The KPMG study had pointed to the likelihood that some firms would be attracted to the more complex cases in view of their higher returns and despite their longer duration, particularly where the firm was specialised in the type of case and had the financial and human resources to handle it.

N. Economic Impact on Defendants

A frequent criticism of legal aid was that it relieved aided parties from cost pressure if the case was lost. Research indicated that this shifted the balance of bargaining power between litigants in favour of the claimant[152] and that this provided aided parties with an incentive to hold out for as long as possible.[153] Under the new system, defendants benefit overall from the removal of the rule that they could not recover costs against legally aided claimants,[154] but lose out from the new rule that they have to pay claimants' success fees and premiums in addition to normal costs where the defendant loses or settles. These factors, coupled with the impact of claimants' offers to settle,[155] favour claimants' bargaining power.

11.82

---

[149] See White Paper, *Modernising Justice* (HMSO, 1998) and Legal Aid Board, *The Funding Code* (1999).
[150] Legal Week, 4 Mar 1999.
[151] Letter by G Hoon MP, *The Times*, 22 Mar 1999.
[152] H Genn, *Hard Bargaining: Out of Court Settlement in Personal Injury Actions* (OUP, 1988).
[153] P Fenn and N Rickman, 'Delay and Settlement in Litigation' (July 1999) 109 *The Economic Journal* 457–491.
[154] *Hansard*, HC Standing Committee E Access to Justice Bill [Lords], col 263 (11 May 1999).
[155] CPR, Part 36.

However, the impact of the Civil Procedure Rules should be to lower transactional costs of litigation by shortening and simplifying the process and making costs proportional to sums in dispute. The CFA system should inhibit cases which do not have good chances of success, reducing the number of claims previously funded by legal aid, but permitting more citizens to bring claims.[156] The refocusing of public funding on housing and welfare cases, particularly through Citizens Advice Bureaux (CAB), on the basis of regional funding priorities, will alter the nature of cases brought. The development of the Community Legal Service through agencies such as CAB will obviously threaten another retraction in locally-based solicitors' firms. Indeed, research for the Lord Chancellor's Department indicated that Legal Aid Board franchised contracts for civil litigation which involved 1,000 cases would only need to be issued to six firms in the London legal aid area to satisfy demand.[157] Availability of public funding for expensive cases and public interest cases will obviously be a factor in multi-party actions: much depends on policy and interpretation of the Funding Code. The overall effects of all these changes may be detailed and complex. Any overall increase in costs to defendants' insurers will be borne by their major customers—motorists, employers, household insureds.

O. The International Context

11.83 CFAs remain illegal or contrary to professional rules throughout most of the rest of Europe. Given that increasing access to justice is a formal policy of the European Commission,[158] and competition from US lawyers has forced the Council of Bars and Law Societies of Europe (CCBE) to initiate a review of the ban on contingency fees in Europe in 1996,[159] there may be widespread and swift change. The position will be affected by the response to the European Commission's proposals to move towards harmonisation of EU Member State rules on cross-border legal aid.[160] The CCBE's Code of Conduct 1998 only prohibits a fee agreement between a lawyer and his client which is entered into prior to final conclusion of a matter in which the client undertakes to pay the lawyer a share of the result upon conclusion of the matter (*Pactum de Quota Litis*) if it is not

---

[156] The Minister was reported as saying: 'The effect of extending conditional fee deals may be a surge of new cases, but at least the tax payer would not have to foot the bill.' *Mail on Sunday*, 28 Sept 1997.
[157] T Goriely, *Contracting for civil litigation: modeling volumes, access and regional distributions for certificated non-matrimonial civil legal aid* (TPR Social and Legal Research, 1997).
[158] European Commission, *Consumer Action Plan 1999–2001* COM(98) 696 final, 2 Dec 1998.
[159] LS Gaz, 19 June 1996.
[160] *Green Paper from the Commission: Legal aid in civil matters: The problems confronting the cross-border litigant* COM (2000) 51 final, 9 Feb 2000.

in accordance with an officially approved fee scale or not under the control of a competent authority having jurisdiction over the lawyer. In other words, CCBE considers that regulated contingency fees are permissible. South Africa introduced contingency fees (in fact UK-style conditional fees) in 1999.[161]

---

[161] The Contingency Fees Act, No 66, 1997, which came into force on 23 Apr 1999.

12

PUBLIC FUNDING

A.	Public Funding: The Statutory Framework	12.01	F.	Community Legal Service Contracts	12.35
	Factors affecting the Funding Code	12.06	G.	Wider Public Interest Cases	12.37
	Payments	12.08		No cost-benefit ratio: valuing public interest	12.45
	Costs protection	12.09		Public Interest Advisory Panel	12.49
B.	Funding Service Levels	12.17		Financial eligibility	12.52
C.	Funding Excluded Services	12.28		Not a public inquiry: consistency	12.53
				Competing interests	12.58
D.	Multi-Party Action Funding	12.30		Possible future restriction on public interest funding	12.62
E.	MPA Procedures	12.33	H.	Representations by Defendants	12.64

A. Public Funding: The Statutory Framework

The system of public funding of civil litigation was reformed by the Access to Justice Act 1999.[1] The Legal Services Commission (the Commission) was created to oversee the Community Legal Service (CLS), which assumed the functions of the Legal Aid Board.[2] The CLS funds services out of the Community Legal Service Fund (the Fund), which is itself funded at the discretion of the Lord Chancellor.[3]

12.01

---

[1] The intention was to increase access to justice by, first, reforming the legal aid scheme in order to ensure that limited resources can be allocated in a way to reflect priorities and to secure better value for money; secondly, co-ordinating central government funding with funding from other sources, in particular local authority grants to advice centres, to ensure that the available resources are used to the best effect overall; and thirdly, extending the scope and operation of conditional fees to enable more people to fund litigation privately. *Explanatory Notes: Access to Justice Act 1999* (The Stationery Office Limited, 1999) para 21.

[2] Access to Justice Act 1999, ss 1, 4.

[3] Access to Justice Act 1999, s 5.

12.02 The Commission sets priorities in its funding of services as it considers appropriate, but in accordance with any directions given by the Lord Chancellor, and after taking into account the need for services of descriptions specified in the Act.[4] The Lord Chancellor has directed the Legal Services Commission to give top priority to child protection cases and cases where a client is at risk of loss of life or liberty. The Commission is instructed to deploy available resources so that all cases in these categories that meet appropriate merits criteria can be funded. After that, the Commission should give high priority to:

- other cases concerning the welfare of children;
- domestic violence cases;
- cases alleging serious wrongdoing or breaches of human rights by public bodies; and
- 'social welfare' cases, including housing proceedings and advice about employment rights, social security entitlements, and debt.[5]

12.03 The Commission may not fund services specified in Schedule 2 of the Act.[6] Proscribed services within Schedule 2 include services consisting of the provision of help in relation to:

- allegations of negligently caused injury, death, or damage to property, apart from allegations relating to clinical negligence;[7]
- conveyancing;
- boundary disputes;
- matters of trust law, defamation, or malicious falsehood;
- matters of company or partnership law.

12.04 However, services proscribed under Schedule 2 are to be funded where the Lord Chancellor directs the Commission to do so in the circumstances he specifies.[8] This power of the Lord Chancellor was intended to be used only in 'exceptional' circumstances,[9] an example of which would be personal injury cases where exceptionally high investigative or overall costs are likely to be necessary, or where issues of wider public interest are involved.

---

[4] Access to Justice Act 1999, s 6.
[5] Lord Chancellor's Department, *Community Legal Service Fund: Funding Priorities* (2 Feb 2000).
[6] Access to Justice Act 1999, s 6(6).
[7] These categories are excluded because the Lord Chancellor considers that the great majority are suitable for funding under CFAs: Lord Chancellor's Guidance on Scope of the Community Legal Service Fund (2 Feb 2000) para 4.
[8] Access to Justice Act 1999, s 6(8)(a). See further paras 12.28 *et seq* below.
[9] *Access to Justice Bill [HL] Explanatory Notes* (HMSO, 1998); *Hansard,* HL (Series 5) vol 595, col 1113 (14 Dec 1998). But Lord Irvine of Lairg LC indicated that as the market develops and solicitors become more confident about which cases they can handle on a CFA, he expects not to make public funding available for higher cost cases. The Lord Chancellor does not have power to direct that an individual case be funded but may respond to an approach from the Commission. *Hansard,* HL (Series 5) vol 597, cols 421 and 422 (11 Feb 1999).

A. The Statutory Framework

Further, the Lord Chancellor may authorise the Commission to fund any Schedule 2 services in circumstances he specifies or, if the Commission requests him to do so, in an individual case.[10] The effect of a direction by the Lord Chancellor under section 6(8)(a) is to order the Commission to fund specified services, whereas under section 6(8)(b) the Commission is granted a discretion. The Lord Chancellor may give guidance to the Commission as to the manner in which he considers it should discharge its functions and the Commission shall take any such guidance into account when considering the manner in which it is to discharge its functions. Guidance may not, however, be given under that provision in relation to individual cases.[11] The second part of section 6(8)(b) may be highly important in a Group Litigation Order (GLO). Under it, an applicant must persuade the Commission to request the Lord Chancellor to authorise a given case, although the Commission would still have discretion to refuse.

12.05

Factors affecting the Funding Code

Public funding is available for individuals whose financial resources are limited but in addition certain services are available irrespective of financial resources.[12] The detailed criteria which apply to decisions on funding, or continuing to fund, CLS services are set out in The Funding Code, which is published by the Commission after approval by the Lord Chancellor and being laid before Parliament.[13] In settling the criteria to be set out in the Code the Commission shall consider the extent to which they ought to reflect the following factors:[14]

12.06

(a) the likely cost of funding the services and the benefit which may be obtained by their being provided,
(b) the availability of sums in the Community Legal Service Fund for funding the services and (having regard to present and likely future demands on that Fund) the appropriateness of applying them to fund the services,[15]
(c) the importance of the matters in relation to which the services would be provided for the individual,
(d) the availability to the individual of services not funded by the Commission and the likelihood of his being able to avail himself of them,
(e) if the services are sought by the individual in relation to a dispute, the prospects of his success in the dispute,

---

[10] Access to Justice Act 1999, s 6(8)(b).
[11] Access to Justice Act 1999, s 23.
[12] Access to Justice Act 1999, s 7.
[13] Access to Justice Act 1999, ss 8 and 9.
[14] Access to Justice Act 1999, s 8.
[15] Legal advice must compete with other government-funded welfare programmes (including education, health, housing, and social security) and is not the only way of delivery of justice. AA Paterson and T Goriely, *A Reader on Resourcing Civil Justice* (1996).

(f) the conduct of the individual in connection with services funded as part of the Community Legal Service (or an application for funding) or in, or in connection with, any proceedings,
(g) the public interest, and
(h) such other factors as the Lord Chancellor may by order require the Commission to consider.

12.07 The Lord Chancellor expressed concern in 1999 that a small number of very expensive cases used to take up a disproportionately large share of the legal aid fund and has given directions under section 5(6) of the Act specifying a maximum amount which the Commission may spend each year on cases likely to exceed a prescribed cost threshold.[16]

Payments

12.08 An individual for whom services are funded by the CLS shall not be required to make any payment in respect of the services except where regulations otherwise provide.[17] Regulations may, however, require him to make contributions:[18] the rules on financial assessment of the financial resources of a person are contained in the Community Legal Service (Financial) Regulations 2000.[19] This continues the pre-existing means-tested system, including tapering financial contributions depending on available income and capital. These details are outside the scope of this book.

Costs protection

12.09 The liability of a person funded by the CLS for an order for costs in favour of opponents in litigation shall not, except in prescribed circumstances, exceed the amount (if any) which is a reasonable one for him to pay having regard to all the circumstances including:[20]

(a) the financial resources of all the parties to the proceedings, and
(b) their conduct in connection with the dispute.

12.10 In assessing the financial resources of an individual for whom services are funded, his clothes and household furniture and the tools and implements of his trade shall not be taken into account, except so far as may be prescribed.[21]

---

[16] Letter from Lord Irvine of Lairg LC to Sir Tim Chessells, reproduced in Legal Aid Board, *A New Approach to Funding Civil Cases* (1999). For the details, see n 39 below.
[17] Access to Justice Act 1999, s 10(1).
[18] Access to Justice Act 1999, s 10(2).
[19] SI 2000/516. See amendment proposals to take effect on 1 Apr 2001 in Lord Chancellor's Department, *Financial conditions for funding by the Legal Services Commission (2000)*.
[20] Access to Justice Act 1999, s 11(1).
[21] Access to Justice Act 1999, s 11(2). This was a change from the previous exclusion of assets, notably a dwelling house under Legal Aid Act 1988, s 17.

A. The Statutory Framework

12.11 Where the court makes a section 11(1) costs order, it shall consider whether, but for costs protection, it would have made a costs order against the client and, if so, whether it would have specified the amount to be paid: detailed provisions apply under either eventuality.[22]

12.12 Costs protection only applies to costs in funded proceedings incurred after the issue of the CLS certificate.[23] If a certificate is revoked (as opposed to withdrawn) costs protection does not apply in relation to work done either before or after the revocation.[24]

12.13 Costs protection of a funded person does not apply in relation to certain types of funding, including Litigation Support or Investigative Support,[25] except where proceedings in respect of which Investigative Support was given are not pursued after the certificate for Investigative Support is discharged.[26]

12.14 Where costs protection applies, the court may order the whole or part of the costs of a successful non-party to be paid by the Commission where the funded person is not ordered to pay the full costs, the non-party makes a request for a costs hearing within three months of the costs order being made, the proceedings were instituted by the funded person, the non-funded party would suffer severe financial hardship, and it is just and equitable to pay such costs out of public funds.[27]

12.15 Where a costs order is made against a non-funded party, the court shall order that the Commission shall pay the amount of the excess part of such costs, not to exceed a reasonable amount, by which the person's liability exceeds his maximum insurance limit, where that maximum has been approved by the Commission.[28]

---

[22] The Community Legal Service (Costs) Regulations 2000, SI 2000/441, reg 9.
[23] The Community Legal Service (Cost Protection) Regulations 2000, SI 2000/824, reg 3(4).
[24] The Community Legal Service (Cost Protection) Regulations 2000, SI 2000/824, reg 3(1).
[25] See para 12.22 below.
[26] The Community Legal Service (Cost Protection) Regulations 2000, SI 2000/824, reg 3(4). With effect from 1 Apr 2001 it is proposed to relax the 'severe financial hardship' rule to plain 'financial hardship' and to reduce the figure disregarded in relation to the funded person's home from £100,000 to £3,000 plus any contribution from equity due to the Commission. The stated rationale was: 'The rules governing costs between parties in funded cases seek to balance competing objectives. On the one hand, funded clients would be deterred from pursuing worthwhile cases if they risked facing an unknown and effectively open-ended liability for costs. If the Fund faced this liability, there would be fewer resources available for other priorities. On the other hand, it is undesirable that funded clients are placed in a more favourable position than their unfunded opponents (who may be only slightly better off). [It is argued above] that funded clients should, so far as practicable, be placed in an equivalent position to private litigants; this would include accepting some of the discipline inherent in the risk of costs.' Lord Chancellor's Department, *Financial conditions for funding by the Legal Services Commission* (2000). This issue is highly significant and the Law Society said that the treatment of equity in homes would effectively abolish public funding for virtually all owner-occupiers, with a catastrophic effect on access to justice: SJ, 4 Aug 2000, 718.
[27] The Community Legal Service (Cost Protection) Regulations 2000, SI 2000/824, reg 5.
[28] The Community Legal Service (Cost Protection) Regulations 2000, SI 2000/824, reg 6. Research by the Consumers' Association found a strong public perception that the quality of advice obtained through legal aid was second-rate and sub-standard: *Consumer Policy Review* July/Aug 2000, vol 10 no 4.

12.16 It is recognised by the government that the cost protection rule creates an advantage in litigation for the funded person.[29] In this connection, the Legal Aid Board stated that the scheme should not fund cases which only have high prospects of success because the very existence of public funding gives them such prospects of success.[30]

B. Funding Service Levels

12.17 Before considering the details of the various different types of public funding, it is important to understand the essential difference between public funding and private funding. Where a case has some private funding, perhaps under a conditional fee agreement (CFA), public support funding may supplement this. Further, whether the basic funding is either public or private, two kinds of funding may be available: for investigation of a case and for the litigation once commenced. The position and terminology for the available levels of service specified in The Funding Code[31] are illustrated in Figure 12.1.

12.18 Thus, where no CFA exists, a client might, subject to assessment of means and to any applicable contribution, receive

- Investigative Help to investigate the strength of a proposed claim, up to the point of being able to carry out a risk assessment and decide whether the case either has sufficiently strong prospects of success and should be undertaken on a CFA, or has insufficient chance of success and should be dropped.
- Full Representation in relation to proceedings.

12.19 Where a CFA or other private funding exists, the equivalent options would be Investigative Support and Litigation Support, perhaps to cover particularly high disbursements, especially experts' fees. Thus, certain public funding might be available for certain aspects of a multi-party action run on CFAs.[32]

12.20 A case which has characteristics that would make it suitable for a CFA would not

---

[29] *Access to Justice Bill [HL] Explanatory Notes* (HMSO, 1998) para 90.
[30] Legal Aid Board, *The Funding Code: A New Approach to Funding Civil Cases* (1999) para 2.15. The system was changed so that regulations could specify the principles to be applied in determining the amount of costs which may be awarded against a funded party, the circumstances in which an order for costs could be enforced against him, and the circumstances for payment of costs by the Commission (Access to Justice Act 1999, s 11(3)). The mechanism of making these provisions under regulations, rather than under primary legislation as previously, was said to provide greater flexibility to deal with problems that may be caused by the protection from costs creating too great an advantage for the funded person.
[31] *The Funding Code* (The Stationery Office, 2000) Part 1.
[32] A multi-party action might not go before the courts without public funding. However, 'from a management point of view, the [Australian] research does not answer the question of why legal aid

B. Funding Service Levels

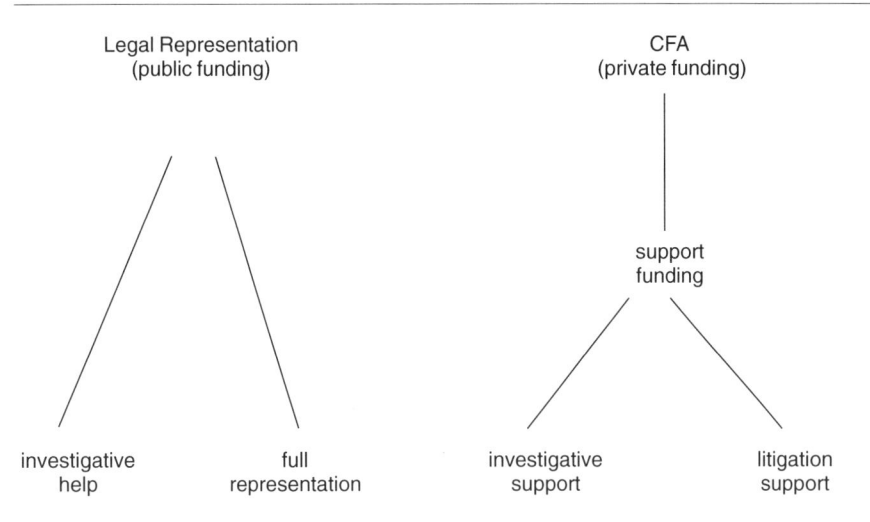

Figure 12.1

```
Legal Representation                    CFA
  (public funding)                (private funding)
       /\                                |
      /  \                               |
     /    \                          support
    /      \                         funding
   /        \                          /\
  /          \                        /  \
 /            \                      /    \
investigative  full            investigative  litigation
    help    representation       support       support
```

generally receive public funding. One aspect might be funding (called Investigative Help) or partial funding (called Investigative Support). The principle that public funds should not be used to support litigation which is capable of being pursued privately is central to the Act.[33]

A client who is publicly funded must be financially eligible under regulations, except where exemptions apply,[34] and an application may be refused if it appears unreasonable to grant funding in the light of the conduct of the client.[35]   **12.21**

The criteria for the relevant differing categories of support are that funding will be   **12.22**
refused:[36]

for Full Representation

    (a) where prospects of success are (i) unclear, (ii) borderline and the case does not appear to have a significant wider public interest or to be of overwhelming importance to the client, or (iii) poor (less than 50 per cent);

---

is necessarily the most appropriate option to fund such cases. Why should scarce public resources give priority to these civil actions and not the large number of other individual actions? . . . Alternative funding sources might be more appropriate in a time of scarce resources.' D Fleming, 'Responding to New Demands: Legal Aid and Multi-Party Actions' in F Regan, A Paterson, T Goriely and D Fleming (eds), *The Transformation of Legal Aid* (OUP, 1999).

[33] Legal Aid Board, *A New Approach to Funding Civil Cases* (1999) para 6.5.
[34] *The Funding Code* (The Stationery Office, 2000) Part 1–4.9.
[35] ibid, Part 1–4.10.
[36] ibid, Part 1–5. Financial thresholds are based on research data: Legal Aid Board Research Unit, *Testing the Code* (1999).

(b) if the claim is primarily a claim for damages and does not have a significant wider public interest, unless the following cost-benefit criteria[37] are satisfied:

  (i) if prospects of success are very good (80 per cent or more), likely damages must exceed costs;
  (ii) if prospects of success are good (60–80 per cent), likely damages must exceed costs by a ratio of 2:1;
  (iii) if prospects of success are moderate (50–60 per cent), likely damages must exceed costs by a ratio of 4:1;

(c) if the claim is not primarily a claim for damages but does not have a significant wider public interest, unless the likely benefits to be gained from the proceedings justify the likely costs, such that a reasonable private paying client would be prepared to litigate, having regard to the prospects of success and all other circumstances;[38]

(d) if the claim has a wider public interest, unless the likely benefits of the proceedings to the applicant and others justify the likely costs, having regard to the prospects of success and all other circumstances;

for Litigation Support

(e) unless the form of the CFA agreement is satisfactory and complies with Code procedures;

(f) unless satisfactory insurance cover or an equivalent arrangement is available to the client;

(g) unless the reasonable costs of the litigation, including the costs of the investigative stage but excluding any sums already funded by the Commission or other bodies, are such that:[39]

---

[37] The cost-benefit criteria are intended to replicate the profile of merits, costs, and damages under which a private client would be prepared to litigate using his or her own money. The Board calculated that, at these ratios, one-third of the good and 55% of the moderate categories of cases previously funded on legal aid would be excluded: Legal Aid Board, *A New Approach to Funding Civil Cases* (1999) paras 7.46 and 7.49.

[38] The inclusion of the private client test was thought important and supported on consultation. In categories like personal injury, in the Legal Aid Board's view, the aim of funding should be to create a level playing field between pure CFA cases and those funded partially by the Commission: Legal Aid Board, *A New Approach to Funding Civil Cases* (1999) para 6.3.

[39] The Board's research indicated that 0.7% of personal injury cases have gross costs of £25,000 or more and that disbursements typically account for roughly 25% of overall costs: Legal Aid Board, *A New Approach to Funding Civil Cases* (1999) para 10.18. The Lord Chancellor subsequently gave a direction to the Legal Services Commission that out of its 2000–1 budget of £749 million it should spend no more than £1 million net on cases commencing after 1 Apr 2000 which individually are likely to cost more than £25,000 (ie an estimate of 40 cases if the costs of each were £25,000). He indicated that he was minded to increase the central budget of £1 million to £4.5 million in 2001–2 and £13.5 million in 2002–3, to take account of the annual build-up in very high cost cases, which would be expected to last a number of years. He anticipated that these budgets would allow the

(i) disbursements[40] are or are likely to exceed £5,000;
(ii) the costs of the case at prescribed rates,[41] excluding disbursements, have reached or are likely to exceed £15,000;[42]

but the Commission may vary the above thresholds if satisfied that the case has a significant wider public interest;

(h) if the prospects of success are unclear, borderline (not possible to say that they are better than 50 per cent), or poor (less than 50 per cent);
(i) save where the case has a significant wider public interest,[43] unless the cost-benefit criteria set out at (b) above are satisfied;
(j) as (d) above.

Investigative Support[44] may only be granted where the prospects of success are uncertain and the reasonable costs of investigating the claim to determine prospects of success are such that **12.23**

(i) disbursements (including counsel's fees) are, or are likely to exceed, £1,000; or
(ii) investigative costs at prescribed rates other than disbursements have reached or are likely to exceed £3,000.[45]

Investigative support will be refused unless the damages are likely to exceed £5,000, and may only be granted if there are reasonable grounds for believing that when the investigative work has been carried out the claim will be strong enough, in terms of prospects of success and cost benefit, to proceed privately, together with Litigation Support if appropriate. **12.24**

Investigative Help[46] may only be granted where the prospects of success of the claim are uncertain and substantial investigative work is required before those prospects can be determined. It may be refused if the nature of the case and circumstances of the client are such that investigative work should be carried out privately with a view to a CFA or that funding should take the form only of **12.25**

Commission to grant funding to all high cost cases that meet the normal Funding Code criteria if future demand reflects past trends. However, he indicated his expectation in future to set the central budget at a lower level so as to limit the proportion of overall spending on the few most expensive cases.

[40] This would not apply if an insurance policy covered disbursements, but would otherwise include the premium of an after-the-event insurance policy. Legal Aid Board, *A New Approach to Funding Civil Cases* (1999) para 10.21.
[41] £70 per hour for solicitors, £50 per hour for junior counsel, and £90 for senior counsel.
[42] Previously proposed as £20,000.
[43] This is to enable the Commission to fund such a case where the individual's chances of success exceed 50% but damages and risk of irrecoverable costs make a CFA unattractive: Legal Aid Board, *A New Approach to Funding Civil Cases* (1999) para 10.34.
[44] *The Funding Code* (The Stationery Office, 2000) Part 1–5.8.
[45] Previously proposed as £5,000.
[46] *The Funding Code* (The Stationery Office, 2000) Part 1–5.6.

Investigative Support. If the client's claim is primarily a claim for damages and has no significant wider public interest, Investigative Help will be refused unless the damages are likely to exceed £5,000. Investigative Help may only be granted if there are reasonable grounds for believing that when the investigative work has been carried out the claim will be strong enough, in terms of prospects of success and cost benefit, to satisfy the relevant criteria for Full Representation.

12.26 It is intended that Support Funding, which is essentially a limited banking and insurance function, should concentrate on funding disbursements above certain thresholds. The Commission considers that Support Funding is particularly appropriate for investigating a potential multi-party action.[47] The success fee would be apportioned between the lawyers and the Commission according to the degree of risk borne by each.

12.27 Funding may be withdrawn,[48] *inter alia*, where the criteria under which funding was originally granted are no longer satisfied, or where it is unreasonable for funding to continue in all the circumstances of the case, taking into account the interests of the client, any wider public interest, and the interest of the Community Legal Service Fund. Investigative Help or Investigative Support will cease where it appears that sufficient work has been carried out to enable prospects of success to be determined.

C. Funding Excluded Services

12.28 The effect of Schedule 2 to the Act is that only basic information and advice will be publicly funded for the proscribed categories, notably negligence claims (see paragraph 12.04 above). Claims alleging strict product liability under Part 1 of the Consumer Protection Act 1987 are not excluded under Schedule 2. The reason for this different approach to the obviously closely linked causes of action of negligence and strict liability appears to have been an oversight on the part of the Lord Chancellor's Department.[49]

12.29 The Lord Chancellor has, however, given directions under section 6(8) of the Act to fund certain excluded services,[50] including the following 'expensive personal injury cases':

---

[47] Legal Aid Board, *A New Approach to Funding Civil Cases* (1999) ch 10. Lord Kingsland said that cases such as the Gulf War veterans and organophosphate sheep farmers' actions are extremely complex and require a great deal of money to be paid up front before a proper assessment can be made of the likelihood of success or failure: *Hansard*, HL (Series 5) vol 613, col 1110 (6 June 2000).
[48] *The Funding Code* (The Stationery Office, 2000) Part 1–14.
[49] Correspondence between the Lord Chancellor's Department and the author.
[50] *Scope of the Community Legal Service Fund, Lord Chancellor's Direction* (2000). See Legal Aid Board, *A New Approach to Funding Civil Cases* (1999).

1. Investigative Support in relation to allegations of negligently caused injury or death, where the costs of investigating the circumstances of the case to the point where it is possible to assess whether and on what terms it could be funded under a CFA exceed the relevant threshold set out in the Code;
2. Litigation Support in relation to allegations of negligently caused injury or death where the overall costs of the case exceed the relevant threshold set out in the Code;

and Investigative Support, Litigation Support, or Legal Representation (as it considers appropriate) in relation to any of the proscribed issues listed in paragraph 1 of Schedule 2 to the 1999 Act (referred to at paragraph 12.03 above), in cases that have a wider public interest or in proceedings against public authorities (including judicial review) alleging serious wrongdoing, abuse of position or power, or significant breach of human rights.

D. Multi-Party Action Funding

From 1994 to mid-1997 the Legal Aid Board entered into thirteen group action contracts[51] and a further three in 1998–9.[52] Cases which meet the criteria for the Legal Services Commission's 'very expensive' category are also subject to criteria which take into account the resources available in the central budget: funding will be refused or deferred unless it appears reasonable for funding to be granted in the light of the resources available in the Central Budget and likely future demands on those resources.[53] The Legal Aid Board acknowledged that multi-party actions were the most expensive cases which it funded.[54] Accordingly, in its initial proposals for the Funding Code, the Board expressed a strong presumption in favour of funding a test case and against funding a full multi-party action (MPA) procedure.[55] After consultation, the Board recognised that this might not be appropriate

12.30

---

[51] Depo-Medrone (steroid); Femodene and Minulet (oral contraceptives); Gulf War Syndrome; Human Growth Hormone; Infant Drinks; Lariam (anti-malarial drug); MMR Vaccine; Norplant (contraceptive implant); Nottingham District Heating Scheme; Radiotherapy breast cancer treatment (medical negligence, failure to diagnose); sheep dip pesticide; Smoking (the contract for which was terminated in 1996); and Vibration White Finger (industrial injury): Legal Aid Board, *Annual Report 1996–97* (1997). Since then contracts have been awarded for Minocin (1998) and Roaccutane (1999).

[52] BSE (contamination of the food chain); BCCI (employees); Persona (contraceptive system): Legal Aid Board, *Annual Report 1998–99* (1999).

[53] *The Funding Code* (The Stationery Office, 2000) Part 1, para 6.4; Legal Aid Board, *A New Approach to Funding Civil Cases* (1999) para 3.10; a separate fund for multi-party actions is not available.

[54] Legal Aid Board, *When the price is high: Consultation paper on draft MPA contract and tendering documents* (1999) para 7.12.

[55] Legal Aid Board, *A New Approach to Funding Civil Cases* (1999) para 12.4. See also Lord Chancellor's Department, *Financial conditions for funding by the Legal Services Commission* (2000) para 2.17.

where, for example, limitation issues arise which require all other individual claims to issue proceedings or under the then forthcoming draft rule of court on GLOs.[56] The Board stated that the extent to which it is appropriate to fund an MPA rather than an individual test case will depend on how the rule operates in practice and in particular:

1. whether orders will be made requiring significant amounts of work to be carried out on individual cases when they are entered on the register;
2. whether funding an MPA will reduce the chances of the Commission recovering generic costs if successful. In line with the general approach to costs in the new rules the Board believes that generic costs should be recovered according to the outcome of the generic issues, and that the extent of recovery should not be reduced according to the outcome of the individual claims. Resolution of this issue of principle could have a major impact on the extent to which the Commission will be able to fund MPAs in the future.

12.31 The Commission wishes to ensure that staff resources and costs in MPAs are not unnecessarily devoted to investigation of individual claims and are instead concentrated on generic issues.[57] However, proceeding too far down this line might run into problems under the Human Rights Act 1998. The following comments were made:

> In a personal injury MPA we consider it essential for the Commission to have a discretion as to which elements of cost to fund. Funding by the Commission will concentrate on the generic work, including the co-ordination of the claim by the lead solicitors and bringing to trial lead cases and lead issues. The usual approach to individual cases should be that only minimal work is necessary to register claims as part of the action. There is no reason why such work as is necessary should not be done under conditional fee agreements. Unless the Commission agrees otherwise, the approach will therefore be that the Commission will fund generic work from the outset, but will provide no funding towards other individual costs.[58]

12.32 Accordingly, on the policy that the Commission would only fund generic work which was not suitable for CFAs, the Commission proposed a new approach to financial eligibility for MPAs. The approach would apply only where:

1. The Commission is funding an MPA on the basis that it has a significant public interest. Obviously for this purpose a case will still be treated as having significant public interest even if large numbers of clients join the action, thereby reducing the number of potential people outside the litigation who could benefit.
2. The court had certified the case as a multi-party situation in accordance with the new rules.

---

[56] Legal Aid Board, *A New Approach to Funding Civil Cases* (1999) para 12.4.
[57] Legal Aid Board, *A New Approach to Funding Civil Cases* (1999) para 12.10.
[58] Legal Aid Board, *A New Approach to Funding Civil Cases* (1999) para 12.14.

3. The Commission is satisfied that the great majority of those who would benefit from the MPA are eligible for support under the normal eligibility rules, and that any other funder of claimants in the litigation (such as, for example, a trade union) is making an appropriate contribution to the generic costs.

Where these conditions apply, there would be no upper eligibility limit in relation to generic costs in the MPA. In practice, the approach would be that:

1. The generic work would be funded by the Commission on behalf of the clients as a whole, whatever their individual financial circumstances.
2. All clients above the free eligibility level for funding would pay a contribution towards the generic costs. This would be calculated from income or capital in accordance with regulations, but it would not exceed a sum determined by the Commission to be a reasonable contribution by the individual towards the generic work.
3. All clients in the litigation would enjoy cost protection under section 11 of the Act in relation to orders for the payment of generic costs. Under the rules in section 11, this protection would of course be less effective for clients with more substantial assets.
4. There would be no cost protection for clients in relation to individual costs. If necessary, these would usually be covered by insurance arrangements against an inter partes order negotiated for the particular action. A number of insurers have been interested in providing such cover in actions under the present system. The Commission would have a discretion if necessary to contribute to the funding of premiums for clients at income support levels to the extent that such payments could not be borne entirely by the firms involved.[59]

E. MPA Procedures

12.33 Funding for MPAs is controlled from a central budget by the Community Legal Service's Special Cases and Multi-Party Actions Unit, based in its London Area Office. An application or an existing certificate shall be referred by the Regional Director to the Special Cases Unit where it appears to the Regional Director that either:[60]

- the actual or likely costs under the certificate exceed £25,000;[61]
- if the case were to proceed to a contested trial or final hearing the likely costs under the certificate might exceed £75,000;
- the application is for Litigation Support; or
- the application or certificate relates to a multi-party action or potential multi-party action.

---

[59] Legal Aid Board, *A New Approach to Funding Civil Cases* (1999) paras 12.17 and 12.18.
[60] *The Funding Code* (The Stationery Office, 2000) Part 2 C.23.
[61] It had been earlier proposed that this figure be £50,000, at which threshold it was estimated in 1999 that somewhere between 1,000 and 2,000 applications would be made to this fund per year: Legal Aid Board, *A New Approach to Funding Civil Cases* (1999) para 7.2.

12.34 All decisions as to the scope or continuation of work under an MPA contract are made by the CLS's MPA Unit, save where the Unit decides to refer any matter to the MPA Committee, in which case the decision of the MPA Committee shall be final.[62] All applications to the CLS on behalf of clients in the MPA must be made through the lead solicitor.

F. Community Legal Service Contracts

12.35 The CLS enters into a contract with the solicitors that it funds in relation to an MPA.[63] Competitive price tendering for MPA contracts was introduced by the Legal Aid Board from 1 February 1999. The basis of contracting rests on tenders which include a detailed case plan for progressing the litigation and binding cost limitations on stages of the work. Quality is the most important criterion in assessing tenders. Tenders are initially assessed against quality criteria: if more than one tender demonstrates sufficient quality, price will be a factor in choosing between them,[64] by assessing value for money (a costed case plan, with at least the first stage costed in detail) and comparison of hourly rates (either differentiated rates for grades of personnel or a single rate for all). Risk is shared between the Commission and its contractors, such that hourly rates would be lower than commercial market rates and similar to (or less than) legal aid hourly rates, without any 'mark-up'. At the end of the case, if it is successful, the contractor would have the option of whether to accept only the *inter partes* costs or only the contract payment: the former would be more advantageous in most cases. If the contractor chooses to accept only the contract payment (probably when an action is unsuccessful) any *inter partes* costs which are payable to the claimants will be paid into the CLS fund and the statutory charge will apply to any damages which might be recovered, to the extent of the contract payment, reduced by any *inter partes* costs paid into the CLS fund and any clients' contributions. The contract will, therefore, be similar to a CFA but with an assurance of payment at the contract rate if the claim is not successful, rather than no payment. Payments may be made on account. Payments for counsel and experts are 'ring fenced' within contract prices: it is not appropriate to specify experts' fees in a GLO contract, but the Commission considers that hourly rates of contracted solicitors and counsel should be the same, in order to implement the risk-sharing principle.

---

[62] *The Funding Code* (The Stationery Office, 2000) D.2.
[63] *The Funding Code* (The Stationery Office, 2000) Part 2 C26.
[64] Normal maximum rates prescribed for public funding under the Legal Advice and Assistance Regulations 1989, SI 1989/340, are disapplied in relation to group litigation or potential group litigation by the Community Legal Service (Funding) Order 2000, SI 2000/627, reg 5.

G. Wider Public Interest Cases

12.36 An MPA Solicitors Panel was established on 1 February 1999 of firms who are considered to have pre-qualified on certain aspects of MPA tenders and to act as a consultative panel to alert the Commission to emergent MPAs at an early stage and to raise any concerns about the Commission's contract and tender procedures. Criteria for joining the panel[65] include: possession of a Legal Aid Board franchise; recent substantial involvement in co-ordinating or managing generic work in at least three MPAs over the previous five years; sufficient fee-earning staff and an adequate infrastructure to conduct a moderately sized MPA; and demonstrated financial and corporate stability. The first eighteen firms to be appointed to the panel are listed in Appendix D and the Commission's Multi-Party Action Arrangements are at Appendix H.

G. Wider Public Interest Cases

12.37 A case which can be said to be in the public interest would attract priority for public funding from the central CLS Fund[66] but it must first come within an eligible category—public interest *per se* does not attract funding. It has been recognised that public interest is a concept open to a wide range of different interpretations and it is difficult to define with precision.[67] The Funding Code uses the term 'wider public interest', which is defined to mean:

> the potential of the proceedings to produce real benefits for individuals other than the client (other than benefits to the public at large which normally flow from proceedings of the type in question).[68]

12.38 This would include two distinct types of case. First, there are judicial review cases and cases alleging serious wrongdoing by public authorities, such as the police. The 1998 White Paper also mentioned cases of failure to act, of public bodies (including cases under the Human Rights Act), or alleging that public servants, such as the police, have abused their position or power.[69] All cases in these categories are considered to have an inherent public interest. Secondly, there are individual cases, in any category of law, which 'have the potential to produce real benefits for a significant number of people or which raise an important new legal issue'. This second category is what is meant by 'wider public interest' when it appears as a separate criterion in the Code.[70]

---

[65] Legal Aid Board, *Multi-Party Solicitors' Panel: Membership Criteria and Guidance* (1998), available from the Legal Services Commission, Multi-Party Action Unit, 29–37 Red Lion Street, London WC1R 4PP.
[66] See Access to Justice Act 1999, s 8(2)(g).
[67] Legal Aid Board, *A New Approach to Funding Civil Cases* (1999); P Pleasance and S Maclean, *Research Briefing: The Public Interest* (Legal Aid Board, 1998).
[68] *The Funding Code* (The Stationery Office, 2000), Part 1 Section 2.4.
[69] Lord Chancellor's Department, *Modernising Justice* (The Stationery Office, 1998 Cm 4155).
[70] Legal Aid Board, *A New Approach to Funding Civil Cases* (1999) para 8.2.

12.39 The 1998 Consultation Paper stated that to justify funding a case would 'have to demonstrate the potential to produce *tangible* benefits for a *significant* number of people in a *definable* category' (original emphasis). This would include cases involving novel points of law likely to have a real impact, but not points only of academic interest.[71]

12.40 Some proposed examples were given in the 1998 Consultation Paper of what would be considered to be public interest cases. First, a test case about a novel point of law which had no more than a 50 per cent chance of success but where the decision might impact on numerous future cases (such as a recent decision extending the duty of care owed by a sports referee to players[72]). Secondly, a claim for a relatively small sum but where many others had similar claims: use of pharmaceutical products and pollution cases were mentioned, which were very expensive because novel and complex.[73] Further suggestions made during the parliamentary debates in late 1997 for cases which might justify legal aid funding as being in the public interest included medical negligence cases; cases against the police, prison or immigration authorities, or other officials for abuse of power; failure to obtain informed consent in medical treatment; sterilisation of the mentally ill; human rights; claims against public authorities or servants for mistakes or abuse of power; clarification of the law. All these views were, however, expressed before publication of the Lord Chancellor's directions to the Legal Services Commission on priorities for funding,[74] which did not prioritise, for example, personal injury cases.

12.41 In 1988 the Legal Action Group[75] sought to draw a distinction between fundamental rights, for which it argued that legal aid should be granted on a non-means-tested basis, and non-fundamental rights, for which it thought that legal aid should continue to be means-tested. Family, housing, dismissal, and personal injury claims were given a high ranking; consumer disputes and defamation were given a low ranking. However, it has been said that:

> the more specific the examples, the more arbitrary the lists became. Personal injury claims may be seen as preserving 'the right to health'—and would therefore score high. However, personal injury claims do not prevent injuries, they only provide compensation after the event and the £2,000 one receives for a small personal injury claim looks very similar to the £2,000 one may receive in a consumer dispute. Tenancy disputes over repairs were ranked as fundamental ('the right to housing') but owner-occupiers fighting builders or surveyors were non-fundamental. Given that most legal disputes are in the end about money, the distinction between a fundamental and non-fundamental right proves difficult to draw in practice.[76]

---

[71] Lord Chancellor's Department, *Access to Justice with Conditional Fees* (1998) para 3.32.
[72] *Smoldon v Whitworth* [1997] PIQR 133, [1997] ELR 249.
[73] Lord Chancellor's Department, *Access to Justice with Conditional Fees* (1998).
[74] See para 12.02 above.
[75] Legal Action Group, *Legal Services: A Blueprint for the Future* (1977).
[76] AA Paterson and T Goriely (eds), *A Reader on Resourcing Civil Justice* (OUP, 1996).

G. Wider Public Interest Cases

The Consultation Paper proposed a minimum threshold of 40 per cent chance of success in order to justify public interest funding, although after consultation this was restated as 'a little below 50%':[77]

12.42

> Funding for some public interest cases might be justified even if prospects of success were a little below 50%. Whilst cases which were 50–50 might be allowed to continue we do think it important even for public interest cases that cases with low chances of success should not be funded. Therefore the threshold we suggest should be set at something like 40%. However in our view funding for a case with under 50% prospect of success should be truly exceptional. Beyond meeting the criteria for public interest it should be necessary for the case to demonstrate very substantial benefits to the public.[78]

It was originally proposed that the Funding Code should define a minimum number of people who must benefit from a case (twenty or fifty were initially suggested) and the nature of the benefit they would receive. The earlier consultation had suggested that a number of different types of benefit may come to people through litigation brought by others:

12.43

1. Direct financial benefit—for example where a challenge to welfare benefit entitlements leads to the government thereafter making higher payments to a whole class of claimants.
2. Potential financial benefit—this is usually the situation for most test cases or group actions, such as those which establish liability of a manufacturer for harm caused by a dangerous product. Success in litigation will not usually guarantee compensation for those outside the litigation, who may still need to bring their own claims and prove their own issues on liability, causation, and quantum.
3. Protection of life or other basic human rights—for example a challenge to a government immigration policy concerning a class of asylum seekers, who allege that they face persecution or death if not allowed to remain in the country.
4. Cases concerning intangible benefits such as health, safety, and quality of life.

On further consideration, the Board concluded that it would not be advisable to attempt to set precise thresholds and that cases could qualify which concern unquantifiable benefits such as health, safety, and quality of life. However, since almost any worthwhile case could be said to have *some* public interest, the test in the Code requires that a case demonstrates 'significant' wider public interest 'in the sense of securing real benefits'.[79]

12.44

---

[77] Legal Aid Board, *A New Approach to Funding Civil Cases* (1999) para 8.19.
[78] Legal Aid Board, *A New Approach to Funding Civil Cases* (1999) para 4.17.
[79] Legal Aid Board, *A New Approach to Funding Civil Cases* (1999) para 8.9.

Chapter 12: Public Funding

No cost-benefit ratio: valuing public interest

12.45 The Commission does not apply a cost-benefit ratio in cases which have a significant public interest. However, the general principle that the benefits of the proceedings must justify the likely costs still applies and in this the Commission will value the extent of the public interest.[80] In performing this task, guidance is provided on the application form to include estimates of:

1. how many people might benefit from the case;
2. how much they will benefit by;
3. how directly they will benefit.

12.46 Cases which have borderline prospects of success need to demonstrate very strong public interest. Cases concerning only indirect or intangible benefits will only be cost-effective if very substantial numbers of people can be shown to benefit. Applications must provide sufficient information to quantify so far as possible the nature of the public benefit.

12.47 In assessing cost-benefit ratios, the Commission would consider whether there might be alternative sources of funding, such as from an interested organisation, and consider the reasonableness of a grant in the light of that information.

12.48 In the Consultation Paper the Board gave the illustration of two MPAs, in one of which up to 100 claimants have claims for damages up to £100,000 each and in the other 10,000 people might claim on average £1,000 each. The Board asserted that although the cost-benefit and public interest assessment of each MPA might be the same, the former would be a more deserving piece of litigation, partly because of the added cost and complexity of administration of the latter, or because of the greater public interest in compensating those with more substantial losses.

Public Interest Advisory Panel

12.49 Since the fund available to the CLS will be a budget rather than an unlimited fund, the CLS will make its decisions on which cases to fund on the basis of its assessment of the relative priorities of different cases to receive public funding. It recognises that a degree of subjectivity is unavoidable.[81] In evaluating the public interest of an application for funding, the Commission has a wide discretion to obtain advice on the relative weight of public interest cases from a Public Interest Advisory Panel, combined with advice from specialist interest groups where appropriate. This mechanism is aimed at adopting a consistent and more independent approach to evaluating public interest in a wide range of cases. Reasons are to

---

[80] Legal Aid Board, *A New Approach to Funding Civil Cases* (1999) para 8.11.
[81] Legal Aid Board, *A New Approach to Funding Civil Cases* (1999) para 7.8.

G. Wider Public Interest Cases

be given by the Panel for its decisions but it is unclear whether such advice would be transparent. The Board considers that members of the Panel should predominantly be those who can represent consumer interests. This is open to criticism as the consumer interest is not synonymous with the public interest.

The CLS has stated that wherever possible it will make objective comparisons between cases, and that decisions on funding are likely to depend in particular on: **12.50**

1. the likely cost of the case and
2. the degree of merit of the case.

Assessment of the relative merit of a case may be assisted by a points or banding system, but this will be used as a secondary aid until the Commission is confident that it can be applied fairly and reasonably.[82] **12.51**

Financial eligibility

The normal eligibility rules apply in wider public interest cases, at least for the time being.[83] However, a different approach may apply to multi-party cases. The Commission does, nevertheless, have power to waive some or all of any contribution assessed as payable under the regulations, and has power to waive all or part of the statutory charge on damages and costs recovered. The aim of this is to permit an individual test case to be pursued to resolve an issue of principle, without the need for an expensive group action involving large numbers of other claims sharing the costs of the lead case, but increasing the costs of the litigation. In return, a client funded on a test case basis would need to agree not to settle his or her claim without the consent of the Commission. **12.52**

Not a public inquiry: consistency

There are serious difficulties with a public interest test. First, it is strongly subjective, as the Board accepted,[84] and therefore open to change over time. Secondly, it is easy to confuse the questions of whether a case is of interest to the public with whether it is genuinely in the public interest that the case be pursued.[85] The former question raises issues of numerosity, media attraction, and manipulation and the second question raises issues of public policy. **12.53**

---

[82] Legal Aid Board, *When the price is high: Consultation paper on draft MPA contract and tendering documents* (1999).
[83] Legal Aid Board, *A New Approach to Funding Civil Cases* (1999) para 8.17.
[84] Legal Aid Board, *A New Approach to Funding Civil Cases* (1999) para 8.8.
[85] 'There is a world of difference between what is in the public interest and what is of interest to the public': *Lion Laboratories Ltd v Evans* [1984] 2 All ER 417, 435 per Griffiths LJ. The Board's Research Unit concluded that a high-profile case, ie one which is or has the potential for attracting media attention, does not have an inherent public interest: P Pleasance and S Maclean, *Research Briefing: The Public Interest* (Legal Aid Board, 1998).

12.54 The mere numerical existence of sufficient claimants who might arguably be affected is clearly an insufficiently reliable test on its own and could only be an indicator. Numbers can easily be manipulated by publicity, often attracting claims which are subsequently shown to be weak or hopeless.[86] The initial impression may be of large numbers and this may give the illusion of substance to claims—and hence of public interest. However, it cannot be in the public interest to fund actions which fail, particularly where the costs of failure are extensive. The structural problems of bias and self-interest within the system are largely removed under the CFA system, but are not removed under the continuing arrangements for public funding of very expensive cases.

12.55 There is, therefore, concern that an MPA about product liability or environmental damage, ostensibly involving a large number of potential claimants, can be presented as having public interest, and so deserve public funding, when the reality is quite different. Those advocating funding of such a case would stress issues of public safety, public health, a need to hold major corporations 'accountable', and the potentially large numbers of claimants.[87]

12.56 Various points are made in response. It is said that the function of a civil claim for damages is solely compensatory: it is not a public inquiry into the activities of a manufacturer but a judicial determination of whether money shall be paid to an individual.[88] On this basis, the public's interest in knowing whether one citizen is liable to pay damages to another or others cannot intrinsically be as significant a matter as the public interest in providing a mechanism for this to be decided, which is the function of the courts. It would follow that the function of the court is here limited to its traditional role of deciding issues of civil liability and payment of damages.

12.57 The argument that it should be the function of the civil courts seised of a compensation claim to examine the affairs of a company or industry in a quasi-public inquiry runs into the danger of producing conflict and inconsistency between the decisions of the courts and regulatory authorities. If the function of the civil courts were to be to adopt a public inquiry approach into the activities of a company or industry, this would involve such courts setting standards of conduct for industry. This would be both to usurp and duplicate the function of regulatory authorities. Over the past thirty years, more and more product sectors have become regulated, increasingly under EU legislation and authorities. It is those regulatory authorities which have the function of investigating and controlling

---

[86] See ch 2.
[87] References were made in the tobacco litigation to potential claimants of 1,000 (P Furness, interview on *The Financial World Tonight*, Radio 4, 5 Aug 1996) whereas the membership of the group before the court at the final hearing was 53.
[88] See *AB and Others v John Wyeth & Brother Ltd* [1994] 5 Med LR 149, 153 per Stuart-Smith LJ.

G. Wider Public Interest Cases

companies' activities in the public interest. It is suggested that complex issues of public safety are inappropriate for resolution in civil compensation claims. Instead, sophisticated and stringent regulatory mechanisms precisely designed to ensure public safety must be considered. Further, the courts have declared that they will not interfere with the exercise of discretion on safety issues by regulatory authorities save in limited situations such as procedural irregularity or *Wednesbury* unreasonableness.[89] The double jeopardy point arises for defendants, but the main point is that the civil courts are simply an inappropriate and unsophisticated forum for deciding regulatory issues on, for example, pharmaceuticals, pollution, or industrial processes. Those are the functions of the Medicines Control Agency, the Environmental Protection Agency, the Health & Safety Executive, the Vehicles Inspectorate, the Medical Devices Agency, and many other similar agencies and local Trading Standards Departments. It would be against public policy to permit the possibility of the civil courts setting different standards of conduct or product safety from those set by regulators. This would largely be because of the ignorance of the former but the process is also wasteful of public expenditure, because of its duplication through cost of regulation and cost of civil justice.

Competing interests

12.58 Consideration of double standards between civil courts and regulatory authorities leads on to the problem of competing interests. It may not be in the general public interest that a particular case is pursued since the consequences of doing so might do harm to other public interests. This is because, as the Consultation Paper recognised, public interest 'is not an absolute interest. Benefits to one section of the public may well directly or indirectly result in harm to another section. This is best illustrated by litigation relating to the health service.'[90] Whether a case is won or lost, finite public resources are prevented from being devoted to other ends which are, by definition, being pursued in the public interest. The point does in fact apply to some extent also to private enterprise defendants, where consequences relating to employment, innovation, or insurance may affect a wider section of the public than just the specific defendant. Indeed, some have argued that the macroeconomic or social consequences of supporting a culture of litigation are so serious that litigation should be discouraged.[91]

12.59 The Law Society recognised the effects of unjustified allocation of resources on public interest cases in 1995:

---

[89] See *R v Medicines Control Agency, ex p Pharma Nord* [1998] 3 CMLR 109; *Upjohn Ltd v The Licensing Authority established by the Medicines Act 1968 and Others* [1999] 1 WLR 927; see also *Albery & Budden v BP Oil & Shell UK*, CA (Megaw, Bridge, Cumming-Bruce LJJ), 2 May 1980.
[90] Legal Aid Board, *A New Approach to Funding Civil Cases* (1999) para 4.6.
[91] F Furedi, *Courting Mistrust* (Centre for Policy Studies, 1999).

[The legal aid merits test is not suitable] to the more novel multi-party actions, nor to some of the test cases instituted by individuals, especially where they do not have a direct personal interest. The uncertainty of success, the very large potential costs, or the absence of a direct personal interest in the outcome make it at best doubtful whether these cases should qualify for legal aid on the normal merits test. Nevertheless, many of the cases have obvious social importance, or implications beyond the individual action concerned. It would be undesirable for there to be no means of funding such cases, yet without public funds it is difficult to see how they could be pursued. On the other hand, it would be inappropriate for these cases to use so much of the money available for legal aid that they led to restrictions on the availability of legal aid in ordinary cases.[92]

12.60 In any event, the Commission ignores competing or contrary interests (such as the publicly funded health, educational, and housing services) when deciding whether a case has public interest, on purely pragmatic grounds. However, it may take competing interests into account in valuing the public interest in either deciding on the cost-effectiveness of a case and/or deciding on whether a high cost public interest case justifies funding out of the limited resources available, where the decision would be borderline if considerations of competing interests were not considered.[93]

12.61 An MPA can lead to adverse consequences outside its limited contents which are not in the public interest. This can be illustrated by the benzodiazepine and Norplant case histories (chapters 22 and 31). In the benzodiazepine claims, drugs which satisfied every regulatory requirement were the subject of litigation which cost the taxpayer £40 million without a penny being obtained in compensation by any claimant. It was asserted that the litigation had changed the nature of medical practice for legal rather than scientific reasons in relation to the prescription of such drugs. The prescription of benzodiazepines, which are safe and cheap, has generally been replaced by prescription of drugs which are often more costly and, in some cases, less safe. Norplant, including its labelling, was approved by the regulatory authorities and used by some 55,000 women in the country but the claims by 267 women and the resultant 400 adverse media reports were largely blamed by the defendant manufacturer for the commercial failure of the product and its withdrawal after the claims collapsed.[94]

Possible future restriction on public interest funding

12.62 What conclusions can be drawn from the above discussion on public funding of MPAs? Given a policy of 'privatisation' of funding of civil litigation through the CFA mechanism, what justification is there for the continuation of public fund-

---

[92] Law Society, *A Better Way Forward* (1995) paras 12.1.4 and 12.1.2.
[93] Legal Aid Board, *A New Approach to Funding Civil Cases* (1999) para 8.10.
[94] See *Hansard*, HL (Series 5) vol 606, col WA 249 (11 Nov 1999) and ch 31 below.

ing for very expensive cases? The answer is purely pragmatic—the financial burden and risk of such cases are thought to be too great to be carried by solicitors' firms within the country in their current state of capitalisation and profitability. They simply do not have the resources of, and their partners are not as rich as, their American counterparts. But this may change. When it does, the thresholds and policy of public funding should be reassessed accordingly. After the collapse in 1999 of the first MPA run on a CFA (albeit after initial investigations funded by legal aid) it was said that it was impossible for any firm to fund an MPA. There were extensive press reports that Leigh Day & Co had lost £2.5 million in the litigation but their senior partner was also reported as saying that his firm had fully reserved against the risk that that sum might not be recovered and the sum represented a small amount of the firm's total turnover over several years.[95]

12.63 Funding of cases on a public interest basis raises serious problems. On the one hand, many would agree that certain issues are of genuine public interest and would otherwise be difficult for individuals to fund so that the wider public could benefit from their resolution.[96] Such issues might include equal pay or retirement age, or questions of public administration. On the other hand, there are strong arguments for great care being taken in funding certain types of cases where the public interest may be illusory or outweighed by other interests which may be damaged.

H. Representations by Defendants

12.64 There was some debate around 1992 as to whether it was proper for defendants to make representations to the Legal Aid Board against the grant or continuation of funding, whether of an action as a whole or of individual actions. It was said that relations between claimants and the Board were confidential. This principle was not, however, undermined merely by the making of voluntary representations. The argument for representations was clearly correct, particularly when information contained in them led the Board to re-examine cases and withdraw funding. Courts,[97]

---

[95] See ch 32 below.
[96] The Law Commission has proposed that public interest challenges should be explicitly recognised as a category of case. It recommends the adoption of a two-track system for judicial review: the first to cover applicants who have been personally adversely affected by the decision, and the second to cover public interest challenges. Law Commission, *Administrative Law: Judicial Review and Statutory Appeals* (Law Com No 226, 1994) paras 5.20–5.22. See also *A matter of public interest: Reforming the law and practice on interventions in public interest cases* (JUSTICE and the Public Law Project, 1996).
[97] *A B and Others v John Wyeth and Brother Ltd* [1994] 5 Med LR 149, 153.

commentators,[98] and the Legal Aid Board[99] recognised the validity of representations on the merits of actions.[100] In 1995, the Law Society's Report proposed the introduction of a challenge procedure so that decisions could be based on 'the fullest possible information'. The Working Party accepted that 'Legal aid is sometimes granted in cases where, had the full facts been available to the Board, it is unlikely that it would have been'. By 1997, the Board said that it welcomed representations, especially where they are cogent and considered and enabled funding decisions to be made on better information.[101] Essentially, therefore, the Board was accepting that defendants should be notified of an impending funding decision so as to afford them an opportunity to contribute. This has long been the position in Scotland.[102] The Law Society also at length accepted that opponents of those funded by legal aid should be able to challenge its grant.[103]

12.65 The Funding Code[104] entitles any person, including an opponent or potential opponent of a client who has applied for or has received a certificate, to make representations to the appropriate Regional Director, who must consider such representations, although there is a discretion not to consider them if they relate to proceedings which are not currently being pursued, for example if an individual case in an MPA is stayed. On receipt of representations, the Regional Director may, if appropriate, place limitations on any certificate, but shall not take steps to discharge or revoke a certificate on the basis of representations received unless the solicitor has been given an opportunity to respond to issues raised by the representations. If a certificate is in force it shall be deemed to cover reasonable work done in responding to representations, but such work must be carried out within the cost limitation.[105]

12.66 The Regional Director may also at any stage invite an opponent, potential opponent, or other person or body to make representations where he or she considers that it is appropriate to do so before deciding whether to provide or continue to provide public funds to support the case.

---

[98] Law Society, *A Better Way Forward* (1995) para 12.37. Legal Aid Board, *Issues arising for the Legal Aid Board and the Lord Chancellor's Department from Multi-Party Actions* (1994) para 4.39. Representations by opponents were envisaged in the White Paper *Legal Aid in England and Wales: A New Framework* (1987) para 37, which formed the basis of the Legal Aid Act 1988, and were supported when the Bill was considered in the House of Lords: *Hansard*, HL (Series 5) Vol 491, col 624 (15 Dec 1987).
[99] Letter by R Green, LS Gaz, 28 Oct 1992 and subsequent Legal Aid Board *Annual Reports*.
[100] Pursuant to the Civil Legal Aid (General) Regulations 1989, Rule 28.
[101] Legal Aid Board, *When the price is high* (1997) para 6.2.
[102] Civil Legal Aid (Scotland) Regulations 1987, regs 7 and 8.
[103] The Law Society, *Scales of Justice* (1997) para 7.
[104] *The Funding Code* (The Stationery Office, 2000) Part 2 section 11.
[105] It was at one stage an objection to representations by defendants that claimants would be put to expense in responding to them. P Balen, 'Multi-Party Actions and the Legal Aid Board' [1996] JPIL 231, 244. This was solved by the restoration of legal aid or the making of special grants.

H. Representations by Defendants

12.67 In what circumstances might it be appropriate to operate this discretion? On the one hand, many small publicly funded cases conform to a straightforward type with predictable chances of success and for which it can be ascertained whether the relevant facts have been verified and what the chances of success are. It would be unnecessary and uneconomic to seek initial evidence or views from the prospective defendant. The change to pre-action disclosure of the case of both parties through protocols should assist in the discontinuation of poor cases which are funded. On the other hand, there are complex or novel cases where the complete facts and prospects of success will be uncertain for the claimant and the CLS Fund and, as experience has shown, seeking the views of the prospective defendant as to relevant facts and/or analysis of the case can be beneficial, particularly before a decision is made to commit large sums of public money. In these situations, particularly, the Commission would seek representations from an opponent before making the funding decision.[106] This is a discretionary power for the Commission rather than a procedure to be followed in every case. However, it is likely to apply to most major MPAs.

12.68 In some instances, it is not possible to evaluate a case since certain key facts relevant to the assessment are in the hands of the opponent. It is suggested that the Commission could not, therefore, validly make a decision without filling this information gap. This would be the case with, for example, a product liability MPA, where the claimant has details of his injury and medical history but it is only the defendant who has evidence of the design and manufacture of the product. Both the defendant and a regulatory body may have evidence of regulatory information. It is difficult to see how a rational decision could be made on funding without a complete picture of this information and representations should be sought. Defendants in nearly all the major cases have positively wished to be given the opportunity to submit representations, as many did voluntarily. In other cases, representations may be valuable in providing an analysis of the weaknesses of the legal case rather than new factual information.[107]

12.69 A difficulty arises for defendants to be in a position to provide relevant representations unless they have been provided with a reasonable statement of what case is being put against them. It was always a problem for defendants in the 1990s that, in drafting voluntary representations, they were drafting blind and dependent on any public statements which might have been made by claimants or their lawyers and on guesswork. The Board was under a duty not to breach claimants' confidentiality,[108] although it was argued that there was no absolute ban on disclosure and that anonymised information could be provided for the purposes of assisting

---

[106] Legal Aid Board, *A New Approach to Funding Civil Cases* (1999) para 7.15.
[107] This was the case in the tobacco litigation: see ch 32 below.
[108] Legal Aid Act 1988, s 38.

decision making. The Board had a discretionary power to inform a person, who brings to the Board's attention information relevant to a certificate, whether or not that certificate had been revoked or discharged.[109] Such a person was entitled as far as practicable to be satisfied that the Regional Director had applied his mind appropriately to the issue. In practice, he would probably be able to disclose little, if anything, because of the confidentiality restrictions. The prudent course, however, would be for the Regional Director to give such reasons as he could, consistent with the duty of confidentiality.[110]

12.70 The Legal Aid Board revealed in 1997 that, in the last eleven months of its 1996–7 year, a total of 14,181 representations had been received. Of the 8,605 which related to merits, or to both merits and means, some 26 per cent led to the application for legal aid being refused or the certificate being amended, discharged (18 per cent), or revoked.[111]

12.71 Whilst the above discussion relates to the issue of public funding, it is accepted that the court's decision on the certification of an MPA, for example, can only be on the basis of involving all relevant parties.[112] That acceptance in turn illustrates the need for an open discussion on issues relevant to funding.

---

[109] Civil Legal Aid (General) Regulations 1989, reg 82(5).
[110] *R v The Legal Aid Board, ex p Owners Abroad (Tour Operator,* Queen's Bench Division (Crown Office List), col 843/96 (Transcript: Smith Bernol), 31 July 1997.
[111] Legal Aid Board, *Annual Report 1996–97* (1997). The figures in the following two years were respectively 14,213 and 13,589 total representations leading to change in 35% and 32% of cases.
[112] Lord Chancellor's Department, *Access to Justice. Multi-Party Situations: Proposed New Procedures. A Consultation Paper* (1997).

Part IV

Multi-Party Rules in Other Jurisdictions

13

CLASS ACTIONS: AN AMERICAN PERSPECTIVE

Laurel J Harbour, Sarah Croft, Thomas Sheehan[1]

A.	Introduction	13.01	D.	Conclusion	13.42
B.	The Theory of Class Actions	13.04	**Appendix**		
C.	Class Actions in Practice	13.14			

A. Introduction

Class actions in the United States federal courts are 'an exception to the usual rule that litigation is conducted by and on behalf of the individual named parties only'.[2] The procedure allows one or more individuals (class representatives) to sue on behalf of themselves and class members who are similarly situated. If the class representatives prevail, the defendant will be liable to each member in the class. Likewise, if the defendant prevails, the judgment binds all the members of the class.[3] **13.01**

While some cases, such as transport disasters, may be well suited for class treatment because of the commonality of the issues and comparatively small numbers of plaintiffs involved, other cases, such as those involving product liability claims, **13.02**

---

[1] Laurel Harbour and Sarah Croft are partners in Shook, Hardy & Bacon MNP, in London. Thomas Sheehan is of Counsel to Shook, Hardy & Bacon LLP, Kansas City, Missouri.

[2] *Califano v Yamasaki*, 442 US 682, 700–701 (1979). The court system in the United States is made up of federal and state courts. In the federal system, trials are conducted in the district courts. Appeals are taken to the twelve circuit courts of appeals, from which the United States Supreme Court hears a very small percentage of cases. The state court systems are generally similar in that they involve a trial court level and usually an intermediate court of appeals and supreme court.

[3] Class actions in United States federal courts are governed by Federal Rule of Civil Procedure 23. The attempted use of class actions under that rule has flourished since the Supreme Court liberalised the requirements in 1966.

present significant problems. In the 1980s, however, plaintiffs sought certification for increasingly large classes involving thousands or even millions of putative class members nationwide, many of whom would not have sued on their own. The putative class members become litigants not by choice, but rather by virtue of being part of a class filed by someone else. These huge class actions have placed unprecedented demands on an already overstretched judiciary.

13.03 Since the early to mid-1990s, the trend has been for the federal courts to refuse to certify so-called 'mass tort' cases,[4] culminating in a decision of the US Supreme Court which held that when plaintiffs' claims turn on facts unique to each class member, certification is not appropriate.[5]

B. The Theory of Class Actions

13.04 In order for a case to proceed as a class action, the trial court must enter an order certifying it as such. To obtain class certification, the plaintiffs must show that the proposed class satisfies all the requirements of Federal Rule of Civil Procedure 23(a) and the requirements of either Rule 23(b)(1), 23(b)(2), or 23(b)(3) (see Appendix to this chapter).[6] Here, the requirements of Rule 23 are explained and in Section C below the practical application of the rule is reviewed and illustrated through various examples.

13.05 Rule 23(a) requires plaintiffs to show, among other things, that the class is so numerous that joinder of all class members is impracticable (the 'numerosity' requirement), that common questions of law or fact exist ('commonality'), that the claims of the class representatives are typical of those of the unnamed class members ('typicality'), and that the class representatives will adequately represent the interests of the class ('adequacy of representation'). The court must also apply Rule 23(b), as to which see further below.

13.06 For the commonality requirement to be fulfilled there has to be one or more issues of law or fact that affect every class member's claim. Commonality is closely linked with predominance of issues (see below). The typicality requirement focuses on the claims of the class representatives and is satisfied when the class

---

[4] According to Professor Coffee, all mass tort litigation shares the following characteristics: '1) a predictable evolutionary cycle during which the value and volume of individual claims starts low and then spirals upward; 2) high case interdependency so that litigated outcomes in any mass tort area quickly impact on the settlement value of other pending cases in that same field; 3) a highly concentrated plaintiffs' bar, in which individual practitioners control exceptionally large inventories of cases, sometimes totaling in the tens of thousands; and 4) a capacity to place logistical pressure on individual courts that is simply unequaled by any other form of civil litigation'. John C. Coffee, Jr, 'Class Wars: The Dilemma of the Mass Tort Class Action' (1995) 95 Colum L Rev 1343, 1358–1359.
[5] *Amchem Prods, Inc v Windsor*, 821 US 591, 117 S Ct 2231 (1997).
[6] Rule 23 also allows certification of defendant classes.

B. The Theory of Class Actions

representatives 'possess the same interest and suffer the same injury as the class members'.[7]

13.07 In determining whether the requirement of 'adequacy of representation' has been met, the courts will examine such factors as whether the class representatives are financially able to pursue the case, whether the interests of the class members are sufficiently aligned with those of the class representatives so that no conflicts of interest will arise, and whether the class representatives' lawyers are qualified to handle the case.[8] Taken together, the elements of Rule 23(a) establish a threshold that, broadly speaking, requires plaintiffs to show that there will be some benefit to proceeding as a class.[9]

13.08 Once plaintiffs establish the Rule 23(a) requirements, the court will next analyse the case under Rule 23(b). This subsection is designed to ensure that the goal of promoting judicial economy is met. Rule 23(b)(3), under which most plaintiffs in mass tort cases seek certification, requires plaintiffs to show that common questions of law or fact predominate over individual issues and that a class action is superior to other methods of adjudication. Rule 23(b)(3) lists several matters that are pertinent to the issue of superiority, including the difficulties likely to be encountered in the management of a class action. These 'predominance' and 'superiority' requirements will not be satisfied where the factual and legal issues differ dramatically from individual to individual or where the case is so large or complex that the court cannot, as a practical matter, try it as a class action (see below).[10]

13.09 Class actions require far more judicial attention than ordinary individual cases.[11]

---

[7] See *Harding v Tambrands, Inc*, 165 FRD 623, 628 (D Kan 1996).
[8] See *Georgine v Amchem Prods, Inc*, 83 F 3d 610, 630 (3d Cir 1996); *aff'd Amchem Prods, Inc v Windsor*, 521 US 591, 117 S Ct 2231 (1997); *Brooks v Southern Bell Tel & Tel Co*, 133 FRD 54, 58–59 (SD Fla 1990).
[9] 'The requirements of Rule 23(a) are meant to assure both that class treatment is necessary and efficient and that it is fair to the absentees under the particular circumstances.' *Barnes v The American Tobacco Corp*, 161 F 3d 127, 140 (3d Cir 1998).
[10] See *Georgine*, 83 F 3d at 626–634; *Brooks*, 133 FRD at 58–59.
[11] A judge presiding over a class action must perform tasks not required in single party cases. The court should generally:

1. Develop a special schedule for resolving Rule 23 issues, including issue of class certification;
2. Hold pre-certification conferences;
3. Narrow the issues, eg through ordering requests for admissions or stipulations of fact;
4. Manage Rule 23-related discovery;
5. Decide, usually after hearing, whether to certify a class, and prepare written findings and conclusions supporting that decision;
6. Decide periodically whether good cause exists to decertify a case as a class action;
7. Determine and adopt a precise class definition;
8. Periodically define and redefine common issues;
9. Determine the content and method of communicating initial notices to class members;
10. Consolidate any pending related cases in the same court, choose one as the class vehicle, and select lead class counsel;

Studies have shown that class actions consume almost five times as much judicial time as traditional cases.[12] Their median life span can be more than three times as long as individual civil cases.[13] The average number of docket entries[14] per class action is often as many as seven times the number for other cases.[15]

13.10 If a Rule 23(b)(3) class action is certified, the court will require the class representatives to provide notice of the existence of the class action to the class members. Providing adequate notice can be quite expensive and the class representatives must bear the cost.[16] Rule 23(c)(2) provides that 'the court shall direct to the members of the class the best notice practicable under the circumstances, including individual notice to all members who can be identified through reasonable effort'. In mass tort cases, unlike employment or business cases, providing notice to class members can be difficult. Businesses regularly keep records of their employees and so giving notice to such class members can be accomplished in most cases. Providing notice in mass tort cases is generally more difficult because there may be no records of, or means of determining, who the potential class members are.[17]

13.11 In an asbestos case, the court of appeals reversed the trial court's order certifying a class consisting generally of all persons and relatives of persons exposed to asbestos manufactured by the defendants.[18] The court reversed in part because giving adequate notice to these individuals would present an insurmountable burden. The court reasoned that many of the putative class members may not even know that they were exposed to asbestos. Even those with knowledge of exposure would

---

11. Order replacement or supplement action of class representatives;
12. Rule on motions to intervene by class members;
13. Create subclasses, if appropriate, after identifying intraclass conflicts;
14. Supervise attorney communications with class members (including certification notices and settlement notices), and supervise record keeping on these matters;
15. Determine how long class members should have to withdraw from the class ('opt out') if they do not wish to participate in the case, decide requests for late opt-outs, maintain inventory, and deal with communications to the court by class members;
16. Approve settlement proposals after notice and usually after hearing;
17. Determine attorney fees, often after notice and hearing; and
18. Supervise distribution of judgments to class members.

Manual for Complex Litigation (Third) §§ 24, 30 (1995).

[12] The Federal Judicial Center, 'An Empirical Study of Class Actions in Four Federal District Courts: Final Report to the Advisory Committee on Civil Rules', 17 Jan 1996, at 9.
[13] ibid.
[14] Interlocutory applications.
[15] The Federal Judicial Center, 'Preliminary Report on Time Study Class Action Cases', 9 Feb 1995, at 19.
[16] *Eisen v Carlisle & Jacquelin*, 417 US 157, 179 (1974).
[17] For the same reasons, it is often difficult to even define the class in mass tort cases. In *Smith v Brown & Williamson Tobacco Corp*, 174 FRD 90 (WD Mo 1997), for example, the court labelled the class definition proposed by plaintiffs 'flawed', because mini-trials would be necessary to determine exactly who was in the class. Ibid at 92 n 2.
[18] *Georgine v Amchem Prods*, 83 F 3d 610, 633 (3rd Cir 1996).

likely pay little attention to the class notice if they had no physical disease. The court reasoned that the problem with the class action procedure and, specifically, the notice requirements was that 'plaintiffs may become bound to the settlement even if they are unaware of the class action or lack sufficient information to evaluate it'.[19] Although the Supreme Court did not decide the issue of notice when it affirmed *Georgine*, the Court did acknowledge the gravity of the question 'whether class action notice sufficient under the Constitution and Rule 23 could ever be given to legions so unselfconscious and amorphous'.[20]

13.12 The notice to the class members will also include an explanation that they can 'opt out' of (exclude themselves from) the class and how to do so, which they will need to do within a specified deadline. Individuals who opt out are free to pursue individual claims against the defendant or defendants. Those who do not opt out within the allotted time remain part of the class and will be bound by the outcome of the case.

13.13 After notice has been given, the class representatives proceed with the case and will eventually present their claims in court, typically to a jury rather than a judge alone. Absent class members generally have no role in the trial; their interests are intended to be protected by the class representatives. The finding on the merits binds all parties, including the unnamed class members. If the case settles before trial and the trial court approves the settlement,[21] the agreement has the force of a judgment on the merits.[22] If the court denies certification, the former class representatives are allowed to proceed if they so desire to separate, individual trials as if they never requested a class.

C. Class Actions in Practice

13.14 Class actions are effective tools in some cases: some employment cases, for example. The Supreme Court has acknowledged that 'suits alleging . . . discrimination

---

[19] ibid. See also *Valentino v Carter-Wallace, Inc*, 97 F 3d 1227, 1234 (9th Cir 1996) (notice problematic where putative class members may not be aware that they are part of class); *Harding*, 165 FRD at 631 (same).
[20] *Amchem Prods, Inc v Windsor*, 521 US 591, 117 S Ct 2231, 2252 (1997).
[21] Pursuant to Rule 23(e), a 'class action shall not be dismissed or compromised without the approval of the court'. Class members may object to the settlement, but approval ultimately lies in the trial court's discretion.
[22] There has been a recent trend in the federal courts toward certification of class actions filed for the sole purpose of obtaining trial court approval of a settlement agreement. In the typical scenario, class counsel and defence counsel agree to a settlement before suit is filed. The attorneys for the class then file suit and both sides jointly move for class certification and approval of the settlement agreement. Until recently, there was disagreement in the courts as to whether these so-called 'settlement classes' were required to satisfy all the applicable requirements of Rule 23. The United States Supreme Court put an end to the conflict in *Amchem Prods, Inc*, 117 S Ct 2231 (1997), where it held that settlement classes must satisfy the Rule 23 prerequisites. See also *Ortiz v Fibreboard*, 119 S Ct 2295 (1999).

are often by their very nature class suits, involving class-wide wrongs. Common questions of law or fact may be present.'[23] For example, a business's refusal to promote women to management positions could be appropriate for class-wide adjudication if the refusal stemmed from a written company policy that applied to all class members and was found to be discriminatory. Again, the liability issues may be common to every member of the class because the company's discriminatory policy would uniformly affect each class member.[24]

13.15 Class actions are also effective in certain types of tort cases. A single catastrophe like a hotel fire may injure many people, but the defendant's liability to each person may be identical; only the amount of damages suffered by each plaintiff will differ. If there is a finding that the defendant's negligence caused the fire, the causation issue is determined for every member of the class. Individual issues of causation do not arise. In this way, a single class action lawsuit can effectively determine whether the defendant is liable to all the injured guests.[25]

13.16 The economies of scale associated with the types of class actions discussed above are not realised when plaintiffs file class actions in personal injury product liability cases. These massive lawsuits present numerous individual cases with different, rather than common, questions of fact. In product liability cases, the fact finder must determine in each individual's case whether and to what extent the defendant's product caused the plaintiff's injuries. In such a case, each plaintiff tells a unique story about the product and warnings at issue, the period of exposure, and the resulting consequences.

13.17 Take a lawsuit in which 100 plaintiffs sue a manufacturer alleging that its product injured them. While each potential class member may have ingested or used the same product and may allege similar injuries, these similarities do not justify trying a case as a class action that would only splinter into individual trials as the case proceeds. Fundamentally, consideration of such issues will not establish causation or any other liability issues in each individual's case.

---

[23] *East Texas Motor Freight v Rodriguez*, 431 US 395, 405 (1977); see also *General Tel Co v Falcon*, 457 US 147, 159 n 15 (1982) ('Significant proof that an employer operated under a general policy of discrimination conceivably could justify a class . . . if the discrimination manifested itself in . . . the same general fashion').

[24] Rule 23(b)(2), which allows class-wide injunctive relief when the defendant 'has acted or refused to act on grounds generally applicable to the class', is commonly used in employment and other civil rights cases. See Advisory Committee's Notes to Subdivision (b)(2); see also *Amchem Prods, Inc*, 117 S Ct at 2245 ('Civil rights cases against parties charged with unlawful, class-based discrimination are prime examples [of Rule 23(b)(2) classes]'); *Selzer v Board of Educ*, 112 FRD 176, 179 (SDNY 1986) (class certified in case challenging defendant's discrimination in employment against women. Evidence showed that class representatives were discriminated against 'in the same general fashion' as the class members).

[25] See *Coburn v 4-R Corp*, 77 FRD 43 (ED Ky 1977) (claims of hotel fire victims susceptible to class-wide treatment).

C. Class Actions in Practice

13.18 Typically, many fact issues will arise that are not common to each class member. These include, for example: how often each plaintiff was exposed to the product; how long each was exposed; whether any plaintiffs had pre-existing medical conditions; and what type of injury each plaintiff allegedly suffered. Other individual issues that will need to be adjudicated in each case include whether some other possible cause produced the alleged injuries, whether the alleged warning would have made any difference in preventing the plaintiff's claimed injury, whether the plaintiff's own negligence contributed to the injuries, and whether the plaintiff knew of and assumed any risks of using the defendant's product. These individual fact issues are not susceptible to class-wide adjudication.

13.19 Mass tort cases alleging product liability causes of action often involve thousands of putative class members, straining the court system in ways not foreseen by the drafters of Rule 23. In fact, the Advisory Committee's Notes to Rule 23 make plain that it was not designed for mass accidents, much less mass product liability cases:

> A 'mass accident' resulting in injuries to numerous persons is ordinarily not appropriate for a class action because of the likelihood that significant questions, not only of damages but of liability and defenses to liability, would be present, affecting the individuals in different ways. In these circumstances, an action conducted nominally as a class action would degenerate in practice into multiple lawsuits separately tried.[26]

13.20 Despite this clear statement of intent, the number and size of proposed mass tort class actions rose steadily from the 1970s to the present.[27]

13.21 One cause of the increase in filings was the proliferation of suits involving asbestos. Courts responded to the perceived crisis in asbestos litigation by certifying large class actions to ease their crowded dockets.[28] Following the bankruptcies of numerous asbestos manufacturers due to asbestos litigation, other, non-asbestos, manufacturers became targets.

13.22 Publicity regarding huge class settlements led to increased filings that, in turn, generated more publicity.[29] This 'bandwagon' effect means that class members

---

[26] See Advisory Committee Notes to 1966 Amendments to Rule 23(b)(3).
[27] See *Amchem Prods, Inc*, 117 S Ct at 2250 ('district courts, since the late 1970s, have been certifying such cases in increasing numbers').
[28] See, eg, ibid at 2237 ('[t]he settlement-class certification we confront evolved in response to an asbestos-litigation crisis'); *Georgine*, 83 F 3d at 618–619 (describing demands placed on courts by asbestos litigation); John C Coffee, above n 4 at 1356 (courts certified asbestos class actions to avoid flooded dockets).
[29] This phenomenon was also described in a class action involving the defoliant 'Agent Orange'. *In re Agent Orange Prod Liab Litig*, 818 F 2d 145, 165 (2d Cir 1987) ('[t]he drum-beating that accompanies a well-publicized class action claiming harm from toxic exposure and the speculative nature of the exposure issue may well attract excessive numbers of plaintiffs with weak to fanciful cases'), *cert denied*, 484 US 1004 (1988).

attracted by publicity possess claims that should not, and probably would not, have been filed individually.[30] As Professor Miller has noted, '[e]nthusiasm for the class action fed upon itself, and the procedure fell victim to overuse by its champions and misuse by some who sought to exploit it for reasons external to the merits of the case'.[31]

13.23 With the possible exception of asbestos cases, courts have become increasingly reluctant to certify mass tort class actions.[32] The courts have learned from their experience with asbestos that mass tort class actions are simply not manageable. Several recent cases make plain that mass tort cases are not appropriate for class-wide treatment.

13.24 In *In re American Medical Systems, Inc*,[33] plaintiffs proposed a nationwide class consisting of between 15,000 and 120,000 men who had been implanted with penile prostheses manufactured by the defendant. After the trial court certified the class, the court of appeals reversed, holding that the class did not satisfy the requirements of Rule 23(a) or 23(b). As to commonality, the court of appeals held that because the defendant had manufactured at least ten models of penile implants, plaintiffs' claims would necessarily vary depending on the particular model used. Moreover, factual differences existed between plaintiffs based on 'a variety of factors, including surgical error, improper use of the device, anatomical incompatibility, infection, device malfunction, or psychological problems'.[34]

13.25 Factual differences among plaintiffs' claims also defeated the typicality requirement of Rule 23(a)(3). The court stated that the claims of the class representatives were not even similar to each other, much less to those of the putative class members.[35] Finally, the court of appeals held that the plaintiffs had failed to establish that the class representatives would adequately represent the interests of the class.

---

[30] For example, at the time of class certification in *In re Rhone-Poulenc Rorer, Inc*, 51 F 3d 1293 (7th Cir), *cert denied*, 116 S Ct 184 (1995), only thirteen cases had been tried involving the product at issue. Ibid at 1300. The class certified by the district court, however, contained thousands of members. In *Smith v Brown & Williamson*, 174 FRD at 98, the court rejected the plaintiff's suggestion that class certification was needed to handle the volume of individual cases that would be filed. The court stated that while the circumstances that might lead to such a 'judicial crisis' have existed for some time, the 'flood of suits' has not arrived.

[31] Arthur A Miller, 'Of Frankenstein Monsters and Shining Knights: Myth, Reality, and the "Class Action Problem"' (1979) 92 Harv L Rev 664, 678.

[32] See, eg, *In re American Med Sys, Inc*, 75 F 3d 1069, 1089 (6th Cir 1996) (citing 'national trend to deny class certification in drug or medical product liability/personal injury cases') (citing numerous cases); Coffee, above n 4 at 1345, n 2 ('federal courts remain largely unreceptive to mass tort class actions that are not presented to them as pre-arranged settlements in the form of "settlement classes." Attempts to certify a mass tort class action over the objections of defendants still regularly fail.').

[33] 75 F 3d 1069 (6th Cir 1996).

[34] ibid at 1081.

[35] ibid at 1082.

C. Class Actions in Practice

The trial court's failure to make an adequate finding on this element was also fatal to the class certification order.[36]

Regarding the Rule 23(b)(3) requirements, the trial court's certification order fared no better. The court of appeals held that mass tort cases are particularly unsuited for class certification and that this case was no exception to that rule.[37] The court acknowledged that mass tort cases arising out of a single accident may be appropriate for class-wide treatment, but held that: **13.26**

> in medical device products liability litigation of the sort involved here the factual and legal issues often *do* differ dramatically from individual to individual because there is no common cause of injuries.[38]

The court further held that: **13.27**

> In this situation, the economies of scale achieved by class treatment are more than offset by the individualization of numerous issues relevant only to a particular plaintiff.[39]

A single lawsuit addressing design and manufacturing issues arising over more than twenty-two years along with the individual problems of thousands of plaintiffs 'would present a nearly insurmountable burden on the district court'.[40] For these and other reasons the court ordered the class decertified. **13.28**

In another case, the Ninth Circuit Court of Appeals reversed an order certifying a mass tort class action.[41] The court held that the class of persons allegedly injured by a drug used to treat epilepsy failed to satisfy the Rule 23 requirements because plaintiffs could not show how the case could be tried as a class action or that class-wide treatment was superior to other methods of adjudication.[42] **13.29**

A similar holding was reached in several other mass tort cases. In *In re Norplant Contraceptive Prods Liab Litig*,[43] for example, the court refused to certify a class of individuals allegedly injured by the defendant's product because class certification was not superior to other methods of adjudication.[44] Similarly, in *Harding v Tambrands, Inc*,[45] plaintiffs moved for certification of a class consisting of all United States residents who suffered toxic shock syndrome as a result of using the defendant's tampons. The court denied class certification because the issue **13.30**

---

[36] ibid at 1083.
[37] ibid at 1084–1085.
[38] ibid at 1084 (emphasis in original).
[39] ibid at 1085.
[40] ibid at 1085.
[41] *Valentino v Carter-Wallace, Inc*, 97 F 3d 1227 (9th Cir 1996).
[42] ibid at 1234–1235.
[43] 168 FRD 577 (ED Tex 1996).
[44] ibid at 578.
[45] 165 FRD 623 (D Ken 1996).

whether the defendant's product caused toxic shock syndrome was individual to each member of the class.[46] In addition, the court held that any advantage gained by class-wide adjudication would be outweighed by case management difficulties.[47]

13.31 In another case, possibly the largest class action ever filed in federal court, plaintiffs sued a number of tobacco companies on behalf of a class of essentially all persons in the United States who were allegedly addicted to nicotine and their estates and close relatives.[48] The trial court certified certain 'core liability' issues for class treatment, but held that other issues, including injury-in-fact, proximate cause, reliance, affirmative defences, and compensatory damages, were individual to each class member and could not be certified for class treatment.[49]

13.32 The Fifth Circuit Court of Appeals reversed the certification order, holding first that plaintiffs had not satisfied the predominance requirement because they failed to show how their 'addiction claims could be tried, individually or on a class basis'.[50] The court also stated that class actions are not superior to other methods of adjudication in mass tort cases. Plaintiffs' claims were large enough to justify individual suits. Moreover, the court was concerned 'that a mass tort cannot be properly certified without a prior track record of trials from which the district court can draw the necessary information to make the predominance and superiority analysis required by Rule 23.'[51] Since the court decertified the class in *Castano*, plaintiffs have filed numerous new class actions each purportedly on behalf of all residents of the state in which the suit was filed. At press time all federal courts that have considered class certification of smoker class actions have refused to certify them.[52]

---

[46] ibid at 630.
[47] ibid at 632.
[48] *Castano v American Tobacco Co*, 84 F 3d 734 (5th Cir 1996).
[49] *Castano v American Tobacco Co*, 160 FRD 544, 559 (ED La 1995).
[50] *Castano v American Tobacco Co*, 84 F 3d at 744.
[51] ibid at 747.
[52] See *Barnes v American Tobacco Co*, 161 F 3d 127, 143 (3rd Cir 1998), *cert denied*, 119 S Ct 1760 (1999); *Arch v American Tobacco Co*, 175 FRD 469, 486 (ED Pa 1997); *Ruiz v American Tobacco Co*, 180 FRD 194 (DPR 1998); *Smith v Brown & Williamson Tobacco Corp*, 174 FRD 90 (WD Mo 1997); *Emig v American Tobacco Co*, 184 F 3d 379 (D Kan 1998); *Insolia v Philip Morris Inc*, 186 FRD 535 (WD Wis 1998); *Hanson v The American Tobacco Co*, Case No LR-C-96-881, 1999 US Dist LEXIS 16277 (ED Ark 21 July, 1999), *Clay v American Tobacco Co*, Case No 97-CV-4167-JPG, 1999 WL 688437 (SD Ill, 9 July 1999); *Chamberlain v The American Tobacco Co*, Case No 196 CV 2005, 1999 WL US Dist LEXIS 5843 (ND Ohio 12 Apr 1999); and *Thompson v Philip Morris*, 189 FRD 544 (D Minn 1999). The court in *Smith v Brown & Williamson Tobacco Corp*, 174 FRD 90 (WD Mo 1997), refused to certify a class of Missouri smokers because the issues of causation, failure to warn, negligence, comparative fault, and damages were peculiar to each individual plaintiff.

C. Class Actions in Practice

In *Barnes v The American Tobacco Co*, 161 F 3d 127 (3d Cir, 1998), the trial court denied the plaintiffs' motion for class certification for many of the same reasons cited by the *Castano* court. The court of appeals affirmed the trial court, holding that common issues did not predominate over individual issues because, among other things, plaintiffs' 'addiction' claims would require individual inquiry into each plaintiff and class member's reasons for smoking cigarettes, amount and duration of smoking, reaction to the cigarettes, and knowledge of the alleged risks of smoking. The *Barnes* court noted that 'no federal appeals court has upheld the certification of a class of cigarette smokers or reversed a District Court's refusal to certify such a class'.[53]

13.33

Courts have closely scrutinised cases where the putative class members purport to have large claims for damages. The aggregation of thousands or even millions of claims can put enormous pressure on defendants to settle, regardless of the merits of individual claims. Take, for example, a case decided by the United States Court of Appeals for the Seventh Circuit.[54] The plaintiffs in *Rhone-Poulenc* were haemophiliacs who allegedly were infected with the AIDS virus when they used the defendants' products. The plaintiffs sued on behalf of thousands of AIDS victims nationwide, challenging the defendants' failure to detect the AIDS virus in blood used for manufacturing clotting factors. At the time the district court certified the class, thirteen similar individual lawsuits had been tried in various courts throughout the country. The defendants had won twelve of them.

13.34

---

[53] 161 F 3d at 143 n 19. In addition, numerous state courts have rejected certification of smoker class actions. See *Brown v American Tobacco Co*, Case No JCCP-4042, slip op (San Diego Sup Ct 10 Apr 2000); *Taylor v The American Tobacco Co Inc*, Case No 97715975 NP, slip op (Cir Ct Wayne Cty Mich 10 Jan 2000). *Small v Lorillard Tobacco Co*, 679 NYS 2d 593 (NY App Div 1998), *aff'd*, 94 NY 2d 43, 698 NYS 2d 615 (NY 1999); *Geiger v The American Tobacco Co*, 696 NYS 2d 345 (NY Sup Ct 1999); *Reed v Philip Morris Inc*, 1997 WL 538921 (Super Ct DC 18 Aug 1997); *Consentino v Philip Morris Inc*, NO MID-L5135-97, slip op (NJ Super Ct Law Div 22 Oct 1998), *recon denied* (NJ Super Ct Law Div 11 Feb 1999). Most recently the Maryland Court of Appeals, on a writ of mandamus, ordered the circuit court to vacate class certification. *Philip Morris, Inc v The Honorable Edward S Angeletti*, Misc No 2, September Term, 1998 slip op (Md 16 May 2000), *vacating, Richardson v Philip Morris, Inc*, No 961450/CE212596 (Baltimore City Cir Ct 28 Jan 1998). One state court has also refused to certify an environmental tobacco smoke class action. See *Avallone v American Tobacco Co*, CA No MID-L-4883-98MT (Sup Ct NJ 13 Apr 1999). Three state courts have certified tobacco class actions. See *RJ Reynolds Tobacco Co v Engle*, 672 So 2d 39 (Fla App 3rd District 1996); *Broin v Philip Morris Cos*, 641 So 2d 888 (Fla Ct App 1994); *rev denied* 654 So 2d 919 (Fla 1995); *Scott v The American Tobacco Co*, No 96-8461 (Orleans Parish, La, 16 Apr 1997). The *Engle* and *Scott* certifications have been criticized by other courts. Eg *Geiger*, slip op at 13 (noting that contrary to *Scott*, 'most jurisdictions are of the view that addiction is a highly individualized issue ... and the Louisiana Court's impression that the tobacco case involved a mass tort arising from a common cause finds no support in other reported cases'); *Philip Morris v The Honorable Judge Angeletti*, slip op at 84 n 35 ('As for the two state cases allowing a tobacco class action to proceed [*Engle* and *Scott*], we find their reasoning unpersuasive for the same reasons that two New York courts [*Small* and *Geiger*] have discredited their authority').

[54] *In re Rhone-Poulenc Rorer, Inc*, 51 F 3d 1293 (7th Cir), *cert denied*, 116 S Ct 184 (1995).

13.35 The trial court certified for class-wide treatment several distinct issues relating to the defendants' liability. The court envisaged that if the defendants were found liable, the class members would be permitted to file individual lawsuits in which the defendants would be precluded from contesting liability. The court of appeals reversed this finding, and ordered the trial court to decertify the class. The court first noted the intense pressure to settle that class actions exert on defendants:

> Suppose that 5,000 of the potential class members are not yet barred by the statute of limitations. And suppose the named plaintiffs . . . win the class portion of this case to the extent of establishing the defendants' liability under either of the two negligence theories. It is true that this would only be prima facie liability, that the defendants would have various defenses. But they could not be confident that the defenses would prevail. They might, therefore, easily be facing $25 billion in potential liability (conceivably more), and with it bankruptcy. They may not wish to roll these dice . . . They will be under intense pressure to settle.[55]

13.36 The *Rhone-Poulenc* court noted that defendants in class actions will feel enormous pressure to settle regardless of whether plaintiffs' claims are strong or weak. Even meritless claims can bankrupt a business, if enough of them are joined. As the court noted, class actions force 'defendants to stake their companies on the outcome of a single jury trial, or to be forced by fear of the risk of bankruptcy to settle even if they have no legal liability'.[56]

13.37 The court also expressed dissatisfaction with the prospect of allowing a single jury to 'hold the fate of an industry in the palm of its hand', when the court system lacked sufficient experience to decide the validity of plaintiffs' claims.[57] The court could not allow the lone jury hearing the class action case potentially to throw the entire industry into bankruptcy when defendants had won twelve of the thirteen individual cases previously taken to judgment. Given the interest of the individual class members in their own lawsuits, the court held that it would not be a waste of judicial resources to require them to try their cases individually.[58]

13.38 Individual trials may be fairer to plaintiffs with large claims. In class actions, the plaintiffs with the strongest claims frequently receive the least relative value for their injuries. In the *Agent Orange* litigation, the court stated:

> If plaintiffs with strong claims remain members of the class, they may see their claims diluted because a settlement attractive to the defendants will in all likelihood occur. Weak plaintiffs, who may exist in very large numbers, stand to gain from even a small settlement.[59]

---

[55] 51 F 3d at 1298.
[56] ibid.
[57] ibid at 1300.
[58] ibid.
[59] *In re Agent Orange*, 818 F 2d at 166.

C. Class Actions in Practice

13.39 These examples make clear that class actions—as opposed to individual lawsuits—are not superior to other methods of litigation in mass tort cases. Litigation is not streamlined and there is no saving of judicial resources when separate mini-trials are required to resolve individual liability. These separate trials frequently take many years to complete, if they ever occur at all.

13.40 The school asbestos cases are a good example of the delays that can result from class certification. In 1986 the United States Court of Appeals for the Third Circuit reluctantly affirmed the trial court's order certifying a class of school districts claiming that their buildings had been contaminated by asbestos.[60] This case was pending for more than ten years. In another asbestos case claiming property damage, the plaintiffs filed suit in 1987 and moved for class certification in 1988. Four years later the district court conditionally certified the class. The Fourth Circuit Court of Appeals affirmed in 1993, some six years after the case was filed, but with some reservations. The court identified a number of potential problems with the class and instructed that '[i]f just some of these issues seem to the district court upon reflection not to lend themselves to class treatment, the district court should decertify the class'.[61]

13.41 Even in cases where some common issues can be decided on a class-wide basis, often resolution of those issues does not materially advance the litigation or justify the additional time and cost caused by class certification. While American courts have allowed the use of mini-trials to determine plaintiffs' damages,[62] they have often refused to certify classes where mini-trials are needed to determine liability.[63] Plaintiffs sometimes propose trial of common issues first, such as so-called 'generic causation' issues, and leave individual issues to be resolved at a later point in the litigation. Federal courts have rejected such plans as inherently unmanageable because individual follow-up trials would still be necessary to address individual issues.[64] Such cases offer no prospect of achieving the judicial economy promised by the class action procedure.[65]

---

[60] *In re School Asbestos Litig*, 789 F 2d 996 (3rd Cir), *cert denied*, 479 US 852 (1986).
[61] *In re Agent Orange*, 818 F 2d at 190, a case involving exposure to a defoliant.
[62] See Advisory Committee Notes to 1996 Amendments to Rule 23(b)(3).
[63] See, eg, *Kurczi v Eli Lilly & Co*, 160 FRD 667, 681 (ND Ohio 1995) (certification denied where separate hearing required for each plaintiff on issues of choice of law, causation, and damages).
[64] 'A finding of "general causation" would do little to advance this litigation. Liability will depend on whether cigarettes are generally capable of causing disease; liability will depend upon whether cigarettes caused a particular plaintiff's disease. The latter inquiry will depend on numerous individual factors rendering the causation factor inappropriate for common disposition.' *Smith v Brown & Williamson Tobacco Corp*, 174 FRD at 96.
[65] If the net effect of certification is not to resolve the claims of any putative class members, but instead 'to bring in thousands of possible claimants whose presence will in actuality require a multitude of mini-trials, . . . then the justification for class certification is absent'. *State of Ala v Blue Bird Body Co*, 573 F 2nd 309, 328 (5th Cir 1978).

D. Conclusion

13.42 Class actions in America are facing issues unforeseen by the drafters of Rule 23. Designed as a vehicle for resolving fundamentally similar claims, the class action is viewed by some as a panacea for all claims involving numerous plaintiffs. Experience has shown that while the purposes of class actions can be served in some cases, in other types the use of the class action is counter-productive. In practice, mass tort cases, particularly mass product liability cases, have proven unsuitable for class-wide treatment. These cases have numerous factual issues that make a single trial impossible. They frequently attract plaintiffs with weak claims who would not have sued on their own, and result in forced settlements that overvalue some claims to the detriment of others. The economies of scale at the heart of any class action are simply not achieved when thousands of plaintiffs unite to pursue their divergent claims in a single lawsuit.

APPENDIX

2000 Edition
[extract]
Federal Civil Judicial Procedure and Rules

[as amended to January 28, 2000]

Rules of Civil Procedure
Rules of Judicial Panel on Multidistrict Litigation
Rules—Habeas Corpus Cases
Rules—Motion Attacking Sentence
Rules of Evidence
Rules of Appellate Procedure
Rules of the Supreme Court

Includes laws through the close of the 106th Congress, First Session (1999)

Title 28, Judiciary and Judicial Procedure
Act June 25, 1948, c 646, §§ 2 to 39
Appendix:
   Judicial Personnel Financial Disclosure
      Requirements [Repealed]
   Development of Mechanisms for Resolving Minor
      Disputes [Codified]
Constitution of the United States
Title 5, Government Organization and Employees
   App 4—Financial Disclosure Requirements of Federal
      Personnel
Consolidated Index
. . .

RULE 23. CLASS ACTIONS

(a) Prerequisites to a Class Action

One or more members of a class may sue or be sued as representative parties on behalf of all only if (1) the class is so numerous that joinder of all members is impracticable, (2) there are questions of law or fact common to the class, (3) the claims or defenses of the representative parties are typical of the claims or defenses of the class, and (4) the representative parties will fairly and adequately protect the interests of the class.

(b) Class Actions Maintainable

An action may be maintained as a class action if the prerequisites of subdivision (a) are satisfied, and in addition:

(1) the prosecution of separate actions by or against individual members of the class would create a risk of

    (A) inconsistent or varying adjudications with respect to individual members of the class which would establish incompatible standards of conduct for the party opposing the class, or

    (B) adjudications with respect to individual members of the class which would as a practical matter be dispositive of the interests of the other members not parties to the adjudications or substantially impair or impede their ability to protect their interests; or

(2) the party opposing the class has acted or refused to act on grounds generally applicable to the class, thereby making appropriate final injunctive relief or corresponding declaratory relief with respect to the class as a whole; or

(3) the court finds that the questions of law or fact common to the members of the class predominate over any questions affecting only individual members, and that a class action is superior to other available methods for the fair and efficient adjudication of the controversy. The matters pertinent to the findings include: (A) the interest of members of the class in individually controlling the prosecution or defense of separate actions; (B) the extent and nature of any litigation concerning the controversy already commenced by or against members of the class; (C) the desirability or undesirability of concentrating the litigation of the claims in the particular forum; (D) the difficulties likely to be encountered in the management of a class action.

(c) Determination by Order Whether Class Action to be Maintained; Notice; Judgment; Actions Conducted Partially as Class Actions

(1) As soon as practicable after the commencement of an action brought as a class action, the court shall determine by order whether it is to be so maintained. An order under this subdivision may be conditional, and may be altered or amended before the decision on the merits.

(2) In any class action maintained under subdivision (b)(3), the court shall direct to the members of the class the best notice practicable under the circumstances, including individual notice to all members who can be identified through reasonable effort. The notice shall advise each member that (A) the court will exclude the member from the class if the member so requests by a specified date; (B) the judgment, whether favorable or not, will include all members who do not request exclusion; and (C) any member who does not request exclusion may, if the member desires, enter an appearance through counsel.

(3) The judgment in an action maintained as a class action under subdivision (b)(1) or (b)(2), whether or not favorable to the class, shall include and describe those whom the court finds to be members of the class. The judgment in an action maintained as a class action under subdivision (b)(3), whether or not favorable to the class, shall include and specify or describe those to whom the notice provided in subdivision (c)(2) was directed, and who have not requested exclusion, and whom the court finds to be members of the class.

(4) When appropriate (A) an action may be brought or maintained as a class action with respect to particular issues, or (B) a class may be divided into subclasses and each subclass treated as a class, and the provisions of this rule shall then be construed and applied accordingly.

(d) Orders in Conduct of Actions

In the conduct of actions to which this rule applies, the court may make appropriate orders: (1) determining the course of proceedings or prescribing measures to prevent undue repetition or complication in the presentation of evidence or argument; (2) requiring, for the protection of the members of the class or otherwise for the fair conduct of the action, that notice be given in such manner as the court may direct to some or all of the members of any step in the action, or of the proposed extent of the judgment, or of the opportunity of members to signify whether they consider the representation fair and adequate, to intervene and present claims or defenses, or otherwise to come into the action; (3) imposing conditions on the representative parties or on intervenors; (4) requiring that the pleadings be amended to eliminate therefrom allegations as to representation of absent persons, and that the action proceed accordingly; (5) dealing with similar procedural matters. The orders may be combined with an order under Rule 16, and may be altered or amended as may be desirable from time to time.

(e) Dismissal or Compromise

A class action shall not be dismissed or compromised without the approval of the court and notice of the proposed dismissal or compromise shall be given to all members of the class in such manner as the court directs.

(f) Appeals

A court of appeals may in its discretion permit an appeal from an order of a district court granting or denying class action certification under this rule if application is made to it within ten days after entry of the order. An appeal does not stay proceedings in the district court unless the district judge or the court of appeals so orders.

(As amended Feb 28, 1966, eff July 1, 1966; Mar 2, 1987, eff Aug 1, 1987; Apr 24, 1998, eff Dec 1, 1998.)

14

CLASS ACTIONS IN THE COMMON LAW PROVINCES OF CANADA

JA Prestage, S Gordon McKee[1]

A.	Introduction	14.01	F.	Resolution of Individual Issues and Damages	14.35
B.	Certification of a Class Action	14.05	G.	Fees and Funding	14.37
	Cause of action	14.08	H.	Limitation Periods	14.46
	Size and identification of class	14.09	I.	Conclusion	14.47
	Common issues	14.13			
	Preferable procedure	14.18		Appendix 1	
	Class representative	14.27		Appendix 2	
	Examples	14.29		Appendix 3	
C.	Notice to Class Members	14.30			
D.	Judicial Control	14.31			
E.	Representation of Class Members	14.34			

A. Introduction

Of the nine common law provinces in Canada, only Ontario and British Columbia have legislation permitting class proceedings.[2] In Ontario, the Class Proceedings Act 1992[3] came into force on 1 January 1993. It followed by a decade

14.01

---

[1] Partners, Blake, Cassels & Graydon, Toronto.
[2] Virtually all of the provinces have had for many years rules permitting 'representative actions' in a narrow set of circumstances such as a dispute by a group over a common fund. These rules, however, have been held to be insufficient to support a general right to group actions where there are merely common issues in the claims of the group members: *Naiken v General Motors of Canada Ltd* [1983] SCR 72. In addition to Ontario and British Columbia, Quebec also has class proceedings legislation (Quebec Civil Code, Book IX). Quebec was the first jurisdiction in Canada to adopt class proceedings legislation, having done so in 1978. The Quebec statute is also broadly based on Federal Rule 23 from the United States of America. Quebec is a civil law rather than a common law jurisdiction and it is outside the scope of this chapter.
[3] Class Proceedings Act 1992, SO 1992, c 6 ('Ontario CPA').

a 1982 report of the Ontario Law Reform Commission recommending such legislation.[4] In British Columbia, the Class Proceedings Act 1995[5] was adopted in August 1995. The two enactments are similar in many respects, but not identical. Both are modelled in a general way on Federal Rule 23 from the United States of America.

14.02 As in other jurisdictions, the purpose of the class proceedings legislation in Ontario and British Columbia is to permit one or more parties to advance or defend claims on behalf of a group of similarly situated parties in such a way that the members of the group are bound by the result of the proceeding.

14.03 In order to proceed with a class action in either Ontario or British Columbia, certification by the court is required. If certification is granted, the statutes require that notice be given to class members and that class members be given an opportunity to opt out of the proceeding. Members of the class who do not opt out within the prescribed period of time will be bound by the disposition of the common issues in the class proceeding. Those common issues in appropriate cases may be defined so as to fully dispose of all claims by or against the members of the class; in other cases the common issues may be defined so as to finally resolve only one or some of the issues in the proceedings and leave the other issues to be resolved in subsequent proceedings involving individual class members. The legislation in both provinces not only prescribes procedures and requirements for certification, but also contains an array of other provisions relating to the conduct, settlement, and funding of class proceedings.

14.04 In both Ontario and British Columbia, there is a growing body of jurisprudence at lower court levels interpreting the statutes, particularly as they relate to the criteria for certification. The jurisprudence continues, however, to develop. As of mid-1999, only two Ontario class proceedings have proceeded through trial.[6] The issue of certification has been considered on only one occasion by the Ontario Court of Appeal[7] and on only three occasions by the British Columbia Court of Appeal.[8] The Supreme Court of Canada has yet to address any issue under either statute.

---

[4] Ontario Law Reform Commission, Report on Class Actions (1982).
[5] Class Proceedings Act 1995, SBC 1995, c 21 ('BC CPA').
[6] *Windisman v Toronto College Park Ltd* (1996), 28 OR (3d) 29 (Gen Div); *Peppiatt v Nicol* [1998] OJ No 3370 (Gen Div).
[7] *Anderson v Wilson* [1999] 175 DLR (4th) 409 (Ont CA).
[8] *Tiemstra v Insurance Corp of BC* [1997], 149 DLR (4th) 419 (BCCA); *Chace v Crane CanadaInc* [1997], 44 BCLR (3d) 264 (BCCA); *Campbell v Flexwatt Corp* (1997), 44 BCLR (3d) 343 (BCCA).

B. Certification of a Class Action

14.05 Both the Ontario and British Columbia statutes provide for certification of both plaintiff and defendant class actions. To date, the experience in both jurisdictions has been almost exclusively in relation to actions on behalf of plaintiff classes.[9]

14.06 The motion to certify is the key event in any proposed class proceeding. Only if the court grants a certification order can the matter continue as a class proceeding.

14.07 Although not framed in identical terms, both the Ontario and British Columbia statutes provide for a similar five-part test for certification of class proceedings.[10] Both statutes make certification of a proceeding mandatory if:

(1) the pleadings disclose a cause of action;
(2) there is an identifiable class of two or more persons;
(3) the claim or defence of the class members raises common issues;
(4) a class proceeding would be the preferable procedure for resolution of the common issues; and
(5) there is a representative who would fairly and adequately represent the interests of the class, has provided a plan for the proceeding that sets out a workable method of advancing the proceeding on behalf of the class and notifying other members of the proceeding, and does not have, on the common issues, an interest in conflict with the other class members.

On a certification motion, each of these criteria will be considered by the court.

Cause of action

14.08 The requirement that the pleadings disclose a cause of action has been held to create a very low threshold. The issue is determined on the assumption that the facts pleaded are true. The test applied is whether it is 'plain and obvious' on the face of the pleading that no claim exists.[11] Very few, if any, serious class actions will fail on this element of the certification test. Rather than placing significant reliance on this element, defendants in Canada wanting to attack the merits of the claim have tended to bring motions for summary judgment either before or after the certification motion.

---

[9] *Chippewas of Sarnia Band v Canada* [1996], 137 DLR (4th) 239, supplementary reasons 138 DLR (4th) 574 (Gen Div) is an example of a defendant class action. In that case, a native land claim was certified against a class of defendants consisting of others with potential claims to the property in question. *Cooper Industries (Canada) Inc v Babin* (Ontario Court File No B173/95) and *Cooper Industries (Canada) Inc v Adam* (Court File No B172/95) were cases in which a class of defendants consisting of pension plan members was certified on consent in a proceeding initiated by an employer relating to entitlement to surplus in terminated pension plans.

[10] Ontario CPA, s 5; BC CPA, s 4.

[11] *Anderson v Wilson*, n 7 above.

Size and identification of class

14.09 Both of the Ontario and British Columbia statutes require as a condition of certification that there be an identifiable class but both statutes provide that a class may consist of as few as two persons.[12] While a two-person class would be unlikely to satisfy the further requirement that the class proceeding be the preferable procedure for resolving the common issues, it is clear that the absence of a large number of potential class members is not in and of itself a bar to certification.

14.10 The requirement that there be an 'identifiable' class does not incorporate a requirement that the number of class members or their identity be ascertainable.[13] It appears simply to require that it be possible to define the class in a way which allows an objective determination of whether a particular person falls inside or outside the class.[14]

14.11 Because of Canada's federal nature, class actions raise some constitutional and jurisdictional issues in Canada. The administration of justice is a matter within the jurisdiction of the provincial legislatures. Class proceeding legislation in Canada has been enacted by provincial legislatures. The ability of the courts, acting under authority granted to them by a provincial statute, to certify class actions affecting people outside the provincial boundaries has been raised in a number of certification motions. The British Columbia statute addresses this issue by providing that non-residents of British Columbia are bound by class actions certified in British Columbia only if they opt into the proceeding.[15] The Ontario statute does not specifically address participation by non-residents in the class. On a number of occasions the Ontario courts have been prepared to certify classes which have been extra-provincial in scope.[16] No appellate court has considered the extent to which Ontario courts have jurisdiction to certify classes with non-resident members. Further, it remains to be seen whether non-residents of Ontario will in fact be foreclosed from further proceedings by the disposition of a class action certified in Ontario.

14.12 In *Robertson v The Thomson Corporation*[17] the Ontario court defined a class sufficiently broadly so as to potentially include some non-Canadian residents. Since the court concluded that virtually all of the members of the proposed class were subject to Ontario's jurisdiction, it was prepared to certify the class despite the

---

[12] Ontario CPA, s 5(1)b; BC CPA, s 4(1)b.
[13] Ontario CPA, s 6.4; BC CPA, s 7(d).
[14] *Bywater v Toronto Transit Commission* [1998] OJ No 4913 (Gen Div).
[15] BC CPA, ss 2(1) and 16.
[16] *Nantais v Telectronics Propriety Ltd* (1995), 25 OR (3d) 331 (Gen Div) leave to appeal denied 129 DLR (4th) 110 (Gen Div); *Carom v Bre-X Minerals Ltd* (1999), 43 OR (3d) 441 (Gen Div); *Webb v K-Mart Canada Ltd* [1999] OJ No 2268 (OSCJ).
[17] *Robertson v The Thomson Corporation* (1999), 43 OR (3d) 161 (Gen Div).

B. Certification of a Class Action

possibility of an atypical foreign class member. The court recognised that the question of whether or not the foreigner would be bound by the result of the Ontario class proceeding if he or she initiated proceedings elsewhere would be a matter for the foreign court hearing such proceeding to decide.

Common issues

14.13 The requirement that the proposed class action raise common issues has proved to be the focal point of many certification motions.

14.14 Common issues are defined in both statutes[18] as:

(1) common but not necessarily identical issues of fact; or
(2) common but not necessarily identical issues of law that arise from common but not necessarily identical facts.

14.15 It is now well established in both Ontario and British Columbia that the common issues need not be the predominant issues in the litigation or even be issues which would establish liability. It is sufficient that the common issues be ones which, when resolved, will move the litigation forward.[19]

14.16 In some cases, the common issues have been defined broadly as 'liability and punitive damages'.[20] In other circumstances, the issues have been defined more narrowly with a recognition that resolution of the common issues would not in fact determine liability. In *Anderson v Wilson*, the claim pertained in part to dental patients who had contracted hepatitis. The court recognised that issues related to causation and damages were individual to each member of the class but determined that the issues of the appropriate standard of care and whether or not the defendant clinic had fallen below that standard of care were nevertheless common issues which would move the litigation forward. With respect to this portion of the claim, the court defined the common issues solely with relation to the standard of care even though, if successful on those common issues, the individual members of the class would have to pursue the issues of causation and damages in individual proceedings.[21]

14.17 The statutes in Ontario and British Columbia require that the certification order emanating from a successful certification motion set out the common issues. In

---

[18] Ontario CPA, s 1; BC CPA, s 1.
[19] *Anderson v Wilson*, n 7 above; *Campbell v Flexwatt Corp*, n 8 above.
[20] *Anderson v Wilson*, n 7 above with respect to one of the subclasses.
[21] See also *Harrington v Dow Corning* [1996], 22 BCLR (3d) 97 (BCSC), a case relating to breast implants, in which the common issue was defined as whether or not silicone gel implants were fit for their purposes, leaving for resolution in individual proceedings other issues relating to negligence of individual suppliers, causation, and damages.

Allen v CIBC Trust Corp[22] the court held that persons who had been class members in an earlier class proceeding could advance alternative theories of liability in subsequent litigation where the common issues in the class action that had been dismissed only asserted one theory of liability. Because the disposition of the class action only binds members of the class to the extent that the judgment determines the common issues identified in the certification order, the definition of the common issues is crucial to both the plaintiff and the defendant.

Preferable procedure

14.18   A class proceeding does not have to be the preferable procedure for resolving the whole controversy between the parties but merely for resolving the common issues.

14.19   Although it is well established that, in contrast to the US Federal Class Action Rule, the common issues do not have to predominate over the individual issues, in *Carom v Bre-X Minerals*[23] the fact that the individual issues overwhelmed the alleged common issues, such that complex individual trials were going to be required in any event, was a factor considered by the court in determining that a class proceeding was not the preferable procedure for addressing some of the claims advanced.

14.20   In its 1982 report, the Law Reform Commission of Ontario identified the three goals of class proceedings as being:

(1) promoting judicial economy and the efficient handling of potentially complex cases of mass wrong;
(2) improving access to justice for those whose actions might not otherwise be asserted because the cost of proceeding with an action on an individual basis would be disproportionate to the amount of each claim;
(3) modifying the behaviour of actual or potential wrongdoers who might otherwise be tempted to ignore public obligations.

14.21   In determining whether a class proceeding is the preferable procedure for resolution of the common issues, Canadian courts have turned to these purposes and have sought to weigh the extent to which these purposes would be advanced if certification were granted.[24] A class proceeding is the preferable procedure where it presents a fair, efficient, and manageable method of determining the common issues which arise from the claims of multiple plaintiffs and where such determination will advance the proceeding in accordance with the goals of judicial economy, access to justice, and the modification of the behaviour of wrongdoers.[25]

---

[22] (1998), 39 OR (3d) 675 (Gen Div).
[23] *Carom v Bre-X Minerals* (1999), 44 OR (3d) 173 (Gen Div).
[24] *Abdool v Anaheim Management Ltd* (1995) 21 OR (3d) 453 (Div Ct).
[25] *Carom v Bre-X Minerals*, n 23 above.

B. Certification of a Class Action

In considering whether a class proceeding is the preferable procedure, the courts will have regard to other alternatives available to resolve the common issues.[26] 14.22

Unlike the Ontario statute, which is silent on this point, the British Columbia statute lists specific factors to be considered by the court in assessing the preferable procedure. It provides in section 4(2): 14.23

> In determining whether a class proceeding would be the preferable procedure for the fair and efficient resolution of the common issues, the court must consider all relevant matters including
>
> (a) whether questions of fact or law common to the members of the class predominate over any questions affecting only individual members,
> (b) whether a significant number of the members of the class have a valid interest in individually controlling the prosecution of separate actions,
> (c) whether the class proceeding would involve claims that are or have been the subject of any other proceedings,
> (d) whether other means of resolving the claims are less practical or less efficient, and
> (e) whether the administration of the class proceeding would create greater difficulties than those likely to be experienced if relief were sought by other means.

The Ontario courts have given weight to these types of considerations and any other consideration relevant to whether the class action proposed is likely to advance the three goals of the legislation. 14.24

Both the Ontario and British Columbia statutes specifically identify factors which will *not*, at least individually, constitute bars to certification.[27] The statutes provide that the courts must *not* refuse to certify a proceeding on the grounds that: 14.25

(1) the relief claimed includes a claim for damages that would require individual assessment after determination of the common issues;
(2) the relief claimed relates to separate contracts involving different class members;
(3) different remedies are sought for different class members;
(4) the number of class members or the identity of each class member is not known;
(5) the class includes a subclass whose members have claims or defences that raise common issues not shared by all class members.

The language in the Ontario and British Columbia statutes is somewhat different. In British Columbia the court cannot refuse to certify the class proceeding by reason of one *or more* of the above five grounds. In Ontario, the language of the statute is less clear but the prevailing view is that the presence of more than one of the enumerated factors may be considered in determining whether a class 14.26

---

[26] ibid; *SR Gent (Canada) Inc Ontario* [1999] OJ No 3362 (OSCJ).
[27] Ontario CPA, s 6; BC CPA, s 7.

proceeding is the preferable procedure, although their presence is by no means determinative of the issue.[28] In *Bywater v Toronto Transit Commission*, for example, the action was certified despite the presence of four of the five enumerated factors.[29]

Class representative

14.27 The last requirement for certification relates to the adequacy of the proposed class representative. The courts have held that a representative plaintiff need not be typical so long as he or she has no conflict of interest and has demonstrated that he or she will fairly and adequately advance the class claims.[30]

14.28 Both the Ontario and British Columbia Acts[31] provide that where a class includes a subclass whose members have claims that raise common issues not shared by all of the class members, a subclass may be certified, if that is necessary to protect the interests of the subclass. Where a subclass is certified, a separate representative will be appointed and separate counsel may be retained. Subclasses may be created at the time of the original certification motion, or may be created later in the proceedings when differences among the class members manifest themselves.[32]

Examples

14.29 The Courts in Ontario and British Columbia have certified class actions involving product liability claims (medical devices,[33] blood products,[34] and toilets[35]), transportation (a Toronto subway collision[36]), financial services (claims related to syndicated mortgages and other investments[37]), employment claims (for statutory benefits,[38] pension surplus,[39] and wrongful dismissal[40]), and breach of copyright[41] among others. Many applications for certification have been contested, although some have been certified on consent, particularly for the purpose of

---

[28] *Bywater v Toronto Transit Commission*, n 14 above; *Robertson v The Thomson Corporation*, n 17 above.
[29] ibid.
[30] *Abdool v Anaheim Management Ltd*, n 24 above.
[31] Ontario CPA, s 5(2); BC CPA, s 6.
[32] *Peppiatt v Royal Bank of Canada* (1996), 27 OR (3d) 462 (Gen Div).
[33] *Nantais v Telectronics Propriety Ltd*, n 16 above; *Harrington v Dow Corning*, n 21 above; *Bendall v McGhan Medical Corp* (1993), 14 OR (3d) 744 (Gen Div).
[34] *Endean v Canadian Red Cross Society* [1997], 147 DLR (4th) 158 (BCSC).
[35] *Chace v Crane Canada*, n 8 above.
[36] *Bywater v Toronto Transit Commission*, n 14 above.
[37] *Maxwell v MLG Ventures Ltd* [1995] OJ No 1136 (Gen Div); *Nash v CIBC Trust Corp* [1996] OJ No 1460 (Gen Div); *Peppiatt v Royal Bank of Canada* (1993), 16 OR (3d) 133 (Gen Div); *Carom v Bre-X Minerals*, n 23 above.
[38] *Wicke v Canadian Occidental Petroleum* (1998), 40 OR (3rd) 731 (Gen Div).
[39] *Cooper Industries (Canada) Inc v Adam*, n 9 above.
[40] *Webb v K–Mart Canada Ltd*, n 16 above.
[41] *Robertson v The Thomson Corporation*, n 17 above.

settling the class action. Although there have been some exceptions,[42] Ontario courts have generally shown reluctance to certify cases involving allegations of misrepresentation on the basis that resolution of the common issues, if there were any, would not meaningfully advance the case given the number of individual issues related to liability (such as reliance and causation) which would remain.[43]

C. Notice to Class Members

Where an action is certified, the statutes in both Ontario and British Columbia require that, unless dispensed with by the court, notice of certification must be given to members of the class. The general content of the notice is prescribed by the statutes and the form of the notice must be approved by the court. In the process of obtaining approval of the notice to class members, the defendants will have an opportunity to make submissions to the court regarding its contents. The court has discretion to determine the manner in which notice is to be given and who is to bear the costs of the notice. The Ontario courts will preserve the integrity of the notice procedure by penalising those who give notices to potential class members without court approval, although limited publication of information on the status of the proceeding is permissible.[44]

14.30

D. Judicial Control

If the class action is certified, one judge will be appointed to hear all interlocutory motions in the action.[45] In Ontario, a judge who hears interlocutory motions in the proceeding shall not, unless the parties agree otherwise, preside at the trial. In British Columbia, however, a judge who hears interlocutory applications may, but need not, preside at the trial. Under both statutes, the court is given a broad discretion to make any order it considers appropriate respecting the conduct of a class proceeding to ensure its fair and expeditious determination and, for that purpose, may impose such terms on the parties as the court considers appropriate.[46]

14.31

Once a proceeding has been certified, it cannot be settled or discontinued without approval of the court.[47] The courts have recognised that since a settlement will

14.32

---

[42] *Maxwell v MLG Ventures Ltd*, n 37 above; *Peppiatt v Nicol*, n 26 above.
[43] *Abdool v Anaheim Management Ltd*, n 24 above; *Carom v Bre-X Minerals*, n 23 above; *Monhteros v Devry Canada Inc* (1998), 41 OR (3d) 63 (Gen Div).
[44] *Mangan v Inco Ltd* (1998), 38 OR (3d) 703 (Gen Div); *Bywater v Toronto Transit Commission* (1999), 43 OR (3d) 367 (Gen Div).
[45] Ontario CPA, s 34; BC CPA, s 14.
[46] Ontario CPA, s 12; BC CPA, s 12.
[47] Ontario CPA, s 29; BC CPA, s 35.

bind all members of the class, the court must be satisfied that it is fair and reasonable and in the best interests of the class. In *Dabbs v Sun Life Assurance Co of Canada*,[48] the Ontario court enumerated the criteria to be considered in assessing the reasonableness of a settlement as follows:

(1) likelihood of recovery or likelihood of success;
(2) amount and nature of discovery evidence;
(3) the settlement terms and conditions;
(4) recommendation and experience of counsel;
(5) future expense and likely duration of litigation;
(6) recommendations of neutral parties (if any);
(7) the number of objectors and nature of the objections;
(8) the presence of arm's length bargaining and absence of collusion.

14.33 The court in the *Dabbs* case indicated that class action settlements must be seriously scrutinised by the court to ensure that they do not sell short the rights of unrepresented parties, but recognised that settlements are the product of compromise and that the test is one of fairness and not perfection. The court must, however, be satisfied that the settlement delivers adequate relief for the class in exchange for the surrender of litigation rights against the defendants.[49] The courts have to date approved almost all settlements for which approval has been sought, although they have on occasion imposed conditions[50] or indicated that the settlement is approved if modified in an identified manner.[51]

E. Representation of Class Members

14.34 Under both statutes the court may at any time permit one or more class members to participate in a class proceeding in order to ensure the fair and adequate representation of the interests of the class or any subclass or for any other appropriate reason. The court has a broad discretion with respect to the terms under which such participation will be permitted, including terms as to costs.[52]

F. Resolution of Individual Issues and Damages

14.35 Once a proceeding has been certified as a class action, both the Ontario and

---

[48] (1998), 40 OR (3d) 429 (Gen Div). The *Dabbs* case has been cited with approval in British Columbia: *Haney Iron Works v Manufacturers Life Ins Co* [1998], 169 DLR (4th) 565 (BCSC).
[49] *Ontario New Home Warranty Program v Chevron Chemical Co* [1999] OJ No 2245 (Gen Div).
[50] ibid.
[51] *Parsons v Canadian Red Cross Society* [1999] OJ No 3572 (OSCJ).
[52] Ontario CPA, s 14; BC CPA, s 15.

British Columbia statutes prescribe that it will generally proceed first to determination of the common issues of the class, followed by determination of the common issues for a subclass, followed by determination of any individual issues that require participation of individual class members.[53] Both statutes clearly contemplate that, following resolution of the common issues, further proceedings involving individual class members may be necessary to determine liability and/or quantify damages. The statutes confer considerable jurisdiction on the court to choose an expeditious and cost-effective method for determining such individual issues.

Both the British Columbia and Ontario statutes contemplate that if liability is established through resolution of the common issues, the court may in appropriate circumstances make an aggregate award of damages in favour of class members rather than requiring individual assessments of damages. Where it would be impractical or inefficient to identify class members or to determine the exact share that should be allocated to each of them, the court is permitted to allocate the award on an average or proportional basis. The court is given wide discretion to direct the means of distribution of amounts awarded.[54] **14.36**

G. Fees and Funding

Both the Ontario and British Columbia statutes specifically address the issues of costs in and financing of class proceedings. **14.37**

In most civil proceedings in Ontario, unlike proceedings in British Columbia, contingency fees are not permitted.[55] When Ontario adopted class proceedings legislation, it specifically excepted class proceedings from this general prohibition. Section 33 of the Ontario statute permits an agreement between a solicitor and a representative party providing for payment of fees only in the event of success in the class proceeding. The Ontario statute contemplates that such an agreement may provide for the solicitor to make a motion to the court to have his or her base fees increased by a multiplier, and provides that the court, on motion, may determine the amount of the solicitor's base fee and the appropriate multiplier to be applied to provide 'fair and reasonable compensation to the solicitor for the risk incurred in undertaking and continuing the proceeding under an agreement for payment only in the event of success'. In *Gagne v Silcorp Ltd*,[56] the Ontario Court of Appeal considered the factors relevant to determining the appropriate **14.38**

---

[53] Ontario CPA, ss 11, 25; BC CPA, ss 11, 27.
[54] Ontario CPA, ss 24, 26; BC CPA, ss 29, 31, 33.
[55] An Act Respecting Champerty, RSO 1897 c 327; Solicitor's Act, RSO 1990, c S-15, s 28; Law Society of Upper Canada, *Rules of Professional Conduct*, Commentary 10.
[56] (1998), 41 OR 3d (417) (CA).

multiplier. The court held that both the degree of risk assumed by the lawyers and the degree of success achieved were relevant considerations. In that case, the court applied a multiplier of 2 to a base fee consisting of the hours worked by the solicitors at their usual hourly rates. In this decision, the Ontario Court of Appeal indicated that the maximum multiplier in the 'most deserving case' would be 3 or 4.

14.39 Although the Ontario statute, on its face, contemplates only multiplier-type arrangements, the lower courts of Ontario have given the statute a liberal interpretation and have approved, both before and after completion of the proceeding, other types of contingency arrangements, including fees based on a percentage of the amount recovered[57] and a fixed amount per member of the class.[58]

14.40 Even where a fee arrangement between the representative party and the solicitor is not contingent upon success in the proceedings, the agreement is enforceable only if approved by the court.

14.41 The adoption of the Class Proceedings Act 1992 in Ontario was accompanied by the establishment of a Class Proceedings Fund and a Class Proceedings Committee. Under the applicable provisions of the Law Society Act,[59] a plaintiff in a class proceeding may apply to the Committee for funds from the Class Proceedings Fund in respect of disbursements related to the proceeding. In deciding whether or not to provide such funding, the Committee is directed to have regard to:

(1) the merits of the plaintiff's case;
(2) whether the plaintiff made reasonable efforts to raise funds from other sources;
(3) whether the plaintiff has made a clear and reasonable proposal for use of the funds; and
(4) whether the plaintiff has appropriate financial controls to ensure that the funds are spent for the purpose of the grant.

14.42 In Ontario an unsuccessful representative plaintiff (but not members of the class) may be subject to an award of costs in favour of a successful defendant.[60] The provisions in the Law Society Act relating to the Class Proceedings Fund, however, provide that where a plaintiff has sought and received funding from the Fund, a successful defendant cannot enforce any award of costs in its favour from the representative plaintiff but rather has a claim for such costs against the Fund.

---

[57] *Crown Bay Hotel Ltd Partnership v Zurich Indemnity Insurance Company of Canada* (1998), 40 OR (3d) 83 (Gen Div). In this case, fees of 20% of the settlement amount were approved.
[58] *Nantais v Telectronics Proprietary (Canada) Ltd* (1996), 28 OR (3d) 523 (Gen Div).
[59] RSO 1990, c L-8 s 59.1.
[60] Ontario CPA, s 31. The court is given discretion to consider the special nature of class actions in determining cost awards. The court may consider whether the action was a test case raising a novel point of law or involves a matter of public interest.

An Ontario plaintiff who seeks and receives support from the Fund, if successful in the proceeding, is required to pay 10 per cent of any damage award to the Fund.[61]

14.43

Although a creative attempt to facilitate financing class actions, there has, as yet, been limited resort to the Class Proceedings Fund. Many plaintiffs and their counsel have tended to resort to other methods of financing proceedings rather than resorting to the Fund.

14.44

The British Columbia cost regime is different. British Columbia has no equivalent to the Class Proceedings Fund and, barring frivolous, vexatious, or abusive conduct, or other exceptional circumstances, no costs will be awarded to either party in a British Columbia class proceeding.[62] Contingency fees were permissible in British Columbia before class proceedings legislation was adopted in that province and the British Columbia statute has no special rules in that regard. Like its Ontario counterpart, the British Columbia statute provides that an agreement between a representative plaintiff and a solicitor respecting fees is enforceable only if approved by the court.

14.45

H. Limitation Periods

Limitation periods applicable to a cause of action asserted in a class proceeding are suspended in favour of class members on the commencement of a class proceeding until that person is no longer a member of the class proceeding.[63] It has not been decided as yet whether 'commencement' means when the claim sought to be certified was issued or when the claim was certified as a class action.

14.46

I. Conclusion

The full impact of the introduction of class proceedings legislation in Ontario and British Columbia has yet to be fully realised. There has, however, been a growing realisation among litigants and their counsel in both jurisdictions that class proceedings can provide an effective means of litigating and resolving controversies which affect large groups of people. As the number of class proceedings increases, many of the currently unresolved issues under both statutes will no doubt be decided.

14.47

---

[61] Law Society Act, s 59.S, Ontario Regulation 771/92, s 10.
[62] BC CPA, s 37.
[63] Ontario CPA, s 28; BC CPA, s 39.

APPENDIX 1—ONTARIO

An Act respecting Class Proceedings
Assented to June 25th, 1992

CHAPTER 6

CONTENTS

1. Definitions
2. Plaintiff's class proceeding
3. Defendant's class proceeding
4. Classing defendants
5. Certification
6. Certain matters not bar to certification
7. Refusal to certify: proceeding may continue in altered form
8. Contents of certification order
9. Opting out
10. Where it appears conditions for certification not satisfied
11. Stages of class proceedings
12. Court may determine conduct of proceeding
13. Court may stay any other proceeding
14. Participation of class members
15. Discovery of parties
16. Examination of class members before a motion or application
17. Notice of certification
18. Notice where individual participation is required
19. Notice to protect interests of affected persons
20. Approval of notice by the court
21. Delivery of notice
22. Costs of notice
23. Statistical evidence
24. Aggregate assessment of monetary relief
25. Individual issues
26. Judgment distribution
27. Contents of judgment on common issues
28. Limitations
29. Discontinuance and abandonment
30. Appeals
31. Costs
32. Agreements respecting fees and disbursements
33. Agreements for payment only in the event of success
34. Motions
35. Rules of court
36. Crown bound

37. Application of Act
38. Commencement
39. Short title

HER MAJESTY, by and with the advice and consent of the Legislative Assembly of the Province of Ontario, enacts as follows:

Definitions

1. In this Act,
   'common issues' means,
      (a) common but not necessarily identical issues of fact, or
      (b) common but not necessarily identical issues of law that arise from common but not necessarily identical facts; ('questions communes')

   'court' means the Ontario Court (General Division) but does not include the Small Claims Court; ('tribunal')
   'defendant' includes a respondent; ('défendeur')
   plaintiff' includes an applicant. (demandeur')

Plaintiff's class proceeding

2.—(1) One or more members of a class of persons may commence a proceeding in the court on behalf of the members of the class.

(2) A person who commences a proceeding under subsection (1) shall make a motion to a judge of the court for an order certifying the proceeding as a class proceeding and appointing the person representative plaintiff.

(3) A motion under subsection (2) shall be made,
   (a) within ninety days after the later of,
      (i) the date on which the last statement of defence, notice of intent to defend or notice of appearance is delivered, and
      (ii) the date on which the time prescribed by the rules of court for delivery of the last statement of defence, notice of intent to defend or a notice of appearance expires without its being delivered; or
   (b) subsequently, with leave of the court.

Defendant's class proceeding

3. A defendant to two or more proceedings may, at any stage of one of the proceedings, make a motion to a judge of the court for an order certifying the proceedings as a class proceeding and appointing a representative plaintiff.

Classing defendants

4. Any party to a proceeding against two or more defendants may, at any stage of the proceeding, make a motion to a judge of the court for an order certifying the proceeding as a class proceeding and appointing a representative defendant.

Certification

5.—(1) The court shall certify a class proceeding on a motion under section 2, 3 or 4 if,
   (a) the pleadings or the notice of application discloses a cause of action;
   (b) there is an identifiable class of two or more persons that would be represented by the representative plaintiff or defendant;
   (c) the claims or defences of the class members raise common issues;
   (d) a class proceeding would be the preferable procedure for the resolution of the common issues; and

- (e) there is a representative plaintiff or defendant who,
    - (i) would fairly and adequately represent the interests of the class,
    - (ii) has produced a plan for the proceeding that sets out a workable method of advancing the proceeding on behalf of the class and of notifying class members of the proceeding, and
    - (iii) does not have, on the common issues for the class, an interest in conflict with the interests of other class members.

(2) Despite subsection (1), where a class includes a subclass whose members have claims or defences that raise common issues not shared by all the class members, so that, in the opinion of the court, the protection of the interests of the subclass members requires that they be separately represented, the court shall not certify the class proceeding unless there is a representative plaintiff or defendant who,

- (a) would fairly and adequately represent the interests of the subclass;
- (b) has produced a plan for the proceeding that sets out a workable method of advancing the proceeding on behalf of the subclass and of notifying subclass members of the proceeding; and
- (c) does not have, on the common issues for the subclass, an interest in conflict with the interests of other subclass members.

(3) Each party to a motion for certification shall, in an affidavit filed for use on the motion, provide the party's best information on the number of members in the class.

(4) The court may adjourn the motion for certification to permit the parties to amend their materials or pleadings or to permit further evidence.

(5) An order certifying a class proceeding is not a determination of the merits of the proceeding.

Certain matters not bar to certification

6. The court shall not refuse to certify a proceeding as a class proceeding solely on any of the following grounds:
    1. The relief claimed includes a claim for damages that would require individual assessment after determination of the common issues.
    2. The relief claimed relates to separate contracts involving different class members.
    3. Different remedies are sought for different class members.
    4. The number of class members or the identity of each class member is not known.
    5. The class includes a subclass whose members have claims or defences that raise common issues not shared by all class members.

Refusal to certify: proceeding may continue in altered form

7. Where the court refuses to certify a proceeding as a class proceeding, the court may permit the proceeding to continue as one or more proceedings between different parties and, for the purpose, the court may,
    - (a) order the addition, deletion or substitution of parties;
    - (b) order the amendment of the pleadings or notice of application; and
    - (c) make any further order that it considers appropriate.

Contents of certification order

8.—(1) An order certifying a proceeding as a class proceeding shall,
   - (a) describe the class;
   - (b) state the names of the representative parties;
   - (c) state the nature of the claims or defences asserted on behalf of the class;
   - (d) state the relief sought by or from the class;
   - (e) set out the common issues for the class; and

(f) specify the manner in which class members may opt out of the class proceeding and a date after which class members may not opt out.

(2) Where a class includes a subclass whose members have claims or defences that raise common issues not shared by all the class members, so that, in the opinion of the court, the protection of the interests of the subclass members requires that they be separately represented, subsection (1) applies with necessary modifications in respect of the subclass.

(3) The court, on the motion of a party or class member, may amend an order certifying a proceeding as a class proceeding.

Opting out

9. Any member of a class involved in a class proceeding may opt out of the proceeding in the manner and within the time specified in the certification order.

Where it appears conditions for certification not satisfied

10.—(1) On the motion of a party or class member, where it appears to the court that the conditions mentioned in subsections 5 (1) and (2) are not satisfied with respect to a class proceeding, the court may amend the certification order, may decertify the proceeding or may make any other order it considers appropriate.

(2) Where the court makes a decertification order under subsection (1), the court may permit the proceeding to continue as one or more proceedings between different parties.

(3) For the purposes of subsections (1) and (2), the court has the powers set out in clauses 7 (a) to (c).

Stages of class proceedings

11.—(1) Subject to section 12, in a class proceeding,
  (a) common issues for a class shall be determined together;
  (b) common issues for a subclass shall be determined together; and
  (c) individual issues that require the participation of individual class members shall be determined individually in accordance with sections 24 and 25.

(2) The court may give judgment in respect of the common issues and separate judgments in respect of any other issue.

Court may determine conduct of proceeding

12. The court, on the motion of a party or class member, may make any order it considers appropriate respecting the conduct of a class proceeding to ensure its fair and expeditious determination and, for the purpose, may impose such terms on the parties as it considers appropriate.

Court may stay any other proceeding

13. The court, on its own initiative or on the motion of a party or class member, may stay any proceeding related to the class proceeding before it, on such terms as it considers appropriate.

Participation of class members

14.—(1) In order to ensure the fair and adequate representation of the interests of the class or any subclass or for any other appropriate reason, the court may, at any time in a class proceeding, permit one or more class members to participate in the proceeding.

(2) Participation under subsection (1) shall be in whatever manner and on whatever terms, including terms as to costs, the court considers appropriate.

Discovery of parties

15.—(1) Parties to a class proceeding have the same rights of discovery under the rules of court against one another as they would have in any other proceeding.

(2) After discovery of the representative party, a party may move for discovery under the rules of court against other class members.

(3) In deciding whether to grant leave to discover other class members, the court shall consider,
  (a) the stage of the class proceeding and the issues to be determined at that stage;
  (b) the presence of subclasses;
  (c) whether the discovery is necessary in view of the claims or defences of the party seeking leave;
  (d) the approximate monetary value of individual claims, if any;
  (e) whether discovery would result in oppression or in undue annoyance, burden or expense for the class members sought to be discovered; and
  (f) any other matter the court considers relevant.

(4) A class member is subject to the same sanctions under the rules of court as a party for failure to submit to discovery.

Examination of class members before a motion or application

16.—(1) A party shall not require a class member other than a representative party to be examined as a witness before the hearing of a motion or application, except with leave of the court.

(2) Subsection 15 (3) applies with necessary modifications to a decision whether to grant leave under subsection (1).

Notice of certification

17.—(1) Notice of certification of a class proceeding shall be given by the representative party to the class members in accordance with this section.

(2) The court may dispense with notice if, having regard to the factors set out in subsection (3), the court considers it appropriate to do so.

(3) The court shall make an order setting out when and by what means notice shall be given under this section and in so doing shall have regard to,
  (a) the cost of giving notice;
  (b) the nature of the relief sought;
  (c) the size of the individual claims of the class members;
  (d) the number of class members;
  (e) the places of residence of class members; and
  (f) any other relevant matter.

(4) The court may order that notice be given,
  (a) personally or by mail;
  (b) by posting, advertising, publishing or leafleting;
  (c) by individual notice to a sample group within the class; or
  (d) by any means or combination of means that the court considers appropriate.

(5) The court may order that notice be given to different class members by different means.

(6) Notice under this section shall, unless the court orders otherwise,
  (a) describe the proceeding, including the names and addresses of the representative parties and the relief sought;
  (b) state the manner by which and time within which class members may opt out of the proceeding;
  (c) describe the possible financial consequences of the proceeding to class members;
  (d) summarize any agreements between representative parties and their solicitors respecting fees and disbursements;
  (e) describe any counterclaim being asserted by or against the class, including the relief sought in the counterclaim;
  (f) state that the judgment, whether favourable or not, will bind all class members who do not opt out of the proceeding;

(g) describe the right of any class member to participate in the proceeding;
(h) give an address to which class members may direct inquiries about the proceeding; and
(i) give any other information the court considers appropriate.

(7) With leave of the court, notice under this section may include a solicitation of contributions from class members to assist in paying solicitor's fees and disbursements.

Notice where individual participation is required

18.—(1) When the court determines common issues in favour of a class and considers that the participation of individual class members is required to determine individual issues, the representative party shall give notice to those members in accordance with this section.

(2) Subsections 17 (3) to (5) apply with necessary modifications to notice given under this section.

(3) Notice under this section shall,
(a) state that common issues have been determined in favour of the class;
(b) state that class members may be entitled to individual relief;
(c) described the steps to be taken to establish an individual claim;
(d) state that failure on the part of a class member to take those steps will result in the member not being entitled to assert an individual claim except with leave of the court;
(e) give an address to which class members may direct inquiries about the proceeding; and
(f) give any other information that the court considers appropriate.

Notice to protect interests of affected persons

19.—(1) At any time in a class proceeding, the court may order any party to give such notice as it considers necessary to protect the interests of any class member or party or to ensure the fair conduct of the proceeding.

(2) Subsections 17 (3) to (5) apply with necessary modifications to notice given under this section.

Approval of notice by the court

20. A notice under section 17, 18 or 19 shall be approved by the court before it is given.

Delivery of notice

21. The court may order a party to deliver, by whatever means are available to the party, the notice required to be given by another party under section 17, 18 or 19, where that is more practical.

Costs of notice

22.—(1) The court may make any order it considers appropriate as to the costs of any notice under section 17, 18 or 19, including an order apportioning costs among parties.

(2) In making an order under subsection (1), the court may have regard to the different interests of a subclass.

Statistical evidence

23.—(1) For the purposes of determining issues relating to the amount or distribution of a monetary award under this Act, the court may admit as evidence statistical information that would not otherwise be admissible as evidence, including information derived from sampling, if the information was compiled in accordance with principles that are generally accepted by experts in the field of statistics.

(2) A record of statistical information purporting to be prepared or published under the authority of the Parliament of Canada or the legislature of any province or territory of Canada may be admitted as evidence without proof of its authenticity.

(3) Statistical information shall not be admitted as evidence under this section unless the party seeking to introduce the information has,

(a) given reasonable notice of it to the party against whom it is to be used, together with a copy of the information;
(b) complied with subsections (4) and (5); and
(c) complied with any requirement to produce documents under subsection (7).

(4) Notice under this section shall specify the source of any statistical information sought to be introduced that,
(a) was prepared or published under the authority of the Parliament of Canada or the legislature of any province or territory of Canada;
(b) was derived from market quotations, tabulations, lists, directories or other compilations generally used and relied on by members of the public; or
(c) was derived from reference material generally used and relied on by members of an occupational group.

(5) Except with respect to information referred to in subsection (4), notice under this section shall,
(a) specify the name and qualifications of each person who supervised the preparation of statistical information sought to be introduced; and
(b) described any documents prepared or used in the course of preparing the statistical information sought to be introduced.

(6) A party against whom statistical information is sought to be introduced under this section may require, for the purposes of cross-examination, the attendance of any person who supervised the preparation of the information.

(7) Except with respect to information referred to in subsection (4), a party against whom statistical information is sought to be introduced under this section may require the party seeking to introduce it to produce for inspection any document that was prepared or used in the course of preparing the information, unless the document discloses the identity of persons responding to a survey who have not consented in writing to the disclosure.

Aggregate assessment of monetary relief

24.—(1) The court may determine the aggregate or a part of a defendant's liability to class members and give judgment accordingly where,
(a) monetary relief is claimed on behalf of some or all class members;
(b) no questions of fact or law other than those relating to the assessment of monetary relief remain to be determined in order to establish the amount of the defendant's monetary liability; and
(c) the aggregate or a part of the defendant's liability to some or all class members can reasonably be determined without proof by individual class members.

(2) The court may order that all or a part of an award under subsection (1) be applied so that some or all individual class members share in the award on an average or proportional basis.

(3) In deciding whether to make an order under subsection (2), the court shall consider whether it would be impractical or inefficient to identify the class members entitled to share in the award or to determine the exact shares that should be allocated to individual class members.

(4) When the court orders that all or a part of an award under subsection (1) be divided among individual class members, the court shall determine whether individual claims need to be made to give effect to the order.

(5) Where the court determines under subsection (4) that individual claims need to be made, the court shall specify procedures for determining the claims.

(6) In specifying procedures under subsection (5), the court shall minimize the burden on class members and, for the purpose, the court may authorize,
(a) the use of standardized proof of claim forms;
(b) the receipt of affidavit or other documentary evidence; and
(c) the auditing of claims on a sampling or other basis.

(7) When specifying procedures under subsection (5), the court shall set a reasonable time within which individual class members may make claims under this section.

(8) A class member who fails to make a claim within the time set under subsection (7) may not later make a claim under this section except with leave of the court.

(9) The court may give leave under subsection (8) if it is satisfied that,
   (a) there are apparent grounds for relief;
   (b) the delay was not caused by any fault of the person seeking the relief; and
   (c) the defendant would not suffer substantial prejudice if leave were given.

(10) The court may amend a judgment given under subsection (1) to give effect to a claim made with leave under subsection (8) if the court considers it appropriate to do so.

Individual issues

25.—(1) When the court determines common issues in favour of a class and considers that the participation of individual class members is required to determine individual issues, other than those that may be determined under section 24, the court may,
   (a) determine the issues in further hearings presided over by the judge who determined the common issues or by another judge of the court;
   (b) appoint one or more persons to conduct a reference under the rules of court and report back to the court; and
   (c) with the consent of the parties, direct that the issues be determined in any other manner.

(2) The court shall give any necessary directions relating to the procedures to be followed in conducting hearings, inquiries and determinations under subsection (1), including directions for the purpose of achieving procedural conformity.

(3) In giving directions under subsection (2), the court shall choose the least expensive and most expeditious method of determining the issues that is consistent with justice to class members and the parties and, in so doing, the court may,
   (a) dispense with any procedural step that it considers unnecessary; and
   (b) authorize any special procedural steps, including steps relating to discovery, and any special rules, including rules relating to admission of evidence and means of proof, that it considers appropriate.

(4) The court shall set a reasonable time within which individual class members may make claims under this section.

(5) A class member who fails to make a claim within the time set under subsection (4) may not later make a claim under this section except with leave of the court.

(6) Subsection 24 (9) applies with necessary modifications to a decision whether to give leave under subsection (5).

(7) A determination under clause (1) (c) is deemed to be an order of the court.

Judgment distribution

26.—(1) The court may direct any means of distribution of amounts awarded under section 24 or 25 that it considers appropriate.

(2) In giving directions under subsection (1), the court may order that,
   (a) the defendant distribute directly to class members the amount of monetary relief to which each class member is entitled by any means authorized by the court, including abatement and credit;
   (b) the defendant pay into court or some other appropriate depository the total amount of the defendant's liability to the class until further order of the court; and
   (c) any person other than the defendant distribute directly to class members the amount of monetary relief to which each member is entitled by any means authorized by the court.

(3) In deciding whether to make an order under clause (2) (a), the court shall consider whether distribution by the defendant is the most practical way of distributing the award for any reason, including the fact that the amount of monetary relief to which each class member is entitled can be determined from the records of the defendant.

(4) The court may order that all or a part of an award under section 24 that has not been distributed within a time set by the court be applied in any manner that may reasonably be expected to benefit class members, even though the order does not provide for monetary relief to individual class members, if the court is satisfied that a reasonable number of class members who would not otherwise receive monetary relief would benefit from the order.

(5) The court may make an order under subsection (4) whether or not all class members can be identified or all of their shares can be exactly determined.

(6) The court may make an order under subsection (4) even if the order would benefit,
- (a) persons who are not class members; or
- (b) persons who may otherwise receive monetary relief as a result of the class proceeding.

(7) The court shall supervise the execution of judgments and the distribution of awards under section 24 or 25 and may stay the whole or any part of an execution or distribution for a reasonable period on such terms as it considers appropriate.

(8) The court may order that an award made under section 24 or 25 be paid,
- (a) in a lump sum, forthwith or within a time set by the court; or
- (b) in instalments, on such terms as the court considers appropriate.

(9) The court may order that the costs of distribution of an award under section 24 or 25, including the costs of notice associated with the distribution and the fees payable to a person administering the distribution, be paid out of the proceeds of the judgment or may make such other order as it considers appropriate.

(10) Any part of an award for division among individual class members that remains unclaimed or otherwise undistributed after a time set by the court shall be returned to the party against whom the award was made, without further order of the court.

Contents of judgment on common issues

27.—(1) A judgment on common issues of a class or subclass shall,
- (a) set out the common issues;
- (b) name or describe the class or subclass members;
- (c) state the nature of the claims or defences asserted on behalf of the class or subclass; and
- (d) specify the relief granted.

(2) A judgment on common issues of a class or subclass does not bind,
- (a) a person who has opted out of the class proceeding; or
- (b) a party to the class proceeding in any subsequent proceeding between the party and a person mentioned in clause (a).

(3) A judgment on common issues of a class or subclass binds every class member who has not opted out of the class proceeding, but only to the extent that the judgment determines common issues that,
- (a) are set out in the certification order;
- (b) relate to claims or defences described in the certification order; and
- (c) relate to relief sought by or from the class or subclass as stated in the certification order.

Limitations

28.—(1) Subject to subsection (2), any limitation period applicable to a cause of action asserted in a class proceeding is suspended in favour of a class member on the commencement of the class proceeding and resumes running against the class member when,
- (a) the member opts out of the class proceeding;

(b) an amendment that has the effect of excluding the member from the class is made to the certification order;
(c) a decertification order is made under section 10;
(d) the class proceeding is dismissed without an adjudication on the merits;
(e) the class proceeding is abandoned or discontinued with the approval of the court; or
(f) the class proceeding is settled with the approval of the court, unless the settlement provides otherwise.

(2) Where there is a right of appeal in respect of an event described in clauses (1) (a) to (f), the limitation period resumes running as soon as the time for appeal has expired without an appeal being commenced or as soon as any appeal has been finally disposed of.

Discontinuance and abandonment

29.—(1) A proceeding commenced under this Act and a proceeding certified as a class proceeding under this Act may be discontinued or abandoned only with the approval of the court, on such terms as the court considers appropriate.

(2) A settlement of a class proceeding is not binding unless approved by the court.

(3) A settlement of a class proceeding that is approved by the court binds all class members.

(4) In dismissing a proceeding for delay or in approving a discontinuance, abandonment or settlement, the court shall consider whether notice should be given under section 19 and whether any notice should include,
(a) an account of the conduct of the proceeding;
(b) a statement of the result of the proceeding; and
(c) a description of any plan for distributing settlement funds.

Appeals

30.—(1) A party may appeal to the Divisional Court from an order refusing to certify a proceeding as a class proceeding and from an order decertifying a proceeding.

(2) A party may appeal to the Divisional Court from an order certifying a proceeding as a class proceeding, with leave of the Ontario Court (General Division) as provided in the rules of court.

(3) A party may appeal to the Court of Appeal from a judgment on common issues and from an order under section 24, other than an order that determines individual claims made by class members.

(4) If a representative party does not appeal or seek leave to appeal as permitted by subsection (1) or (2), or if a representative party abandons an appeal under subsection (1) or (2), any class member may make a motion to the court for leave to act as the representative party for the purposes of the relevant subsection.

(5) If a representative party does not appeal as permitted by subsection (3), or if a representative party abandons an appeal under subsection (3), any class member may make a motion to the Court of Appeal for leave to act as the representative party for the purposes of subsection (3).

(6) A class member may appeal to the Divisional Court from an order under section 24 or 25 determining an individual claim made by the member and awarding more than $3,000 to the member.

(7) A representative plaintiff may appeal to the Divisional Court from an order under section 24 determining an individual claim made by a class member and awarding more than $3,000 to the member.

(8) A defendant may appeal to the Divisional Court from an order under section 25 determining an individual claim made by a class member and awarding more than $3,000 to the member.

(9) With leave of the Ontario Court (General Division) as provided in the rules of court, a class member may appeal to the Divisional Court from an order under section 24 or 25,
(a) determining an individual claim made by the member and awarding $3,000 or less to the member; or

(b) dismissing an individual claim made by the member for monetary relief.

(10) With leave of the Ontario Court (General Division) as provided in the rules of court, a representative plaintiff may appeal to the Divisional Court from an order under section 24,
- (a) determining an individual claim made by a class member and awarding $3,000 or less to the member; or
- (b) dismissing an individual claim made by a class member for monetary relief.

(11) With leave of the Ontario Court (General Division) as provided in the rules of court, a defendant may appeal to the Divisional Court from an order under section 25,
- (a) determining an individual claim made by a class member and awarding $3,000 or less to the member; or
- (b) dismissing an individual claim made by a class member for monetary relief.

Costs

31.—(1) In exercising its discretion with respect to costs under subsection 131 (1) of the *Courts of Justice Act*, the court may consider whether the class proceeding was a test case, raised a novel point of law or involved a matter of public interest.

(2) Class members, other than the representative party, are not liable for costs except with respect to the determination of their own individual claims.

(3) Where an individual claim under section 24 or 25 is within the monetary jurisdiction of the Small Claims Court where the class proceeding was commenced, costs related to the claim shall be assessed as if the claim had been determined by the Small Claims Court.

Agreements respecting fees and disbursements

32.—(1) An agreement respecting fees and disbursements between a solicitor and a representative party shall be in writing and shall,
- (a) state the terms under which fees and disbursements shall be paid;
- (b) give an estimate of the expected fee, whether contingent on success in the class proceeding or not; and
- (c) state the method by which payment is to be made, whether by lump sum, salary or otherwise.

(2) An agreement respecting fees and disbursements between a solicitor and a representative party is not enforceable unless approved by the court, on the motion of the solicitor.

(3) Amounts owing under an enforceable agreement are a first charge on any settlement funds or monetary award.

(4) If an agreement is not approved by the court, the court may,
- (a) determine the amount owing to the solicitor in respect of fees and disbursements;
- (b) direct a reference under the rules of court to determine the amount owing; or
- (c) direct that the amount owing be determined in any other manner.

Agreements for payment only in the event of success

33.—(1) Despite the *Solicitors Act* and *An Act Respecting Champerty*, being chapter 327 of Revised Statutes of Ontario, 1897, a solicitor and a representative party may enter into a written agreement providing for payment of fees and disbursements only in the event of success in a class proceeding.

(2) For the purpose of subsection (1), success in a class proceeding includes,
- (a) a judgment on common issues in favour of some or all class members; and
- (b) a settlement that benefits one or more class members.

(3) For the purposes of subsections (4) to (7),
'base fee' means the result of multiplying the total number of hours worked by an hourly rate; ('honoraires de base')
'multiplier' means a multiple to be applied to a base fee. ('multiplicateur')

(4) An agreement under subsection (1) may permit the solicitor to make a motion to the court to have his or her fees increased by a multiplier.

(5) A motion under subsection (4) shall be heard by a judge who has,
   (a) given judgment on common issues in favour of some or all class members; or
   (b) approved a settlement that benefits any class member.

(6) Where the judge referred to in subsection (5) is unavailable for any reason, the regional senior judge shall assign another judge of the court for the purpose.

(7) On the motion of a solicitor who has entered into an agreement under subsection (4), the court,
   (a) shall determine the amount of the solicitor's base fee;
   (b) may apply a multiplier to the base fee that results in fair and reasonable compensation to the solicitor for the risk incurred in undertaking and continuing the proceeding under an agreement for payment only in the event of success; and
   (c) shall determine the amount of disbursements to which the solicitor is entitled, including interest calculated on the disbursements incurred, as totalled at the end of each six-month period following the date of the agreement.

(8) In making a determination under clause (7) (a), the court shall allow only a reasonable fee.

(9) In making a determination under clause (7) (b), the court may consider the manner in which the solicitor conducted the proceeding.

Motions

34.—(1) The same judge shall hear all motions before the trial of the common issues.

(2) Where a judge who has heard motions under subsection (1) becomes unavailable for any reason, the regional senior judge shall assign another judge of the court for the purpose.

(3) Unless the parties agree otherwise, a judge who hears motions under subsection (1) or (2) shall not preside at the trial of the common issues.

Rules of court

35. The rules of court apply to class proceedings.

Crown bound

36. This Act binds the Crown.

Application of Act

37. This Act does not apply to,
   (a) a proceeding that may be brought in a representative capacity under another Act;
   (b) a proceeding required by law to be brought in a representative capacity; and
   (c) a proceeding commenced before this Act comes into force.

Commencement

38. This Act comes into force on a day to be named by proclamation of the Lieutenant Governor.

Short title

39. The short title of this Act is the *Class Proceedings Act, 1992*.

APPENDIX 2—BRITISH COLUMBIA

Class Proceedings Act

CHAPTER 21

Assented to June 21, 1995

CONTENTS

PART 1
DEFINITIONS

1. Definitions

PART 2
CERTIFICATION

2. Plaintiff's class proceeding
3. Defendant's class proceeding
4. Class certification
5. Certification application
6. Subclass certification
7. Certain matters not bar to certification
8. Contents of certification order
9. Refusal to certify
10. If conditions for certification not satisfied

PART 3
CONDUCT OF CLASS PROCEEDINGS

Division 1—Role of Court

11. Stages of class proceedings
12. Court may determine conduct of proceeding
13. Court may stay any other proceeding
14. Applications

Division 2—Participation of Class Members

15. Participation of class members
16. Opting out and opting in
17. Discovery
18. Examination of class members before an application

Division 3—Notices

19. Notice of certification

20. Notice of determination of common issues
21. Notice to protect interests of affected persons
22. Approval of notice by the court
23. Giving of notice by another party
24. Costs of notice

Part 4
Orders, Awards and Related Procedures

Division 1—Order on Common Issues and Individual Issues

25. Contents of order on common issues
26. Judgment on common issues is binding
27. Determination of individual issues
28. Individual assessment of liability

Division 2—Aggregate Awards

29. Aggregate awards of monetary relief
30. Statistical evidence may be used
31. Average or proportional share of aggregate awards
32. Individual share of aggregate award
33. Distribution
34. Undistributed award

Division 3—Termination of Proceedings and Appeals

35. Settlement, discontinuance, abandonment and dismissal
36. Appeals

Part 5
Costs, Fees and Disbursements

37. Costs
38. Agreements respecting fees and disbursements

Part 6
General

39. Limitation periods
40. Rules of Court
41. Application of Act
42. *Offence Act*
43. Power to make regulations
44. Consequential Amendment
45. Commencement

HER MAJESTY, by and with the advice and consent of the Legislative Assembly of the Province of British Columbia, enacts as follows:

Chapter 14: Class Actions in Canada

PART 1
DEFINITIONS

Definitions

1. In this Act:

'**certification order**' means an order certifying a proceeding as a class proceeding;

'**class proceeding**' means a proceeding certified as a class proceeding under Part 2;

'**common issues**' means
   (a) common but not necessarily identical issues of fact, or
   (b) common but not necessarily identical issues of law that arise from common but not necessarily identical facts;

'**court**', except in sections 36 (4) and 37, means the Supreme Court;

'**defendant**' includes a respondent;

'**plaintiff**' includes a petitioner.

PART 2
CERTIFICATION

Plaintiff's class proceeding

2. (1) One member of a class of persons who are resident in British Columbia may commence a proceeding in the court on behalf of the members of that class.
   (2) The person who commences a proceeding under subsection (1) must make an application to a judge of the court for an order certifying the proceeding as a class proceeding and, subject to subsection (4), appointing the person as representative plaintiff.
   (3) An application under subsection (2) must be made
      (a) within 90 days after the later of
         (i) the date on which the last appearance or statement of defence was delivered, and
         (ii) the date on which the time prescribed by the Rules of Court for delivery of the last appearance or statement of defence expires without its being delivered, or
      (b) at any other time, with leave of the court.
   (4) The court may certify a person who is not a member of the class as the representative plaintiff for the class proceeding only if it is necessary to do so in order to avoid a substantial injustice to the class.

Defendant's class proceeding

3. A defendant to 2 or more proceedings may, at any stage of one of the proceedings, make an application to a judge of the court for an order certifying the proceedings as a class proceeding and appointing a representative plaintiff.

Class certification

4. (1) The court must certify a proceeding as a class proceeding on an application under section 2 or 3 if
      (a) the pleadings disclose a cause of action,
      (b) there is an identifiable class of 2 or more persons,
      (c) the claims of the class members raise common issues, whether or not those common issues predominate over issues affecting only individual members,
      (d) a class proceeding would be the preferable procedure for the fair and efficient resolution of the common issues, and
      (e) there is a representative plaintiff who
         (i) would fairly and adequately represent the interests of the class,
         (ii) has produced a plan for the proceeding that sets out a workable method of advancing

the proceeding on behalf of the class and of notifying class members of the proceeding, and
   (iii) does not have, on the common issues, an interest that is in conflict with the interests of other class members.
(2) In determining whether a class proceeding would be the preferable procedure for the fair and efficient resolution of the common issues, the court must consider all relevant matters including
   (a) whether questions of fact or law common to the members of the class predominate over any questions affecting only individual members,
   (b) whether a significant number of the members of the class have a valid interest in individually controlling the prosecution of separate actions,
   (c) whether the class proceeding would involve claims that are or have been the subject of any other proceedings,
   (d) whether other means of resolving the claims are less practical or less efficient, and
   (e) whether the administration of the class proceeding would create greater difficulties than those likely to be experienced if relief were sought by other means.

Certification application

5. (1) An application for a certification order under section 2 (2) or 3 must be supported by an affidavit of the applicant.
   (2) A copy of the notice of motion and supporting affidavit must be filed and
      (a) delivered to all persons who are parties of record, and
      (b) served on any other persons named in the style of proceedings.
   (3) Unless otherwise ordered, there must be at least 14 days between the delivery or service of a notice of motion and supporting affidavit and the day named in the notice of motion for the hearing.
   (4) Unless otherwise ordered, a person to whom a notice of motion and affidavit is delivered under this section or on whom a notice of motion and affidavit is served under this section must, not less than 5 days or such other period as the court may order before the date of the hearing of the application, file an affidavit and deliver a copy of the filed affidavit to all persons who are parties of record.
   (5) A person filing an affidavit under subsection (2) or (4) must
      (a) set out in the affidavit the material facts on which the person intends to rely at the hearing of the application,
      (b) swear that the person knows of no fact material to the application that has not been disclosed in the person's affidavit or in any affidavits previously filed in the proceeding, and
      (c) provide the person's best information on the number of members in the proposed class.
   (6) The court may adjourn the application for certification to permit the parties to amend their materials or pleadings or to permit further evidence.
   (7) An order certifying a proceeding as a class proceeding is not a determination of the merits of the proceeding.

Subclass certification

6. (1) Despite section 4 (1), if a class includes a subclass whose members have claims that raise common issues not shared by all the class members so that, in the opinion of the court, the protection of the interests of the subclass members requires that they be separately represented, the court must not certify the proceeding as a class proceeding unless there is, in addition to the representative plaintiff for the class, a representative plaintiff who
   (a) would fairly and adequately represent the interests of the subclass,
   (b) has produced a plan for the proceeding that sets out a workable method of advancing the

proceeding on behalf of the subclass and of notifying subclass members of the proceeding, and
  (c) does not have, on the common issues for the subclass, an interest that is in conflict with the interests of other subclass members.
 (2) A class that comprises persons resident in British Columbia and persons not resident in British Columbia must be divided into subclasses along those lines.

Certain matters not bar to certification

7. The court must not refuse to certify a proceeding as a class proceeding by reason only of one or more of the following:
   (a) the relief claimed includes a claim for damages that would require individual assessment after determination of the common issues;
   (b) the relief claimed relates to separate contracts involving different class members;
   (c) different remedies are sought for different class members;
   (d) the number of class members or the identity of each class member is not known;
   (e) the class includes a subclass whose members have claims that raise common issues not shared by all class members.

Contents of certification order

8. (1) A certification order must
   (a) describe the class in respect of which the order was made by setting out the class's identifying characteristics,
   (b) appoint the representative plaintiff for the class,
   (c) state the nature of the claims asserted on behalf of the class,
   (d) state the relief sought by the class,
   (e) set out the common issues for the class,
   (f) state the manner in which and the time within which a class member may opt out of the proceeding,
   (g) state the manner in which and the time within which a person who is not a resident of British Columbia may opt in to the proceeding, and
   (h) include any other provisions the court considers appropriate.
 (2) If a class includes a subclass whose members have claims that raise common issues not shared by all the class members so that, in the opinion of the court, the protection of the interests of the subclass members requires that they be separately represented, the certification order must include the same information in relation to the subclass that, under subsection (1), is required in relation to the class.
 (3) The court, on the application of a party or class member, may at any time amend a certification order.

Refusal to certify

9. If the court refuses to certify a proceeding as a class proceeding, the court may permit the proceeding to continue as one or more proceedings between different parties and, for that purpose, the court may
   (a) order the addition, deletion or substitution of parties,
   (b) order the amendment of the pleadings, and
   (c) make any other order that it considers appropriate.

If conditions for certification not satisfied

10. (1) Without limiting section 8 (3), at any time after a certification order is made under this Part, the court may amend the certification order, decertify the proceeding or make any other

order it considers appropriate if it appears to the court that the conditions mentioned in section 4 or 6 (1) are not satisfied with respect to a class proceeding.

(2) If the court makes a decertification order under subsection (1), the court may permit the proceeding to continue as one or more proceedings between different parties and may make any order referred to in section 9 (a) to (c) in relation to each of those proceedings.

Part 3
Conduct of Class Proceedings

Division 1—Role of Court

Stages of class proceedings

11. (1) Unless the court otherwise orders under section 12, in a class proceeding,
    (a) common issues for a class must be determined together,
    (b) common issues for a subclass must be determined together, and
    (c) individual issues that require the participation of individual class members must be determined individually in accordance with sections 27 and 28.

    (2) The court may give judgment in respect of the common issues and separate judgments in respect of any other issue.

Court may determine conduct of proceeding

12. The court may at any time make any order it considers appropriate respecting the conduct of a class proceeding to ensure its fair and expeditious determination and, for that purpose, may impose on one or more of the parties the terms it considers appropriate.

Court may stay any other proceeding

13. The court may at any time stay any proceeding related to the class proceeding on the terms the court considers appropriate.

Applications

14. (1) The judge who makes a certification order is to hear all applications in the class proceeding before the trial of the common issues.
    (2) If a judge who has heard applications under subsection (1) becomes unavailable for any reason to hear an application in the class proceeding, the chief justice of the court may assign another judge of the court to hear the application.
    (3) A judge who hears applications under subsection (1) or (2) may but need not preside at the trial of the common issues.

Division 2—Participation of Class Members

Participation of class members

15. (1) In order to ensure the fair and adequate representation of the interests of the class or any subclass or for any other appropriate reason, the court may, at any time in a class proceeding, permit one or more class members to participate in the proceeding.
    (2) Participation under subsection (1) must be in the manner and on the terms, including terms as to costs, that the court considers appropriate.

Opting out and opting in

16. (1) A member of a class involved in a class proceeding may opt out of the proceeding in the manner and within the time specified in the certification order.
    (2) Subject to subsection (4), a person who is not a resident of British Columbia may, in the manner and within the time specified in the certification order made in respect of a class

proceeding, opt in to that class proceeding if the person would be, but for not being a resident of British Columbia, a member of the class involved in the class proceeding.
(3) A person referred to in subsection (2) who opts in to a class proceeding is from that time a member of the class involved in the class proceeding for every purpose of this Act.
(4) A person may not opt in to a class proceeding under subsection (2) unless the subclass of which the person is to become a member has or will have, at the time the person becomes a member, a representative plaintiff who satisfies the requirements of section 6 (1) (a), (b) and (c).
(5) If a subclass is created as a result of persons opting in to a class proceeding under subsection (2), the representative plaintiff for that subclass must ensure that the certification order for the class proceeding is amended, if necessary, to comply with section 8 (2).

Discovery

17. (1) Parties to a class proceeding have the same rights of discovery under the Rules of Court against one another as they would have in any other proceeding.
(2) After discovery of the representative plaintiff or, in a proceeding referred to in section 6, one or more of the representative plaintiffs, a defendant may, with leave of the court, discover other class members.
(3) In deciding whether to grant a defendant leave to discover other class members, the court must consider
   (a) the stage of the class proceeding and the issues to be determined at that stage,
   (b) the presence of subclasses,
   (c) whether the discovery is necessary in view of the defences of the party seeking leave,
   (d) the approximate monetary value of individual claims, if any,
   (e) whether discovery would result in oppression or in undue annoyance, burden or expense for the class members sought to be discovered, and
   (f) any other matter the court considers relevant.
(4) A class member is subject to the same sanctions under the Rules of Court as a party for failure to submit to discovery.

Examination of class members before an application

18. (1) A party must not require a class member, other than a representative plaintiff, to be examined as a witness before the hearing of any application, except with leave of the court.
(2) Section 17 (3) applies to a decision whether to grant leave under subsection (1) of this section.

Division 3—Notices

Notice of certification

19. (1) Notice that a proceeding has been certified as a class proceeding must be given by the representative plaintiff to the class members in accordance with this section.
(2) The court may dispense with notice if, having regard to the factors set out in subsection (3), the court considers it appropriate to do so.
(3) The court must make an order setting out when and by what means notice is to be given under this section and in doing so must have regard to
   (a) the cost of giving notice,
   (b) the nature of the relief sought,
   (c) the size of the individual claims of the class members,
   (d) the number of class members,
   (e) the presence of subclasses,
   (f) whether some or all of the class members may opt out of the class proceeding,
   (g) the places of residence of class members, and
   (h) any other relevant matter.

(4) The court may order that notice be given by
  (a) personal delivery,
  (b) mail,
  (c) posting, advertising, publishing or leafleting,
  (d) individually notifying a sample group within the class, or
  (e) any other means or combination of means that the court considers appropriate.
(5) The court may order that notice be given to different class members by different means.
(6) Unless the court orders otherwise, notice under this section must
  (a) describe the proceeding, including the names and addresses of the representative plaintiffs and the relief sought,
  (b) state the manner in which and the time within which a class member may opt out of the proceeding,
  (c) state the manner in which and the time within which a person who is not a resident of British Columbia may opt in to the proceeding,
  (d) describe the possible financial consequences of the proceeding to class members and subclass members,
  (e) summarize any agreements respecting fees and disbursements
    (i) between the representative plaintiff and the representative plaintiff's solicitors, and
    (ii) if the recipient of the notice is a member of a subclass, between the representative plaintiff for that subclass and that representative plaintiff's solicitors,
  (f) describe any counterclaim being asserted by or against the class or any subclass, including the relief sought in the counterclaim,
  (g) state that the judgment on the common issues for the class, whether favourable or not, will bind all class members who do not opt out of the proceeding,
  (h) state that the judgment on the common issues for a subclass, whether favourable or not, will bind all subclass members who do not opt out of the proceeding,
  (i) describe the rights, if any, of class members to participate in the proceeding,
  (j) given an address to which class members may direct inquiries about the proceeding, and
  (k) give any other information the court considers appropriate.
(7) With leave of the court, notice under this section may include a solicitation of contributions from class members to assist in paying solicitors' fees and disbursements.

Notice of determination of common issues

20. (1) When, in a class proceeding, the court determines common issues for the class or a subclass, the representative plaintiff for the class or subclass must give notice to the members of the class or subclass in accordance with this section.
  (2) Section 19 (3) to (5) applies to notice given under this section.
  (3) Notice under this section must
    (a) state that common issues have been determined,
    (b) identify the common issues that have been determined and explain the determinations made,
    (c) if common issues have been determined in favour of the class or subclass,
      (i) state that members of the class or subclass may be entitled to individual relief,
      (ii) describe the steps that must be taken to establish an individual claim, and
      (iii) state that failure on the part of the member of the class or subclass to take those steps will result in the member not being entitled to assert an individual claim except with leave of the court,
    (d) give an address to which members of the class or subclass may direct inquiries about the proceeding, and
    (e) give any other information that the court considers appropriate.

Notice to protect interests of affected persons

21. (1) At any time in a class proceeding, the court may order any party to give notice to the persons that the court considers necessary to protect the interests of any class member or party or to ensure the fair conduct of the proceeding.
    (2) Section 19 (3) to (5) applies to notice given under this section.

Approval of notice by the court

22. A notice under this Division must be approved by the court before it is given.

Giving of notice by another party

23. The court may order a party to give the notice required to be given by another party under this Act.

Costs of notice

24. (1) The court may make any order it considers appropriate as to the costs of any notice under this Division, including an order apportioning costs among parties.
    (2) In making an order under subsection (1), the court may have regard to the different interests of a subclass.

PART 4
ORDERS, AWARDS AND RELATED PROCEDURES

Division 1—Order on Common Issues and Individual Issues

Contents of order on common issues

25. An order made in respect of a judgment on common issues of a class or subclass must
    (a) set out the common issues,
    (b) name or describe the class or subclass members to the extent possible,
    (c) state the nature of the claims asserted on behalf of the class or subclass, and
    (d) specify the relief granted.

Judgment on common issues is binding

26. (1) A judgment on common issues of a class or subclass binds every member of the class or subclass, as the case may be, who has not opted out of the class proceeding, but only to the extent that the judgment determines common issues that
    (a) are set out in the certification order,
    (b) relate to claims described in the certification order, and
    (c) relate to relief sought by the class or subclass as stated in the certification order.
    (2) A judgment on common issues of a class or subclass does not bind a party to the class proceeding in any subsequent proceeding between the party and a person who opted out of the class proceedings.

Determination of individual issues

27. (1) When the court determines common issues in favour of a class or subclass and determines that there are issues, other than those that may be determined under section 32, that are applicable only to certain individual members of the class or subclass, the court may
    (a) determine those individual issues in further hearings presided over by the judge who determined the common issues or by another judge of the court,
    (b) appoint one or more persons including, within limitation, one or more independent experts, to conduct an inquiry into those individual issues under the Rules of Court and report back to the court, or

(c) with the consent of the parties, direct that those individual issues be determined in any other manner.

(2) The court may give any necessary directions relating to the procedures that must be followed in conducting hearings, inquiries and determinations under subsection (1).

(3) In giving directions under subsection (2), the court must choose the least expensive and most expeditious method of determining the individual issues that is consistent with justice to members of the class or subclass and the parties and, in doing so, the court may
   (a) dispense with any procedural step that it considers unnecessary, and
   (b) authorize any special procedural steps, including steps relating to discovery, and any special rules, including rules relating to admission of evidence and means of proof, that it considers appropriate.

(4) The court must set a reasonable time within which individual members of the class or subclass may make claims under this section in respect of the individual issues.

(5) A member of the class or subclass who fails to make a claim within the time set under subsection (4) must not later make a claim under this section in respect of the issues applicable only to that member except with leave of the court.

(6) The court may grant leave under subsection (5) if it is satisfied that
   (a) there are apparent grounds for relief,
   (b) the delay was not caused by any fault of the person seeking the relief, and
   (c) the defendant would not suffer substantial prejudice if leave were granted.

(7) Unless otherwise ordered by the court making a direction under subsection (1) (c), a determination of issues made in accordance with subsection (1) (c) is deemed to be an order of the court.

Individual assessment of liability

28. Without limiting section 27, if, after determining common issues in favour of a class or subclass, the court determines that the defendant's liability to individual class members cannot reasonably be determined without proof by those individual class members, section 27 applies to the determination of the defendant's liability to those class members.

Division 2—Aggregate Awards

Aggregate awards of monetary relief

29. (1) The court may make an order for an aggregate monetary award in respect of all or any part of a defendant's liability to class members and may give judgment accordingly if
   (a) monetary relief is claimed on behalf of some or all class members,
   (b) no questions of fact or law other than those relating to the assessment of monetary relief remain to be determined in order to establish the amount of the defendant's monetary liability, and
   (c) the aggregate or a part of the defendant's liability to some or all class members can reasonably be determined without proof by individual class members.

(2) Before making an order under subsection (1), the court must provide the defendant with an opportunity to make submissions to the court in respect of any matter touching on the proposed order including, without limitation,
   (a) submissions that contest the merits or amount of an award under that subsection, and
   (b) submissions that individual proof of monetary relief is required due to the individual nature of the relief.

Statistical evidence may be used

30. (1) For the purposes of determining issues relating to the amount or distribution of an aggregate monetary award under this Act, the court may admit as evidence statistical information that

would not otherwise be admissible as evidence, including information derived from sampling, if the information was compiled in accordance with principles that are generally accepted by experts in the field of statistics.

(2) A record of statistical information purporting to be prepared by or published under the authority of the Parliament of Canada or the legislature of any province or territory of Canada may be admitted as evidence without proof of its authenticity.

(3) Statistical information must not be admitted as evidence under this section unless the party seeking to introduce the information
   (a) has given to the party against whom the statistical evidence is to be used a copy of the information at least 60 days before that information is to be introduced as evidence,
   (b) has complied with subsections (4) and (5), and
   (c) introduces the evidence by an expert who is available for cross-examination on that evidence.

(4) Notice under this section must specify the source of any statistical information sought to be introduced that
   (a) was prepared or published under the authority of the Parliament of Canada or the legislature of any province or territory of Canada,
   (b) was derived from market quotations, tabulations, lists, directories or other compilations generally used and relied on by members of the public, or
   (c) was derived from reference material generally used and relied on by members of an occupational group.

(5) Except with respect to information referred to in subsection (4), notice under this section must
   (a) specify the name and qualifications of each person who supervised the preparation of the statistical information sought to be introduced, and
   (b) describe any documents prepared or used in the course of preparing the statistical information sought to be introduced.

(6) Unless this section provides otherwise, the law and practice with respect to evidence tendered by an expert in a proceeding applies to a class proceeding.

(7) Except with respect to information referred to in subsection (4), a party against whom statistical information is sought to be introduced under this section may require the party seeking to introduce it to produce for inspection any document that was prepared or used in the course of preparing the information, unless the document discloses the identity of persons responding to a survey who have not consented in writing to the disclosure.

Average or proportional share of aggregate awards

31. (1) If the court makes an order under section 29, the court may further order that all or a part of the aggregate monetary award be applied so that some or all individual class or subclass members share in the award on an average or proportional basis if
   (a) it would be impractical or inefficient to
      (i) identify the class or subclass members entitled to share in the award, or
      (ii) determine the exact shares that should be allocated to individual class or subclass members, and
   (b) failure to make an order under this subsection would deny recovery to a substantial number of class or subclass members.

(2) If an order is made under subsection (1), any member of the class or subclass in respect of which the order was made may, within the time specified in the order, apply to the court to be excluded from the proposed distribution and to be given the opportunity to prove that member's claim on an individual basis.

(3) In deciding whether to exclude a class or subclass member from an average distribution, the court must consider
   (a) the extent to which the class or subclass member's individual claim varies from the average for the class or subclass,
   (b) the number of class or subclass members seeking to be excluded from an average distribution, and
   (c) whether excluding the class or subclass members referred to in paragraph (b) would unreasonably deplete the amount to be distributed on an average basis.
(4) An amount recovered by a class or subclass member who proves that member's claim on an individual basis must be deducted from the amount to be distributed on an average basis before the distribution.

Individual share of aggregate award

32. (1) When the court orders that all or a part of an aggregate monetary award under section 29 (1) be divided among individual class or subclass members on an individual basis, the court must determine whether individual claims need to be made to give effect to the order.
(2) If the court determines under subsection (1) that individual claims need to be made, the court must specify the procedures for determining the claims.
(3) In specifying the procedures under subsection (2), the court must minimize the burden on class or subclass members and, for that purpose, the court may authorize
   (a) the use of standard proof of claim forms,
   (b) the submission of affidavit or other documentary evidence, and
   (c) the auditing of claims on a sampling or other basis.
(4) When specifying the procedures under subsection (2), the court must set a reasonable time within which individual class or subclass members may make claims under this section.
(5) A class or subclass member who fails to make a claim within the time set under subsection (4) must not later make a claim under this section except with leave of the court.
(6) Section 27 (6) applies to a decision whether to grant leave under subsection (5) of this section.
(7) The court may amend a judgment given under section 29 (1) to give effect to a claim made with leave under subsection (5) of this section if the court considers it appropriate to do so.

Distribution

33. (1) The court may direct any means of distribution of amounts awarded under this Division that it considers appropriate.
(2) In giving directions under subsection (1), the court may order that
   (a) the defendant distribute directly to the class or subclass members the amount of monetary relief to which each class or subclass member is entitled by any means authorized by the court, including abatement and credit,
   (b) the defendant pay into court or some other appropriate depository the total amount of the defendant's liability to the class or subclass members until further order of the court, or
   (c) any person other than the defendant distribute directly to each of the class or subclass members, by any means authorized by the court, the amount of monetary relief to which that class or subclass member is entitled.
(3) In deciding whether to make an order under subsection (2) (a), the court
   (a) must consider whether distribution by the defendant is the most practical way of distributing the award, and
   (b) may take into account whether the amount of monetary relief to which each class or subclass member is entitled can be determined from the records of the defendant.

(4) The court must supervise the execution of judgments and the distribution of awards under this Division and may stay the whole or any part of an execution or distribution for a reasonable period on the terms it considers appropriate.

(5) The court may order that an award made under this Division be paid
 (a) in a lump sum, promptly or within a time set by the court, or
 (b) in instalments, on the terms the court considers appropriate.

(6) The court may
 (a) order that the costs of distributing an award under this Division, including the costs of any notice associated with the distribution and the fees payable to a person administering the distribution, be paid out of the proceeds of the judgment, and
 (b) make any further or other order it considers appropriate.

Undistributed award

34. (1) The court may order that all or any part of an award under this Division that has not been distributed within a time set by the court be applied in any manner that may reasonably be expected to benefit class or subclass members, even though the order does not provide for monetary relief to individual class or subclass members.

(2) In deciding whether to make an order under subsection (1), the court must consider
 (a) whether the distribution would result in unreasonable benefits to persons who are not members of the class or subclass, and
 (b) any other matter the court considers relevant.

(3) The court may make an order under subsection (1) whether or not all the class or subclass members can be identified or all their shares can be exactly determined.

(4) The court may make an order under subsection (1) even if the order would benefit
 (a) persons who are not class or subclass members, or
 (b) persons who may otherwise receive monetary relief as a result of the class proceeding.

(5) If any part of an award that, under section 32 (1), is to be divided among individual class or subclass members remains unclaimed or otherwise undistributed after a time set by the court, the court may order that that part of the award
 (a) be applied against the cost of the class proceeding,
 (b) be forfeited to the government, or
 (c) be returned to the party against whom the award was made.

Division 3—Termination of Proceedings and Appeals

Settlement, discontinuance, abandonment and dismissal

35. (1) A class proceeding may be settled, discontinued or abandoned only
 (a) with the approval of the court, and
 (b) on the terms the court considers appropriate.

(2) A settlement may be concluded in relation to the common issues affecting a subclass only
 (a) with the approval of the court, and
 (b) on the terms the court considers appropriate.

(3) A settlement under this section is not binding unless approved by the court.

(4) A settlement of a class proceeding or of common issues affecting a subclass that is approved by the court binds every member of the class or subclass who has not opted out of the class proceeding, but only to the extent provided by the court.

(5) In dismissing a class proceeding or in approving a settlement, discontinuance or abandonment, the court must consider whether notice should be given under section 20 and whether the notice should include
 (a) an account of the conduct of the proceeding,

(b) a statement of the result of the proceeding, and
(c) a description of any plan for distributing any settlement funds.

Appeals

36. (1) Any party may appeal to the Court of Appeal from
   (a) an order certifying or refusing to certify a proceeding as a class proceeding,
   (b) an order decertifying a proceeding,
   (c) a judgment on common issues, and
   (d) an order under Division 2 of this Part, other than an order that determines individual claims made by class or subclass members.
(2) If a representative plaintiff does not appeal as permitted by subsection (1) within the time limit for bringing an appeal set under section 14 (1) (a) of the *Court of Appeal Act* or if a representative plaintiff abandons an appeal under subsection (1), any member of the class or subclass for which the representative plaintiff had been appointed may apply to a justice of the Court of Appeal for leave to act as the representative plaintiff for the purposes of subsection (1).
(3) An application by a class or subclass member for leave to act as the representative plaintiff under subsection (2) must be made within 30 days after the expiry of the appeal period available to the representative plaintiff or by such other date as the justice may order.
(4) With leave of a justice of the Court of Appeal, a class or subclass member, a representative plaintiff or a defendant may appeal to that court any order
   (a) determining an individual claim made by a class or subclass member, or
   (b) dismissing an individual claim for monetary relief made by a class or subclass member.

PART 5
COSTS, FEES AND DISBURSEMENTS

Costs

37. (1) Subject to this section, neither the Supreme Court nor the Court of Appeal may award costs to any party to an application for certification under section 2 (2) or 3, to any party to a class proceeding or to any party to an appeal arising from a class proceeding at any stage of the application, proceeding or appeal.
(2) A court referred to in subsection (1) may only award costs to a party in respect of an application for certification or in respect of all or any part of a class proceeding or an appeal from a class proceeding
   (a) at any time that the court considers that there has been vexatious, frivolous or abusive conduct on the part of any party,
   (b) at any time that the court considers that an improper or unnecessary application or other step has been made or taken for the purpose of delay or increasing costs or for any other improper purpose, or
   (c) at any time that the court considers that there are exceptional circumstances that make it unjust to deprive the successful party of costs.
(3) A court that orders costs under subsection (2) may order that those costs be assessed in any manner that the court considers appropriate.
(4) Class members, other than the person appointed as representative plaintiff for the class, are not liable for costs except with respect to the determination of their own individual claims.

Agreements respecting fees and disbursements

38. (1) An agreement respecting fees and disbursements between a solicitor and a representative plaintiff must be in writing and must
   (a) state the terms under which fees and disbursements are to be paid,

(b) give an estimate of the expected fee, whether or not that fee is contingent on success in the class proceeding, and
(c) state the method by which payment is to be made, whether by lump sum or otherwise.

(2) An agreement respecting fees and disbursements between a solicitor and a representative plaintiff is not enforceable unless approved by the court, on the application of the solicitor.

(3) An application under subsection (2) may,
   (a) unless the court otherwise orders, be brought without notice to the defendants, or
   (b) if notice to the defendants is required, be brought on the terms respecting disclosure of the whole or any part of the agreement respecting fees and disbursements that the court may order.

(4) Interest payable on fees under an agreement approved under subsection (2) must be calculated
   (a) in the manner set out in the agreement, or
   (b) if not so set out, at the interest rate, as that term is defined in section 7 of the *Court Order Interest Act*, or at any other rate the court considers appropriate.

(5) Interest payable on disbursements under an agreement approved under subsection (2) must be calculated
   (a) in the manner set out in the agreement, or
   (b) if not so set out, at the interest rate, as that term is defined in section 7 of the *Court Order Interest Act*, or at any other rate the court considers appropriate, on the balance of disbursements incurred as totalled at the end of each 6 month period following the date of the agreement.

(6) Amounts owing under an enforceable agreement are a first charge on any settlement funds or monetary award.

(7) If an agreement is not approved by the court, the court may
   (a) determine the amount owing to the solicitor in respect of fees and disbursements,
   (b) direct an inquiry, assessment or accounting under the Rules of Court to determine the amount owing, or
   (c) direct that the amount owing be determined in any other manner.

Part 6
General

Limitation periods

39. (1) Subject to subsection (2), any limitation period applicable to a cause of action asserted in a proceeding that is certified as a class proceeding under this Act is suspended in favour of a class member on the commencement of the proceeding and resumes running against the class member when
   (a) the member opts out of the class proceeding,
   (b) an amendment is made to the certification order that has the effect of excluding the member from the class proceeding,
   (c) a decertification order is made under section 10,
   (d) the class proceeding is dismissed without an adjudication on the merits,
   (e) the class proceeding is discontinued or abandoned with the approval of the court, or
   (f) the class proceeding is settled with the approval of the court, unless the settlement provides otherwise.

(2) If there is a right of appeal in respect of an event described in subsection (1) (a) to (f), the limitation period resumes running as soon as the time for appeal has expired without an appeal being commenced or as soon as any appeal has been finally disposed of.

Rules of Court

40. The Rules of Court apply to class proceedings to the extent that those rules are not in conflict with this Act.

Application of Act

41. This Act does not apply to
    (a) a proceeding that may be brought in a representative capacity under another Act,
    (b) a proceeding required by law to be brought in a representative capacity, and
    (c) a representative proceeding commenced before this Act comes into force.

Offence Act

42. Section 5 of the *Offence Act* does not apply to this Act.

Power to make regulations

43. The Lieutenant Governor in Council may make regulations as referred to in section 41 of the *Interpretation Act*.

Consequential Amendment

Crown Proceeding Act

44. Section 4 (1) of the *Crown Proceeding Act*, RSBC 1979, c 86, is amended by adding 'and, where applicable, under the *Class Proceedings Act*' **after** 'the *Supreme Court Act*'.

Commencement

45. (1) This Act comes into force on August 1, 1995 unless the Lieutenant Governor in Council, by regulation, brings it into force on an earlier date in which case it comes into force on that earlier date.
    (2) The Lieutenant Governor in Council may make a regulation under subsection (1) bringing this Act into force on a date that is earlier than August 1, 1995.

APPENDIX 3—QUEBEC

Code de procédure civile du Quebec (Arts 999–1030)

BOOK IX
CLASS ACTION

TITLE I
INTRODUCTORY PROVISIONS

999. In this book, unless the context indicates a different meaning,
   (*a*) 'judgment' means a judgment of the court;
   (*b*) 'final judgment' means the judgment which decides the questions of law or fact dealt with collectively;
   (*c*) 'member' means a natural person who is part of a group on behalf of which a natural person brings or intends to bring a class action;
   (*d*) 'class action' means the procedure which enables one member to sue without a mandate on behalf of all the members.

P 954

1000. The Superior Court hears exclusively, in first instance, suits brought under this book.

P 31, 954, 1026

1001. Unless the chief justice decides otherwise, the same judge designated by him hears the entire proceedings relating to the same class action.
   Where the chief justice considers that the interest of justice so requires, he may designate such judge notwithstanding articles 234 and 235.

P 234, 235

TITLE II
AUTHORIZATION TO INSTITUTE A CLASS ACTION

1002. A member cannot institute a class action except with the prior authorization of the court, obtained on a motion.
   The motion states the facts giving rise thereto, indicates the nature of the recourses for which authorization is applied for, and describes the group on behalf of which the member intends to act; the allegations of the motion are supported by an affidavit. It is accompanied with a notice of at least ten days of the date of presentation and is served on the person against whom the applicant intends to exercise the class action.

P 76

1003. The court authorizes the bringing of the class action and ascribes the status of representative to the member it designates if of opinion that:
   (*a*) the recourses of the members raise identical, similar or related questions of law or fact;
   (*b*) the facts alleged seem to justify the conclusions sought;
   (*c*) the composition of the group makes the application of article 59 or 67 difficult or impracticable; and
   (*d*) the member to whom the court intends to ascribe the status of representative is in a position to represent the members adequately.

P 59, 67, 753

1004. If the court grants the motion, it refers the record to the chief justice who, taking into account the interest of the parties and of the members, fixes the district in which the class action is brought.

1005. The judgment granting the motion:
   (*a*) describes the group whose members will be bound by any judgment;
   (*b*) identifies the principal questions to be dealt with collectively and the related conclusions sought;
   (*c*) orders the publication of a notice to the members.

The judgment also determines the date after which a member can no longer request his exclusion from the group; the delay for exclusion cannot be less than thirty days nor more than six months after the date of the notice to the members. Such delay is peremptory; the court may nevertheless permit the exclusion of a member who shows that in fact it was impossible for him to act sooner.

P 9, 1007, 1013, 1022

1006. The notice to the members indicates:
   (*a*) the description of the group;
   (*b*) the principal questions to be dealt with collectively and the related conclusions sought;
   (*c*) the right of a member to intervene in the class action;
   (*d*) the district in which the class action is to be brought;
   (*e*) the right of a member to request his exclusion from the group, the formalities to be followed and the delay for requesting his exclusion;
   (*f*) the fact that a member who is not a representative or an intervener cannot be called upon to pay the costs of the class action; and
   (*g*) any other information the court deems it useful to include in the notice.

P 68s, 208s, 477s

1007. A member may request his exclusion from the group by notifying the prothonotary of his decision, by registered or certified mail, before the expiry of the delay for exclusion.

A member who has requested his exclusion is not bound by any judgment on the demand of the representative.

P 1005, 1008

1008. A member is deemed to have requested his exclusion from the group if he does not, before the expiry of the delay for exclusion, discontinue a suit he has brought which the final judgment on the demand of the representative would decide.

P 1007

1009. In the case of an application for a declaratory judgment, the notice replaces, with respect to the members, the service provided for by article 454.

P 454

1010. The judgment dismissing the motion is subject to appeal *pleno jure* by the applicant or, by leave of a judge of the Court of Appeal, by a member of the group on behalf of which the motion had been presented. The appeal is heard and decided by preference.

The judgment granting the motion and authorizing the exercise of the recourse is without appeal.

P 29, 511

1010.1 Unless inconsistent therewith, Title III applies, *mutatis mutandis*, to this title.

P 1011s

Title III
Conduct of the Action

1011. The representative brings his demand in accordance with the ordinary rules. If he does not do so within three months of the authorization, the court may declare it perempted upon motion by any interested party served on the representative and accompanied with a notice of at least thirty days of its presentation. The notice must also be published at least fifteen days before the date of presentation of the motion, in the same manner as the notice of the judgment granting the motion to authorize the bringing of the class action, unless the court orders another mode of publication.

So long as the motion is not decided, the representative or another member requesting to be substituted for him may still avoid the declaration of peremption of the authorization by bringing his demand; in such case, the court grants the motion, but for the costs only.

P 110s, C 1237a, 2230

1012. Except in the case where he claims to have a recourse in warranty, the defendant cannot urge a preliminary exception against the representative unless it is common to a substantial part of the members and bears on a question dealt with collectively.

P 159s, 216, 1040, C 2230

1013. Proof or hearing of the demand brought by the representative cannot take place before the expiry of the delay for exclusion.

P 1005

1014. An admission by a representative binds the members unless the court considers that the admission causes them prejudice.

C 1243

1015. The representative is deemed to have a sufficient interest notwithstanding his acceptance of the defendant's offers respecting his personal claim. However, another member may request to be substituted for him.

P 55, 187s

1016. The representative cannot amend a proceeding, or discontinue, in whole or in part, the action, a proceeding or a judgment, without the permission of the court and except on the conditions it deems necessary.

P 199s, 262s

1017. A member cannot intervene voluntarily in demand except to assist the representative, to aid his demand or to support his pretensions.

The court admits the intervention if of opinion that it is useful to the group.

P 208s, 1006

1018. In the case of conservatory intervention, the court may at any time limit the right of an intervener to produce a proceeding or to participate in the proof or hearing, if it is of opinion that the intervention is prejudicial to the conduct of the action or is contrary to the interest of the members.

P 1017

1019. A party cannot, before the final judgment, submit a member other than a representative or an intervener to an examination on discovery or a medical examination unless the court considers the examination on discovery or medical examination useful to the adjudication of the questions of law or fact dealt with collectively.

P 397, 398, 399

1020. A witness cannot be heard out of court without the permission of the court.

P 404

1021. A member cannot be examined on articulated facts.

P 405s

1022. The court may, at any time, upon the application of a party, revise the judgment authorizing the bringing of the class action if it considers that the conditions set forth in paragraph *a* or *c* of article 1003 are no longer met.

The court may then amend the judgment authorizing the bringing of the class action or annul it, or allow the representative to amend the conclusions sought.

In addition, if the circumstances so require, the court may, at any time, and even *ex officio*, change or divide the group.

P 1003, 1005

1023. The person wishing to waive his status of representative can only do so with the authorization of the court.

The court accepts the waiver if it is able to ascribe the status of representative to another member.

1024. A member may, by motion, apply to the court to have himself or another member substituted for the representative.

The court may substitute the applicant or another member consenting thereto for the representative if it is of opinion that the latter is no longer in a position to represent the members adequately.

The substituted representative accepts the trial at the stage it has then reached; he may, with the authorization of the court, refuse to ratify the proceedings already had if they have caused an irreparable prejudice to the members. He cannot be bound to pay the costs and other expenses for proceedings prior to the substitution, unless the court orders otherwise.

1025. Transaction, acceptance of a tender or acquiescence, except where it is unconditional in the whole of the demand, is valid only if approved by the court. This approval cannot be given unless a notice has been given to the members.

The judgment determines, if such is the case, the terms and conditions of application of articles 1029 to 1040.

P 187s, 1029s

1026. If, after the demand of the representative is brought, the court annuls the judgment authorizing the bringing of the class action, the suit continues between the parties in accordance with the ordinary rules; where such is the case, the record is returned to the competent court.

Chapter 14: Class Actions in Canada

P 1000

Title IV
Judgment

Chapter 1
Content and Effect
of the Final Judgment

1027. Every final judgment describes the group and binds the member who has not requested his exclusion from the group.

1028. Every final judgment condemning to damages or to the reimbursement of an amount of money orders that the claims of the members be recovered collectively or be the object of individual claims.

P 1031s, 1037s

1029. The court may, *ex officio* or upon application of the parties, provide measures designed to simplify the execution of the final judgment.

P 1025

1030. When the final judgment acquires the authority of *res judicata*, the court of first instance orders the publication of a notice.

The notice contains a description of the group and indicates the tenor of the judgment.

If the final judgment provides that a member may file his claim, the notice also indicates the questions remaining to be determined, the information and documents that must accompany the claim and any other information the court deems it useful to include in the notice.

15

MULTI-PARTY ACTIONS IN AUSTRALIA

Dr Jocelyn Kellam,[1] *S Stuart Clark*[2]

A.	Introduction	15.01	Opt-out procedure	15.46
B.	Traditional Mechanisms	15.08	Further individual or group proceedings	15.49
	Joinder	15.09	Order that proceedings not continue as representative proceedings	15.50
	Test cases	15.13		
	Consolidation	15.16	Notice provisions	15.56
	Representative actions	15.21	Determination of non-common issues	15.60
C.	Class Actions under Part IVA Federal Court Act 1992		Settlement	15.64
			Judgment	15.68
	Generally	15.26	Costs	15.73
	Requirements for a representative action	15.31	D. Representative Actions by the Australian Competition and Consumer Commission	15.77
	Commencement of proceedings	15.34		
	Identification of the applicants	15.36		
	Issues common to all the applicants arising from like circumstances	15.40	E. Conclusion	15.80
	A claim against the same respondent	15.45	Appendix	

A. Introduction

Multi-party litigation in Australia is going through a period of intense development. Over the past two years, there has been an unprecedented increase in the level of class action litigation. Indeed, Australia has now gained the unenviable reputation of being the most likely place, outside the United States, for such a suit to be brought.

15.01

---

[1] Partner, Clayton Utz, Sydney. The authors thank Kirstie Howard for her assistance in the preparation of this chapter.
[2] Partner, Clayton Utz, Sydney.

15.02 Certain celebrated controversies—for example, in relation to financial services, toxic torts, and product liability claims—have highlighted the potential for such proceedings to be brought in instances of 'mass wrongs'. It is also no coincidence that the rising sophistication of such litigation has paralleled improvements in technology, in particular, computer litigation support.[3]

15.03 The Australian legal system[4] has traditionally recognised the notion of multi-party or grouped proceedings. Historically, however, Australian courts have appeared reluctant to encourage such litigation. Until the decision of the High Court of Australia (the High Court) in *Carnie v Esanda Finance Corp Limited*[5] in 1995, it was difficult for plaintiffs to maintain such an action since the traditional 'common interest' requirements in the Rules of the State Supreme Courts and the Federal Court of Australia (the Federal Court) were interpreted narrowly. Further, the traditional mechanisms for bringing multi-party or group proceedings suffer from the disadvantage that the judgments are only binding upon the individual litigants named in the proceedings rather than determining the rights of a class.

15.04 Recent years, however, have seen dramatic changes to this area of the law for a number of reasons. First, there has been a liberalisation of judicial attitudes in Australia towards procedural matters generally,[6] including multi-party actions as recognised in *Carnie v Esanda Finance Corp Limited*.

15.05 Secondly, there have been statutory reforms expanding the scope for multi-party actions to be brought in Australia. Most importantly, the enactment of Part IVA of the Federal Court of Australia Act (FCA) in 1992 gave plaintiffs access to an effective class action mechanism. Part IVA allows seven or more persons whose claims arise out of the same, similar, or related circumstances and which give rise to substantial common issues of law or fact to commence a representative action. Subject to members of the group being given a right to 'opt out' of the proceedings, any judgment is binding upon all persons falling within the class description.

---

[3] See R Davis, 'Complex Litigation' in J Kellam, R Travers and R Davis (eds), *Product Liability—Law and Practice* (looseleaf) (Sydney, Legal Books 1996) 18–39.

[4] Australia comprises a federation of six states (New South Wales, Victoria, Queensland, South Australia, Western Australia, and Tasmania) and two self-governing territories (Northern Territory and Australian Capital Territory). The Australian parliamentary system is governed by the Constitution, which assigns the Federal Government responsibility for certain matters, generally those of national significance, and assigns the balance to the various States. The Australian court system consists of a hierarchy of courts in each State and Territory, with the highest court in each being the Supreme Court, and a parallel Federal Court which deals with matters over which the Commonwealth has power. The highest court of appeal from both the State and Federal systems is the High Court of Australia.

[5] (1995) 182 CLR 398; (1995) 127 ALR 76; (1995) 69 ALJR 206 discussed below.

[6] A feature of the administration of justice in Australia in recent times has been a general disfavour towards procedural rigidities and a preference for a more flexible approach to statutory preconditions where these are of a procedural character (see Kirby J in *Emanuele v Australian Securities Commission* (1997) 188 CLR 114, 146–147).

Further, in 1986, reforms were also made to the Trade Practices Act allowing the Trade Practices Commission (now the Australian Competition and Consumer Commission) (ACCC) to bring a representative suit. Its powers were supplemented in 1992 in relation to product liability actions with the introduction of Part VA into the Trade Practices Act. **15.06**

Set out below is a discussion of the traditional mechanisms for bringing a multi-party action suit in Australia, the reforms contained in Part IVA FCA, and a summary of the ACCC's power to bring a representative suit. **15.07**

B. Traditional Mechanisms

Part IVA of the FCA does not provide a general right to bring a class action. It applies only to those plaintiffs whose causes of action arise under Federal jurisdiction and whose causes of action arose after the date of amendment of the FCA, namely 4 March 1992. Plaintiffs who wish to bring a multi-party suit but who cannot bring their case within the ambit of Part IVA of the FCA, for example because of the long latency period associated with their injuries or damage, must use traditional mechanisms to bring multi-party litigation. These include: **15.08**

- joinder of actions;
- test cases;
- consolidation of actions; and
- representative actions.

Joinder

Joinder is a court procedure available in all Australian jurisdictions which allows a number of plaintiffs whose claims have common issues of law or fact to join as parties to the litigation. The parties must have the same cause of action. **15.09**

The Federal Court Rules are typical: **15.10**

> Two or more persons may be joined as applicants or respondents in any proceeding—
>
> (a) where—
> (i) if a separate proceeding were brought by or against each of them, as the case may be, some common question of law or of fact would arise in all the proceedings; and
> (ii) all rights to relief claimed in the proceeding (whether they are joint, several or alternative) are in respect of or arise out of the same transaction or series of transactions; or
> (b) where the court gives leave so to do.[7]

---

[7] Federal Court Rules O 6 r 2. See also High Court Rules O 16 rr 1, 7; ACT Supreme Court Rules O 19 rr 1, 5; NT Supreme Court Rules r 9.02; NSW Supreme Court Rules Pt 8 r 2; QLD

15.11 There are significant limitations on the operation of joinder. It is difficult to satisfy the requirements of sub-paragraph (a). It was held in *Payne v Young*[8] that joinder is not allowed in cases arising from separate transactions, even where those transactions are substantially similar or even identical in nature.[9] In that case, the High Court held that even though all seven plaintiffs were challenging the validity of the regulations allowing the inspecting authorities to levy slaughter fees, the plaintiffs had entered into separate transactions with the authorities and thus could not properly be joined. The Court found that, whilst a common question of law or fact did arise, the rights to relief did not arise out of the same transaction or series of transactions.

15.12 It may also be difficult to convince the court of the merits of exercising its discretion to grant leave under sub-paragraph (b) since it may be impractical or inconvenient to do so in situations where the court is required to consider the plaintiffs' different injuries and individual circumstances.[10] It is also likely that dealings between the defendant and each plaintiff may vary and that questions of alternative causation will arise.

Test cases

15.13 Plaintiffs may rely on test cases to resolve common issues whereby one or more cases are heard before others of a similar nature in an attempt to narrow the issues between the parties. Test cases in Australia are not analogous to the English practice of lead actions,[11] in which one case is chosen to precede other similar proceedings and to raise issues common to all proceedings.

15.14 Test cases have no basis in the Federal Court or State and Territory Supreme Court Rules (save for the courts' broad discretion to give directions and formulate procedures).[12] Accordingly, test cases suffer from the disadvantage of only binding the actual parties to the test case. For the result to be of benefit, there must be an agreement between all the parties in all of the claims to be bound by the decision in the test case.

Rules of the Supreme Court O 3 rr 1, 5; SA Supreme Court Rules R 27.01; TAS Rules of the Supreme Court O 18 rr 1, 4; VIC Rules of the Supreme Court Ch 1 r 9.03; and WA Rules of the Supreme Court O 18 r 4.

[8] (1980) 145 CLR 609; (1980) 54 ALJR 448; (1980) 30 ALR 557.
[9] See also *Bishop v Bridgelands Securities* (1990) 25 FCR 311.
[10] *TPC v Queensland Aggregates Pty Ltd* (1981) 51 FLR 356.
[11] For comparison with lead actions, see M Aronson and J Hunter, *Litigation: Evidence and Procedure* (6th edn, Sydney, Butterworths, 1998) 90.
[12] For example, Part 26 r 1 of the NSW Supreme Court Rules provides: 'The Court may, at any time and from time to time, give such directions and make such orders for the conduct of any proceedings as appears convenient (whether or not inconsistent with the Rules) for the just, quick and cheap disposal of the proceedings'. Order 10 r 1 of the Federal Court Rules provides that 'the Court shall give such directions with respect to the conduct of the proceeding as it thinks proper'.

B. Traditional Mechanisms

There are also other disadvantages. For example, there is no suspension of the limitation period for bringing the action.[13] As a result, if the test case proceedings are lengthy, then plaintiffs who have not commenced proceedings may lose their right to bring suit.

Consolidation

Consolidation of actions is another method by which a grouped proceeding may arise. Consolidation is a procedure by which several actions are united into one trial where it is in the 'interests of justice'[14] to do so.

Generally proceedings will not be consolidated unless the separate proceedings might have been brought in the one statement of claim.[15] Consolidation differs from joinder in that there may be multiple causes of action. Hence, proceedings may be consolidated despite the fact that they have completely different parties.[16] Another possibility is that the court may consolidate several actions for the purpose of making a separate decision on one particular issue[17] (such as the admissibility of scientific evidence or a preliminary issue) although the remainder of each trial is heard separately.

Again, however, consolidation of actions is entirely at the court's discretion.

The Federal Court Rules are typical:

15.15

15.16

15.17

15.18

15.19

---

[13] Compare the position under Part IVA FCA. Section 33ZE states that:
 (1) Upon the commencement of a representative proceeding, the running of any limitation period that applies to the claim of a group member to which the proceeding relates is suspended.
 (2) The limitation period does not begin to run again unless either the member opts out of the proceeding under section 33J or the proceeding, and any appeals arising from the proceeding, are determined without finally disposing of the group member's claim.

[14] *Re Ling: Ex parte Ling v Commonwealth of Australia* (1995) 58 FCR 129, 134 per Hill J: 'The rule confers upon the Court a broad discretion to make orders for consolidation where it is in the interests of justice to do so. Relevant to the exercise of discretion would be the desirability of avoiding multiple actions, the saving of time and expense and whether the parties would be prejudiced by such a course: *Cameron v McBain* [1948] VLR 245, 247. There is no reason to interpret the rule so that consolidation is to be confined to cases where there are several actions brought which could have been joined in the one writ . . .'

[15] *Cameron v McBain* [1948] VLR 245; *Horwood v British Statesman Publishing Co Ltd* (1929) 45 TLR 237; *Todd v Jones* [1969] VR 169; *Bolwell Fibreglass Pty Ltd v Foley* [1984] VR 97.

[16] See P Taylor (ed), *Ritchie's Supreme Court Procedure New South Wales* (looseleaf) (Sydney, Butterworths, 1984) vol 1, 2666.

[17] For instance, Order 29 r 2 of the Federal Court Rules provides that:
 The Court may make orders for—
 (a) the decision of any question separately from any other question, whether before, at or after any trial or further trial in the proceedings; and
 (b) the statement of a case and the question for decision.
 There is an identical provision (Part 31 r 2) in the NSW Supreme Court Rules.

> Where several proceedings are pending in the same Division, then, if it appears to the Court:
> (a) that some common question of law or fact arises in both or all of them;
> (b) that the rights to relief claimed therein are in respect of, or arise out of, the same transaction or series of transactions; or
> (c) that for some other reason it is desirable to make an order under this rule,
>
> the Court may order those proceedings to be consolidated or may order them to be tried at the same time or one immediately after another or may order them to be stayed until after the determination of any of them.[18]

15.20 The Australian consolidation provisions are broadly comparable with the US methods of congregation[19] such as multi-district litigation (MDL), which involves the 'joint procedural administration and management of otherwise individual matters through orders for judicial consolidation'[20] and with the Federal Rule of Civil Procedure 42.[21]

Representative actions

15.21 A representative action is one in which the plaintiff who commences the action represents all those with a common interest in the proceedings. It is important to distinguish this form of representative action from the representative action procedure established by Part IVA of the FCA. The NSW Supreme Court Rules are typical:

> Where numerous persons have the same interest in any proceedings the proceedings may be commenced, and, unless the Court otherwise orders, continued, by or against any one or more of them as representing all or as representing all except one or more of them.[22]

15.22 The test for a representative action used to be whether the representative and those represented had (a) the same interest; (b) a common grievance; and (c) whether the relief sought was beneficial to them all.[23]

---

[18] Federal Court Rules O 29 r 5. See also: High Court Rules O 31 r 7; ACT Supreme Court Rules O 51 r 1; NT Supreme Court Rules r 9.12; NSW Supreme Court Rules Pt 31 r 7; QLD Rules of the Supreme Court O 17 r 13 and O 61 r 5; SA Supreme Court Rules r 73.01; TAS Rules of the Supreme Court O 55; VIC Rules of the Supreme Court Ch 1 r 9.12; and WA Rules of the Supreme Court O 83 r 1.

[19] For more detailed discussion, see P Rheingold, *Mass Tort Litigation* (looseleaf) (New York, Clark, Boardman and Callaghan, 1996).

[20] R Davis, 'Complex Litigation' in J Kellam, R Travers and R Davis (eds), *Product Liability—Law and Practice* (looseleaf) (Sydney, Legal Books, 1996) 18-23 to 18-25.

[21] FRCP 42(a) provides for consolidation 'when actions involving a common question of law or fact are pending before the court'.

[22] NSW Supreme Court Rules Pt 8 r 13. Provision for representative proceedings is also made in High Court Rules O 16 r 12; ACT Supreme Court Rules O 19 r 10; NT Supreme Court Rules r 18.01, 18.02; Federal Court Rules O 6 r 13 (1); QLD Rules of the Supreme Court O 3 r 10; SA Supreme Court Rules r 34.01; TAS Rules of the Supreme Court O 18 r 9; VIC Rules of the Supreme Court Ch 1 rr 18.02 and 18A; and WA Rules of the Supreme Court O 18 rr 12, 13.

[23] *Duke of Bedford v Ellis* [1901] AC 1, 8.

C. Class Actions

Until 1995, owing to the restrictive interpretation of the 'same' or 'common interest' in the English decision of *Markt & Co Limited v Knight Steamship Co Ltd*,[24] the representative action was of limited use in Australia. In particular, it could only be used where the relief sought did not include damages.

15.23

The decision in the *Markt* case was overruled by the High Court in 1995. In *Carnie v Esanda Finance Corp Limited*,[25] Mason CJ and Deane and Dawson JJ noted that:

15.24

> All that this sub-rule requires is numerous parties who have the same interest. The sub-rule is expressed in broad terms and it is to be interpreted in the light of the obvious purpose of the rule, namely to facilitate the administration of justice by enabling parties having the same interest to secure a determination in one action rather than in separate actions.

This is a key decision in the development of multi-party actions in Australia. In its decision, the High Court reinterpreted the 'same interest' requirement of the Court Rules which had acted as a fetter on the development of representative action procedure in Australia, thereby signalling to State Courts to develop multi-party actions.[26]

15.25

C. Class Actions under Part IVA Federal Court Act 1992

Generally

The class action introduced in the Federal Court of Australia, described in the legislation as a 'representative proceeding', was originally drafted with the intention of avoiding the limitations imposed by Rule 23 of the US Federal Rules of Civil Procedure, in particular to allow claims involving drugs and medical devices to be litigated as class actions.

15.26

As a result, there are significant differences between the Australian and US procedures. First, there is no certification procedure in Australia. Unlike the USA, once a class action has been commenced it will continue unless and until the respondent can convince the Court that it should be terminated.

15.27

Secondly, there is no requirement that common issues should predominate over individual ones. This has led to class actions being commenced and being allowed to proceed, notwithstanding an apparently overwhelming preponderance of individual issues.

15.28

---

[24] [1910] 2 KB 1021. In the *Markt* case, it was held that consignors who had signed separate but identical contracts with the same shipowner did not have a common interest since they had different individual damages claims.
[25] (1995) 182 CLR 398.
[26] *Carnie v Esanda Finance Corp Limited* (1995) 182 CLR 398, 78.

15.29 Thirdly, specific provision is made in the rules for the Court to deal with sub-group or even individual issues when hearing a class action.

15.30 It should be noted that Part IVA is a Federal law. As such, it has already been the subject of a challenge to its constitutional validity. While that challenge failed,[27] it is possible that similar challenges will be made.[28]

Requirements for a representative action

15.31 Part IVA creates a procedure which is available where seven or more persons have claims which arise out of the same, similar, or related circumstances provided that they give rise to a substantial common issue of law or fact. The procedure is available irrespective of the type of damages claimed.

15.32 Section 33C, the central provision in Part IVA of the FCA, provides:

(1) Subject to this Part, where:
   (a) 7 or more persons have claims against the same person; and
   (b) the claims of all those persons are in respect of, or arise out of, the same, similar or related circumstances; and
   (c) the claims of all those persons give rise to a substantial common issue of law or fact;

a proceeding may be commenced by one or more of those persons as representing some or all of them.

(2) A representative proceeding may be commenced:
   (a) whether or not the relief sought:
      (i) is, or includes, equitable relief; or
      (ii) consists of, or includes, damages; or
      (iii) includes claims for damages that would require individual assessment; or
      (iv) is the same for each person represented; and
   (b) whether or not the proceeding:
      (i) is concerned with the separate contracts or transactions between the respondent in the proceeding and individual group members; or
      (ii) involves separate acts or omissions of the respondent done or omitted to be done in relation to individual group members.

15.33 Hence, the three elements of a representative proceeding under Part IVA are:

---

[27] *Bright v Femcare Limited* [1997] FCA 1377.

[28] A challenge was made to the validity of Chapter 1 Order 18A of the Victorian Supreme Court Rules in *Schutt Flying Academy (Australia) Pty Ltd v Mobil Oil Australia Ltd* [2000] VSCA 103, 8 June 2000. Order 18A replicates the substance of Part IVA of the FCA. The plaintiffs argued that it was beyond the power of the Court to enact Order 18A since it diminished plaintiffs' common law rights to recover damages and wrongly gave the Court power to extend its jurisdiction over parties who had not consented to be joined as plaintiffs and power to bind conclusively all group members. The majority upheld the validity of Order 18A.

C. Class Actions

1. Seven or more persons must have a claim or claims against the same person (or persons);
2. The claims of all those persons must arise out of the same, similar, or related circumstances; and
3. The claims of all those persons must give rise to a substantial common issue of law or fact.

Commencement of proceedings

It is not necessary to obtain the consent of group members[29] before commencing a representative proceeding unless the group member is the Commonwealth, a State or Territory, or a Minister or officer of the Commonwealth, a State, or a Territory.[30] **15.34**

The representative applicant[31] will have sufficient standing to commence a representative proceeding where they have sufficient interest to commence the proceeding on their own behalf.[32] The representative applicant retains a sufficient interest either to continue the proceeding or to bring an appeal from a judgment even though he/she may cease to have a claim against the respondent. **15.35**

Identification of the applicants

At the commencement of the proceedings, it is not necessary to provide any specific details about the group members. Hence, it is not necessary to name or even specify the number of group members.[33] **15.36**

In *Tropical Shine Holdings Pty Ltd v Lake Gesture Pty Ltd*,[34] the Court dealt with the problem of reconciling the requirement of section 33C(1)(a) that there be at least seven persons with the lack of a need for specificity in section 33H. *Tropical Shine Holdings Pty Ltd v Lake Gesture Pty Ltd* concerned an action for misleading and deceptive advertising. The applicant, a furniture wholesaler, claimed that the respondent's advertisements for 'liquidation sales' misled or deceived potential purchasers as to the value and quality of the respondent's furniture. The applicant described the group members as: **15.37**

> all those persons who have suffered or are likely to suffer loss or damage by reason of the Respondent's conduct alleged in the Statement of Claim being all those persons

---

[29] s 33E(1).
[30] s 33E(2).
[31] In the Federal Court the plaintiff is referred to as the 'applicant' while the defendant is referred to as the 'respondent'.
[32] s 33D.
[33] s 33H(2).
[34] (1993) 45 FCR 457, (1993) 118 ALR 510, [1993] ATPR 41, 766.

who bought furniture at the sales advertised, promoted and conducted by the First Respondent as set out below.

15.38 Wilcox J held that the effect of section 33C(1)(a) was to restrict 'the use of Part IVA to claims that, by their nature and assuming that they have substance, are shared by at least seven persons'.[35] Based on the number of sales and advertisements, and the period of time over which the sales were advertised, he held that this description of the class satisfied the section 33C requirement as it was clear that at least seven people must have had a potential claim.[36]

15.39 The pleadings must identify both the basis upon which the representative applicant alleges that his or her case arises, what the rights of those represented claim to be, and how they are said to arise. While the provisions of Part IVA of the FCA impose no requirements with respect to the provision of information about group members, the Federal Court has, pursuant to the general rules of procedure of the Court, made it clear that the pleadings must clearly articulate the basis of the claims of those whom the representative applicant purports to represent.[37] This is of some importance in Australia where there is a system of fact pleading rather than, for example, issue pleadings as in the United States. Thus, for example, in a case involving allegations of misrepresentation, the Federal Court has emphasised the importance of the pleadings specifying precisely the representations that were allegedly made to individuals within the group.[38]

Issues common to all the applicants arising from like circumstances

15.40 Under section 33C of the FCA, the applicants must have in common substantial issues of fact or law and their claims must arise from the same, similar, or related circumstances.[39]

---

[35] *Tropical Shine Holdings Pty Ltd v Lake Gesture Pty Ltd* (1993) 45 FCR 457, 462.
[36] For further discussion, see P Lynch, 'Representative Actions in the Federal Court of Australia' (1994–1995) 12 *Australian Bar Review* 159, 159–161.
[37] *Harrison v Lidoform Pty Limited* (24 Nov 1998, Federal Court of Australia); *Cameron v Qantas Airways Limited* [1993] ATPR 41-251.
[38] *Connell v Nevada Financial Group Pty Limited* (1996) 139 ALR 723.
[39] In *Zhang de Yong v Minister for Immigration, Local Government and Ethnic Affairs* (1993) 118 ALR 165, French J recommended a purposive approach to determining whether this requirement was satisfied. For an example of a case where the factual and legal issues were discrete, see *Soverina Pty Ltd v Natwest Australia Bank Ltd* (1993) 118 ALR 298; (1993) 40 FCR 452 (defamation and conversion). In *Philip Morris (Australia) Ltd v Nixon* [2000] FCA 229; (2000) 170 ALR 487, the Full Federal Court held that the claims of all group members did not arise out of the 'same, similar or related circumstances' since the conduct complained of was that of three cigarette maufacturers over a period of 40 years. The Court held that the group members' claims were so disparate and involved such varied conduct on the part of the respondents that they could not be said to arise out of related circumstances. The Full Federal Court also doubted whether there were any questions of law or fact common to all the group members.

C. Class Actions

15.41 What degree of 'commonality' is required has been the subject of judicial disagreement which has recently been considered by the High Court in *Wong v Silkfield Pty Limited*.[40]

15.42 In that case, the respondent argued that there was no 'substantial common issue of law or fact' in issue between the parties within the meaning of section 33C(1)(c). When the matter had been considered by the Full Federal Court, the majority had held that a common issue was not 'substantial' unless it was likely to have 'a major impact on the conduct and outcome of the litigation' to such an extent that it was likely to 'resolve wholly or to any significant degree the claims of all group members'.[41]

15.43 The High Court rejected this analysis in the unanimous judgment. Rather, they held that 'substantial' meant:

> ... when used to identify the threshold requirements of section 33C(1), 'substantial' does not indicate that which is 'large' or 'of special significance' or would 'have a major impact on the ... litigation' but, rather, it is directed to issues which are 'real or of substance'.

The High Court went on to observe that: 'It was not necessary to show that litigation of this common issue would be likely to resolve, wholly, or to any significant degree, the claims of all group members.'

15.44 Thus, it would seem that, provided there is a real common issue to be decided—regardless of whether or not that common issue is of significance in terms of the overall litigation—it will be sufficient to satisfy the requirements of section 33C(1)(c).

A claim against the same respondent

15.45 By virtue of the interaction of sections 33C and 33D of the FCA, a representative action requires that there be at least seven people who have a claim against the same respondent and, where there is more than one respondent in the proceedings, against each respondent.[42]

---

[40] [1999] ATPR 41-713; (1999) 165 ALR 373; (1999) 15 LegRep 7; (1999) 73 ALJR 1427.
[41] *Silkfield Pty Limited v Wong* (1998) 159 ALR 329. The Full Court suggested that a comparison of common and non-common issues should also be considered.
[42] *Symington v Hoechst Schering Agrevo and Ors* (1997) 78 FCR 164; (1997) 149 ALR 261 and *Ryan v Great Lakes Council and Ors* (1997) 78 FCR 309; (1997) 149 ALR 45. See also *Nixon v Philip Morris (Australia) Ltd* [1999] FCA 1107, [1999] ATPR 41-707; (1999) 165 ALR 515 and *Philip Morris (Australia) Ltd v Nixon* [2000] FCA 229; (2000) 170 ALR 487. In the latter decision, the Full Federal Court noted that the applicants' case was not based on the collective conduct of the respondents but rather was that each group member was influenced by the conduct of *one or other* of the respondents to smoke, to continue smoking, or to fail to quit smoking. Therefore, not every group member had a claim against each respondent.

Opt-out procedure

15.46 The class action procedure created by the FCA is an 'opt-out' procedure. That is to say, every person falling within the description of the group will continue as a group member and be bound by the outcome of proceedings unless they take steps to opt out.

15.47 Section 33J provides that:

(1) The Court must fix a date before which a group member may opt out of a representative proceeding.
(2) A group member may opt out of the representative proceeding by written notice given under the Rules of Court before the date so fixed.
(3) The Court, on the application of a group member, the representative party or the respondent in the proceeding, may fix another date so as to extend the period during which a group member may opt out of the representative proceeding.
(4) Except with leave of the Court, the hearing of a representative proceeding must not commence earlier than the date before which a group member may opt out of the proceeding.

15.48 The opt-out procedures are considered beneficial because they achieve finality. Under section 33ZB of the FCA, any group member who fails to opt out is bound by the result of the case. This will be so even if the group member was unaware of the existence of the proceedings. On the other hand, this creates the unusual position that a person may be in dispute with another without knowing anything of the proceedings.[43] This in turn appears to give rise to a constitutional difficulty under the terms of the Australian Constitution though the Full Federal Court has upheld the validity of section 33ZB under the Constitution.[44]

Further individual or group proceedings

15.49 New members may be added to the group at any stage in the proceedings. This can occur by way of an amendment to the group description. Section 33K provides:

(1) The Court may at any stage of a representative proceeding, on application made by the representative party, give leave to amend the application commencing the representative proceeding so as to alter the description of the group.
(2) The description of the group may be altered so as to include a person:

---

[43] This argument was raised in *Schutt Flying Academy Pty Ltd v Mobil Oil Australia Ltd* [2000] VSCA 103, 8 June 2000 and *Femcare Ltd v Bright* [2000] FCA 512, 19 Apr 2000. Both the Victorian Court of Appeal in the *Mobil* case and the Full Federal Court in the *Femcare* case rejected the notion that s 33ZB or its Victorian equivalent were invalid as being beyond the power of the Court.

[44] *Femcare Ltd v Bright* [2000] FCA 512, 19 Apr 2000. (See also *Nixon v Philip Morris (Australia) Ltd* [1999] FCA 1107, [1999] ATPR 41-707; (1999) 165 ALR 515.)

C. Class Actions

(a) whose cause of action accrued after the commencement of the representative proceeding but before such date as the Court fixes when giving leave; and
(b) who would have been included in the group, or, with the consent of the person would have been included in the group, if the cause of action had accrued before the commencement of the proceeding.

Order that proceedings not continue as representative proceedings

In certain circumstances, it may be impractical or inappropriate for the action to continue as a representative proceeding. Section 33L gives the Federal Court the discretion to order that proceedings be discontinued as representative proceedings in circumstances where it appears likely that there are fewer than seven group members. Section 33M affords the Court the same discretion in circumstances where it appears likely that the amount of damages per group member will be exceeded by the cost of notification to group members and distribution of the damages. 15.50

As has already been noted, the FCA class action rules do not include a certification procedure. Rather, it is left to the respondent to move the Court to terminate the proceedings where the respondent believes it is not appropriate to have the matter dealt with as a representative proceeding. Where this occurs, the respondent will generally launch a multi-faceted attack asserting that: 15.51

(1) the proceedings do not satisfy the requirements of commonality prescribed by section 33C; and
(2) that, for one or more of the reasons set out in subsection 33N(1), the proceedings should be terminated.

Subsection 33N(1) provides that: 15.52

(1) The Court may, on application by the respondent or of its own motion, order that a proceeding no longer continue under this Part where it is satisfied that it is in the interests of justice to do so because:
   (a) the costs that would be incurred if the proceeding were to continue as a representative proceeding are likely to exceed the costs that would be incurred if each group member conducted a separate proceeding; or
   (b) all the relief sought can be obtained by means of a proceeding other than a representative proceeding under this Part; or
   (c) the representative proceeding will not provide an efficient and effective means of dealing with the claims of group members; or
   (d) it is otherwise inappropriate that the claims be pursued by means of a representative proceeding.

To date, the outcome for respondents who pursue this course has been mixed. Some judges of the Federal Court have taken the view that, wherever possible, the rules should be interpreted so as to maintain proceedings.[45] Others have taken a 15.53

---

[45] In *Tropical Shine Holdings Pty Ltd v Lake Gesture Pty Ltd* (1993) 118 ALR 510; [1993] ATPR 41-283, Wilcox J allowed an action to proceed notwithstanding the fact that the group representa-

stricter view and terminated the proceedings.[46] In yet other cases, the applicants have abandoned the proceedings in the face of such an application.

15.54 In *Zhang de Yong v Minister for Immigration Local Government and Ethnic Affairs*,[47] French J concluded that there should be a determination of the common issue and a judgment in accordance with section 33ZB. His Honour also ordered that thereafter the proceeding no longer continue as a representative proceeding and that decisions affecting individual group members should be pursued individually.[48] In *Schanka & Ors v Employment National (Administration) Pty Ltd*,[49] Moore J contemplated the same course of action as was taken in *Zhang*. However, there is also a line of authority to suggest that the Federal Court ought to determine at the outset whether there is a 'substantial common issue of law or fact' rather than adopting a 'wait and see' approach and then making an order under section 33N and thereby increasing the cost for the litigants.[50]

15.55 Section 33N was also considered in *Gui Sen Huang v Minister for Immigration and Multicultural Affairs*.[51] In that case, Lehane J held that it would not be in the 'interests of justice' to order that the proceedings no longer continue as representative proceedings because the practical result would be that the represented applicants would be time barred from bringing individual actions. In *Australian Competition and Consumer Commission v Internic Technology Pty Ltd & Anor*,[52] Lindgren J ordered that proceedings not continue under Part IVA because the cost of calling all 2,000 or so group members to prove inducement would exceed the likely amount of damages (estimated at a maximum of Aus$150 per group member).

Notice provisions

15.56 Under section 33X(1) of the FCA, notice must be given to group members of the following matters:

(a) the commencement of the proceeding and the right of the group members to opt out of the proceeding before a specified date, being the date fixed under subsection 33J(1);

---

tive was a business competitor of the respondent, while the other group members were persons who purchased furniture from the respondent and thus had different claims. See also *Johnson Tiles Pty Ltd v Esso Australia Pty Ltd* [1999] FCA 1645, 25 Nov 1999.

[46] See *Gold Coast City Council v Pioneer & Ors* [1997] ATPR 44-076 and *Australian Competition and Consumer Commission v Giraffe World Australia Pty Ltd & Others* [1998] ATPR 41-648; (1998) 156 ALR 273; (1998) 84 FCR 512.

[47] (1993) 45 FCR 384, (1993) 118 ALR 165.

[48] s 33Q.

[49] (1998) 86 IR 283.

[50] See the discussion on this issue under the heading of 'Issues common to the applicants arising from like circumstances' above.

[51] (1997) 50 ALR 134.

[52] [1998] ATPR 41-646.

C. Class Actions

(b) an application by the respondent in the proceeding for the dismissal of the proceeding on the ground of want of prosecution;
(c) an application by a representative party seeking leave to withdraw under section 33W as a representative party.

However, if the relief sought in the proceeding does not include damages, then the Federal Court may dispense with the requirements of section 33X(1).[53] The Court may also order that notice be given where the respondent pays money into court in answer to the claim,[54] where the Court is to determine an application for approval of a settlement,[55] or at any other stage in the proceedings.[56] Notice must be given as soon as is practicable after the occurrence of the event to which the notice relates.[57] Additionally, notice must be given where the Court orders that a constitution fund be established to distribute money to group members.[58]

15.57

Section 33Y prescribes the form and content of the notices to be given to group members. The notice must be as approved by the Court.[59] The section also provides that:

15.58

(3) The Court must, by order, specify:
  (a) who is to give the notice; and
  (b) the way in which the notice is to be given;
  and the order may include provision:
  (c) directing a party to provide information relevant to the giving of the notice; and
  (d) relating to the costs of the notice.
(4) An order under subsection (3) may require that notice be given by means of a press advertisement, radio or television broadcast, or by any other means.
(5) The Court may not order that notice be given personally to each group member unless it is satisfied that it is reasonably practicable, and not unduly expensive, to do so.
(6) A notice that concerns a matter for which the Court's leave or approval is required must specify the period within which a group member or other person may apply to the Court, or take some other step, in relation to the matter.
(7) A notice that includes or concerns conditions must specify the conditions and the period, if any, for compliance.
(8) The failure of a group member to receive or respond to a notice does not affect a step taken, an order made, or a judgment given, in a proceeding.

---

[53] s 33X(2).
[54] s 33X(3).
[55] s 33X(4).
[56] s 33X(5).
[57] s 33X(6).
[58] s 33ZA(3).
[59] s 33Y(2).

15.59 The giving of notice to group members can be expensive and time-consuming[60] and it is for this reason that the Federal Court retains the power under section 33N to order that the proceeding not continue as a representative proceeding where the costs of giving notice are excessive.

Determination of non-common issues

15.60 In any representative proceeding, there will arise issues which are not common to all the group members since there may be differences, for example, in:

- the injuries or other loss suffered by individual applicants;
- representations made by the respondents;
- the reliance of group members on any statements made to them;
- the circumstances of individual group members;
- the causes of the group members' loss, damage, or injury.

15.61 Where there are issues common to only some of the group members, the Federal Court may establish a sub-group and appoint a representative party on behalf of the sub-group.[61] Where that occurs, that person, and not the representative party, is liable for the costs associated with the determination of the issue/s common to the sub-group members.[62]

15.62 Where there is an issue which relates only to an individual group member, the Federal Court may permit that individual to appear in the representative proceeding for the purpose of determining the issue.[63] Once again, that group member is liable for the costs associated with the determination of the issue.[64]

15.63 The Court also retains the power to order that separate proceedings be commenced to determine the issue of an individual group member[65] or that separate representative proceedings be commenced to determine the issue/s common to the sub-group.[66]

---

[60] For instance, V Morabito, 'Class Actions: The Right to Opt Out Under Part IVA of the Federal Court of Australia Act 1976 (Cth)' (1994) 19 Melbourne University Law Review 615, 630 reports a study of a case in the United States, commonly known as the 'second antibiotics settlement', in which over $800,000 was spent in postage alone to distribute the first two notices in the early stages of the litigation; yet nearly one-half of the potential class members who were surveyed could not remember receiving, or stated that they did not receive, either of the two notices. For further discussion, see T Bartsh, F Boddy, B King, and P Thompson, *A Class Action Suit That Worked: The Consumer Refund in the Antibiotic Antitrust Litigation* (Massachusetts, Lexington Books, 1978) 101–116.
[61] s 33Q(2).
[62] s 33Q(3).
[63] s 33R(1).
[64] s 33R(2).
[65] s 33S(a).
[66] s 33S(b).

C. Class Actions

Settlement

15.64 Any settlement must be approved by the Federal Court.[67] Section 33V provides that:

> (1) A representative proceeding may not be settled or discontinued without the approval of the Court.
> (2) If the Court gives such approval, it may make such orders as are just with respect to the distribution of any money paid under a settlement or paid into the Court.

15.65 Section 33V was considered by Branson J in *ACCC v Chats House Investments Pty Limited & Ors*,[68] where he held (at 258) that:

> The purpose served by s33V(1) is obvious. It is appropriate for the Court to be satisfied that any settlement or discontinuance of representative proceedings has been undertaken in the interests of group members as a whole, and not just in the interests of the applicant and the respondent. In my view, s33V proscribes not only complete settlement of proceedings without the approval of the Court, but also settlement of claims against a joint respondent, or settlement of any substantive claim against a respondent.

15.66 Similarly, section 33W allows representative parties to settle individual claims in whole or in part at any stage in the representative proceeding so long as the Court grants leave to do so.

15.67 Section 33P provides that if the Court does make an order that proceedings no longer continue as representative proceedings under sections 33L, 33M, or 33N, then the proceeding may be continued against the respondent by the representative party on his/her own behalf and group members may apply to be joined as applicants in the proceeding.

Judgment

15.68 Section 33Z sets out the powers of the Federal Court in relation to judgment:

> (1) The Court may, in determining a matter in a representative proceeding, do any one or more of the following:
>
>   (a) determine an issue of law;
>   (b) determine an issue of fact;
>   (c) make a declaration of liability;
>   (d) grant any equitable relief;

---

[67] For consideration of factors to be taken into account in granting approval, in particular where the group members include persons under a disability, see *Lopez v Star World Enterprises Pty Ltd* [1997] FCA 104.

[68] (1996) 71 FCR 250; (1996) 142 ALR 177. See also the comments of Finkelstein J in *Lopez v Star World Enterprises Pty Ltd (in liq)* [1999] ATPR 41-678.

(e) make an award of damages for group members, sub-group members or individual group members, being damages consisting of specified amounts or amounts worked out in such a manner as the Court specifies;
(f) award damages in an aggregate amount without specifying amounts awarded in respect of individual group members;
(g) make such other order as the Court thinks just.

(2) In making an order for an award of damages, the Court must make provision for the payment or distribution of the money to the group members entitled.

(3) Subject to section 33V, the Court is not to make an award of damages under paragraph (1)(f) unless a reasonably accurate assessment can be made of the total amount to which group members will be entitled under the judgment.

(4) Where the Court has made an order for the award of damages, the Court may give such directions (if any) as it thinks just in relation to:

(a) the manner in which a group member is to establish his or her entitlement to share in the damages; and
(b) the manner in which any dispute regarding the entitlement of a group member to share in the damages is to be determined.

15.69 As has already been noted, section 33ZB provides that a judgment binds all the parties to the proceeding unless they opted out under section 33J.

15.70 The Federal Court considered the effect of section 33Z in *ACCC v Golden Sphere International Inc & Ors*,[69] a case in which the applicant, the ACCC, amended its original application to seek relief as a representative party pursuant to Part IVA of the FCA, on behalf of a class of persons who had lost money as a result of participating in a pyramid selling scheme. O'Loughlin J held that the FCA does not require each and every group member to give evidence about their loss and damage. Rather, he held that section 33Z(1) gives the Court 'wide discretionary powers to fix awards of damages consistent with the circumstances of a particular action' and that 'the group who may ultimately enjoy the benefit of a judgment and an award of damages will most likely be indeterminate at the time of judgment'.

15.71 The Federal Court considered the operation of section 33ZB in *Jenkins v NZI Securities Australia Ltd & Ors*,[70] and held, in setting aside the declaration made at first instance, that:

> In our view the direction to make a declaratory order, even if otherwise to be supported despite the applicability of the reasoning in the cases discussed above, will miscarry if there is failure to consider its impact upon the group members whose substantive rights will be bound by it. One purpose of s 33ZB is to make it plain on the face of the record that such matters have entered into the decision-making process leading to the grant of a declaratory order.

---

[69] (1998) 83 FCR 424; [1998] ATPR 41-638.
[70] (1994) 52 FCR 572; (1994) 124 ALR 605.

However, even though the Federal Court must consider the impact of any judgment on all group members, not all group members will necessarily receive the same relief:

> Nothing in Part IVA assimilates all represented persons so that because some only apply for specific relief, all others are deemed to have applied for that relief.[71]

Costs

In Australia, the general rule is that costs follow the event. The expression 'costs' includes both the lawyers' professional fees and out of pocket expenses, referred to as 'disbursements'.

In the case of representative proceedings, the situation is more complicated since the unsuccessful representative applicant must bear the costs of both sides: in the absence of an agreement between group members to share the costs, the representative must pay personally. A costs order cannot be made against group members.

The problem of costs was discussed in *Woodlands & Anor v Permanent Trustee Co Ltd & Ors*:[72]

> The problem that has arisen in this case comes as no surprise to me. It is a problem inherent in representative proceedings. In a nutshell, the problem is that a representative party is exposed to the risk of an order to pay the costs of a respondent or respondents (the amount of which will usually be increased by the very fact that the proceeding is a representative one), without gaining any personal benefit from the representative role. So there is little or no incentive for a person to act as a representative party. Unless the person's potential costs are covered by someone else, there is a positive disincentive to taking that course.

From the applicants' perspective, the obvious answer is to put up a 'person of straw' or person without assets as the representative applicant. If the case fails, there will be nothing for the respondent to pursue. When this occurs in traditional proceedings, the defendant may move for security for costs. However, in the case of representative proceedings, the Federal Court has been reluctant to place any barriers in the path of the commencement of representative actions and hence will not order security for costs as readily as in individual actions.[73]

---

[71] *Harjanto v Minister for Immigration & Multicultural Affairs* (1998) 88 FCR 411.
[72] (1995) 58 FCR 139.
[73] In *Woodlands & Anor v Permanent Trustee Co Ltd & Ors* (1995) 58 FCR 139, Wilcox J rejected the application for security for costs, stating that 'it be particularly unfortunate if that factor caused the abandonment of litigation that made claims having the potential, if successful, to benefit many thousands of people, most of them likely to be of limited means'. See also *Ryan v Great Lakes Council and Others* (1998) 154 ALR 584 and *Woodhouse v McPhee* (1998) 80 FCR 529, as discussed in K Howard and J Kellam, 'Ryan v Great Lakes Council' (1999) 10 *Australian Product Liability Reporter* 81, 82.

D. Representative Actions by the Australian Competition and Consumer Commission

15.77 Historically, the promotion or support of litigation by a third party with no direct concern in the case has constituted the tort of maintenance in Australia. Over time this rule has been relaxed to take into account the reality that few individual litigants bring or defend suits now without the backing of an insurer, union, or some other organisation with a legitimate interest.

15.78 The Trade Practices Act 1974 (Cth) (TPA) makes provision for the commencement of representative actions by the ACCC. Under section 87(1B) of the TPA, where a person has contravened a provision of Part V, for example, a breach of section 52 (which prohibits misleading or deceptive conduct by a corporation), the ACCC may make an application for relief on behalf of those who have suffered or who are likely to suffer loss or damage as a result of the contravening conduct. The ACCC may only make such an application with the prior written consent of the persons on whose behalf the application is made. This means in effect that the ACCC is not entitled to pursue a representative action on behalf of a general class of aggrieved persons but only on behalf of those who have been identified and who have consented to the action.

15.79 The ACCC is given a similar power under section 75AQ(1) to bring an action in reliance upon the strict liability regime on behalf of persons who have suffered loss as a result of a defective product. Section 75AQ(2) imposes the same limitation of prior written consent. To date, just one decision has been reported concerning a representative action by the ACCC[74] under the product liability provision of the TPA. Nevertheless, the potential remains for the ACCC to bring a representative suit to clarify contentious areas of law or in difficult cases.

E. Conclusion

15.80 Multi-party actions are a burgeoning area of practice in Australia. After a slow start prior to the mid-1990s, representative proceedings or class actions are becoming a hallmark of the Australian litigation landscape, particularly in the financial services, product liability, and toxic tort areas. The past two years have seen an extraordinary growth in the figures for commencement of class actions, in particular involving product claims. Some of these have been linked to litigation that has its origins in other countries, for example, breast implants, the fen-phen litigation, and tobacco. Others have involved purely local issues, such as claims

---

[74] *Australian Competition and Consumer Commission v Glendale Chemical Products Pty Ltd* (1998) 40 IPR 619; [1998] ATPR 41-632.

E. Conclusion

arising out of the contamination of Sydney's water supply by *giardia* and *cryptosporidium* or contaminated food products.

Perhaps the main purpose of Part IVA of the FCA is to deal efficiently with the situation where a large number of persons wish to bring a claim against a respondent and the damages sought by each claimant are large enough to justify an individual action. In this sense, its aim is to ensure that groups of persons are able to obtain redress more cheaply and efficiently than would be the case with individual actions.[75]

15.81

Increasingly, Australian courts are grappling with how individual cases can best be gathered in a class action for efficient handling. The US experience is that common issues must predominate over individual issues for class actions to be certified. The approach taken by Part IVA is different—the common issues are determined at a common hearing and then the individual issues are separated for individual determination, either through the sub-group procedure or individually. A representative proceeding will only be abandoned if it does not prove an efficient and effective means of dealing with the claims of group members. In this respect, the Australian approach is similar to the new English rule.

15.82

When the first class actions came before the Federal Court, the decisions considering the new law and procedure appeared to demonstrate a reluctance on the part of the Court to limit the scope of legislation. Classes were defined in the broadest of terms and actions were allowed to continue as class actions notwithstanding what many saw as only tenuous common issues. However, more recently the Federal Court has become more active in obliging plaintiffs to restrict the scope of their claims and plead their allegations with greater precision. At the end of the day, it is a question of balance and fairness. However, fairness is a 'two-way' concept which must include fairness for defendants as well as plaintiffs.

15.83

---

[75] Second Reading Speech to FCA, *Hansard*, at 3174 (14 Nov 1991).

APPENDIX

Federal Court of Australia Act 1976 (Cth)

PART IVA—REPRESENTATIVE PROCEEDINGS

Division 1—Preliminary

33A Interpretation
33B Application

Division 2—Commencement of representative proceeding

33C Commencement of proceeding
33D Standing
33E Is consent required to be a group member?
33F Persons under disability
33G Representative proceeding not to be commenced in certain circumstances
33H Originating process
33J Right of group member to opt out
33K Causes of action accruing after commencement of representative proceeding
33L Situation where fewer than 7 group members
33M Cost of distributing money etc excessive
33N Order that proceeding not continue as representative proceeding where costs excessive etc
33P Consequences of order that proceeding not continue under this Part
33Q Determination of issues where not all issues are common
33R Individual issues
33S Directions relating to commencement of further proceedings
33T Adequacy of representation
33U Stay of execution in certain circumstances
33V Settlement and discontinuance—representative proceeding
33W Settlement of individual claim of representative party

Division 3—Notices

33X Notice to be given of certain matters
33Y Notices—ancillary provisions

Division 4—Judgment etc

33Z Judgment—powers of the Court
33ZA Constitution etc of fund
33ZB Effect of judgment

Division 5—Appeals

33ZC Appeals to the Court
33ZD Appeals to the High Court—extended operation of sections 33ZC and 33ZF

Appendix

Division 6—Miscellaneous

33ZE Suspension of limitation periods
33ZF General power of Court to make orders
33ZG Saving of rights, powers etc
33ZH Special provision relating to claims under Part VI of the Trade Practices Act 1974
33ZJ Reimbursement of representative party's costs

Division 1—Preliminary

33A Interpretation

In this Part, unless the contrary intention appears:
group member means a member of a group of persons on whose behalf a representative proceeding has been commenced;
representative party means a person who commences a representative proceeding;
representative proceeding means a proceeding commenced under section 33C;
respondent means a person against whom relief is sought in a representative proceeding;
sub-group member means a person included in a sub-group established under section 33Q;
sub-group representative party means a person appointed to be a sub-group representative party under section 33Q.

33B Application

A proceeding may only be brought under this Part in respect of a cause of action arising after the commencement of the *Federal Court of Australia Amendment Act* 1991.

Division 2—Commencement of Representative Proceeding

33C Commencement of proceeding

(1) Subject to this Part, where:
  (a) 7 or more persons have claims against the same person; and
  (b) the claims of all those persons are in respect of, or arise out of, the same, similar or related circumstances; and
  (c) the claims of all those persons give rise to a substantial common issue of law or fact;

a proceeding may be commenced by one or more of those persons as representing some or all of them.

(2) A representative proceeding may be commenced:
  (a) whether or not the relief sought:
    (i) is, or includes, equitable relief; or
    (ii) consists of, or includes, damages; or
    (iii) includes claims for damages that would require individual assessment; or
    (iv) is the same for each person represented; and
  (b) whether or not the proceeding:
    (i) is concerned with separate contracts or transactions between the respondent in the proceeding and individual group members; or
    (ii) involves separate acts or omissions of the respondent done or omitted to be done in relation to individual group members.

33D Standing

(1) A person referred to in paragraph 33C(1)(a) who has a sufficient interest to commence a proceeding on his or her own behalf against another person has a sufficient interest to commence a representative proceeding against that other person on behalf of other persons referred to in that paragraph.

(2) Where a person has commenced a representative proceeding, the person retains a sufficient interest:
  (a) to continue that proceeding; and
  (b) to bring an appeal from a judgment in that proceeding;
even though the person ceases to have a claim against the respondent.

33E Is consent required to be a group member?

(1) The consent of a person to be a group member in a representative proceeding is not required unless subsection (2) applies to the person.
(2) None of the following persons is a group member in a representative proceeding unless the person gives written consent to being so:
  (a) the Commonwealth, a State or a Territory;
  (b) a Minister or a Minister of a State or Territory;
  (c) a body corporate established for a public purpose by a law of the Commonwealth, of a State or of a Territory, other than an incorporated company or association; or
  (d) an officer of the Commonwealth, of a State or of a Territory, in his or her capacity as such an officer.

33F Persons under disability

(1) It is not necessary for a person under disability to have a next friend or committee merely in order to be a group member.
(2) A group member who is under disability may only take a step in the representative proceeding, or conduct part of the proceeding, by his or her next friend or committee, as the case requires.

33G Representative proceeding not to be commenced in certain circumstances

A representative proceeding may not be commenced if the proceeding would be concerned only with claims in respect of which the Court has jurisdiction solely by virtue of the *Jurisdiction of Courts (Cross-vesting) Act* 1987 or a corresponding law of a State or Territory.

33H Originating process

(1) An application commencing a representative proceeding, or a document filed in support of such an application, must, in addition to any other matters required to be included:
  (a) describe or otherwise identify the group members to whom the proceeding relates; and
  (b) specify the nature of the claims made on behalf of the group members and the relief claimed; and
  (c) specify the questions of law or fact common to the claims of the group members.
(2) In describing or otherwise identifying group members for the purposes of subsection (1), it is not necessary to name, or specify the number of, the group members.

33J Right of group member to opt out

(1) The Court must fix a date before which a group member may opt out of a representative proceeding.
(2) A group member may opt out of the representative proceeding by written notice given under the Rules of Court before the date so fixed.
(3) The Court, on the application of a group member, the representative party or the respondent in the proceeding, may fix another date so as to extend the period during which a group member may opt out of the representative proceeding.
(4) Except with the leave of the Court, the hearing of a representative proceeding must not commence earlier than the date before which a group member may opt out of the proceeding.

33K Causes of action accruing after commencement of representative proceeding

(1) The Court may at any stage of a representative proceeding, on application made by the representative party, give leave to amend the application commencing the representative proceeding so as to alter the description of the group.
(2) The description of the group may be altered so as to include a person:
   (a) whose cause of action accrued after the commencement of the representative proceeding but before such date as the Court fixes when giving leave; and
   (b) who would have been included in the group, or with the consent of the person would have been included in the group, if the cause of action had accrued before the commencement of the proceeding.
(3) The date mentioned in paragraph (2)(a) may be the date on which leave is given or another date before or after that date.
(4) Where the Court gives leave under subsection (1), it may also make any other orders it thinks just, including an order relating to the giving of notice to persons who, as a result of the amendment, will be included in the group and the date before which such persons may opt out of the proceeding.

33L Situation where fewer than 7 group members

If, at any stage of a representative proceeding, it appears likely to the Court that there are fewer than 7 group members, the Court may, on such conditions (if any) as it thinks fit:
   (a) order that the proceeding continue under this Part; or
   (b) order that the proceeding no longer continue under this Part.

33M Cost of distributing money etc excessive

Where:
(a) the relief claimed in a representative proceeding is or includes payment of money to group members (otherwise than in respect of costs); and
(b) on application by the respondent, the Court concludes that it is likely that, if judgment were to be given in favour of the representative party, the cost to the respondent of identifying the group members and distributing to them the amounts ordered to be paid to them would be excessive having regard to the likely total of those amounts;

the Court may, by order:
(c) direct that the proceeding no longer continue under this Part; or
(d) stay the proceeding so far as it relates to relief of the kind mentioned in paragraph (a).

33N Order that proceeding not continue as representative proceeding where costs excessive etc

(1) The Court may, on application by the respondent or of its own motion, order that a proceeding no longer continue under this Part where it is satisfied that it is in the interests of justice to do so because:
   (a) the costs that would be incurred if the proceeding were to continue as a representative proceeding are likely to exceed the costs that would be incurred if each group member conducted a separate proceeding; or
   (b) all the relief sought can be obtained by means of a proceeding other than a representative proceeding under this Part; or
   (c) the representative proceeding will not provide an efficient and effective means of dealing with the claims of group members; or
   (d) it is otherwise inappropriate that the claims be pursued by means of a representative proceeding.

(2) If the Court dismisses an application under this section, the Court may order that no further application under this section be made by the respondent except with the leave of the Court.
(3) Leave for the purposes of subsection (2) may be granted subject to such conditions as to costs as the Court considers just.

33P Consequences of order that proceeding not continue under this Part

Where the Court makes an order under section 33L, 33M or 33N that a proceeding no longer continue under this Part:
(a) the proceeding may be continued as a proceeding by the representative party on his or her own behalf against the respondent; and
(b) on the application of a person who was a group member for the purposes of the proceeding, the Court may order that the person be joined as an applicant in the proceeding.

33Q Determination of issues where not all issues are common

(1) If it appears to the Court that determination of the issue or issues common to all group members will not finally determine the claims of all group members, the Court may give directions in relation to the determination of the remaining issues.
(2) In the case of issues common to the claims of some only of the group members, the directions given by the Court may include directions establishing a sub-group consisting of those group members and appointing a person to be the sub-group representative party on behalf of the sub-group members.
(3) Where the Court appoints a person other than the representative party to be a sub-group representative party, that person, and not the representative party, is liable for costs associated with the determination of the issue or issues common to the sub-group members.

33R Individual issues

(1) In giving directions under section 33Q, the Court may permit an individual group member to appear in the proceeding for the purpose of determining an issue that relates only to the claims of that member.
(2) In such a case, the individual group member, and not the representative party, is liable for costs associated with the determination of the issue.

33S Directions relating to commencement of further proceedings

Where an issue cannot properly or conveniently be dealt with under section 33Q or 33R, the Court may:
(a) if the issue concerns only the claim of a particular member—give directions relating to the commencement and conduct of a separate proceeding by that member; or
(b) if the issue is common to the claims of all members of a sub-group—give directions relating to the commencement and conduct of a representative proceeding in relation to the claims of those members.

33T Adequacy of representation

(1) If, on an application by a group member, it appears to the Court that a representative party is not able adequately to represent the interests of the group members, the Court may substitute another group member as representative party and may make such other orders as it thinks fit.
(2) If, on an application by a sub-group member, it appears to the Court that a sub-group representative party is not able adequately to represent the interests of the sub-group members, the Court may substitute another person as sub-group representative party and may make such other orders as it thinks fit.

33U Stay of execution in certain circumstances

Where a respondent in a representative proceeding commences a proceeding in the Court against a group member, the Court may order a stay of execution in respect of any relief awarded to the group member in the representative proceeding until the other proceeding is determined.

33V Settlement and discontinuance—representative proceeding

(1) A representative proceeding may not be settled or discontinued without the approval of the Court.
(2) If the Court gives such an approval, it may make such orders as are just with respect to the distribution of any money paid under a settlement or paid into the Court.

33W Settlement of individual claim of representative party

(1) A representative party may, with leave of the Court, settle his or her individual claim in whole or in part at any stage of the representative proceeding.
(2) A representative party who is seeking leave to settle, or who has settled, his or her individual claim may, with leave of the Court, withdraw as representative party.
(3) Where a person has sought leave to withdraw as representative party under subsection (2), the Court may, on the application of a group member, make an order for the substitution of another group member as representative party and may make such other orders as it thinks fit.
(4) Before granting a person leave to withdraw as a representative party:
 (a) the Court must be satisfied that notice of the application has been given to group members in accordance with subsection 33X (1) and in sufficient time for them to apply to have another person substituted as the representative party; and
 (b) any application for the substitution of another group member as a representative party has been determined.
(5) The Court may grant leave to a person to withdraw as representative party subject to such conditions as to costs as the Court considers just.

DIVISION 3—NOTICES

33X Notice to be given of certain matters

(1) Notice must be given to group members of the following matters in relation to a representative proceeding:
 (a) the commencement of the proceeding and the right of the group members to opt out of the proceeding before a specified date, being the date fixed under subsection 33J(1);
 (b) an application by the respondent in the proceeding for the dismissal of the proceeding on the ground of want of prosecution;
 (c) an application by a representative party seeking leave to withdraw under section 33W as representative party.
(2) The Court may dispense with compliance with any or all of the requirements of subsection (1) where the relief sought in a proceeding does not include any claim for damages.
(3) If the Court so orders, notice must be given to group members of the bringing into Court of money in answer to a cause of action on which a claim in the representative proceeding is founded.
(4) Unless the Court is satisfied that it is just to do so, an application for approval of a settlement under section 33V must not be determined unless notice has been given to group members.
(5) The Court may, at any stage, order that notice of any matter be given to a group member or group members.
(6) Notice under this section must be given as soon as practicable after the happening of the event to which the notice relates.

33Y Notices—ancillary provisions

(1) This section is concerned with notices under section 33X.

(2) The form and content of a notice must be as approved by the Court.
(3) The Court must, by order, specify:
   (a) who is to give the notice; and
   (b) the way in which the notice is to be given;

and the order may include provision:
   (c) directing a party to provide information relevant to the giving of the notice; and
   (d) relating to the costs of notice.

(4) An order under subsection (3) may require that notice be given by means of press advertisement, radio or television broadcast, or by any other means.
(5) The Court may not order that notice be given personally to each group member unless it is satisfied that it is reasonably practicable, and not unduly expensive, to do so.
(6) A notice that concerns a matter for which the Court's leave or approval is required must specify the period within which a group member or other person may apply to the Court, or take some other step, in relation to the matter.
(7) A notice that includes or concerns conditions must specify the conditions and the period, if any, for compliance.
(8) The failure of a group member to receive or respond to a notice does not affect a step taken, an order made, or a judgment given, in a proceeding.

Division 4—Judgment etc

33Z Judgment—powers of the Court

(1) The Court may, in determining a matter in a representative proceeding, do any one or more of the following:
   (a) determine an issue of law;
   (b) determine an issue of fact;
   (c) make a declaration of liability;
   (d) grant any equitable relief;
   (e) make an award of damages for group members, sub-group members or individual group members, being damages consisting of specified amounts or amounts worked out in such manner as the Court specifies;
   (f) award damages in an aggregate amount without specifying amounts awarded in respect of individual group members;
   (g) make such other order as the Court thinks just.

(2) In making an order for an award of damages, the Court must make provision for the payment or distribution of the money to the group members entitled.
(3) Subject to section 33V, the Court is not to make an award of damages under paragraph (1)(f) unless a reasonably accurate assessment can be made of the total amount to which group members will be entitled under the judgment.
(4) Where the Court has made an order for the award of damages, the Court may give such directions (if any) as it thinks just in relation to:
   (a) the manner in which a group member is to establish his or her entitlement to share in the damages; and
   (b) the manner in which any dispute regarding the entitlement of a group member to share in the damages is to be determined.

33ZA Constitution etc of fund

(1) Without limiting the operation of subsection 33Z(2), in making provision for the distribution of money to group members, the Court may provide for:
   (a) the constitution and administration of a fund consisting of the money to be distributed; and

(b) either:
  (i) the payment by the respondent of a fixed sum of money into the fund; or
  (ii) the payment by the respondent into the fund of such instalments, on such terms, as the Court directs to meet the claims of group members; and
(c) entitlements to interest earned on the money in the fund.
(2) The costs of administering a fund are to be borne by the fund, or by the respondent in the representative proceeding, as the Court directs.
(3) Where the Court orders the constitution of a fund mentioned in subsection (1), the order must:
  (a) require notice to be given to group members in such manner as is specified in the order; and
  (b) specify the manner in which a group member is to make a claim for payment out of the fund and establish his or her entitlement to the payment; and
  (c) specify a day (which is 6 months or more after the day on which the order is made) on or before which the group members are to make a claim for payment out of the fund; and
  (d) make provision in relation to the day before which the fund is to be distributed to group members who have established an entitlement to be paid out of the fund.
(4) The Court may allow a group member to make a claim after the day fixed under paragraph (3)(c) if:
  (a) the fund has not already been fully distributed; and
  (b) it is just to do so.
(5) On application by the respondent in the representative proceeding after the day fixed under paragraph (3)(d), the Court may make such orders as are just for the payment from the fund to the respondent of the money remaining in the fund.

33ZB Effect of judgment

A judgment given in a representative proceeding:
(a) must describe or otherwise identify the group members who will be affected by it; and
(b) binds all such persons other than any person who has opted out of the proceeding under section 33J.

Division 5—Appeals

33ZC Appeals to the Court

(1) The following appeals under Division 2 of Part III from a judgment of the Court in a representative proceeding may themselves be brought as representative proceedings:
  (a) an appeal by the representative party on behalf of group members and in respect of the judgment to the extent that it relates to issues common to the claims of group members;
  (b) an appeal by a sub-group representative party on behalf of sub-group members in respect of the judgment to the extent that it relates to issues common to the claims of sub-group members.
(2) The parties to an appeal referred to in paragraph (1)(a) are the representative party, as the representative of the group members, and the respondent.
(3) The parties to an appeal referred to in paragraph (1)(b) are the sub-group representative party, as the representative of the sub-group members, and the respondent.
(4) On an appeal by the respondent in a representative proceeding, other than an appeal referred to in subsection (5), the parties to the appeal are:
  (a) in the case of an appeal in respect of the judgment generally—the respondent and the representative party as the representative of the group members; and
  (b) in the case of an appeal in respect of the judgment to the extent that it relates to issues common to the claims of sub-group members—the respondent and the sub-group representative party as the representative of the sub-group members.

(5) The parties to an appeal in respect of the determination of an issue that relates only to a claim of an individual group member are that group member and the respondent.
(6) If the representative party or the sub-group representative party does not bring an appeal within the time provided for instituting appeals, another member of the group or sub-group may, within a further 21 days, bring an appeal as representing the group members or sub-group members, as the case may be.
(7) Where an appeal is brought from a judgment of the Court in a representative proceeding, the Court may direct that notice of the appeal be given to such person or persons, and in such manner, as the Court thinks appropriate.
(8) Section 33J does not apply to an appeal proceeding.
(9) The notice instituting an appeal in relation to issues that are common to the claims of group members or sub-group members must describe or otherwise identify the group members or sub-group members, as the case may be, but need not specify the names or number of those members.

33ZD Appeals to the High Court—extended operation of sections 33ZC and 33ZF

(1) Sections 33ZC and 33ZF apply in relation to appeals to the High Court from judgments of the Court in representative proceedings in the same way as they apply to appeals to the Court from such judgments.
(2) Nothing in subsection (1) limits the operation of section 33 whether in relation to appeals from judgments of the Court in representative proceedings or otherwise.

Division 6—Miscellaneous

33ZE Suspension of limitation periods

(1) Upon the commencement of a representative proceeding, the running of any limitation period that applies to the claim of a group member to which the proceeding relates is suspended.
(2) The limitation period does not begin to run again unless either the member opts out of the proceeding under section 33J or the proceeding, and any appeals arising from the proceeding, are determined without finally disposing of the group member's claim.

33ZF General power of Court to make orders

(1) In any proceeding (including an appeal) conducted under this Part, the Court may, of its own motion or on application by a party or a group member, make any order the Court thinks appropriate or necessary to ensure that justice is done in the proceeding.
(2) Subsection (1) does not limit the operation of section 22.

33ZG Saving of rights, powers etc

Except as otherwise provided by this Part, nothing in this Part affects:
(a) the commencement or continuance of any action of a representative character commenced otherwise than under this Part; or
(b) the Court's powers under provisions other than this Part, for example, its powers in relation to a proceeding in which no reasonable cause of action is disclosed or that is oppressive, vexatious, frivolous or an abuse of the process of the Court; or
(c) the operation of any law relating to:
　(i) vexatious litigants (however described); or
　(ii) proceedings of a representative character; or
　(iii) joinder of parties; or
　(iv) consolidation of proceedings; or
　(v) security for costs.

Appendix

33ZH Special provision relating to claims under Part VI of the Trade Practices Act 1974

(1) For the purposes of subsection 87 (1) of the *Trade Practices Act* 1974, a group member in a representative proceeding is to be taken to be a party to the proceeding.

(2) An application under subsection 87 (1A) of the *Trade Practices Act* 1974 by a representative party in a representative proceeding is to be taken to be an application by the representative party and all the group members.

33ZJ Reimbursement of representative party's costs

(1) Where the Court has made an award of damages in a representative proceeding, the representative party or a sub-group representative party, or a person who has been such a party, may apply to the Court for an order under this section.

(2) If, on an application under this section, the Court is satisfied that the costs reasonably incurred in relation to the representative proceeding by the person making the application are likely to exceed the costs recoverable by the person from the respondent, the Court may order that an amount equal to the whole or a part of the excess be paid to that person out of the damages awarded.

(3) On an application under this section, the Court may also make any other order it thinks just.

Part V

CASE STUDIES

Introduction to Case Studies	303
Pertussis Vaccine Litigation	319
Opren Litigation	327
HIV Haemophilia Litigation	341
Gravigard IUD	349
Myodil Litigation	357
Benzodiazepine Litigation	369
Lloyd's Litigation	393
Reay v BNFL; *Hope v BNFL*	405
Manufacturing Operations: Mixed Claims: *B & ors v X Co*; *D & ors v X Co*	415
Docklands Nuisance Class Actions	425
Lockton Litigation	437
Creutzfeldt-Jakob Disease (Human Growth Hormone) Litigation	445
British Coal: Vibration White Finger Litigation	455
British Coal: Respiratory Disease Litigation	465
Norplant Litigation	475
Tobacco Litigation: 1992–1999	489

16

INTRODUCTION TO CASE STUDIES

A. The Historical Context	16.01	D. The Difficulties in Succeeding in a Pharmaceutical Claim	16.16
B. The Funding Background: Legal Aid	16.05	E. The Future of Group Litigation	16.22
C. Underlying Success Rates	16.10		

This Part contains case histories of many of the major multi-party actions which lawyers and the courts have had to manage since the phenomenon emerged in its modern form in the 1980s. The cases which have been included here have been chosen not only as major multi-party cases but also to represent some range of subject matter. The majority of complex cases have involved product liability claims, principally medicines (a list of those known to the editor is at Table 16.1), but there have been environmental cases (Sellafield; *X Co*; Docklands) and financial cases (Lockton, Lloyd's). The total number of claimants and outcome of the case histories is at Table 16.2. Various points need to be made in order to understand the case histories.

A. The Historical Context

16.01 It must be emphasised that particular management techniques were used in the circumstances of a particular case at a particular time. This may mean that an attempt to impose a technique on another case may be inappropriate because of the differences in circumstances. One reason for this is that an understanding of the advantages and disadvantages of particular techniques was developing and being debated as time progressed, so that with hindsight different approaches might now appear to have been better. A second reason is that these cases occurred in a legal environment that was different in two major respects from today.

16.02 First, funding of litigation was influenced by the legal aid system. Conditional fee agreements (CFAs) were only introduced towards the end of this period, and are discussed in detail in chapter 11. The approach required under the rules relating to the Community Legal Service and its Funding Code did not exist. Secondly, no

Table 16.1: Multi-claimant product cases and alleged damage

1960s
- Thalidomide—phocomelia (UK, Germany)

1970s
- Practolol—eye and other defects (UK)
- Hormone pregnancy tests—teratogenic effects (UK)

1980s
- Opren (benoxaprofen)—liver damage, photosensitivity (UK)
- Pertussis vaccine—neurological problems (UK, Ireland)
- Blood products—HIV in haemophiliacs (eg UK, Ireland, Italy, Germany, Denmark)
- Contrast media—arachnoiditis (UK, Australia)
- Benzodiazepines—dependence (UK, Sweden, Ireland, Australia)
- IUCDs—PID and infertility (UK, Australia, New Zealand)

1990s
- Human insulin—hypoglycaemic unawareness (UK)
- DES—carcinoma (UK, Netherlands)
- Sheep dip—neurological problems (UK)
- Baby drinks—dental caries (UK, Germany)
- Fluoride products—dental damage (UK)
- Human Growth Hormone: CJD (UK)
- Vaccines (MMR)—neurological problems (UK)
- Injectable hormonal contraception (UK)
- Injectable anti-inflammatory steroids—arachnoiditis after epidural use (UK)
- Anti-malaria tablets (Lariam)—psychiatric problems (UK)
- Oral contraceptives—thrombo-embolic disorders (UK)
- Pancreatic enzymes—fibrosing colonopathy (UK)
- Contraceptive implant (Norplant)—various (UK)
- Breast implants—auto-immune disease (UK and Australia)
- Pesticides—(benomyl)- anophthalmia and microphthalmia (UK)
- Tobacco—lung cancer (UK)
- BSE—new variant Creutzfeldt-Jakob Disease (UK)
- Persona—pregnancy (UK)
- LSD—psychiatric problems
- Oral steroids—side effects
- Hormone replacement—venous thromboembolism
- Minocin—acne

Table 16.2 Outcome of Case Studies

Product liability cases

Product	Alleged defect	Total number of claimants	Outcome
DTP (whooping cough) vaccine	Brain damage	200	Cases collapsed in 1988 after a preliminary court ruling in a test case that the product was not capable of causing the damage
Benoxaprofen (Opren)	Hepatic damage and other adverse effects	2,000	1,200 cases settled with total payment reported to be £2,275,000 and £4m costs in 1987: most of further 587 cases ruled barred for limitation in 1992
Blood products	Transmission of HIV virus	1,200	Settled by the Department of Health in 1990 with the establishment of a £42m fund
Contrast media (Myodil)	Arachnoiditis	4,000	Settled in 1995 with £7m divided amongst the 426 then continuing plaintiffs
Benzodiazepine tranquillisers	Dependency	17,000	Case collapsed in 1994 when the Legal Aid Board withdrew funding after spending £30–35m in legal and expert costs: defendants made no payments to any plaintiffs
Intrauterine device (Gravigard)	Infection and infertility	100	Cases were successively discontinued or withdrawn until legal aid was withdrawn from the remaining 17 cases in 1996 after some 8 years' funding. Defendants made no payments
Norplant	Difficult extraction	324	All cases discontinued in 1999 against the manufacturer after legal aid was withdrawn from the claimants just before trial on the advice of their counsel
Human growth hormone	Viral contamination	98+	As at end of 1999, 32 cases with Creutzfeldt-Jakob disease had been compensated and 45 out of a further 111 with claims for mental injury
Tobacco	Lung cancer	50	All claims discontinued in 1999 after 9 cases failed on a preliminary issue on limitation

Table 16.2 continued

Other personal injury cases

Product	Alleged defect	Total number of claimants	Outcome
British Coal	Respiratory disease	75,000	Following judgment for the plaintiffs on generic issues in 1998, a scheme was agreed for settlement of individual claims
British Coal	Vibration White Finger	50,000+	Following judgments for the plaintiffs in lead cases on breach of duty and causation, a settlement scheme was established in 1999 involving total payments estimated at £500 million

Financial cases

Case	Issue	Total number of claimants	Outcome
Lockton	Misrepresentation in BES prospectuses	200	Settled before trial
Lloyd's	Non-disclosure, misrepresentation, etc	12,300	Settlement scheme agreed 1996—£3.2 billion

Environmental cases

Case	Issue	Total number of claimants	Outcome
X Co	Atmospheric release/carcinoma/nuisance	39	Settled before trial
Sellafield	Leukaemia in children	2+40	Cases failed to prove generic causation at trial

rule of court explicitly dealt with multi-party actions, and none of these cases were subject to either the principles or specifics of the Civil Procedure Rules, or Rule 19.III, which they preceded.

16.03 The cases are arranged in roughly chronological order so that the emergence of a coherent approach to managing multi-party actions can be seen as it developed towards the system adopted in Rule 19.III and described in Parts I and II of this book. Despite these caveats, the case histories are nevertheless valuable as illustrations of the problems which arise in this type of litigation and some solutions which might, or might not, work. Some editorial comments have been added in an introduction to each case history in order to give a flavour to the background in which each case occurred and the managerial issues which arose, but these are limited in order not to hinder the imagination of readers who may wish to develop their own ideas on what might work in future.

16.04 It should also be said that the following case histories are not presented as complete records of the cases. Their focus is on the managerial aspects rather than on the issues of substantive law. Fascinating as the underlying facts and legal issues may be, complete presentation of these would detract from the managerial issues and in some cases be inordinately long.

B. The Funding Background: Legal Aid

16.05 As stated above, almost all of the claimants in the cases discussed here, apart from part of the tobacco case, were funded by legal aid.[1] Indeed, it may be argued that they were only possible because of the particular arrangements of the legal aid system.[2] This is particularly true of the product liability cases, in which up to 98 per

---

[1] See Legal Aid Act 1988; Civil Legal Aid (General) Regulations 1989; *Legal Aid Handbook* (Annual editions).

[2] In support of this, it can be said that the existence of a funding mechanism which reduces claimants' payment obligations to pay their own lawyers and risk of paying successful opponents' costs, coupled with the financial incentives for claimants' lawyers, are major factors why multi-party actions have developed in some jurisdictions of the world (notably North America and the UK) but not in others (such as other EU states). See *Product Liability Rules in OECD Countries* (OECD, 1995); J Stapleton, 'Products Liability in the United Kingdom: The Myths of Reform' (1999) 34 Tex Int LJ 45, 66. During the 1980s and 1990s availability and expenditure on legal aid has been greater in the UK than other European jurisdictions. See M Cousins, 'The Politics of Legal Aid—A Solution in Search of a Problem' [1994] CJQ 111. E Blankenburg, 'Access to Justice and Alternatives to Courts: European Procedural Justice Compared' [1995] CJQ 176; T Goriely, *Legal Aid Delivery Systems: Which offer the best value for money in mass casework? A summary of international experience*, Lord Chancellor's Department Research Series No 10/97 (Dec 1997); A Paterson, 'Financing Legal Services: A Comparative Perspective' in DL Carey Miller and P Beaumont (eds), *The Option of Litigating in Europe* (UK National Committee of Comparative Law, 1992). E Blankenburg, 'The Lawyers' Lobby and the Welfare State: The Political Economy of Legal Aid' in F Regan, A Paterson, T Goriely and D Fleming (eds), *The Transformation of Legal Aid* (OUP, 1999).

cent of claimants were funded by legal aid.[3] Until CFAs were introduced in the later 1990s, the principal feature of the major multi-party actions was that both the funding requirement and risk of an adverse costs order were almost entirely removed from those claimants who qualified for funding under the legal aid scheme. A claimant who had the benefit of legal aid funding would have to contribute either nothing or a limited contribution to his legal costs as the case progressed, and would be very unlikely to have to pay his opponent's legal costs if he lost.[4] This phenomenon was described as 'legal aid blackmail',[5] since the defendant would be unable to recover his costs if he won and was therefore in an adverse bargaining position and under pressure to settle even cases whose merits would not normally justify settlement, or to agree a settlement which was more favourable to the claimant than would normally be justified. This situation was widely criticised as unfair to the unassisted party and to the taxpayer who paid the costs if the case was lost.[6]

16.06 Legal aid began as a post-war welfare benefit[7] covering 80 per cent of the population on income grounds. Its scope expanded to the mid-1980s but then reached a crisis up to the mid-1990s, by which time eligibility had fallen to 48 per cent of households, due to growing numbers of litigants using the scheme and increases in the cost per case, which resulted in a rapid increase in overall and net costs.[8]

16.07 In the five years from 1985 to 1990, the number of civil legal aid certificates for non-matrimonial cases increased by 22 per cent, gross expenditure rose by 120 per cent to £153 million and net expenditure by 145 per cent to £76 million.[9] Over the same period, the average legal aid bill rose by 60 per cent from £950 to £1,526.

---

[3] Legal Aid Board, *Issues arising for the Legal Aid Board and the Lord Chancellor's Department from multi-party actions* (1994).

[4] The costs order would be made but subject to the restriction that it should not be enforced without leave of the court, which would only be granted where the defendant showed that he would otherwise suffer severe financial hardship: Legal Aid Act 1988, s 18(4). The Board contributed to the costs of only 158 successful unassisted defendants in 1994–5 and 186 in 1993–4.

[5] Lord Chancellor's Department, *Legal Aid: Targeting Need* (1995) Cm 2854; *Manley v Law Society* [1981] 1 All ER 401, 411; RS Jandoo and WA Harland, 'Legal Aid Blackmail' (27 Apr 1984) NLJ; Hansard, HC (series 6) vol 280, col 875 (2 July 1996).

[6] Lord Chancellor's Department, *Legal Aid: Targeting Need* (1995) Cmd 2854; General Council of the Bar, *Response to the Government's Green Paper: 'Legal Aid: Targeting Need'* (1995); the Bar called for a reversal of the position under s 17 of the Legal Aid Act 1988, so that there would be a presumption that an unsuccessful assisted person should be liable for the other party's costs but could be relieved by the court to the extent that he showed that it would not be reasonable for him to pay them having regard to all the circumstances, including the financial resources of the parties and their conduct in connection with the dispute. The Law Society accepted that when legal aid continued after it should have been terminated, it is unreasonable to leave a successful unassisted party out of pocket: The Law Society, *Better Justice Better Value* (1996).

[7] Legal Aid and Advice Act 1949.

[8] House of Commons Library Research Paper, *The Access to Justice Bill: Legal Aid* (1999) 99/33.

[9] Lord Chancellor's Department, *Review of Financial Conditions for Legal Aid: A Consultation Paper* (1991).

Introduction to Case Studies

In 1990, 36 million people, or 64 per cent of the population, were eligible on income grounds for non-matrimonial civil legal aid. For personal injury claims it was estimated that 38 million or 69 per cent of the population were eligible.[10] There was a sharp increase in legal aid in 1990–1. In the four years from 1990–1 to 1993–4, there was no change in GDP and total government expenditure increased by 12 per cent, but legal aid expenditure increased by 55 per cent. Of this increase, 74 per cent was accounted for by Civil Legal Aid, 11 per cent by Criminal Higher, 11 per cent by Green Form, and 5 per cent by the two Duty Solicitor schemes. For Civil Legal Aid within this period, total real spend increased by 91 per cent, unit cost by 51 per cent, and volume by 27 per cent. In 1993–4 expenditure on legal aid was *five* times the level in 1979–80 (in real terms as deflated by the Treasury GDP deflator). In contrast, total government expenditure had increased in that period by 29 per cent and GDP by 24 per cent.[11] From 1990 to 1997, the cost of civil and family legal aid tripled to £671 million. Perhaps most significantly, the average cost of a case increased by 53 per cent above inflation, and the number of people helped fell by almost 30 per cent.[12]

16.08 In interpreting this data, some have argued that the problem was a structural one over access to justice:[13] first, litigation costs were so high that many people could not afford them (only the very rich or the very poor who qualified for legal aid), secondly, that the risk of losing included the risk of paying opponents' costs, which would be not only high but unquantifiable in advance. The converse interpretation was that individuals who could not obtain legal aid did not sue because they did not consider the expenditure and risk of legal costs to be sufficient to justify the potential benefit which might be achieved by proceeding. Also, on this view, those cases which did proceed were often speculative, being brought by people for whom the legal system provided full support and who faced no risk. On this theory, the system was flawed in giving unconditional support to some, but correct in presenting risk for others, who took correct cost-benefit decisions.

16.09 Deficiencies in the legal system which restricted access to justice were addressed by the government in two ways. First, procedural reforms originally proposed by Lord Woolf[14] were introduced from April 1999 through the Civil Procedure Rules

---

[10] *Hansard*, HC (series 6) vol 191, cols 490–491W (22 May 1991).
[11] G Bevan, 'Has There Been Supplier-Induced Demand for Legal Aid?' [1994] CJQ 98.
[12] *Hansard*, HC (series 6) vol 307, col 1060 (4 Mar 1998); *Explanatory Notes: Access to Justice Act 1999* (The Stationery Office Limited, 1999).
[13] Lord Mackay of Clashfern when Lord Chancellor stressed that access to justice is not synonymous with access to lawyers and that 'whilst justice is priceless, it cannot be at any price. As with any other human endeavour the cost and benefits need to be considered . . . Affordability is the key to improved access to justice.' Speech by the Rt Hon Lord Mackay of Clashfern on 'Access to Justice' at the Royal Society of Arts, 27 July 1992.
[14] Lord Woolf, *Access to Justice: Interim Report* (1995) and *Final Report* (1996); Lord Chancellor's Department, *Access to Justice: The Way Forward* (1996); Lord Chancellor's Department, *Access to Justice: Judicial Case Management: The Fast Track and Multi Track: A Working Paper* (1997); Lord

1998 (CPR). These were aimed at making litigation costs lower, more predictable, more transparent, and more proportionate to the sums in dispute. Secondly, access to justice was extended from July 1995 and 1998 to those termed 'middle income not eligible for legal aid' (MINELAs) by the introduction of CFAs plus insurance policies to cover the costs risk.[15] For the implications of this for funding a multi-party action, see chapter 11.

C. Underlying Success Rates

16.10 Despite the apparent advantages enjoyed by claimants funded by legal aid, however, a number of major multi-party actions have not only failed but collapsed before trial, as appears from Table 16.2, frequently on the ground that they were not financially viable because the cost-benefit risk was unfavourable.

16.11 There has been much debate as to the reason for such pre-trial failures.[16] On the one hand, it has been said that the individual cases pursued have been weak or speculative.[17] It is argued that the cases were bound to fail and should not have been pursued at all. In these instances, it was said that there was a failure of the legal aid system, and those responsible for operating it, properly to scrutinise, screen, and weed out these cases sufficiently early. In particular, the following combination of factors has been suggested:[18]

- in permitting and encouraging lawyers to advertise, the system has been unable to regulate advertising of speculative claims which can result in a public perception that liability and compensation are already established.[19]

Chancellor's Department, *Access to Justice: Civil Procedure Rules about Costs: Consultation Paper* (1997); although a single procedural code for civil business, covering all courts, had been proposed in Lord Chancellor's Department, *Civil Justice Review: General Issues* (1988) recommendation 16; see also Lord Chancellor's Department, *Rights of Audience and Rights to Conduct Litigation in England and Wales: The Way Ahead* (1998).

[15] Lord Chancellor's Department, *Modernising Justice* (1988); Access to Justice Act 1999; *Explanatory Notes: Access to Justice Act 1999* (The Stationery Office Limited, 1999).

[16] See C Hodges, 'Factors influencing the incidence of multiple claims' [1999] JPIL 284.

[17] Lord Chancellor's Department, *Legal Aid: Targeting Need* (1995) Cm 2854, para 1.12; *Striking the Balance* (1996) Cm 3305; Law Society, *Ensuring Justice?* (1998).

[18] See AA Zuckerman, *Civil Justice in Crisis* (OUP, 1999) 37.

[19] This issue is discussed in ch 6 above. The quality of solicitors' advice was attacked by the Consumers' Association as being 'inadequate, incomplete or plain wrong': Consumers' Association, *Which?* (Oct 1997). The Law Society responded that this was based on a small survey of firms and 'a sideshow in the wider debate about legal services': SJ, 3 Oct 1997. Research has shown first, that claimants are primarily motivated by money and the proclivity to claim varies regionally: P Pleasance, S Maclean and A Morley, *Profiling Civil Litigation: The Case for Research* (Legal Aid Board Research Unit, 1996); and secondly, that the severity of a claimant's injuries is the most useful general predictor available which increases chance of success, costs, damages, and duration in personal injury cases: P Pleasance, 'The Hazards of Litigation: A Study of Legally Aided Personal Injury Claims' [1999] JPIL 34.

- the phenomenon of lawyer-led litigation.[20] The argument here is whether some claimants' lawyers are more motivated to encourage litigation out of which they can make money than with the objective rights and expectations of their clients. This profit motive can be masked where leading claimant lawyers are portrayed in the media as motivated by concern to champion individuals' rights against large, well-resourced companies.[21]
- the legal aid system has paid the lawyers of claimants which it supports whether they win or lose.[22]
- the legal aid system has not encouraged independent or objective scrutiny of the merits of individual cases and has not separated the agency function (prescribing the possible cure to the problem) from the service function (delivering the cure).[23]

---

[20] R Abel, 'The Paradoxes of Legal Aid' in J Cooper and R Dhavan (eds), *Public Interest Law* (Basil Blackwell, 1986); C Harlow and R Rawlings, *Pressure Through Law* (1992) 296; M Cousins, 'The Politics of Legal Aid—A Solution in Search of a Problem?' [1994] CJQ 111–132; G Bevan, T Holland, M Partington, *Organising cost-effective access to justice* (Social Market Foundation, 1994); G Bevan, 'Has There Been Supplier-Induced Demand for Legal Aid?' [1994] CJQ 98; 'The nub of the problem is that, aside from plaintiffs or defendants themselves, the people who benefit from legal aid are the same as those who largely determine whether it should be granted: lawyers. The result is supplier-induced demand': *The Economist*, 22 June 1996; 'The lawyers have not helped. Some have treated legal aid as a blank cheque. Fees have risen sharply and cases have been brought before the courts for no other reason than to enrich the legal profession': *Financial Times*, 23 July 1996; Lord Woolf, *Access to Justice: Final Report* (1996) ch 17; E Blankenburg, 'The Lawyers' Lobby and the Welfare State: The Political Economy of Legal Aid' in F Regan, A Paterson, T Goriely and D Fleming (eds), *The Transformation of Legal Aid* (OUP, 1999); but see AA Paterson and T Goriely (eds), *A Reader on Resourcing Civil Justice* (OUP, 1996).

[21] *International Commercial Litigation* (Oct 1997) 19; SJ (16 Oct 1998) 944; Legal Business (Feb 1999) 42; a study of legal aid cases noted the optimistic predictions of chances of success and costs, advantageous to those giving them: Legal Aid Board, *Testing the Code* (1999).

[22] It has been said: 'Attorney compensation is a critical determinant of consumer access [to justice and compensation]': Organization for Economic Co-operation and Development, *Product liability rules in OECD countries* (1995) 45. It was said that the benzodiazepine litigation was 'run for the benefit of lawyers . . . The Legal Aid Board spent about £2000–£3000 per plaintiff to prove there was no case.' G Pulman QC, 'Funding for multi-party actions' in R Smith (ed), *Shaping the Future: New directions for legal services* (Legal Action Group, 1995). The Deputy Vice-President of the Law Society said: 'To some people who read only the tabloid press, legal aid must look like a racket—promising support for those of moderate means, but in practice providing it only to the poorest of the poor—and to some wealthy exploiters of the system': NLJ, 23 June 1995; 'too many lawyers are assiduously milking the system . . . Too many weak cases are backed': *The Economist*, 16 Sept 1995; 'under legal aid there were cases where solicitors ran up significant fees on investigative costs and then "turned down the case" ': RCA White and R Atkinson, 'Personal Injury Litigation, Conditional Fees and After-the-Event Insurance' [2000] CJQ 118, 127.

[23] The Legal Aid Board pointed out its frustration in the efficiency of the screening process where it had to rely on lawyers who have a financial interest in the outcome. Legal Aid Board, *Issues for the Legal Aid Board and the Lord Chancellor's Department in multi-party actions* (1994); in July 1997 Chancery Division judges wrote to the Lord Chancellor expressing concern at a significant number of wasteful and undeserving cases funded by legal aid 'that no-one in their right minds would pursue if they were paying for them themselves', granted on the advice of lawyers who are then paid to run them. The judges proposed that lawyers who advise on legal aid should not then act in the case and that opponents should have the right to ask the Board to seek a second opinion on the merits of

- neither the civil litigation system nor the legal aid system have always required the parties to investigate their individual cases at an early stage, so as to enable them to take an objective view of the merits.[24] This has been particularly fatal to many individual cases which have been permitted to join multi-party cases which have been run on 'generic' theories that liability exists, such as that a particular product is dangerous and causes injuries.

16.12 It has further been argued that the above factors led to a number of socially undesirable consequences. First, there may be a waste of judicial and publicly-funded resources on speculative or unjustified claims. Secondly, useful products may be forced off the market by commercial failure as a result of adverse publicity surrounding a multi-party action.[25] Thirdly, there are issues of manipulation of citizens' expectations,[26] particularly when the claimants' lawyers have a financial interest which is directly related to the continuation of the group litigation and the number of claimants involved. A citizen may be induced to enter a group in the belief that he has a right to compensation when this is far from established.[27] Subsequent media publicity of the progress of the litigation, particularly when it involves large numbers of claimants, can give the impression that the claims have more validity than is really the case. If the case collapses, expectations will be dashed. The issue of advertising is discussed further in chapter 6.

16.13 Most people would support the proposition that lawyers should not create false expectations in their clients.[28] This is an issue of professional ethics requiring

---

the case: *The Times*, 28 July 1997, and see the *Guardian*, 29 Jan 1999. This issue motivated the Board's introduction of quality controls and assurance in the latter 1990s: B Main and P Peacock, *What Price Civil Justice?* (The Institute of Economic Affairs, 2000).

[24] 'It is easy for a lawyer to stand up and say there are no grounds for a legal action, having done next to no research on either the science or the law . . . that seems wrong': M Day, *The Times*, 14 Feb 1995; 'legal aid is sometimes granted in cases where, had the full facts been available to the Board, it is unlikely that it would have been': Law Society, *A Better Way Forward* (1995) para 10.3; Law Society, *Better Value Better Justice* (1996) para 46.

[25] This was cited by Hoechst Marion Roussel as one reason for their withdrawal of Norplant: see ch 31.

[26] See *AB and Others v John Wyeth & Brother Ltd* [1997] 8 Med LR 57, 73, 74 per Brooke LJ; J Millington, 'Breast Cancer Radiation Claims' (Sept 1999) Medical Litigation 7.

[27] Most members of the public are not skilled buyers of legal services, lacking both knowledge and economic power; G Hanlon, 'A Profession in Transition?—Lawyers, the Market and Significant Others' [1997] MLR 798. 'Legal aid is a social reform that begins with a solution—lawyers—and then looks for a problem it might solve, rather than beginning with the problem—poverty, or oppression, or discrimination, or capitalism—and exploring solutions': R Abel, 'The Paradoxes of Legal Aid' in J Cooper and R Dhavan (eds), *Public Interest Law* (1986); 'The expertise of Legal Aid Board staff is legal and administrative, rather than medical or technical': *Hansard*, HC (Series 5) vol 254, col 845W (17 Feb 1995).

[28] In an action for negligence over the manner in which information was communicated (informing patients of the very remote risk of infection from an obstetric health care worker who had tested HIV positive), the Court of Appeal said: 'both plaintiffs' advisers and legal aid authorities will need to identify evidence of a psychiatric illness or injury properly so called before people who have suffered distress as a result of being told some worrying piece of news in an incompetent manner are

client care and communication. Accordingly, lawyers should take great care in multi-party actions that clients are fully apprised of the objective chances of success, particularly if the claim is speculative. The issue of a financial conflict of interest was a structural feature of the legal aid system, where claimants' lawyers would be paid whether they won or lost. Conflict also arises on a conditional fee system.[29] The conflict may be particularly acute in a multi-party case because of the size of the sums involved, because the lawyers are acting for many different individuals whose interests may diverge, and because the lawyers may have a larger financial stake in the outcome than any of their individual clients.[30] Accordingly, it may be wise for claimants' lawyers to devise mechanisms under which their objectivity can be verified and be seen to operate. One possibility is for an independent trustee to be appointed to represent the interests of multiple claimants.[31]

In response to the above points, it has been argued that: 16.14

- There is an imbalance of resources between individual claimants and multinational defendants with extensive resources.[32] A 'David and Goliath' perception can exist.[33] One aspect of this is an imbalance of legal resources as between smaller solicitors acting for claimants and large City firms acting for defendants. This imbalance does not arise in the USA, where claimant lawyers can have huge resources garnered from successful contingency fees. One approach to the imbalance problem has been for claimants' solicitors to pool the resources of several firms, dividing responsibility for different aspects among them.[34] Indeed, consolidation of lawyers into units which are larger, more efficient, and more effective business units with increased specialisation was a policy of the government's access to justice reform programme.[35]

---

permitted and encouraged to embark on litigation which may be doomed to failure from the start, and which may only serve to increase their distress': *AB and Others v Tameside and Glossop Health Authority and another* (1997) 35 BMLR 79, 94, CA.

[29] As discussed at paras 11.63 *et seq*.

[30] This is often the position in US class actions run on contingency fees, where attorneys can be the primary stakeholders: see MD Green, *Bendectin and Birth Defects* (University of Pennsylvania Press, 1996) 252.

[31] See para 5.33 above.

[32] After the collapse of the benzodiazepine group action, the Legal Aid Board announced the suspension of funding for those 1,700 claimants in the benzodiazepine group action involving three of the six drugs concerned (Mogadon, Librium, and Valium). It was reported that the decision stemmed from a lack of sufficient medical evidence in many of the claims: SJ, 22 Jan 1993. This was followed by claims by plaintiffs' lawyers that 'big companies were killing off ordinary people's attempts to sue them by persuading the authorities to refuse financial assistance with the huge cost of the cases': *Independent on Sunday*, 7 Feb 1993.

[33] M Day, P Balen, G McCool, *Multi-Party Actions* (Legal Action Group, 1995) 8; LS Gaz, 96/10 (10 Mar 1999); R Barr, 'Of bananas, tobacco and Denning' (12 Mar 1999) SJ; this comment was made by the mother of a child suing over MMR vaccine: The Lawyer, 19 Apr 1999.

[34] Supreme Court Rules Committee, *Guide for use in Group Actions* (1991).

[35] See Lord Chancellor's Department, *Regulatory impact assessment: Improvement in the availability and use of conditional fees* (1998).

The counter-argument to the imbalance suggestion is that the legal aid system has created a powerful financial force for claimants to challenge corporate resources, through the deployment of the limitless resources of the State, and the suspension of the 'loser pays' rule. These conditions created the well-recognised 'legal aid blackmail' phenomenon where defendants felt under pressure to settle cases irrespective of merit and to settle for higher amounts than might be justifiable.[36]

- Claimants should be allowed their day in court to have a judicial determination on all substantive issues of liability (freedom of expression) rather than being defeated at a preliminary stage such as on issues of limitation and perhaps viability.[37] Yet there may be a confusion between whether the function of civil litigation should be to resolve a claim for compensation or to constitute a public inquiry into the historic conduct of an industry or manufacturer.[38] It is difficult to see how the above 'freedom of expression' argument fits with the principles of resolving litigation swiftly, speedily, and with proportionate cost, which are enshrined in the CPR and designed to afford efficient resolution in the interests not only of the parties but also of other litigants and of society's limited resources.
- Scarce resources should be saved by focusing them on pursuing a generic case rather than on investigating the potentially large number of individual claims. Investigating individual claims can be an expensive process, particularly where complex issues of liability arise involving fact, causation, and a need for expert evidence, as was shown in the benzodiazepine litigation, where the bulk of the legal aid costs were spent in investigating individual issues and in particular on screening of medical records by psychiatric experts and barristers.[39] The difficulty with this approach, however, as discussed in Part II, is that problems can arise in some cases where individual claims are not verified but are assumed to be valid on their individual facts and worth pursuing, when these assumptions are incorrect. In these circumstances, the scarce resources are wasted by not

---

[36] See *Hansard*, HC (series 6) vol 280, col 875 (2 July 1996).

[37] After the collapse of the tobacco cases in 1999 following the court's determination that a number of cases were statute barred, John Pickering was quoted as saying: 'The sadness is that in none of these instances the actual merits of the issues have been tested. One queries whether the system affords a vehicle for testing issues': LS Gaz, 96/10 (10 Mar 1996). In response, defence interests would no doubt argue that limitation was one of the central merits issues in these cases.

[38] The civil courts seem to view their role as being limited to the former function: see *AB and Others v John Wyeth & Brother Ltd* [1994] 5 Med LR 149, 153 per Stuart-Smith LJ and ch 22 below. Various points are relevant in this debate, including the existence and breadth of regulatory and commercial constraints on business, and whether these complex mechanisms are sufficiently understood: see C Hodges, *Report for the Commission of the European Communities on the Application of Directive 85/374/EEC on Liability for Defective Products* (McKenna & Co, 1994); C Hodges, *Unknown Risks and the Community Interest: The Development Risks Defence in the Product Liability Directive* (McKenna & Co, 1996).

[39] Legal Aid Board, *Issues arising for the Legal Aid Board and the Lord Chancellor's Department from multi-party actions* (1994).

undertaking verification but paying for the resolution of generic issues and possibly then also particularly expensive individual resolutions.

16.15 Given the evidence from the case studies in Part V and summarised in Table 16.2 of such large numbers of claimants whose claims then failed, it is difficult to avoid the conclusion that the system that was operated prior to the reforms of funding and procedural rules around 1998–2000 contained serious design and operational flaws. There were two major weaknesses. The first concerned the funding aspects: financial incentives for claimants' lawyers to err on the side of advising the instigation and continuation of cases for which they would be paid irrespective of outcome; failure to separate the functions of assessment for public funding from the partisan representation of the client, with the resulting conflict of interest; and suspension for a publicly funded litigant of the normal rule that the loser should pay the costs. Some but not all of these lessons have been taken into account in the funding reforms. The second major problem arose out of the absence of a requirement for initial verification and assessment of individual claims. This issue may have been addressed under the CPR and Group Litigation Order procedures and pre-action protocol requirements but the extent to which this may be so remains to be seen.

D. The Difficulties in Succeeding in a Pharmaceutical Claim

16.16 It is striking that the pharmaceutical claims in particular have a low success rate (under 7 per cent of claims against manufacturers on the figures in Table 16.2). This prompts further enquiry. It is a common view that the chance of success in a product liability case is good, particularly since the introduction of strict liability.[40] Whilst this may be true in many simple cases, other cases involve inherently complex and difficult issues, notably causation. This is particularly true of cases involving medicinal or other products which are highly regulated, may involve inherent side effects, and present difficulties of deciding on causation, particularly distinguishing between effects associated with underlying disease, the product in question, and other alternative possible agents.[41] Many recognised adverse drug reactions are indistinguishable, clinically, pathologically, or biochemically, from conditions which can occur spontaneously.[42] Such claims are fraught with difficulties.[43]

---

[40] Consumer Protection Act 1987 Part I, implementing Directive 85/374/EEC.
[41] C Newdick, 'Special Problems of Compensating Those Damaged by Medicinal Products' in S McLean (ed), *Compensation for Damages* (Dartmouth, 1993); I Dodds-Smith and M Spencer, 'Product Liability for Medicinal Products' in M Powers and N Harris (eds), *Medical Negligence* (Butterworths, 3rd edn, 2000).
[42] WHW Inman, 'The United Kingdom' in WHW Inman (ed), *Monitoring for Drug Safety* (2nd edn MTP, 1986) 30.
[43] M Mildred, 'Group Actions Present and Future' [1994] JPIL 276.

16.17 The following are some of the background regulatory factors which generate the grave difficulties in succeeding in a design defect claim or a failure to warn claim against a medicinal product in the EU. First, to obtain a marketing authorisation for a product[44] an extended sequence of toxicology studies and clinical trials need to be carried out in order to provide specified data to the licensing authority.[45] Secondly, marketing of the product is subject to approval by a licensing authority on the basis that the data provided establishes that the product satisfies the criteria of safety, quality, and efficacy.[46] Thirdly, the labelling and package leaflets for each product must satisfy specified criteria and be approved by the competent authority.[47] Fourthly, the advertising of medicinal products is subject to regulation.[48] Fifthly, the reporting of adverse reactions to the competent authorities by marketing authorisation holders is subject to regulation. Sixthly, all new chemical entities or innovative products are likely to be classed as prescription only medicines.

16.18 Moreover, a plaintiff will have difficulty in establishing causation where a learned intermediary, such as a doctor, is interposed between manufacturer and consumer. The choice of the product may be that of the learned intermediary rather than of the consumer. In any event, it is more the advice of the learned intermediary that in fact affects the consumer's choice, understanding of the risks, and use of the product than, for example, any failure to warn by the manufacturer. Under English law, at any rate, a plaintiff would have to show that the actions of both himself and his doctor would have been different if he had been told of the alleged defect in the labelling information.

16.19 All this means that it would be unusual for a responsible manufacturer to be held to be negligent. It would normally be equally difficult, under strict liability, to show that a product did not provide the level of safety which persons generally would expect, given the fact that it had been extensively researched, was subject to an extremely stringent regulatory system, and that the product information and promotion were subject to regulatory control. Success in a design defect or failure to warn claim under strict liability involving a modern pharmaceutical product would be unlikely. Medicinal products, like any other, might be subject to a manufacturing defect claim if particular items or batches do not satisfy quality assurance standards, but the standards of pharmaceutical manufacturing are high and subject to regulatory authorisation.[49]

---

[44] Directive 65/65/EEC.
[45] Directive 75/318/EEC, Annex, as amended by Directive 92/318/EEC.
[46] Directive 65/65/EEC, as amended.
[47] Directive 92/27/EEC.
[48] Directive 92/28/EEC.
[49] Directive 75/319/EEC and Directive 91/356/EEC.

16.20 It is obviously conceivable that a medicinal product could be marketed where the post-marketing pharmacovigilance system established by the legislation revealed amongst the ADR (alternative dispute resolution) reports either a number of serious events or a large number of less serious events which in themselves might be viewed as acceptable but which occurred in sufficient numbers and frequency as to alter the risk-benefit equation operated by the competent authorities in deciding on whether a product conforms to the requisite level of safety.

16.21 In a negligence claim, the question would then be whether the manufacturer and/or the competent authority had acted reasonably in the research, marketing, and surveillance of use of the product. In a strict liability claim, the issues would be whether the product was defective and, if so, whether the development risk defence applied. There may be an issue that the product was not defective even though it caused injuries which were not warned about. Assuming, however, for the sake of argument, that the product was held to be defective, many theoretical difficulties arise in interpreting and establishing the development risks defence.[50] In practice, the enquiry under both negligence and strict liability would take place against the background of decisions taken by the regulatory authority and in many cases the civil courts would be unlikely to want to substitute their judgment on complex scientific and regulatory issues for those of a competent authority.

E. The Future of Group Litigation?

16.22 It is noticeable how many of the group cases have been brought by lawyers on a speculative or attemptedly innovative basis. As Lord Steyn has said in the context of rejecting a claim for the costs of bringing up a child conceived after negligent advice that the father was infertile, it is possible to view some cases simply from the perspective of corrective justice. This principle requires somebody who has harmed another without justification to indemnify the other. However, Lord Steyn rejected that principle and claim, preferring the principle of distributive justice, which 'requires a focus on the just distribution of burdens and losses among members of a society'.[51] Lord Steyn expanded upon this approach in comments at a conference on class actions, stating that the House of Lords had decided that 'we do not want a litigation-driven society'.[52]

---

[50] Directive 85/374/EEC, Art 7(e); Consumer Protection Act 1987, s 4(1)(e); T Bourgoignie, 'The 1985 Council Directive on Product Liability and its implementation in the Member States of the European Union' in M Goyens (ed), *Directive 85/374/EEC on product liability: ten years after* (Louvain-La-Neuve, 1996).

[51] *McFarlane v Tayside Health Board (Scotland)* [2000] AC 59.

[52] Remarks made at the conference 'Debate Over Group Litigation in Comparative Perspective: What Can We Learn From Each Other?' organised by Duke University and the University of Geneva at Geneva, Switzerland, 21–22 July 2000.

17

PERTUSSIS VACCINE LITIGATION

Simon Pearl[1]

> This product liability litigation arose in the mid-1980s before the development of more sophisticated and formal arrangements. The key point is that both plaintiffs and defendants regarded the issue of general causation as being the paramount issue. Accordingly, the co-ordinating judge was enabled to resolve this issue and, since he did so in the defendant's favour, the litigation was effectively resolved. The issue was resolved as a preliminary issue in the context of a single test case, although there was an expensive lesson that selection of only a single test case leads to problems if it collapses on its particular facts.
>
> The issue of general causation was far from simple and was only resolved after consideration of extensive and detailed scientific evidence. The most significant interlocutory issue related to the extent to which success could be obtained as a result of the data and workings of a major scientific study.
>
> Given the failure of the allegations in the case, it is particularly relevant to note the effect on public attitudes and on the generation of litigation itself of initial adverse publicity about the safety of the products.

The Pertussis Vaccine litigation remains the only pharmaceutical product liability test case to have gone to a full trial on general causation issues, and is a prime example of the effectiveness of a carefully selected preliminary issue. The outcome of *Loveday v Renton*[2] effectively resulted in the disposal of all Pertussis Vaccine litigation in England and Wales.   **17.01**

A. Background

After a widely reported retrospective study of children who were treated in Great Ormond Street Hospital was published in 1974 (Kulenkampff and Wilson), which reported on thirty-six children who apparently suffered neurological complications following the   **17.02**

---

[1] Partner, Davies Arnold Cooper.
[2] [1990] 1 MLR 117.

receipt of a triple vaccine (DTP) containing a Pertussis (whooping cough) element, it became widely accepted that in rare cases Pertussis Vaccine could cause brain damage.

17.03 The publicity given to the Great Ormond Street Hospital study by the mass media coincided with the formation of the Association of Vaccine Damaged Children in 1973 to campaign to press the government to set up a scheme of compensation for alleged vaccine damaged children. A number of senior doctors allied themselves with this campaign and went so far as to suggest that the risk of damage to a child from vaccination was greater than that of the disease itself. The *Sunday Times* ran a series of highly emotive stories. Not surprisingly, vaccination rates fell dramatically. In England, in 1972, 79 per cent of children of vaccination age completed their course of immunisation. By 1976, the rate had fallen to 38 per cent and the fear was affecting the uptake of other vaccines also.

17.04 The intense pressure and decline in vaccination rates persuaded the government to accept that there should be a scheme of compensation for vaccine damaged children and indeed the Royal Commission on Civil Liability and Compensation in Personal Injury (the Pearson Report) published in 1978 devoted an entire chapter to the question of their compensation. Although the Pearson Report proposals were not adopted, Parliament passed the Vaccine Damage Payments Act 1979 under which any child assessed as 80 per cent disabled or greater by the vaccine would receive a lump sum (then £10,000, now £30,000).

17.05 In the Act, the burden of proof of damage was expressly stated to be determined on the balance of probability, yet it is clear that the Act starts from the premise that vaccination can cause brain damage and envisaged that assessments on specific cases would be based on diagnostic criteria such as evidence of temporal association between the onset of symptoms and vaccination. The presumption that the vaccine could cause brain damage was by this time generally held by the public at large and also the majority of the medical profession. However, there remained considerable doubt amongst a minority of the medical community as to the validity of this assumption.

B. Litigation

17.06 The awards being made under the Act were plainly insufficient for the needs of severely handicapped children and it became inevitable that the issue of whether they were entitled to greater compensation would have to be resolved in the courts.

17.07 In the United States, hundreds of cases were being brought and several resulted in jury findings that the manufacturers had been negligent and huge damages were awarded. In the United States, the causal link between vaccine and permanent brain damage was never fully challenged.

17.08 In Scotland, in 1985, the court dismissed a claim by Richard Bonthrone because of the particular facts of that case. The court found no evidence of a causal link between Pertussis Vaccine and his condition, infantile spasms, although it accepted the general proposition that the vaccine had the capacity to cause brain damage. The manufacturers of the vaccine were not a party and the issue of general causation was not fully ventilated.

In 1985 all English cases concerning Pertussis Vaccine were assigned to Stuart-Smith J (as he then was) and the cases in the District Registries were ordered to be transferred to the Royal Courts of Justice. Because it was recognised that general causation issues were common to all cases and hotly contested, in October 1985 the Judge decided to try a 'test case' to determine the issues of causation. The case of Johnnie Kinnear was selected and the rest were stayed. In fact, the stay was appealed in the case of *Loveday* but on 14 November 1985 that appeal was dismissed. Lloyd LJ, giving the leading judgment of the Court of Appeal refusing to lift the stay, observed that Counsel for the manufacturers had assured the Court that general causation would be a live issue. The essence of the manufacturers' case was to be 'that there is no evidence at all that the brain damage is caused, or can be caused, by any of the vaccines from whomsoever manufactured and at whatsoever date'; 'that being so', concluded Lloyd LJ, 'there is at the very least a chance that a decision on the question of general causation in the Kinnear case will save costs in all the other cases. If the question is answered no—in other words, if it is held that the Pertussis vaccine cannot cause brain damage—there is more than a chance; there is a virtual certainty that costs will be saved.' So all cases remained stayed and the Legal Aid Board placed a moratorium on all expenditure pending the trial of the *Kinnear* case. This case was treated as a genuine test case. Specific causation as well as general causation was to be tried. The reason that it failed to serve its purpose was a hard and expensive lesson. After almost a month of evidence, the case collapsed because the mother's evidence in relation to the onset of the child's condition revealed inconsistencies with the medical records, and the plaintiff's advisors came to the conclusion that the case would not succeed, resulting in legal aid being withdrawn. The fact that the mother was giving evidence at such an early stage of the trial at all was only due to the fact that after a number of wasted days of trial due to the non-availability of expert witnesses, the Court ordered the plaintiff to call a witness and the only one available was the plaintiff's mother.

17.09

Loveday v Renton then had its stay lifted, and was effectively substituted as the test case. In order to avoid any risk of a collapse of the second case, it was decided that there should be a preliminary issue on the question of general causation so that the specific facts relating to Susan Loveday's condition would not be considered until after a judgment had been delivered. The preliminary issue was defined as: '[C]an or could Pertussis Vaccine cause permanent brain damage in young children?'

17.10

The procedures for co-ordination were fairly unsophisticated. No attempt was made to bind in other either actual or potential cases. Stays were in place in relation to issued cases, and an informal register was kept of known cases but was far from comprehensive. The Legal Aid Board had suspended authorisation of expenditure on the stayed cases, but there did not appear to be a great deal of co-ordination between the representatives of the various plaintiffs, despite the involvement of the pressure group. The selection of Kinnear and Loveday as the vehicles for the generic causation issue owed more to the determination of the individual plaintiff's solicitor, than to any grand plan. It was recognised that, as all of these cases were subject to legal aid funding, and the outcome would inevitably have significant impact, since the Legal Aid Board was unlikely to wish to fund cases if there was a negative outcome to the *Loveday* causation trial, there remained a substantial degree of informality regarding these arrangements. The fact that none of the claims were ever likely

17.11

to be affected by limitation difficulties avoided problems which were encountered in other cases, such as the need for cut-off dates or a formal register.

17.12 The role of The Wellcome Foundation Limited needs explanation. Although they were originally sued in negligence in the *Kinnear* action, along with the DHSS, the doctor, and the Health Authority, by the time the matter came on for trial in March 1986, it was recognised that there was no prospect in showing that the manufacturers were negligent and the action against the DHSS and the manufacturers had been discontinued. The Wellcome Foundation Limited applied to be joined as a necessary party to the action under Order 15, Rule 6(2)(a). They had an important interest, as the only manufacturer still making Pertussis Vaccine in the United Kingdom at the time, in establishing that the plaintiff's contention that the vaccine could cause permanent brain damage was wrong and in order to protect the reputation of the vaccine. They were joined as a necessary party to the trial of the general causation issues on the terms they undertook to pay their costs, whatever the outcome. When the *Kinnear* case collapsed, Wellcome applied successfully to be joined as a defendant to the *Loveday* case, which had been proceeding as a pure medical negligence case against the doctors only. No allegations of negligence were ever made against Wellcome at any stage in that case, and indeed it was not known who the manufacturers of the vaccine given to Susan Loveday actually were. Again, they undertook to bear their own costs, and they became the active defendant in preparation of the case 'defending the vaccine'. Comprehensive pleadings were served which set out the competing cases on general causation and they were amended to take into account the views expressed in experts' reports, once served. The Judge scheduled a number of interlocutory hearings and the parties issued Summonses fixed for those dates to seek orders that they desired. The Judge was not proactive in the sense of the activities of assigned Judges in later cases, but he did endeavour to keep the case moving forward to a preset trial date.

17.13 During the interlocutory stages applications were made for discovery under Order 24, Rule 7A of the raw data of the Kulenkampff paper and also of the National Childhood Encephalopathy (NCES) Study which had been set up by the DHSS in the aftermath of the vaccine damage campaign. This latter study, which had been conducted over a three-year period, was the only epidemiological study that attempted to deal directly with the question before the Court. The NCES had concluded that there was a statistically significant relative risk of developing brain damage within seven days of vaccination and calculated that the attributable risk was one in approximately 330,000 vaccinations, a figure which was universally quoted and accepted. Because of the overriding importance of the case, the Judge ordered that the raw data of those studies be made available to the parties, despite concern about the confidentiality of the materials. An Order was made that no reference should be made to medical records which would enable an identification to be made.

17.14 The NCES raw data was reanalysed by the experts and a great deal of Court time was spent in hearing evidence about it. The availability of this data was crucial because if the findings of the study had been accepted at their face value, then the plaintiffs were likely to win the preliminary issue. Obtaining the data, against some considerable resistance by the NCES team, represented by the MDU (Medical Defence Union), was the most significant interlocutory order in the litigation.

17.15　The trial took place over some 63 days and a total of 18 experts from the United Kingdom, the United States, and Europe were called to give evidence. The transcripts of the experts' evidence in the *Kinnear* case was also read into evidence. The experts spanned the fields of neurology, paediatrics, medical statistics, epidemiology, immunology, neuropharmacology, and microbiology. Each expert prepared a detailed report which was submitted in advance and their views were tested through cross-examination, most at length, and also by the Judge. The world literature spanning some 50 years was examined and analysed. At its time, it was the most expensive action ever funded by the Legal Aid Authorities in England. The estimate of the expenditure of the Legal Aid Board was given at £2 million. It is significant that the plaintiff's solicitors had publicly stated that they had no difficulty in getting approval for any expenditure requested. Any suggestion that there was an imbalance in resources available to the parties is not justified.

17.16　The judgment of Stuart-Smith LJ was delivered in March 1988. He held that the plaintiff had failed to prove that Pertussis Vaccine causes brain damage in young children, and that effectively brought to an end the prospect of any claim for brain damage succeeding before a UK court in any Pertussis Vaccine case, unless there was a significant development in the medical or scientific evidence such that the decision would be affected.

17.17　It is not the purpose of this chapter to review the evidence and the findings of fact made by the Judge in reaching his conclusion, as we are dealing here with procedural issues. Suffice it to say that the Judge laid down a framework for the evidence required by a court to establish causation. The relevant evidence falls into six main heads:

1. A distinct and specific clinical syndrome.
2. A specific pathology.
3. Temporal association.
4. Plausible biological mechanisms.
5. Animal experimentation.
6. Epidemiological evidence.

17.18　Having examined in detail the evidence under these six heads and accepting that the burden of proof was on the plaintiff, the Judge concluded that the plaintiff failed on the balance of probabilities to show that Pertussis Vaccine can cause permanent brain damage in young children.

17.19　He also held, obiter, that even if the plaintiff had established the proposition that the vaccine was capable of causing brain damage, insuperable difficulties in establishing negligence under the Bolam principle existed.

17.20　As a result of the *Loveday* judgment, stays which had been placed on all Pertussis Vaccine cases were not lifted by the courts and the Legal Aid Certificates were discharged. At the time there were some 181 Legal Aid Certificates issued, and around two dozen further applications which were made were subsequently rejected. The Legal Aid Authorities had taken the view that although the *Loveday* case created no binding precedent, or issue estoppel, it was a decision of the greatest importance in considering the future of Pertussis Vaccine litigation and that there was no realistic prospect of establishing to the required standard of proof any causative link between Pertussis Vaccine and any Legal Aid applicants' injuries.

17.21 It appeared to dispose of all English Pertussis Vaccine litigation, as there is little possibility of any claim proceeding without the benefit of Legal Aid, but the conclusions cannot be free from doubt, first because of the Judicial Review Application made by a number of plaintiffs, challenging the Legal Aid Board blanket approach, and secondly because of the outcome of the *Kenneth Best* case in Eire.

C. The Judicial Review: *R v The Legal Aid Board No 8 Appeals Committee, Ex Parte Angell et al*

17.22 In March 1990 an Application for Judicial Review of the Legal Aid Authority's decision to revoke Legal Aid Certificates in seven cases was heard before Simon Brown J. The Judge did grant the review and referred these cases back to the Legal Aid Board for consideration of the specific facts. As far as the writer is aware, the reconsideration did not lead to the issue of any new certificates. Certainly, with the exception of a few cases involving the very early vaccines used in the Medical Research Council trials in the 1950s, no further claims have been pursued.

17.23 Simon Brown J's judgment records that four counsel appearing for the plaintiff in the *Loveday* case wrote a joint opinion on the prospects of an appeal but they could not agree on all aspects. Part 1 was signed by the two leading counsel and it emphasised the difficulty that had become apparent during the trial in proving negligence and specific causation quite apart from general causation. On the facts of the *Loveday* case it advised against an appeal. Junior counsel took a different view and later wrote their own somewhat more optimistic advice on an appeal. Part 2 of the joint opinion contained a detailed and vigorous critique of Stuart-Smith LJ's judgment and then Part 3 recited the central conclusion of that opinion that the judgment should not be treated as a ground for refusing Legal Aid in suitable cases in future. It was this opinion which the Judge held was not given sufficient weight.

17.24 The Legal Aid Board had assigned consideration of all applications for Legal Aid to its Area no 8 and one individual officer. He deposed on affidavit that whilst recognising that the *Loveday* case created no binding precedent or issue estoppel, it was an indication of how the same issue might be expected to be resolved in future and the Legal Aid Board issued on all existing certificates a 'Show Cause Notice' under the regulations requiring representations to be made and, following that, all certificates were discharged barring four which dealt with an early experimental vaccine. All pending and fresh applications were refused. This Show Cause Notice had stated 'there does not appear to be any realistic prospect of establishing to the required standard of proof any causative link between Pertussis Vaccine and the assisted person's illness and present conditions' following the judgment in the *Loveday* case. Appeals against the discharge were refused. The Judicial Review was granted, in effect, because the Judge accepted the contention that the Legal Aid Board Appeal Committee did not give adequate reasons for their refusal of the appeals and did not appear to take counsel's opinion properly into account, although the Judge did comment that in his doing so applicants should not be optimistic in the final outcome of such appeals.

D. The Irish Litigation

17.25 No review of the Pertussis Vaccine litigation can be complete without some reference to the situation in Ireland in the case of *Kenneth Best v The Wellcome Foundation Ltd*. In January 1991 Hamilton J decided at first instance that if there had been a temporal connection (which he held on the facts there was not) then he would have been satisfied that the plaintiff's brain damage had been caused by the whooping cough vaccine. The plaintiff appealed to the Irish Supreme Court on the finding that there had been no temporal connection and succeeded. The Supreme Court upheld the Judge's decision that Wellcome had been negligent in releasing a particular batch which was held to have exceeded recommended potency and toxicity levels. The Supreme Court reversed the Judge's findings that the convulsions which the plaintiff suffered occurred months after the vaccination and, having made the temporal connection between the administration of the vaccine and the convulsions, the Supreme Court held Wellcome liable and referred the case back to the trial court on the issue of damages. Although, therefore, there is an Irish Supreme Court case which by implication accepts the whooping cough vaccine can cause brain damage, and at the time the case was decided it was suggested by commentators that this would open up the opportunities for a re-trial of the issue in England, the position remains that the *Best* case has been treated as a 'hot batch case' and as the scientific evidence was not analysed in any depth, and the judgment contains no substantive reasoning justifying the acceptance of the causal connection, the case has not had the impact which was originally anticipated.

E. Conclusions

17.26 The resolution of the Pertussis Vaccine litigation in England and Wales was achieved by the means of a single trial of a preliminary issue as to general causation. This question inevitably arose in each case, and despite the judicial review challenge made to the Legal Aid Board's response to the judgment, the judgment remains as valid today as it was when it was first delivered. It has effectively brought to an end the Pertussis Vaccine litigation in England and Wales and in doing so has resulted in a significant overall saving in costs not only to the Legal Aid Board but to potential defendants.

17.27 The test case concept subsequently fell out of fashion and is certainly not appropriate in all cases. It remains an option which has the potential to resolve multi-party litigation by the determination of one issue which if decided in one particular way will dispose of all of the cases.

18

OPREN LITIGATION

Anne Ware[1]

This product liability litigation was the dominant multi-party action during the late 1980s and early 1990s. A number of important management issues arose and the decisions adopted were influential in later cases. First, a steering committee was formed to co-ordinate the activities of over 200 firms representing plaintiffs. Secondly, the Judge ordered a cut-off date so as to clarify the numbers involved. This was also important in relation to cost-benefit analysis under Legal Aid. Thirdly, the case throughout attracted extensive media publicity which continued to draw new claimants wishing to join. As a result, a succession of cut-off dates and groups of claimants were created, with later groups ultimately being held to be out of time on limitation grounds.

Fourthly, a Master Statement of Claim was adopted as being the most efficient mechanism of avoiding unnecessary repetition in individual pleadings. However, the document contained wide-ranging allegations, a number of which were subsequently not supported by the evidence which later emerged. Short form individual statements of claim were ordered to be served in individual cases, containing information under relevant headings which were agreed by the parties. Fifthly, the case was moved forward by the selection of a small number of lead actions with the remainder being stayed.

Sixthly, important cost-sharing orders were made, notably clarification that plaintiffs shared responsibility for costs equally irrespective of whether they were or were not publicly funded. Seventhly, this was one of the few product liability cases involving voluntary settlement of some of the claims: it was based on payment of a global sum by the defendant which was allocated amongst claimants in accordance with a scheme with a provision for arbitration in the event of disagreement.

The Opren litigation was active from the Autumn of 1982 until the end of 1993, when the last legal aid certificates were discharged. It comprised a fluctuating group of plaintiffs, which exceeded 2,000 at one point. The original group of Opren plaintiffs was represented by a steering committee of five (later six) firms of solicitors. The

---

[1] Partner, Davies Arnold Cooper.

> second plaintiffs' group, whose cases were the subject of preliminary issues on limitation, was co-ordinated by two different firms of solicitors.
>
> The original proceedings named seven defendants, the first five being collectively known as 'the Lilly defendants' and included, as the first defendant, Eli Lilly and Company of Indianapolis. The sixth and seventh defendants were the Attorney-General on behalf of the Committee on Safety of Medicines and the Attorney-General on behalf of the Licensing Authority under the Medicines Act 1968. Proceedings were eventually discontinued by the second group of Opren plaintiffs against the sixth and seventh defendants.

A. The Product

18.01 In March 1980 a new non-steroidal anti-inflammatory drug, for the treatment of arthritis, Benoxaprofen, was licensed under the Medicines Act 1968. It was made available on prescription in the UK under the name 'Opren'.

18.02 Opren had a novel mode of action and from experimental studies it seemed to have the potential to arrest the progress of painful arthritic disease. It also had the benefit of a single daily dosage recommended at 600mgs. As with all effective pharmaceutical products it had adverse effects. The most common of these were transient photosensitivity (a redness and rash on the skin when exposed to sunlight) and onycholysis (the lifting of the nail from the nail bed) in some patients. Caution was advised when prescribing the product to patients with impaired liver or kidney function.

18.03 In May 1980 Lilly introduced Opren for use by consultant physicians in hospitals and in October 1980 it was introduced for use by general practitioners.

B. Background

18.04 In May 1982 a short piece appeared in the *British Medical Journal* by a doctor reporting that six of his elderly patients who had been taking Opren had died of a rare hepato-renal complication. In June 1982 Lilly sent a letter to all doctors recommending that the daily dose of Opren in the elderly be reduced to 300mgs (half the usual recommended dose) because of possible decreased renal function. In July 1982 further reports of alleged side effects associated with Opren appeared in the *British Medical Journal*. On 3 August 1982 the UK Licensing Authority imposed a three-month suspension on the promotion and supply of Opren and on 5 August 1982 Lilly decided voluntarily to cease marketing Opren worldwide.

18.05 These events were followed by an unprecedented publicity campaign in the press and media which concentrated on describing the side effects that had been reported to the Committee on Safety of Medicines (CSM). The most common complaints were the warned against effects of photosensitivity and onycholysis. The media widely publicised the intention of 'victims' to sue the company. This campaign lasted until the settlement of the original litigation in 1988.

C. The Opren Action Group

18.06 In August 1982 the Opren Action Group was formed, supported by leading plaintiffs' personal injury solicitors. In October 1982 a letter before action was sent to Lilly in Indianapolis stating that five (later six) co-ordinating firms of lawyers had been asked to advise the Committee of the Opren Action Group. The letter stated that they believed they already had sufficient evidence to establish the company's liability and demanded a no fault compensation scheme. Despite requests, the solicitors refused to identify those for whom they acted or to provide information about the claims.

D. The US Litigation

18.07 Instead of commencing legal proceedings in England, however, the Opren Action Group's lawyers commenced litigation in the United States. On 5 June 1984 in the Indiana District Court McKinney J declined to hear the claims in the United States on the ground that the proper forum for the English litigants was in England. There followed more demands in the UK that the Lilly defendants should settle the claims. Despite references to 'thousands' of claimants no information had been provided to the Lilly defendants in the UK and only one or two writs had been served in this jurisdiction.

E. The English Litigation—Part 1

18.08 On 11 February 1985 a writ was served in the case of Joseph Owen Davies, who subsequently became the nominal 'lead action'. He was the plaintiff named in a number of the reported judgments.

18.09 Following an Order of the High Court in London in May 1985, an 85-page Master Statement of Claim with appendices was served by the plaintiffs' Group on 9 July 1985. This made wide-ranging allegations involving every aspect of the product's research, clinical trials, and post-marketing surveillance. On 30 October 1985 the Lilly defendants served a 70-page Master Defence with 100 pages of appendices covering in detail all the allegations made against them.

18.10 Thus it was only at this point, some three years after the product was withdrawn, that proceedings commenced in earnest. In January 1986 Hirst J (as he then was) was appointed by the Lord Chief Justice to co-ordinate the litigation. There followed a number of landmark decisions by Hirst J which laid down guidelines in a flexible format for conducting multi-party litigation in England and Wales which have been adopted and adapted in many subsequent cases.

The timetable [2]

18.11 In his judgment of 23 July 1986 Hirst J laid down the timetable for progressing the claims. He was handicapped by the fact that even by July 1986, some four years after the product had been withdrawn, there was no finite group of plaintiffs. In the judgment he refers to some 679 actual or potential plaintiffs represented by the co-ordinating firms of solicitors, and another 210 firms of solicitors representing clients and with whom they were liaising.

18.12 He outlined the 'Opren Scheme', which set up co-ordinated arrangements for the conduct of the claims. The intention of the Court was to select lead actions and stay all other cases pending the conclusion of the main trial on liability. He encouraged claimants to issue and serve writs if they wished to participate in the process of selection of lead actions and to benefit from the costs saving that co-ordinated arrangements would bring.

18.13 He warned of claims being statute barred under the Limitation Act 1980 and highlighted that:

> the longer the delay, the greater the risk of becoming statute barred and also . . . the weaker the prospect of persuading the Court to exercise its powers to override the limitation period in any specific case.

18.14 He laid down a timetable for service of writs no later than 1 October 1986 and for service of a short form statement of claim to be served by 1 November 1986. The information to be included on this form had been agreed between the parties and included basic details such as the dates of ingestion of Opren; other medication prescribed; allegations of injury suffered. The defendants were to serve a short form defence in the prescribed format. The plaintiffs had to notify their intention to join the Opren Scheme by 1 December 1986 and the defendants could object to any individual plaintiff being included by 1 January 1987. He ordered that lead actions be selected by 1 March 1987 and that applications for further directions and summonses to stay the remaining actions should be issued by 1 April 1987. He commented:

> It will be appreciated that this is the most unusual procedure devised to fit the special needs of this litigation. The intention is to be fair to all interested parties. . . . it is equally just both to the present plaintiffs and to all the defendants, that the final shape of the litigation should be established as soon as possible, and for the actions to proceed thereafter as speedily as possible to their conclusion.

18.15 Despite the Order of 23 July 1986 there followed a second hearing before Hirst J in which a subsequent group of Opren plaintiffs called 'Schedule 2' or 'Group B' were co-ordinated. These plaintiffs had to serve their writs by 31 January 1987. Even with this extension there were still many plaintiffs who did not comply (see below, 'Schedule 3' or 'Group C' litigation).

18.16 The criteria for selection of lead actions and issues were never identified as the litigation did not proceed (see below).

---

[2] *Davies v Eli Lilly & Co and Others*, The Times, 2 Aug 1996.

Discovery

Meanwhile discovery was being undertaken by the parties and lists of documents were exchanged. The plaintiffs sought to have the Lilly defendants' documents inspected by a medical journalist who had been assisting them with the litigation. The Lilly defendants objected to this and Hirst J accepted that he was an inappropriate person to undertake this task. This judgment was given on 23 July 1986.[3] It was appealed to the Court of Appeal on 22 January 1987.[4] The Appeal was resolved by the plaintiffs' solicitors and the individual in question giving specific undertakings not to divulge any information obtained during the course of discovery outside the litigation.

18.17

Costs

The plaintiffs had argued that they should be entitled to select lead cases only from the cohort of legally aided plaintiffs which comprised two-thirds of the claims, thus protecting non-legally aided plaintiffs from exposure to costs. The defendants successfully argued that the Legal Aid Fund could not be burdened in this way and that the test cases should be selected from the whole cohort of plaintiffs irrespective of their funding. On 8 May 1987 Hirst J delivered a landmark judgment allocating costs liabilities between all plaintiffs equally.[5]

18.18

This decision was upheld by the Court of Appeal on 3 June 1987. Lord Donaldson, then Master of the Rolls, said:

18.19

> Trying 1500 cases together is much cheaper than trying 1500 cases separately, so the plaintiffs as a group can spend more before they can reach the economic limit. However you arrange things and whether there are 1500 plaintiffs or only one there is always some economic limit. That is the long and short of the problem. Whether that limit will be reached in the present cases is not for me to say, but I see no grounds for thinking that these cases are an exception to the general rule that settling genuine disputes by agreement between the parties is almost always in the interest of all the parties.

Medical evidence

There were a number of important applications relating to medical evidence. Hirst J gave the following judgments:

18.20

> *Walker v Eli Lilly*[6]—Related to the production of medical records and this judgment in Open Court urged the co-operation of doctors and Health Authorities in promptly providing medical records on request.
>
> *Pozzi v Eli Lilly*[7]—The plaintiff served a medical report in support of his allegations but it was apparent on the face of the document that it was incomplete. The Lilly defendants successfully argued that the whole report must be disclosed.

---

[3] *Davies v Eli Lilly & Ors (No 2)*, The Times, 2 Aug 1986.
[4] [1987] 1 All ER 801.
[5] *Davies v Eli Lilly & Ors*, The Times, 11 May 1987.
[6] The Times, 3 Dec 1986.
[7] The Times, 1 May 1986.

A judgment of 6 November 1986 related to medical examinations. It was held that plaintiffs were not entitled to have an observer present when being examined and photo tested by an eminent photobiologist instructed by the Lilly defendants.

18.21 The Lilly defendants had been carefully reviewing such medical reports and records as had been served in the plaintiffs' cases. In many cases the evidence did not support the wide-ranging allegations of the many and varied side effects claimed to have been caused by Opren, including light and heat sensitivity which, uniquely, persisted for months or years after the ingestion of the product had ceased. There were few contemporaneous references to the plaintiffs' alleged complaints in the majority of their medical records.

18.22 Despite allegations of skin related effects, few, if any, had sought the advice of a consultant dermatologist either prior to or after commencing legal proceedings. Following a rigorous examination of the medical evidence available payments into court were made by the Lilly defendants in respect of a small number of claims which the Lilly defendants' medical advisers considered could have been causally related to the ingestion of Opren.

18.23 At no time during the course of the litigation then or since has any independent medical or scientific evidence been served to support the plaintiffs' allegations that Opren could cause persistent photosensitivity or heat sensitivity.

Settlement

18.24 The Court of Appeal's decision on costs allocation and the payments into court generated an even more virulent press and media campaign against the Lilly defendants, verging on contempt of court, which Hirst J alluded to on a number of occasions in court. This campaign included an offer by a wealthy individual to fund the claims of non-legally aided plaintiffs.

18.25 Against the background of this campaign and despite the fact that the plaintiffs' lawyers had served no independent medical or scientific evidence to support the more serious claims being made as to non-warned against side effects, negotiations were carried out between the Steering Committee advising the plaintiffs and the Lilly defendants' solicitors. These negotiations culminated in a settlement of the Schedule I and II claims which was approved by Hirst J in December 1987.

18.26 The specific terms of the settlement were and remain confidential. Although judgment was not given in Open Court inaccurate speculative reports as to its terms were widely publicised in the media. Broadly the terms of the offer comprised a global sum offered to the plaintiffs by the defendants with no admission as to causation or liability. The sum was to be allocated by the plaintiffs' legal advisers on the basis of levels of common law damages then applicable. There had to be some medical evidence to support the alleged symptoms. The exceptions were side effects wholly warned of by Lilly or where the symptoms were of too minor a nature to justify legal proceedings. An independent scheme of arbitration was to be set up to review the awards of any plaintiffs who were dissatisfied. The Lilly defendants took no part in the arbitration process.

Randall v Eli Lilly & Ors[8]

18.27 Hirst J clarified the principles and procedures to be applied in the arbitration process. He outlined the arbitration procedure, which would be non-adversarial, and included a review by Hirst J of a plaintiff's claim on the basis of written submissions following which a short reasoned award would be made. Any plaintiff dissatisfied with that award would then have the right to an oral hearing at which arguments could be addressed but no further evidence submitted.

The Arbitration Report 28 July 1988

18.28 Following the arbitrations Hirst J reported on 28 July 1988. He stated that over 1,300 plaintiffs participated in the settlement scheme and of those forty-four had applied for arbitration. At the time of giving his report forty cases had been concluded. In the majority of arbitration cases he upheld the assessors' awards. In nearly all these cases the plaintiffs had asked the Judge to find, contrary to the expert evidence, that a condition from which they suffered should be attributed to Opren, but the Judge had not been satisfied of this.

18.29 This hearing concluded the original Opren claims. It is of note that despite claims of 'thousands' of litigants, early in the case, approximately 1,300 participated in the settlement.

F. The English Litigation—Part 2

18.30 In March 1987, within two months of the cut-off date ordered by Hirst J for the Schedule II claims, a request was made for a third group of Opren claimants to join the co-ordinated arrangements. This was declined by the Lilly defendants because of the concessions that had already been granted in agreeing to the co-ordinated agreements for Schedules I and II. This new group comprised some 400 individuals by the end of 1987. On 29 March 1988 Hirst J gave directions, for further co-ordinated arrangements for the Schedule III (or Group C) claims under the lead plaintiff name of *Beale*. The cut-off date was 9 May 1988 and those who served writs after this date should await the determination of the Schedule III or Group C cases. The plaintiffs' solicitors had 350 claims which qualified when this date expired. The Lilly defendants received further claims and on 15 June 1989 Hirst J gave orders in respect of these late claims which fell outside Schedule III under the lead plaintiff name of *Ainslie*. This Group were to await the outcome of the *Beale* litigation.

The preliminary issue of limitation

18.31 Because most of these claimants had come forward so late and after generous extensions of

---

[8] Judgment (3 Feb 1988); The Times, 4 Feb 1988.

time ordered by Hirst J, it was agreed between the parties that there should be a preliminary issue on the question of limitation. In the meantime Hirst J had been appointed to the Court of Appeal and Hidden J took his place as the Judge appointed to co-ordinate the remaining litigation.

18.32 The claims had to be pleaded by service of a short form statement of claim and medical records and reports. The defendants did not have to serve a formal defence at that stage. The information served by the plaintiffs enabled the parties to consider an appropriate selection of claims to cover the categories of circumstances of individual plaintiffs to ensure that the preliminary issue could be as determinative as possible. The criteria for selection of lead actions, from the defendants' perspective, included looking at cases which identified different types of side effect; different dates of knowledge as to when plaintiffs asserted that their side effects occurred; when they took medical and/or legal advice on those side effects.

18.33 Fifteen claims were selected by the plaintiffs and two by the defendants. These were ordered by Hidden J to be lead actions. All remaining plaintiffs' claims were stayed meanwhile.

First trial on limitation—15 October 1990–2 November 1990 [9]

18.34 During this hearing evidence was given in nine of the lead cases. The remaining eight cases were not heard as the plaintiffs' lawyers agreed they raised no different issues. The evidence consisted of the plaintiffs themselves and in the majority of cases one or more of their medical advisers. It quickly became apparent in almost every case that the lack of contemporaneous medical evidence, allied with the testimony of the plaintiffs' doctors (who in most cases could not recall either specific complaints about Opren or the many and varied side effects alleged to have been caused by the drug), were not supportive of the plaintiffs' cases.

The Limitation Act 1980

18.35 Having heard the evidence Hidden J undertook a detailed review of the law. He was required to consider the relevant provisions of the Limitation Act 1980, in particular section 11(4), which states that the relevant limitation period is three years from:

(a) The date on which the cause of action accrued; or
(b) The date of knowledge (if later) of the person injured.

18.36 He held the date on which the cause of action accrued to be the first ingestion of Opren and that that date was the date of knowledge under section 11(4)(b) from which the primary limitation period ran.

18.37 Section 14(1) of the Act states that the plaintiff must have had knowledge of the following:

(a) That the injury in question was significant;
(b) That the injury was attributable in whole or in part to the act or omission which is alleged to constitute negligence, nuisance or breach of duty;
(c) The identity of the defendant.

---

[9] *Nash v Eli Lilly* [1991] 2 Med LR 169.

18.38 The word 'significant' in section 14(1)(a) has to be construed in accordance with the provisions of section 14(2), which read:

> For the purposes of this section an injury is significant if the person whose date of knowledge is in question would reasonably have considered it sufficiently serious to justify instituting proceedings for damages against the defendant who did not dispute liability and was able to satisfy judgment.

Hidden J thus followed the decision in *McCafferty v Metropolitan Police Receiver*.[10]

18.39 Hidden J also referred to the definition of 'knowledge' in section 14(3) of the Limitation Act:

> For the purposes of this section a person's knowledge includes knowledge which he might reasonably have been expected to acquire:
>
> (a) From facts observable or ascertainable by him or;
> (b) From facts ascertainable by him with the help of medical or other appropriate expert advice which it is reasonable for him to seek.
>
> But a person shall not be fixed under this sub-section with knowledge of a fact ascertainable only with the help of expert advice so long as he has taken all reasonable steps to obtain (and, where appropriate, to act on) that advice.

18.40 The Judge held that it was not only the plaintiff's individual actual knowledge which had to be considered but, in appropriate circumstances, the knowledge of others which he might reasonably have obtained.

18.41 The Judge considered what 'knowledge' the plaintiff needed, to know that the injury was attributable in whole, or in part, to the act or omission of the defendants alleged to constitute negligence. He held that the word 'attributable' is defined as 'capable of being attributed to'. Knowledge was given its ordinary and natural meaning.

18.42 Because of the voluminous allegations made by the plaintiffs the parties had difficulty in identifying what was considered to be the act or omission for the purpose of section 14(1)(b). The Judge considered the case law and in particular the case of *Wilkinson v Ancliff*.[11]

18.43 He stated that there must be a degree of specificity in defining the act or omission which constituted negligence or breach of duty, bearing in mind an individual plaintiff's knowledge as well as the knowledge he might reasonably have been expected to acquire from an appropriate expert. He held that a solicitor could be such an expert. He expressed himself to be quite satisfied that a plaintiff should be fixed with the knowledge of a solicitor whom he might reasonably be expected to consult.

18.44 The Judge considered that the act or omission relevant in the present cases for the purpose of section 14(1)(b) can be best expressed in the following words: 'providing for the use of patients a drug which was unsafe in that it was capable of causing persistent photosensitivity in those patients and/or in failing to discover such was the case and to properly protect all patients'.

---

[10] [1977] 1 WLR 1073.
[11] [1986] 1 WLR 1352.

18.45 In summary, the question to which the Judge addressed himself in respect of each individual plaintiff was:

> What was the date when that particular plaintiff either had knowledge or might have reasonably been expected to acquire knowledge, either by himself or through his solicitors or his doctors or through others, that his photosensitivity was capable of being attributed as a possible cause in whole or in part to the act or omission of the defendants in exposing him to a drug which was unsafe in that it was capable of causing persistent photosensitivity and/or in failing to take reasonable and proper steps to protect him from such a condition.

18.46 In the light of this the Judge considered the nine individual cases (out of the seventeen) in which he had heard evidence. In all cases, save one, he found that the plaintiffs' claims were statute barred.

Discretion

18.47 The Judge then turned his attention to each plaintiff individually in order to decide whether his discretion should be exercised to disapply the provisions of the Limitation Act under section 33. In particular section 33(3) provides guidance for the court on the approach it should take in exercising its discretion. The court should consider the length of, and reasons for, the delay on the part of the plaintiff; the extent to which, having regard to the delay, the evidence is likely to be less cogent; the conduct of the defendants; the extent to which the plaintiff acted promptly and reasonably after he knew his injury might be attributable to the defendants; the steps taken by the plaintiff to obtain expert advice and the nature of that advice. Overall, the court must look at the individual circumstances of the case.

18.48 Hidden J carefully reiterated the arguments submitted by the parties. In each case he held that the plaintiffs' delay had increased the difficulty in establishing his or her claim and he was satisfied that it would not be appropriate to exercise his discretion under the Act to disapply its provisions.

18.49 In his conclusion Hidden J stated that the judgment was much longer than he had wished because he was aware of the number of claims standing behind these lead actions. He concluded by saying:

> It is a matter of regret to me having seen and heard from all these plaintiffs that I have had to rule against so many of them. I can only give them this reassurance, that if a case is bound to be lost, then the earlier it is lost the better. Those words are in no wise meant to sound callous or unfeeling; rather are they meant to offer a crumb of comfort in what is, no doubt, otherwise a dispiriting situation.

18.50 Following this judgment in July 1991 Hidden J dismissed the remaining Opren Schedule III and late actions. In November 1991 the plaintiffs' solicitors served a Notice of Appeal in the *Nash* case.

Second trial on limitation[12]

18.51 Despite the *Nash* trial, which comprised the plaintiffs' solicitors' selection of those cases

---

[12] *Berger v Eli Lilly & Ors* [1992] 3 Med LR 233.

they considered to be representative and the detailed judgment of Hidden J, with only one case overcoming the limitation hurdle on its own particular facts, the plaintiffs' solicitors claimed that there were nine further cases which fell into that category. These came before Hidden J in September 1991. Judgment was given on 2 and 3 March 1992. The trial followed the same format as the *Nash* case and the evidence given was similar.

Hidden J incorporated large sections of his judgment in the *Nash* case within the *Berger* judgment. He reviewed the nine cases before him on their individual facts, as he had done in the *Nash* case, and held that all, save one, were time barred. In only one case was discretion sought under section 33 and Hidden J refused to exercise discretion as there was little to distinguish these claims from the original nine. 18.52

The Court of Appeal[13]

All plaintiffs whose claims had failed before Hidden J in both the *Nash* and *Berger* trials appealed to the Court of Appeal at a hearing which took place between 23 June and 9 July 1992 and judgment was given on 28 August 1992. 18.53

The Court confirmed the relevant enquiries which had to be made under section 14 of the Limitation Act and upheld Hidden J's judgment in the definition of 'significant injury'. They confirmed that the test is partly a subjective test and partly an objective test, ie what would a particular plaintiff have considered to be a serious injury, and what would have been reasonable to regard as a serious injury. The Court confirmed that it had to look at the circumstances of each plaintiff's case to assess this. 18.54

The Court of Appeal defined the test as: 18.55

> A condition of mind which imports a degree of certainty and that degree of certainty justifies embarking upon the preliminaries to the making of a claim for compensation.

Factors that the Court of Appeal took into account in assessing whether a plaintiff had knowledge included the nature of the information that the plaintiff received, the extent to which he paid attention to it, and his capacity to understand it. The Court decided that it should assess the intelligence of the plaintiff and determine whether he or she did in fact have 'knowledge' as required by the statute. 18.56

It concluded that photosensitivity continuing for an unacceptable period after the patient had ceased to take a drug would clearly be a 'significant injury'. 18.57

Importantly the Court confirmed that: 18.58

> If the plaintiff held a firm belief which was of sufficient certainty to justify the taking of the preliminary steps for proceedings by obtaining advice about making a claim for compensation, then such belief is knowledge and the limitation period would begin to run.

The Court of Appeal supported Hidden J's definition of attributability. 18.59

With regard to constructive knowledge, the Court held that they should consider *subjectively* what a particular plaintiff should have observed or ascertained; but must judge his or her observations by a standard of reasonableness which is *objective*. This objectivity 18.60

---

[13] *Nash v Eli Lilly and Ors* [1992] 4 All ER 383.

should, however, be 'qualified to take into consideration the position and circumstances and character of the plaintiff'.

18.61 The Court accepted that 'other appropriate expert advice' referred to in section 14(3)(b) extended to other experts and included legal and medical advice.

18.62 Turning to the identity of the defendants, the Court of Appeal found that in the circumstances of this case they were 'satisfied that . . . once attributability has been established against one or more of the defendants, identity of the remaining defendants was reasonably ascertainable'.

18.63 The Court of Appeal considered each case afresh on its own facts for the purposes of both section 14 and section 33 discretion and the Court placed great emphasis on the merits of a particular claim, stating: 'if it is shown that the claim is a poor case lacking in merit there may be significant and relevant prejudice to the defendants if the limitation provisions are disapplied'.

18.64 The Court of Appeal made a number of comments in considering generally section 33 discretion, referring to the 'startling absence 'of contemporaneous records of complaint and rejecting:

> The assertion that the defendants suffered no real prejudice in any one of these particular cases which is rightly regarded as a poor case and in which the time bar is disapplied. If the case is rightly regarded as a poor case, having regard to the contrast between complaints now advanced and the absence of any record of complaints by a plaintiff, who is properly regarded as a plaintiff who would have reported such complaints to his doctor if his condition was then as he now recalls it, then, by the disapplication of the bar the defendants are put to the expense of defending, upon its merits, a poor case, which may well cost, upon the issues, apart from liability, far more to defend than the case would be held to be worth.

18.65 The Court went on to say:

> Although each case must be considered in the context of its own particular circumstances, there are a number of features which arise in many of the cases which have common attributes. The drug Opren was withdrawn in August 1982. The Writs upon which the present cases are based were all issued some six years or so later. The nature of the complaints was to a large extent subjective, eg: irritation, pain, dizziness etc, and in most cases there was little to be seen by way of organic damage. During the later stages of the much publicised history of the drug, risk of self deceiving or exaggerated claims was obvious.

18.66 The Court acknowledged that:

> The main method of testing the claims available, therefore, to the defendants was a comparison of contemporary records with the present complaints for the purpose of establishing the date at which the plaintiff had, or should have had, knowledge within the meaning of section 11 of the Act and of testing the credibility of the claim.

18.67 The Court rejected the defendants' submissions that because of the special nature of group litigation section 33 discretion should not be available. It stated:

> There may well be a strong case for legislative action to provide a jurisdictional structure for the collation and resolution of mass product liability claims, particularly in the pharmaceutical field, but this Court cannot devise such rules.

18.68 The Court of Appeal dismissed all the appeals save for three cases where, on their particular facts, they found that the plaintiffs' date of knowledge was within the primary limitation period.

18.69 The Court of Appeal also gave the plaintiffs' group a deadline for notifying the defendants of any claims which they considered fell within the guidelines set out in their judgment in that their cases would be similar to those who succeeded in establishing that their claims were not time barred.

18.70 The plaintiffs' solicitors notified the defendants of forty-eight claims that they still considered not to be statute barred despite the judgments of Hidden J and the Court of Appeal. These included a lead plaintiff from the first limitation trial whose individual case had not been put before the Judge as it was not considered to differ significantly from the other cases, and the named lead plaintiff of the second limitation trial.

18.71 At this point the Lilly defendants wrote a detailed letter to the Legal Aid Board setting out the entire history of the litigation and drawing their attention to the lack of supporting medical and scientific evidence for these claims, and the comments made by Hidden J and the Court of Appeal. In due course the Lilly defendants were informed that legal aid had been withdrawn.

18.72 On 13 March 1996 all remaining claimants were struck out by Hidden J on the ground of inordinate and inexcusable delay which rendered them vexatious and an abuse of the process of the Court.

19

HIV HAEMOPHILIA LITIGATION

Simon Pearl[1]

> The most important factor in this negligence litigation from around 1990 was speed. The parties and the court recognised an overwhelming need to achieve resolution of all of the individual cases in view of the serious risk of impending death to the 1,000 plaintiffs. As a result, no preliminary issues were selected and although it was intended to proceed by way of resolution of generic issues through lead cases, preparatory work on all the other individual cases was continued rather than their being stayed. Steering committees were formed quickly amongst the plaintiffs' solicitors' firms and also, albeit not without some argument, amongst groups of defendants. One useful technique adopted by the Judge was to give non-binding, preliminary indications of his views on points which might become the subject of future Orders, thereby enabling the parties to plan accordingly. Pressure from the Judge on the parties to settle, particularly when this was leaked to the media, is thought to have had a significant impact on achieving settlement.

A. Haemophilia

Haemophilia is a rare hereditary condition which results from a reduced level of Factor VIII or Factor IX blood clotting factors. This leads to abnormal bleeding and bruising. The condition is so serious that internal bleeding into muscles and joints led to an actuarial survival of twenty-three years for a severe Haemophiliac prior to the advent of Factor VIII and Factor IX concentrate. Concentrate so improved the treatment of Haemophiliacs that, prior to AIDS, life expectancy was around that of an average person. **19.01**

The development of Factor VIII concentrate led to its rapid introduction in the 1970s. The concentrate pooled plasma from many donations, and indeed it has been reported that in the 1980s American fractionators were using pools of up to 20,000 donations whilst the NHS pools were up to 8,000. The increased demand for Factor VIII concentrate could not be met by the NHS, from volunteer donated blood, and the shortfall was **19.02**

---

[1] Partner, Davies Arnold Cooper.

resolved by acquiring commercial concentrate from the USA. Donors of blood from commercial fractionators were often paid for their donations. By 1983 the annual usage of concentrate was over 70 million units of which about 30–40 million units were commercial concentrate. Demand for Factor IX concentrate was always satisfied by the NHS.

B. AIDS

19.03 AIDS is due to infection with a virus, HIV. It is now known that the virus is mainly spread through sexual contact and by blood. The first reports of a condition now recognised as AIDS were within the homosexual community in California and New York in the early 1980s. The first reports of Haemophiliacs with these conditions which suggested a possible agent transmissible through blood products were in July 1982. In September 1982 the Centre for Disease Control in the USA defined AIDS and gave the first breakdown of at risk groups which included Haemophiliacs. In November 1983 the first AIDS case in the UK was reported in the literature and by the end of 1983 there was much epidemiological and circumstantial evidence to suggest that AIDS was transmitted by an unknown virus.

19.04 In April 1984 a leading article in *Nature* recorded that Gallo's Group in the USA had isolated the AIDS virus called HTLVIII (later changed to HIV), and research immediately intensified to develop a heat treated product which inactivated the virus and an antibody test. A test for HIV antibodies became available in 1985 at which time it became possible to screen out infected donors. Most Haemophilia Centres started using heat treated Factor VIII in December 1984 but they were variable up to about March/April 1985.

C. The Effect of AIDS on UK Haemophiliacs

19.05 By that time 1,321 individuals with Haemophilia in Britain were infected with HIV, of which 560 were currently alive in 1997.[2] Approximately 1,000 Haemophiliacs or close family relatives commenced legal proceedings against the Department of Health, the Licensing Authority, the Committee of Safety of Medicine, The Central Blood Laboratories Authority, and treating NHS bodies, which included virtually all Regional Health Authorities and District Health Authorities, along with various special Health Authorities throughout England and Wales.

19.06 At the same time the Haemophilia Society and the lawyers representing the plaintiffs pressed for no fault compensation from the Government on the basis that the circumstances were unique. The Government set up a £10 million Trust Fund on an *ex gratia* basis in November 1987 but refused to pay full compensation on a no fault basis as it feared that it would set a precedent (a further £24 million was added in 1990). As the sums available from the Trust to each individual would be so modest compared with the amount of damages that would be expected on a full liability basis, the legal proceedings took their course.

---

[2] Lee, Sabin, and Miners (18 Oct 1997) British Medical Journal.

D. First Interlocutory Hearing

19.07 A Steering Committee of solicitors representing plaintiffs was formed consisting of Pannone Napier, J Keith Park & Co, and Deas Mallen Souter. All cases were transferred to the Royal Courts of Justice and assigned to Ognall J. Throughout the litigation, the Judge was 'hands on' in the manner which Lord Woolf now wishes all judges to be. The first summons came before him in June 1989. The significant Orders made on that occasion included that the title of all individual claims, and the names of the plaintiffs, be omitted from the writs and that the address of the plaintiff be given 'care of' their solicitor. This was to avoid press intrusion as a result of writ room searches. A register of plaintiffs' codes was kept by the Steering Committee and provided to the defendants. The Order also provided that all HIV Haemophilia plaintiffs, both those where proceedings had already been issued and those in proceedings to be issued, would be bound by Orders made and to be made. The Judge ordered that the main statement of claim should be served which would set out a compendium of allegations against the defendants and that all plaintiffs would be bound by these pleadings. The conduct of individual pleadings would remain with the plaintiffs' solicitors on the record but individual pleadings should be in a short form, the details of which were to be fixed at the second interlocutory hearing.

19.08 Ognall J gave various 'Indications', a feature of his interlocutory Orders which became common practice throughout the litigation. Indications were appended to the formal Order and, whilst not binding on the parties, were intended to represent the strong wishes of the Judge. The indications made on the first occasion included that the Health Authorities should make every effort to co-ordinate representation, because, at that hearing, the Court was packed to the rafters with solicitors representing various Health Authorities.

19.09 The Judge also gave indications in respect of publicity, asking the Haemophilia Society to bring the litigation to the notice of all Haemophiliacs to encourage them to act quickly if they wanted to join the litigation as he intended, on a future occasion, to consider cut-off dates.

E. Second Interlocutory Hearing

19.10 The second interlocutory hearing was held a month later. At that time the Judge ordered that the main statement of claim should be served later that week, on or before 31 July 1989, with the balance of the timetable for other pleadings and directions to be heard at a further interlocutory hearing in late October 1989.

19.11 The Judge also ordered that individual statements of claim required information of a relatively general nature, including information to identify the plaintiff, the types of blood products he received, and the date that he became HIV positive, then cross-references into the Master Statement of Claim and details of particular circumstances. The Judge also made provision for disclosure of medical records and importantly made provision that all medical records disclosed at any time be subject to the proviso of Order 24, rule 14A and remain confidential notwithstanding disclosure of such documents in open court.

19.12 A Cost-Sharing Order was made so that save where Orders solely related to particular plaintiffs, generic costs ordered to be paid by the plaintiffs were to be borne proportionately by each of the plaintiffs in the co-ordinated arrangements. An opportunity was given to plaintiffs to discontinue without cost if they did so by 29 September 1989.

19.13 The Judge's indications included an indication that any decision to join blood product manufacturers into the proceedings should be taken by 23 October 1989 (they were not joined) and that the defendants should proceed with their preparation of their Defence with all due expedition.

19.14 As a result of these two initial Orders, the procedures for a co-ordinated action were firmly put into place. The various government defendants co-ordinated their defence with the solicitor to the Department of Health. The Health Authority defendants appointed Davies Arnold Cooper as co-ordinating solicitors. Davies Arnold Cooper did not represent any of the individual defendants and the various Health Authorities retained their own solicitors to plead to the individual statements of claim but Davies Arnold Cooper dealt with all generic matters, and instructed counsel on the co-ordinated summonses. Their position as co-ordinating solicitor was recognised in all the court Orders. Health Authority co-ordinating solicitors have subsequently been appointed in other litigation, and this has now become a common feature with the advent of the National Health Service Litigation Authority's powers to call in repercussive cases. At the time it was regarded as quite revolutionary and met with a not inconsiderable degree of opposition amongst Health Authorities' solicitors.

19.15 The Master Statement of Claim was duly served and was almost 200 pages in length and each defendant served a main Defence.

F. Subsequent Interlocutory Orders

19.16 At the Summons on 20 December 1989 Ognall J decided that there should be no preliminary issues tried in the litigation, deadlines were set for service of the individual statements of claim, and defendants were required to plead limitation specifically if they intended to rely on it. There was no attempt to delay the progress of individual claims by the process of pushing forward on generic issues only, although it was accepted that generic issues would be identified and tried by selecting example cases as lead cases.

19.17 At a further hearing on 22 January 1990 a trial date for the generic issues of the litigation was fixed for one year later, ie 14 January 1991, a very tight timetable indeed, but one intended to reflect the judicial response to the tragedy. A Master (originally Master Warren, later Master Turner) was assigned to deal with applications in individual cases to amend writs, substitute parties, etc, and discovery orders were made against the defendants on the generic cases. The Judge's indications included the statements 'any deferral of the trial date will not be lightly countenanced and will require very compelling reasons. Any application for such deferral must be supported by written reasons served on the Court and on the other parties.' In fact the trial date was subsequently deferred to March 1991 and subsequently adjourned generally at a time when the settlement negotiations were in their final stages.

19.18 It had been intended that the generic issues would be determined by trials of a number of selected test cases. The process of choosing these cases was well under way at the time of the settlement. The system which was agreed to by all the parties was that if any side chose to include a case as a test case, there would be no right of veto, although if one party regarded a chosen case as being an unnecessary case to include, then there was to be a degree of compromise. All parties agreed that it was desirable to cover the widest of issues arising by way of the test case trials, so it was agreed that once selected a plaintiff could not discontinue the action and equally the defendant could not make a payment into court or offer to settle it.

G. The Court of Appeal Rules on Public Interest Immunity

19.19 The next and most significant interlocutory matter that came before the Court was in relation to specific discovery against the central defendants. With hindsight, this can be seen to have been the turning point in the case. The application was made not to Ognall J but to Rougier J on 31 July 1990, concerning certain categories of documents where the Minister had issued a Public Interest Immunity Certificate to prevent disclosure. Neither plaintiffs nor the Government were happy with Rougier J's judgment and the matter came before the Court of Appeal (Lord Justices Ralph Gibson and Bingham, and Sir John Megaw) on 20 September 1990. The Government's main argument was that the allegations made against the defendants were such that they could not succeed on matters of policy and therefore discovery was not necessary.

19.20 The essence of the plaintiffs' case against the Government was that it took inadequate steps in the 1970s to make this country self-sufficient in blood products and allowed the Blood Products Laboratory to decline. The Government's position was that they owed no duty of care to individual NHS plaintiffs and that, even if they did, they could not be liable unless they had been 'Wednesbury' unreasonable as well as negligent and that personal injury resulted. It was the Department's position that since the law required that documents subject to public interest immunity could only be disclosed if the Court was satisfied that it was necessary in the interests of justice to do so, the Court had to decide whether it was arguable that the plaintiffs had in law a cause of action. Hence, before the Court of Appeal, the scope of the Department's duty was canvassed as if it were a preliminary issues or strike-out application. The Court of Appeal held that the plaintiffs had a strongly arguable case in negligence in respect of the Department's acts and omissions in performance of their functions under the National Health Service Act 1977, and whatever difficulty in terms of proof might exist, the Department was ordered to disclose documents for inspection by the Judge, who would then decide whether or not the plaintiffs would be deprived of a means of a proper presentation of their case without disclosure of the documents. This ruling gave great impetus to the settlement discussions which had by that time commenced. At the same time there was Prime Ministerial change, which enabled the political lobbying to start afresh.

H. Ognall J's Statement

19.21 In parallel with the Court of Appeal decision, Ognall J had, at an interlocutory hearing in chambers, encouraged the parties, in the unique circumstances of the litigation, to endeavour to resolve the case, pointing out the fact that neither side could be assured of victory. Some months later, in circumstances which have never become clear, the Judge's observations were published in a national Sunday newspaper.

I. The Settlement of the Main Action

19.22 These events intensified the already substantial media and political pressure which the Government was under to find a solution to the action going to trial, it being estimated that the trial of the selected lead cases would require some twenty-six weeks to be heard. It was not lost on the media that every side in the litigation was funded publicly. Perhaps as a result of this pressure, the Government decided to offer an additional £42 million for all Haemophiliacs and other plaintiffs with the substantial extra benefit that such payment would not be taken into account for Social Security. As a result of this additional injection of money, the plaintiffs agreed to accept the Government's offer and discontinued all claims except for pure medical negligence cases.

19.23 At the announcement in Open Court of the settlement, statements were read out by the Leading Counsel representing the plaintiffs, Rupert Jackson QC and Daniel Brennan QC, and also Andrew Collins QC representing the Government. The essence of the agreement was that plaintiffs would discontinue their litigation against all defendants, and the Department of Health would pay a further £42 million into the Trust Fund for the benefit of all infected Haemophiliacs to be divided up into broad categories of claimants. The payments would not affect recipients' entitlement to state benefit. In addition, the plaintiffs would receive their costs from the Government. The proposals applied to all infected Haemophiliacs whether in the litigation or not. A special provision was also made to permit plaintiffs to continue the medical negligence claims against Health Authorities if they considered they had a claim for pure medical negligence.

19.24 The categories of claimants, and the amount of money that they were to receive, were as follows:

(1) Infants—£21,500 each.
(2) Single adults—£23,500 each.
(3) Married adults (including stable relationships) without dependent children—£32,000.
(4) Married adults (including stable relationships) with dependent children—£60,500.
(5) Infected intimates:
   (a) adults or married infants—£23,500
   (b) unmarried infants—£21,500
(6) Family members at risk—£2,000.

Ognall J then made the following statement at the conclusion of the hearing: **19.25**

> I wish to pay clear tribute to all Counsel, solicitors and their staff involved in this litigation for their expertise, efficiency, co-operation, good sense and a great deal of hard work that they have invested in these complex and emotionally exacting proceedings.
>
> Group litigation of this type does not, in my view, fit easily into the existing structure of our legal system. Without the co-operation previously referred to, I do not believe we would have been able to overcome the practical difficulties which beset litigation of this character.
>
> As you are aware some of my earlier observations conducted in chambers concerning the progress of this litigation were published. At the time I made my views of that publication known. I consider that all parties have been well advised to compromise these actions on the terms before me and I acknowledge their goodwill in doing so.
>
> There are still a number of clinical mismanagement claims to decide. I do not think, however, that these outstanding cases preclude me from saying the following. The plaintiffs' tragic circumstances have excited great concern and sympathy. It is therefore gratifying to know that those who have survived to date had been relieved of the weight of protracted uncertain litigation. I extend my sympathy and good wishes to them all.

J. The Medical Negligence Cases

After the settlement of the main action, 118 claimants originally gave notice that they intended to pursue medical negligence claims against their Health Authority for full compensation. The terms of the settlement agreement permitted the Health Authorities to claim credit for the monies received from the government settlement, and required the claims to be based on 'pure medical negligence' allegations, without the right to pursue 'generic' allegations regarding self-sufficiency or national policy. Davies Arnold Cooper then came on the record in relation to these cases and the Court continued to co-ordinate these claims with a view to fixing a tight timetable for the trial of them. **19.26**

In order to progress the cases, independent Haematologists for the defendants and the plaintiffs set about analysing the medical records of each case. Through Court approved procedures agreed between the parties, informal notes were exchanged, and cases were broadly categorised as ones where there was (a) no negligence, (b) negligence, (c) doubtful negligence. The defendants, subject to agreement on quantum, settled the negligence claims on a full liability basis and assuming the categorisation was agreed the doubtful cases were also settled, taking account of the risks of litigation, effectively on a 50/50 basis. Many of the no-negligence cases were withdrawn. Ultimately there were nine cases unresolved which were fixed to be tried consecutively in October 1992. By this time the assigned Judge had become Alliott J, having passed briefly to Brooke J. By the date of trial, there was only one case left, JKP109, and this was settled prior to judgment. There were a number of cases which had not been included in the trial listing for particular reasons and most of these have now been concluded, although there are two claims which have yet to be resolved. Nevertheless, it can be stated that the negotiations in relation to the medical negligence cases subsequent to the government settlement were conducted in an open spirit and in the main this led to satisfactory and speedy conclusions to these highly emotional and public proceedings. **19.27**

20

GRAVIGARD IUD

Christopher Hodges[1]

> This product liability case was solved in the earlier 1990s by the passing of time: the court unusually permitted time to pass rather than impose interventionist management techniques. Claimants' concern was generated by media stories, particularly following a US jury decision, but over time it became clearer that scientific understanding had evolved from the possibility of supporting a case on general causation to a position where such a case was not supported. After an initial extended period in which the court was not called upon to manage the litigation, but a draft Master Statement of Claim was nevertheless produced in advance of investigation of individual cases, it was clear by the time that the court became involved that claimants were dropping out and that the number of those who wished to remain in the group should be clarified. The court was not asked to and did not impose a cut-off date, but claimants continued to drop out and Legal Aid was ultimately withdrawn after representations by the defendant.

A. The Product

20.01 Interest in the use of intrauterine contraceptive devices (IUCDs), known to have been used since ancient times, was revived in the first half of the twentieth century. Further interest arose with the availability of plastics, which enabled easier insertion and removal, and with the addition of a tail-string to facilitate removal. A considerable number of modern 'second generation' devices were marketed from the late 1960s with the addition of copper to a plastic frame. From the 1980s, frames could incorporate a hormone for slow release. Use of devices grew in the 1970s with the publication of literature concerning possible risks of thrombo-embolic disorders associated with long-term use of combined hormonal contraceptives. Some risks have been associated with each of the different available forms of contraception. The perceived advantages of the IUCD method to the patient are high compliance (after fitting the device the patient need do nothing to ensure efficacy),

---

[1] Partner, CMS Cameron McKenna.

long length of action, independence from the act of coitus, and the lack of a need to take hormones long term. Serious side effects with IUCD use are very rare and most problems arise from inadequate insertion technique. Serious effects are generally accepted to be less with this contraception method than any other, irrespective of the age of the patient.

20.02 A device in the shape of a plastic 7, around which copper wire was wound and with a tail-string to facilitate sterile removal, was designed by a leading clinician and developed in the USA by GD Searle & Co in the early 1970s. The device was classified as a drug by the US regulatory authority, the Food and Drug Administration (FDA), in 1971 and subject to production of research data to and approval of the FDA as being safe and effective. At that time, there was no regulation of devices *per se*. The product was marketed in the USA in 1974 as 'Copper 7'. The UK licensing authority also considered the product to be subject to the Medicines Act 1968 (the then only available regulatory system[2]) and, after considering data, granted a product licence in November 1973 on satisfaction of the requirements of safety, quality, and efficacy. The product was marketed in the UK as 'Gravigard'. In December 1980 a UK product licence was granted for a smaller version of the device, known as 'Mini-Gravigard'. Ongoing clinical studies on the product were continued by Searle for some years.

B. Assumption of Guilt through Association: Folklore and Publicity

20.03 In 1974 there was considerable public concern following reports of mid-trimester septic abortion being associated with use of a different design of inert IUD, the Dalkon Shield, marketed by AH Robins Company. The theory of causation was believed to be the ascension of microbes up the multi-filament tail-string of the Dalkon Shield by a 'wicking' process. Even though other IUDs had different designs of device and tail-string, much subsequent medical literature proceeded on the thesis that IUDs as a class were dangerous products and caused injury. By the 1990s, however, medical opinion had evolved to recognise that a product could not spontaneously cause the injuries which had been associated with IUD use. The main injury that was said to be associated with IUD use was pelvic inflammatory disease (PID), which might lead to scarring and occlusion of the fallopian tubes and hence infertility. However, the prevailing medical opinion developed that such injuries were generally caused by sexual activity and that a proximate cause of injury was generally the lifestyle of the woman (and her partner(s)) rather than the product itself. Modern epidemiological studies confirm that there is, in all probability, no device-related increased risk of PID due to the use of IUCDs such as Gravigard.

20.04 During the 1980s, the manufacturer had successfully defended a succession of product liability suits brought in the USA. In 1986 a users group, the Cu-7 Association, had been formed in the UK. The first letter before action in England was written by solicitors Pannone Napier to the company holding the UK product licence, GD Searle & Co Ltd,

---

[2] Comprehensive regulation of medical devices in Europe was only introduced pursuant to Directive 93/42/EEC, which became mandatory on 14 June 1998.

in January 1988. In September 1988 a US jury in *Kociemba v GD Searle & Co*[3] awarded compensatory and punitive damages of some US$8 million. Publicity of this in the UK, including a TV programme in 1989, led to an increasing number of women seeking legal advice on claiming compensation. They were advised not to proceed in the USA.

C. The Allegations

20.05 The general allegations in the Master Statement of Claim were that the manufacturer had been negligent in the design of the product (the tail-string), in its initial research (allegedly inadequate), in subsequent follow-up, and in failing to warn of the risk of PID/infertility. There were inherent difficulties with these allegations. They covered the entire lifetime of the product, some thirty years. The product had at all times been prescription only status in the USA and the UK and the text of data sheets required to be supplied to doctors required regulatory approval, as did the revisions which were made from time to time. Differences of text and timing between jurisdictions might, therefore, be expected. The UK data sheet had mentioned, since 1980, reports of an association between use of the product and increased incidence of PID and that PID might result in infertility. Searle contended that this information and all other relevant developing knowledge was reported in the medical literature and its current state should have been known to inserting physicians. The exact state of knowledge of each physician and whether he/she and each patient would have reacted differently if they had read a different warning on the product would have had to have been a matter for evidence.

D. Procedural History

20.06 Pannone Napier wrote again to Searle in January 1989 on behalf of thirty-two women who each had a Legal Aid certificate to commence proceedings. The Legal Aid Area Office had designated one case as the lead file. A considerable volume of documentation disclosed in US proceedings was made available to Pannone Napier by US lawyers. In August 1989 the plaintiffs obtained an order against the Department of Health for disclosure of documents concerning the regulatory history of the product. An application was issued for extensive pre-action discovery against GD Searle & Co Ltd in August 1989 and dismissed in March 1990. Pannone Napier stated in November 1991 that they were in a position to commence proceedings and wrote to the Senior Master requesting a single judge to be assigned, in accordance with the procedure recommended in the Supreme Court Procedure Committee's *Guide for use in Group Actions*. On 2 December 1991 the Senior Master issued a Practice Direction assigning Master Miller to co-ordinate proceedings, and stating that all claims should be transferred to the Central Office of the High Court, even if the claimed amount was less than £50,000. Most proceedings had been issued in the Sheffield County Court and were then transferred. Some eighteen firms of solicitors

---

[3] USDC, District of Minnesota, Third Division, 3–85 CIV 1599 (civil information).

were involved at this stage, most representing only one plaintiff, although by the time of the first directions hearing in May 1992 proceedings were only served on behalf of twenty-five women and at least nine women had given notice of intention to discontinue their claims. The plaintiffs' counsel indicated that some seventy women were expected to proceed. Most plaintiffs provided consents for the defendants to inspect their medical records when requested at an early stage. This enabled considerable progress to be made in examining individual claims.

20.07 The next directions hearing took place on 28 May 1993. By this time, not more than some forty-five women were wishing to proceed, all but two of whom had legal aid (and these two dropped out shortly afterwards), but some fifty-one were no longer proceeding. However, only seventeen had served individual writs. It was not clear how many individuals would be in a position to serve individual statements of claim and by when. There was also uncertainty as to whether all those claimants who might wish to proceed were represented at the hearing. The draft Master Statement of Claim which had been served was a very long document with extensive allegations, apparently prepared in advance of scrutiny of individual claims, and it was not clear how much of the document would be adopted in individual claims. It was accepted implicitly that no progress could be made unless and until the individual claims had been pleaded. However, Pannone Napier experienced some difficulty in co-ordinating a number of other firms, some of whom had their own ideas in relation to strategy or timing.

20.08 The Master adjourned the summons generally, not to be restored until all of the forty-five or so women had either issued proceedings or indicated their withdrawal. In an effort to make some progress, the defendants indicated that if draft individual statements of claim and medical reports were served within two months in the fifteen or so cases in which the plaintiffs were apparently ready to proceed, the defendants would within three months thereafter supply a Commentary on the draft Master Statement of Claim and on each of the individual cases. The Master refrained at that stage from ordering 'standard' directions, which had been provisionally agreed between Pannone Napier and McKenna & Co, including matters such as cost sharing between plaintiffs and the keeping of a register of plaintiffs.

20.09 Subsequent progress continued at a slow pace. The next hearing took place on 21 December 1994. By this time, seventy-four women had dropped out, still only seventeen women had issued proceedings (all but two having both issued and served proceedings), and six had not issued proceedings. It was only recently that a total of fifteen had supplied draft individual statements of claim. Accordingly, the defendants agreed to provide their Commentaries by February 1995. The Master indicated that the summons should be restored at that stage and that any claimants who had not caught up should show cause why they should not be excluded from the group.

20.10 There had been an issue as to the extent of information to be provided by plaintiffs in or with individual statements of claim. The defendants requested information not only on particulars of injury, special damage, case on negligence, on causation, and on limitation, but also details of use of the product, advice and warnings received, and gynaecological, reproductive, sexual, and medical history. At the next hearing in April 1995, at which dates were set for further service of pleadings, all these matters were ordered by the Master to be covered by plaintiffs either in individual statements of claim or in a supplementary document. The Master Statement of Claim was formally served at the end of April but no further procedural steps were taken.

Meanwhile, in February 1995, the defendants served their Commentary on the draft Master Statement of Claim. They followed this by submitting detailed written representations to the Legal Aid Board, in both the generic and the individual cases, that funding should be withdrawn. After detailed consideration of the representations and comments from the plaintiffs' advisers, plus the opinion of Queen's Counsel, the Board withdrew funding in June 1996. Appeals by nine women against the discharge of funding were dismissed by the Board's Area Committee in October 1996. **20.11**

E. Commentary

The principal procedural feature of this case was its slow progress. A major source of problems was the existence of too many firms of solicitors representing plaintiffs, often with a firm representing only one or two plaintiffs. This gave rise to administration difficulties, cost, and potential disagreements over strategy. Whilst the Legal Aid Board was able to decree that generic work should only be undertaken by a single firm, there was no power to rationalise this piecemeal representation. **20.12**

Overall, the case is a classic example of the incompatibility between the popular or media assumption that certain injuries were caused by a product and prevailing scientific opinion to the contrary. The result was some eight and a half years of public expenditure through legal aid on legal and medical experts with no tangible result for any claimant. **20.13**

The main legal difficulty which the plaintiffs faced was that of proving causation, both generic and individual. Detailed scrutiny of individual medical records frequently revealed either a failure to establish that the plaintiff suffered from the injury complained of (for example PID), or one or several alternative causes for the injury which were more likely to have been the cause than 'the product'. This problem manifested itself in the phenomenon of the floating plaintiff population. A total of just over 100 women, almost all of whom had legal aid, were notified to the defendants by solicitors. The drop-out rate was consistent throughout the period. By the end, only about fifteen were continuing. **20.14**

A significant impetus for this litigation was one successful case in the USA (amongst many unsuccessful) and certain documentary evidence which was used in it. The English Master Statement of Claim was served in draft at an early stage and was based on an analysis of those documents which had become available in US proceedings. This volume of documentation was not representative of the totality of the US manufacturer's documentation or evidence. The Master Statement of Claim was written before the medical evidence in individual claims was properly analysed, rather than vice versa. This inevitably led to difficulties. For example, the Master Statement of Claim included wide-ranging allegations against a different product, the Mini-Gravigard. Some two women who used this product were initially in the cohort but by the time the pleading was served neither they nor anyone else was proceeding in respect of Mini-Gravigard. **20.15**

20.16 These points underline the necessity, first, of examining each individual claim at the start before it is allowed to join the group and, secondly, of not allowing the tail to wag the dog in relation to pleadings or the supposed issues in the case. The products and allegations involved can only be determined after scrutiny of the individual cases in which they arise.

20.17 This case also illustrates the difficulty of cases succeeding where products are prescribed by learned intermediaries. Plaintiffs can face great difficulty in establishing that both the doctor and the plaintiff would have acted differently if the assumed negligence of the manufacturer had not occurred.

20.18 One innovative feature concerned the issue of jurisdiction and defendants. The plaintiffs stated in November 1991 that they wished to sue GD Searle & Co Ltd (the English subsidiary company which manufactured the product and marketed it in this country under a product licence granted by the licensing authority under the Medicines Act 1968), GD Searle & Co (the American parent company), and possibly another company in the group. The parties then negotiated an agreement which simplified the English litigation in a number of respects, the major aspects being as follows. Those plaintiffs who had named any company other than GD Searle & Co Ltd agreed, first, to serve notice of discontinuation against any such other company and not to join it subsequently. Searle agreed that no defence would be raised on the basis that any allegation made related to the activities of a Searle company other than GD Searle & Co Ltd, secondly, to accept liability in the litigation on behalf of any other Searle company, and, thirdly, to provide specified access to certain US documentation. A relevant consequence was that, in the light of this agreement, the Legal Aid Board made clear that it would not fund any claim against a US company. It should be said that the defendants proposed this agreement since they regarded the circumstances of this case as unusual. An agreement along these lines would not necessarily commend itself in other circumstances.

20.19 If the case had arisen a few years later so that the claims could have been based on the new law of strict liability for a defective product under the Consumer Protection Act 1987, causation would still have been a major difficulty. The issue of whether the manufacturer's conduct had been reasonable over the extended time period would have metamorphosed under strict liability into an issue of whether the product was defective. The development risk defence (section 4(1)(e) of the Consumer Protection Act) would probably not have been significant since the fact that PID was *associated* with IUD use was known—or postulated—almost throughout the marketed lifetime of the products. The issue was whether the product caused PID, when the association should have been warned about, and what strength of wording was appropriate at different times.

F. Postscript

20.20 Proceedings were issued in Australia in 1987, but not served until 1991, after contact between plaintiffs' lawyers in the USA, England, and Australia, and further statements of claim were issued in 1989, 1990, 1991, and then from time to time thereafter, which encompassed at the peak claims by some 300 women. The Australian actions proceeded to a trial of nine cases which ran from 29 January 1996 to 13 September 1996 with further submissions until 23 December 1997.

20.21 On 22 February 1999 Bruce J found in favour of the defendant, Searle, in each case, holding that 'the Plaintiffs have not established that the Defendant(s) were negligent in any material way nor that the actions of the Defendant(s) caused or materially contributed to the injuries to the Plaintiffs'. The judge said that this was 'the longest and most complex product liability litigation in Australian legal history'.

21

MYODIL LITIGATION

John Kelleher[1]

> This product liability litigation ran in the first half of the 1990s. Although vigorously contested, it was marked by the level of co-operation between the plaintiffs and defendant on procedural matters and active, firm, and efficient management by the Court. Given the complexity of the medical issues, the resolution of the litigation was achieved relatively quickly. It was one of the few cases in which settlements were agreed and this result was largely facilitated by the management decisions taken during the litigation.
>
> A single judge was appointed relatively early in the proceedings. All claimants were required to serve individual statements of claim, but this process was made more efficient by the adoption of a Master Statement of Claim—rather than the Master being adopted on its own. The Court ordered service of writs and individual statements of claim by a cut-off date, together with service of medical records, radiological images, and a medical report. Importantly, the parties had previously agreed both the format of medical reports and diagnostic criteria which were used to define the criteria for admission of individual claimants to the group. Despite the fact that the imposition of a cut-off date resulted in some delay caused by the logistical problems in processing the volume of individual claims, this mechanism resulted in the cohort of 4,000 potential claimants being reduced to 426. The parties were then able to reach a settlement which took account of the relative strengths and weaknesses of their positions and was thought to be cost-effective in avoiding the potential costs of a trial. Overall, therefore, the mechanism of requiring all individual claims to meet admission criteria which were set at an early stage proved effective, not only in weeding out those claims which did not meet proper criteria for the group but also in enabling the parties to reach an economic settlement. This result would not have been possible if a test case or lead case approach had been adopted.

---

[1] Partner, Theodore Goddard.

A. Description of the Parties

21.01 The Myodil litigation commenced in early 1990—although there had been earlier indications that claims would be made—and was ultimately settled in July 1995. During that period, over 4,000 individuals notified the defendant, Glaxo Laboratories Limited (Glaxo), of a potential claim.

21.02 On examination of medical records, it transpired that Myodil had not been used during the medical treatment of about 50 per cent of these potential claimants: as a result of steps taken in the proceedings which are described in more detail below, a significant majority of the remaining claimants did not proceed. Individual statements of claim with accompanying documentation were ultimately served by 426 plaintiffs. The Regional Health Authorities were initially named as additional defendants but the plaintiffs' advisers gave notice at an early stage that they did not intend to pursue generic allegations of negligence against them.

21.03 The plaintiffs, most of them legally aided, were represented by Alexander Harris, which chaired a Steering Committee of six firms. Glaxo was represented by Theodore Goddard.

B. Description of the Product

21.04 Myodil was an oil-based contrast medium used in myelography as a diagnostic, not a therapeutic, agent, by hospital specialists. Myelography is a radiological investigation of the contents of the spinal canal, which contains the spinal cord and the nerve roots leaving it. It is an invasive procedure involving the introduction of a needle into the sub-arachnoid space, as in simple lumbar puncture. Through this needle a contrast medium is introduced. The clinical indications for myelography were the confirmation or exclusion of a surgically treatable lesion. Until the availability of techniques such as CT scanning and MRI there was no other procedure by which surgically treatable lesions such as, for example, tumours or prolapsed intervertebral discs could be excluded, confirmed, or located with precision and confidence. Failure to diagnose such lesions at an early stage could cause irreparable damage that could lead to quadriplegia, paraplegia, incontinence, and death. Thus, although its primary purpose was diagnostic, myelography was an essential adjunct to treatment for many years.

21.05 Myodil was developed during the Second World War and was first supplied by Glaxo in 1944. The product was initially used by neurologists and neurosurgeons but in the 1960s and early 1970s was increasingly used by orthopaedic surgeons as an essential part of their practice.

21.06 Alternative contrast media were available. In particular, a number of water-based contrast media were introduced in the 1960s and 1970s but were withdrawn because of concern about their neuro-toxic side effects. Eventually a newer generation of safer water-based products was developed which in time displaced Myodil as the preferred contrast medium of the medical profession in the United Kingdom. Sales of Myodil were discontinued by Glaxo in 1987 for commercial reasons and myelography has now been largely superseded by MRI.

C. The General Nature of the Allegations

Each of the plaintiffs alleged that they had contracted adhesive arachnoiditis as a result of their undergoing at least one myelogram in which the contrast medium used was Myodil. Arachnoiditis is an inflammation causing the arachnoid membrane to become thickened and adherent to adjacent tissues. The inflammatory response consists mainly of exudation of fluid which may cause nerve roots (within the sub-arachnoid space) to adhere to each other and to the spinal theca. Arachnoiditis most often is and remains asymptomatic. In its most severe form it is capable of causing very severe pain. That pain is often difficult to distinguish from pain attributable to the underlying condition for which the diagnosis was applied.   21.07

The principal generic allegations of negligence listed in the original Master Pleading were as follows: 21.08

- Glaxo failed to carry out adequate research and development and sufficient clinical studies and/or trials;
- Glaxo failed to give adequate warnings to the medical profession of the risks of post-myelography arachnoiditis occurring;
- Glaxo failed to give an adequate warning that Myodil should be aspirated (removed) from the sub-arachnoid space after use;
- Glaxo should not have supplied Myodil and/or should have rigorously limited its use.

It became clear during the course of the litigation that the allegation that Myodil should never have been supplied at all by Glaxo was completely incompatible not only with the rest of the plaintiffs' generic case but also with the individual medical circumstances of the plaintiffs. As a result of intense interlocutory pressure over a period of six months the plaintiffs eventually amended their case to plead as their principal allegation that: 21.09

- up until 1977, the use of Myodil should only have been indicated in presenting patients in whom there was a significant prospect of finding a structural lesion which merited resolution by surgery, specific circumstances being cited, for example suspected spinal cord compression.

Glaxo denied these allegations, on the following basis: 21.10

- the risk of symptomatic arachnoiditis occurring after Myodil myelography was rare;
- it had given proper and adequate warnings at all times both as to the risk of arachnoiditis occurring and on the practice of aspiration;
- the decision as to whether or not myelography was indicated was always a serious and important clinical decision: where necessary, it would be performed in hospital by a doctor who could be expected to possess the necessary degree of expertise.

D. Outline Description of the Litigation

- *October 1989*—A letter before action was sent to Glaxo by Alexander Harris on behalf of six of their clients alleged to be suffering from adhesive arachnoiditis.   21.11

- *7 February 1990*—First writ issued and served on Glaxo.
- *22 February 1990*—The plaintiffs obtained an Order that one judge be appointed to deal with all the claims in the Myodil litigation (Steyn J) and that there be a costs-sharing Order as between the individual plaintiffs.
- During *1990* there was publicity about the Myodil claims, particularly in the local press throughout England and Wales. Little progress was made in the legal proceedings except that Glaxo began to receive a number of standard letters before action.
- *7 January 1991*—*World in Action* programme on Myodil was broadcast on national television for which there was a viewing figure of 4.8 million, giving new impetus to the publicity relating to the Myodil litigation.
- On *8 July 1991*, Steyn J gave directions for the framework of the Myodil Solicitors Group, the Myodil Scheme, and the litigation in general. The Order also made provision for the service of generic and individual pleadings. Considerable discussion had taken place between counsel, Alexander Harris, and Theodore Goddard prior to the hearing at which this Order was made and most of the matters were dealt with by consent.
- On *25 November 1991*, the plaintiffs served their Master Statement of Claim. No individual statements of claim had been served at this stage.
- At a hearing on *19 December 1991*, by which time 735 Legal Aid Certificates had been granted and 520 requests for medical records were outstanding, Glaxo raised the question of cut-off dates formally for the first time, submitting that it would soon be appropriate for an Order to be made.
- In *January 1992* a without prejudice meeting took place between legal and medical representatives instructed by the plaintiffs and Glaxo. The purpose of this meeting was to explore whether agreement could be reached on clinical and diagnostic criteria for assessing whether claimants were suffering from symptomatic Myodil-induced arachnoiditis. Following the meeting, detailed clinical and radiological criteria were drawn up and agreement was reached on these criteria in *May 1992*. At the same time, agreement was reached on the format of a standard medical report to be adopted by clinicians charged with the responsibility of examining individual claimants (see section below entitled 'Medical Criteria').
- The hearing which took place on *23 November 1992* was an important landmark in the Myodil litigation because cut-off dates were set for the applications for legal aid (*1 February 1993*), notification to Theodore Goddard on behalf of Glaxo of potential claims (*1 March 1993*), and the service of a Writ and Statement of Claim (*1 March 1994*). A formal structure was put in place whereby each plaintiff had to serve all relevant medical records and radiological images and a medical report in accordance with the form agreed between the parties. Glaxo's time for service of individual defences did not run until all the necessary information had been supplied. Generic issues were also identified by agreement between the parties and it was ordered that a trial of those generic issues take place on a date to be fixed in *October 1994*. As with most of the hearings on procedural matters, these details were largely agreed between the parties. A press release was agreed by the plaintiffs and Glaxo and approved by May J, who had taken over responsibility for the litigation from Steyn J on his promotion to the Court of Appeal: this press release clearly set out the cut-off dates and explained their effect.
- The purpose of the hearing which took place on *7 June 1993* was to administer the first

cut-off dates of 1 February 1993, by which date applications for legal aid had to be made, and 1 March 1993, by which date all potential claimants had to notify Glaxo of their claims. May J permitted a number of potential claimants to join the group litigation although they had not technically complied with the cut-off dates. By this stage, Glaxo had only received a total of thirty-six statements of claim.

- By the next hearing which took place on *26 November 1993*, seventy-six statements of claim had been served with only four months remaining before the expiry of the second cut-off date of 1 March 1994. Alexander Harris explained the difficulties faced by the Myodil Solicitors Group in processing individual claims: these difficulties were principally caused by a massive backlog in obtaining appointments for examination and, subsequently, medical reports from the plaintiffs' team of clinicians. The possibility of extending cut-off dates was discussed.

- At a hearing which took place on *21 December 1993*, May J agreed to the parties' joint request that the cut-off date for service of statements of claim be postponed to 1 September 1994 and that the trial date be similarly postponed for six months until April 1995.

- At the next hearing on *7 March 1994*, directions were given for a hearing date to be fixed for applications to join the group litigation on the part of any potential claimants who had missed the first cut-off date.

- At the subsequent hearing which took place on *20 May 1994*, May J heard an application by 'latecomers' represented by a separate firm, Nelsons, to join this litigation. After reviewing the progress of the litigation, May J stated:

> Glaxo's position is that essentially they do not oppose the introduction of the [latecomers]. The short reason why they take this, at first sight perhaps, strange position is that they see the practical advantages of having all potential claimants in relation to Myodil within the same group and they say that it is inherently desirable that all potentially valid Myodil claims should be determined within one piece of litigation . . .

> The Court is faced with a *huge* problem in devising procedures which are just and effective for this kind of litigation. One thing that stands out above all others, from the experience of this case, is that it is no use extending general time limits simply because people find it difficult to comply with them. If the Court were to take that attitude I am quite sure that this litigation would be perpetuated almost literally into the 21st century . . .

> . . . I think it is only fair to indicate that it is my assessment of the balance of justice between all concerned in this case and that assessment takes account of the fact, albeit the majority of these applicants [the latecomers] deposed to the fact that they were unaware of the existence of the possibility of bringing a claim, the two things nevertheless pertain. Firstly, there has been, as Mr Kelleher's Tenth Affidavit shows, wide publicity about these proceedings over a long period of time and secondly, the existence of the group and thereby the obligation to abide by the directions applying for the group probably provide the means whereby potential plaintiffs can bring proceedings which would otherwise, in all probability, be beyond the practical ability of most of them.

May J allowed the latecomers to join this litigation on the terms that they should serve their statements of claim in accordance with the Orders previously made no later than *20 November 1994*.

- At a hearing on *15 July 1994*, the Judge was asked by Glaxo to make a peremptory Order that any plaintiff who failed to meet the cut-off dates set at the previous hearing should be debarred from bringing a claim in respect of the use of Myodil. The Judge did not feel it appropriate to make this Order, but in his judgment once again reiterated the importance of plaintiffs adhering to cut-off dates.

The main cut-off date for service of statements of claim and accompanying documentation expired at the end of August 1994. During August 1994, in excess of 250 statements of claim were served, that is to say over one-half of the claims in the Myodil litigation. In many cases there appeared to be a genuine reason for the delay, largely because of the difficulty in getting medical reports but one firm alone served all their statements of claim (30) on the final date in August, notwithstanding that many of these had been ready for service several months before.

- Between *July 1994* and *January 1995* a number of interlocutory hearings took place, the net effect of which was as follows:
  - After Glaxo had applied to strike out the plaintiffs' Amended Master Statement of Claim, that pleading was further amended to focus on the two remaining generic issues of importance.
  - Each of the plaintiffs was required to serve a detailed schedule stating whether Myodil myelography had been properly indicated in the light of their medical circumstances. Given the way the plaintiffs' generic case had moved, this was absolutely essential since it required plaintiffs' advisers to address whether each plaintiff really had a case on individual causation, even assuming that their allegations of negligence were established.
  - The trial was adjourned until October 1995. A selection of lead cases was agreed by the parties' legal representatives and approved by the Court.
- On *3 April 1995* the parties exchanged all evidence and subsequently three without prejudice meetings took place between appropriate experts. At a final pre-trial hearing on *19 May 1995*, May J allowed two further claimants to join the litigation on strict terms as to service of their statement of claim and accompanying documentation and payment of costs. Glaxo had, by this time, served its 'Schedule of Indications' stating, in each case, its understanding of why plaintiffs had undergone Myodil myelography. The plaintiffs were ordered to give full particulars of their individual cases, for example, what surgery it was alleged should have been undertaken in the absence of Myodil myelography.

E. Settlement

21.12 During *June and early July 1995*, negotiations took place between the parties' legal representatives leading to the settlement of the Myodil litigation. The terms of the settlement involved the payment to the 425 plaintiffs of a lump sum of £7 million (on average £6,431.92 per plaintiff) to be allocated and distributed at the sole discretion of the Steering Committee of the Myodil Solicitors Group. Their allocation was based on an assessment of a variety of factors, including the strength of the individual case, the injuries claimed, the date when the myelogram took place, and Glaxo's own Defence. This allocation was based only on an assessment of general damages. The lump sum payment was made shortly after the settlement was announced.

On costs, Glaxo paid just over £2.7 million towards the plaintiffs' generic costs and the individual costs have either been negotiated or taxed and paid by Glaxo. Whilst the reasonable generic costs of the plaintiffs were paid, the costs of individual claimants who did not serve statements of claim were not paid by Glaxo. To a large extent those costs were met by the Legal Aid Board. 21.13

There have been no further Myodil proceedings in England and Wales (although at the time of writing, there are claims in other jurisdictions, notably Scotland and Australia). However, little progress has been made in resolving those claims, partly as a result of the absence of group action procedures in those jurisdictions. 21.14

F. The Relationship between Generic and Individual Proceedings

There is always a danger, well-recognised in the submissions to Lord Woolf's Inquiry, that if generic issues are not pleaded by reference to the circumstances of the individual plaintiffs, two separate actions develop, making the group action unmanageable. This could easily have occurred in the Myodil litigation since the Master Statement of Claim and Glaxo's Defence to that document were served by the Summer of 1992 by which time no individual statements of claim had been served and little investigation of individual claims had taken place. As Glaxo began to receive the individual statements of claim and, far more importantly, medical reports prepared by reference to the agreed medical criteria, it became increasingly apparent that the plaintiffs' generic case that Myodil should never have been on the market was completely at odds with the views of clinicians charged with the responsibility of examining and reporting on individual plaintiffs. This fact would have been flushed out far earlier had a significant proportion of the statements of claim been served at an earlier date. It was only when Glaxo's advisers were able to carry out a very detailed review of individual reports and medical records that it became apparent that most of the plaintiffs would have an uphill struggle to persuade the Court that Myodil myelography was not properly indicated given their medical circumstances involving serious back pain over a number of years and the real likelihood that surgery would be required. That had a dramatic effect on the value of the claim and the parties' readiness to reach a resolution. Although this review process was later than one would have wished, it was achieved in time for a sensible compromise to be reached and there could be no doubt that a settlement would have been far harder to achieve had this exercise not been carried out. 21.15

One point which this litigation demonstrates above all is that with most group actions the court should be extremely reluctant to adopt the approach of taking one 'test' or 'lead' case to investigate generic issues, while staying all the remaining claims, for these reasons: 21.16

- The Myodil settlement could not have been contemplated if claims had not been fully investigated and Glaxo given an opportunity to make an assessment of their potential

merit: without such investigation, the parties would have been left with the impression that the number of claims with potential merit was far in excess of 426.
- As May J said at a hearing in May 1994, justice would not be served by letting the claims of individual plaintiffs, some of them old, drag on indefinitely and the Judge felt that this consideration extended to Glaxo's interests as well.
- The investigation of the generic case and only some of the individual cases could have led to a recognition that settlement was an appropriate solution. However, quantification of the value of individual claims would have been impossible without investigation of all or most of the claims. Thus it would have been impossible for either party to put forward realistic proposals for settlement.
- As described above, the 'proper indications for the use of Myodil myelography' were a central issue and the plaintiffs' case changed dramatically in the last year of the litigation. There can be little doubt that it would have been impossible to have had a fair trial on this issue if there had not been a full investigation of all the claims, not least because expert evidence exchanged before the trial would not have fully addressed the issue. It is quite probable that the Court would have addressed issues which were not relevant to any of the cases and missed issues which were essential for the resolution of some cases.

G. Trial of Generic Issues and Selection of Lead Cases

21.17 At a relatively early stage in the litigation the parties agreed that the most effective way of proceeding would be to work towards a trial of generic issues with a selection of cases being chosen which would best illustrate those generic issues. Both parties adopted a pragmatic approach to the choice of lead cases, using factors such as the date when the myelogram was administered, the seriousness of the injury claimed, the possibility that surgery might be required, and other critical issues. The parties managed to agree on all but one of the lead cases ultimately selected. This process took place relatively late in the litigation but this was an advantage to both parties because it enabled them to take witness statements from specialists originally responsible for treating the lead case plaintiffs at the same time as expert evidence was being finalised. Sixteen lead cases were selected. This number was necessary to reflect the generic issues and the wide variations within the group of plaintiffs.

H. Cut-off Dates and Admittance to the Group: Latecomers and One Group

21.18 As described above, there were two separate dates set for cut-off purposes. The first merely required the potential claimant to notify Glaxo that he might be bringing a claim, the principal intention being to give the parties and the Court an idea of how many cases might be involved. This proved to be misleading as over 4,000 notifications resulted in 426 statements of claim. The second cut-off date required the plaintiff to serve the statement of claim, medical report prepared in accordance with an agreed pro forma (see below), and all available radiology and medical records. These latter requirements were rigorously enforced by Glaxo such that many claims were sent back to the individual plaintiffs' solicitors because, for example, documents had not been properly presented or radiology was missing. Although this resulted in additional 'front-end' expenditure for both parties, it saved considerable costs later. The cut-off date for service of statements of claim had to be extended twice and this led to two postponements of the (potential) trial of generic issues.

Given the complexity of the issues, the difficulties inherent in co-ordinating a large number of potential claims, and, most importantly, the problems involved in getting medical reports from medical practitioners, it was a considerable achievement to have all but two of the eventual plaintiffs' claims investigated several months before the generic trial was due to take place. Two lessons emerged from this. First, as May J emphasised on several occasions, cut-off dates, even if extended, must ultimately be adhered to. Secondly, a balance has to be struck between the interests of the parties and justice as a whole so that, if possible, there is only one group of plaintiffs in the Myodil litigation. A number of latecomers were admitted to the group at various stages in the proceedings. Whilst concerned about the expanding group, Glaxo was anxious to deal with one co-ordinated action and wished to avoid the development of separate groups of plaintiffs. This has not been possible in other jurisdictions which have less developed systems for multi-party actions. In the final analysis, there was only one group and no further focus for claims has emerged following the settlement in July 1995. Notwithstanding the understandable reluctance to bar an individual for all time from bringing a claim, it might be essential to make peremptory orders in actions different from the Myodil litigation where more plaintiffs might be involved. 21.19

I. Medical Criteria: A Common Approach to Causation

One of the undoubted successes of the Myodil litigation was the co-operation between the parties in agreeing, at a very early stage, a standard approach for assessing whether individual claimants were suffering from Myodil-induced, symptomatic arachnoiditis. It took the form of detailed clinical criteria, which the parties' neurologists and neurosurgeons were asked to address, and radiological criteria. These criteria went some way to ensuring that a common approach was taken by neuroradiologists representing both parties. (The total number of doctors involved on both sides numbered well over fifty.) By way of example, it was recognised by doctors advising both parties that arachnoiditis is frequently asymptomatic and, even when it causes symptoms, could have been caused by a range of other factors, including disease, surgery, or other interventions. The criteria required the examining physicians to consider all possible alternative causes and the contribution made to the symptoms by the underlying disease. This message was reinforced by a pro forma medical report also agreed by the parties. 21.20

Plainly, there were often different approaches taken and there was disagreement on many occasions between the two parties as to whether individual plaintiffs were truly suffering from symptomatic arachnoiditis caused by Myodil. However, as a result of these initiatives, which were not imposed by the Court: 21.21

- The majority of the claims were weeded out at an early stage, thereby saving costs for the Legal Aid Board.
- Discipline was imposed on the medical experts and a framework for instructions was available for solicitors acting for individual claimants.

J. Registration of Plaintiffs

21.22 At an early stage in the litigation, a Register of plaintiffs was set up and maintained by Alexander Harris, the lead solicitors for the plaintiffs. The guiding provisions were embodied in a court Order agreed between the parties.

21.23 The Register was a list of all plaintiffs bound by any Orders made within the context of the Myodil litigation. The Register was reviewed and brought up to date by Alexander Harris on a quarterly basis. Following this review, Alexander Harris would provide Theodore Goddard with a copy of the current version of the Register which Theodore Goddard would check against its records. Theodore Goddard would notify Alexander Harris of any amendments, additions, or deletions within fourteen days of receipt of the Register and, once such amendments were agreed, a final version of the Register would be prepared by Alexander Harris for the relevant quarter.

21.24 Plaintiffs would be entered on the Register following notification to the Steering Committee of plaintiffs' firms. Notification was required to be given within fourteen days of service of the writ by the plaintiffs' solicitors.

21.25 Plaintiffs continued on the Register until such time as their solicitors served a Notice of Discontinuance, accepted a payment into court, or following an Order of the Court.

21.26 The consequence of inclusion on the Register for the plaintiff was threefold. First, he was thereby deemed to be subject to the provisions made in the Myodil litigation; secondly, his solicitors were deemed to be a member of the Myodil Solicitors' Group; and, thirdly, the plaintiff was then subject to the Costs-Sharing Order. Generic costs and disbursements could be apportioned between the plaintiffs by taking the total incurred by or on behalf of the plaintiffs in respect of any quarter and dividing that sum by the number of plaintiffs on the Register and therefore responsible for the costs of that quarter.

K. The Role of the Legal Aid Board

21.27 It was noticeable that the Legal Aid Board had no visible presence at the later hearings, which was surprising at a time when the plaintiffs' generic case was under attack and the Board must have committed significant funds to investigating both generic issues and individual claims.

21.28 There were well over 100 firms acting for the plaintiffs. This was unfortunate for a number of reasons. First, familiarity with medical criteria was a great advantage and it was noticeable that, in the main, those lawyers acting for a number of plaintiffs were more skilful in 'processing' claims. It would have been cheaper for the Legal Aid Board to have given, say, twenty firms of solicitors around the country responsibility for handling all the cases.

L. Action Groups/Media

There was no effective action group to influence the conduct of the proceedings generally. It is possible that a focus for the formation of an effective action group did not arise because of the relatively speedy progress which was made, and the degree of co-operation between the parties. Also, the media interest did not influence the procedures adopted except when considering cut-off dates, when the coverage was used to demonstrate that individuals should have been aware of the action. **21.29**

22

BENZODIAZEPINE LITIGATION

Gary Hickinbottom[1]

This product liability litigation dominated consideration of group actions throughout the first half of the 1990s. The case was vast by any standards. Over 15,000 claimants came forward, of whom 5,500 issued proceedings, represented by approximately 3,000 firms of solicitors. The Legal Aid Board spent £40 million,[2] before the litigation collapsed.

Although judges had been assigned to previous cases, Ian Kennedy J took charge of the benzodiazepine litigation in a true case management sense, presaging the Woolf reforms and the new Civil Procedure Rules. Lest such huge litigation become entirely unmanageable, he used a number of robust case management techniques, including cut-off dates supported by 'unless' orders, pleadings in the form of schedules, and a willingness to strike out cases that could not succeed.

Media attention and advertising by lawyers played a role in attracting claimants. Large numbers of claimants came forward but, whether because of the constraints of the legal aid system or otherwise, the screening of claimants was insufficiently rigorous to prevent many claims of dubious merit proceeding. Whilst the claimants pressed for a 'generic' attack on the products, with Master pleadings and a public inquiry approach, the Court permitted the defendants to have access to information on individual cases which revealed that many were bound to fail on their own facts, because causation was an insuperable hurdle or because the claimants' factual allegations were not supported when tested against the evidence of their own medical practitioners.

Virtually all claimants were legally aided. When it became apparent to the Legal Aid Board that many cases had insufficient merit to proceed (and, indeed, they were being regularly struck out), they required the claimants' own legal team to 'audit' each claim: which resulted in the discontinuation of the majority of cases and ultimately in the withdrawal of public funding from the entire litigation.

---

[1] District Judge, Welsh Circuit, formerly partner, CMS Cameron McKenna.
[2] Legal Aid Board, *The Funding Code: A New Approach to Funding Civil Claims* (1999) 16.

> The collapse of the claim had major consequences. The Legal Aid Board issued a paper analysing the difficulties which had led to the expenditure of public funds on investigating a claim which had failed very early in the procedural course[3]—and it encouraged the Board in future to pursue a policy of funding generic or test cases, despite the lesson of the benzodiazepine litigation being that it was an initial failure properly to screen individual cases which was the source of the problem. The litigation also indirectly resulted in the establishment of a working party on group actions by the Law Society's Civil Litigation Committee, which published its report 'Group Actions Made Easier' in September 1995. This report was relied upon by Lord Woolf in his consideration of multi-party actions.[4]
>
> The benzodiazepine litigation raised many problems of group actions which had not been faced before. Overall, the case showed how the Court Rules, flexibly applied, could accommodate even the most difficult group case management problems.

A. The Products

22.01 Stressful situations provoke anxiety, which can be an appropriate and even useful response to life events which may stimulate achievement. However, where anxiety occurs without apparent cause, or out of proportion to the cause with respect to intensity or duration, or where the cause cannot be removed (for example, because it is related to social conditions), it can become a problem for the sufferer and medical treatment may have to be considered.

22.02 The treatment of anxiety has always been controversial, with some experts arguing that psychotherapy or cognitive therapy is more likely to be successful in the long term than drug treatment. However, historically, drugs have been the usual therapy for most patients with anxiety, and insomnia associated with anxiety. Opiate-based anxiolytics and hypnotics have been in use for over 2,000 years, a solution of opium and alcohol (laudanum) becoming particularly popular in the eighteenth and nineteenth centuries. These narcotic drugs have well-known, serious side effects, notably dependence with severe effects on withdrawal. Furthermore, with higher doses, there is an increasing effect of central nervous system depression that can lead to coma and eventually death. Death from overdose with these drugs was commonplace.

22.03 As an alternative treatment, barbiturates were introduced in the first decade of the twentieth century, and remained in widespread use until the introduction of the benzodiazepines. By the end of the 1960s, there were over 12 million annual prescriptions for barbiturates on the NHS. Although effective anxiolytics and hypnotics, and safer than opiates which they largely replaced, barbiturates too have many disadvantages, including

---

[3] Legal Aid Board, *Issues Arising for the Legal Aid Board and Lord Chancellor's Department from the collapse of the Benzodiazepine litigation* (1994).

[4] Lord Chancellor's Department, *Access to Justice: Consultation Paper on Multi-Party Actions* (1996); and *Access to Justice: Final Report* (1996).

a similar general central nervous system depressant effect by which overdose readily causes respiratory failure and death. Both accidental death and suicides were common in barbiturate users, particularly as the effects of the drugs are potentiated by alcohol. Less than ten times the therapeutic dose may be lethal. In addition, barbiturates are potent inducers of drug metabolising enzymes in the liver and, therefore, result in a range of dangerous drug interactions. Both physical and psychological dependence occur; and, at the peak of barbiturate use, perhaps 100,000 people in Britain were dependent on barbiturates.

22.04 Because of the serious side effects and potentially lethal effect of overdose with barbiturates, safer alternatives were sought.

22.05 The first benzodiazepine (chlordiazepoxide) was synthesised in 1947 by chemists of Hoffman-LaRoche, who were searching for novel compounds with tranquillising activity. The risk-benefit balance of the product was found to be superior to existing tranquillisers, and it was licensed in the UK in 1960 under the name 'Librium', by Roche Products Limited ('Roche'). Roche licensed a second benzodiazepine (diazepam (Valium)), three years later. Other companies were also conducting research, and John Wyeth & Brother Limited ('Wyeth') introduced oxazepam (Serenid) into the UK in 1966, and lorazepam (Ativan) in 1972. A third company, Upjohn Limited ('Upjohn'), introduced the sedative Halcion. Other companies came into the market with both brand name, and generic, products. A considerable range of benzodiazepine products was available from the end of the 1970s.

22.06 Benzodiazepines have hypnotic, sedative, anxiolytic, anticonvulsant, and muscle relaxant actions, and consequently they were regarded as being particularly suitable for the treatment of anxiety and insomnia. One of their striking features, in comparison with the tranquillisers which preceded them, is that they are remarkably safe in acute overdosage, and even ten times the therapeutic dose merely induces sleep from which the subject is easily roused.

22.07 From their introduction, the number of prescriptions for benzodiazepines in Britain increased rapidly, reaching a peak of 31 million prescriptions by 1979—whilst prescriptions of barbiturates fell by over 80 per cent during the 1970s.

B. The Claims

22.08 Throughout the 1960s and 1970s, benzodiazepines were used in clinical practice without any apparent problems. However, in the early 1980s, widespread public concern followed adverse publicity about the products on television programmes such as *That's Life*, and in newspapers. Although the scope of the reports was wide-ranging (and included, for example, criticism of doctors for mis- and over-prescribing), the primary concern was that longer term use of the products led to dependency, which, in its turn, led to withdrawal symptoms upon cessation of therapy.

22.09 Manufacturers received their first claims in 1987. The number of solicitors who had been approached by potential claimants was such that, in the following year, a formal 'Benzodiazepine Solicitors Group' ('BSG') was formed, with a 'Steering Committee' (which varied over time, from between five and eight firms). In May 1988, letters before action were sent by the Steering Committee's correspondent firm (Pannone Napier) to the two primary target manufacturer companies, Wyeth and Roche. Even at that stage, it was clear to those advising the claimants that 'even by recent standards the scale of the litigation [would] be vast'.

22.10 During the next three years, over 17,000 potential claimants came forward, instructing approximately 3,000 firms of solicitors and 40 counsel. Of these claims, some 5,000 fruited into proceedings, with Wyeth and Roche facing over 3,500 and over 2,000 actions respectively (some plaintiffs suing more than one manufacturer). Fifty sets of proceedings were served on other manufacturers, the vast majority on Upjohn in relation to Halcion.

22.11 In addition to the manufacturers, a substantial number of prescribers (general practitioners and hospital authorities) were also joined into the litigation; and, further, in the early stages of the proceedings, a number of plaintiffs also sued the various regulatory bodies, although these claims were never actively pursued.

22.12 The claim against the manufacturers was made in negligence only, most claims pre-dating the Consumer Protection Act 1987. Many issues were raised by the plaintiffs, who made broad allegations of negligent research and marketing (their Master pleading being nearly 100 pages long); but it was the plaintiffs' primary case in respect of all products except Halcion that the manufacturer ought to have included a warning in the product literature that the product should not be used for more than 2–4 weeks; and, if there had been such a warning, then the product would not have been prescribed for longer than four weeks with the result that the plaintiff would not have become dependent and suffered injury. The case against Halcion was different. The plaintiffs alleged that Halcion was so inherently unsafe that no warning would have rendered it marketable, and it should never have been marketed. The case against the prescribers was that, in various ways, there was negligent prescription (for example, because the product was prescribed for a condition for which it was not indicated).

C. The Approach of the Court

22.13 On 20 June 1990, Ian Kennedy J was assigned to deal with all interlocutory matters arising from benzodiazepine claims. The appointment was followed by a Practice Note of the Lord Chief Justice on 6 December 1990, which confirmed that Ian Kennedy J would deal with all summonses in all actions in which the plaintiff alleged personal injury to have resulted from the taking of a benzodiazepine drug—and seventeen such drugs (by brand and generic names) were scheduled to the Note.

22.14 Judges who had been assigned to earlier group actions had been encouraged by the Court of Appeal to be bold and innovative,[5] but it was in the benzodiazepine litigation that the Court broke away from the usual adversarial nature of proceedings and the strict constraints of the Rules of the Supreme Court, to take charge in a case management sense, presaging the Woolf reforms and the new Civil Procedure Rules. In upholding a particular

---

[5] See *Horrocks v Ford Motor Co*, The Times, 15 Feb 1990.

exercise of discretion by Ian Kennedy J in relation to a procedural matter in the litigation,[6] Steyn LJ said:

> The Rules of Court were devised to control the ordinary run of actions. Those Rules are more often than not silent on the problems which beset the modern phenomenon of group actions and other complex multi-party litigation. There are no Rules of Court or even Practice Directions to provide a procedural framework for such cases. Inevitably, High Court judges assigned to the control of such litigation must depart from transitional procedures and adopt interventionist case management techniques. If the judges charged with the control of such actions did not undertake this innovative role, the system of justice in respect of such cases would break down entirely. That result could not be tolerated . . .
>
> Subject to the duty to act fairly, the judge may and often must improvise: sometimes that will involve the adoption of entirely new procedures. The judge's procedural powers in group actions are untrammelled by the distinctive features of the adversarial system. The judge's powers are as wide as may be necessary to control the litigation fairly and efficiently.[7]

22.15 Because of the wide discretion allowed to the judge in a group action, the Court of Appeal made it clear that, in a group action, the rulings of the assigned judge should not normally be the subject of an appeal.[8]

22.16 How did the assigned Judge use this newly appropriated, wide procedural discretion, in this case?

22.17 It was clear from the outset that the Court faced the prospect of huge numbers of individual actions, but the damages in any individual case were likely to be small. At the first hearing, Leading Counsel for the plaintiffs indicated that quantum in individual claims would rarely, if ever, get to five figures. In the circumstances, in terms that were novel then (although commonplace now, since the introduction of the concept of proportionality into litigation by the Civil Procedure Rules 1998 (CPR)), the Judge made clear the purpose of his appointment, namely to bring the determinative issues to trial 'as quickly, efficiently and economically as possible'.[9] He particularly stressed the importance of matters being dealt with economically.[10]

22.18 In fulfilling these broad aims, Ian Kennedy J used a number of novel case management techniques, for example:

(1) Although the Court had no power to order that cases be issued in, or transferred to, a specific Court, except on the application of a party, in his first judgment he stressed the importance and good sense of issuing in, or transferring cases to, the Central Office as efficiently as possible, and the possible cost consequences of a failure to do so.[11] The Practice Note indicated that delays in parties transferring cases to the

---

[6] ie in refusing to extend the cut-off date for Halcion claimants to join the scheme of litigation: discussed further in Section G, below.
[7] Court of Appeal Transcript, 13 Oct 1992, 15–16.
[8] Court of Appeal Transcript, 6 Dec 1991, 15B, per Woolf LJ.
[9] Judgment 9 Nov 1989, 2.
[10] ibid: 'In this series of cases the latter consideration [ie economy] is as important as any, for I have been told that the damages likely to be attracted by any one complainant will only rarely reach or exceed five figures.'
[11] Judgment 9 Nov 1990, 1–2.

Central Office 'would in all probability be treated as culpable delay' for costs purposes. By this threat of potential costs sanctions, those representing plaintiffs were encouraged to issue in the Central Office (with a consequent saving of the costs of transfer).

(2) He required applications to be made in the form of a 'Travelling Summons', ie 'in a schedule (in the form of a Scott Schedule) listing the applications brought on summons by each of the parties, with columns for concise comments by way of argument for each party'.[12]

(3) In addition to formal orders, in a practice begun by Ognall J in the HIV Haemophilia litigation, he made less formal 'indications' to 'serve as a guide to parties in their conduct of this litigation', where formal orders were inappropriate or impossible.[13]

(4) In terms of pleadings, at the request of the plaintiffs, he adopted the technique, first used in the Opren litigation, of having 'Master pleadings' which set out pleas common to all or at least a substantial proportion of the plaintiffs, with separate individual pleadings or schedules which (i) identified the parts of the Master pleading adopted in the individual case, and (ii) set out the uniquely individual pleas. He also ordered the defendants to serve a 'Commentary' on the Master pleadings, at a stage before the plaintiffs' pleadings were finalised (and before formal Defences were appropriate), to enable the plaintiffs to understand that which was likely to be common ground and the areas upon which they would need to do further work.[14]

(5) In addition to ordering each plaintiff to serve a mandate to enable the defendant to obtain medical records from treating physicians (already, by the Benzodiazepine litigation, a usual order in such actions), he ordered each plaintiff to waive confidentiality in those treating physicians, to allow the defendants to take evidence from them. That evidence was likely to be crucial at trial, but the plaintiffs' legal advisers indicated that they did not intend to seek it. Because no doctor was likely to speak to either party without a waiver of any claim against him (and because the claims over against the prescribers could be worth little in practice), the Judge required such a waiver to be given by each plaintiff and, in default, he ordered a stay.[15]

(6) The Judge was concerned that, without discipline, such huge proceedings could founder under their own weight. Consequently, he made clear early on that, although adequate periods would be given for service of procedural documents, where dates were not met without good cause, 'unless orders' would be made. In addition to this type of 'cut-off date'—well known in all litigation—he also novelly required claimants to apply for legal aid by a specific date, if they were to be included in the scheme of litigation before him. The sanction for a failure to comply was not that a claim was struck out in default, but merely that it would not be considered as part of the scheme of litigation which he proposed should move to trial first. Subject to obtaining any necessary funding from the Legal Aid Board, cases which failed to meet the date would have to wait; and he indicated that claimants may face difficulties (for example, in relation to limitation or legal aid funding) if they did not come forward

---

[12] Order 6 Dec 1999, para 17(c); and Order 28 June 1991, para 1.
[13] Judgment 9 Nov 1990, 1.
[14] For further discussion, see Section E below.
[15] For further discussion, see para 22.47 below.

promptly. The imposition of such a cut-off date on potential (as opposed to actual) parties was expressly endorsed by the Court of Appeal, and was described by Hoffman LJ as 'a very sensible' innovation.[16]

(7) Ian Kennedy J made clear that, although traditionally in litigation the parties determined the issues that needed to be tried, in the Benzodiazepine litigation, because of the potential drain on court resources, the Court must have input into the issues that should be tried, and how those issues should be identified and tried.[17] Again, this approach of the Court managing group cases (rather than simply allowing the parties alone to dictate procedure, timetable, identification of issues to be tried, and the manner of trial) is now reflected in the CPR, as applicable to all litigation.

(8) At all stages, approximately 95 per cent or more of the claimants were legally aided. The Judge invited, and at times required, the Legal Aid Board to be represented at administrative hearings at which costs were particularly central, for example, to give evidence as to how applications were being dealt with in practice.

(9) In striking out individual cases and classes of case within the group, the Judge took a broad-brush approach, not just considering whether a cause of action was disclosed on the face of the pleadings, but taking into account the risk-benefit balance inherent in the litigation, and the difficulties faced by the plaintiffs if they were to proceed. This novel approach was expressly approved by the Court of Appeal.[18]

D. The Course of the Litigation[19]

Following service of letters before action in May 1988, the plaintiffs' legal representatives prepared Master pleadings in respect of Valium and Ativan, which they served in draft on Roche and Wyeth respectively. These documents set out the allegations that were to be adopted in all individual cases, and set out in some detail the epidemiology and learned literature relied upon by the plaintiffs. Those Master pleadings were served in draft in January 1990, and formally served after the first directions hearing in November 1990.   22.19

In addition, individual statements of claim (in agreed form) were prepared, setting out the specific allegations in each particular case, and the individual pleadings were ordered to be served with a medical report as defined in RSC Order 18, Rule 12(1C), copies of all medical records in the plaintiff's possession, and a form of authority for release of medical records. Because of problems in identifying the particular injuries claimed by specific plaintiffs (and, in particular, precisely when it was alleged these injuries occurred), it was   22.20

---

[16] Court of Appeal Transcript, 13 Oct 1992, 19. For further discussion of cut-off dates in this litigation, see Section G below.
[17] Judgment 6 May 1992, 8–9.
[18] In two separate judgments, *AB & Others v John Wyeth & Brother Limited* [1994] 5 Med LR 149 (which concerned the striking out of claims against the general practitioner and health authority prescribers) and *AB & Others v John Wyeth & Brother Limited* [1997] 8 Med LR 57 (which concerned the striking out of the balance of claims against the manufacturers, following the withdrawal of legal aid). For a further discussion of the strike-out principles used, see Section I below.
[19] It is unnecessary here to set out the full history of the litigation, which can be found in the judgment of Ian Kennedy J at [1996] 7 Med LR 267.

eventually ordered that injuries be pleaded in an agreed form in a schedule appended to the individual statement of claim.

22.21 The Judge indicated from the outset that he proposed to impose 'cut-off dates' by which claimants who intended to join the litigation must issue and serve proceedings. In the event, in June 1991, he fixed two cut-off dates for each claimant, namely a date by which application for legal aid had to be made (ie 20 September 1991) and a subsequent date by which proceedings, pleadings, and supporting documents had to be served (ie 15 April 1992).

22.22 Whilst the Judge was prepared to (and did) extend the cut-off date for applications for legal aid by a few days, he was not prepared to extend it further, notably in relation to a cohort of several hundred Halcion claimants who came forward after that date as the result of Halcion-specific publicity. These cases were left out of the first group (and eventually foundered).

22.23 With regard to the date for service of proceedings, pleadings, and supporting documents, that date was extended to 31 August 1992 on a 'final' basis but, after the event, claimants who served proceedings between 1 September and 3 November 1992 were allowed to proceed within the group, but subject to a costs penalty. But the Judge was not prepared to allow any further extension to this 'final' order; nor was he prepared to allow the service of amended pleadings and medical reports to cure significant defects in the documents as served by the cut-off date, on the basis that to allow such amendments would be to defeat the purpose of fixing such a final date.

22.24 In March 1992, the Judge indicated that, once the cases had come in and been reviewed, efforts must be made to identify the determinative issues and then lead cases illustrative of those issues. Having been led through some of the individual cases on various interlocutory applications, he also expressed concern about the merits and viability of at least some of the cases.

22.25 Perhaps as a result of these comments—and representations made to the Legal Aid Board by the defendants—shortly afterwards the Legal Aid Board ordered an 'audit' to assess the merits and viability of all individual pleaded cases, and the viability of the litigation as a whole. In January 1993, the Steering Committee announced that the audit of cases against Roche had been suspended, which was a prelude to funding of those cases being withdrawn by the Board. In respect of the Wyeth cases, the Steering Committee undertook to notify Wyeth within fourteen days of the case being audited as fit to proceed, and Wyeth agreed not to apply to strike out individual cases unless they had 'passed' the audit. However, they began issuing strike-out applications against audited cases which, to a large extent, were successful.

22.26 In the meantime, first the general practitioner prescribers and then the Health Authority prescribers successfully applied to have all actions against them struck out, on the basis that they were oppressive and an abuse. The Court of Appeal upheld the strike outs in both cases, in November 1993.

22.27 Within six weeks, the Legal Aid Board had come to the conclusion that further public funding of the case against Wyeth—the only remaining litigation—was not warranted, and they had sent letters to the plaintiffs requiring them to show why their legal aid certificates should not be discharged. The next month, the Board notified the Court that it had reached the conclusion that further public support of the litigation against Wyeth could not be justified: and, in the following months, the Area Committee of the Board dismissed the plaintiffs' appeal against the discharge of certificates, finally in November 1994.

After final discharge of funding, both Roche and then Wyeth obtained an order from the Court that any plaintiff intending to proceed—now, of course, without the benefit of legal aid—should serve a notice to that effect by a given date, failing which their case should automatically be struck out. This was designed to ensure that only plaintiffs who were determined to proceed should remain in the litigation. **22.28**

In February 1995, Roche applied to strike out the remaining forty-one cases against it, and Master Prebble struck out the claims on the basis that they were an abuse of process. Wyeth issued a similar application in respect of the thirty-nine cases against it, which was set down before Ian Kennedy J, and heard in April 1995. At the end of Wyeth's submissions, that application was adjourned, so that it could be consolidated with the plaintiffs' appeal against the Master's strike out of the Roche cases. These consolidated matters were heard by the Judge in May and October 1995, and February 1996, Ian Kennedy J giving judgment striking out the balance of the Wyeth and Roche cases on 19 July 1996. **22.29**

A number of plaintiffs (sixteen against Wyeth and twenty against Roche) appealed the strike out, but the Court of Appeal refused the appeal in December 1996. Both the Court of Appeal and House of Lords refused leave to appeal further. **22.30**

E. Pleadings

As indicated above, the claimants served a draft Master Statement of Claim in respect of Ativan and Valium in January 1990. At the first hearing for directions (November 1990), they proposed that that pleading be served formally, thereby setting out the common pleas of the plaintiffs; but, so far as individual claims were concerned, they would select eight individual cases (four against Wyeth and four against Roche) which they would fully plead. They suggested that full Defences would be served in these cases, and then the litigation could be reviewed. The plaintiffs intended that no information on the thousands of other cases be disclosed to the defendants or to the Court. **22.31**

However, Ian Kennedy J was particularly concerned that any trial should cover all of the main issues raised by individual cases in the cohort, so that, even if the trial would not technically be determinative of every individual case in the cohort, it would give very clear guidance as to whether those cases would succeed or not. Consequently, he was not prepared to allow the claimants to serve pleadings in a very limited number of cases, selected themselves, without the Court (and the defendants) being satisfied that they were representative of the cohort as a whole. Therefore, he ordered the service of the Master Statement of Claim (which had already been prepared) and individual statements of claim (or schedules of information) in agreed, short form in relation to each of the individual cases, together with a **22.32** medical report and medical records, so that all parties and the Court could be satisfied that any illustrative cases chosen for trial would cover all of the relevant issues.

22.33 In response, in respect of Valium, Roche were ordered to serve a Defence, and did so. Wyeth never served a formal Master Defence prior to the collapse of the litigation, although they did serve a 'Commentary' on the Ativan Master Statement of Claim. The Judge ordered that this be served, 'no more than an informal foreshadow of the Defence which will ultimately be delivered',[20] at a time when the plaintiffs' own pleading was insufficiently final to warrant a Defence being served, but to enable the parties to progress the identification of matters that would ultimately be in issue between them. At the first hearing, the Judge said:

> The Commentary will serve a useful purpose in that it will enable the plaintiffs' advisers to know at an early stage what are the main areas where more detailed research may be necessary and those where there is, if not common ground, at least a measure of agreement.[21]

22.34 In addition, Wyeth served approximately 1,000 defences in individual cases, technically in draft form, but only because final defences could not at that stage be settled because the plaintiffs had not finally determined the form of the Master Statement of Claim (adopted in each individual statement of claim) upon which they wished to proceed.

F. Medical Evidence

22.35 A number of procedural issues arose concerning medical evidence.

Production of documents relied upon by examining psychiatrists

22.36 Each claimant alleged that he had become dependent upon benzodiazepines, and as a result had suffered symptoms from various psychiatric conditions during therapy and on withdrawal. One frequent allegation was that the product caused memory loss.

22.37 Although many claimants alleged that they were continuing to suffer withdrawal symptoms, the alleged injuries had often begun ten years or more before commencement of proceedings. With his individual statement of claim, each plaintiff had to serve a medical report as defined in RSC Order 18, Rule 12(1C), substantiating the injuries claimed. Because of the nature of the injuries, psychiatrists were employed by the plaintiffs to prepare these reports. Many of the alleged injuries occurred many years before examination—and were psychiatric in nature—and, consequently, the basis of the psychiatric opinion was particularly important. Early on in the litigation, Ian Kennedy J said:

> An expert's report is nothing if it states its conclusions without setting out the facts upon which those conclusions are based. This is particularly so when a doctor is dealing with non-organic complaints because then it is essential to know precisely upon what history he is advising and giving his opinion.[22]

---

[20] Judgment 9 Apr 1991, 9.
[21] Judgment 9 Nov 1990, 4.
[22] Judgment 9 Apr 1991, 15.

22.38 A number of cases were then taken to the Judge for him to give guidelines as to when the defendants were entitled to have produced to them the statement of a particular plaintiff or supporting witness which was available to and seen by the reporting psychiatrist. He held that the test was:

> wherever there appears to be a material reliance upon the information furnished by the solicitors then that information should be disclosed . . . It is only where, on a fair reading of the medical report, the statement of the solicitors has been merely treated as background reading that I would not require its production.

22.39 The judgment of Ian Kennedy J consequently adopted the orthodox approach to documents relied upon in pleadings, particulars, or in medical reports (which, by virtue of RSC Order 18, Rule 12, were tantamount to particulars).

22.40 However, the matter went to the Court of Appeal, where Woolf LJ, giving the judgment of the Court, used a different approach. Presaging his later procedural reforms, he said that a test was required that was clear, could be complied with economically and expeditiously, and which would 'assist in achieving justice in this scale of litigation'.[23] The report should set out 'the full relevant medical history of the plaintiff relied on by the plaintiff's doctor for the purpose of preparing the report'.[24] That test—which the Court of Appeal clearly thought was a practical solution to a difficult problem—unfortunately did not assist the defendants in assessing the reports, because the basis of each report was still not known. It was still unclear from where information about the medical history, upon which the psychiatrist relied, was derived. Consequently, the defendants adopted a different approach.

Access to medical records and prescribers

22.41 It was clear from the outset that the evidence from the prescribers would be crucial. As had been the case in previous group actions, at the first hearing for directions it was ordered that each plaintiff serve, with his individual statement of claim, copies of all medical records in his possession, and a signed consent to enable the defendant to have access to the original medical records.[25] Therefore, the legal representatives of both plaintiff and defendant had ready access to all available medical records.

22.42 However, the medical records alone were insufficient. First, it was readily apparent that the many claimants had given to their legal representatives a different version of their medical history from that which appeared in the written records. Only a reference to the actual health care providers would resolve which version presented the truer picture. Secondly, it was the plaintiffs' primary case in respect of all products except Halcion that the manufacturer ought to have included a warning in the product literature that the product should not be used for more than 2–4 weeks; and, if there had been such a warning, then the product would not have been prescribed for longer than 4 weeks, with the result that the plaintiff would not have become dependent and suffered injury. Therefore, to succeed, each plaintiff had to prove not only that the product had physically caused the

---

[23] Transcript, 6 Dec 1991, 5.
[24] ibid, 10.
[25] 9 Nov 1990 Order, para 8(i) and (ii). The form of the consent was agreed between the parties and attached to the Order (as Schedule 7).

injuries claimed, but that, had the warning been as it was claimed it ought to have been, the prescriber would not have prescribed the product for more than 4 weeks. The role of the prescriber—as 'learned intermediary'—was consequently crucial. But the medical records did not of course show what the particular prescriber would have done had the warnings been different, ie had they been as the plaintiffs alleged they ought to have been.

22.43 Nevertheless, the plaintiffs' legal representatives made no attempt to make enquiries of any specific prescriber. So far as the medical history of each plaintiff was concerned, they indicated that they would rely upon the personal recollection of the plaintiff himself and medical records alone. So far as the hypothetical question of what a particular prescriber would have done had the warnings been different is concerned, they said they would rely upon expert evidence as to what a reasonable practitioner would have done had the warnings been as the plaintiffs claimed they ought to have been.

22.44 Although the plaintiffs' legal representatives did not make any enquiry of any practitioner of any plaintiff, the defendants were anxious to obtain evidence from the practitioners, which they regarded as potentially crucial.[26] They consequently made a number of applications.

22.45 On 10 December 1992, on an application by Roche, Ian Kennedy J considered a preliminary issue as to whether, in discharging the burden of proof so far as causation was concerned, a plaintiff should be required to serve a statement from any relevant treating physician covering the issue of whether any omission from the warnings had any operative effect on the practitioner's prescribing in a particular case; or whether that causal link could be made by any other evidence. The Judge held that 'causation can be proved by any relevant and admissible evidence, a plaintiff cannot be *required* to call the physician who was treating him at the relevant time'[27] (emphasis in the original). However, he went on 'to highlight the practical problems' in seeking to prove causation in this way. As he pointed out:

> [I]t could be thought by some to be an unsatisfactory and wasteful procedure to have rival experts debate the various courses that might be taken by the treating physician, when that treating physician was able to be called. He could give an account, albeit hypothetical, of what his reaction to any improved warning would have been; and he could speak directly of his experience and knowledge of the relevant drugs, and of his assessment of the particular patient and his complaint...

22.46 At that hearing, the plaintiffs' Leading Counsel 'was disposed to agree that where a plaintiff had decided not to call his treating physician, that plaintiff must at an appropriate stage release the physician from professional confidentiality' to allow the defendant to approach the doctor to obtain the relevant evidence. The Judge commented: 'I cannot myself see how the matter could be otherwise, and indeed were the contrary suggested there would be a strong argument for that claim to be stayed.'[28]

---

[26] In the circumstances of the benzodiazepine claims, the failure of the plaintiffs' legal representatives to make enquiries of the relevant general practitioners was described by Ian Kennedy J as 'extraordinary' and 'inexplicable': judgment 20 Oct 1993, 6.
[27] Judgment 15 Dec 1992, 3.
[28] ibid, 5.

However, when Wyeth made an application for such a waiver, it was opposed by the plaintiffs as being premature, and the terms of any waiver were also disputed. The Judge nevertheless allowed the application, requiring each plaintiff to provide a waiver of confidentiality to allow the relevant defendant(s) to approach the treating doctors, within a fixed period, failing provision of which the case be stayed.[29] He held that such an order was not premature, because it would allow the defendants to investigate individual cases in a more efficient way than having to review cases twice: 'it would save Wyeth money and limit delay if they could evaluate the cases in the round as they wished to do'. He also held that, as doctors would not speak to the defendant unless they were assured that they were not going to be a party to the litigation themselves, each plaintiff should waive any rights he may have against any treating doctor.[30] This order applied to all claimants who made complaints against Wyeth and Roche; and, later, it was extended to claims against Upjohn implicating Halcion.[31] Although there was no proximate causation issue involving prescribers in respect of Halcion (because the allegation was that that product ought never to have been on the market), nevertheless, there remained issues relating to the medical history of the plaintiffs in respect of which the physicians could give crucial evidence and, as to this, the Judge considered '[t]hey have a lot they can say'.[32]

22.47

Attribution of verified symptoms

One problem faced by the plaintiffs was to verify the symptoms they alleged as injuries, ie to prove on the balance of probabilities that these symptoms were suffered. However, of course, to succeed in a claim, each plaintiff would have to go on to prove on the balance of probabilities that the verified symptoms were caused by the product complained of.

22.48

An important procedural issue arose concerning the failure of many medical reports to attribute these symptoms to the product. The defendants contended that a report did not substantiate injuries in accordance with RSC Order 18, Rule 12(1A) unless it both recorded it and attributed it to the product of which the plaintiff complained. The plaintiffs contended that recording was sufficient, and whether the condition was attributable to the relevant events was a matter for evidence at the trial.

22.49

---

[29] Judgment 15 Mar 1993, reported as *Nur v John Wyeth & Brother Limited* [1996] 7 Med LR 300.

[30] In the same judgment, the Judge struck out all claims against general practitioners; and found that a 'plaintiff was highly unlikely to be discarding any worthwhile right by agreeing not to sue those who prescribed him the drug'.

[31] Judgment 20 Oct 1993, 40–41.

[32] Although Ian Kennedy J refused to allow the defendants to rely upon statements from the treating doctors on applications to strike out, the evidence obtained proved to be valuable and, in many cases, fatal to the claim. Statements in many cases were disclosed to the plaintiff's legal advisers, and the Legal Aid Board (which was considering whether funding for the claims should be continued). In respect of many claims, evidence from the doctor did not support the history given by the plaintiff himself (which was relied upon for pleading purposes and, to a large extent, by examining psychiatrists); and in many cases it was clear that the physicians were very experienced in both treating the particular patient and in prescribing the particular benzodiazepine product(s), and that, irrespective of what warnings there might have been, the prescribing pattern would have been similar.

22.50 Ian Kennedy J held that the report must substantiate injuries, in the sense that it must (on the balance of probabilities) attribute them to the product:

> What is required is a report which substantiates all the injuries with sufficient particularity that one is not left in any doubt what is and what is not attributed to the accident or other event.[33]

22.51 Indeed, he considered the use of the term 'injuries' in the Rules itself suggested that there must be attribution.

22.52 This judgment disclosed a significant (indeed, fatal) flaw in very many of the individual cases, so far as causation was concerned. Although the group claim began as one exclusively focused on dependency, and consequent adverse effects upon withdrawal, the withdrawal symptoms claimed as injuries were very similar in nature to the symptoms of anxiety for which the drugs were prescribed. On investigation of individual cases, it became apparent that, in the vast majority of cases, the withdrawal symptoms alleged were similar to symptoms suffered by the plaintiff patient during the course of therapy and, indeed, before benzodiazepines were ever prescribed. No doubt as a result of this consistency of symptomatology before, during, and after therapy, the plaintiff's examining psychiatrist in very many cases was unable or unwilling to say that, on the balance of probabilities, the symptoms after cessation of therapy were caused by the use of benzodiazepines, rather than being (for example) a recrudescence of the plaintiff's underlying anxiety condition.

22.53 Consequently, as a result of this judgment (which was not appealed), many cases—which would, of course, have failed at any trial in any event, because of an inability to prove causation—discontinued, or were struck out as bound to fail.

G. Cut-off Dates

22.54 At the outset of the litigation, it was clear that the case was going to be very large indeed. Ian Kennedy J was concerned from the beginning that, unless procedural discipline was maintained, the case may founder under its own weight and not proceed to an ultimate determination at all: with the result that justice would be done to none of the parties. Therefore, throughout the litigation, whilst giving very generous time for procedural steps to be undertaken, he eventually imposed a date for each crucial step on an 'unless' basis, sometimes called in group actions a 'cut-off date'. Therefore, for example, having given earlier indications that it was his intention to fix dates for service of individual pleadings and supporting documents, on 28 June 1991 the Judge fixed the date for service as 15 April 1992 (giving the claimants nine months to issue proceedings and serve pleadings etc: the date was four years after service of the letter before action). On 26 March 1992, the plaintiffs' legal representatives indicating that they needed until June to finalise the pleadings and supporting documents in each of the individual cases, the date for service was extended to 31 August 1992, on a 'final' basis. Even then, after the event, the Judge acceded to an application to extend that date: on 7 October 1992, he ordered

---

[33] Judgment 6 May 1992, 10.

that all plaintiffs' proceedings and documents served in proper form by 3 November 1992 be deemed served by 31 August 1992, provided that the case was audited as fit to proceed by 15 December 1992,[34] and subject to a costs penalty.[35]

22.55 The imposition of an 'unless order' as the second order for time for a procedural step was usual in both High Court and county court. Indeed, the time given to the plaintiffs with the resources at their disposal was somewhat more generous than would normally have been granted by a Master or District Judge in a unitary action. However, the real development in respect of procedural, timetabling orders was in Ian Kennedy J's order that, to enable a claimant to join the scheme of litigation that would move to trial first, any application for legal aid had to be made by a particular date.[36] This Order bound not actual but potential plaintiffs in the litigation—but the sanction for non-compliance was merely that the claimant could not join the first group of the litigation.

22.56 If justice was to be done to anyone, the need for discipline in the proceedings (including the need to 'ring-fence' a group to proceed to trial) was recognised by not only the Judge, but all parties, and from the time of the first hearing. At that hearing, Ian Kennedy J said:

> It is my intention, and it is recognised by all of the parties who have appeared before me, that a time will come within the next few months when a 'shutter' will come down, and lately arriving plaintiffs will be unable to have their cases carried forward until the lead actions have been decided. Solicitors consulted by claimants will, I am sure, bear well in mind that it is strongly in their client's interests to be numbered among the claimants within the scheme before that happens, particularly since the relatively small amounts that are likely to be recovered by individual plaintiffs make it difficult for them to persuade the legal aid board that a small number of claims, even taken collectively, have reasonable prospects of success.[37]

22.57 Indeed, this was reflected in the first Order, as an indication: 'It is essential that the group of plaintiffs in this litigation should be finalised and to that end there should be movement towards a cut-off date although it is not yet possible to define it.'[38]

22.58 The purpose and effect of the imposition of a cut-off date was expanded by the Judge at the second hearing:

> My duty, as the Judge nominated to monitor the progress of these actions and to hear the interlocutory summonses which arise, is to secure the orderly progress of this litigation... A time must come when doing justice between the parties requires that the doors to the scheme be closed so that an ascertained body of claimants becomes defined, lead cases are chosen to illustrate particular points, and that body of cases goes forward to trial. The effect of my imposing a cut-off date is not to bar a claimant's right: I have no power to do that. The effect of a cut-off date is only that a claimant may be too late to join the group the claimants to which the Scheme applies. It may be that there will be a second group to which late claimants may gain admittance, but of necessity the cases within the present group will be heard and determined

---

[34] See Section H below.
[35] 'In respect of every [such] case ... no plaintiff will recover from any defendant any costs incurred before the service of the said [positive audit] statement unless, upon application to Master Prebble, relief from this costs order is granted' (Order 23 Oct 1992, para 8.3).
[36] Originally 20 Sept 1991 (Order 28 June 1991), but later retrospectively extended to 24 Sept 1991 (Order 8 Nov 1991).
[37] Judgment 19 Dec 1990, 4–5.
[38] Order 19 Dec 1990, para 17(d).

first, and so at the very lowest a claimant who does not join the present Scheme before the cut-off greatly delays the resolution of his complaint. But, and this is the danger that I must stress, the Limitation Act can extinguish a claimant's right and bar him altogether... What is absolutely certain is this: it is not possible for potential claimants to wait to see the outcome of the scheme litigation, and only then, if the scheme plaintiffs succeed, to advance their own claims. Such inaction would effectively be fatal.[39]

22.59 The ability to fix such a cut-off date in respect of people who (by definition) had not commenced proceedings was challenged by 563 Halcion claimants who had not applied for legal aid before the relevant date, but who came forward because of significant adverse publicity with regard to Halcion after that date. In May 1992, the Judge refused to extend the cut-off date which he had imposed as a condition for eligibility to participate in the first group case. That judgment was upheld by the Court of Appeal.[40] The Court of Appeal held that, although these latecomers may have found it difficult to obtain funding for their cases, the Judge both had jurisdiction to impose such a deadline, and properly exercised his discretion to do so and not to extend it. If the claimants had any complaint about the way in which the legal aid authorities had dealt with applications for funding, then their proper course would be to pursue the Legal Aid Board by way of judicial review. In the words of Hoffman LJ:

> The constitution of a class by reference to the date of the application for legal aid as well as by reference to the commencement of proceedings was an innovation but in my view a very sensible one and well within the judge's powers.[41]

H. Legal Aid, Funding, and Costs Issues

22.60 Throughout the litigation, Ian Kennedy J was concerned about the potential level of costs, compared with the potential level of damages. At the first hearing in November 1990, Leading Counsel for the plaintiffs said that the upper limit for damages in any case was in the order of £10,000. It was later explained that this was the maximum for general damages only, but it was clear that the vast majority of cases would not have any significant loss of earnings or other claim for special damages.[42] Such likely quantum figures had to be compared with the actual and potential costs of seeking to prove the case. It was clear that such costs would be enormous. In December 1991, the Judge indicated that generic costs through to trial would amount to at least £12.5 million. In addition, there were individual costs. The plaintiffs indicated that the costs up to and including service of proceedings alone were, on average, £2,000.[43]

---

[39] Judgment 9 Apr 1991, 1–4.
[40] Judgment 13 Oct 1992.
[41] ibid, 19.
[42] See judgment 6 Dec 1991, 4 *et seq.*
[43] ibid, 7. 'If the case is authorised to proceed, the cost up to and including service of proceedings is an average of £2000... The implications are appalling: if 10,000 claimants are to be screened, the cost is £7.5m on the lower estimate: the 150 "approved" psychiatrists stand to earn £5m between them. The scheme's solicitors have an approved list of psychiatrists and Counsel (and so a patronage which is astonishing). If the advice is that proceedings are justified, every thousand sets of proceed-

22.61 The Legal Aid Board played a major part in the litigation, being the funder of almost all claimants. They were closely involved with the proceedings and, to assist the parties in the Court, agreed to circulate in agreed form details of the flow of applications and certificates as they were granted.[44] Indeed, the Board were invited to (and required to attend) some hearings, that were particularly concerned with costs aspects. They attended by way of separate counsel.

22.62 The litigation also saw the development of the opponent of a legally assisted person submitting representations to the Board against the grant or continuation of funding. Such representations were made in Scotland, where the Scottish Legal Aid Board invited submissions from an opponent before any certificate was granted. In England, such invitations were unknown: but, as the Board were required to take into account 'all circumstances' when granting or continuing funding, Wyeth considered the Board would be bound to take into account any representations submitted by the defendants, when considering funding issues. Indeed, they considered that such representations may assist the Board in coming to an informed decision, by filling considerable gaps of knowledge about the claims, under which the Board were clearly labouring.

22.63 In their representations, the defendants expressed concern about the apparent problems in individual cases faced by the plaintiffs. Some plaintiffs appeared never to have been prescribed the product of which they complained. In many more cases, the symptoms which they alleged as withdrawal effects were very similar in nature to the symptoms suffered before first prescription, and for which the products were indicated and prescribed. In relatively few cases did the plaintiff's examining psychiatrist positively attribute the symptoms, alleged as injuries, to the product of which complaint was made.

22.64 As the Judge saw more of the individual cases, he too expressed concern about their merits. In his judgment of 6 May 1992, he specifically referred to these concerns and, perhaps as a result of this (and the defendants' representations), the following month, the Legal Aid Board confirmed that an 'audit' of all pleaded cases was to take place, to assess the merits and viability of the individual cases and the viability of the litigation as a whole. Each individual case was to be reviewed by a different counsel, and it would only be allowed to proceed if it 'passed' this audit.

22.65 In January 1993, the Steering Committee wrote to Roche's solicitors, giving notice of the suspension of the audit of all Roche cases. Although at the time cryptic, this was the beginning of the withdrawal of funding for the cases against Roche; and the Roche claimants played no further part in the procedural activity of the group action, before Roche made their final strike-out application.

22.66 So far as Wyeth were concerned, the audit reduced the number of cases against them from over 3,000 to approximately 1,200. Even these cases were the subject of regular strike-out applications by Wyeth, who took cases to the Master on a monthly basis. Eventually, in

---

ings will cost at least another £1m. I must look anxiously at and endeavour to moderate this expenditure.' The final expenditure of public funds was over £40m, which included the investigation of 13,000 claims and the commencement of over 5,000 actions.

[44] Judgment 9 Apr 1991, 12.

January 1994, the Legal Aid Board determined that further funding of the Wyeth claimants was unwarranted and would be unreasonable, and they sent letters to the Wyeth plaintiffs requiring them to show cause why the certificates should not be discharged. The following month, the Board notified the Court that it had reached the conclusion that further public support of the litigation against Wyeth could not be justified. However, there was a lengthy funding appeal process brought by the plaintiffs. The Area Committee of the Board dismissed the Appeal in March 1994 but agreed to review their own decision, following the threat of a judicial review. However, the Area Committee again dismissed the appeal in November 1994.

22.67 The withdrawal of funding was followed by offers from Roche and Wyeth to agree to a discontinuance of an action on the basis of no order for costs and an agreement that the plaintiff would not seek to pursue any action in the future. They also obtained orders that, where a claimant had not accepted the 'costs holiday' offer, he should be required to serve a notice of intention to proceed, so that the Court and the defendants knew precisely how many plaintiffs wished to proceed further, without the benefit of funding. The withdrawal of funding and the 'costs holiday' offer resulted in the reduction of numbers of plaintiffs from over 1,200 to under 100.[45]

I. Striking out

22.68 The litigation saw a number of developments in relation to the summary striking out of claims. Of course, the litigation was heard before the introduction of the CPR, with its specific procedure for the summary disposal of claims.[46] The only grounds available for the striking out of a case were procedural default, abuse of process (under RSC Order 18, Rule 19), or under the Court's inherent jurisdiction.

22.69 However, the Judge made it clear that he was not prepared for cases of no or dubious merit to continue in the group, baselessly supporting the cases with some merit. There was no room for 'passengers', who could distort the whole balance of the group so far as potential damages, potential costs, and merits were concerned.

Individual cases

22.70 Therefore, despite the huge numbers of claimants in the group, both the Master and Judge were prepared to entertain applications for the striking out of individual cases, and the defendants brought these on a monthly basis. Very many cases were struck out because of procedural default (for example, a failure to serve a medical report that properly substantiated the claimed injuries, in accordance with RSC Order 18, Rule 12(1C)), or because, on their face, they disclosed no cause of action or were bound to fail.

---

[45] Roche and Wyeth then applied to strike out the remaining claims (discussed below, Section I).
[46] CPR Part 24.

22.71 Because of the deficiencies in the individual cases, the Legal Aid Board instituted a full-scale review of all cases.[47] Whilst this audit was in progress, the defendants agreed that they would not seek to strike out individual cases that had not been audited. However, as the results of the audit came through, it appeared to them that many of the cases even with a positive audit still lacked sufficient merit to survive a strike-out application. Wyeth selected six cases from the first hundred 'positively audited' claims and applied to the Judge to have them struck out. Four were discontinued when identified, prior to the hearing. The other two were both struck out by Ian Kennedy J at a hearing in October 1992. Of the proper tests for the strike out of claims in a group action, he said:

> It is well settled now that the judge in charge of group litigation has a more intraventionist role than is otherwise the case, and that he must where necessary innovate in order to control the litigation fairly and efficiently . . .
>
> I am satisfied that in order to make my control fair to both parties and effective in securing that costs and (let it not be forgotten) Court time are not wasted, I should entertain [strike-out] applications such as the present. I am perfectly well aware that the defendants' motive is to whittle away at the passed-audit cases until the [legal aid] board is persuaded that the balance tips against continuing to fund the plaintiff. This is not improper: the question is whether a case is fit to continue or not.
>
> The tests must be two-fold: does the medical report substantiate the injuries pleaded: if so (or to the extent that it does), is the case such that 'the plaintiff has no reasonable chance of success in (his) action on the facts alone and that consequently his claim is truly frivolous and vexatious and should be struck out'?
>
> . . .[I]mplicit in any assessment must be not just whether a particular case has any reasonable chance of success with the generic issues already decided as the plaintiffs would have them, but whether it has such a reasonable chance of success in its own facts that it can be said to contribute to, and not just be a passenger upon, the generic issues.
>
>> If this is not the test, too much turns on the Court's assent to group litigation. If any other approach than this were to be adopted it would entail that once group litigation starts the need to consider whether overall the action has a reasonable chance of success ceases. In my opinion the Court must be willing to take an overview of the individual cases contributing to the whole picture. In the unitary action, payment-in provides a defendant with some defence against an exaggerated claim even where he intends to contest liability: payment-in against, say, five hundred individual actions or their total is a difficult concept. The assessment is not easy and the jurisdiction must be exercised cautiously.
>>
>> How is such a jurisdiction to be exercised? Plainly, one can look to the pleading and the supporting medical report. In my view, one can look also to the general practitioner notes and the correspondence disclosed with them, not to make fine judgments on matters of medical expertise, but to see whether the report relied upon ignores matters which grossly must be relevant or runs counter to the plain thrust of all the contemporaneous material.
>>
>> The defendants, having taken statements from the general practitioners, ask me to take them into account . . . I have refused to allow the statements to be used in that way . . .[48]

22.72 Applying these tests, Ian Kennedy J struck out the remaining two Wyeth cases before him. He found that the first 'could never justify an action of the complexity that would be entailed in examining her complaints and their origins, let alone afford support to the

---

[47] The 'audit', referred to in Section H above.
[48] Judgment 20 Oct 1993, 25–28.

generic case'.[49] With regard to the second, he said: 'This case has no reasonable chance of success, and is struck out. Cases such as this bedevil this litigation. When I find they have been positively audited my concern increases.'[50]

22.73 Following this judgment, Wyeth continued to take striking-out applications to Master Prebble on a monthly basis (who applied the criteria identified by the Judge), with almost complete success, until the Legal Aid Board notified the Court that it had reached the conclusion that the further public support of the litigation against Wyeth could not be justified, in February 1994.

Strike out of prescriber cases

22.74 At the same hearing at which Ian Kennedy J dealt with the strike out of audited individual Wyeth cases, he also struck out the plaintiffs' actions against the health authority prescriber defendants. In March 1993, he struck out all of the approximately 150 cases against the general practitioner prescribers. In doing so, he took account of the facts that (i) the proportion of cases in which the prescribers were defendants was only about 3.4 per cent of the total claims against manufacturers; and (ii) the claims against the prescribers were brought in the alternative—they were only to be pursued if the claims against the manufacturers failed, and in this sense they were contingent.

22.75 The Judge found that it would be unjust and an abuse of process for the prescribers to remain in the litigation. In respect of the health authority prescribers, he gave the following reasons:

(i) They cannot properly defend the claims against them without being present at the generic trial;
(ii) The claims made against them could not reasonably have been brought if the primary claims were not being advanced; and
(iii) The cost to the health authorities taking as limited a part in the generic trial as they can fairly take would bear no sensible relationship to any benefit that the plaintiffs might hope to obtain from their inclusion.[51]

22.76 In addition, in striking out the general practitioner prescriber cases, he added two more reasons:

(iv) The proposal that these claims should stand over for perhaps another 4 years would involve a delay which is bound to cause injustice in that it will then be necessary to examine the details of presentations, impressions, diagnoses and treatments 15 or more years in the past, and when the passage of time will involve that more prescribers are dead and more still disabled in their recollection.[52]
(v) Since the hypothesis upon which the claims against the prescribers are to be pursued is that the actions will have failed against the manufacturers, any damages that legally aided plaintiffs might recover against the prescribers and health authorities would be consumed by the legal aid charges for the costs of the unsuccessful claims against the

---

[49] ibid, 34.
[50] ibid, 36–37.
[51] Judgment 20 Oct 1992, 10: set out in the Court of Appeal judgment of Stuart-Smith LJ reported as *AB & Others v John Wyeth & Brother Limited* [1994] 5 Med LR 149, 151.
[52] Judgment 15 Mar 1993, 21: set out in the Court of Appeal judgment of Stuart-Smith LJ reported as *AB & Others v John Wyeth & Brother Limited* [1994] 5 Med LR 149, 151.

manufacturers . . . [T]here would be no benefit to the plaintiffs in pursuing the litigation against the prescribers.[53]

22.77 Both judgments were appealed, and both appeals were dismissed. The Court said:

> In most cases it will be quite inappropriate for the Court to enter upon the sort of costs benefits analysis which the Judge undertook here. The Court cannot weigh the plaintiff's prospect of receiving £1,000 against the defendants' costs of £10,000 which may be irrecoverable; this can only be done at the trial; alternatively it is a matter for the commercial judgment of the defendant whether he attempts to reach a settlement with the plaintiff: and in so doing he has to take into account as part of the equation that the plaintiff is legally aided or impecunious. But this case is quite different. One can see at a glance that the prescriber defendants will be put to astronomical expense in defending these contingent claims. And to what end? If the plaintiffs stood to obtain a substantial benefit, the position might well be different. But here the benefit is at best extremely modest, and in all probability nothing. That involves great injustice to the defendants. It is no answer that they are public authorities or insurance associations that are footing the bill. The National Health Service has better things to spend its money on than lawyers' fees and the cost of medical insurance is a matter of public concern. Group actions involve great advantage to plaintiffs, who are able to join together to bring actions which, on their own, would never be possible. But they must be conducted in such a way that they do not involve injustice to other parties . . . In such litigation this Court will be especially reluctant to interfere with a Judge's exercise of his discretion, since he knows far more about the litigation than we do. Far from being persuaded that the Judge was wrong here, we are entirely satisfied that he was right, for the reasons which he gave . . .[54]

22.78 Therefore, the Court of Appeal confirmed that, in applying the traditional rules concerning strike out (under RSC Order 18, Rule 19, at the inherent jurisdiction of the Court), the Court was entitled to take into account the fact that the action before it was a group action. Indeed, the Court said: 'the question whether, and if so, to what extent, these principles apply to non-group litigation, may have to be considered hereafter'.[55]

Strike out of manufacturer cases

22.79 Following the withdrawal of legal aid funding, a small number of Roche and Wyeth claimants sought to proceed further, the balance of claimants (well over 3,000) having discontinued or been struck out. Master Prebble struck out the *Roche* cases as constituting an abuse of process, but not on grounds of inordinate and inexcusable delay. A number of plaintiffs appealed that decision, and Roche appealed against his refusal to find in favour of them on the second ground. In the meantime, Wyeth applied direct to the Judge who, having heard Wyeth's submissions, adjourned to allow the *Roche* appeal to be consolidated. He then went on to hear submissions from the plaintiffs and both manufacturer defendants over several days, and gave the plaintiffs a number of opportunities to formulate their case, and bring forward further evidence, particularly on their ability to proceed to trial. However, on 19 July 1996, Ian Kennedy J struck out all of the actions both on the basis that they were an abuse of process of the Court, and for want of prosecution.[56]

---

[53] Paraphrase of the Judge's fifth ground, from the judgment of Stuart-Smith LJ in the Court of Appeal reported as *AB & Others v John Wyeth & Brother Limited* [1994] 5 Med LR 149, 151.
[54] ibid, at 153, per Stuart-Smith LJ.
[55] ibid. Of course, consideration of the principles would now be under the CPR, and particularly CPR Part 24.
[56] Reported as *AB & Others v John Wyeth & Brother Limited* [1996] 7 Med LR 267.

22.80 In the prescriber strike-out judgment, the Judge did not refer to many of the difficulties clearly faced by the plaintiffs in their actions, for example that in over 90 per cent of the cases there was a limitation defence, there were very considerable problems on causation, and there was the difficult question of balancing the benefits of the drug against the possible undesirable consequences of taking it.[57]

22.81 However, in striking out the manufacturer claims, the Judge did take the broad overall context of the litigation into account. He bore in mind that an individual plaintiff could only have brought an action as part of group litigation and, without funding, there was no prospect of the case even being brought to trial, let alone to a successful outcome for the plaintiff. He found that the plaintiffs were incapable of proceeding to trial; and, further, he found that a fair trial was by then impossible because of the prejudice to the defendants that delay had brought.

22.82 The judgment was strongly supported by the Court of Appeal.[58] The Court effectively found that the delay was part of the abuse of process, and struck out the claims as an abuse. They found not only that the Judge had properly exercised his discretion to strike out the claims, but 'he was plainly right to do so',[59] taking the broad-brush approach which he did and taking into account the various difficulties faced by the plaintiffs in attempting to pursue the cases to trial.

J. Conclusion

22.83 The history of this litigation was described by Brooke LJ in the Court of Appeal as an 'expensive disaster'.[60] Clearly, as frequently stressed by Ian Kennedy J, something went wrong in the process of screening claimants prior to their issuing proceedings.[61] The Legal Aid Board have also been criticised for spending over £40 million[62] on litigation which, certainly with the benefit of hindsight, was always bound to fail.[63]

---

[57] Referred to in the judgment of Stuart-Smith LJ [1994] 5 Med LR 149, 153. He said: 'We accept . . . that the Judge did not take these matters into account in reaching his decision. He did not need to do so because there was ample other material upon which he could act. But, in our judgment, he would have been entitled to take them into consideration had he wished to . . .'

[58] Reported as *AB & Others v John Wyeth & Brother Limited* [1997] 8 Med LR 57.

[59] ibid, per Stuart-Smith LJ, 69.

[60] *AB & Others v John Wyeth & Brother Limited* [1997] 8 Med LR 57, 74.

[61] This point was also referred to by Brooke LJ in the Court of Appeal: 'Solicitors involved in group litigation like this, where a critical mass of plaintiffs is required to permit the litigation to go forward, must always remember that they should not allow their clients to get involved in such proceedings without fully explaining to them what the litigation may involve. There must have been many thousands of vulnerable people who had their hopes raised by this litigation, only to see them cruelly dashed by the withdrawal of legal aid and, now, by the dismissal of the proceedings. It is only if lessons like this are learned for the future that expensive disasters such as the one represented by the history of the litigation can be in any way justified.' (*AB & Others v John Wyeth & Brother Limited* [1997] 8 Med LR 57, 73–74.)

[62] Legal Aid Board, *The Funding Code: A New Approach to Funding Civil Claims* (1999) 16.

[63] For example, see the comment of Margaret Puxon QC at [1997] 8 Med LR 74.

22.84 However, criticisms of how the Court handled the case[64] are not well founded. As can be seen from the history of the case, throughout, faced with enormous numbers of individual cases with limited financial value, Ian Kennedy J was sensitive to the issue of costs and made it clear that he would do everything he could to mitigate them. With respect to those who hold a contrary view, the Judge cannot be criticised for the expenditure of taxpayers' money on an action which, upon proper consideration, proved to be without merit. His view that it is not appropriate to allow a very small number of cases out of a potentially very large cohort to go forward, with the balance being subject to no investigation whatsoever, has been proved correct in subsequent cases, which have also shown the value of investigating a sufficient number of individual cases to ensure that the litigation focuses on the real, determinative issues. At every opportunity, he was willing to give guidelines in respect of the cohort, based on applications made only in a number of specific cases. In many respects, his handling of the case presaged the Woolf reforms and the CPR, which require the cost of litigation steps to be taken into account before any directions are given, and require a flexible and robust approach to court management of cases.

22.85 The Benzodiazepine litigation was enormous by any standards, and raised many problems of group actions which had not been faced before. During the course of it, inevitably, many lessons were learned by the legal representatives of the parties and, no doubt, by the Court itself. However, in retrospect, far from illustrating shortcomings of the court system, overall the case showed how the Court Rules, flexibly applied, could accommodate even the most difficult group case management problems.

---

[64] See, eg, M Day, P Balen and G McCool, 'Multi-Party Actions' (Legal Action Group, 1995) 26: '[t]he shortcomings of the legal system in England and Wales were very fully illustrated by the Benzodiazepine Litigation . . .'.

23

LLOYD'S LITIGATION

Gary Wakinshaw[1]

> This enormous litigation was active in the early and mid-1990s and related to the arrangements between different members of the Lloyd's insurance market. There were many individual actions, although they can be grouped into eight broad categories.
>
> A succession of judges was appointed to co-ordinate the actions, which were all dealt with within the Commercial Court. At an early stage, the Court called the parties together for a two-day discussion of the nature of the actions and the management issues which would arise, which resulted in adoption of a test case approach generally based on preliminary issues and a general timetable. This approach was successfully adopted in progressing the various categories of cases: a sequence of appeals may have reversed findings of substantive law but not the essential management approach. The lawyers involved faced enormous challenges of disseminating information to the tens of thousands of clients involved, and the liaison committee approach was adopted to deal with this.
>
> These types of cases did not give rise to issues of attracting potential litigants who might not qualify for inclusion, since the identity of names and other parties could be established by reference to previously published lists. There were, however, problems over the need to issue writs promptly as names came forward in order to avoid limitation problems: this issue would now be solved by the register system. Potentially enormous discovery was agreed to be limited to a sample number of names and agencies so as to avoid expensive duplication. As most of the cases moved towards settlement, the Court assisted by deferring trial dates in order to facilitate settlement discussions and avoid unnecessary costs.

A. Background

23.01 The Lloyd's litigation is the general term which was given to a group of actions brought by Lloyd's names against their members' agents, managing agents, syndicate auditors, and

---

[1] Kwelm Management Services Limited.

actuaries. The bulk of the litigation was commenced between 1992 and 1994 and in total some 2,000 writs were issued by about 12,000 names against 300 defendants.

23.02　Lloyd's of London is an institution made up of a number of syndicates offering insurance. Syndicates are made up of a number of 'names', who are private individuals who put up a certain amount of their assets to guarantee the insurance policies sold by the syndicates. In addition, for the last four years Lloyd's has accepted corporate capital. Until 1989 a name's contractual relationship was only with his members' agent. It was the members' agent who dealt with all of the administration, advised names which syndicates they should join, collected the profits from the syndicates, and redistributed them to the names. Whilst the contractual relationship between the name and the member's agent was such that the members' agent would undertake the underwriting on behalf of the name, in reality this was usually subcontracted to managing agents. Each syndicate would have a managing agent who employed the active underwriter of the syndicate who is the person who chooses which risks to take on and what premium to charge. Accordingly, the vast majority of the litigation involved alleged acts committed where there was no direct contractual relationship with the managing agent. The names sued the members' agents in contract as being vicariously liable for the negligence of the managing agent and also the managing agent in tort.

B. Causes of the Litigation

23.03　There were two main causes of the Lloyd's litigation:
1. Asbestosis and pollution claims arising from the USA; and
2. Thirteen man-made and natural disasters of over US$1 billion in value which occurred between 1988 and 1990 including the Piper Alpha explosion, the *Exxon Valdez* Oil Spill, Hurricane Hugo, and an earthquake in San Francisco.

C. The Syndicate

23.04　A syndicate is not a legal entity. It is made up of a number of names who participate on it for a particular year. There is a syndicate for each year, as every year certain names may join or leave the syndicate or increase or decrease the value of their participation on it (known as the name's 'line' on that syndicate). Whilst participation on a syndicate is an annual venture each syndicate has a three-year accounting period. At the end of the three-year period a calculation is performed by the managing agent to assess the Reinsurance To Close (RITC). The RITC is essentially an unlimited reinsurance premium paid for by the names on the year to be closed to the names on the subsequent year in order to allow, if they wished, the names on the year to be closed to leave the syndicates. The RITC is therefore the amount needed to reinsure any risks which are still outstanding at the end of thirty-six months, not only the reported claims which have not yet been paid, but also the incurred but not reported claims (IBNR), ie those losses which will be suffered by the syndicate but of which the syndicate has at that time no notice. The intention of the RITC calculation is to attain equity between the reinsuring and reinsured names. The negligence of the managing agent in preparing the IBNR calculation proved to be one of the main reasons for the downfall of a number of the syndicates involved in the Lloyd's litigation.

If the managing agents are unable to calculate a figure for the RITC which is 'a true and fair figure', then they are obliged to leave that year of account open. This means that any losses which are reported to the syndicate for that year of account will be paid by the names on the syndicate for that year. **23.05**

D. Causes of Action

The easiest way to split the various types of case is to adopt a characterisation given to the various cases by Cresswell J, who was appointed by the Commercial Court to oversee all of the Lloyd's litigation, in a statement dated 4 March 1994 giving a review of the progress of the Lloyd's litigation. The six categories are as follows. **23.06**

LMX spiral cases

The London market excess of loss spiral came about when one reinsurer reinsured some or all of its own risks with another reinsurer which then repeated the process. Whilst this further diluting of particular risks would usually be to the benefit of the names who participated on an LMX syndicate the difficulty arose at Lloyd's when, through a series of these reinsurances, the first reinsurer found itself reinsuring part of its own risk. This arrangement therefore ultimately concentrated losses on those syndicates accepting reinsurance business which did not then have their own reinsurance cover. The most notable of the LMX syndicates was the Gooda Walker Syndicate, which lost its names, by the end of 1993, an average of £500,000. **23.07**

Long-tail cases

Long-tail business is where the nature of the risk underwritten is such that claims can be made upon a particular policy over an extended period of time. The losses suffered by long-tail syndicates arose mainly from asbestosis and environmental pollution claims in the USA from the 1940s to the 1980s. **23.08**

In 1980, the US Government passed the Comprehensive Environmental Response Compensation Liability Act (CERCLA) to ensure that, in relation to any sites which were found to be polluted, the company responsible was forced to pay for the clean-up irrespective of cost. **23.09**

In relation to asbestosis the dangers were for those employees working in industries where asbestos was commonly used. It is estimated that between 8 and 11 million US workers have been exposed to asbestos based products since 1940. As an example, by 1990 Johns-Manville, one of the largest asbestos producers, was involved in 149,000 liability claims. **23.10**

The companies against whom pollution clean-up orders were made and against whom employees or their estates were claiming for asbestosis in turn claimed through third **23.11** party/employee liability insurance policies. The claims which were subsequently brought by the names in the Lloyd's litigation on long-tail syndicates were then split into two different but closely related types.

Run-off contract cases

23.12   In the early 1980s a number of Lloyd's syndicates took over, by way of reinsurance, the contingent liabilities of other syndicates. Many of the contingent liabilities were in respect of insurances or reinsurances of US asbestos and pollution risks. The names alleged that at the time the run-off contracts were written by the syndicates upon which they were placed, the members' and managing agents were or should have been aware of the potentially enormous losses which could be suffered by virtue of the run-off contracts written. Accordingly, the names alleged that the members' and managing agents had been negligent in writing that business.

Reinsurance to close cases (RITC)

23.13   These cases concerned the closing of each of the year's account from about 1978 onwards. The names contended that from that time the managing agents should have been aware that it was impossible to calculate a true and fair figure for the RITC. Instead of leaving the year of account open (which would result in significant adverse publicity) the managing agent closed each of the years of account into the next year and, in the case of some syndicates, up until 1989. Accordingly, whereas losses should have been suffered by the names on the syndicate in the 1978 or 1979 or 1980 etc (whichever should have been properly left open) year account, in fact, they were suffered by names on the year of account which was eventually left open with an RITC premium paid to them from the previous year which was entirely insufficient.

23.14   In a number of those cases names not only sued their managing agents, and the members' agents, but also the auditors and actuaries of the syndicate who had been instructed to advise, in the case of the actuaries on the appropriate level of the RITC and, in relation to the auditors, that it reflected a true and fair figure. Accordingly, apart from the question of whether or not a particular year should have been closed, the question arose as to the existence and scope of any duty owed by auditors and actuaries to the names.

Personal stop loss cases

23.15   Stop loss insurance is an insurance policy available to names which can be purchased to indemnify them personally for any losses they may suffer on the syndicates which they have placed up to a particular limit with the application of an excess. This category of case was concerned with syndicates who wrote personal stop loss insurance for names on other syndicates. The plaintiffs were the names on stop loss syndicates who contended that the writing of the stop loss policies involved indirect reinsurance of both LMX and long-tail business and that the managing agents should not have taken on such business or at least should have arranged adequate reinsurance.

Portfolio selection cases

23.16   In this category the names alleged that their respective members' agents failed to advise them properly as to which syndicates they should join, or put them on unsuitable syndicates, or failed to advise them to leave a syndicate when, the names alleged, it was, or should have been, apparent that the syndicate was not suitable for the name concerned. Those cases in the main concerned names that were put on syndicates operating in the LMX market.

Central fund litigation

In those cases the Society of Lloyd's claimed against the names under the central fund by-law for reimbursement of payments made from the central fund when a name refused to pay his losses or in the case of a name's failure to maintain the required level of security at Lloyd's. 23.17

Other cases

There were a number of other cases which concerned the workings of Lloyd's. None became of any major importance or involved significant numbers of plaintiffs or defendants. 23.18

E. The Outhwaite Syndicates

The first major piece of Lloyd's litigation was in relation to the Outhwaite Syndicates. Disputes arose between the Outhwaite Syndicates and a number of other syndicates which they reinsured by way of run-off contracts. Outhwaite disputed payments under these run-off contracts due to material non-disclosure. The Outhwaite names, irrespective of the Outhwaite Syndicates' success in managing to dispute the vast majority of the run-off contracts, were still facing losses of approximately 450 per cent of their line. In early 1988 about two-thirds of the 1,500 plus Outhwaite names paid an initial subscription of £250 plus 4 per cent of their premium line to commence litigation. It should be noted that unlike many other types of class actions there was no difficulty identifying potential plaintiffs and defendants. The plaintiff names and their members' agents were easily identifiable from lists produced by the Syndicate; the managing agent was also easily identifiable as the company that ran the Syndicate in question. 23.19

So far as the cost for the names was concerned of entering into litigation this was generally a drop in the ocean compared to the losses on the Syndicates. Taking an average line for a name on the Outhwaite Syndicate of, say, £20,000 the initial subscription amounts to only £1,050 compared to that name's losses of £90,000. At, say, £1,000 for each of the initial 1,000 names this gives a fighting fund of £1,000,000. Proceedings were commenced against the managing agent and also the eighty or so members' agents who had been responsible for placing the names on the Outhwaite Syndicates. The main reason for this was, as later indicated by Cresswell J, that there was a limited pot of funds available from the various managing and members' agents' errors & omissions insurers from whom damages could be sought. The names could therefore be assured of receiving a far greater proportion of their losses on a judgment against over eighty defendants each with errors & omissions insurance than in a judgment against only the one managing agent with one limit on its policy. 23.20

23.21 Of the remaining one-third of the Outhwaite names who did not commence the litigation there were a number of reasons, particularly in respect of working names (ie people who worked in Lloyd's) who were under great pressure not to commence litigation against the wishes of Lloyd's and be seen to be disloyal. During trial the defendants became increasingly concerned about the possible adverse outcome and, after pressure was brought to bear by Lloyd's, negotiated a settlement. The amount of the settlement was generally considered to be a success for the names. However, names who had not participated in the Outhwaite litigation were not entitled to any of the settlement monies.

23.22 Following this settlement, names who had previously been reluctant to join action groups in relation to other syndicates, as they had been told by Lloyd's and their members' agent that any action was doomed to failure, gained confidence.

F. Commercial Court Administration

23.23 The total value of the claims for all of the action groups was estimated to be in the region of £3–4 billion. This, together with the number of writs, plaintiffs and defendants, meant that the problems at Lloyd's are thought to have been the largest single cause of litigation in this country. Saville J, who was then sitting in the Commercial Court, was originally appointed to manage the Lloyd's litigation. He took the initiative in June 1993 by taking the unprecedented step of inviting all lawyers in the Lloyd's litigation to a meeting to debate how the Court should handle the Lloyd's litigation. Saville J was keen to ensure that the cases did not swamp the Court and clog it up for decades to come. Solicitors for anyone being sued or suing in the Lloyd's litigation were invited to attend to put ideas to Saville J and to consider which test cases should be chosen to go through the Court first and whether mediation or arbitration could play a role. At that time legal proceedings had been commenced in relation to *Feltrim, Gooda Walker, Wellington, Poland, Merrett, Pulbrook*, and a number of others. Saville J also asked for a number of further Commercial Court judges to deal with the increase in litigation. At the end of the two-day meeting which, whilst technically held in chambers, was widely publicised, Saville J had established a timetable of bringing the various actions to trial and also to obtain the agreement of the parties to participate in a number of preliminary issue hearings. Soon afterwards Saville J was appointed to the Court of Appeal and Cresswell J was appointed to replace him.

23.24 In his statement of 4 March 1994 on the Commercial Court's approach to the case management of the Lloyd's litigation Cresswell J stated:

1. The Commercial Court would try to balance the demands of the Lloyd's litigation and the demands of other litigants who brought domestic and international commercial disputes to the Court. He said, however, that he wished to impress upon the parties to the Lloyd's litigation that there was the distinct possibility, even if the plaintiffs' claims were sound in law, that there may be insufficient funds to satisfy them all. The reasons for this were threefold:

   - Insufficient insurance cover. One of the main reasons for this was that errors &

omissions insurance for members' and managing agents had become prohibitively expensive due to the escalating losses;
- Defendants with few real assets;
- Policy points taken by errors & omissions insurers as a means for avoiding payment under a policy, for example avoidance for fraud (Gooda Walker).

2. Cresswell J said that it was the Court's intention to continue to select, from cases in a particular category, lead or pilot cases for trial as to liability and principles relating to quantum (if appropriate) in the hope that decisions in these cases may provide broader guidance in relation to other cases in the same category. He also said that where appropriate in group cases the claims of sample names would be considered in order to save expenses. Whilst the Court recognised that, for example, each of the LMX cases raised certain common issues it would not be feasible to list them all for hearing at the same time, as each defendant contended that it would be necessary to look at the circumstances of each individual underwriter's method of doing business to decide definitively whether there was negligence and if so in what respect. Any attempt to bring all the actions together for a full trial would produce a case of unmanageable proportions. In addition, some action groups were further advanced than others.

3. A liaison committee would be set up to facilitate distribution of information to parties involved in the Lloyd's litigation. Cameron Markby Hewitt (now CMS Cameron McKenna) was chosen to distribute information to firms of solicitors acting for other defendants as it was involved in more of the Lloyd's litigation, on behalf of defendants, than any other firm.

23.25 The Commercial Court also went to some lengths to ensure that all of the Lloyd's litigation was dealt with by that Court to ensure efficient management. In *Deeny v Littlejohn & Co & Others* Cresswell J held that overall case management of Lloyd's litigation could only be achieved in an efficient and consistent manner if all future cases were commenced in the Commercial Court. In 1992 Evans J, then in charge of the Commercial List, made provision for management of 'all existing and future cases concerning conduct or management of business at Lloyd's and involving either the Society of Lloyd's or disputes between parties involved in the business of Lloyd's including underwriting members, their members and underwriting agents and brokers'.

G. Proceedings

Writs and points of claim

23.26 The Outhwaite settlement in 1992 gave a good incentive to names on other syndicates to join the action groups for fear that if they did not and actions brought against those syndicates' managing and members' agents were successful they would still not benefit. As mentioned, the formation of the action groups themselves was relatively easy as the names of each of the participants on the syndicate are readily available.

23.27 Once action groups had been formed it was important to issue proceedings as soon as possible. In many of the actions there were substantial limitation problems. For example, in

RITC cases where many of the actions were not commenced until 1993 the names were claiming negligence in relation to the closure of the 1979 year of account in 1982. Whilst many contracts between the members' agent and the name were under seal, giving a twelve-year limitation period in respect of any cause of action, this was not always the case. In a lot of cases, whether or not the contract was under seal was also an issue as the original contracts could not be found. Accordingly, in many of the cases a number of writs were issued so that as soon as a number of names had joined a writ was issued including not only the ones who were already litigating but also including the new names.

23.28 With separate interests for each of the groups of defendants, separate firms of solicitors were instructed on behalf of each. In some of the actions over 150 members' agents were named as defendants. A similar method of invoicing to that used by the names' solicitors was used by the solicitors acting on behalf of the members, agents, ie the percentage of premium income of the members' agents litigating names pro rata to the total premium income of all of the litigating names on the syndicate. This method was subsequently approved by the Court on taxation of costs.

23.29 When Points of Claim were served by the names' solicitors, at least in the later actions, the plaintiffs appended a schedule identifying which name was claiming against which members' agent and for which year or years of account. This made the calculation of each members' agent's potential liability and share of costs easier.

23.30 In a number of the long-tail actions commenced by the names a representative name in relation to each of the years of account which was allegedly negligently closed purported to sue on his own behalf and on behalf of all names on the syndicate who either joined the syndicate for the first time in a particular year of account or increased their line on the syndicate for that year of account. The intended effect was therefore that not only were the named plaintiffs intending to seek recovery but all names who were placed on the syndicate were potentially able to recover (unlike in the Outhwaite litigation). There were arguments in each of these cases that the represented names did not share the same interest as the litigating names as, for example, any name who left a syndicate prior to any loss-making year of account could not be said to have the same interest as a name exposed to the open year.

23.31 In a large number of cases the names' solicitors made errors as to the identity of the members' agent who had placed a particular name on the syndicate. This was especially true in relation to names placed many years before the proceedings were commenced by one members' agent where the names then changed members' agent some time later. In those cases there were novation agreements which sometimes transferred liability to a new members' agent and sometimes did not. Questionnaires were sent out by the solicitors for the members' agents to the members' agents asking for confirmation that the names identified as bringing an action against them were indeed names who had been placed on the syndicate by that members' agent for that year of account and also to establish the name's line. The name's line was important not only for billing purposes but also in trying to establish the quantum of any judgment which could be brought against a particular members' agent should the name be successful.

23.32 In addition, applications were made in a number of cases seeking to strike out names' claims where the name could not show any loss due to the negligent underwriting. For example, a name joined a syndicate in 1978 with a £10,000 line which he maintained until 1989 when the year of account was left open. If the court found that the 1987 year should have been left open, that name has not suffered any increased loss by virtue of the 1987 and 1988 years having negligently been left open. Accordingly he has no cause of action.

Law firm administration

23.33 There were substantial practical difficulties in acting on behalf of vast numbers of plaintiff names and defendant members' agents. As a rule, a particular law firm only acted for one 'type' of defendant due to potential conflicts of interest.

23.34 One of the most complex matters for the members' agents' solicitors was billing their clients. Whilst the percentage of each members' agent's participation in the litigation could be calculated from the alleged loss suffered by the names who were suing them, there were also a number of sub-groups who had separate defences available to them, for example novations of contract. Work was done on behalf of those members' agents to extricate them from the litigation which had to be billed separately. Also, as mentioned, some of the members' agents were insured and some were not. Work was done at the request of insurers which could only be billed to insured members' agents. There was also work done on behalf of each individual members' agent. Accordingly there could be three or four separate calculations to be done to produce a bill for one members' agent.

23.35 Similarly, reporting to and obtaining instructions from the names and members' agents caused great difficulties. Whilst the names generally agreed to the formation of a steering committee to give instructions this was not true of the members' agents. It seems that the members' agents were reluctant to give up any power to direct the litigation and therefore could not agree to the constitution of a steering committee. This had a knock-on effect on reporting; whereas the names were content with a 'newsletter' the members' agents required full reports. Where instructions were required these were obtained by way of negative responses only, ie where a client agreed with the recommended course of action no response was required; however, if they did not they had to respond. On some occasions an acceptance form was appended to a report asking for a 'yes' or 'no' to the suggested course of action.

Limitation

23.36 The question of whether or not each of the names named as a plaintiff was a working (ie someone who works at Lloyd's) or non-working name was also important from a limitation point of view, particularly in relation to allegations of deliberate concealment of relevant facts and where the relevant facts were not known. Such arguments were inevitably going to be more difficult to be brought by a working name than a non-working name.

23.37 These arguments were considered in *Hallam-Eames & Others v Merrett Syndicates & Others* in which Gatehouse J held that some of the names' claims were statute barred. He considered the extension of the primary limitation period provided by the Limitation Act 1980 which is the special time limit for negligence actions where facts relevant to the cause of action are not known at the date of accrual of the cause of action. The Court of Appeal held that Gatehouse J had unduly restricted the facts which section 14(A) requires to be known and found that he could not decide as a preliminary point of law or as a preliminary issue whether or not names' claims were statute barred. Accordingly the claims remained open until trial.

23.38 Also in relation to limitation, in the case of *Aitken & Others v Pulbrook & Others* the defendants argued that contracts under seal should not entitle a party to a twelve-year limitation period. The Court found against this argument.

Points of defence

23.39 Following the House of Lords' decision on the preliminary issue in *Gooda Walker*, *Feltrim*, and *Merrett* regarding members' agents' vicarious liability for the acts of the managing agent it was inevitable that there was going to be an identity of interest between the members' and the managing agents. To a large extent the members' agents' defence simply mirrored that of the managing agent. The solicitors on the record for the members' agents and managing agents in the various actions were also advising on strategy etc to the secretariat to their errors & omissions insurers (Clyde & Co) who were involved in almost all of the actions. Accordingly there was a great flow of information between the solicitors for the members' agents and the solicitors for the managing agents which substantially reduced costs and pooled resources and expertise.

Summonses for directions

23.40 It was clear from the outset of all of the long-tail and LMX actions and, to a lesser extent, the stop loss actions, that discovery was going to be one of the most costly and time-consuming parts of the actions. In relation to both the LMX and long-tail actions, many of them had more than 1,000 plaintiff names and in the *Gooda Walker* case, for example, there were over 3,000. In view of the fact that the vast majority of documents in the possession of the names would essentially be the same (except so far as quantum was concerned) it was obvious that there was little point in requiring each of them to provide full discovery. Accordingly, in a number of the actions it was agreed that discovery would be limited to a sample of names from each of a number of various groups which were split as follows:

1. Working names, ie people involved in Lloyd's;
2. Accountants, lawyers, financial advisers, and other similar professionals and such persons who were retired at the relevant time;
3. Business persons and retired business persons; and
4. Those who had no significant experience in any of the aforementioned categories.

23.41 A questionnaire was devised by agreement between all of the parties' solicitors to be sent to each of the names to discover which of the categories they fell into together with obtaining various other items of information as to whether the contracts were under seal, which members' agents they thought had placed them on the syndicate, for which years of account, and their line. From the responses a number of names were chosen by each of the groups of defendants and plaintiffs themselves to provide discovery. In addition, the members' agents who had placed each of the chosen names on the syndicate were then also to give discovery of all of the documents in their possession. What the sampling would not be sufficient for would be a finding on quantum where the individual circumstances of every name would have to be taken into account.

23.42 Despite this limitation, discovery of documents going back thirty, forty, and even fifty years was inevitably problematic. Whilst the members' agents had relatively little documentation directly relevant to the issues in question, the managing agents and the names were asked to produce a vast quantity of documents. Not surprisingly, it transpired that the majority of names had thrown away most of their documents. The courts were generally sympathetic to this.

23.43 There were also issues concerning loss of privilege in relation to attorneys' reports, particularly in relation to pollution and asbestos claims arising out of the USA. Outside the Lloyd's litigation there was (and still is) a vast amount of litigation against companies which had produced asbestos and had caused pollution and also between those companies and their insurers. The insurers had attorneys acting for them to defend claims by their insureds and also to keep a watching brief on claims against the insureds. These reports became discoverable in the Lloyd's litigation. In order to protect the attorney/client privilege in these documents, an order was obtained from the Court confirming that any privilege in these reports would not be deemed waived, nor would there be any reading from the reports in open court.

23.44 So far as witness statements were concerned similar considerations were applied as for discovery of documents. A sample of names was selected by the plaintiffs' solicitors and by each of the firms of solicitors acting on behalf of the various groups of defendants, ie members' agents, managing agents, actuaries, and accountants.

23.45 Expert reports were dealt with as normal as there was no reason to restrict these beyond the usual restrictions of ensuring that no more experts' reports were served than were necessary.

Adjournments

23.46 Whilst the names were successful in each case which went before the courts at first instance, in most cases this did not result in any payments being made to them. In each case quantum was usually reserved and even in relation to liability the defendants invariably appealed to the Court of Appeal and subsequently to the House of Lords. Accordingly, when the proposals for Lloyd's Reconstruction and Renewal (R & R) were published in May 1995 together with individual statements for each of the names as to how much they would receive under the settlement proposals by way of debt credits there was a general desire from within the names to accept. One of the other main reasons was a point mentioned earlier that there was a limited fund from which judgment monies could be paid to the names. Once the first few cases had gone to trial and quantum had been determined and paid out to the names there was inevitably going to be very little left for each of the subsequent actions. Accordingly, whilst two of the earliest actions, *Gooda Walker* and *Feltrim* (both LMX actions), between them accounted for some 4,500 names, there was a willingness amongst the names in other action groups to accept the Lloyd's settlement proposals. What they did not wish was to be halfway through trial or close to trial and incurring significant costs, which, if the settlement proposals were to be accepted, would be a waste of money. Accordingly a number of the names' action groups applied to the Court for adjournments until after the outcome of R & R was known. For example, in the *Wellington* case an application for an adjournment was made only four days before the commencement of the trial. There was an obvious concern amongst the solicitors acting for the defendants that this may be replicated in other actions. Accordingly, McKenna & Co (as it then was), acting on behalf of Ernst & Young and Ernst & Winney, who had been auditors of a number of syndicates, made an application to the Court to impose a general moratorium on all names' action group cases. Cresswell J held that it would be contrary to principle to impose a moratorium on all parties to the Lloyd's litigation, irrespective of their wishes. He did, however, indicate that if the parties to a case with a hearing date in 1996 (towards the end of which the names were to vote on the R & R) wished to defer the start of the case, the Court would assist by revising the current timetable. If some of the parties to an action wished to adjourn and some did not the Court said that it would weigh the competing considerations.

23.47 Following the names' application in the *Wellington* case the defendants' solicitors in a number of the other actions wrote to the plaintiffs asking whether they had the intention of making an application for an adjournment. In one of the long-tail actions, *Secretan*, even though the response came back from the names that they did not intend to seek an adjournment, they subsequently did so. When the hearing came before the Court it allowed the adjournment without imposing any costs penalty on the names irrespective of their previous confirmation that they had no intention of seeking an adjournment pending the outcome of R & R.

Settlement

23.48 The settlement offer of £3.2 billion was made up of debt credits and a settlement fund which was offered to all names, not only those litigating, as a package. Each name who wished to accept the settlement offer was required to give up his rights to litigate against Lloyd's, the members' and managing agents, and the other contributors to the settlement fund. The intention of the settlement was to reinsure all of Lloyd's 1992 and prior years of account into a new company, Equitas Limited, who would take over the run-off of all of the syndicates whose risks had been reinsured. On 30 August 1996 R & R became unconditional, with 90 per cent of names having accepted the terms of it. Cresswell J made various orders for disposing of what was left of the litigation. So far as those names who were plaintiffs who had not accepted the offer were concerned, he ordered that each must provide an address for service and details of the solicitors who would be acting for him and that each had to apply to the Court for further directions, failing which his action would be stayed.

24

REAY v BNFL; HOPE v BNFL

Aidan Thomson[1]

> These cases from the early 1990s concerned allegations of personal injury attributed to exposure to radiation of those alleging personal injury and their parents. They were resolved by a trial of two lead cases, selected by the plaintiffs' lawyers from a pool of cases, which determined that general causation was not established. The parties co-operated to reach agreement on most procedural issues, particularly limiting discovery. The case involved one of the earliest examples of solicitors' advertising, which successfully attracted claimants to a single firm, thereby avoiding co-ordination issues.

A. Factual Background

Sellafield

British Nuclear Fuels plc, and its predecessor, the UK Atomic Energy Authority, have operated nuclear reprocessing plants at Sellafield in West Cumbria since the early 1950s. The plants are used for the commercial reprocessing of spent nuclear fuel from nuclear reactors as part of the 'nuclear fuel cycle'. The operations produce very low level radioactive discharges into the atmosphere and to sea. These discharges have been authorised over the years of the plant's operation by the environmental regulators. 24.01

Investigations into the plant's effects

In 1983, a TV documentary pointed to anecdotal evidence of a higher than expected incidence of childhood leukaemia in the vicinity of the Sellafield plant. Particular attention was focused on an apparent 'cluster' of leukaemias in the village of Seascale, situated two miles from the Sellafield plant. Scientific research work was undertaken over the following ten years, much of it devoted to investigating a possible link between the plant's environmental discharges of radioactivity and the childhood leukaemia cases (the hypothesis being that exposure to radioactivity from Sellafield present in the local environment had caused some or all of the leukaemias in question). 24.02

The Gardner Study

In February 1990 Professor Martin Gardner, who was one of the independent researchers 24.03

---

[1] Partner, Freshfields.

engaged by a Government Committee to investigate the incidence of leukaemia and lymphoma among young people near the Sellafield site, published the results of a case-control study. The study results showed a statistically significant association between certain types of childhood leukaemia and the occupational exposure to radiation of fathers who had worked at the Sellafield plant before their children were conceived.

Case facts

24.04 The cases of *Reay v BNFL* and *Hope v BNFL* (together with a number of other factually similar cases) were launched some time before the publication of the Gardner Study. The *Reay* and *Hope* cases were the two cases ultimately pursued to trial as 'lead cases' effectively selected by the plaintiffs' lawyers. Their brief facts were as follows.

Reay v BNFL

24.05 Dorothy Reay was born in October 1961 and was diagnosed as suffering from acute lymphatic leukaemia in August 1962. She died in September 1962. Her father George Reay was a radiation worker at BNFL's plant at Sellafield in Cumbria from 1948 until 1977. The family lived throughout the relevant period in Whitehaven, a town approximately ten miles north of Sellafield. The claim was brought by Dorothy Reay's mother Elizabeth Reay:

(a) on her own behalf, for loss of ability to mother a normal healthy child, for pain and anguish at Dorothy's early death, and for loss of dependency;
(b) as administratrix of the estate of Dorothy Reay (under the Law Reform (Miscellaneous Provisions) Act 1934); and
(c) as widow and administratrix of the estate of George Reay (under the Law Reform (Miscellaneous Provisions) Act 1934) in respect of his loss of ability to father a normal healthy child and his pain and anguish at Dorothy's early death.

Hope v BNFL

24.06 Vivien Hope was born in 1965 and diagnosed as suffering from non-Hodgkins lymphoma (NHL) in June 1988. She was treated and was, at the time the case was proceeding, in remission, though with permanent disabilities. Her father David Hope was a radiation worker at the Sellafield plant from 1956 to 1988. Vivien Hope herself worked at Sellafield prior to diagnosis of, and after treatment for, her disease. The family lived in Drigg, a small village near Seascale, until 1971 and from 1971 onwards they lived in Seascale. Her claim was brought in her own name. No claims were brought by her parents.

B. Procedural History

24.07 The procedural history of the *Reay* and *Hope* actions is summarised briefly below.[2]

---

[2] The principal reason for the cases' complex procedural history was because, as noted above, the cases were commenced prior to the publication of the report by Professor Gardner (in Feb 1990) but came to trial after the report had been published.

Event	Date
Legal Aid applications	Late 1988
Pleadings	
Writs issued	Late 1989–early 1990
Writs served with Statements of Claim	March 1990
Defences served	March 1990
Requests for Further and Better Particulars/Still Further and Better Particulars served and Replies given	April 1990–June 1991
Amended Statements of Claim/Amended Defences served	June–July 1991
Interrogatories served by both sides and Answered	April 1991–October 1991
Discovery	
(a) General Discovery provided by Defendant on a rolling basis (Four Lists)	April 1990–April 1991
(b) Specific Discovery provided by Defendant (again on a rolling basis—Four Further Lists)	October 1991–April 1992
(c) Third Party Discovery orders sought and obtained against various Government departments, hospitals, and other third parties	May 1991–March 1992
Evidence	
Medical evidence (diagnosis and prognosis where relevant) exchanged	November 1991
Non-medical evidence	
First Exchange	June 1992
Second Exchange	September 1992
Witness Statements exchanged	July 1992
Trial	
Hearing	Commenced on 29 October 1992 Ended on 30 June 1993
Judgment	8 October 1993

C. Key Aspects of the Cases

Advertising for plaintiffs

24.08 The starting point of the Sellafield cases was an advertisement placed in the *Whitehaven Gazette*, a local newspaper, in July 1988 by the plaintiffs' solicitors. They used the (then very recent) changes in the Law Society's rules permitting them to advertise for plaintiffs. The advertisement read as follows:

> Official surveys have demonstrated that there is a significant excess of leukaemia amongst children living in the vicinity of the Sellafield and Dounreay nuclear reprocessing plants. Scientific opinion now accepts that there may well be a link between the leukaemia and the nuclear plants.
>
> Under the Nuclear Installations Act, British Nuclear Fuels are required to compensate any individual who has suffered injury as a result of their operations. We believe that there may now be sufficient scientific evidence to persuade the Courts in this country that some leukaemias are caused by the action of British Nuclear Fuels, which would enable the victims to be compensated.
>
> Our firm is experienced in dealing with radiation cases and have been involved in a number of cases against British Nuclear Fuels and the United Kingdom Atomic Energy Authority. We ensure that, wherever possible, our clients are financially protected by a legal aid certificate.
>
> If your child suffered or is still suffering from leukaemia, if you live in the surrounding area of Sellafield and if you are interested in making a claim against British Nuclear Fuels then why not telephone us. Your case will be treated in absolute confidence.
>
> Please telephone MARTYN DAY on 01-242 1775 and he will arrange to visit you at your house on one of his regular visits to Cumbria. We can guarantee that whether or not you are eligible for legal aid the first appointment will cost you nothing.

A number of potential plaintiffs came forward. Where eligible, the plaintiffs' solicitor applied for and obtained legal aid for their new clients.

Challenging legal aid

24.09 BNFL wrote to the Legal Aid Board, challenging the decision to grant legal aid. At the time, there was no express provision in the relevant legal aid legislation dealing with the making of representations by a prospective defendant. However, the Civil Legal Aid (General) Regulations then in force envisaged information coming to the attention of the Legal Aid Area Director otherwise than via the assisted person or his solicitor and that if such information did come to the Area Director's attention he would be under an obligation to consider it.

24.10 BNFL's representation advanced arguments to the effect that the plaintiffs had no reasonable grounds for bringing their case (ie the plaintiffs failed to satisfy the 'merits' test) and that the case circumstances were such that it was not reasonable for the applicant to be granted legal aid (ie the plaintiffs failed to satisfy the 'reasonableness' test). The Legal Aid Board reversed their earlier decision and withdrew legal aid. The plaintiffs appealed the decision to withdraw funding and the appeal was allowed.

Selection of plaintiffs

24.11 The plaintiffs' solicitors had a pool of legally aided plaintiffs from which to choose. Three plaintiffs originally went forward as 'lead' cases. These included the *Reay* and *Hope* cases.[3] The connection with the Gardner Study made the *Reay* and *Hope* actions appropriate cases to be tried first. The fathers in these cases had both worked for considerable periods of time at Sellafield prior to the conception of their child and had been included in the statistics of Professor Gardner's Study.

24.12 A further seven cases were prepared and commenced, with a view to them running procedurally behind the lead actions. These were called the 'Follow on' actions. When the lead actions were at trial, the Follow on cases had reached the discovery stage.

24.13 The structure of these multi-party proceedings was determined consensually and informally. The 'lead' and 'Follow on' case approach described above emerged as the obvious and sensible means of case management. The defendant was content to leave lead case selection to the plaintiffs. The only formal case management order made by the Court was that the *Hope* and *Reay* cases should be heard at the same time and by the same judge.

Pleaded case

24.14 In each of the *Reay* and *Hope* cases, the essence of the claim ultimately brought by or on behalf of the child was that radiation emanating from the Sellafield plant caused or materially contributed to the child's personal injury by one or more of four alleged mechanisms working either alone or in interaction with each other:

(a) the occupational exposure to ionising radiation of the child's father working at Sellafield damaged the father's sperm cells to the extent that his child, when born, was predisposed to developing leukaemia;
(b) the exposure of the father and mother to radiation discharged from Sellafield into the environment resulted in damage to the father's sperm cells and the mother's ova to the extent that the child, when born, was predisposed to developing leukaemia;
(c) the exposure of the child herself (both *in utero* and once born) to radiation discharged from Sellafield into the environment caused her to develop leukaemia; and/or
(d) the exposure of the father, mother, and child to radioactive contamination carried home from Sellafield by the father on his body and his clothing caused her leukaemia.

24.15 Originally, Reay and Hope had only pleaded mechanisms (c) and (d). The Gardner Study was published some time after the plaintiffs' actions had been commenced. When that study was published, and relied on by the plaintiff, amendments to the statement of claims were required to incorporate mechanisms (a) and (b) set out above.[4]

24.16 The claims were brought under the strict liability provisions of the Atomic Energy Authority Act 1954 and the Nuclear Installations Act 1965 which impose a duty on the operator of nuclear installations, such as the Sellafield site, to ensure that no ionising radiations from anything on the site or from any waste discharged from the site cause any hurt to any person or any damage to any property. Under the strict liability regime there is a thirty-year limitation period for the bringing of a claim after the date of the last

---

[3] The third case, *D'Arcy*, was, in the event, pursued as a Follow on action.
[4] Mechanism (a) was ultimately the only mechanism relied upon by the plaintiffs at trial.

occurrence giving rise to damage. (Thus, although the last possible alleged radioactive exposure which could have been relevant to the *Reay* case took place before 1962, a claim could be brought in 1990 under this rule.)

24.17 Although the periods of exposure varied between the cases, the overall time span of exposures material to the cases was 1948 to 1988. BNFL was incorporated in 1971 and only had direct liability as operator from 1971 onwards. However, it had inherited, under the statutory nuclear liability regime, the past liabilities of previous operators (principally the UK Atomic Energy Authority) for their operations between 1948 and 1971. Therefore the claims were effectively against BNFL alone.

Evidence

Pre-Gardner Study

24.18 The evidence that was required to support the pleaded case changed markedly during the course of the cases. Prior to the publication of the Gardner Study, the issues (and the discovery) were focused on the environmental dose of radiation received by the plaintiffs themselves and on whether these somatic exposures were more likely to have caused the plaintiffs' two diseases than other competing causes. From an early stage, the plaintiffs consented to access by the defendant to medical records, including pathology samples held by hospitals.

24.19 Far too little radioactivity had been discharged from Sellafield during its period of operation for mainstream science to support the view that radiation from Sellafield was the cause. The plaintiffs therefore needed to adduce evidence to show either that the environmental doses were actually high enough to have caused the diseases or that there was something special about the doses received by the plaintiffs in order to cause the diseases.

24.20 The plaintiffs' task was not straightforward. It was common ground that childhood leukaemia clusters have occurred spontaneously in a number of other locations around the country and without any apparent cause, radiation or otherwise, being capable of being attributed to them. The defendant sought further and better particulars as to the alleged causation mechanisms—ie as to why radiation in the environment had caused (a) the cluster of cases in Seascale and (b) these particular cases of the plaintiffs. The defendant also asked the plaintiffs detailed interrogatories as to their lifestyles so that a complex scientific modelling exercise could be conducted by the defendant's environmental and radiation dosimetry experts to determine with a high degree of accuracy each plaintiff's lifetime environmental dose of radioactivity.

Sequential exchange of expert reports

24.21 The defendant also considered that due to the uncertainty of the scientific case that the plaintiffs would ultimately bring, expert evidence should be exchanged sequentially rather than mutually. The defendant argued that the plaintiffs should disclose their expert evidence before the defendant disclosed its expert evidence so that the defendant's experts could deal with it, rather than have to speculate as to the possible causative mechanisms that the plaintiffs' experts may be running. Ultimately, and likely due to the relative novelty of sequential orders for exchange at that time, no order for sequential exchange was made by the Judge.

Post-Gardner Study

24.22 The Gardner Study changed the entire direction of the case. Experts were used by both sides to analyse the report for its strengths and weaknesses. As discovery became available to demonstrate that the worker doses used by Professor Gardner were not accurate (thus undermining the study's conclusions),[5] the plaintiffs undertook to carry out a complete reanalysis of his work using more accurate dose figures that had been agreed with the defendant. The reanalysis still showed that there was a statistically significant association between childhood leukaemia and the pre-conception exposure of the relevant fathers to radiation whilst working at Sellafield.

24.23 Ultimately, the plaintiffs' evidence was based entirely on the statistical association shown by the reanalysed Gardner Study. They did not put forward any evidence as to the alleged link between environmental radiation levels around the plant and leukaemia.[6] The defendant recognised the statistical association demonstrated by the reanalysed Gardner data but sought to show that the pre-conception exposure hypothesis was:

- unsupported by other relevant studies,[7] and
- genetically implausible.

24.24 The defendant's other key arguments were that:

- NHL (from which Vivien Hope suffered) was a different condition, medically and aetiologically, from acute lymphatic leukaemia, and
- the excess of childhood leukaemias observed in Seascale had only existed for a relatively few years, and by far the greatest proportion of the 'collective' pre-conception radiation doses received by the Sellafield workforce was to be found amongst company employees living in the larger urban areas to the north of the site and not in the small community of Seascale. There was no excess of leukaemias in those other areas. Further, during the course of preparing expert evidence, a raised incidence of childhood leukaemia was identified as also having occurred in Egremont, another village near to the Sellafield site, but with no statistical association between the Egremont cases and pre-conception parental radiation exposure, and
- the conclusion urged by the defendant was that the 'cluster' in Seascale was more likely to have occurred by a combination of chance and some other factor active in the local environment.[8]

---

[5] See 'Discovery' below.

[6] This, as mentioned above, was the only allegation upon which the plaintiffs' pre-Gardner Study case was originally based.

[7] The defendant relied on the orthodox science which was based on 40 years of analysis and reanalysis of follow-up studies on the survivors of the atomic weapons dropped in Japan and on the learning based on the observed effects on patients treated with radiotherapy. Neither of these study groups showed any inherited effect of childhood leukaemia from parental exposure to radiation.

[8] There were other recent studies suggesting that viral agents operating in conditions where there had been 'population mixing' (ie rapid demographic change resulting from an influx of new settlers into previously remote areas) could be such a factor. The industrial history of West Cumbria fitted this model.

24.25 In all, 60 expert witnesses prepared evidence amounting to 180 expert reports in the areas of occupational dose, environmental dose,[9] epidemiology, genetics, and medical science.

Discovery

24.26 Due to the sheer volume of potentially relevant documents held mainly at Sellafield but also at other locations, including the Public Records Office, agreement was very quickly reached between the plaintiffs and the defendant to limit the scope of the discovery exercise so as to eliminate documents which, whilst relevant, would serve no purpose to either side.

24.27 Discovery was aimed at finding documents relevant to:

- the doses of environmental radiation received by the plaintiffs and their parents, and
- occupational radiation doses received by the workers involved in the Gardner Study, which included David Hope and George Reay.

24.28 Most effort was ultimately devoted to locating documents in the second category, both sides knowing that the accuracy of these doses was vital to the accuracy of the Gardner Study conclusions. This meant that the discovery, unlike in so many other cases, became a very real exercise for the defendant as well as the plaintiffs. It was not a case of producing what might be relevant for Order 24 but a proactive exercise to produce every document which shed light on what the true doses to industrial worker fathers were.

24.29 The relevant records were not necessarily in the possession, custody, or power of BNFL. Both sides took advantage of the third party discovery procedures available in personal injury actions to search, inter alia, BNFL's predecessor's archives over the past forty years and the archives of the Medical Research Council (the body with which Professor Gardner had worked to produce his study).

24.30 The discovery exercise in itself was a monumental task, involving up to twelve paralegals performing the initial document trawl and further teams of more senior lawyers and technical experts to subject the documents to a legal and technical review. The exercise was one of the first to involve the use of an electronic discovery database, which proved to be of enormous value during the long, complicated, and voluminous review process.

Assigned judge

24.31 The parties agreed at an early stage that a judge should be assigned to the case as soon as possible. An application that the Senior Master approach the Lord Chief Justice to have a judge assigned was made. Though the Senior Master agreed that a judge should be assigned to the case at an early stage, the Lord Chief Justice, then Lord Widgery, refused. Subsequently, Lord Taylor (Lord Chief Justice after Lord Widgery) issued a specific practice direction on his own motion and French J was assigned to the case.

The trial

24.32 At the trial, both sides presented evidence in the areas of dosimetry (dealing with the likely

---

[9] Only the defendant presented evidence at trial in this area.

dose of radiation to the plaintiffs and their parents), epidemiology, and genetics. It was agreed between the parties and the Judge that rather than hear the whole of one side's evidence followed by the whole of the other side's evidence, there would be a series of tranches of evidence whereby the plaintiffs and the defendant would be heard before moving on to the next tranche. At the end of each expert's evidence, both sides prepared and submitted interim submissions on that expert's evidence and then at the end of each main tranche, further submissions on that section were presented.

After ninety days of trial the Judge, in a 220-page judgment, held that he preferred 'decisively' BNFL's case which, on the whole range of evidence before him, had the 'greater internal consistency and logic'. The Judge produced for the benefit of the press and the general public his 'Layman's Guide to the Judgment' which contained the following conclusions: 24.33

1. The Gardner Study stands virtually alone and unsupported by other studies. The Gardner theory of PPI[10] predisposing a child to leukaemia cannot explain the excesses round Dounreay or in Egremont North. It cannot explain the excesses near proposed nuclear sites where no installations were built. On the other hand, the 'population mixing' theory could explain not only Dounreay and Egremont North but also Seascale.
2. The Gardner Study is inconsistent with the huge follow up study of the children of Japanese A bomb victims which showed no excess of leukaemias in the children of irradiated fathers.
3. The Gardner Study, when closely examined, has shortcomings which reduce considerably the confidence which can properly be placed in it.
4. The evidence of the 'genetics' experts does show that the Gardner theory of PPI cannot be excluded on 'mechanistic' grounds. On the other hand, the mechanisms which the experts propose to explain the operation of PPI are, at this stage of scientific knowledge, speculative and do not carry the Plaintiffs' case forward.
5. The Plaintiffs have failed to prove that PPI is a material contributory cause of Dorothy's leukaemia or of Vivien's NHL.
6. The Plaintiffs have failed to prove that leukaemia and NHL are properly to be regarded as one disease rather than as different disease entities.

There must be judgment for the Defendants.

Follow on cases

The lead cases had failed, but the Follow on actions were still proceeding. Following the judgment in the *Reay* and *Hope* actions, the plaintiffs applied to the Court to have the Follow on actions stayed for a period of one year pending the possible emergence of fresh evidence during that period. The plaintiffs conceded that their actions had no prospect of success if based on the evidence presented in the *Reay* and *Hope* actions. Legal aid, however, was to be maintained notwithstanding this position. The defendant applied to the Court to have the actions struck out. In May 1994, French J, considering the prospect of fresh evidence emerging over the proposed twelve-month stay period to be entirely speculative, ordered that the Follow on actions be struck out. 24.34

---

[10] PPI stands for Paternal Preconception Irradiation. It was Professor Gardner's theory that the likelihood of leukaemia in the child of a father who had worked at Sellafield was linked to the amount of radiation that the father had received prior to conception of the child.

25

MANUFACTURING OPERATIONS: MIXED CLAIMS
B & ORS v X CO; D & ORS v X CO

Aidan Thomson[1]

This case from the mid-1990s concerned alleged environmental damage (nuisance, health effects, property devaluation, and loss of enjoyment of property). The litigation management aspects of the case were relatively conventional, with consolidation of two sets of multiple proceedings and standard orders.

The interest of the case lies in the wider implications of the use of a multi-party action. First, the case was instigated following public concern over a television programme which included scientific allegations that were subsequently investigated and found to be incorrect. Moves towards civil proceedings were commenced promptly by solicitors, on the basis of public funding, whilst other public authorities pursued the scientific investigations which proved decisive but took some time to complete. (A point could be made about possible duplication of public funds, although the claimants may not have expended funds on expert evidence at this stage.) Secondly, the details of individual cases seem generally not to have been investigated at the start. There were several consequences. First, some cases which were very weak were included. Secondly, subsequent failure to produce evidence led to adverse costs orders. Further, the focus of the allegations altered as the case progressed. The cases were settled on a restricted basis midway in their procedural progress, after mechanisms such as interrogatories and witness statements for *each* claimant had helped clarify the position.

A. The Background to the Proceedings

The defendant, X Co, owned and operated a plant in North London which produced and packaged garden products. The plant had been in continuous operation since the Second World War, carrying on various blending processes of chemically inactive ingredients.   **25.01**

---

[1] Partner, Freshfields.

The TV programme

25.02 In January 1993, a television programme alleged that there was a higher than normal incidence of cancer both amongst workers at the X Co plant and amongst residents living in the vicinity of the plant, in particular in two streets close to the plant. It was alleged that these cancers were due to the exposure of both workers and residents to substances which had been handled at X Co's plant over the years. In addition, the programme drew attention to two specific incidents at the plant, one in May 1989 and the other in May 1992, during which there had been atmospheric releases from the plant into the local environment. The programme caused considerable public concern.

The two incidents

25.03 The first of the two incidents referred to above (the 1989 incident) was a fire in the fertiliser section of the plant. The material involved in the fire was a dried ground coffee bean residue. The fire itself was quickly brought under control and smoke that blew off the site quickly dispersed. No toxic fumes were released. The fire caused limited damage to the X Co site and attracted only limited public interest at the time. X Co reimbursed one local resident, without admission of liability, shortly after the incident in respect of the loss of pet birds kept in an open cage at the bottom of his garden.

25.04 The second of the two incidents (the 1992 incident) involved the accidental atmospheric release of a solvent vapour called dimeothoate, and the subsequent release into the atmosphere of a breakdown product of dimeothoate called methyl mercaptan. Methyl mercaptan has a strong and unpleasant odour not unlike rotting cabbage. On this occasion the odour was perceptible throughout the town in North London where the plant was situated but, in the concentrations arising from the incident, there was no toxic or harmful effect. The release was swiftly brought under control and the contaminated area of the plant was cleaned up. As a result of this second incident, local residents were sent a letter from X Co apologising for the incident and giving information on the substance released. In addition to this, an open meeting was held at which nearly 200 local residents were given an explanation of the incident and the opportunity to ask questions. Payments were made by X Co to the few local residents who made claims for out-of-pocket expenses, mainly comprising the costs of overnight accommodation elsewhere and bills for fabric cleaning.

25.05 The Health and Safety Executive (HSE) investigated the 1992 incident and concluded that, whilst there was considerable public concern, it had not involved a blatant or reckless disregard for health and safety. The HSE decided not to take legal proceedings against X Co.

The grant of legal aid

25.06 In the wake of the television programme there was a considerable amount of legal activity. A firm of solicitors announced in a press release at the beginning of February 1993 that it was acting for a number of clients who had been granted legal aid:

- to investigate occupational and residential cancer claims, and
- to pursue private nuisance claims against X Co.

25.07 There was no suggestion that the two categories of claim were linked, although the anecdotal reports of increased cancer incidence in the TV programme and the occurrence of the two recent accidental releases were both relied on generally in the making of a subsequent legal aid application and in the attempted formation of a group of plaintiffs, albeit with widely differing claims.

The scientific studies

25.08 The publicity and concern generated by the television programme gave rise to two studies, one carried out by the HSE Epidemiology and Medical Statistics Unit, which investigated the incidence of cancer within the X Co workforce, and the other carried out by the Small Area Health Statistics Unit (SAHSU) acting under the auspices of the Department of Health, which investigated the incidence of cancer in the local population.

25.09 The HSE Study was published in March 1995. The Study concluded that 'although the results of this investigation do show that in this workforce more men than expected had died from cancer, there is no convincing evidence that working at X Co was a cause for this'. In addition, the HSE concluded that 'the findings do not indicate a need for HSE to call for any new action in the workplace'.

25.10 SAHSU was asked by the Department of Health to investigate whether the reported cancer cluster in the immediate vicinity of the X Co plant existed and whether it could be associated with the plant's operations. The SAHSU Study was published in early 1997 and 'provided limited and inconsistent evidence for a localised excess of cancer in the vicinity of the X Co plant'. It further stated that 'at present, a further investigation does not appear to be warranted other than continued surveillance of mortality and cancer incidence in the locality'.

25.11 In addition to the SAHSU Study and the HSE Study mentioned above, in July 1995 the local authority, Z District Council (ZDC), carried out an evaluation of the processes and procedures employed at X Co's plant for odour abatement. ZDC confirmed to X Co that:

(a) In general terms best practicable means were used to control odours from the plant;
(b) There was no evidence to suggest that technologies in use had, are, or were likely to give rise to statutory nuisance; and
(c) ZDC has not been able to attribute any odour nuisance to X Co.

B. Procedural History

25.12 As stated above, legal aid was granted, prior to the publication of the HSE, SAHSU, and ZDC reports, to investigate the possibility of occupational and residential cancer claims and to bring nuisance proceedings.

Procedural history of the cancer claims

25.13 In September 1993, prior to the publication of the HSE Study, the plaintiffs requested pre-action discovery of various X Co documents relating to four individuals who had at one time or another been members of the X Co workforce and who had allegedly contracted various forms of cancer as a result of X Co's activities. Occupational, personnel, and medical records were sought, and disclosed, to the extent that they existed. Further information relating to the plant's operational history and practices sought by the prospective plaintiffs was refused.

25.14 Ultimately, no occupational or residential claims were brought against X Co in respect of cancer. The early intervention of the government bodies (HSE and SAHSU) in investigating, and concluding that there was no substance to, the anecdotal claims of health effects is an illustration of how important the role of such independent agencies can be in influencing the course of multi-party actions. It also demonstrates the benefits to a potential defendant in many cases of not only co-operating with such investigative bodies, but actively encouraging their involvement.

Procedural history of the nuisance proceedings

25.15 In late 1995, two sets of identically pleaded nuisance proceedings were eventually launched against X Co—*B and others v X Co* and *D and others v X Co*. There were thirty-nine plaintiffs in all, each having legal aid. In the main, the plaintiffs in the *D* action were the children of the plaintiffs in the *B* action. The two actions were consolidated in a joint Order for Directions. It is likely that the thirty-nine plaintiffs constituted *all* of the individuals represented by the plaintiffs' solicitors who had legal aid to pursue nuisance actions. In other words, the plaintiffs' solicitors had not held any claims back.

25.16 The procedural history of the two actions was as follows:

- Writ issued (*B* case): 25 May 1995
- Writ served (*B* case): 15 September 1995
- Defence served (*B* case): 12 October 1995
- Defendant's Request for Further and Better Particulars (*B* case) served: 3 November 1995
- Plaintiffs' Replies to Requests for Further and Better Particulars (*B* case) served: 30 November 1995
- Plaintiffs' Requests for Further and Better Particulars of the Defence (*B* case) served: 30 November 1995
- Writ and Statement of Claim (*D* case) served: 8 December 1995
- Defence (*D* case) served: 12 January 1996
- Orders for Directions made: 22 March 1996
- Discovery lists exchanged: May 1996
- Interrogatories served: 5 June 1996
- Order for the answering of Interrogatories: 26 July 1996
- Unless Order re answering of Interrogatories: 23 August 1996
- Order for the exchange of Witness Statements made: 20 August 1996
- Witness Statements exchanged: 30 August 1996
- Settlement approved by Court: 18 March 1997

C. Key Aspects of the *B* and *D* Proceedings

Legal aid

In March 1993, shortly after the announcement that legal aid both for the cancer claims and the nuisance claims had been granted but well before the commencement of any legal proceedings or the publication of the SAHSU, HSE, and ZDC studies, the defendant made representations to the Legal Aid Board that funding should be withdrawn for all claims relating to the plant. The representations were based on the three kinds of potential claim which could be identified from the plaintiffs' solicitor's press reports, as follows: **25.17**

- Cancer claims for or on behalf of X Co workers and/or local residents;
- Personal injury/damage to property/nuisance claims in respect of the 1989 and 1992 incidents at the plant;
- Nuisance claims as a result of chronic alleged long-term exposure to fumes/dust/smells emanating from the plant.

The weaknesses identified in respect of each of these claims, in terms of legal merit and their failure to satisfy the cost-benefit analysis which the Legal Aid Board had to apply, were as follows: **25.18**

- The substances released in the two incidents were non-toxic, caused no illness (although they may have caused some temporary minor irritation), and any compensation which could conceivably be ordered by a court to be paid out to any individual for nuisance based on either or both incidents would be very small.
- There was no evidence of any chronic nuisance emanating from X Co's plant, nor any sufficiently particularised allegation of such nuisance from any of the prospective plaintiffs.
- The defendant *had* compensated residents who had made legitimate claims for out-of-pocket expenses at the time of the incidents.
- The HSE/SAHSU studies were being undertaken to establish whether or not there was any higher than normal incidence of cancer among the residential and occupational groups in question. Until such time as the findings of these studies were published it would be inappropriate and premature to grant legal aid in respect of any claim, investigative or otherwise, based on these matters.

The Legal Aid Board took no action in relation to these submissions.

By early 1996, the HSE Study had been published (concluding that there was no convincing evidence that working at X Co was a cause of cancer), the ZDC audit report had been completed (with findings that there was no odour or other statutory nuisance resulting from plant operations), and none of the potential plaintiffs with cancer claims had issued proceedings. There were, however, the *B* case and *D* case nuisance actions which had been commenced that previous summer. In these circumstances, X Co made a second set of representations to the Legal Aid Board to the effect that: **25.19**

- the funding for the nuisance claims should be removed, and
- (if it had not already been withdrawn) the funding for the occupational and residential cancer claims should be withdrawn.

25.20 The Board informed X Co that it was not prepared to change its view that legal aid was appropriately granted, even in the light of the important, and apparently determinative, new evidence from official bodies.[2]

The pleaded allegations of nuisance

25.21 In both actions, the plaintiffs claimed damages (including for personal inconvenience, loss of enjoyment, damage to property, and diminution in house values) alleged to have been suffered as a result of nuisance occasioned by the fumes, vapours, dust, and smells produced at X Co's plant. An injunction was also claimed to prevent the alleged nuisance from continuing.

25.22 The nuisance was alleged to have arisen as a result of:

- three specific alleged incidents, being: the 1989 incident; the 1992 incident; and a further incident in January 1994 (the 1994 incident) in which odours were said to have been released again from the plant;
- constant and continuing (ie chronic) emissions of odour and noise from the plant over the period from May 1989 to February 1994.

25.23 The defendant considered that the chronic nuisance allegations were unfounded and it denied them. In relation to the 1989 incident and the 1992 incident, the defendant's position was that both had occurred but did not amount to actionable nuisances and that, in any event, the few local residents who claimed to have suffered loss or inconvenience at the time had already been compensated on an *ex gratia* basis.

Evidence

25.24 The key aspect of the case was the extent to which the individual plaintiffs could demonstrate their loss as a result of the alleged nuisance emanating from the three specific incidents and the alleged chronic nuisance.

Difficulties in proving chronic nuisance

25.25 By the time the *B* and *D* actions had been commenced, ZDC had already published the results of its odour abatement study at X Co's facility (which were firmly in X Co's favour). The defendant considered the specificity of the nuisance pleading, especially in relation to chronic nuisance, to be inadequate and was, therefore, keen to take every opportunity to pin down precisely what suffering and loss had been suffered by the plaintiffs and how it was alleged to have occurred. For example: the defendant twice requested further and better particulars of the Statement of Claim, focusing especially on the alleged incident in 1994 and on the allegation of chronic nuisance.[3]

---

[2] Legal aid was eventually withdrawn for the occupational and residential cancer claims but seemingly not in direct response to any representations made to the Legal Aid Board by the defendant.

[3] The defendant also applied to the Court for a limit on its obligation to give automatic discovery. It was argued that it was unnecessary and oppressive for discovery to be given in relation to issues of chronic nuisance and the 1994 incident, without more specific particulars. The issue was resolved by agreement.

25.26 The Orders for Directions in the *B* and *D* actions (ultimately made with the consent of both parties) *only* gave directions in relation to the allegations of nuisance arising out of the three pleaded specific incidents. No directions were made in relation to the chronic nuisance issue. The chronic nuisance allegations were, by consent, put 'on hold' in the proceedings.[4]

Difficulties in proving nuisance as a result of the three specific incidents

25.27 After the Order for Directions in March 1996, the plaintiffs' task was to demonstrate that they had suffered loss of enjoyment of their properties as a result of the three specific incidents. The evidence they supplied varied considerably from individual to individual.

25.28 Many of the plaintiffs did not manage to serve factual witness statements. The factual statements that were served showed that the only incident that was the subject of any complaint was the 1992 incident. However, even in relation to the 1992 incident, the plaintiffs' evidence was conflicting as to how intense and how long the incident lasted, with some plaintiffs claiming that the odour had persisted for up to 8 weeks and others claiming that it lasted only for 2–3 days. Very few plaintiffs remembered anything about an incident in 1994. Most of the plaintiffs recalled the 1989 incident but did not consider it to have caused anything other than a brief period of anxiety. No witness statements were served on behalf of the plaintiffs from any medical attendants relating to the alleged physical effects of any of the incidents.

25.29 The defendant took steps to investigate the extent to which each of the plaintiffs had suffered as a result of the three specific incidents by serving interrogatories on each defendant. The answers that were provided confirmed that some of the plaintiffs were not even present in the locality during all of the alleged incidents (though all were present for the main 1992 incident). They also confirmed that only a small handful sought medical advice following the incidents or complained to X Co or ZDC.

Costs orders against the plaintiffs

25.30 The plaintiffs were slow to answer the interrogatories served by the defendant. The defendant applied to the Court for and obtained an order that the interrogatories be answered, with the costs of the application to be paid by the plaintiffs in any event. As a result of still further delays, the defendant obtained an order that unless each plaintiff answered the interrogatories by a certain date, their claim would be dismissed. Again, the costs of the application were to be paid by the plaintiffs in any event. Three plaintiffs failed to meet the deadline and their claims were dismissed with costs to be paid by the plaintiffs to the defendant. The plaintiffs also failed to serve their witness statements on time, prompting the defendant to obtain a further order that no evidence could be called at trial unless contained in a witness statement exchanged on or before a certain date. Once again, the costs of the application were to be paid by the plaintiffs in any event.

---

[4] The plaintiffs did not formally withdraw the chronic nuisance allegations, but conceded that they could not be tried until fuller particulars and facts were pleaded.

25.31 The defendant's costs in each application were relatively small. Crucially, however, so were the amounts that the plaintiffs could expect to get if they won at trial.[5] The costs awards meant that, even if the plaintiffs were to have pursued the matter through to trial and won with costs in their favour, the defendant would have been able to offset the interlocutory costs awards against the final costs order. The Legal Aid Board would therefore have been faced with a shortfall which it would have sought to make good from the plaintiffs' damages. Assuming that the level of damages per plaintiff was low, the plaintiffs put themselves at risk of recovering very little and possibly nothing at the end of the day, even if they won.

Settlement initiatives

25.32 Attempts were made to settle the *B* and *D* actions from a very early stage. Both parties wanted to settle the case before trial. However, the plaintiffs and the defendant had very different views at an early stage as to the prospects of success of the action.

25.33 The defendant was keen to restrict any settlement sum to the absolute minimum, not just because it did not believe that the plaintiffs' claim could be demonstrated or that it merited any sums but also because of the risk of 'copy cat' actions in the event that substantial sums were awarded to the plaintiffs. Claims for diminution in the value of the plaintiffs' houses as a result of the alleged chronic nuisance were pleaded. The defendant was conscious of the fact that multiple claims of this sort could have been beyond their financial resources to meet and would have posed serious questions as to the company's future. Moreover, there was no obvious geographical limit to the area said to have been affected by the alleged incident, and, accordingly, the pool of prospective plaintiffs was very difficult to quantify. The X Co plant was in a highly developed residential area with several thousand homes within a half-mile radius. Even a payment of £1,000 per house (on whatever basis it was made) would have amounted to a seven-figure sum.

25.34 For their part, the plaintiffs initially sought substantial sums on the basis that they could prove all of the allegations in the Statement of Claim.[6] They were looking for thousands of pounds per plaintiff. There was no common ground. Early attempts at settlement were unsuccessful.

25.35 The plaintiffs' stance changed when they:

- recognised that the chronic nuisance claim could not be sustained without far more detailed pleading and evidence,
- could not obtain any substantial evidence as to the 1989 and 1994 incidents,

and, most importantly,

- incurred costs awards against them 'in any event'.

25.36 The cases were settled shortly thereafter under a global arrangement, which provided for each plaintiff, regardless of the case he or she pleaded, receiving a few hundred pounds,

---

[5] Even on the basis of the particulars of suffering and loss of enjoyment set out in their witness statements and answers to interrogatories.

[6] ie that they could prove that there had been chronic nuisance and nuisance arising out of the specific incidents and that their properties had been devalued as a result.

with lower sums for plaintiffs who were minors.[7] Due to the small size of the amounts involved and the lack of any compelling evidence to support any part of the plaintiffs' claim, no attempt was made to tailor settlement amounts to the alleged loss of each individual plaintiff.

25.37 In hindsight, it is clear that the X Co litigation (actual and potential) was 'kick started' by the television broadcast in 1993. On the back of the public concern generated by this, legal aid was granted to investigate the very serious allegations made. Over the course of the next four years, independent scientific studies demonstrated the allegations to be false. The public concern and potential claims died away as each study was published and the eventual settlement of the cases received very little attention locally. In the end, the only things that the parties were arguing over was the scale of compensation for one or two isolated incidents which, considering the scale of the original allegations, demonstrated that the whole episode was a 'storm in a teacup' and that the legal activity was premature. This case emphasises the need right from the start for the careful management of the issue in the media until proper scientific opinion has been formed—and, when the issue is in the public eye, the sooner it can be formed, the better.

25.38 Another issue worth highlighting is the fact that weaker cases were not 'weeded out' by the plaintiffs' solicitors. It seemed to be the case that *all* of the plaintiffs' solicitors' clients were joined in the *B* and *D* actions without an investigation of each plaintiff's claim. Interrogatories and witness statements revealed differing levels of alleged suffering. Some had not suffered at all as a result of the alleged incidents. Thus, their evidence lacked the necessary amount of coherence and this weakened the plaintiffs' claim. The plaintiffs would have been better advised to select their claims carefully before launching proceedings. As it was, the group of plaintiffs was large and clearly difficult to manage. In the end, it seemed that some plaintiffs had lost their interest in the proceedings and this enabled X Co to obtain the costs orders in its favour which were instrumental in bringing an end to the cases.

---

[7] This was due to the fact that the *Canary Wharf* case was then on appeal. One issue in the appeal was whether or not a plaintiff with no interest in property could bring an action in nuisance in respect of enjoyment of that property. The lower settlement figure in respect of the minor plaintiffs reflected the uncertainty of their claim.

26

DOCKLANDS NUISANCE CLASS ACTIONS

John Evans[1]

This chapter describes two groups of claims against different defendants arising out of similar circumstances based on differing allegations relating to environmental nuisance in the mid-1990s. The two groups were managed in similar fashion although independently. There were orders in both for cut-off dates for claimants to join the group, and cost-sharing arrangements as between claimants. Early selection of legal issues and their resolution as preliminary issues proved dispositive of at least one group of claims and also cost-effective in both groups by avoiding expensive discovery and expert reports. Issues were raised over the novelty of the causes of action, whether these claims were 'lawyer driven', and whether they were financially viable—the balance between costs (high) and possible damages (low). A lack of financial viability proved decisive in the second group and was the subject of vigorous and successive representations by the defendants to the Legal Aid Board.

A. Background

On 23 October 1991, London Docklands Development Corporation (LDDC) was convicted of eight offences contrary to sections 61(5) and 74 of the Control of Pollution Act 1974 in that they permitted work to be carried out at the Ming Street, Ropemaker Field, J, Dundee Wharf, and Emmet Street sites of the Limehouse Link construction project in contravention of a condition attached to a section 61 Consent issued by the London Borough of Tower Hamlets (LBTH) on 20 March 1990. LDDC succeeded in having one charge dismissed because the prosecution called no evidence and a second dismissed on the basis that there was no case to answer. 26.01

The prosecution was commenced long before the so-called 'class actions'[2] were threatened. The threat of civil proceedings did, however, influence LDDC's conduct of its defence. First, having regard to an assessment that LDDC had a genuine prospect of success, 26.02

---

[1] Partner, Ashurst Morris Crisp.
[2] The plaintiffs' lawyers described them as 'class actions' rather than 'group actions' in pre-action publicity and the label stuck.

a 'not guilty' verdict, if secured, was thought likely to discourage prospective plaintiffs and their advisers; secondly, LDDC did not wish in any way to compromise their insurance by pleading guilty in circumstances where any convictions secured by LBTH might have prejudicial value in a subsequent civil action.

26.03 Representatives from Leigh Day & Co, the solicitors representing the putative class action plaintiffs, were present throughout the Limehouse Link Control of Pollution Act trial from 21–23 October 1991. Letters before action had by then been written by Leigh Day & Co (on 30 August 1991) to both LDDC and Olympia & York Canary Wharf Limited (O&Y). As against LDDC, damages were claimed in relation to 'loss of quality of life and quiet enjoyment of their homes, and in some cases damage to health', with the nuisances complained of having allegedly 'caused illnesses such as sleeplessness, distress and respiratory problems'. Identical claims were notified to O&Y in respect of the building of Canary Wharf and these were supplemented by the novel claim that interference with television reception constituted an actionable nuisance.

26.04 Legal aid was applied for but was initially refused on the basis that the claims were adjudged not to have a reasonable prospect of success. That decision was appealed against and LDDC's conviction (albeit in relation to 'noise nuisance' rather than 'dust nuisance') may have played a significant part in persuading the Legal Aid Board to revisit its original decision. Leigh Day & Co's press release of 15 November 1991 asserted, no doubt *in terrorem*, that 'there are some 10,000 people affected by the development, and with their claims being valued at an average of £10,000, success in the cases would mean a bill for the LDDC and Olympia & York of £100 million'.

B. Relevant Considerations

26.05 Generally, as regards nuisance, the allegation that lives had been disrupted would have to be balanced against factors such as the cost and size of the projects (and the statutory authority for the regeneration of London's Docklands), associated benefits, the need for the projects to be completed, the fact that most of the materials used had been moved by river rather than by road, and the considerable effort and expense on the part of LDDC to improve the welfare of residents by relocating deserving cases, installing secondary glazing, and participating, with O&Y, in community projects initiated by O&Y. Allied to this, it was anticipated that dust levels in the Limehouse Link and Canary Wharf areas would be no worse than in other parts of London.

26.06 As regards interference with television reception, it was acknowledged that even though existing case law did not support the plaintiffs, it was not beyond the bounds of possibility that a court in 1992 would hold that there existed a right to television reception.

26.07 Finally, as to the environmental personal injury claims, any defence would have to have regard to issues of general and specific causation. With respect to general causation, the plaintiffs would need to prove a statistical connection between exposure to dust (and particular types of dust) and the incidence of disease. To counter such arguments, the defendants would need evidence to support a phenomenon of declining air quality standards in

London and elsewhere and a consequent increase in morbidity and mortality. An important confounding variable was the presence and effect of exhaust fumes in inner-city areas, an issue highlighted, for example, following publication of the report by the City of Edinburgh District Council in relation to an investigation into nitrogen dioxide levels in the City of Edinburgh for the period October 1990–September 1991. On the subject of specific causation, it would be necessary to explore the medical background and work history of each individual plaintiff in order to determine whether or not there existed other factors, for example exposure to asbestos, which were in some way associated with the disease or condition complained of.

C. Subsequent Developments Leading to the Submission of Representations

26.08 The Legal Aid Certificate originally granted permitted pre-action preparation and investigation of 'generic' issues only without defining that term. In the circumstances of the threatened class actions, this was interpreted by the prospective defendants as encompassing the obtaining of preliminary scientific advice leading to the procurement of counsel's opinion. The issue of further Legal Aid Certificates permitting the issue of proceedings was thought to be dependent upon the Legal Aid Authority being satisfied that the causes of action arising were ones which they should support.

26.09 Even before the legal aid position crystallised, a further letter before action dated 4 March 1992 was written by Leigh Day & Co to London Regional Transport claiming damages on behalf of residents in relation to the loss of quality of life and quiet enjoyment of their homes and, in many cases, damage to health that had allegedly resulted from the building, alteration, maintenance, and operation of the Docklands Light Railway (DLR), with the various alleged nuisances having led to many prospective plaintiffs 'suffering from stress related illnesses such as sleeplessness, distress and respiratory problems'.

26.10 On 4 November 1992 the LDDC, O&Y, and DLR submitted representations to the Legal Aid Board for the purpose of drawing the Board's attention to matters which were relevant to the issue of whether or not to grant further legal aid funding for claims which were then in contemplation for nuisance and/or what was described as loss of quality of life and quiet enjoyment of the home and community and/or personal injury and/or loss of television reception, all allegedly caused by construction works in London's Docklands. The memorandum submitted to the Board could not be regarded as exhaustive. No particulars were available in relation to any one or more specific claims and the memorandum's purpose was to provide the Board with a framework for the assessment of any application for further funding. It was written against the background of press publicity afforded to certain categories of claims and by reference to letters before action written in the broadest of terms (see above).

26.11 The executive summary at the beginning of the memorandum submitted to the Board was couched in the following terms:

1. The cost of conducting the litigation will be such that no Plaintiff will be able to show his

action as viable, particularly bearing in mind the effect of the statutory charge on any damages awarded.
2. Any analysis of what constitutes reasonable or unreasonable activity or user in London's Docklands must have regard to the fact of regeneration in fulfilment of the statutory objectives stipulated in S 136 of the Local Government, Planning and Land Act, 1980 and the immunity from suit thereby afforded the LDDC and other prospective Defendants.
3. The law of nuisance is a 'law of relativity'. A measure of inconvenience and disruption is inevitably associated with the implementation of works for the general public good and is not of itself an actionable nuisance.
4. In relation to the threat of claims for personal injury, an assertion of a cause and effect relationship between exposure to dust emanating from construction works in London's Docklands and a particular disease or condition can only be regarded with extreme scepticism in the absence of scientific and medical evidence capable of identifying the initiators and/or promoters of any such disease or condition, particularly in circumstances where so-called confounding variables abound and where diseases with long lead times between exposure and the onset of disease are likely to involve exposures occurring before the redevelopment of London's Docklands.
5. Interference with TV reception is not an actionable wrong.
6. Legal aid should not be granted for costly research of any so-called 'generic' issues or for any wide-ranging socio-economic enquiry into the reasons for, the methodology of and the results obtained through the regeneration of London's Docklands.
7. Olympia & York Canary Wharf Limited is in administration [as was by then the case] and the value of secured claims exceeds the value of its assets.

26.12 It was submitted that the threatened litigation had arisen out of advertising and public meetings and had been 'lawyer driven' rather than 'resident driven'. Public meetings had been held and had attracted potential claimants and pronouncements (as above) had been made with a view to raising expectations to an unrealistic level. Against this background, the representations urged that the Board should very carefully scrutinise each individual case and should only grant legal aid if the means, merits, and overall reasonableness tests were satisfied.

26.13 The primary objective was to persuade the Board not to fund personal injury type claims which, more than any other, would raise the profile of the litigation and persuade others (possibly thousands) to join the putative classes because such claims were potentially of significantly higher value than what may be described as the more straightforward nuisance claims. In this the representations were successful.

D. The Judicial Review Proceedings

26.14 In April 1993, the LDDC and DLR (by then a subsidiary of LDDC) applied for leave to institute judicial review proceedings challenging the Legal Aid Board's decision to amend the Legal Aid Certificates originally granted to the Docklands residents so as to then permit them to issue proceedings for damages for nuisance against the LDDC and DLR. O&Y were not party to the judicial review proceedings as they were by then in administration.

26.15 The application for leave referred to the representations submitted to the Legal Aid Board on 4 November 1992. Specifically, it was emphasised that the purpose of the representations was to draw to the attention of the Board a number of matters which were relevant to the decision as to whether or not to grant further legal aid funding for potential claims against the three parties submitting the representations. The representations had emphasised that applications for legal aid were required to be considered separately in each individual case and, for the purpose of the judicial review proceedings, the Court's attention was drawn to paragraph 16 of the *1992 Legal Aid Handbook*, and specifically to paragraph 16–02: 'In most respects legal aid as regards a multi-party action operates in the same way as in any other case. *Any person applying for civil legal aid in a multi-party action must still satisfy the usual means and merits tests* [emphasis added].'

26.16 The Area Committee of the Legal Aid Board had decided, on or about 25 January 1993, that Certificates should be granted to the would-be plaintiffs so as to permit the issue of proceedings against LDDC, DLR, and O&Y. Contemporaneous *inter partes* correspondence suggested, however, that in taking the decision to extend the ambit of the Legal Aid Certificate the Board had not considered each of the cases individually. This was highlighted after legal aid was granted for the issue of proceedings when it became apparent that the plaintiffs' solicitors had, prior to the grant, been unable to take instructions from their clients on an individual basis, with the result that legal proceedings could not in fact be issued for some time.

26.17 As an aside, DLR had been operated by London Regional Transport prior to its becoming a subsidiary of LDDC. However, there existed no clear statutory authority defence for activities undertaken by the DLR, even including those undertaken pursuant to section 86 of the Railway Clauses Consolidation Act 1845, as incorporated into the DLR legislation. This may not seem immediately relevant to the judicial review proceedings but, contemporaneously, a Bill was to be drafted which would include a clause providing the DLR with clear statutory authority defences in respect of its activities. Once the necessary legislation was in place, no additional nuisance claims could be pursued as against the DLR; moreover, for as long as the judicial review proceedings were ongoing, the focus of the plaintiffs' lawyers, and of the Legal Aid Board, would be upon resisting those judicial review proceedings, more specifically the application in due course made for leave to serve interrogatories upon Mr Richard Green, Legal Director of the Legal Aid Board, and for discovery. That of necessity meant that very little effort (if any) was expended in seeking to persuade additional plaintiffs to become members of the putative 'DLR class' and, so far as the defendants are aware, the issue of a substantive DLR class action was postponed, never to be revived. In other words, the limitation statute was tolling in relation to historic claims and no new claims could be pursued once section 122 of the Railways Act 1993 came into force on 1 April 1994, thus impacting upon any cost-benefit analysis or viability test from both ends of the chronology. The putative 'DLR class' was to be an ever-diminishing class and the fact that the judicial review proceedings were, in due course, abandoned was of no real consequence in circumstances where the overall strategic objective was achieved.

26.18 By way of amplification, the application for leave to serve interrogatories and for discovery arose out of an inability to comprehend how the Board, upon reviewing a large body of evidential material and correspondence, counsel's opinions, reports from expert witnesses, and representations from the prospective defendants, had concluded that such material, confined as it was to six individual claims, could be extrapolated so as to lead the

Board to conclude that up to 800 individuals had reasonable grounds to bring proceedings. No application was made to cross-examine Mr Green because, by reference to his own Affidavit, he had not been at the meeting on 25 January 1993 and was not himself a party to the decision challenged in the judicial review proceedings.

26.19 The application for leave to serve interrogatories and for discovery was carefully framed so as not to seek disclosure of material that would tend to show the strengths and weaknesses of the prospective plaintiffs' arguments against LDDC, DLR, and O&Y so as to offend the confidentiality provision of section 38 of the Legal Aid Act 1988. They were simply designed to establish what kind of information was before the Board on 25 January 1993 and to ascertain whether there was any legitimate basis on which the Board could conclude, by examining detailed material about six cases, that up to 800 individuals should be given legal aid to commence proceedings.

26.20 The application failed, both at first instance and in the Court of Appeal. The Courts declined to grasp an opportunity to scrutinise more closely the decision-making processes of the Legal Aid Board and to highlight the accountability of the Board in relation to the expenditure of public funds.

E. Proceedings as Issued against LDDC and Canary Wharf Limited (CW), the Successor to O&Y

26.21 Proceedings were issued on 16 December 1993. The generally endorsed writs made plain that the plaintiffs claimed as occupiers of and/or persons with a legal estate in property (thus challenging the traditional position that only plaintiffs with a proprietary interest in land had standing to sue in private nuisance). As against CW, interference with television reception was alleged either to be a nuisance or the result of the defendant's negligence. As against the LDDC, the plaintiffs gave notice of their intention to pursue nuisance and *Rylands v Fletcher* type claims and also asserted a claim in negligence arising out of the fact that the LDDC caused or permitted large quantities of dust to leave their land and enter the plaintiffs' dwellings. There were over 500 named plaintiffs in the LDDC litigation and very nearly 700 in the CW litigation (with considerable overlap between the two).

26.22 As illustrated in Table 26.1, the actions proceeded through service of Master Statements of Claim and Master Defences. It was notable, in the case of the LDDC action, first that no adverse health effects were pleaded (presumably the representations submitted to the Legal Aid Board had been successful in persuading the Board not to fund speculative claims of that nature); secondly, that what were perceived to be the more difficult, *Rylands v Fletcher* type, claims were abandoned (presumably because of a reluctance on the part of the Board to fund the same). Although never abandoned (there were references, from time to time, to the possibility that adverse health claims might be resurrected), such claims did not feature in the litigation proper on any meaningful basis.

26.23 The procedural timetable in the two actions differed slightly for reasons which are no longer relevant. There were separate hearings in which the management of each action was debated at some length, the first of which, in each action, established that there

Table 26.1: The chronology of both actions summarised

Date	LDDC	CW
16.12.1993	Writ of Summons	Writ of Summons
11.02.1994		Order of His Honour Judge James Fox Andrews QC (for sub-trial)
24.02.1994		Master Statement of Claim
25.03.1994		Master Defence
17.05.1994	Master Statement of Claim	
26.05.1994	Order of His Honour Judge James Fox Andrews QC (for sub-trial)	
27.06.1994		Order of His Honour Judge James Fox Andrews QC (identifying the preliminary issues to be tried)
04.07.1994	Master Defence	
18.07.1994		Amended Master Statement of Claim
05.09.1994		Judgment and Order of His Honour Judge Richard Havery QC
11.10.1994		Notice of Appeal on behalf of plaintiffs
14.10.1994	Order of His Honour Judge Richard Havery QC identifying the Preliminary Issues to be tried	Notice of Appeal on behalf of defendants
01.11.1994	Judgment and Order of His Honour Judge Richard Havery QC	
23.11.1994	Notice of Appeal on behalf of the plaintiffs	
07.12.1994	Notice of Appeal on behalf of the defendant	
12.10.1995	Judgment and Order of Court of Appeal as reported in Part 12 of The Weekly Law Reports, 29 March 1996	Judgment and Order of Court of Appeal as reported in Part 12 of The Weekly Law Reports, 29 March 1996
02.02.1996	Petition of Appeal	
23.04.1996		Petition of Appeal / Petition of Cross Appeal
24.04.1997	Judgment of the House of Lords in relation to all appeals[a]	

[a] 1997 AC 655 and 1996 2 WLR 684.

should be a defined group, with joining and leaving rules including the imposition of a cut-off date, as well as a form of cost-sharing order, and the second of which, again in both cases, identified questions of law suitable for determination at an early stage in the litigation. Such issues were identified by the parties, and agreed upon with the Court's blessing, as capable of cutting short the litigation because of their potentially dispositive nature. These hearings were essentially 'case management conferences', the first identifying the potential for a cost-effective result and the second defining the issues. At the risk of stating the obvious, the potential cost savings could be measured in millions, given that no discovery would have to be given and no expert reports commissioned in relation to two of the UK's largest ever development and infrastructure projects pending final determination of the preliminary questions of law.

26.24 The preliminary questions of law, together with the decisions given at first instance, in the Court of Appeal, and in the House of Lords are set out in Table 26.2.

F. Further Representations

26.25 At appropriate intervals throughout the litigation both the LDDC and CW submitted further representations to the Legal Aid Board, both by way of formal memoranda and through correspondence. Examples are referred to below and the overriding purpose on each occasion was to convey to the Board, and to the plaintiffs' representatives, that the defendants would rely upon and advance any and all legitimate arguments available to them, whether in the context of funding or in the substantive litigation.

26.26 On 22 June 1994, CW submitted a memorandum in which it was forcefully argued that the existing Legal Aid Certificates should be discharged. It was submitted, *inter alia*, that the cut-off date having passed, the Board need no longer be concerned with a hypothetical question concerning whether a solicitor could properly advise a privately funded plaintiff to proceed; on the contrary, it was by then known that each of the 676 plaintiffs with extant claims was legally aided, a fact which was significant and entirely consistent with the argument that no solicitor could properly advise a would-be plaintiff privately to pursue the proceedings against CW even though he (the plaintiff) had means which were adequate to meet the likely costs of the case or would make payment of the likely costs possible although something of a sacrifice. The absence of a single privately paying plaintiff amongst the plaintiffs in the CW action provided the strongest prima facie evidence that the claim failed the 'privately paying client' test. By way of reinforcement, two plaintiffs who had had their eligibility for legal aid reassessed had immediately chosen to discontinue rather than press ahead with claims in circumstances where they would have been responsible for a proportion of their own costs if successful and for the whole of their costs as well as a proportion of the defendant's costs if unsuccessful.

26.27 By way of a further memorandum submitted on 19 December 1995 it was submitted that, in light of the Court of Appeal's unanimous decision that the television interference pleaded by the plaintiffs was not capable of constituting an actionable nuisance and the Court's further observation that the performance by the BBC of its statutory duty to deal with problems caused by interference would usually provide any plaintiff with the relief

Table 26.2: Summary of issues of law

	The Questions of Law	The Answers Given by His Honour Judge Havery QC (1993)	The Answers Given by the Court of Appeal (1995)	The Answers Given by the House of Lords (1996–1997)
	In relation to the claim of *private* nuisance:			
1.	*Damage* Is interference with television reception capable of constituting an actionable private nuisance?	Yes	No	No
2.	*Proprietary Interest* Whether it is necessary to have an interest in property to claim in private nuisance and, if so, what interest in property will satisfy this requirement	Yes; a plaintiff must have a right to exclusive possession of the property	No; a plaintiff is qualified to bring an action in private nuisance through occupation of property as a home	Yes; an action in private nuisance will only lie at the suit of a person who has a right to the land affected. Ordinarily, such a person can only sue if he has the right to exclusive possession of the land such as a freeholder or tenant in possession or even a licensee with exclusive possession
3.	*Statutory Authority Defence* On the assumption that the interference complained of was a direct consequence of the statutory scheme and consents referred to in paragraph 17 of the Master Defence and that the interference occurred without want of care on the part of the defendant whether the defence of statutory authority arises	No	No	Issue not addressed

433

Table 26.2: *continued*

	The Questions of Law	The Answers Given by His Honour Judge Havery QC (1993)	The Answers Given by the Court of Appeal (1995)	The Answers Given by the House of Lords (1996–1997)
	In relation to the claim of *public nuisance*:			
4.	*Public Nuisance—Damage* Is interference with television reception capable of constituting an actionable public nuisance?	Yes, in the case only of plaintiffs who can show that they have suffered particular damage beyond that suffered by the relevant public generally	No	Issue not addressed
5.	*Statutory Authority Defence* On the assumption that the interference complained of was a direct consequence of the statutory scheme and consents referred to in paragraph 17 of the Master Defence and that the interference occurred without want of care on the part of the defendant whether the defence of statutory authority arises	No	No	Issue not addressed
6.	Whether it is open to the plaintiffs or any of them to maintain this action against the defendant in respect of those periods of time during which they did not without	A plaintiff cannot recover consequential damages (defined in the judgment of the Court as damages for loss of use of television signals for watching	Issue not addressed	Issue not addressed

434

	reasonable justification hold a valid television licence	television programmes) in respect of any period of time during which he did watch or would have watched unlicensed television at the relevant premises	
	In relation to the claim in negligence:		
7.	Can annoyance and discomfort found an action in negligence?	No; annoyance and discomfort are not sufficient damage to found an action in negligence. However, annoyance/discomfort together with other actionable damage may found such an action	Issue not addressed because finding at first instance was not challenged
8.	Whether the deposition of dust on property mentioned in paragraph 3 of the pro forma individual statement of claim is capable of constituting damage to that property	Yes	Yes; a deposit of dust is capable of giving rise to an action in negligence—whether it does depends on proof of physical damage and that depends on the evidence and the circumstances. Damage is in the physical change which renders the article less useful or less valuable. Dust is an inevitable incident of urban life, and the claim arose on the assumption that the defendants cause 'excessive deposits'
9.	Whether the matters alleged in paragraph 3 of the pro forma individual statement of claim are capable of founding an action in negligence	Yes	See item 8 above

435

sought, the statutory criteria for funding were not capable of being satisfied and any meaningful cost-benefit analysis required funding to be withdrawn.

G. Conclusion

26.28 A dispositive ruling having been handed down by the House of Lords in the CW litigation (interference with television reception caused by the mere presence of a building in line of sight between transmitter and receiver was held not to be an actionable nuisance), the action was at an end. The same could not be said of the LDDC action even though the House of Lords had confirmed, by a majority of 4–1, that only plaintiffs with a proprietary interest in land had standing to sue in private nuisance. Further representations were subsequently delivered in that action to the Legal Aid Board submitting that, with almost exactly two-thirds of the putative plaintiffs having fallen by the wayside, an action which could, at best, have been regarded as but marginally viable was no longer capable of satisfying the overall reasonableness test and was unviable and ought to be discontinued. Following this, funding was withdrawn, and the action was discontinued by the remaining plaintiffs shortly thereafter.

27

LOCKTON LITIGATION

Christopher Vigrass, Eleanor Boddington[1]

> This litigation from 1992–6 was possibly the first major financial services multi-party action. Procedurally, the case only became managed as a multi-party action after a period of some delay and lack of progress. These problems would almost certainly have been alleviated if a rule of court had been available to have been applied. Given that the case involved some 233 actions and nine firms representing plaintiffs, the case strongly illustrates the tactical importance of selection of issues, timing of discovery, and costs where there is an imbalance of financial resources between the parties. Six lead cases were selected as representative of different fact situations. The fact situations were agreed between the parties, thereby forming criteria for selection of the lead cases. It was accepted that the lead cases would be determinative of some common issues and other cases, but only indicative of others, and that individual issues would ultimately be determinative in most individual cases: it might therefore have been necessary to investigate all individual facts. However, in the circumstances of this litigation, it was possible to define the criteria for selection of lead cases in such a way that would not require prior investigation or verification of individual facts. Issues of the amount and distribution of costs among claimants were important: the Court of Appeal decision that liability of individual investors be limited to their proportionate share of overall costs, and be several and not joint, was significant for them in relation to viability. The amount of managerial power assumed by the Court in this case was somewhat tentative, given the developing debate about rules on multi-party actions.

A. Background to the Litigation

From 1985 the merchant bank Guinness Mahon (GM) acted as sponsor to various start-up companies which were set up under the Business Expansion Scheme (BES). One of the attractions of a BES company was that shareholders could claim tax relief at the higher rate   **27.01**

---

[1] Ashurst Morris Crisp.

of tax (if appropriate) on the monies which they invested in BES companies. In the instant litigation GM acted as sponsor to three BES companies, each of which bore the name 'Lockton'.

27.02 At the beginning of 1986, 1987, and 1988 prospectuses were issued by, respectively, Lockton Retail Stores Plc, Lockton Shops Plc, and Lockton Superstores Plc. Each of the Lockton companies was a newly formed BES company raising capital by the issue of shares to the public. Each of the companies proposed to undertake some sort of retail business. The prospectus issued by each of the companies was more or less in identical form, and similar in content, to that issued by each of the other companies. In each case GM offered to provide subscribers of shares with loan finance for the amount of the subscription. Many of the investors took advantage of the offer. In the early 1990s each of the Lockton companies failed, being placed in receivership or liquidation.

B. The Facts

27.03 The investors individually brought proceedings against GM from 1992 to 1994. There were approximately 99 actions relating to Lockton Shops, approximately 15 relating to Lockton Retail Stores, and 119 relating to Lockton Superstores. Some of the investors had invested in more than one Lockton company.

27.04 The vast majority of investors were represented by the firm of solicitors, Leon Kaye, Collin & Gittens (LK). Each of the investors who instructed LK instituted proceedings in an identical form, other than specific personal details. They alleged that the prospectuses for each issue contained material misrepresentations by GM, that GM was in breach of its duty of care in preparation of the prospectuses, that the investors subscribed for shares in reliance on incorrect statements in the prospectus, and, in the case of those investors who borrowed from GM, that the borrowing was induced by the incorrect statements. It was also alleged that the prospectuses should have contained warnings that an investment in the Lockton companies was speculative and high risk. In three claims there were additional allegations of specific misrepresentations.

27.05 The investors claimed as damages their losses from their investment. Those who borrowed from GM also claimed rescission of their loan agreements, and hence that they were under no liability to repay GM any amounts borrowed or outstanding interest thereon. GM, for its part, claimed repayment of any outstanding loans and interest, and defended the claims against it on a variety of grounds, including that the statements in the prospectuses were true. In some actions a defence under the Limitation Act was also pleaded. GM also contended that claims were only made by the investors because of the failure of the Lockton companies, which was not attributable to GM's conduct but was, in fact, attributable to the change in market conditions both in the property and retail market sector in the late 1980s, which was not, and could not have been, anticipated when the prospectuses were issued. GM was represented by Ashurst Morris Crisp (AMC).

C. Proposal for a Group Action

27.06 The proposal for a group disposal of the actions was first made by LK in early 1994, almost two years after it first began issuing proceedings on behalf of investors.

27.07 At the beginning of 1994 correspondence passed between LK, AMC, and the Court about the proposals for a group disposal of the actions. The investors initially took the view that lead actions should be drawn from all three Lockton issues. The correspondence between the parties culminated in an informal conference before Master Tennant in July 1994. The Court's approach was that it wished to aim for the most efficient way of dealing with the largest number of cases to keep down costs. The investors were particularly concerned to avoid unnecessary cost as they had limited resources. At the conference, it was agreed, in principle, that a number of sample actions should be selected, which were to be broadly representative of the whole group of investors. It was also agreed between the parties that the selected lead cases should all be selected from just one of the Lockton companies, rather than selecting from all the issues. This was on the basis that there were different questions of fact and different considerations needed for each Lockton company and that the litigation would be considerably protracted by having to address each company. For the purposes of efficiency and costs it was therefore agreed that it would be preferable to try the issues in relation to one Lockton company first.

27.08 GM was of the view, however, that, whilst the conclusion of the lead cases would be determinative of some issues, they would only be indicative of others. Master Tennant held that some issues common to each action could be decided absolutely by trying a number of lead actions, for example, whether GM was indeed responsible for any misrepresentations in the prospectuses. The Master pointed out that, if it were determined that GM was not so responsible, that would be the end of the matter and the entirety of the litigation would come to an end.

27.09 Subsequent to the conference the parties agreed that the lead actions should be chosen from the Lockton Shops ('Shops') issue on the basis that Master Tennant had said that the most important factor in deciding which Lockton company should be tried first was that the group with the largest number of common issues should be chosen.

27.10 In November 1994 there was a further directions hearing before Master Tennant. This was to hear Summonses for Directions for all of the actions, including actions in which the relevant investor was represented by solicitors other than LK (including eight other firms of solicitors in twenty-nine separate actions) or in which the investors were unrepresented. At this hearing the Master gave directions staying the non-Shops-related actions and also ruled on a timetable for the selection of lead actions from the Shops issue. The hearing for further directions was adjourned until December 1994.

D. Selection of Lead Actions

27.11 The selection of the lead actions was not as uncontroversial as the selection of Shops. There remained a question between the two sides as to what sort of test cases should be selected. GM considered it would be preferable if a small number of cases which had characteristics that each side considered important could be identified. The parties, however, fundamentally disagreed about what the key issues were. GM asserted that it was only possible to assess the standing of the investors, and their state of mind when they invested, by undergoing a limited discovery exercise in respect of all investors. An issue which concerned GM was the extent to which, if at all, each individual investor had relied on the statements in the prospectuses. In GM's view the reason why investors had subscribed for shares and had entered into agreements with GM was of fundamental importance in proceedings where the investors' case was one based on misrepresentation. Also, the individual investor's tax position had a bearing on the issues of liability because some investors would have decided simply to invest to use up their BES tax relief with little or no regard, and therefore reliance, for the 'investment'. One particular issue between the parties was whether the Court should consider the typical investor or whether it should divide up the investors into a number of different categories. GM asserted that, in respect of each individual category, a different approach would be required. In considering the suitability of the proposed lead litigants, GM conducted an examination of the occupations for each of the investors to seek to assess each investor's degree of sophistication.

27.12 The investors contended that there were common elements to each claim and that the issues needed to be decided first before dividing the investors into categories in this way. The issue common to all the prospectuses was whether the statements in them were misleading, according to the investors. GM had to consider whether to insist that it should be provided with witness statements from each of those investors for whom LK were instructed so as to enable it to make an informed decision as to whether the proposed lead litigants put forward by LK were appropriate.

27.13 The investors argued that a vast amount of costs would be wasted as a result of having a full discovery process prior to the selection of lead cases. They contended that if the investors were to lose at trial of the lead actions they could not conceive of a situation whereby LK would be in a position to proceed with the litigation on behalf of the remaining investors. The investors argued that if, on the other hand, they were to win at trial, then GM could reassess their position as to how it wanted to proceed in terms of further discovery and, therefore, GM would in no way be prejudiced if full discovery was not undertaken in respect of all investors. They argued that the balance of convenience in terms of costs savings overwhelmingly favoured their line of argument.

27.14 The Master decided that the investors should put forward a selection of proposed lead cases and limit discovery to such a 'team'. GM could then address whether the 'team' was acceptable and raise possible deficiencies with it at the next directions hearing. The investors were of the view that there ought to be four categories of investors represented by the lead actions, namely:

(1) those investors suing GM who purchased shares without the assistance of a loan from GM;
(2) those investors suing GM who purchased shares with the assistance of a loan from GM but who had repaid their loans;
(3) those investors suing GM who purchased shares with the assistance of a loan from

GM which had not been repaid and against whom GM was counter-claiming for repayment of the loan;

(4) those investors being sued by GM for repayment of a loan who purchased shares with the assistance of the loan and were counter-claiming damages.

GM was of the view that the lead actions should also represent the following categories of investors: **27.15**

(1) an investor who did not read the offer document;
(2) an investor who did read the offer document;
(3) an investor who had a financial adviser who introduced him or her to the issue;
(4) an investor who was considered to be a 'sophisticated investor';
(5) an investor who, having settled his or her dispute with GM, subsequently commenced proceedings; and
(6) an investor who entered into a refinancing agreement with GM.

AMC pointed out that each of the categories of investor which LK suggested could be accommodated within the categories of investors suggested by GM. Ultimately the investors agreed to this approach. **27.16**

GM wanted at least one of the lead actions to raise the question of limitation. However, the Master indicated that limitation should be dealt with after the lead actions had been tried. **27.17**

At the adjourned hearing in December 1994 the Master made a provisional selection of six lead actions. He also gave directions, at GM's request, aimed at simplifying the pleadings in the lead actions so that the common allegations were set out once only. He contemplated that, at the conclusion of the process of confirming the selection of the lead actions, the assigned trial judge would be asked by the parties to consider a proposal for disposing of the proceedings by way of group action—for example, would determination of a lead case be binding on other cases? **27.18**

E. Costs Issues[2]

The issue of costs was a central one in the litigation. Only about six of the total number of investors were legally aided, so that the incidence of legal aid was not a major feature of the costs argument as it had been in previous multi-party actions. **27.19**

GM did not wish to be involved in any arrangements which might have been made as between the investors *inter se* for dealing with their own or indeed GM's costs. However, in principle, it believed that any arrangement which had been put in place by the investors ought to allow for investors to withdraw from the group action at any time. **27.20**

However, GM took the view that, if Court intervention as to costs were unavoidable, its costs should be borne either solely by the investors in the lead actions, or, alternatively, by **27.21**

---

[2] See ch 8 above.

all the investors jointly and severally. It believed that it would be wrong in principle for the Court to order that it should only be entitled to recover costs from each investor severally, as suggested by LK. Also, in so far as investors had loan agreements with GM, these made provision for GM's costs. GM argued that the Court could not interfere with GM's contractual right to recover from investor-borrowers the costs incurred by GM in enforcing its agreements with those borrowers.

27.22 GM, however, accepted that the Court did have jurisdiction to make a costs order prior to trial. In June 1995, Alliott J ruled that GM was correct in its contention that the model costs order devised in the case of *Davies v Eli Lilly & Co*[3] was limited to the costs position as between the group of plaintiffs *inter se* and was not an *inter partes* order. Alliott J held that, on that basis, any *inter partes* costs order should be made by the trial judge.

27.23 The investors appealed Alliott J's decision, which appeal was heard in early 1996.

27.24 The crux of the investors' argument on appeal was that no individual investor should be disadvantaged by being part of a group litigation scheme which, they argued, an investor would be if Alliott J's decision were upheld, in that that investor could become liable for the whole of GM's costs.

27.25 The investors argued that it was in the nature of the Lockton group litigation that there were common issues shared in all cases. The same issues would have to be tried in *any* action brought by any of the investors and therefore GM would not be prejudiced by the costs order which they were seeking. They also argued that it was appropriate for the Court to make a costs-sharing order in advance of the trial so that they knew where they stood.

27.26 The investors contended that it would be unfair to give GM an advantage—ie the threat of recovering all of its costs against a 'substantial' investor, leaving that investor to seek contribution from others. If this were to be the position, the whole development of group litigation by lead actions would be threatened, in the investors' submission.

27.27 GM argued that the order proposed by the investors on appeal went beyond the costs order made in the *Davies* case (upon which the investors were seeking to rely) in that the investors' proposed order did not merely govern contribution amongst the plaintiffs *inter se* but sought to limit the potential liability of each of the investors to GM by providing that they should be liable for only a proportionate fraction of the costs.

27.28 GM was of the view that the investors had the organisation of the matter, and that they could, without undue difficulty, organise a fund or a guarantee which would ensure that the lead investors were adequately protected.

27.29 GM argued that if the order proposed by the investors were made, the investors would be placed in a substantially better position. Under the order proposed by the investors, the mere fact that there were investors with common issues to be tried would have entailed that each investor's liability to pay costs would have been limited to $1/n$. This would be a fortuitous and arbitrary advantage in favour of the investors, according to GM.

---

[3] [1987] 1 WLR 1136; see para 18.18 above.

27.30 GM argued that it might be placed in a worse position since, instead of being entitled to look to any given unsuccessful investor for recovery of costs, GM might have to institute recovery proceedings against numerous investors for comparatively small sums and might find itself out of pocket to the extent that sums were irrecoverable from some investors.

27.31 In any event, GM contended that, in so far as the group litigation affected the amount of GM's costs as against a given investor, those were matters which turned on future events and could only be properly dealt with by the trial judge. Therefore no anticipatory order could fairly or sensibly be made as to costs sharing.

27.32 On hearing the investors' appeal as to costs, the Court of Appeal was particularly swayed by the Law Society's report published in September 1995 (ie after Alliott J's first instance judgment). The report considered, amongst other things, the incidence of *inter partes* costs in group actions. It stated:

> One point on which there is general agreement is that if defendants win on common issues and costs are ordered against the plaintiffs, the liability of plaintiffs should be several rather than joint.... Any other arrangement would make the risk inherent in group actions so great as to limit access to justice solely to those plaintiffs with nothing at all to lose.

27.33 The Court of Appeal was persuaded, therefore, that it was appropriate to make an order that the liability of the individual investors be limited to the proportionate share of the overall costs, whether incurred by the investors *inter se* or payable by the investors to GM, and that such liability be several and not joint. The Court of Appeal believed that the purpose of selecting lead cases would be vitiated if regard had to be had not to the issues in particular actions but to the means or willingness of the particular investors to accept a high degree of risk as to costs.

27.34 The Court of Appeal's decision given in February 1996 was undoubtedly a considerable comfort to the investors given that the trial of the lead actions had, by the time the costs appeal was heard, been listed to be heard for four weeks in the summer of 1996; the lead litigants had faced the real prospect of being liable for all of GM's costs in the matter to date if their costs appeal had failed and they had been unsuccessful at trial.

27.35 The parties settled the litigation before the trial got under way. Therefore the issue of whether the judgment in respect of the lead actions could have been binding on the losing party in respect of the non-lead actions was never established. However, in the four years leading up to trial, it was evident that, for both parties, the issues of identifying the key issues to be tried, the method of selection of lead actions, and the issue of costs sharing were of fundamental importance.

28

CREUTZFELDT-JAKOB DISEASE (HUMAN GROWTH HORMONE) LITIGATION

David Body[1]

This negligence claim from the mid-1990s was a notable overall success for the claimants. One very important management lesson emerged. As discussed at chapter 2, there had been controversy arising in many of the product liability claims of the previous five years or so of whether it was appropriate in a multi-party action either to proceed immediately to trial solely on the issue of one or some supposedly common issues and to defer all other matters, or alternatively to proceed on a broader basis. In this case, there was an initial trial of breach of duty and general causation but with no evidence of the facts of any individual cases. The approach was seen to have serious drawbacks and subsequent cases adopted instead the 'trial of lead cases' approach.

The litigation also illustrates other management points. First, no cut-off date was ordered, because cases were continuing to emerge (and may continue to do so for the next twenty years), so the group had not crystallised and could not be crystallised. Nevertheless, the existence of litigation was very well known and publicised by other means amongst the community of those potentially affected, so there was a high degree of confidence that potential claimants would be aware of the litigation, and leave was required for latecomers to join. Furthermore, the claimants and their advisers repeatedly made the point that they were uncomfortable about any form of publicity in addition to that which occurred naturally since there was anecdotal evidence that this was accentuating the problems of those who had received treatment but who were not claimants. Accordingly, the advisers closely followed guidance given by the Child Growth Foundation. Secondly, a small steering committee functioned effectively. Thirdly, there were the costs aspects, which included the Court preferring a solution of providing for certainty of accounting during the litigation as it proceeded, rather than including all future claimants, which would have been theoretically more just but impracticable.

---

[1] Partner, Irwin Mitchell.

A. The Human Growth Hormone Programme 1959–1985

28.01 Some children suffer from a defective pituitary gland which fails to secrete sufficient human growth hormone (hGH). As a consequence they suffer from extreme short stature. Serious ill health may result in about 10 per cent of such children and possibly a life-threatening condition such as hypoglycaemia. Since 1986, these children have received a synthetic hormone to make them grow. Before that date the only treatment possible was with pituitary growth hormone, a biological product derived from pituitaries harvested at post-mortem from cadavers.

28.02 From the 1930s to the 1950s attempts were made by medical scientists to repeat the success in producing insulin for treatment of diabetes. Many animal pituitary hormones were extracted for research and used with mixed success; in the late 1950s use of extracted pituitary hormones to stimulate growth and fertility was first attempted. By 1959 the Medical Research Council had started clinical trials in which hGH was processed into therapeutic dosage quantities and administered to growth deficient children. Between 1960 and 1971 an extensive trial at Great Ormond Street had established the therapeutic value of this treatment.

28.03 This trial of pituitary or 'cadaveric' growth hormone had developed by the mid-1970s into a large-scale therapeutic programme (1,800 plus patients); the UK programme was one of many national programmes. The USA had a major pituitary hormone programme for children (5,000 plus patients); Australia used pituitary hormones in a fertility programme (2,000 plus patients). European countries had their own programmes, in particular France (1,300 plus) where the treatment continued until 1988.

28.04 Early in 1985 three cases of Creutzfeldt-Jakob Disease (CJD) were established at post-mortem amongst American recipients of hGH; a British case of CJD in a recipient was confirmed in June 1985. The UK programme was terminated on 9 May 1985 on the basis of the US evidence, by which time about 940,000 pituitaries had been harvested in the UK and more than 1,800 children treated. By the time of the generic trial in mid-1996 sixteen UK recipients had died of CJD. As at December 1999 that number had risen to thirty-four deaths.

28.05 Two lead issues faced the children and their parents. First, was it possible to establish a generic breach of duty by the Medical Research Council and Department of Health in causing this identifiably novel, 'iatrogenic' variant of CJD which had been classified by neuropathological assessment at the National CJD Surveillance Unit at Edinburgh? Secondly, if generic liability could be established, was it possible to show individual causation arising by that date, so as to prove individual breach of duty?

B. Prelude to the Litigation

28.06 Claims were first identified in 1990 when the Newman family, whose son, Terry, was then dying of CJD, contacted solicitors. Further claims began to emerge in 1991 when the Department of Health, acting through the follow-up study (established at the

Institute of Child Health), started a programme of warnings to patients about the risk of contracting CJD. Terry Newman's case was the fifth British iatrogenic CJD death and others followed.

28.07 As the numbers of claims notified grew, media attention increased, particularly after a series of articles in the *Today* newspaper and documentaries made by *World in Action* and *Panorama*. The families' liaison group, the Child Growth Foundation, made early contact with Irwin Mitchell and became a referral point for claims.

28.08 A Steering Committee was constituted on 6 October 1992 initially following the traditional model but this was superseded when the first Legal Aid Contract Tender was issued by the Legal Aid Board. After this tendering the Legal Aid Board awarded the Contract for the Generic Litigation to Irwin Mitchell and Smith Llewelyn. The small size of the Steering Committee subsequently constituted (David Body and Andrew Tucker (Irwin Mitchell), Peter Llewelyn and Mark Mildred (Smith Llewelyn)) greatly simplified the task of assembling the outline of the case.

28.09 Pre-action disclosure did not take place; proceedings were issued from 1993 onwards (adopting the date of death or a date of knowledge in 1991 as the trigger for limitation). Disclosure was sought in January 1993, in the form of a generic request to the Department of Health, and it soon became apparent that there was agreement between the parties that the issues to be tried were sufficiently generic to justify the institution of a multi-party action. It is important to stress this because the aftermath of the generic trial (see below) has tended to blur this agreement and the acceptance by the parties that, having dealt with generic issues, those findings would need to be applied to individual cases.

28.10 Discovery was voluminous; overall it was estimated that over 1,250,000 documents were examined. A decision was taken early on that the most coherent way for those documents to be organised was into 'Yearbooks' for each year of the programme 1959 to 1985; this enabled the contemporaneity of documentation to be obvious and the dissemination of information to be understood. Inclusion in these Yearbooks of the scientific literature of the year was also a powerful assistance to establishing knowledge to be imputed to those in charge of aspects of the programme.

28.11 Three calls for a public inquiry as a substitute for this litigation were rejected by the Department of Health, notwithstanding the support of a large number of MPs for this proposal expressed in a Parliamentary Early Day Motion.

C. The Litigation

28.12 The litigation commenced in November 1994 with a consent directions order constituting the litigation made by Otton J. A timetable of directions was established, culminating in a trial on generic issues fixed (by agreement in November 1994) for April 1996. This timetable for preparation, although tight, was met.

28.13 To simplify the action, two groups of plaintiffs were identified: Group A (patients who had contracted CJD or their families on behalf of their estates) and Group B (those patients fearful that they might contract the disease ('the worried well')). Group B was stayed whilst the generic trial proceeded on the basis of the facts of the Group A cases.

28.14 No cut-off dates were ordered. However, the leave of the Court was required for claimants to join one group of claimants (Group A, comprising some eleven plaintiffs at the beginning of the trial) after 1 December 1995. Group B remained, comprising those who had received the growth hormone in the programme and remained apparently uninfected by CJD but who claimed for psychiatric injury after being told between 1991 and 1993 that they were at risk of developing CJD in the future (some eighty-seven plaintiffs). It has been said that:

> The reason for this in relation to Group A was presumably that the number of patients falling ill with CJD was likely to increase with the passage of time. None could have limitation difficulties since none would have a complete cause of action unless and until symptoms of the illness occurred. To this extent the case was quite different from the usual case of the product in mass circulation withdrawn from the market. Since the Group B cases were stayed until the conclusion of the Group A trial there was no prejudice to the defendants in allowing plaintiffs to join until that time.[2]

28.15 Interlocutory hearings were few, the substantive exception being a strike-out application by the defendants decided by May J in April 1995. The two issues at large here were the questions of:

(a) whether there was a single remedy available to all plaintiffs (whether fatal accident or worried well) based in battery. It later became clear that those clinicians who had consented patients' parents about treatment in the programme (ie the paediatric endocrinologists) had been unable to warn of risks in the administration of the product because they were themselves in ignorance of the risks until April 1985 as they had not been told about them;
(b) a declaration whether the removal of pituitaries without consent was illegal.

28.16 Both these elements were struck out. In the light of the later generic finding the strike out of (a) above may seem ironic. Success on this footing would have obviated the causation arguments which separated wholly successful plaintiffs from 'straddlers'. In particular, it would have enfranchised those Group B 'straddlers', whose claims had ultimately to be discontinued. It is clear that the clinicians administering the product not only knew nothing of its potential risks but would have stopped using it if they had been told of those risks. There arose an inevitable artificiality in the distinction between negligent and non-negligent treatment (for the determination of entitlement to compensation) when it was clear that none of the treating clinicians knew anything of the risk until the programme had to be stopped.

---

[2] M Mildred, 'The Human Growth Hormone (Creutzfeld-Jacob [sic] Disease) Litigation' [1998] JPIL 251.

D. The Inadvisability of a Generic Trial and Ignoring the Facts of Individual Cases

The case proceeded with a trial of 'generic' issues of liability with no evidence from individual cases.[3] For the purpose of the action, the defendants conceded (belatedly) medical causation, ie that CJD had been transmitted by the injection of growth hormone. They maintained a denial of duty obligations towards those who had been growth hormone recipients. The trial began on 15 April 1996. Judgment was given on 19 July 1996.

28.17

Discovery continued throughout the trial as the defendants were gradually persuaded to disclose the full extent of their stored paper. One important aspect of the trial itself was the success of the 'live note' system, which enabled a clear check to be kept on evidence and which was invaluable in preparing closing submissions. It is hard to imagine undertaking a case of this size in the future without this system.

28.18

The Judge held[4] those responsible for the hGH programme to have been in breach of a duty of care owed to patients in:

28.19

- failure to bring before the two expert controlling committees (one controlled production, one dealt with clinical treatment: these committees had only one member in common) initial evidence of possible risk provided in Autumn 1976;
- failure by the production committee to obtain timely independent expert advice, and apply it more quickly than they eventually did;
- later failure to put before the production committee expert views warning of the real but unquantifiable risk of death to patients and recommending urgent laboratory testing and in that committee's failure to make full disclosure to the clinicians committee who had full responsibility for the treatment programme: thus denying them the opportunity to stop the programme;
- failure, as a result, to suspend by 1 July 1977 the programme for all new patients who had begun treatment. However, the judge found that the continuation of the programme of treatment for patients which had already started by 1 July 1977 was not negligent.

E. After the Generic Trial

Both parties were on novel ground at the end of the generic trial. Factual liability and causation issues in individual cases were left undecided. Application of the generic findings to those cases had no agreed mechanism. In the event, application of the findings was effected by agreement between the parties in those cases which were 'clear' winners; this

28.20

---

[3] The litigation involved a series of nine substantive judgments at first instance and one decision in the Court of Appeal. These are reported at Volume 49 of Butterworths Medical Law Reports. This includes the Practice Direction of 30 July 1998 which inaugurates the CJD List set up to apply the findings of this litigation to any subsequently occurring Group A or B claim.

[4] *N and Others v United Kingdom Medical Research Council and Secretary of State for Health*, 'The Creutzfeldt Jakob Disease Litigation' [1996] 7 Med LR 309.

process revealed five cases which had succeeded. There was then a need to deal with various distinct categories. These were:

(a) Those cases in which the majority of treatment took place after 1 July 1977, in which no evidence had been heard of what decisions would have been taken as to the continuation of treatment by
   (i) treating clinicians,
   (ii) parents properly warned of the risk involved.

These cases became known as 'straddlers'.

(b) Other Group A fatal cases now seeking to join the litigation. A particular factor in this case was that deaths have continued and will continue for many years after the cessation of the products' use.
(c) The effect of the findings on the psychiatric injury cases. For example, whilst it was possible readily to agree directions for trial of causation issues in those cases in which all treatment could be seen to have taken place after 1 July 1977, there was a group (the Group B 'straddlers') who, whilst having the majority of their treatment after this date, could not take refuge in the argument which eventually enabled the Group A 'straddlers' to succeed, namely the likelihood that the infective dose was non-cumulative and that one dose was as likely as any other to introduce the infection. This was thought not to be sustainable as an approach to competing causes of psychiatric injury.

28.21 Looking more closely at Category A, in five of the Group A cases in which treatment had begun after 1 July 1977, but also in at least six more, the majority of treatment, and therefore arguably, on the balance of probabilities, infection, had occurred after that date. The problem was:

> No oral or written evidence had been given at trial of the treatment history of any individual plaintiff and no attempt had been made to do other than try the generic issues between the parties. This omission was, in the light of the judge's findings (and in particular the manner in which they were expressed), to prove costly of time and effort. Indeed, there is an irony in the fact that the first truly generic trial in a multi-plaintiff case had gone some way to vindicate those who stood out against resolution of group actions by the generic approach and to change judicial approaches to the management of these cases.[5]

F. Litigation after the Generic Trial

28.22 In December 1996 an application was made to the Judge for directions as to whether or not the issue of 'straddling' plaintiffs could be settled simply by asking for clarification of the July 1996 generic judgment. This clarification came in a further determinative judgment given at Cardiff in December 1996, which confirmed the limited extent of the finding and made other Orders about the trial of Group B issues and costs which determined the way in which the residual issues were to be resolved.

---

[5] Mildred, n 2 above.

28.23 In the face of the Judge's reinforcement of the terms of his July judgment, refusing to consider evidence from 'straddling' plaintiffs, an appeal was made to the Court of Appeal. Whilst this was being listed, quantum trials were listed in the five 'clear' winning cases and in relation to the broad issue of psychiatric injury. These trials were listed for September and November 1997 respectively; the decision of the Court of Appeal was handed down in November 1997. During this period the parties were involved in trying several parts of the case in parallel.

28.24 The psychiatric injury causation trial provided a detailed examination of the authorities on primary and secondary victims and the distinction to be drawn in cases like this in which continued deaths amongst the patient cohort provides 'reinforcement' of the injury suffered. When the first of these claims came to quantum trial in April 1998, a record award for psychiatric injury of £340,000 was made.

28.25 The Court of Appeal's determination effectively explored the extent to which the Judge should apply his generic findings to individual cases and will provide a guide in future to the structure of hearings of generic issues. As the Court of Appeal noted, neither side had advanced an argument or anticipated a finding that there would have been a *partial* suspension in the programme which was at the heart of Morland J's finding. The Court of Appeal held that the defendants owed some duty of care to *all* patients involved in the programme. There was an arguable breach of duty to existing patients if their treatment continued without those responsible for their care informing them of the risks so that they (or their parents) could decide whether to continue with their treatment. All claims by those whose treatment straddled 1 July 1977 were not bound to fail on the basis that the information given to clinicians by the hypothetical deliberations of the committees and their experts would have been a recommendation that treatment for existing patients should continue. Judge LJ continued:

> This is not a case about fresh evidence being put before the court which should have been canvassed earlier. At the first hearing generic questions only were tried but one of the difficulties about group litigation is that there will be occasions—of which this is one—when the judgment does not in fact decide all the issues which it was hoped or expected should be decided. Those claims require further analysis. Each side should be entitled to advance evidence and argument about the effect of the decision at the hypothetical meeting on the patients whose treatment straddled July 1, 1977. The plaintiffs' evidence should be directed to the issues whether in their individual cases treatment with hGH would for any reason have continued or been brought to a halt, and whether on balance of probabilities the infecting dose or doses were received on or before July 1, 1977.

28.26 Accordingly, as Mildred later commented:

> In this case the question whether the trial judge did elide questions of breach and causation is unresolved as is the consequence of failure on the part of plaintiffs in a 'generic issue' trial to lead evidence on the causative outcome of an (unanticipated) finding of fact. The latter may provide cogent support for the addition to generic issues of at least a sample of individual cases fully pleaded on the issue of breach and of causation. The advantage of such an approach appears to have been accepted by the judges presently supervising the interlocutory stages of Norplant, Larium and tobacco litigation.[6]

---

[6] Mildred, n 2 above, 260.

28.27 Having been instructed by the Court of Appeal to revisit the claims of straddling plaintiffs, Morland J approached the problem by determining first that since there was no clinical evidence of cumulative infection, it must follow that each injection received represented a separate opportunity for infection; by extension, when a plaintiff had had more injections after 1 July 1977 than before, it must follow, applying a balance of probabilities test, that the greater likelihood was that infection arose after than before that date. In each case involving Group A 'straddlers' an injection count was then undertaken. That was no small undertaking since many recipients had received injections twice a week for ten or more years.

28.28 The question of the patient's parents' choice of whether to be warned and, if so warned, to cease treatment needed a two-stage approach. First, the Judge drafted a hypothetical letter to clinicians based on the advice that should have been tendered by the processing committee in the light of the perceived risk as at Spring 1977. The hypothetical communication referred to 'an immeasurable but exceedingly low risk of contamination', as a result of which it had been decided that no new patients should receive hGH or be included in the programme pending further scientific research.

28.29 With regard to patients already receiving therapy, the hypothetical letter continued:

> the meeting would have decided that although risk could not be entirely discounted hGH may continue to be prescribed but . . . it is the responsibility of the individual clinician to decide in relation to an individual patient whether or not to advise the patient or his parents that hGH therapy should be continued. Before giving such advice a clinician will wish to discuss the matter with the Director of a hGH Centre who was present at the meeting.

28.30 Secondly, it was necessary to examine expert evidence from erstwhile members of that committee as to the warnings they would have given to patients in 1977, if they themselves and parents had been properly warned of the *nature* of the risk.

28.31 The evidence from witnesses who were both expert (in the sense that they were all distinguished paediatric endocrinologists) and factual witnesses (in the sense that they had all treated patients in the pre-1985 hGH programme) was unanimous that if properly warned in 1977 they would have suspended the programme for those then in treatment and would have accepted no further entrants to the programme. This rebutted an assumption central to Morland J's 1996 generic finding.

28.32 Following on from these determinations came a series of quantum trials, the last of which in September 1998 brought the litigation to a close.

28.33 This post-generic trial section of the litigation had strengths and weaknesses: flexible listing and duration of listing ensured that the management was effectively left in the hands of the parties; although delays in response by the Department of Health meant that the process was extended over a three-year period after the generic trial. Even allowing for the Court of Appeal visit these issues could have been timetabled into two years. A shorter litigation time, which would now be uppermost in a Civil Procedure Rules 1998 (CPR) driven Judge's mind, would have translated into a significant reduction in stress for the plaintiffs' families, for whom this was a tortuous process. Evidence of the flexibility adopted can be found in the fact that this was a peripatetic case, with hearings taking place in London (generic trial), Liverpool, Sheffield, Cardiff, Oxford (on commission), and Lincoln.

G. Complications of the Generic Trial Approach

28.34 A clear understanding is needed, first, of the complete sequence of legal issues which can be anticipated to arise in the litigation and, secondly, what evidence it would be necessary to hear in order to decide each issue. The real problem lay in the fact that the Judge was unaware of the relevant facts of individual cases, with the consequence that his attempt to be helpful in deciding what everyone thought was a generic trial on liability, when it was in reality only deciding breach of duty, led to difficulty in applying his findings on causation to the true facts. Thus the moral here was that the attempt to decide a case on a 'generic trial' basis in ignorance of the factual matrix of individual cases was shown to be a management technique which only partially succeeded.

H. Costs

28.35 An order made by consent at the start of the litigation included the provision: 'As between plaintiffs and defendants, any generic costs ordered to be paid by the plaintiffs to the defendants shall be apportioned between them. The plaintiffs' liability shall be several.'

28.36 This was made in November 1994 when consideration of costs issues in multi-party actions was at a relatively early stage.

28.37 The Judge upheld the defendants' argument that each member of Groups A and B should be liable on a several, rather than joint, basis for a share of the generic costs. This was in view of the facts, first, that cost sharing was essential not only as a matter of fairness but also to establish the viability of a group action and, secondly, that those who take the advantage of joining a group must bear the concomitant responsibility and discipline of proportionate liability for the costs to which a defendant should not have been put but for the existence of the group action.

28.38 The Judge refused to impose a liability for generic costs on possible future claimants, who might for example develop CJD, since their number could not be ascertained. The converse result would have postponed finality of accounting indefinitely and given the participants no certainty as the litigation progressed.

28.39 The principle of certainty of accounting as the case progressed was in fact not achieved in this case. As late as 30 April 1998, the Judge ordered that all claimants who had issued proceedings before 1 January 1998 should share the costs of the generic trial and all those whose treatment straddled the 1 July 1977 date plus all psychiatric injury claimants should be liable for their share in all costs relating to the relevant issue. On 19 June 1998 he further ordered that those straddlers who lost should recover from the defendants three-quarters of their share of the party and party generic costs of the 'straddler' issue. The practical consequence of this approach to costs apportionment has been an overwhelming complication of the bill of costs prepared for assessment.

I. Conclusion

28.40 This litigation showed that complex issues of breach and causation can be tried successfully in a multi-party action. The duration of the programme opened up to criticism the absence of key witnesses and the scale of the documentation involved suggested to the Department of Health advisers that this was a case that could not be lost at trial. Perhaps for those reasons any attempt at proposing a no-fault scheme of compensation was rejected.

28.41 Like any case of this scale, issues emerged in the course of the case (mainly to do with the disclosure of documents, 5,000 or so novel pages emerging during the course of the trial) which added to the originally pleaded case. Even at the outset the issues were in a format which argued a traditional negligence case writ large rather than the point of departure for a multi-party action.

28.42 This litigation involved the first full trial of substantive issues in a multi-party action product liability case in this country. It was also the first trial anywhere in the world of liability issues arising from pituitary hormone administration. In a public issue of this importance, however, it may be wondered whether this should really have been the subject of a trial at all. In giving generic judgment Morland J commented: 'Litigation of this scientific complexity on a subject of general public importance might be better resolved by an inquisitorial rather than an adversarial system.'

28.43 In Australia the Allars Committee Investigation into the administration of pituitary hormones was constituted in May 1993 and reported in June 1994. After this report all Australian iatrogenic CJD fatal claims were compensated. Claims for psychiatric injury were initiated and eventually settled after judgments given by Morland J in 1997 were reported in Australia. French fatal claims were immediately compensated and criminal proceedings initiated against responsible clinicians; psychiatric claims were later compromised. No claims have come to trial or been compromised in the United States.

28.44 In many respects the generic trial itself was a form of public inquiry, which ranged over the subject matter of the claim, eventually highlighting areas of greater concern than others which by the end of the trial became the particular focus of the plaintiffs' submissions. This, of course, is what the families wanted: findings of fact and the dispelling of the many misunderstood elements of the previously only partially told story were in themselves a good thing. The findings in negligence which followed from the findings of fact were for some of the families almost incidental.

28.45 A public inquiry is what was originally sought in 1992 and 1993, a suggestion pointedly refused by successive Secretaries of State for Health. Furthermore, in those pre-CPR days, an offer to settle in February 1996 was blankly refused—perhaps because at that stage the Secretary of State for Health was turning his attention to the then emerging problem of new variant CJD caused by the BSE epidemic in cattle.

28.46 Ultimately, if slightly inelegantly, the outcome for plaintiffs justified the initiation of proceedings and showed that even before the CPR, the Queen's Bench Division judge had a sufficiently pragmatic approach to a complex issue multi-party action to try it.

29

BRITISH COAL: VIBRATION WHITE FINGER LITIGATION

Andrew Tucker[1]

> This personal injury action arising out of occupational health exposure of coal miners ran from 1993 until the establishment in 1999 of a framework to evaluate the award of compensation in individual claims. The litigation was extremely large and involved over 50,000 claimants, with an estimated total liability of £500 million.
>
> Nine lead cases were selected for a trial of breach of duty and general causation, followed by a subsequent trial on individual causation. Although the other individual claims were stayed pending resolution of the lead cases, a schedule of the available information in the individual claims was prepared which assisted with selection of lead cases. A register of claimants and Master pleadings was utilised.
>
> Particular problems which had to be overcome included initial disagreements over representation of claimants, whether lead cases could be settled and what the costs consequences might be, and the fact that the settlement framework (Handling Agreement) had to be amended when it was recognised that alternative causation issues were relevant in individual cases. Overall, this litigation represented a notable win for the claimants.

A. Introduction

29.01 Vibration white finger is a condition well known in the field of occupational health as explained by Professor CL Welsh, Consultant Vascular Surgeon, in evidence in *Armstrong & Others v British Coal Corporation* as follows:

> Since the second decade of this century it has been recognised that users of hand held powered tools which transmit vibration to the hands complain of a variety of symptoms affecting the hands including whiteness of the fingers, tingling and numbness. The initial reports of Loriga (1911), Hamilton (1918) and Leake (1918) recognised the causal link between

---

[1] Partner, Irwin Mitchell.

exposure to vibration and the symptoms, indeed, Hamilton noted that the severity of symptoms was directly related to the degree of use of the powered tools. These initial reports were concerned only with pneumatically driven tools, but in the 1940s and the 1950s electrically powered rotating tools were implicated (Agate 1949). In the 1960s the advent of the one-man operated petrol driven chainsaw brought vibration related problems to the timber producing countries (Taylor et al 1981). It has been estimated that in British Industry approximately 150,000 workers in manufacturing, agriculture, forestry and the public utilities were exposed to vibration transmitted to the hand and arm (Kyriakides 1988). The essential characteristic is not the occupation nor the tool used, but the frequency, magnitude and duration of the vibration exposure. The condition was initially known as white finger or dead hand, later becoming known as Raynaud's Phenomenon of occupation origin. The terms traumatic vasospastic disease (TVD) and vibration induced white finger (VWF) were introduced in the 1970s but as it became apparent that vibration affected other parts of the hand-arm system than the vascular tree, the term hand-arm vibration syndrome (HAVS) was introduced in 1986 (Gemne et al 1987). There is evidence that hand-transmitted vibration causes changes in the digital vascular tree, the peripheral nerves and the musculo-skeletal system.

Maurice Raynaud (1862) in his Thesis 'De L'Asphyxie et de la Grangrene Symmetrique des Extremeties' described examples of differing conditions in which similar manifestations have appeared. From this unsatisfactory base confusion has arisen and has been compounded by the use of eponymous titles. Vascular disturbances resulting from the handling of powered tools were recognised in a case description by Loriga (1911).

In 1918 an outbreak of hand problems in Indiana lime stone cutters led to an investigation by the United States Department of Labor. Hamilton (1918) called the condition a spastic anaemia. Leake (1918) concluded that 'there exists in the hands of stone cutters who use pneumatic tools a hypertonicity of the blood vessels which shows itself as an exaggerated reaction to low temperatures'. Brocklehurst (1945) labelled the condition 'Pseudo-Raynaud's Disease', while at the same time Telford, McCann and MacCormack (1945) used the name 'Dead Hand'. The term traumatic vasospastic disease was used by Gurdjian and Walker (1945) and this is close to the modern concept of the condition. Agate (1949) preferred Raynaud's Phenomenon of occupational origin. The Industrial Injuries Advisory Council promulgated that in the United Kingdom the name 'Vibration Induced White Finger' should be used. There is now widespread acceptance of this global term but more recently Hand-Arm Vibration Syndrome has been used to cover the problems which occur in the vascular, musculo-skeletal and nervous systems associated with vibration.

B. The Group Action

29.02 By late 1993 several hundred individual actions had been commenced in various county courts and District Registries. The common thread to those actions was that employees and former employees of British Coal Corporation claimed that the routine use of vibratory tools during their occupations as coal miners had induced vibration white finger. Had British Coal Corporation taken appropriate steps, it was alleged, injury would have been avoided and consequently there was a liability to pay damages. In underground coal mining operations a wide variety of tools are used which are hand-held and give rise to vibration. These include rotary and percussive drills, compressed air drills, grinders, pneumatic picks, and pneumatic hammers to name but a few. Some of these tools were also used in surface work where in addition at many collieries there were workshops where pedestal grinders were used which also transmit vibration to the hands of the user.

Many of these early claims were issued out of the Newcastle upon Tyne County Court or District Registry. As a consequence of an initiative by a local district judge the Lord Chief Justice issued a Practice Direction on 12 January 1994 which: **29.03**

(1) assigned claims for vibration white finger (VWF) brought against British Coal Corporation to His Honour Judge Stephenson sitting as a Deputy High Court judge of the High Court of Justice Newcastle upon Tyne District Registry;
(2) directed the transfer of all cases not issued in Newcastle upon Tyne to that District Registry;
(3) directed the transfer of cases issued in the Newcastle upon Tyne County Court to the High Court; and
(4) directed that new actions should be commenced in Newcastle upon Tyne.

This Practice Direction was the catalyst which led to the consolidation of the claims into a group action.

Immediately after the promulgation of the Practice Direction, claimants' solicitors met on two separate occasions to establish whether there was a willingness to co-ordinate the many claims. At the second meeting it was decided that a Solicitors' Group would be formed and that the Group would be represented by a Steering Committee. The Steering Committee would have the responsibility of bringing the litigation to trial on behalf of members of the Solicitors' Group and their clients. At this point, early 1994, approximately 500 cases had been issued. The Solicitors' Group meeting selected a Steering Committee of four firms of solicitors: Thompsons, Irwin Mitchell, Watson Burton, and Hugh James Ford Simey. **29.04**

The Steering Committee commenced work immediately by instructing experts to address common issues and, where appropriate, briefing counsel. Procedurally, the group action was formed by Order of Deputy High Court Judge Stephenson made on 21 July 1994. **29.05**

C. The Steering Committee

However, immediately following selection of the Steering Committee two firms of solicitors, both of whom had been represented at the Solicitors' Group meetings, indicated they thought that the outcome was inappropriate, alleging that there may be a potential conflict of interest between the claimants represented by the Legal Aid Board and those represented by various mining trade unions. It was proposed that there should be two separate committees, representing each client group defined by funder, namely a legal aid group and a trade unions group. **29.06**

The Steering Committee of four firms was endorsed by the Order made on 21 July 1994. That Steering Committee could see no potential for a conflict of interest. Although it was conceivable that there might be a conflict of instruction this was thought unlikely. The Legal Aid Board was accepting of the role of the Steering Committee in this interim phase, as were the mining trade unions. However, subsequently the Legal Aid Board issued an invitation to tender pursuant to the Multi-Party Action Arrangements 1992. The Steering Committee submitted a tender as a group of four firms. One of the two firms that had **29.07** previously objected to the organisation of claimants' representation tendered separately. That firm was a small two-partner practice with little prior experience of multi-party litigation. The Legal Aid Board awarded the contract to that firm in September 1994, misjudging the scale of the litigation and dismissing the democratic process that had given rise to the selection of the existing Steering Committee. That Steering Committee remained in position by reason of the Court Order of 21 July 1994 and commenced judicial review proceedings against the Legal Aid Board. Prior to the determination of those judicial review proceedings the firm to which the contract had been provided dissolved, the two partners choosing to practise separately thereafter. The Legal Aid Board reissued the invitation to tender and on this occasion two members of the existing Steering Committee who represented legally aided claimants tendered together on the basis that, if successful, they would delegate authority under the contract to the other two firms who represented only trade unions funded claimants. One of the two new firms created from the dissolution of the previous contract holder also tendered. The Legal Aid Board, learning from its recent experience, suggested that one of the two firms jointly tendering should hold the contract together with the new firm. Authority to delegate by those two contract holders to the other three members of the Steering Committee was authorised by the Legal Aid Board. The judicial review proceedings were compromised as a consequence and five firms have served on the Steering Committee to date. Thus, the claimants' representation was resolved in April 1995.

D. Pre-Trial Phase

29.08 Despite the sideshow, the Steering Committee continued to progress the action to trial. By mid-1994 several hundred cases had been formally pleaded and many were the subject of detailed requests for further and better particulars and interrogatories. The first group directions Order made on 21 July 1994 sought to address the question of pleadings, formulate a group action, and provide directions through to trial. The Order provided for the formation of a group, defining the litigation as the 'British Coal Vibration White Finger Litigation', and defining the claimants and the defendants. It is noteworthy that there were actions brought against British Coal Corporation and various mining contractors as second defendants. Claims against these other defendants were stayed at this stage pending resolution of the 'main event' against British Coal Corporation. The Solicitors' Group and Steering Committee were also defined by the Order. Common issues and common costs were identified. A register, to be brought up-to-date quarterly, was provided for and provision was made for joinder of new actions to the Group.

29.09 The claimants were ordered to serve a Master Statement of Claim and the defendants to respond with a Master Defence. This was to be concluded by late October 1994. Discovery was to be given in relation to common issues identified in those pleadings fourteen days after close of pleadings. The defendants took issue with the pleading of the Master Statement of Claim and appealed to the Court of Appeal which, on 10 November 1994, dismissed the appeal but ordered that the Master Statement of Claim be re-served pleading particulars of the steps the defendants should have taken to avoid injuring its employees.

29.10 Written factual evidence as to those common issues was to be disclosed by 1 March 1995 by which time medical and other expert evidence was also to be exchanged. Lead actions were to be selected by service of a claimants list by 1 April 1995, with the defendant allowed liberty to seek amendment. Lead actions were to be set down on 1 May 1995 and at that point all other actions were to be stayed. It was ordered that the trial of the lead actions would commence on 2 October 1995. Nine lead cases were selected, albeit after a contested hearing.

29.11 The Order provided for costs sharing and by a separate schedule sought to regularise the pleadings in individual cases during the period up to the stay of such actions, which was immediately after selection of lead cases. It was thought that this would allow for provision of relevant details about individual claims to assist in the lead case selection. The further particulars of claims included detail as to periods of employment, tools used, the amount of time tools were used and for what activities, together with detailed particulars of the onset, nature, and extent of injuries, provided for in a standard form of schedule. The procedure for individual cases also determined the broad content required of the medical report served in support of each individual pleading and for the provision of certain particulars that would go to subsequent quantification of special damage and future loss. There was also a provision for detailed, though standardised, particularisation of limitation issues.

E. The Trials and Appeals

29.12 It is believed that this was the first case in which a comprehensive Order for directions has been given in a multi-party action providing for inception of the group through to trial. It is to the credit of those involved that the trial started in October 1995 without appreciable slippage of the timetable. However, the parties agreed immediately prior to that trial that there was a genuine preliminary issue of substance and upon joint application His Honour Judge Stephenson determined to hear that preliminary issue as follows:

> From what date, if at all, ought the defendants to have recognised:
> (i) that the work with the tools complained of in these nine actions gave rise to a foreseeable risk of VWF, and
> (ii) that effective precautions to guard against that risk could and ought to have been taken in respect of that work

29.13 In January 1996, following an eight-week trial of this preliminary issue, His Honour Judge Stephenson handed down a closely typed fifty-two-page judgment in favour of the claimants answering the preliminary issues as follows:

> (1) 1 January 1973;
> (2) In respect of warnings, system and routine examination, 1 January 1975. In respect of rotation of job, 1 January 1976. Of adaptation of tools or eradicating the job, I cannot make any findings save that it would be after 1 January 1976.

29.14 The defendant immediately appealed to the Court of Appeal, arguing that the date provided in answer to the first question was wrong because:

> In essence the defendants assert that they had no reason to 'believe' that their operations

(underground or on the surface) carried with them any significant risk of VWF which required them to take preventative or precautionary action.[2]

29.15 This was the principal issue although the answer to the second question was also subject to appeal. The Court of Appeal dismissed the appeal but indicated that the following matters remained open:

(a) whether he suffered excessive exposure to vibrating tools and equipment;
(b) whether the defendants negligently failed to take effective precautions to prevent, avoid or reduce such excessive exposure;
(c) whether he suffered occupational white finger in consequence of the defendants' negligence.

In each such case all questions of causation, the quantum of damages (if any) and limitation remain open for decision.

29.16 Despite having lost the generic breach of duty and causation arguments and having failed on appeal the defendant determined to fight on, placing substantial faith in the reference made by the Court of Appeal to excessive exposure, and subsequently argued that the claimants had to establish excessive exposure as vibration over and above an established safe limit. As no one knew at the time what exposure was excessive the claimants should fail. The evidence demonstrated that the defendant had failed to co-operate in national research into levels of exposure and the Judge said of its approach to this issue: 'the argument that because they did not know, there was nothing they could do, seems to me to verge on the cynical'.[3]

29.17 The trial of the nine lead actions came back before the Court on 3 March 1997, concluding on 17 June 1997 with judgment delivered on 30 September 1997. The defendant made a payment into court in each of the nine lead actions. The potential consequence of this, if claimants were minded to accept, would have been the collapse of the lead case litigation prior to the further trial to address breach causation, individual causation, and quantum. As a consequence the claimants applied to the Lord Chief Justice seeking Orders that there should be no compromise of lead actions without leave of the Court, that the monies paid into Court should be paid out forthwith, and no further sums should be tendered nor any other form of offer of settlement made without leave of the Court. The Lord Chief Justice said of the lead cases that:

> It is of obvious importance that they should represent a genuine cross-section, in particular so far as the strengths and weaknesses of different cases are concerned. The reason for this is obvious. If the strongest case were to fail, then it would necessarily follow that the plaintiffs would have a very poor chance of success in weaker cases. If, on the other hand, the weakest case were to succeed, the defendants would recognise that they had little chance of successfully defeating the stronger cases.

29.18 He remarked on the benefits of common issues:

> The course of identifying common issues with a Master Statement of Claim and Defence, and the identification of lead cases, should lead to advantages for at least three groups of people. The first is the plaintiffs who are saved the risk, expense and labour of preparing and contesting thousands of individual actions. There should also be a corresponding benefit to the

---

[2] Court of Appeal transcript, 28 Nov 1996 per Judge LJ.
[3] HHJ Stephenson, 30 Sept 1997.

defendants who are themselves saved the risk, expense and labour of resisting thousands of individual actions. There is also—and this is not unimportant—a public benefit since the capacity of the courts to hear and determine thousands of cases is limited and there are obvious implications in terms both of costs and public resources. There is also a public interest in the just resolution of claims of this sort.

29.19 After reciting the usual consequences of failing to beat a payment into court but identifying the overall discretion provided by section 51 of the Supreme Court Act 1981, the Lord Chief Justice held:

It is in my judgment quite clear that a different approach is called for in managed group litigation of this kind. Just as a lead case should not be chosen because the plaintiff is legally aided, but because his or her case is a suitable vehicle for testing certain factual issues, so a lead plaintiff's failure to accept a payment into court in his or her action alone, in the absence of any similar offer applicable to all claims raising similar issues, should not necessarily entitle the defendant to costs if the plaintiff fails both to accept the payment in and to beat it. The correct order for costs depends on the judge's discretion at the end of the day having regard to all relevant circumstances in the context of the group litigation. If the plaintiffs even in this context reject an offer of compromise made across the board which the court felt should have been accepted, then that no doubt will weigh in favour of the defendants who made the offer and against the plaintiffs who reject it. If, on the other hand, the defendants were to be justly suspected of seeking to wreck or obstruct plans for the orderly, efficient and cost-effective conduct of the litigation by means of common issues and group actions, then that is something which the court would undoubtedly and properly bear in mind when the question of costs came to be decided.

29.20 The Lord Chief Justice went on to find that the Court lacked the power to make the Orders sought but that the trial judge had power under section 51 of the Supreme Court Act 1981, balancing the benefit of lead case trial against the interest of individual claimants faced with an offer suggesting that it may be appropriate that should a claimant fail to beat a payment in the usual Order should not be made. The Lord Chief Justice directed that his judgment and the consequent Order should not be made known to the trial judge until after judgment had been delivered but prior to any decision being made as to costs. In the event, recourse to the judgment was not necessary because the claimants who succeeded beat the payments into court tendered.

29.21 At the subsequent trial the remaining common issue of breach of causation was resolved in the claimant's favour and damages were awarded to seven of the nine lead claimants. One lead claimant failed having been unable to establish that his disease progressed beyond the date of guilty knowledge determined on the first trial of the preliminary issue. One other claimant failed for matters entirely idiosyncratic to his case. The judge ordered that the defendant pay all of the common costs despite two lead claimants having lost. The defendant appealed for a second time to the Court of Appeal.

29.22 The defendant's second appeal took issue with virtually every point in respect of the seven successful claimants. By the time the appeal was heard the defendant was facing in total 25,000 similar claims brought by former employees. The defendant changed its counsel team between service of the Notice of Appeal and the hearing. Many of the issues contained within the original Notice of Appeal were dropped. Indeed, by the opening of the appeal the defendant's position as described in the subsequent judgment was as follows:

The defendants were prepared to accept that they had correctly been held liable to the seven individual plaintiffs who were found to have been suffering from VWF consequent on their employment with the defendants and exposure to vibrating tools after January 1973. The main issue which Mr Walker wished this Court to resolve was the basis of the judge's conclusion on exposure on which the outcome of many of the other claims depends. He conceded that in the light of their proved exposure to vibrating equipment after January 1973, arrangements should have been in place to rotate the jobs of all these seven plaintiffs, with the exception of Stokoe, and thus reduce their exposure, and that liability was also established in those cases, including Stokoe, where the judge had found that a warning would have led the individual plaintiff's exposure to be reduced or avoided. Nevertheless Mr Walker contended that further claims could not be sustained merely because the employee could point to some exposure beyond the level properly described as 'de minimis'. This was precisely the test held by the judge to be appropriate, and Mr Walker submitted that he was wrong.[4]

29.23 Following close analysis the defendant's appeal was dismissed. The defendant also sought to challenge the levels of award of general damages and some awards for handicap on the labour market. The Court of Appeal endorsed the awards of general damages and only interfered in two cases in so far as awards for handicap on the labour market were concerned. The levels of general damages approved by the Court of Appeal realigned awards for this condition, which had been low.

F. Handling Agreement

29.24 Without prejudice negotiations had been continuing with the representatives of the defendant since early 1997 with a view to seeking to negotiate an arrangement for the subsequent assessment and resolution of the many outstanding claims. In January 1998 the DTI assumed responsibility for the health care liabilities of the former British Coal which was privatised by the Coal Industry Act of 1994. In 1998 His Honour Judge Stephenson retired from the bench and Smith J was assigned to the Group Action. In view of the slow progress of negotiations after the second Court of Appeal judgment in July 1998 the claimants made application to Smith J in November 1998. At the hearing the Judge indicated a willingness to oversee the litigation and, if necessary, to try and arbitrate any discrete issues that could not be resolved by negotiation. An Order was made that redefined the post-trial continuing group of claims. This judicial impetus subsequently assisted in breaking the logjam and finally, in January 1999, a claims Handling Agreement was put before Smith J and attracted her approval. There are now over 50,000 claimants and the value of claims has been estimated to exceed £0.5 billion.

29.25 Thereafter, the coal mining contractors and other coal mine owners were drawn into the litigation. Following interlocutory application to Smith J with a view to seeking to resolve their liability after a number of hearings and directions and a further Practice Direction (29 July 1999) redefining the scope of that of 12 January 1994, the issue was driven towards trial in default of agreement. However, upon the DTI compromising its contribution to the potential liability of contractors and, where appropriate, subsequent owners, all those defendants accepted the Handling Agreement as the method of resolution of the claims.

---

[4] Court of Appeal transcript, 31 July 1998 per Judge LJ.

29.26 Following approval of the terms of the Handling Arrangement by Smith J in January 1999 the parties encountered practical difficulties in operating that arrangement in the context of subsequent medical evidence that identified potential alternative medical conditions that may have caused the symptoms complained of and also in the appropriate assessment and valuation where appropriate for claims for services. Over the course of a series of interlocutory hearings Smith J managed continuing negotiations that led to agreement which will lead to amendment of the Handling Arrangement to address these particular issues. Presently, the post-trial case management of the continuing claims remains, with Smith J retaining jurisdiction to review from time to time the operation of the Handling Arrangement.

30

BRITISH COAL: RESPIRATORY DISEASE LITIGATION

Andrew Tucker[1]

> This employers' liability case from the second half of the 1990s was a notable win for the claimants, resulting in financial liability estimated at £2 billion to former mineworkers. It was an interesting example of judicial control, not least in relation to timing: some 100 individual cases were commenced between 1989 and 1995 but, following judicial co-ordination through a group mechanism, an enormous discovery and evidence-taking exercise was completed at considerable speed and judgment given by February 1998. The Judge's force of personality also encouraged the twenty-seven firms representing claimants to consolidate into a Steering Committee and resolve their differences. Eight lead actions were selected for trial: this would not have been possible without the fact that all statements of claim and defences, as well as disclosure of medical records, had been undertaken prior to the formation of the group. Given the decisions by the parties on the effect of notifying claims on limitation and the fact that the cohort of mineworkers was identified, questions of cut-off dates were not relevant. The normal techniques of a register and the normal orders on costs were adopted. An interesting factor was that of mobility, with factual evidence being taken in a number of different locations.

A. Background

Of the diseases that have afflicted people as a consequence of the environment in which they have earned a living, pneumoconiosis in coal miners is perhaps the most famous of all, rooted in folklore, and recognised as an adverse consequence of the inhalation of coal mine dust for most of this century.[2] Perhaps surprisingly to the layman the condition, although highly undesirable, is not disabling in the first three categories of classification. However, it is a progressive disease and therefore early identification of onset coupled with a reduction in subsequent dust exposure may avoid the fourth, seriously disabling and

30.01

---

[1] Partner, Irwin Mitchell.
[2] See reports of the Medical Research Council 1942, 1943, and 1945 in response to the high incidence of disease in South Wales.

potentially fatal, category, pulmonary massive fibrosis. This renowned occupational disease (and the risk of explosion presented by coal dust) led to the enactment of statutory duties. The coal industry was nationalised under the Coal Industry Nationalisation Act in 1946, which imposed upon the National Coal Board (as it was then)[3] the express obligation of 'securing . . . the safety, health and welfare of persons in their employment'.[4] This, of course, is no more than a reflection of common law principles, and was followed by the Mines and Quarries Act of 1954, which provided that:

> It shall be the duty of the manager of every mine to ensure that, in connection with the getting, dressing and transporting of minerals below ground in the mine, the giving off of . . . dust of such character and in such quantity as to be likely to be injurious to the persons employed is minimised.[5]

30.02   The recently nationalised industry, as a consequence of legislation and by direction of Government,[6] embarked upon an exercise, probably unique in scale and complexity, in occupational health. In 1952 it launched the process that led to five surveys[7] of twenty-five collieries[8] known as the Pneumoconiosis Field Research (PFR), with the objective of establishing the environmental conditions necessary to avoid disability caused by dust. This was followed in 1956 by a decision to commence the Periodic X-Ray Scheme, a survey by chest X-ray of all of the men employed at all of the collieries in the United Kingdom every five years. This Scheme served the purposes of providing a medical check-up of each miner's health and of assessing the effectiveness of dust suppression by recording the prevalence of disease.[9] These projects also ran in parallel with the collection of data from all collieries as to levels of respirable mine dust. The data was collated by the PFR, which became Institute of Occupational Medicine in 1969, and which, until recent times, was a subsidiary of the nationalised industry. The primary object of the exercise was to seek to correlate respirable dust to the risk of onset of pneumoconiosis and the progression of that disease.

B. The First Cases

30.03   It had been suspected since the early 1970s, based on analyses of the PFR data, that coal mine dust may also be the cause of both chronic bronchitis and emphysema. Indeed, these conditions were first considered for prescription as industrial diseases in 1985 and eventually were prescribed in 1993.[10] In parallel to these developments litigation commenced

---

[3] The NCB became British Coal Corporation by s 1 of the Coal Industry Act 1987.
[4] Section 1(4).
[5] Section 74(1). See also s 74(2).
[6] The Ministry of Fuel & Power established the National Joint Pneumoconiosis Committee in 1947 drawing members from the Ministry, the NCB, and the trade unions.
[7] The first survey began in 1953 and lasted until 1958. The final round was commenced in 1973.
[8] By the fifth round only 10 collieries of the original 25 remained open.
[9] The Scheme began in 1959. The first round lasted until 1963 and X-rayed 462,899 men. The final round ran from 1990 to 1993.
[10] See Industrial Injuries Advisory Council reports 1988 (Cm 379), 1992 (Cm 2091), and 1996 (Cm 3240).

and on 20 December 1989 Philips J (as he then was) gave judgment[11] in an action brought by the personal representatives of John Charles Tanner, a former employee of the nationalised coal industry, who worked for his entire life at Snowdon Colliery in the Kent coalfield. It was alleged that he had suffered from pneumoconiosis, chronic bronchitis, and emphysema arising from tortious exposure to dust at work. In this unitary action Philips J held that although the personal representatives had established relevant breaches of common law and statutory duty at Snowdon colliery they had failed to do so at the higher levels of the NCB and had also failed to establish medical causation in relation to chronic bronchitis and emphysema. The plaintiff appealed to the Court of Appeal and in a judgment handed down on 20 June 1999[12] an award of damages was made for chronic bronchitis during Mr Tanner's life which was not found to have been the cause of death. General damages for chronic bronchitis are modest. Of the conditions, emphysema is significantly disabling and can lead to early death. The industry viewed this result as a considerable success because breach of duty had only been established at a local level and the main disease state, emphysema, had been found not to be caused by exposure to coal mine dust. As there have been approximately 2,000 operational coal mines managed by the nationalised industry over the period since 1946 producing varying types of coal in varying geologies by varying working methods, following the judgment of the Court of Appeal the prospects of any subsequent plaintiffs establishing liability on a comprehensive nation-wide basis must have appeared extremely remote.

However, science moved on and the Industrial Injuries Advisory Council, following consideration of further published studies, reported in 1992 to the Secretary of State for the Department of Social Security in favour of prescription of chronic bronchitis and emphysema as industrial diseases. **30.04**

In 1989 another case was issued in respect of chronic bronchitis and emphysema, this time on behalf of a living plaintiff who had been employed in the industry in South Wales. Over the next six years other cases were issued sporadically throughout England and Wales. **30.05**

C. Steps towards Co-ordination

These claims were not co-ordinated in any way and were brought by firms of solicitors instructed by individuals in all of the main coal fields. By 1995, over 100 cases had been issued and following liaison between the solicitors representing British Coal Corporation and solicitors for some of the plaintiffs a summons was brought before Curtis J sitting in the High Court in Swansea which was heard on 2 October 1995. Amongst other things, the Judge directed that the defendant should issue appropriate summonses to bring all litigants before a High Court judge so that directions might be given 'as to the management and trial of 114 of the current proceedings'. Immediately prior to this hearing a first meeting of the plaintiffs' solicitors had taken place. At that time twenty-seven firms of solicitors were instructed. Following a series of meetings those firms that were prepared to meet **30.06**

---

[11] Unreported.
[12] Unreported.

selected a Co-ordinating Group of five firms to lead the litigation. At this stage there had been no significant advertising for claims although it is believed that one or two members of the Solicitors Group had placed advertisements in regional publications.

30.07 Turner J was nominated as the Judge responsible for the management of the interlocutory phase and for the trial of the litigation. The case first came before him on 10 November 1995. The defendant was seeking a preliminary trial of medical causation only and had persuaded a firm of solicitors representing a number of plaintiffs that this was the appropriate course. Although a Co-ordinating Group of solicitors had been recently formed, various plaintiffs were represented by various counsel and some of the claimants' solicitors were opposed to co-ordination. Those representing the bulk of the English plaintiffs argued that a preliminary trial of medical causation was misconceived and that instead lead actions should be selected with due regard to geographical diversity with a view to determining both liability and causation in one trial. Turner J concurred and directed that 'a number of lead actions be selected which will raise for determination the greatest number of medical and liability issues which can be achieved'. The case was adjourned for further directions on 21 December 1995.

30.08 By December 1995 the co-ordination of plaintiffs had further consolidated but there remained a small number of dissident firms. As a consequence, the Order made on 21 December, whilst otherwise comprehensive, did not go so far as to identify the extent of the Solicitors Group and its Co-ordinating Committee nor did it provide for costs sharing. The Judge made it clear that in his view the issue of representation should be resolved quickly and preferably outside court. He went on to make an Order that formally consolidated the plaintiffs into a group bringing proceedings in respect of chronic obstructive airways disease (an umbrella term including chronic bronchitis, emphysema, small airways disease) and asthma. The group of plaintiffs that had issued proceedings were identified, the defendant named, and the group litigation styled as 'British Coal Corporation Respiratory Disease Litigation'. It was determined that the litigation would be resolved by a trial of lead actions 'selected . . . with a view to disposing, so far as possible, with the issues that arise in this litigation'.

D. Case Management Decisions

30.09 Thereafter, a timetable for the trial of the lead action was directed. The plaintiffs were ordered to propose candidate lead actions by mid-February 1996, the defendant was ordered to either agree and/or propose counter-candidates, and, failing agreement, the matter would return to the Court which would order selection of lead cases at the end of February 1996. Following selection of lead cases the other actions were stayed. Selection of lead cases was facilitated by discovery of medical records having been given to the defendant in the majority of the litigated cases prior to the formation of the group action. Also, in virtually all issued cases medical evidence had been served on behalf of the claimants and in a minority of the cases the defendant had obtained and disclosed condition and prognoses reports. Following imposition of the stay, interlocutory activity, including disclosure of records and service of medical reports, ceased in respect of the non-lead cases. Eight lead cases were selected, seven of which were proposed by the plaintiffs and agreed by the defendant with one case proposed by the defendant and agreed by the plaintiffs. The defendant apparently felt able to make a judgment as to lead cases despite not having obtained its own medical expert opinion upon the entire pool of litigated claims.

Discovery, a colossal exercise which ran into millions of pages of documents, located at a number of different archive centres, was ordered to commence with the service of the defendant's lists of different classifications of documents (four in total) in March 1996. **30.10**

Factual witness statements were to be exchanged mutually at the beginning of June 1996, with medical reports addressing individual issues to be exchanged at the end of April 1996. Experts' reports as to common issues and as to liability were to be exchanged by mid-August 1996. **30.11**

The trial was fixed to commence in Cardiff at the end of October 1996, subsequently to move to Sheffield and then London by the beginning of 1997. **30.12**

The remarkable aspects of the Order of 21 December 1995 are, first, the tight timetable to trial given the vast discovery which had to be inspected, collated, reduced in scale, and made available to experts for the preparation of their reports on the common issues which, in turn, fell to be exchanged within eight months of the date of the Order. Secondly, the mobility between trial centres, the object of which was the convenience of the factual witnesses (primarily but not exclusively the plaintiffs) and the expert witnesses. Five of the eight selected lead cases were from South Wales and the remaining three from the Nottinghamshire, Yorkshire, and Durham coal fields respectively. Factual evidence was therefore taken in Cardiff from the Welsh plaintiffs and in Sheffield from the English plaintiffs. Expert evidence was taken in London. The third significant feature of the Order was a direction that 'any payment into Court in respect of any of the lead actions shall be disregarded for the purpose of determining the costs of the lead actions'. Surprisingly this was an uncontentious provision, the purpose of which was to ensure that a trial of all of the lead actions took place unless the parties arrived at terms of settlement on a comprehensive basis. In other words, the litigation could not be disrupted by 'buying off' the lead plaintiffs. **30.13**

It is notable that, unlike many of the group actions which preceded this litigation, in this case there was no commonality of pleading. The individual cases had been pleaded and defences had been served prior to consolidation of the group. **30.14**

In accordance with the Judge's firm indication given at the hearing in December 1995, the Solicitors Group resolved its few remaining differences, and on 11 January 1996 a further Order was made by Turner J that formally constituted the Solicitors Group and its representative Co-ordinating Group of five firms (which became six in February 1999 when an additional firm joined by consent). This Order went on to provide for a definition of common costs and for the sharing of those costs between plaintiffs who were recorded on a register, brought up-to-date quarterly. Plaintiffs' liabilities for costs *inter partes* were ordered to be several and costs were to be apportioned as between plaintiffs on the register during each quarter. In the event that liability arose whereby plaintiffs had to meet defendant's common costs apportionment would be on a similar basis. **30.15**

30.16 The litigation was funded by the South Wales branch of the National Association of Colliery Overmen, Deputies and Shotfirers (NACODS) and by the Legal Aid Board, apportioned according to respective funding of the group of litigated cases, namely one-third and two-thirds respectively. No other area of NACODS was prepared to fund the litigation, a position adopted by all of the NUM areas.

30.17 Four of the five co-ordinating firms represented solely English plaintiffs and, because all of the documents in respect of the English plaintiffs fell to be inspected during the course of 1996, these four firms concentrated primarily upon completing that task. The one Welsh firm on the Co-ordinating Group had made good progress with the inspection of documents prior to the formation of the group litigation and focused upon concluding that task. One English firm, Irwin Mitchell, briefed counsel in respect of the English litigants' issues and the Welsh firm, Hugh James Ford Simey, briefed a separate counsel team as to the Welsh issues. The two firms worked jointly on the numerous common issues, broadly instructing one counsel team to address liability and the other to focus on medical causation.

E. Limitation, Cut-off, and Publicity

30.18 The parties agreed that the impact of the Limitation Act 1980 would be suspended upon written notification of individual claims to an agreed format. Any limitation defence existing at the time notification was given would remain open to the defendant but the period following notification up to the determination of the limitation amnesty (as it became known) would not be taken into account in calculating the passage of time for the purpose of that Act. The objective was to avoid a proliferation of proceedings after selection of lead cases. This agreement remained in place post-judgment and throughout the subsequent negotiation of a settlement scheme (which is discussed in more detail below). Although the possibility of a cut-off date for closing the group was raised during the interlocutory phase of the litigation it was not pressed by the defendant, perhaps because there was no significant notification of claims in accordance with the agreed process prior to judgment. Thereafter, the number of claims increased rapidly following widespread media coverage of the outcome and consequential advertising by many firms of solicitors. Given the substantial influx of cases post-judgment, it was fortuitous that a cut-off date was not ordered before trial. No doubt a similar influx of cases would have occurred which would have deflected significant resources on both sides from trial preparation.

F. Trial

30.19 One of the most noteworthy features of the litigation is that although there was some slippage in the pre-trial timetable it is not significant in the greater scheme of things and the trial commenced as scheduled. The trial took up 102 days of court time, commencing on 28 October 1996 and concluding in September 1997. Judgment was formally handed down on 6 February 1998, in favour of the plaintiffs in respect of generic issues. The defendant was found to be liable for breach of statutory duty in all of the collieries, in each of the geographic administrative areas into which the nationalised industry was divided, and also at a national level. Medical causation was established in respect of chronic bronchitis and emphysema but on the individual facts of the lead cases no finding was thought necessary by Turner J in respect of small airways disease. With regard to asthma, causation *de novo* was not established but temporary exacerbation was found. Therefore, one plaintiff who was seeking to establish that asthma was caused by exposure to dust failed in his individual claim and a further plaintiff failed in his individual claim because it was not established that he was exposed to sufficient levels of coal mine dust. This was a comprehensive success for the plaintiffs. The defence at all levels was demolished with particular judicial criticism directed towards the nature of the defence of the generic medical issues, based as it was on an attempt to discredit the PFR data.

G. Costs

At the hearing on 6 February 1998, the Judge ordered that all of the costs, both common and individual, be paid by the defendant notwithstanding that two plaintiffs had lost individually. This was because the cases were selected as lead actions representative of others and liability was established in all cases which was of general benefit. The Judge said: 30.20

> Following the resolution of all issues of liability on quantum it now falls for the Court to deal with the question of costs. It will be recalled that in the formal judgments in respect of the individual Plaintiffs all, except Mr Griffiths and Mr Clay, won their actions. The reasons why Mr Griffiths' and Mr Clay's cases failed was not for want of proof of wrong doing on the part of the Defendants but because of their inability to prove that the medical conditions of which they complained had been caused by wrongful exposure to mine dust. It was in the nature of this litigation, once the parties had decided that it would proceed by way of lead actions, that there would be included within the lead actions those which raised the maximum number of issues both in regard to liability and quantum, with a view not just to determining those actions, but insofar as was practicable, issues that would be of benefit to all of the many actions and claims which yet remain to be tried and made respectively . . . it seems to me that the justice of the case requires that the Plaintiffs do recover their costs.

The Judge also ordered that the defendant pay costs on the indemnity basis in respect of the medical causation issue, saying: 30.21

> The generic medical issue in large measure concerned the extent to which the Court should place reliance upon the papers and studies which resulted from the Pneumoconiosis Field Research. It will be recalled that the epidemiological study was set up by the Defendants. It will be recalled that at some stage the management of that study was passed to the Institute of Occupational Medicine, which at its inception was funded entirely by the Defendants and latterly to a partial extent. That study ran for a great number of years and produced a number of papers which, as I said in the course of my judgment, have been regarded not only nationally but internationally as being of high quality. The Defendants have said by way of submission that they are or were fully entitled to challenge the results of that study, if and insofar as their challenge was based upon medical evidence which was not, on its face, obviously to be rejected. In other words, the Defendants were saying that they should not be called to account if they proceeded in the conduct of this litigation on medical evidence which was available to them. In general terms, such an approach can certainly be justified. In the course of my judgment at page 173, I said: 'As has been noted above, the thrust of British Coal's

generic medical report had been to attack the PFR root and branch. At the conclusion of the evidence, both written and oral, by Dr Jacobsen it should have been clear to all, except the blinkered, that the strategy of full frontal attack on the PFR was bound to fail and that if any progress was to be made, a fresh and more focused approach would be required. Doctors Morgan & Pearson, however, attempted to hold the basis of their written reports. This was seriously in error and, in my judgment, resulted in both eminent physicians losing intellectual and professional credibility.' My criticisms, however, do not stop there. For it is not to be overlooked that the PFR studies and papers written on the basis of those studies had, as I have already said, been universally acclaimed. In general terms, it can be said that no serious challenge to those studies and the papers which they generated was made until this litigation was mounted. Before I come to my conclusion, there is another feature which has to be considered, already hinted at, which is that the defendant corporation was a knowledgeable party, in the sense that it maintained its own department concerned with occupational hygiene. Not only that, but to an extent it had itself adopted into its dust standards some of the workings of the PFR, notably the interim standards study conducted by Dr Jacobsen, formerly Deputy Director of the Institute of Occupational Medicine. Those features, in my judgment, mean that it would be erroneous to approach this case on the basis that the defendants were perfectly entitled, without risk, to say, 'We will put the results of the PFR in issue', when until the time of this litigation no serious issue or challenge had been mounted in respect of any of its workings. It is that factor, coupled with the decision to continue the challenge through Dr Morgan and Dr Pearson after Dr Rudd and Dr Jacobsen had completed their evidence, that, in my judgment, amounted to unreasonable conduct of this litigation. It is that feature which, in my judgment, requires that the burden of proof as between standard and indemnity should be reversed in favour of the Plaintiffs at least to some extent.

H. Comments on Case Management

30.22 In an appendix to his judgment Turner J expressed views on case management, making the following observations:

> It is now accepted wisdom that effective case management of litigation on this scale and nature is essential if a speedy and efficient resolution is to be achieved. Here such considerations were of special importance since many of the plaintiffs are dying or enduring serious disability from the disease in respect of which they or their dependants sue. My approach to the management of this case has been to set broad parameters as to the manner in which the litigation should proceed and, wherever possible, leave the detailed aspects of the case management issues to the parties to agree between themselves always subject to the Court retaining an overall power to approve or set alternatives. It has only been necessary to intervene where there has been disagreement between the parties as to the course to follow.
>
> In general this intuitive method can be seen to have been successful in that discovery ... which has been on a massive scale was (almost) completed to time, expert evidence again was (almost) completed within the scheduled programme but, notwithstanding, trial began on the date set. The parties are to be applauded for their efforts to secure these interlocutory goals. It was clearly understood that despite the 'hands off' approach, the parties would have come under much closer supervision and control by the Court had they not delivered as they said they would. One outstanding advantage of this approach was that during the initial interlocutory stages the parties themselves were cognizant of the issues and the resources available to them, in contradistinction to the position of the Court. As will become apparent, most of the interlocutory orders were made by consent and the time set therein was very nearly always observed . . .
>
> On 10 November 1995 I heard argument on this matter from all relevant counsel. The issue

can be put simply as whether the question the Court should be called upon to decide should be 'can coal dust cause any identified medical condition?' I declined to approve the trial of this or any similar issue. The Court is not equipped to deal with or adjudicate upon hypothetical questions. So it was that the parties acceded to the suggestion that there should be trials of not more than twelve lead actions which would raise for determination the greatest number of medical issues and liability issues that could sensibly be achieved with the expressed hope that the decisions reached on those issues would enable the large number of the other waiting claims to be negotiated between the parties if the decision on the generic issues was to be decided broadly in favour of the plaintiff. The alternative course was to likely to lead to prolongation of the litigation rather than its early disposal and would increase the overall cost of disposing of these matters. So it was that on that date the Court ordered that 'a number of lead actions should be selected which would raise for determination the greatest number of medical and liability issues which can be achieved'.

Between the interlocutory hearings and at my request I was kept informed of the progress of the action by monthly reports provided by British Coal, in conjunction with the plaintiffs. Monthly reports were provided for: February/March, April, May and June 1996. This method has the benefit of forcing the two sides to review on a monthly basis the 'state of play' in regard to the interlocutory timetable and allowed me to be informed of any relevant developments or the lack thereof. The Court was therefore in a position to intervene if it perceived the risk of delay as likely to affect the trial date. This approach avoided the need for regular case management hearings and the costs which would have arisen . . .

The Judge retained supervisory control of the litigation post-judgment, encouraging the parties to resolve the outstanding claims by agreement. There followed some seven further case management hearings between February 1997 and 29 July 1999. During this period intensive negotiations took place, resulting in the agreement of a scheme for the settlement of individual claims including the assessment of damages, both general and special, in agreed sums distinguished according to disability and the factual circumstances of individual cases. The Handling Agreement, as it is known, extends to 413 pages. At the inception of the group litigation 167 plaintiffs had commenced proceedings. By the time the Handling Agreement was signed on 24 September 1999, 75,000 claims had been notified, a reflection that at its peak the National Coal Board was the biggest single employer in the Western world, at one time employing 710,000 men. The Judge has retained oversight of the operation of the Agreements with 'review' hearings to take place biannually. **30.23**

This litigation demonstrates that multi-party actions brought raising complex issues of liability and causation by a disparate group of plaintiffs can succeed against a substantial well-resourced defendant. The case also demonstrates that the judicial system in England and Wales is capable, even in the absence of specific rules of court, of managing litigation on this scale to trial within a short period of time and thereafter is able to ensure that the parties conclude a fair and reasonable settlement of the following claims based upon that judgment. **30.24**

31

NORPLANT LITIGATION

Arundel McDougall[1]

In a number of ways the Norplant product liability story illustrates an important change in the courts' attitude towards case management in the later 1990s. The plaintiffs' initial co-ordination of a group and proposals for case management were symptomatic of the absence of a multi-party rule (although the plaintiffs did unsuccessfully attempt to persuade the Nottingham County Court to issue a Case Management Order in respect of all prospective Norplant cases before any proceedings were served) and of the policy of the Legal Aid Board only to fund investigation of a generic case rather than individual cases. The Board's multi-party arrangements did, however, facilitate the emergence of a single firm of solicitors as (in this case a sole) co-ordinating firm.

Initially, the tactics of the co-ordinating solicitors were to suggest case management based on a generic approach to liability and agreement of a 'compensation grid' scheme. The co-ordinating solicitors eventually served a Master Statement of Claim as the pleading in the first case and intended that this should be the format for all future cases, without any requirement to plead individual case details. These and other tactics had the effect of engendering a climate of suspicion rather than co-operation between the opposing sides.

Once the defendant obtained transfer of the cases from the Nottingham County Court to the High Court in London, the co-ordinating judge became actively involved in case management. He rejected the plaintiffs' Master Statement of Claim approach and instead required all plaintiffs to register by a fixed cut-off date so that the numbers, scope, and issues of the litigation would become clear, with each plaintiff serving 'standard minimum requirements' giving sufficiently particularised facts of her individual circumstances, together with medical records and a medical report. Out of the cohort of approximately 280 plaintiffs, ten lead cases were selected (five by each party, in default of agreement) which were theoretically representative of the range of issues involved, although in fact the lead cases were selected for partisan reasons as the parties' 'best' and 'worst' cases out of the cohort

---

[1] Partner, Ashurst Morris Crisp.

> and were not truly representative of all the issues raised. The co-ordinating Judge required the parties to list the 'issues' in the case and it was only following service of the plaintiff's List that the basis of their legal and scientific case became clear. In fact, the allegations had significantly narrowed from the original broad unspecific approach taken in the Master Particulars of Claim although the allegations still suffered from legal weaknesses.
>
> One of the most notable features of the case was the high proportion of privately funded plaintiffs in the cohort: approximately one-third. In previous group actions, the percentage of privately funded as opposed to legally aided plaintiffs had typically been 2–5 per cent. In this action, a large number of individual plaintiffs were at risk of liability for a share of the defendant's costs, which were likely to exceed the cases' individual quantum, which was low. When combined with the relatively small number of plaintiffs, these factors led to an unfavourable cost-benefit balance, something which, despite numerous and lengthy representations, was only recognised by the Legal Aid Board at a very late stage, shortly after exchange of expert evidence and only a few weeks before the trial date, at which point legal aid was withdrawn and the case collapsed.
>
> As a footnote, the product was subsequently withdrawn from the market by the UK distributor who cited one of its reasons as the commercial damage which had been done to the product's reputation as a result of what it strongly felt to be unjustified litigation and the resultant publicity.

A. The Product

31.01 Norplant is a subdermal contraceptive implant. It consists of six silastic capsules filled with levonorgestrel, a synthetic progestogen, designed to give up to five years' contraceptive protection by releasing a low sustained dose of the hormone into the bloodstream. Levonorgestrel has been used for some decades as the active ingredient in several brands of contraceptive pill. The six capsules are inserted in the subcutaneous layer on the inside of the woman's non-dominant arm, between the shoulder and the elbow. Insertion and extraction requires a minor surgical operation, under local anaesthetic, by a health care professional who has been trained in the method.

31.02 The product was developed over a period of twenty years by the Population Council, a US non-profit making organisation devoted to developing the science of population control. The product was licensed in the USA in 1990 and in the United Kingdom by the Medicines Control Agency in May 1993, where it was distributed by Roussel Laboratories Ltd (Roussel) until October 1999 when it was discontinued for commercial reasons. It is currently licensed in over sixty countries.

31.03 The product was a prescription only medicine. It was most commonly prescribed by general practitioners. About 10 per cent of prescriptions were through family planning clinics or dispensing doctors. An insertion kit was supplied for doctors. The great majority of women who used the product obtained a dispensing pack, after prescription, from their pharmacy, and then either arranged for a subsequent appointment for insertion or had it inserted immediately. In addition to the product, the dispensing pack contained a patient leaflet, the 'Patient Guide'. At the date of launch in the UK, Norplant was the most effective contraceptive on the market—being almost as effective as surgical sterilisation.

B. The Pre-Litigation Phase

31.04 The product was launched in October 1993. On 18 May 1995, by which stage some 33,000 prescriptions had been written for the product, a press release announced the formation of the Norplant Action Group (NAG). Its objectives were stated to be:

- to provide an information forum for women who were dissatisfied with the product;
- to force Roussel to change its literature;
- to secure compensation for women users who had been 'harmed' by the product's use.

31.05 A media campaign was organised, involving regular appearances on radio broadcasts and phone-ins. An 'early day motion' was put down in the House of Commons by John Heppell, the MP for Nottingham East (where the Action Group was based) seeking revocation of the product licence on grounds of lack of safety but this failed to attract adequate support. Sales fell as a result of sustained adverse media comment. Doctors became less enthusiastic about prescribing Norplant as a result both of fear of litigation and because of the Department of Health's refusal to allow doctors an appropriate fee for inserting the product.

31.06 Co-ordinating solicitors acting for the plaintiffs, Freeth Cartwright Hunt Dickens of Nottingham (Freeth Cartwright), obtained legal aid from the Nottingham Area Office, which became the Area Office responsible for administering all legal aid applications, to carry out generic work on Norplant claims. Individual legal aid certificates were issued, limited to pursuing a claim for personal injuries and/or other losses against Roussel in respect of a breach of the Consumer Protection Act 1987 (the Act) and limited to obtaining individual medical records and proofing each client. Legal aid was granted on the basis that Freeth Cartwright would successfully persuade the Court controlling Norplant claims to issue their draft Case Management Order. Roussel was not informed of these funding details, nor of Freeth Cartwright's approach in July 1995 to the Circuit Administrator of the Oxford and Midlands Circuit in Birmingham. When Roussel found out about this some months later, and realised that Freeth Cartwright had been trying very early on to get the Court to give an *ex parte* case management direction, a climate of suspicion was engendered which affected the next year and a half and explained in part why there was limited co-operation when the plaintiffs tried to agree generic case management directions in the autumn of both 1995 and 1996.

31.07 Freeth Cartwright wrote a letter before action on 10 May 1995 to Roussel alleging that Norplant was a defective product under Part I of the Act and requesting compensation for personal injuries alleged to arise from its use. The alleged injuries included too much bleeding, too little bleeding, weight gain, weight loss, mood swings, depression, acne, hair loss, hair gain, nausea, and other symptoms. Difficulties arose from the facts that these symptoms were, first, known certainly to medical practitioners to be commonly experienced with any method of hormonal contraception and, secondly, mostly explicitly warned against in the Patient Guide and in the prescribing information available to doctors (the data sheet).

31.08 The claims and their management were throughout subject to the restriction of quantum. The average claim, if liability had been established, was only worth £2,000. Claims would not be viable if pursued as unitary actions. Group litigation would only be viable if a sufficient number of plaintiffs were pooled so as to result in acceptable economies of scale.

31.09 A further consequence of the quantum was the then procedural constraint that individual actions under £50,000 had to be issued in the county courts rather than the High Court. An initial benefit of this for the plaintiffs was that Freeth Cartwright could liaise with their local Legal Aid Area Office in Nottingham, and could issue initial proceedings in the Nottingham County Court, both to the inconvenience of the defendant. Freeth Cartwright approached the courts on the basis that a significant number of actions relating to Norplant were about to be launched in the Nottingham County Court, following which, in November 1995, Latham J, presiding judge of the Midland and Oxford Circuit, issued a memorandum to all Combined and County Courts on that circuit relating to the hand-ling of all Norplant cases on a preliminary basis. His Honour Judge Brunning in the Nottingham County Court was to assume supervisory authority for all cases issued within the confines of that circuit, and he was to be assisted by District Judge Beale. This did not cater for cases already issued elsewhere.

31.10 A meeting organised by Freeth Cartwright was held in November 1995 between Freeth Cartwright, for Roussel, Rowe & Maw, for the medical defence organisations, Hempsons and Le Brasseurs, and for the NHS Trusts, Wansbrough Willey Hargrave. The meeting in November was originally intended to be an 'informal' meeting in front of His Honour Judge Brunning in Nottingham County Court 'to discuss the administrative arrangements for the disposal of claims arising out of the use of Norplant'. The potential defendants objected that this was wholly premature and the meeting instead became one solely for the parties' lawyers, not involving the Judge. Freeth Cartwright indicated that several hundred women had consulted various firms of solicitors around the country, and that quantum in any one claim would be small. They tabled a draft Case Management Order intended to be the vehicle for disposing of all claims in the Nottingham County Court on the basis of an approach geared to the determination of generic issues. The prevailing reaction of the potential defendants' advisers was that, as no proceedings had been issued, considerations of case management were premature until the individual cases had been pleaded. Accordingly, the draft Case Management Order was shelved. Freeth Cartwright also sought to secure easier access to medical records from NHS Trusts and indicated the plaintiffs' case on interpretation of the Act, namely that if one expert's report stated that a particular side effect could be caused by Norplant, that would be sufficient to prove causation in every case, rendering individual causation reports unnecessary. Freeth Cartwright also stated that the Legal Aid Board had not decided whether to award a generic contract.

31.11 The tension which dominated the positions put forward by the parties in this pre-litigation phase were similar to other previous group actions: the plaintiffs strove for a procedural framework so as to give maximum tactical advantage to a group which was not officially in existence, the framework being based on advancing a generic case whilst de-emphasising individual case issues; Roussel was preoccupied with efforts to identify the substance of the case against it before concluding on the appropriate case management techniques.

The situation was complicated by uncertainty over the plaintiffs' best approach to the issue of prescribing doctors. Initial consideration favoured their inclusion (on the basis that the product could only be used on prescription, and the prescribing decisions of each physician, coupled with the knowledge which he or she imparted to each plaintiff, were part of the patient's expectations). There were various counter-arguments. The omission of doctors would avoid having to prove individual allegations of clinical negligence. Attacking doctors might adversely affect ongoing doctor-patient relationships. Restricting the attack to the single product licence holder on the basis of strict liability under the Act had advantages of restricting costs and allowing the plaintiffs to argue a relatively simple case from which both the issue of the potential liability of learned intermediaries and evidence of prescribers could be excluded.[2] However, focusing on Roussel's liability left the plaintiffs with the problem that because Norplant was a prescription only medicine, doctors were inevitably very involved in each woman's choice to use the product. Roussel was not permitted to advertise the product direct to women nor to discuss with them their clinical treatment. In the end, just one claim in the Group proceeded in which a doctor had been joined. It appears that this case, a claim of medical negligence against the doctor, resulted in compensation to the plaintiff but because of the application of the legal aid statutory charge, the plaintiff received nothing.[3] After the demise of the group litigation, eight unitary cases continued against doctors.

31.12

The Legal Aid Board invited tenders for a multi-party contract, but not an all works contract, for Norplant litigation and in March 1996 granted the contract to Freeth Cartwright, just after Rowe & Maw had made representations to the Legal Aid Board against the grant of legal aid in the Norplant claims. On 11 July 1996 the Legal Aid Board confirmed that more than ten people were in receipt of legal aid in respect of Norplant claims.

31.13

C. Transfer and Court Control

In October 1996 the co-ordinating solicitors again tried to kick-start the proceedings in the Nottingham County Court. The first summons was issued—but not served—that

31.14

---

[2] The plaintiffs argued that Art 8.1 of Directive 85/374/EEC precluded a learned intermediary defence. The defendant's response was, first, that doctors' advice was one of the relevant factors in considering all the circumstances under the test of defectiveness under Art 6 and, secondly, that the doctor's intervention constituted a *novus actus* which broke the chain of causation. It was said that the only way for a plaintiff to overcome these objections would have been to allege that the doctor had been misled by the company's prescribing literature, which would have required evidence from each doctor and which was not alleged.

[3] Written Answer: *Hansard* HL (11 Nov 1999).

month. With it was sent another draft Case Management Order, modelled closely on the 1995 version. The proposed directions anticipated a group action tried by reference to generic issues. There was still no Group. Efforts were made by the co-ordinating solicitors, without informing the defendant's lawyers, to persuade the District and Circuit judges in Nottingham to give case management directions, premised on there being a group, in the one issued but unserved case without any form of *inter partes* hearing. When Rowe & Maw requested Freeth Cartwright to provide copies of their correspondence with the Court (including Freeth Cartwright's draft Case Management Order and summary of the case) Freeth Cartwright refused to enter into any discussion with Rowe & Maw on the subject, on the basis that Rowe & Maw had objected that any discussion of case management premised on a viable group was inappropriate and premature. This prompted the Nottingham judges to invite both parties to an informal meeting to discuss case management.

31.15 The meeting took place on 29 January 1997. At this meeting it became apparent that Kennedy LJ had asked His Honour Judge Brunning to require both sides to write with their submissions on case management to allow him to consider making a practice direction as to the future conduct of the Norplant claims. Roussel submitted that the two extant claims should be transferred to the High Court in London, that further discussion of case management was inappropriate at this stage, and that each plaintiff should plead her own case. Roussel's submissions also noted that Freeth Cartwright's position had changed to the extent that Freeth Cartwright were now ignoring the pivotal role of doctors.

31.16 The Master Particulars of Claim had been served on 16 January 1997 as the pleading in the first case. These Master Particulars were in the format which had become standard in previous group actions, namely setting out a wide-ranging series of generic allegations about Norplant, followed by formulaic allegations about women's general expectations of safety. The generic allegations were that: progestogen-only contraceptives such as Norplant are only a suitable contraceptive for a small sub-group of women and cannot be characterised as suitable for women in general; the defendant knew that a high percentage of women discontinued use of the product prematurely due to intolerable side effects; the defendant knew, prior to marketing the product, of the incidence and severity of a range of side effects and of possible difficulties in removal; and the product literature produced by the defendant did not adequately convey this information. Various sections of the Patient Guide were singled out for particular criticism, most notably the description of alterations to the menstrual cycle which was castigated as being 'euphemistic, unbalanced and wholly inadequate'. The allegations concerning women's general expectations were expressed in the negative, ie, that, 'in the absence of information to the contrary', women were reasonably entitled to certain specific expectations, including that: Norplant's side effect profile was no worse than other contraceptives; previous experience indicated a high degree of tolerance of Norplant by users; an overwhelming majority of users had been content to use Norplant for the full five years; it was unnecessary to undergo a prior trial of an oral levo-norgestrel contraceptive; removal would be simple and accomplished in one attempt; their own doctor would not need any special training to carry out insertion and removal.

31.17 The second case (for which legal aid had been granted in February 1996) was also served in January 1997, eighteen months after the first public intimation of a potential group action. The plaintiff adopted wholesale the Master Particulars of Claim. A further eighty or so claims were issued and served over the next four months.

31.18 In March 1997 Roussel applied successfully to transfer the two cases to the High Court in London. This application could not have been made before these proceedings had been issued. Considerations under the County Courts Act 1984 and Article 7(5) of the High Court and County Courts Jurisdiction Order 1991 as to the public importance and complexity of the litigation outweighed the low value of the claims and the increase in the burden of costs to the plaintiffs.

31.19 After transfer of the two sets of proceedings to the Central Office, they were assigned to May J, then judge in charge of the Queen's Bench Lists. Roussel applied to strike out the claims as disclosing no reasonable cause of action. This application was heard by May J in June 1997 and, although it failed, it provided an opportunity for the Judge to become familiar with the issues and to give managerial directions. May J's tight control of the litigation from the outset foreshadowed the implementation of Lord Woolf's suggested reforms to the civil procedure regime two years later. He stated: 'it seems to me that the one thing the Court in the modern era is required to do is to manage litigation'. And: 'The Court is here to provide a service to the public and I can see that that service is best provided if it manages the case so as best to be able to decide it.'[4]

31.20 May J directed that the Master Particulars of Claim should be shelved as being too long and discursive, more in the nature of an expert's report than a pleading, and unsuited to elucidating the real issues in the cases. He required the plaintiffs to plead fewer than ten cases individually and succinctly, stating that: 'I have . . . indicated that I do have initial sympathy with the proposition that to start off with a blanket load of allegations by way of Master Statement of Claim and then add individual things to it . . . do not . . . add up to a sensible way of proceeding . . . it might well be more helpful to have a clutch of individual cases pleaded individually and to find out what common issues there may be.'[5]

D. Directions

31.21 The hearing in June 1997 set the pattern for a subsequent series of pre-trial reviews, at each of which the Judge made further case management directions. May J stated at the 30 June hearing:

> I am not at all keen myself to be bogged down in precedents . . . so as to be diverted from inventing, if necessary, procedures appropriate to this case. Nor would I be deterred from doing so solely because there might be no specific summons before the Court asking for the exact relief which I regard as appropriate. Inventive case management requires the Court to take the steps which it regards as appropriate whether the parties ask for them or not.[6]

31.22 Further significant directions were given following hearings in October which resulted in May J's judgment of 29 October 1997 and his Order of 14 November 1997. May J

---

[4] *Caroline Foster v Roussel Laboratories Limited* (May J, 30 June 1997) 12 and 71.
[5] ibid 12.
[6] ibid 15.

suggested that only one or two individual cases should be tried, but, surprisingly in view of the substantive delay which resulted, this suggestion was rejected by the plaintiffs. May J stated that his priority was to get cases to court and to construct a timetable for doing so which recognised the peculiarities of the dynamics of group litigation: those peculiarities including the necessity of establishing a co-ordinating mechanism for unitary actions.

31.23 May J stated: 'it will be necessary to consider the further selection of cases which are to be taken forward, further pleadings in those cases and discovery and then to map out a timetable towards a trial . . . The parties should think in terms of such a trial happening at the earliest time which is consistent with fair and proper preparation . . . I shall expect to impose a tight programme and require it to be adhered to.' May J was concerned that 'individual plaintiffs with relatively modest individual claims' should not 'have to suffer unconscionable delay' by virtue of the parties' lawyers' tactics.

31.24 His main directions were:

1. A formal determination that there was a Group; some seventeen months after the first case was served and more than a year after some eighty cases had materialised.
2. All plaintiffs who wished to bring proceedings within the Group should put themselves on a Plaintiffs' Register, and that once on the Register a plaintiff was taken to have assented to being part of the Group and to be bound by the Group directions. Furthermore, for any plaintiff on the Register, the co-ordinating solicitors were taken to have received instructions from her to that effect.
3. Plaintiffs within the Group should serve 'standard minimum requirements' and a nucleus of selected cases should go forward for trial. 'Standard minimum requirements' meant: a statement of claim containing sufficiently particularised facts relevant to the plaintiff's own circumstances; medical records; and a medical report.
4. Lead cases should be selected by a set deadline, in the first instance by agreement between the parties, failing which, by nomination of an equal number by each party (the total to be not more than ten).

    As the case developed, the problem for the plaintiffs in defining their way forward was that the factual issues determined the generic issues. So the objective became a subordination of generic issues to a process which tried to encapsulate as many factual features of the litigation as possible. The lesson learnt was that after extensive review of the injuries which were alleged by plaintiffs within the cohort which then existed, the cases selected were illustrative of as many injuries as possible. This led to some unusual results. The injury which was alleged to have occurred albeit rarely, but which led to the largest money claim, benign intracranial hypertension, was omitted from the final selection of lead cases.
5. There should be a cut-off date, to be fixed. May J rejected the argument that since the product remained on the market and continued to be prescribed, creating a cut-off date for entry into the Group (the opt-in) was pointless. He was influenced by the need to force plaintiffs who had been waiting on the sidelines and who had no limitation problem, off-risk, to confront the risk of the action, so as to give the action a defined shape ready for trial. He also took into account the idea that the action would not be manageable nor capable of compromise if the Group remained open. He stated that: 'In my view it is quite unacceptable for the court, let alone the defendants, to be

expected to make decisions about a constituency whose membership was never closed.'

6. A Costs-Sharing Order based on similar versions in previous cases but tailored by the Judge. The Norplant litigation was unusual in that whereas in the previous major actions the percentage of plaintiffs which had not been funded and protected by legal aid was typically only some 2–5 per cent, it was nearly one-third (85) of the eventual cohort of 267 Norplant plaintiffs. This constituted a significant cohort which had a pro-rata exposure to paying the defendant's costs if the former discontinued or lost.

There were three main principles in the Costs-Sharing Order: 31.25

(1) Apportionment: plaintiffs' common costs and defendant's costs were to be apportioned between the members of the Group. Each plaintiff's share was calculated at the end of each calendar quarter by reference to the fraction represented by each plaintiff divided by the number of plaintiffs in the Group (defined by reference to the Plaintiffs' Register) during that quarter. The plaintiffs' liability was to be several; the defendant's liability was to each plaintiff in respect of her share of apportionable costs.
(2) Any plaintiff discontinuing her case became liable for her proportionate share of the defendant's costs; her liability was crystallised by reference to the quarter in which she discontinued; the number of plaintiffs still in the Group as at the end of the quarter was the denominator.
(3) A plaintiff joining the Group accepted responsibility for her fraction of, and she became potentially liable for, or entitled to, her share of the apportionable costs as from the date they started to accrue.

The majority of cases in the cohort never progressed beyond the stage of serving the 'standard minimum requirements' ordered by May J, following which they were held in abeyance. Further pleadings were only ordered in relation to the ten selected lead cases. 31.26

Buckley J took over the Queen's Bench List in May 1998 on May J's elevation to the Court of Appeal and the action in this phase was assigned to him. The parties had failed to resolve the issue of lead case selection within the time frame ordered by May J. Buckley J therefore redirected that ten lead cases should be selected by agreement between the parties (failing which, by nomination of an equal number by each party) and set a new deadline. Buckley J set out the rationale behind lead case selection at a hearing on 30 June 1998: 'If there is to be any purpose in class litigation of this sort, the result of the trial should at the very least cut a substantial swathe through the litigation as a whole . . . what is necessary is somehow to pick out sufficient cases to achieve that, which must mean dealing with the general issues anyway.'[7] 31.27

In the circumstances of this case, the selection of lead cases did not constitute the selection of cases which would have assisted the court in resolving as many issues and cases as possible by providing cases which gave sufficiently wide individual illustrations. In reality, case selection became simply a device in which the parties could put forward what might be 31.28

---

[7] *Caroline Foster v Roussel Laboratories Limited* (Buckley J, 30 June 1998) 14.

five of the best and five of the worst cases, hopefully capturing as many combinations of symptoms as possible—a sort of shop window of alleged side effects of the product.

31.29 Buckley J also ordered that a List of Issues be produced by the plaintiffs. This was intended to identify those issues on which the plaintiffs were to call expert evidence. Leave was given for specific categories of expert evidence (including gynaecological, epidemiological, and psychiatric) and exchange dates set for witness statements and experts' reports, as well as a trial date. A cut-off date of 7 August was mandated.

31.30 The plaintiffs' first List of Issues was unacceptable as it did not assist in identifying matters which they intended to prove at trial nor in identifying expert disciplines and Buckley J ordered them to make a second attempt. The plaintiffs' final List of Issues was served in July 1998, together with further and better particulars of the particulars of claim citing the six scientific documents which formed the basis of the plaintiffs' generic case, and was answered by Roussel in its Response served in August. These two documents, the List and the Response, were the first occasion when the real generic issues materialised. The issues split broadly into two, the science and the law: the expectations of women generally in relation to Norplant; and the conceptual safety issues under the Act.

31.31 The main thrust of the argument under the Act was the suggestion that women were entitled to recover for side effects of which they had been warned. The reasoning behind this surprising proposition was that, as a matter of law, if Norplant were found to be a defective product, and causation of injury were proved, the defendant would be liable for all foreseeable consequences, not those merely related to defectiveness.

31.32 On the science, the nature of the allegations shifted away from emphasis on side effects towards criticism of the manner in which the product was introduced. What was now the nub of the medical complaint was Roussel's training methodology. In place of the formulaic approach culled from the Master Particulars of Claim, the case narrowed down to one main complaint surrounding the inadequacy of the training given to health care professionals (HCPs) on launch, with many satellite claims. This focus ignored the fact that Roussel were not legally permitted to oblige HCPs prescribing Norplant to undergo any training at all: the decision whether or not to undergo training being one of professional judgment for each HCP. However, Roussel did all it could to encourage HCPs to attend its training sessions.

31.33 Training involves: a theoretical session with a trainer which stresses patient counselling, and gives the HCP a practice on a dummy arm; a clinical session attended by a trainer involving observation of at least three actual insertions and participation by the trainee in two of them; and another clinical session involving two actual removals. From launch of the product in October 1993 until October 1995 Roussel provided training in the method free. The training programme was then given accredited status by the Faculty of Family Planning of the Royal College of Obstetricians and Gynaecologists which took over full responsibility for its administration in the UK in October 1996. The Faculty issues Letters of Competence and Letters of Equivalent Experience to doctors trained in the method (which type depending on whether or not the doctor is a member of the Faculty). Criticism of the Roussel training strategy had to contend with the fact that the training cascade had gained prior endorsement by the Johns Hopkins Programme for International

Education in Reproductive Health. The Johns Hopkins Programme has an established reputation in advising and implementing reproductive health training programmes throughout the world.

The standard cluster of side effects was relegated to a subordinate position. The only side effect allegation of any substance at the end of the day was the allegation that mood swings and depression are caused by Norplant, were not warned against, and should have been. 31.34

Following selection of the ten lead cases, Roussel started on the process of having each of the ten plaintiffs interviewed by its gynaecological and psychiatric experts. Buckley J provided in his Order of 30 June 1998 for the defendant to obtain expert reports in relation to individual cases. It was apparent that none of the women expected to have to undergo this experience. One of the ten never submitted to be interviewed—she was the one privately paying plaintiff among the ten lead cases. Her case would have been struck out had the Group Action not collapsed. Several of the plaintiffs experienced serious difficulty in making the simple but necessary travel arrangements. They were unprepared for the rigours of taking their cases to court. 31.35

The approaching cut-off date of 7 August 1998 produced a rush of plaintiffs. One-third of the final cohort of 287 registered within the three days prior to 7 August. 31.36

E. Evidence

Conventional directions were given for discovery and exchange of evidence. A case which revolves around the general expectations of safety of a product would be expected to depend on documents which evidence the design, development, manufacturing, and marketing processes, but, possibly in a bid to minimise costs, the plaintiffs' co-ordinating solicitors indicated during the 1997 hearings that they were not after 'forensic' discovery and would not even seek an Order for discovery save for documents relied upon for the development risks defence. This approach was at odds with the pleadings, which put in issue the entire development of the product, but it remained the strategy until, in mid-1998, the preparation of the List of Issues caused the plaintiffs to focus on matters to be proved by the expert scientific evidence. In the light of the plaintiffs' redefinition of the thrust of their allegations, requests were made for Roussel to produce training and marketing documents. It became apparent that the plaintiffs' experts had turned their attention from the side effect profile of the drug to the methodology of its introduction and marketing in the UK. 31.37

F. Withdrawal of Funding

Factual witness statements were exchanged in October 1998 and experts' reports in November. Following exchange of experts' reports, the plaintiffs' counsel's advice to the Legal Aid Board led the Board to withdraw funding shortly before the start of the trial on 1 February 1999. 31.38

G. Unresolved Funding Issues

31.39 One of the legally aided plaintiffs, with the support of the Legal Aid Board, had sought out of time to appeal the Costs-Sharing Order made by May J on 14 November 1998. Wright J refused leave to appeal, but the Court of Appeal granted leave, on the basis that the point at issue was one of public importance. The appeal was due to be heard on 15 February 1999, together with an appeal on the same issue in the Tobacco litigation, but both cases collapsed and the appeals were never heard.

31.40 The principal argument by the plaintiffs was that the funding arrangements did not reflect the issues-led nature of the litigation. The plaintiffs' concern was that if a plaintiff discontinued, she had to pay her share of Roussel's costs, whether or not the generic issues which she had adopted were ultimately successful. On this analysis, every plaintiff except one could have discontinued, but as long as that one plaintiff continued her action, and then won the generic issues, she would have been awarded the costs of those issues but would only recover her proportion of the plaintiffs' costs. Roussel, on the other hand, would have picked up a windfall because it would have defended unsuccessfully but would have had paid to it all but that one person's share of Roussel's costs of defending the generic issues unsuccessfully. The difficulty posed by this argument was that it cut across the automatic right of the party against whom the plaintiff discontinues to have his costs taxed. That right is subject to the discontinuing plaintiff's right to apply for leave to discontinue as to costs, so the design of the Norplant Order was not breaking any new ground.

31.41 The essence of the argument was that the Legal Aid Board would not be able to recover the apportioned costs of the so-called generic issues attributable to any plaintiff wishing to discontinue, even if the remaining plaintiffs went on to win the generic issues and obtain orders for costs. The Legal Aid Board would have lost that potentially recoverable share of costs when the plaintiff discontinued: it would have paid it out but not recovered it.

H. Some Conclusions

31.42 The above history reveals some dissatisfaction on the part of the judges with two aspects. First, those High Court judges who had some experience of managing group actions were prevented under the then current procedural constraints from assuming managerial direction of the litigation for some two years. Secondly, when they did gain control, they rejected the significant aspects of the 'generic case' and Master pleadings approach which was initially pursued on behalf of the plaintiffs, and which was partly dictated by the requirements of the Legal Aid Board's policy of investigating and pursuing a generic case rather than individual cases.

31.43 The width of the allegations in the Master Particulars of Claim meant that they amounted to a request for a public inquiry into the development, marketing, and use of the product. It put in issue the statutory system for licensing medicinal products and the Licensing Authority's decisions in relation to approval of the product. It is suggested that this approach—at least for a case with such low quantum as this and coming after previous criticism of the public inquiry or 'kitchen sink' approach—was a tactical mistake. The adoption of Master Particulars of Claim, themselves produced at some significant cost, would only be of value if each plaintiff could have simply placed her name on a register and then done nothing further—in other words, if the 'generic case' approach had been 100 per cent successful. Each plaintiff would have had to have avoided pleading details of and producing evidence on her individual facts, and identifying which parts of the Master Particulars of Claim she did not adopt. The inclusion of multiple allegations diverted a case which could not afford this into subsidiary areas, increasing costs and losing time. It is suggested that the 'kitchen sink' approach is an artifice permitted by the legal aid system that would be inappropriate for cases funded under a conditional fee and insurance system. May J was persuaded by Roussel's submissions that *each* individual case should be investigated and pleaded and ordered each plaintiff in the Group to serve 'standard minimum requirements'.

I. Aftermath

The only successful aspect of the story from the viewpoint of the plaintiffs and their lawyers was the initial media campaign. This succeeded in creating a public impression that there was a safety issue associated with the product. This coincided with a completely separate campaign by doctors for discrete payment for insertion and extraction of Norplant, which culminated in 1995 in the British Medical Association advising all doctors not to prescribe Norplant until the minor surgical operations involved had been made subject to an appropriate fee from the NHS. This never happened. As a result of the combination of these publicity and reimbursement issues, the commercial value of the product ebbed away and Roussel announced that the supply of Norplant would be discontinued at the end of October 1999. The final retrospect on the story would be the realisation that so much of the success or failure of this new form of contraceptive technology depended on a perception by individual members of the medical profession of their own skills in providing it, principally skills in counselling and minor surgery.

31.44

32

TOBACCO LITIGATION: 1992–1999

Mark Elvy,[1] Miles Alexander and Tom Keevil[2]

This product liability case illustrates a number of the management issues of a multi-party action which were topical during the 1990s. First, the Court found that the case was lawyer-led and generated by advertising. Secondly, the plaintiffs' lawyers' assertions that the case would involve large numbers of plaintiffs, perhaps hundreds of thousands, did not materialise and the final cohort involved approximately fifty claimants. The Court declined to order a cut-off date for plaintiffs to join, but imposed a restriction on further plaintiffs joining the action without agreement or leave, making their entitlement to do so conditional upon the defendants being given notice and an explanation as to why the claim had not been begun previously. Thirdly, there was an extended period before proceedings were started, then a period during which a succession of claimants commenced proceedings in small numbers. Until the nature and number of the claims being put forward was clarified, the Court was unable to manage the litigation.

Fourthly, during the initial period, investigation of the litigation was funded by the Legal Aid Board and therefore subject to the Board's policy of only funding the investigation of supposedly generic issues and not funding the investigation of individual claims. Furthermore, it was tactically preferable for the plaintiffs to seek to emphasise issues of breach of duty and generic causation. Accordingly, the details of individual cases appear only to have been investigated to the extent of obtaining plaintiffs' unverified answers to a questionnaire and obtaining a pro forma statement from their general practitioners that the plaintiff had been diagnosed as suffering from one specific type of cancer and giving the date of diagnosis. The absence of further investigations and the verification of individual medical histories of plaintiffs before commencing actions (such as by medical examination, considering medical records, and obtaining an independent medical report on each) seems to have resulted in some plaintiffs commencing actions who did not meet their legal advisers' criteria and ultimately led to plaintiffs being ordered to pay defendants' costs when cases were amended or discontinued. Adverse costs orders were also

---

[1] Mark Elvy, Partner, Ashurst Morris Crisp.
[2] Partners, Simmons & Simmons.

ordered when claimants had to amend or discontinue against some defendants after there had been a failure to investigate or verify the identity of the correct defendants. These costs orders may not have mattered if the case had been continued with legal aid funding, since the Court would have been most unlikely to have given leave for the costs orders to be enforced, but became significant after legal aid funding was withdrawn.

Fifthly, the Court rejected the plaintiffs' strategy of putting forward a generic case approach and a Master Statement of Claim, to which pro forma individual statements of claim were appended. Instead the Court concluded that the defendants were entitled to fully pleaded individual statements of claim and subsequently ordered that a number of individual lead cases should be investigated and fully pleaded as being representative of as many of the issues as possible in the other individual cases, which would also be investigated to some extent at that stage.

The case is further significant as the first example of a multi-party case run on a conditional fee agreement basis. This introduced a need for a more focused and commercial approach to running the case than was permissible under the legal aid scheme. For example, proceedings were only issued against two manufacturers and were restricted to a particular type of lung cancer claim. Further, it was agreed that the defendants would undertake and initially fund the collection of plaintiffs' medical records. The collection of medical records was a necessary step towards the Court's preference for proceeding by way of selecting a certain number of lead cases: without this step the parties would not have been able to select five cases each as being representative of others or of the whole, and the selection process was in any event made difficult by the fact that plaintiffs were at that stage continuing to begin claims in tranches.

Since the issue of limitation arose in nearly all of the lead cases and a significant number of the rest of the cohort, the Court proceeded by deciding this issue as a preliminary issue and this turned out to be dispositive of the litigation.

The Costs-Sharing Order was made in the form developed in other cases and although it was appealed, the appeal was abandoned. A very extensive discovery exercise by the defendants was put in train and disclosure of documents was given in tranches.

A. Advertising for Clients

32.01 On 24 June 1992 the Supreme Court of the United States of America gave judgment in *Cipollone v Liggett Group Inc*.[3] The decision was quite complex and gave rise to difficulties of interpretation, although the supporters of both plaintiffs and defendants claimed success in the media. The case concerned an action by Mrs Cipollone (deceased) and her

---

[3] 505 US 504 (1992).

husband for damages arising out of her death from lung cancer allegedly caused by her heavy cigarette smoking.

There was widespread coverage in the media of the *Cipollone* decision, prompting certain English firms of solicitors to consider whether claimants might have any chance of succeeding in negligence claims in England and Wales.[4] It was recognised that anyone with a smoking-associated illness diagnosed more than three years previously would be subject to a prima facie limitation bar and that the health risks associated with smoking have been well known for some decades.[5] However, the solicitors thought that people with a variety of ailments who had started smoking between the 1950s, when epidemiological studies first reported an association between smoking and lung cancer, and 1971, after which warnings were placed on cigarette packets in this country, would stand a chance of success. Mr Martyn Day of Leigh Day & Co (Leigh Day) was reported as saying that possibly hundreds of thousands of claims might fall within the parameters[6] that might lead to a successful claim.

32.02

Accordingly, Bindman & Partners (Bindmans) and Leigh Day, neither of whom at that stage had any such clients, advertised for 'smoking victims' to come forward or attend meetings, to see if they could become 'legal test cases'. One advertisement included the statements

32.03

> the Supreme Court in the United States ruled that the claims by victims of smoking would be allowed to proceed through the courts, notwithstanding the objections of the tobacco industry. It is our view that claims for compensation for smoking related illnesses, in this country, have a reasonable chance of succeeding.[7]

The statements were later criticised by the tobacco companies as being, first, a misleading interpretation of the Supreme Court's decision and, secondly, an unwarranted generalisation in relation to chances of success in litigation. Other lawyers pointed out the difficulties which any smoker would face in succeeding in a claim.[8]

32.04

B. Applying for Legal Aid

Some 300 people contacted the two firms of solicitors as a result of the advertisements, public meetings, and surrounding publicity and, in July 1992, applications on behalf of 227 individuals were made to the Northern Area Office of the Legal Aid Board of England and Wales (Board). The five tobacco companies who were potential defendants (Imperial Tobacco, Gallaher, BAT, Rothmans, and Philip Morris) then submitted representations in writing to the Board setting out the legal difficulties faced by any claimant and the cost and complexity of any litigation. The Board refused to fund the applicants and the subsequent appeal to the Northern Area Committee was unsuccessful.

32.05

---

[4] 'Tobacco firms hit by US health ruling', *The Times*, 25 June 1992.
[5] M Day, R Lewis, SJ, 10 July 1992; LS Gaz, 8 July 1992.
[6] LS Gaz, 8 July 1992.
[7] Advertisement, *Hackney Gazette*.
[8] M Mildred, *The Times*, 20 June 1992.

32.06 In October 1992, Leigh Day, Bindmans, and Freeth Cartwright Hunt Dickens (who had joined them) sought judicial review of the Area Committee's decision on behalf of twenty-nine named individuals and 227 others. After leave to seek judicial review was granted by Laws J on 29 September 1993, the tobacco companies applied to be served with copies of relevant evidence in the application. However, Turner J decided that potential defendants were not 'persons directly affected' under RSC Order 53, Rule 5(3) and they would only become directly affected if legal aid was granted.[9] On 1 July 1994 Popplewell J quashed the decision of the Area Committee on the grounds of procedural irregularity and failure to give proper reasons as to how the decision had been reached.[10]

32.07 The application was then reconsidered by a specially constituted Area Committee in London, which had the benefit of further representations from the tobacco companies. The applicants also submitted further extensive written submissions to the Board (which were later published in a journal in the USA[11]). On 31 January 1995, the Committee decided to grant legal aid to approximately 200 applicants but limited only to a full review of merits, quantum, and total likely costs involved in pursuing an action against the tobacco companies: this authorised work in examining common or so-called 'generic' issues and preparing a set of experts' reports but did not cover work on individual certificates or medical reports.

32.08 The Board entered into an 'all work' contract with three firms of solicitors, Leigh Day, Freeth Cartwright Hunt Dickens, and Bindmans. This was a new mechanism used to ensure that all work was authorised under one contract, rather than under individual Legal Aid Certificates, thereby avoiding the situation which had arisen in previous group actions (such as the Benzodiazepine case) where large numbers of different firms became involved and costs escalated. The review funded by the Board included consideration of certain internal company documents which had become public and consultation with experts. By this stage, the tobacco companies had seen the earlier written submissions of the applicants which were published in the USA and this enabled them to submit further but much more focused and detailed written representations in October 1995.

32.09 Following the completion of the review by the applicants' legal advisers, the Board's Area Committee considered a wealth of information, including counsel's opinion, experts' reports, some publicly available tobacco company documents, and representations from the tobacco companies. They also obtained an independent opinion on the strength of the applicants' cases from Rupert Jackson QC. This was not published but it was subsequently revealed that it had recommended no further funding should be made available. It is understood that this was the first time the Board obtained its own independent opinion on the merits of a claim. On 17 July 1996, the Board issued a press release confirming that legal aid would not be extended for any further preparatory work or litigation as the statutory criteria had not been satisfied. They stated that: 'it is unlikely that public funding will be available for cases of this type in the absence of significant new information affecting the merits of the claims'.

---

[9] *R v The Legal Aid Board, ex p Megarry and Others* (Turner J, 25 Apr 1994).
[10] *R v The number 8 Area Committee of the Legal Aid Board, ex p Megarry & Others* (Popplewell J, 1 July 1994).
[11] Litigation Documents 9.5 TPLR 3.741.

32.10 There were two further matters relating to this pre-action period which were to become relevant in the subsequent proceedings. First, the limitation period relating to one of the lead plaintiffs, Mr Hodgson, who had consulted Leigh Day in 1992, expired during 1995. Wright J later made comments in his judgment on limitation issues that no satisfactory explanation had been given as to why a writ was not issued within three years of his diagnosis, indicating that the proper course was to serve the writ and then obtain from the defendant or the Court an extension of time in which to serve a statement of claim.[12] The second issue, also relevant to limitation, was the acknowledgement in the applicants' submissions to the Board that limitation would be an issue and 'could be dealt with by way of a preliminary issue which would limit the costs exposure'. Later the plaintiffs took exactly the opposite approach before the Court and strenuously opposed the defendants' application to have limitation heard as a preliminary issue. However, Wright J said circumstances demanded that limitation be tried as a preliminary issue.

C. Legal Advisers Decide to Fund Action under Conditional Fee Agreements (CFAs)

32.11 Following the withdrawal of legal aid, Leigh Day issued a press release on 27 September 1996 stating that they proposed to issue proceedings against Imperial Tobacco and Gallaher on behalf of forty individuals who allegedly had been diagnosed with lung cancer. The action was to be the first group action funded on a conditional fee basis and Dan Brennan QC, then president of the Personal Injury Bar Association, and Professor Mark Mildred were to be part of the plaintiffs' legal team.[13] Leigh Day subsequently confirmed that the CFAs provided for an 'uplift', in the event that the plaintiffs' claims were successful, of 100 per cent of their fees subject to a limit of 25 per cent of the damages recovered by each individual plaintiff. This was in accordance with the Law Society guidelines on CFAs. Unsuccessful attempts were made to obtain insurance cover, so none of the prospective plaintiffs would have insurance against the risk of costs orders made against them in the event they were to lose. Further publicity of the solicitors' agreement to act under a CFA ensued. However, the media reports of many hundreds of plaintiffs never in fact materialised.

32.12 Letters before action were served on Ashurst Morris Crisp (solicitors for Imperial Tobacco) and Simmons & Simmons (solicitors for Gallaher) on 26 September 1996. Unlike the claims which were the subject of legal aid applications, the proposed claims would only be against Imperial and Gallaher and would only involve plaintiffs diagnosed with a specific type of lung cancer.

---

[12] *Hodgson v Imperial Tobacco Ltd* (Wright J, 9 Feb 1999).
[13] Press release, Leigh Day, 27 Sept 1996.

D. Collection of Medical Records

32.13 Immediately on receipt of the letters before action, and some four weeks before the first writ was issued, Ashursts and Simmons & Simmons wrote to Leigh Day requesting details of each plaintiff and copies of the medical records relating to each plaintiff on whose behalf proceedings were to be issued. Leigh Day initially replied to the effect that medical records would be provided on the usual terms once they were complete and properly organised. However, the plaintiffs' legal advisers had not at that stage had sight of all the medical records of individual plaintiffs nor, therefore, analysed them, prior to commencing proceedings. The funding restrictions imposed by the Board had limited the preparation to general issues. The individual plaintiffs were assessed on the basis of short questionnaires drawn up by the solicitors to test whether each plaintiff met their criteria. In addition, a short form standard letter from GPs identifying the type of lung cancer and date of diagnosis was produced. In evidence, Mr Day stated that medical examinations did not take place and medical reports were not obtained even for the lead plaintiffs until August 1997 and that the first time the plaintiffs' lawyers looked at the medical records of any of the plaintiffs was from May 1997.

32.14 It was agreed between the parties that Ashursts would collect all medical records (including pathology and X-rays) and then distribute copies and, where necessary, originals to all the other parties. Whilst the defendants bore the cost of collection, copying, and distribution, it was agreed that ultimately these costs were to be 'costs in the cause'. Most hospitals and medical bodies have a document destruction policy and this procedure assisted in safeguarding many of the very old but relevant medical records still in existence. It also saved the plaintiffs' solicitors from incurring the initial expenditure of collection, leaving this to be dealt with as part of the costs of the action. The securing of lifetime medical records and their early analysis was to prove crucial later in the litigation when the plaintiffs and defendants were each directed to select five plaintiffs whose claims were to be fully pleaded.

32.15 The collection and analysis of medical records also allowed the plaintiffs and the defendants to investigate fundamental issues such as diagnosis, smoking history, medical advice, other exposures, and issues relating to limitation. As a direct result, claims (which should never have been commenced even on the plaintiffs' criteria) were discontinued at an early stage. There may be the temptation in group actions, especially where legal advisers are acting under CFAs, for the important but time-consuming and expensive early investigation of claims and medical records to be neglected. This case demonstrated the importance of a thorough and early investigation of claims.

E. Issue of Proceedings

32.16 On 12 November 1996, Leigh Day issued the first of a series of writs against Imperial and Gallaher. It was issued on behalf of twelve plaintiffs who were identified in a schedule attached to the writ. Each writ had a brief general endorsement claiming 'damages for injuries suffered and loss and expense incurred as a result of the negligence and/or breach of statutory duty of the defendants . . . in the manufacture, distribution and/or supply of their tobacco products from the period 1950 . . .' and attached a schedule consisting of one A4 page for each plaintiff setting out brief details of that plaintiff's smoking history and cancer diagnosis. Also served for each plaintiff was a two-line pro forma letter from the plaintiff's GP confirming that the plaintiff had been diagnosed as suffering from a specific type of cancer and giving the date of diagnosis. There was no opinion on causation and no further medical details were provided.

In a number of cases, the alleged dates of diagnosis and the description of the type of alleged lung cancer given in the schedules did not match the information contained in the GP statements. More importantly, in some cases proceedings were brought against both Imperial and Gallaher when the schedule of smoking history served with the writ showed that the individual plaintiff did not smoke one or other of the defendants' cigarettes. This resulted in claims being discontinued and costs orders being made against the relevant plaintiffs in favour of the defendant whose cigarettes they had not smoked. 32.17

F. Plaintiffs' Application for Early Assignment of a Judge

From the start, Leigh Day stated that they would make an application to the Court for a tight time schedule for the progressing of the action on the basis that they were retained under a CFA. On 12 November 1996, Leigh Day wrote to the Senior Master enclosing a copy of the writ and a draft Order for Directions requesting that he consider recommending to the Lord Chief Justice that a judge be assigned to the action and for that assigned judge, or the judge in charge of the non-jury list, to hear the directions application. Leigh Day asserted that the early assignment of a judge to the case was necessary owing to: 32.18

(1) the potential scale of the action and derivative actions being enormous;
(2) the importance of the action;
(3) the likelihood that there would be a large number of complex interlocutory applications;
(4) the need for a disciplined timetable; and
(5) a single judge would be able to become familiar with the underlying scientific and technical themes.

This letter to the Senior Master gave the defendants their first information on the broad outline of the plaintiffs' case. The draft directions proposed a timetable up to and including trial, service of Master pleadings and statements of 'generic' issues, identification of lead cases, discovery, exchange of witness and expert statements, and setting the action down for trial of the 'generic' issues and lead cases. However, no pleadings had yet been served and the size and nature of the group of plaintiffs had yet to be identified. 32.19

Leigh Day stated that the great majority of the issues involved in these cases were generic in that they involved common questions such as a consideration of the steps the tobacco companies took in the face of the scientific evidence emerging in the 1950s and 1960s and of the epidemiological evidence regarding the strength of the link between smoking generally (and tar particularly) and lung cancers. They asserted that individual details would 32.20

be of a very minor nature in comparison to the common issues. Leigh Day also stated that they anticipated a further 20–30 plaintiffs being added to the first group and they asserted it was very likely that this initial number would increase as the action moved toward trial, perhaps involving several tens of thousands.

32.21 Ashursts and Simmons & Simmons both wrote to the Senior Master outlining the uncertainties regarding the nature and scope of the potential litigation, suggesting that more information was required before Leigh Day's request could be properly considered, and requested that he make directions for an *inter partes* hearing to enable the defendants' point of view and proposals to be considered. They contended that the defendants and the Court were being asked to commit to the appointment of a single judge (with its consequences for disruption to court resources), the full panoply of a 'group action', and a rigid set of directions purportedly covering all aspects of the litigation until trial which Leigh Day then estimated would commence on 2 October 1998 with a time estimate of three months. At that time there were only twelve plaintiffs who had issued proceedings and their medical conditions were unknown to the defendants and the Court. The details of the claims of each were equally unknown. The ultimate anticipated size of the 'group' was unknown not only to the defendants and the Court but also to the plaintiffs' lawyers. It was further contended that the draft order for directions had been drawn up by the plaintiffs' lawyers in ignorance of the nature and extent of the plaintiffs' claims and the nature and extent of the defences. It excluded any prospect of case management as necessitated by the litigation as it emerged or developed.

G. First Draft Master Statement of Claim

32.22 On 9 December 1996, Leigh Day produced what was described as a '1st Preliminary Draft of the Master Statement of Claim'. Short details of individual cases were given in schedules. The basic allegations were that the companies were in breach of a duty of care to investigate, warn about, and successively reduce tar levels from the late 1950s onwards.

32.23 On 10 December 1996, Leigh Day issued a second writ on behalf of eleven further plaintiffs who were again listed in a schedule attached to the writ. Schedules of smoking histories and GP statements for each plaintiff which followed the form of those served with the first writ were subsequently supplied.

H. Hearing before the Senior Master

32.24 In November 1996, Leigh Day took out a Summons for Directions but the Senior Master stated that he would prefer to hear the parties regarding the issue of the allocation of a judge to the action before making a decision on what to recommend to the Lord Chief Justice. He asked that draft pleadings and any affidavit evidence be lodged. At the hearing on 11 December 1996, the Senior Master declined the plaintiffs' application for a recommendation to the Lord Chief Justice for the assignment of a judge to manage the actions as a group action, awarding costs to the defendants. He criticised the '1st Preliminary

Draft Master Statement of Claim' as being defective but said that he would review the matter again once there was some clarity over the form and content of the finalised Statement of Claim, the likely size of the group, the identity of the defendants if others were to be joined, and the basis of the liability of individual defendants.

I. Issue of Further Proceedings

32.25 A third writ was issued on 18 April 1997 on behalf of thirteen plaintiffs with the usual schedules. A revised Draft Master Statement of Claim relating to all the plaintiffs who had commenced proceedings in the first three writs was also served which bore little resemblance to the original '1st Preliminary Draft Master Statement of Claim' and came with eighteen appendices. On 7 May 1997, Leigh Day served an Affidavit sworn by Martyn Day exhibited to which were four individual draft statements of claim together with a one and a half page report prepared by the epidemiologist, Sir Richard Doll, relating to those four individual cases.

32.26 On 19 May 1997, a fourth writ was issued against the third defendant on behalf of the twenty-three plaintiffs to the first and second writs. A fifth writ was issued on 19 June 1997 on behalf of eleven plaintiffs against all three defendants. As before, it was served with schedules of smoking history and GP letters in respect of each individual plaintiff.

J. Assignment of a Judge

32.27 On 1 July 1997, the then forty-seven plaintiffs renewed their application before Senior Master Turner and again sought a recommendation for the assignment of a judge. In his judgment on 4 July 1997, the Senior Master noted that the issues had been very considerably refined. However, he was again critical of the plaintiffs' pleading, stating: 'I find the Master Statement of Claim unhelpful and in breach both of the spirit and actual requirements of Order 18, rule 7. It seeks to focus this litigation in the form of a public enquiry into the alleged health risk of smoking and does not recognise that this is *not* the purpose of litigation.' He said that 'large portions of the pleadings, if served, would be struck out by me' and he listed in a two-page schedule to his judgment those passages of the Master Statement of Claim which, in his view, offended Order 18, rule 7. Master Turner rejected the Master Statement of Claim approach and said that 'instead of starting with a generic pleading tacking individual cases on to it, the better course is to plead individual cases and then to see if they raise common issues'.

32.28 The Senior Master again refused the assignment of a judge and suggested that the four individual draft statements of claim be redrafted. He was, however, satisfied that a judge ought to review the claim, and he released the Summons to the judge in charge of the non-jury list to give directions for the further conduct of the actions.

K. Selection of Lead Cases

32.29 By the time the matter came before Popplewell J on 25 July 1997 the plaintiffs' lawyers had served a more fully particularised pleading in one of the cases and parties were able to agree directions.

32.30 The Court rejected the 'general' approach to the conduct of this litigation as exemplified by the various draft Master Statements of Claim and discarded the rigid proposals for directions for the litigation to trial as proposed by the plaintiffs' lawyers in favour of a staged assessment of the needs of the litigation as proposed by the defendants. The directions called for a very tight timetable for exchange of pleadings, with any further directions to be considered by the Court after the close of pleadings.

32.31 With Popplewell J's guidance, it was agreed that the proper way forward would be for the plaintiffs' and the defendants' representatives to each select five cases which were broadly representative of the other cases in the group and for those cases alone to be fully pleaded in the first instance (the plaintiffs having already identified as one of their five choices the person whose individual statement of claim had been served). In addition, the plaintiffs were to provide the defendants with full medical reports and statements of special damages relating to each of the ten plaintiffs to be pleaded. Best available Schedules of Information were to be provided in each of the remaining cases. The defendants contended that it was still difficult to identify cases which were representative of the issues as the group had not yet settled, the issues had not yet been defined, and medical records were still to be collected for many of the plaintiffs who had issued proceedings. The plaintiffs' solicitors were to use their best endeavours to ensure that all plaintiffs should by close of business on 31 July 1997, or as soon as possible thereafter, provide the defendants with written authorisations to enable the defendants to obtain all their medical records and material. Orders were also made safeguarding the medical records and pathology and setting up protocols for any testing of pathology material.

32.32 The parties also agreed that the issues of cost sharing and the disclosure of the CFAs should be addressed at a separate hearing to be arranged before Popplewell J in October 1997. The parties were to continue preparing to give discovery. The Summons for Directions would be restored in December 1997. One week before the hearing, counsel were to meet to discuss whether the lead cases, and if so which, should be selected for trial from the pleaded cases or whether there should be a separate trial of any, and if so which, issues and, in such event, in which pleaded cases.

32.33 In July 1997 it was revealed that a further firm of solicitors, Irwin Mitchell, had been instructed in some individual cases and were working on 'generic' issues with Leigh Day.

L. Further Pleadings

32.34 Individual statements of claim and detailed medical reports for the four remaining cases selected by the plaintiffs were served in August 1997 together with the revised schedules of individual smoking histories for all but a few of the remaining plaintiffs. The information contained in each of the schedules changed (to a lesser or greater extent) from that set out in the schedules served earlier with the writs and included details of each plaintiff's employment history.

In September 1997 Leigh Day advised the defendants that two of the plaintiffs would be applying to discontinue and that in the case of one further action (where the individual plaintiff had died) the executors had decided not to take forward the action on behalf of the estate. These cases were later discontinued, with Costs Orders made against the plaintiffs. It was also about this time that the plaintiffs informed the defendants that there was at least some question regarding the diagnosis of several of the plaintiffs. 32.35

The individual statements of claim, particularly in dealing with limitation and plaintiffs' reasons for delay, adopted a pro forma style. This approach was later criticised by Wright J[14] on the basis that the pleaded reasons for delay were not supported by the plaintiffs themselves but were 'the product of the ingenuity of the Plaintiffs' legal advisers, and do not represent either the reality, or the instructions given by each individual Plaintiff'. He said this was a matter of some concern to him and was 'to be deprecated'. 32.36

On 8 September, the defendants nominated their five plaintiffs to be pleaded and thereafter pleadings were served in relation to the ten pleaded cases in accordance with the timetable. On 6 October, Leigh Day advised the defendants that a further plaintiff would be discontinuing. 32.37

M. Debarring Order

A second directions hearing was held on 10 October 1997 before Popplewell J. The principal matter intended to be resolved was the Costs-Sharing Order in respect of costs liabilities between individual plaintiffs and between the plaintiffs and the defendants. However, the plaintiffs raised a new matter. They sought a pre-emptory Order debarring the defendants from ever seeking costs against the plaintiffs' legal representatives other than under section 51(6) of the Supreme Court Act 1981 (the wasted costs jurisdiction). The effect of the proposed Order would have been that, in the event that the plaintiffs lost outright, it would not be open to the defendants to seek to challenge the CFA, other than for an application for a wasted costs Order. It was understood that the plaintiffs' legal advisers wanted to clarify their position as they and their insurers were concerned that the legal advisers may be liable to a costs order for maintaining the action. 32.38

The media reported this application, but inaccurately. Contrary to how the application was characterised by the plaintiffs' legal advisers in the media,[15] it was never the position of the defendants that they claimed that a properly constituted conditional fee based action amounted to maintenance. What was said was that until the CFA was seen it was impossible for the defendants to form a view on whether or not the CFA was properly constituted. The plaintiffs had refused to produce their CFAs on the basis that they were 32.39

---

[14] *Hodgson v Imperial Tobacco Ltd* (Wright J, 9 Feb 1999) 19.
[15] The *Independent*, 7 Oct 1997.

privileged, a view which the Judge shared and the defendants did not dispute. The Judge refused to make the order sought by the plaintiffs. This was essentially because to do so would have removed from the trial judge his discretion as to costs. The plaintiffs' legal advisers immediately sought and were granted leave to appeal and they applied to adjourn the rest of the hearing on the Costs-Sharing Order. Thus, an issue which primarily concerned the plaintiffs' legal advisers and their liability, rather than that of their clients, had the effect of adjourning the litigation generally until the appeal was heard in January 1998. It also resulted in the issue of cost sharing, which did directly affect the plaintiffs (particularly those who had already discontinued), being left unresolved.

32.40 Popplewell J did deal with various other matters. He confirmed the agreed dismissal of the four plaintiffs' claims with costs orders made against them and gave leave to a further twenty-one plaintiffs to discontinue proceedings against one or two of the three defendants, ordering them to pay the costs thrown away. These individuals discontinued as they had commenced proceedings against one or other of the defendants when they had not in fact at any relevant time smoked their cigarettes. On 24 December 1997 Leigh Day indicated that two further cases (where they had been considering diagnosis issues) would be consenting to an Order being made dismissing their cases with costs.

N. Media Order

32.41 Popplewell J also extended the prohibition on the parties commenting on the litigation in the media. At the previous hearing, an Order restricting media comment had been made by consent. On this occasion, however, the plaintiffs opposed the Order and sought leave to appeal this as well, which was refused by the Judge.

O. Court of Appeal

32.42 On 26 January 1998 the Court of Appeal (Lord Woolf MR, Aldous LJ, Chadwick LJ) granted leave to appeal the Media Order and heard both the appeals. On 12 February 1998 the Court dismissed the plaintiffs' appeal in respect of the Debarring Order and allowed the other appeal, quashing the Media Order of Popplewell J, and ordered the defendants to pay 25 per cent of the plaintiffs' costs of the appeals.

32.43 On the Debarring Order, the Court of Appeal commented that: 'The existence of a CFA should make a legal advisers' position as a matter of law no worse, so far as being ordered to pay costs is concerned... This is unless, of course, the CFA is outside the statutory protection... The Plaintiffs' lawyers were mistaken in thinking that unless they had this protection they could not act for the Plaintiffs.'[16]

32.44 In relation to the Media Order, the Court of Appeal commented: 'Naturally the Court recognises the special problems created by group actions, and we also recognise the fact that it is desirable to see responsible behaviour by those engaged in these actions.'

---

[16] *Hodgson v Imperial Tobacco Ltd* (Wright J, 9 Feb 1999) 19.

32.45 They then went on to say that a case of this type should be heard publicly and to outline proposals for the Court to make arrangements for proceedings in chambers to be made more open to the public when this is requested.

32.46 Despite the fact that the Court of Appeal took the then novel step of issuing its own press release, the decision on the Debarring Order was again misquoted in the media.

32.47 On 12 February 1998, a sixth writ was issued by four plaintiffs against all three defendants, and a seventh writ was issued by five plaintiffs against two defendants alone. However, on 26 February 1998 Leigh Day informed Ashursts that they could not continue to act for one of the plaintiffs as he had been diagnosed with adenocarcinoma (a type of lung cancer which did not fit into their criteria). The plaintiff had refused to discontinue his action and thereafter acted in person. On 13 March, Leigh Day informed the defendants that the administrator of the estate of another of the plaintiffs had decided to withdraw and agreed that the claim be dismissed with costs. In March 1998, three cases were formally dismissed with costs. In addition, a further seven claims were dismissed as against Gallaher alone, with costs thrown away being ordered.

In March 1998 three further writs were issued by Irwin Mitchell on behalf of four plaintiffs against the defendants.

P. Further Directions

32.48 Following the Court of Appeal hearing, the matter was relisted before Buckley J to be heard in April. On 16 March, the defendants put forward their proposed Costs-Sharing Order, which was based on the Order by May LJ in the Norplant litigation and which had also been adopted by the Senior Master in the Lariam litigation. Directions were also proposed which, *inter alia*, provided for limitation to be tried as a preliminary issue, thirty-five of the then fifty-three plaintiffs being prima facie statute barred on date of diagnosis. The hearing before Buckley J took place on 3 April 1998. He declined to impose a cut-off date for plaintiffs to join the group but indicated that the plaintiffs' solicitors should give advance notice to the defendants, with an explanation for the delay in issuing proceedings, and should then apply to the Court to add new plaintiffs where they were unable to obtain the consent of the defendants. Although argument was heard in relation to the cost-sharing issue it was adjourned for further management of the proceedings by a judge to be nominated to try the case. The only order which Buckley J made was that the plaintiffs' liability was to be several and the terms 'common costs' and 'individual costs' should be defined. The defendants' application to have limitation heard as a preliminary issue was also adjourned.

In May 1998 an eleventh writ was issued by Leigh Day on behalf of two plaintiffs against all three defendants.

32.49 Wright J was then appointed to manage and try the cases and a third hearing for directions was held on 22 and 23 June 1998. He ordered that the issue of whether the claims should proceed notwithstanding that they were prima facie statute barred as having been issued more than three years after the respective causes of action arose was to be tried as a preliminary issue in nine of the ten pleaded cases. Of the statute barred lead plaintiffs, the shortest overrun was seventeen months and the longest nearly twenty-five years. The judgment would be binding on all the parties in the actions in relation to the claims made by all other statute barred plaintiffs. It was an issue in nine of the ten pleaded cases and in the majority of all cases.

32.50 The Costs-Sharing Order proposed by the defendants on the basis of the Norplant and Lariam precedents was accepted. This was important in that it clarified the costs position for all plaintiffs, including those who had discontinued who were liable for both their individual costs and their appropriate share of common costs to the date they discontinued. Also, it resulted in the funder, ie the plaintiffs' lawyers under a CFA, not being able to recoup their outlay on that part of the common costs which was attributable to those plaintiffs who had discontinued (and, equally important, losing the opportunity to recover a mark-up on those costs) in the event that any continuing plaintiffs were successful on common issues.

32.51 Although Wright J adopted a Woolf-like management of the litigation in ordering a preliminary issue to be tried, he recognised that litigation of this size needed proper preparation under a realistic timetable, not a guillotine for the sake of it. Discovery was ordered to continue under the timetable agreed by the parties. In view of the fact that the claims related to a period of several decades and the quantity of potentially relevant documents, the defendants had proposed that discovery should be given in stages rather than attempting to provide all discovery in a single, larger list. The plaintiffs and their lawyers gave confidentiality undertakings in relation to the defendants' discovery. The parties were ordered to exchange a preliminary list of experts by speciality upon which they intended to rely at trial. The trial of the pleaded cases was set down for the first day of term in January 2000, with a time estimate of three to six months. All plaintiffs' claims other than those of the ten pleaded cases were stayed.

In June and October 1998 two further cases against the defendants were dismissed with costs.

Q. Limitation Hearing

32.52 On 7 December 1998, the Court heard the plaintiffs' application to exercise its discretion under section 33 of the Limitation Act 1980 to allow the claims of eight of the ten pleaded cases to proceed. At this point, it was announced that one of the lead claims was to be discontinued against all defendants. Oral evidence was given by seven plaintiffs, a further plaintiff being unable to attend court due to illness.

32.53 In his judgment,[17] Wright J refused the plaintiffs' application, holding:

> It is with regret that I have come to the conclusion that none of them should be permitted to continue their claims against the defendant companies. That is not only because of the in-

---

[17] *Hodgson v Imperial Tobacco Ltd* (Wright J, 9 Feb 1999).

Tobacco Litigation

herent difficulties in the successful presentation of their respective cases, or the somewhat speculative nature of their claims, but in particular because in my judgment none of them (save only perhaps Mr Hodgson, in so far as his own personal activity was concerned) acted promptly or reasonably once they knew whether the acts or omissions of the defendant tobacco companies to whose products they claim their injuries are attributable, might be capable of giving rise to an action for damages . . . As I said at the outset of this judgment, the whole purpose of the Limitation Act is to ensure that claims are litigated promptly and that stale claims should be discouraged . . . Applying those principles as I do, I can see no escape from the decisions that I have arrived at in each of these cases. Accordingly, the applications are refused.

32.54 Wright J concluded that the cases were 'to a degree speculative', that the prospects of success were 'by no means self-evident', that defences of *volenti* and contributory negligence would greatly reduce or eliminate any recoveries, and that the potential liability of each plaintiff in the event of losing was 'formidable'. He concluded that the prejudice suffered by any individual by not granting the application was not as great as would otherwise be the case. Unavailability of witnesses and lapse of time would prejudice the defendants. The Judge held that even if sixteen non-statute-barred claims continued, the defendants would still be prejudiced by the statute-barred claims proceeding and the Court noted that there must be a 'real prospect . . . that all those 16 will . . . come to the conclusion that the risks involved in this litigation are simply not worth taking, and will discontinue'.

32.55 Wright J concluded that the proceedings were brought solely because Leigh Day was prepared to act on a conditional fee basis and he expressed concern that the reasons for delay stated in the statements of claim 'are the product of the ingenuity of the plaintiffs' legal advisers and do not represent either the reality or the instructions given by each individual plaintiff. I can only say that this is to be deprecated.' He held that the change in law allowing CFAs did not of itself constitute good reason for the delay. He noted that he was alert to the effect any decisions would have on the many smokers who had been diagnosed with lung cancer who may be considering bringing claims against the tobacco companies.

32.56 The plaintiffs had sought to appeal the Costs-Sharing Order but this was overtaken by events after the judgment of Wright J. On 26 February 1999, an agreement was made between the plaintiffs, the former plaintiffs, the plaintiffs' legal advisers, their firms (Leigh Day and Irwin Mitchell), and the defendants (Imperial, Gallaher, and Hergall) whereby the action was abandoned by forty-six of the fifty-three plaintiffs. An order was made on 3 March 1999 dismissing the claims with costs.

32.57 Seven claims remained outstanding against the defendants and four plaintiffs were given until 16 April 1999 to write to either of the defendants' solicitors identifying any significant parts which would allow them to continue in the action.

The cost-sharing provisions were varied in that all but four of the Limitation Plaintiffs were liable to each of the defendants in respect of his or her due proportion of the limitation costs. Further, each of the plaintiffs were liable to each of the defendants in respect of the individual costs incurred by that defendant in respect of his or her claim and in respect of his or her due proportion of the common costs of that defendant.

32.58 The seven outstanding claims were finally dismissed with costs on 25 April 1999.

APPENDIX A

Civil Procedure Rules 1998 (Extract)

PART 19

III GROUP LITIGATION

Definition

19.10 A Group Litigation Order ('GLO') means an order made under rule 19.11 to provide for the case management of claims which give rise to common or related issues of fact or law (the 'GLO issues').

Group Litigation Order

19.11—(1) The court may make a GLO where there are or are likely to be a number of claims giving rise to the GLO issues.
(The practice direction provides the procedure for applying for a GLO)
  (2) A GLO must—
    (a) contain directions about the establishment of a register (the 'group register') on which the claims managed under the GLO will be entered;
    (b) specify the GLO issues which will identify the claims to be managed as a group under the GLO; and
    (c) specify the court (the 'management court') which will manage the claims on the group register.
  (3) A GLO may—
    (a) in relation to claims which raise one or more of the GLO issues—
      (i) direct their transfer to the management court;
      (ii) order their stay until further order; and
      (iii) direct their entry on the group register;
    (b) direct that from a specified date claims which raise one or more of the GLO issues should be started in the management court and entered on the group register; and
    (c) give directions for publicising the GLO.

Effect of the GLO

19.12—(1) Where a judgment or order is given or made in a claim on the group register in relation to one or more GLO issues—
    (a) that judgment or order is binding on the parties to all other claims that are on the group register at the time the judgment is given or the order is made unless the court orders otherwise; and
    (b) the court may give directions as to the extent to which that judgment or order is binding on the parties to any claim which is subsequently entered on the group register.
  (2) Unless paragraph (3) applies, any party who is adversely affected by a judgment or order which is binding on him may seek permission to appeal the order.
  (3) A party to a claim which was entered on the group register after a judgment or order which is binding on him was given or made may not—

(a) apply for the judgment or order to be set aside, varied or stayed; or
(b) appeal the judgment or order,

but may apply to the court for an order that the judgment or order is not binding on him.

(4) Unless the court orders otherwise, disclosure of any document relating to the GLO issues by a party to a claim on the group register is disclosure of that document to all parties to claims—
(a) on the group register; and
(b) which are subsequently entered on the group register.

Case management

19.13 Directions given by the management court may include directions—
(a) varying the GLO issues;
(b) providing for one or more claims on the group register to proceed as test claims;
(c) appointing the solicitor of one or more parties to be the lead solicitor for the claimants or defendants;
(d) specifying the details to be included in a statement of case in order to show that the criteria for entry of the claim on the group register have been met;
(e) specifying a date after which no claim may be added to the group register unless the court gives permission; and
(f) for the entry of any particular claim which meets one or more of the GLO issues on the group register.

(Part 3 contains general provisions about the case management powers of the court)

Removal from the register

19.14—(1) A party to a claim entered on the group register may apply to the management court for the claim to be removed from the register.

(2) If the management court orders the claim to be removed from the register it may give directions about the future management of the claim.

Test claims

19.5—(1) Where a direction has been given for a claim on the group register to proceed as a test claim and that claim is settled, the management court may order that another claim on the group register be substituted as the test claim.

(2) Where an order is made under paragraph (1), any order made in the test claim before the date of substitution is binding on the substituted claim unless the Court orders otherwise.

APPENDIX B

Practice Direction—Group Litigation

THIS PRACTICE DIRECTION SUPPLEMENTS SECTION III OF PART 19.

Introduction

1 This practice direction deals with group litigation where the multiple parties are claimants. Section III of Part 19 (group litigation orders) also applies where the multiple parties are defendants. The court will give such directions in such a case as are appropriate.

Preliminary Steps

2.1 Before applying for a Group Litigation Order ('GLO') the solicitor acting for the proposed applicant should consult the Law Society's Multi Party Action Information Service in order to obtain information about other cases giving rise to the proposed GLO issues.

2.2 It will often be convenient for the claimants' solicitors to form a Solicitors' Group and to choose one of their number to take the lead in applying for the GLO and in litigating the GLO issues. The lead solicitor's role and relationship with the other members of the Solicitors' Group should be carefully defined in writing and will be subject to any directions given by the court under CPR 19.13(c).

2.3 In considering whether to apply for a GLO, the applicant should consider whether any other order would be more appropriate. In particular he should consider whether, in the circumstances of the case, it would be more appropriate for—
   (1) the claims to be consolidated; or
   (2) the rules in Section II of Part 19 (representative parties) to be used.

Application for a GLO

3.1 An application for a GLO must be made in accordance with CPR Part 23, may be made at any time before or after any relevant claims have been issued and may be made either by a claimant or by a defendant.

3.2 The following information should be included in the application notice or in written evidence filed in support of the application:
   (1) a summary of the nature of the litigation;
   (2) the number and nature of claims already issued;
   (3) the number of parties likely to be involved;
   (4) the common issues of fact or law (the 'GLO issues') that are likely to arise in the litigation; and
   (5) whether there are any matters that distinguish smaller groups of claims within the wider group.

3.3 A GLO may not be made in the Queen's Bench Division without the consent of the Lord Chief Justice or in the Chancery Division or a county court without the consent of the Vice-Chancellor.

Appendix B: Practice Direction

3.4 The court to which the application for a GLO is made will, if minded to make the GLO, send to the Lord Chief Justice or the Vice-Chancellor (as the case may be) a copy of the application notice, a copy of any relevant written evidence and a written statement as to why a GLO is thought to be desirable. These steps may be taken either before or after a hearing of the application.

High Court in London

3.5 The application for the GLO should be made to the Senior Master in the Queen's Bench Division or the Chief Chancery Master in the Chancery Division. For claims that are proceeding or are likely to proceed in a specialist list, the application should be made to the senior judge of that list.

High Court outside London

3.6 Outside London, the application should be made to a Presiding Judge or a Chancery Supervising Judge of the Circuit in which the District Registry which has issued the application notice is situated.

County courts

3.7 The application should be made to the Designated Civil Judge for the area in which the county court which has issued the application notice is situated.
3.8 The applicant for a GLO should request the relevant court to refer the application notice to the judge by whom the application will be heard as soon as possible after the application notice has been issued. This is to enable the judge to consider whether to follow the practice set out in paragraph 3.4 above prior to the hearing of the application.
3.9 The directions under paragraphs 3.5, 3.6 and 3.7 above do not prevent the judges referred to from making arrangements for other judges to hear applications for GLOs when they themselves are unavailable.

GLO made by Court of its Own Initiative

4 Subject to obtaining the appropriate consent referred to in paragraph 3.3 and the procedure set out in paragraph 3.4, the court may make a GLO of its own initiative. (CPR 3.3 deals with the procedure that applies when a court proposes to make an order of its own initiative)

The GLO

5 CPR 19.11(2) and (3) set out rules relating to the contents of GLOs.

The Group Register

6.1 Once a GLO has been made a Group Register will be established on which will be entered such details as the court may direct of the cases which are to be subject to the GLO.
6.2 An application for details of a case to be entered on a Group Register may be made by any party to the case.
6.3 An order for details of the case to be entered on the Group Register will not be made unless the case gives rise to at least one of the GLO issues.
(CPR 19.10 defines GLO issues)
6.4 The court, if it is not satisfied that a case can be conveniently case managed with the other cases on the Group Register, or if it is satisfied that the entry of the case on the Group Register would adversely affect the case management of the other cases, may refuse to allow details of the case to be entered on the Group Register, or order their removal from the Register if already entered, although the case gives rise to one or more of the Group issues.
6.5 The Group Register will normally be maintained by and kept at the court but the court may direct this to be done by the solicitor for one of the parties to a case entered on the Register.
6.6 (1) Rule 5.4 (supply of documents from court records) applies where the register is main-

tained by the court. A party to a claim on the Group Register may request documents relating to any other claim on the Group Register in accordance with rule 5.4(1) as if he were a party to those proceedings.

(2) Where the register is maintained by a solicitor, any person may inspect the Group Register during normal business hours and upon giving reasonable notice to the solicitor; the solicitor may charge a fee not exceeding the fee prescribed for a search at the court office.

6.7 In this paragraph, 'the court' means the management court specified in the GLO.

Allocation to Track

7   Once a GLO has been made and unless the management court directs otherwise:
    (1) every claim in a case entered on the Group Register will be automatically allocated, or re-allocated (as the case may be), to the multi-track;
    (2) any case management directions that have already been given in any such case otherwise than by the management court will be set aside; and
    (3) any hearing date already fixed otherwise than for the purposes of the group litigation will be vacated.

Managing Judge

8   A judge ('the managing judge') will be appointed for the purpose of the GLO as soon as possible. He will assume overall responsibility for the management of the claims and will generally hear the GLO issues. A Master or a District Judge may be appointed to deal with procedural matters, which he will do in accordance with any directions given by the managing judge. A costs judge may be appointed and may be invited to attend case management hearings.

Claims to be Started in Management Court

9.1 The management court may order that as from a specified date all claims that raise one or more of the GLO issues shall be started in the management court.

9.2 Failure to comply with an order made under paragraph 9.1 will not invalidate the commencement of the claim but the claim should be transferred to the management court and details entered on the Group Register as soon as possible. Any party to the claim may apply to the management court for an order under CPR 19.14 removing the case from the Register or, as the case may be, for an order that details of the case be not entered on the Register.

Transfer

10 Where the management court is a county court and a claim raising one or more of the GLO issues is proceeding in the High Court, an order transferring the case to the management court and directing the details of the case to be entered on the Group Register can only be made in the High Court.

Publicising the GLO

11 After a GLO has been made, a copy of the GLO should be supplied—
    (1) to the Law Society, 113 Chancery Lane, London WC2A 1PL; and
    (2) to the Senior Master, Queen's Bench Division, Royal Courts of Justice, Strand, London WC2A 2LL.

Case Management

12.1 The management court may give case management directions at the time the GLO is made or subsequently. Directions given at a case management hearing will generally be binding on all claims that are subsequently entered on the Group Register (see CPR 19.12(1)).

12.2 Any application to vary the terms of the GLO must be made to the management court.

12.3 The management court may direct that one or more of the claims are to proceed as test claims.

12.4 The management court may give directions about how the costs of resolving common issues or the costs of claims proceeding as test claims are to be borne or shared as between the claimants on the Group Register.

Cut-Off Dates

13 The management court may specify a date after which no claim may be added to the Group Register unless the court gives permission. An early cut-off date may be appropriate in the case of 'instant disasters' (such as transport accidents). In the case of consumer claims, and particularly pharmaceutical claims, it may be necessary to delay the ordering of a cut-off date.

Statements of Case

14.1 The management court may direct that the GLO claimants serve 'Group Particulars of Claim' which set out the various claims of all the claimants on the Group Register at the time the particulars are filed. Such particulars of claim will usually contain—
   (1) general allegations relating to all claims; and
   (2) a schedule containing entries relating to each individual claim specifying which of the general allegations are relied on and any specific facts relevant to the claimant.

14.2 The directions given under paragraph 14.1 should include directions as to whether the Group Particulars should be verified by a statement or statements of truth and, if so, by whom.

14.3 The specific facts relating to each claimant on the Group Register may be obtained by the use of a questionnaire. Where this is proposed, the management court should be asked to approve the questionnaire. The management court may direct that the questionnaires completed by individual claimants take the place of the schedule referred to in paragraph 14.1(2).

14.4 The management court may also give directions about the form that particulars of claim relating to claims which are to be entered on the Group Register should take.

The Trial

15.1 The management court may give directions—
   (1) for the trial of common issues; and
   (2) for the trial of individual issues.

15.2 Common issues and test claims will normally be tried at the management court. Individual issues may be directed to be tried at other courts whose locality is convenient for the parties.

Costs

16.1 CPR 48 contains rules about costs where a GLO has been made.

16.2 Where the court has made an order about costs in relation to any application or hearing which involved both—
   (1) one or more of the GLO issues; and
   (2) an issue or issues relevant only to individual claims;

   and the court has not directed the proportion of the costs that is to relate to common costs and the proportion that is to relate to individual costs in accordance with rule [48.6A], the costs judge will make a decision as to the relevant proportions at or before the commencement of the detailed assessment of costs.

APPENDIX C

Civil Procedure Rules 1998 (Extract)

PART 19

II Representative Parties

Representative Parties with same interest

19.6—(1) Where more than one person has the same interest in a claim—
   (a) the claim may be begun; or
   (b) the court may order that the claim be continued,

   by or against one or more of the persons who have the same interest as representatives of any other persons who have that interest.

(2) The court may direct that a person may not act as a representative.

(3) Any party may apply to the court for an order under paragraph (2).

(4) Unless the court otherwise directs any judgment or order given in a claim in which a party is acting as a representative under this rule—
   (a) is binding on all persons represented in the claim; but
   (b) may only be enforced by or against a person who is not a party to the claim with the permission of the court.

(5) This rule does not apply to a claim to which rule 19.7 applies.

Representation of interested persons who cannot be ascertained etc

19.7—(1) This rule applies to claims about—
   (a) the estate of a deceased person;
   (b) property subject to a trust; or
   (c) the meaning of a document, including a statute.

(2) The court may make an order appointing a person to represent any other person or persons in the claim where the person or persons to be represented—
   (a) are unborn;
   (b) cannot be found;
   (c) cannot easily be ascertained; or
   (d) are a class of persons who have the same interest in a claim and—
      (i) one or more members of that class are within sub-paragraphs (a), (b) or (c); or
      (ii) to appoint a representative would further the overriding objective.

(3) An application for an order under paragraph (2)—
   (a) may be made by—
      (i) any person who seeks to be appointed under the order; or
      (ii) any party to the claim; and
   (b) may be made at any time before or after the claim has started.

(4) An application notice for an order under paragraph (2) must be served on—
   (a) all parties to the claim, if the claim has started;

(b) the person sought to be appointed, if that person is not the applicant or a party to the claim; and
(c) any other person as directed by the court.

(5) The court's approval is required to settle a claim in which a party is acting as a representative under this rule.

(6) The court may approve a settlement where it is satisfied that the settlement is for the benefit of all the represented persons.

(7) Unless the court otherwise directs, any judgment or order given in a claim in which a party is acting as a representative under this rule—
(a) is binding on all persons represented in the claim; but
(b) may only be enforced by or against a person who is not a party to the claim with the permission of the court.

Death

19.8—(1) Where a person who had an interest in a claim has died and that person has no personal representative the court may order—
(a) the claim to proceed in the absence of a person representing the estate of the deceased; or
(b) a person to be appointed to represent the estate of the deceased.

(2) Where a defendant against whom a claim could have been brought has died and—
(a) a grant of probate or administration has been made, the claim must be brought against the persons who are the personal representatives of the deceased;
(b) a grant of probate or administration has not been made—
   (i) the claim must be brought against 'the estate of' the deceased; and
   (ii) the claimant must apply to the court for an order appointing a person to represent the estate of the deceased in the claim.

(3) A claim shall be treated as having been brought against 'the estate of' the deceased in accordance with paragraph (2)(b)(i) where—
(a) the claim is brought against the 'personal representatives' of the deceased but a grant of probate or administration has not been made; or
(b) the person against whom the claim was brought was dead when the claim was started.

(4) Before making an order under this rule, the court may direct notice of the application to be given to any other person with an interest in the claim.

(5) Where an order has been made under paragraphs (1) or (2)(b)(ii) any judgment or order made or given in the claim is binding on the estate of the deceased.

Derivative Claims

19.9—(1) This rule applies where a company, other incorporated body or trade union is alleged to be entitled to claim a remedy and a claim is made by one or more members of the company, body or trade union for it to be given that remedy (a 'derivative claim').

(2) The company, body or trade union for whose benefit a remedy is sought must be a defendant to the claim.

(3) After the claim form has been issued the claimant must apply to the court for permission to continue the claim and may not take any other step in the proceedings except—
(a) except as provided by paragraph (5); or
(b) where the court gives permission.

(4) An application in accordance with paragraph (3) must be supported by written evidence.

(5) The—
(a) claim form;
(b) application notice; and
(c) written evidence in support of the application,

must be served on the defendant within the period within which the claim form must be served and, in any event, at least 14 days before the court is to deal with the application.

(6) If the court gives the claimant permission to continue the claim, the time within which the defence must be filed is 14 days after the date on which the permission is given or such period as the court may specify.

(7) The court may order the company, body or trade union to indemnify the claimant against any liability in respect of costs incurred in the claim.

APPENDIX D

COMMUNITY LEGAL SERVICES
MULTI-PARTY ACTION (MPA) SOLICITORS PANEL

On 1 February 1999 the Legal Aid Board, at the request of the Lord Chancellor, launched a panel of specialist firms of solicitors, to whom preference will be given in the contracting of multi-party actions. Members of the MPA Solicitors Panel have demonstrated experience and expertise in group actions. Panel members will be eligible to tender for any MPA contract led by the Board, whether or not they have clients in the action.

Criteria for joining the Panel include: a Legal Aid Board franchise; recent substantial involvement in co-ordinating or managing generic work in at least three MPAs; sufficient fee-earning staff and an adequate infrastructure to conduct a moderately sized MPA.

The first eighteen firms to be appointed to the Panel are:

Alexander Harris
Ashley House
Ashley Road
Altrincham
WA14 2DW
Tel: 0161 925 5555
Fax: 0161 925 5500

Gadsby Wicks
91–99 New London Road
Chelmsford
CM2 0PP
Tel: 01245 494929
Fax: 01245 495347

Hugh James
Arlbee House
Greyfriars Road
Cardiff
CF1 4QB
Tel: 01222 224871
Fax: 01222 388222

John Pickering & Partners
9 Church Lane
Oldham
OL1 3AN
Tel: 0161 633 6667
Fax: 0161 626 1671

Donns
PO Box 41
201 Deansgate
Manchester
M60 1DZ
Tel: 0161 834 3311
Fax: 0161 834 2317

Hay & Kilner
Merchant House
30 Cloth Market
Newcastle upon Tyne
NE1 1EE
Tel: 0191 232 8345
Fax: 0191 221 0514

Irwin Mitchell
St Peter's House
Hartshead
Sheffield
S1 2EL
Tel: 0114 276 7777
Fax: 0114 275 3306

Lawrence Tucketts
Bush House
72 Prince Street
Bristol
BS99 7JZ
Tel: 0117 929 5252
Fax: 0117 929 8313

Freeth Cartwright Hunt Dickens
Willoughby House
20 Low Pavement
Nottingham
NG1 7EA
Tel: 0115 936 9369
Fax: 0115 936 9370

Hodge Jones & Allen
Twyman House
31–39 Camden Road
London
NW1 9LR
Tel: 0207 482 1974
Fax: 0207 267 3476

Jackson & Canter
32 Princes Road
Liverpool
L8 1TH
Tel: 0151 708 6593
Fax: 0151 708 5850

Leigh Day & Co
Priory House
25 St John's Lane
London
EC1M 4LB
Tel: 0207 650 1200
Fax: 0207 253 4433

Appendix D: MPA Solicitors Panel

Nelsons
Pennine House
8 Stanford Street
Nottingham
NG1 7BQ
Tel: 0115 958 6262
Fax: 0115 958 4702

Russel Jones & Walker
Swinton House
324 Gray's Inn Road
London
WC1X 8DH
Tel: 0207 837 2941
Fax: 0207 837 2941

Pannone & Partners
123 Deansgate
Manchester
M3 2BU
Tel: 0161 909 3000
Fax: 0161 909 4444

Smith Llewelyn Partnership
18 Princess Way
Swansea
SA1 3LW
Tel: 01792 464444
Fax: 01792 464726

Raleys
Regent House
Regent Street
Barnsley
S70 2EG
Tel: 01226 211111
Fax: 01226 212227

Wolferstans
Deptford Chambers
60–64 North Hill
Plymouth
PL4 8EP
Tel: 01752 663295
Fax: 01752 672021

APPENDIX E

Costs Rules Relating to a GLO

CIVIL PROCEDURE RULES 1998 (EXTRACT)

Costs where the court has made a Group Litigation Order

48.6A—(1) This rule applies where the court has made a Group Litigation Order ('GLO').

(2) In this rule—
   (a) 'individual costs' means costs incurred in relation to an individual claim on the group register;
   (b) 'common costs' means—
      (i) costs incurred in relation to the GLO issues;
      (ii) individual costs incurred in a claim while it is proceeding as a test claim, and
      (iii) costs incurred by the lead solicitor in administering the group litigation; and
   (c) 'group litigant' means a claimant or defendant, as the case may be, whose claim is entered on the group register.

(3) Unless the court orders otherwise, any order for common costs against group litigants imposes on each group litigant several liability for an equal proportion of those common costs.

(4) The general rule is that where a group litigant is the paying party, he will, in addition to any costs he is liable to pay to the receiving party, be liable for—
   (a) the individual costs of his claim; and
   (b) an equal proportion, together with all the other group litigants, of the common costs.

(5) Where the court makes an order about costs in relation to any application or hearing which involved—
   (a) one or more GLO issues; and
   (b) issues relevant only to individual claims,
the court will direct the proportion of the costs that is to relate to common costs and the proportion that is to relate to individual costs.

(6) Where common costs have been incurred before a claim is entered on the group register, the court may order the group litigant to be liable for a proportion of those costs.

(7) Where a claim is removed from the group register, the court may make an order for costs in that claim which includes a proportion of the common costs incurred up to the date on which the claim is removed from the group register. (Part 19 sets out rules about group litigation).

Extract from Practice Direction: Parts 43–48

SECTION 52 COSTS WHERE THE COURT HAS MADE A GROUP LITIGATION ORDER: RULE 48.6A

52.1 (1) The Practice Direction supplementing Part 19 Section III deals with group litigation. Rule 48.6A(3) Provides that the general rule is that where a group litigant is the paying

party he will, in addition to any costs he is liable to pay to the receiving party be liable for:—
  (a) the individual costs of his claim; and
  (b) an equal proportion, together with all the other group litigants, of the common costs.
(2) The court may require the parties to provide information about the costs that have already been incurred.
(3) Where the court appoints a lead solicitor in accordance with rule 19.13 the court may direct that recoverable costs may include the costs incurred by the lead solicitor in administering the group litigation. This may include costs that are unique to the Group Litigation such as convening meetings of litigants or producing a new sheet for the parties.

52.2 Rule 44.3(4)(b) provides that in deciding what (if any) order to make about costs, the court must have regard to whether a party has succeeded on part of his claim. This will be especially relevant in a group litigation claim. The court may decide, for example, that because the claimants have succeeded on the issue of liability, it would be inappropriate to make a costs order against a particular claimant who happens to have been unsuccessful on issues regarding the amount of damages (eg, because the amount of damages awarded to him was substantially reduced by a successful plea of contributory negligence).

52.3 Rule 48.6A(5) provides that the court will direct the proportion of the costs that is to relate to the common costs and the proportion that is to relate to individual costs. It is the duty of the legal representatives to raise this matter with the court and if the court does not deal with the point the costs officer will make a decision as to the relevant proportions at or before the commencement of the detailed assessment of the costs.

APPENDIX F

Directive 98/27/EC of the European Parliament and of the Council of 19 May 1998 on injunctions for the protection of consumers' interests

THE EUROPEAN PARLIAMENT AND THE COUNCIL OF THE EUROPEAN UNION

Having regard to the Treaty establishing the European Community, and in particular Article 100a thereof,

Having regard to the proposal from the Commission.[1]

Having regard to the opinion of the Economic and Social Committee.[2]

Acting in accordance with the procedure laid down in Article 189b of the Treaty.[3]

(1) Whereas certain Directives, listed in the schedule annexed to this Directive, lay down rules with regard to the protection of consumers' interests;

(2) Whereas current mechanisms available both at national and at Community level for ensuring compliance with those Directives do not always allow infringements harmful to the collective interests of consumers to be terminated in good time; whereas collective interests mean interests which do not include the cumulation of interests of individuals who have been harmed by an infringement; whereas this is without prejudice to individual actions brought by individuals who have been harmed by an infringement;

(3) Whereas, as far as the purpose of bringing about the cessation of practices that are unlawful under the national provisions applicable is concerned, the effectiveness of national measures transposing the above Directives including protective measures that go beyond the level required by those Directives, provided they are compatible with the Treaty and allowed by those Directives, may be thwarted where those practices produce effects in a Member State other than that in which they originate;

(4) Whereas those difficulties can disrupt the smooth functioning of the internal market, their consequence being that it is sufficient to move the source of an unlawful practice to another country in order to place it out of reach of all forms of enforcement; whereas this constitutes a distortion of competition;

(5) Whereas those difficulties are likely to diminish consumer confidence in the internal market and may limit the scope for action by organisations representing the collective interests of

---

[1] OJ C107, 13. 4. 1996, p 3 and OJ C80, 13. 3. 1997, p 10.
[2] OJ C30, 30. 1. 1997, p 112.
[3] Opinion of the European Parliament of 14 November 1996 (OJ C362, 2. 12. 1996, p 236). Council common position of 30 October 1997 (OJ C389, 22. 12. 1997, p 51) and Decision of the European Parliament of 12 March 1998 (OJ C104, 6. 4. 1998). Council Decision of 23 April 1998.

Appendix F: Directive on Injunctions

consumers or independent public bodies responsible for protecting the collective interests of consumers, adversely affected by practices that infringe Community law;

(6) Whereas those practices often extend beyond the frontiers between the Member States; whereas there is an urgent need for some degree of approximation of national provisions designed to enjoin the cessation of the abovementioned unlawful practices irrespective of the country in which the unlawful practice has produced its effects; whereas, with regard to jurisdiction, this is without prejudice to the rules of private international law and the Conventions in force between Member States, while respecting the general obligations of the Member States deriving from the Treaty, in particular those related to the smooth functioning of the internal market;

(7) Whereas the objective of the action envisaged can only be attained by the Community; whereas it is therefore incumbent on the Community to act;

(8) Whereas the third paragraph of Article 3b of the Treaty makes it incumbent on the Community not to go beyond what is necessary to achieve the objectives of the Treaty; whereas, in accordance with that Article, the specific features of national legal systems must be taken into account to every extent possible by leaving Member States free to choose between different options having equivalent effect; whereas the courts or administrative authorities competent to rule on the proceedings referred to in Article 2 of this Directive should have the right to examine the effects of previous decisions;

(9) Whereas one option should consist in requiring one or more independent public bodies, specifically responsible for the protection of the collective interests of consumers, to exercise the rights of action set out in this Directive; whereas another option should provide for the exercise of those rights by organisations whose purpose is to protect the collective interests of consumers, in accordance with criteria laid down by national law;

(10) Whereas Member States should be able to choose between or combine these two options in designating at national level the bodies and/or organisations qualified for the purposes of this Directive;

(11) Whereas for the purposes of intra-Community infringements the principle of mutual recognition should apply to these bodies and/or organisations; whereas the Member States should, at the request of their national entities, communicate to the Commission the name and purpose of their national entities which are qualified to bring an action in their own country according to the provisions of this Directive;

(12) Whereas it is the business of the Commission to ensure the publication of a list of these qualified entities in the *Official Journal of the European Communities*; whereas, until a statement to the contrary is published, a qualified entity is assumed to have legal capacity if its name is included in that list;

(13) Whereas Member States should be able to require that a prior consultation be undertaken by the party that intends to bring an action for an injunction, in order to give the defendant an opportunity to bring the contested infringement to an end; whereas Member States should be able to require that this prior consultation take place jointly with an independent public body designated by those Member States;

(14) Whereas, where the Member States have established that there should be prior consultation, a deadline of two weeks after the request for consultation is received should be set after which, should the cessation of the infringement not be achieved, the applicant shall be entitled to bring an action before the competent court or administrative authority without any further delay;

(15) Whereas it is appropriate that the Commission report on the functioning of this Directive and in particular on its scope and the operation of prior consultation;

(16) Whereas the application of this Directive should not prejudice the application of Community competition rules, have adopted this directive.

Appendix F: Directive on Injunctions

Article 1

Scope

1. The purpose of this Directive is to approximate the laws, regulations and administrative provisions of the Member States relating to actions for an injunction referred to in Article 2 aimed at the protection of the collective interests of consumers included in the Directives listed in the Annex, with a view to ensuring the smooth functioning of the internal market.

2. For the purpose of this Directive, an infringement shall mean any act contrary to the Directives listed in the Annex as transposed into the internal legal order of the Member States which harms the collective interests referred to in paragraph 1.

Article 2

Actions for an injunction

1. Member States shall designate the courts or administrative authorities competent to rule on proceedings commenced by qualified entities within the meaning of Article 3 seeking:
(a) an order with all due expediency, where appropriate by way of summary procedure, requiring the cessation or prohibition of any infringement;
(b) where appropriate, measures such as the publication of the decision, in full or in part, in such form as deemed adequate and/or the publication of a corrective statement with a view to eliminating the continuing effects of the infringement;
(c) insofar as the legal system of the Member State concerned so permits, an order against the losing defendant for payments into the public purse or to any beneficiary designated in or under national legislation, in the event of failure to comply with the decision within a time-limit specified by the courts or administrative authorities, of a fixed amount for each day's delay or any other amount provided for in national legislation, with a view to ensuring compliance with the decisions.

2. This Directive shall be without prejudice to the rules of private international law, with respect to the applicable law, thus leading normally to the application of either the law of the Member State where the infringement originated or the law of the Member State where the infringement has its effects.

Article 3

Entities qualified to bring an action

For the purposes of this Directive, a 'qualified entity' means any body or organisation which, being properly constituted according to the law of a Member State, has a legitimate interest in ensuring that the provisions referred to in Article 1 are complied with, in particular:
(a) one or more independent public bodies, specifically responsible for protecting the interests referred to in Article 1, in Member States in which such bodies exist and/or
(b) organisations whose purpose is to protect the interests referred to in Article 1, in accordance with the criteria laid down by their national law.

Article 4

Intra-Community infringements

1. Each Member State shall take the measures necessary to ensure that, in the event of an infringement originating in that Member State, any qualified entity from another Member State where the interests protected by that qualified entity are affected by the infringement, may seize the court or administrative authority referred to in Article 2, on presentation of the list provided for in paragraph 3. The courts or administrative authorities shall accept this list as proof of the legal capacity of the qualified entity without prejudice to their right to examine whether the purpose of the qualified entity justifies its taking action in a specific case.

2. For the purposes of intra-Community infringements, and without prejudice to the rights granted to other entities under national legislation, the Member States shall, at the request of their qualified entities, communicate to the Commission that these entities are qualified to bring an action under Article 2. The Member States shall inform the Commission of the name and purpose of these qualified entities.
3. The Commission shall draw up a list of the qualified entities referred to in paragraph 2, with the specification of their purpose. This list shall be published in the *Official Journal of the European Communities*; changes to this list shall be published without delay, the updated list shall be published every six months.

Article 5

Prior consultation

1. Member States may introduce or maintain in force provisions whereby the party that intends to seek an injunction can only start this procedure after it has tried to achieve the cessation of the infringement in consultation with either the defendant or with both the defendant and a qualified entity within the meaning of Article 3(a) of the Member State in which the injunction is sought. It shall be for the Member State to decide whether the party seeking the injunction must consult the qualified entity. If the cessation of the infringement is not achieved within two weeks after the request for consultation is received, the party concerned may bring an action for an injunction without any further delay.
2. The rules governing prior consultation adopted by Member States shall be notified to the Commission and shall be published in the *Official Journal of the European Communities*.

Article 6

Reports

1. Every three years and for the first time no later than five years after the entry into force of this Directive the Commission shall submit to the European Parliament and the Council a report on the application of this Directive.
2. In its first report the Commission shall examine in particular:
—the scope of this Directive in relation to the protection of the collective interests of persons exercising a commercial, industrial, craft or professional activity;
—the scope of this Directive as determined by the Directives listed in the Annex;
—whether the prior consultation in Article 5 has contributed to the effective protection of consumers.

Where appropriate, this report shall be accompanied by proposals with a view to amending this Directive.

Article 7

Provisions for wider action

This Directive shall not prevent Member States from adopting or maintaining in force provisions designed to grant qualified entities and any other person concerned more extensive rights to bring action at national level.

Article 8

Implementation

1. Member States shall bring into force the laws, regulations and administrative provisions necessary to comply with this Directive no later than 30 months after its entry into force. They shall immediately inform the Commission thereof.

When Member States adopt these measures, they shall contain a reference to this Directive or shall be accompanied by such reference on the occasion of their official publication. The methods of making such reference shall be adopted by Member States.

2. Member States shall communicate to the Commission the provisions of national law which they adopt in the field covered by this Directive.

Article 9

Entry into force

This Directive shall enter into force on the twentieth day following that of its publication in the *Official Journal of the European Communities*.

Article 10

Addressees

This Directive is addressed to the Member States.

ANNEX

LIST OF DIRECTIVES COVERED BY ARTICLE 1 (*)

1. Council Directive 84/450/EEC of 10 September 1984 relating to the approximation of the laws, regulations and administrative provisions of the Member States concerning misleading advertising (OJ L250, 19.9.1984, p 17).
2. Council Directive 85/577/EEC of 20 December 1985 to protect the consumer in respect of contracts negotiated away from business premises (OJ L372, 31.12.1985, p 31).
3. Council Directive 87/102/EEC of 22 December 1986 for the approximation of the laws, regulations and administrative provisions of the Member States concerning consumer credit (OJ L42, 12.2.1987, p 48), as last amended by Directive 98/7/EC (OJ L101, 1.4.1998, p 17).
4. Council Directive 89/552/EEC of 3 October 1989 on the coordination of certain provisions laid down by law, regulation or administrative action in Member States concerning the pursuit of television broadcasting activities: Articles 10 to 21 (OJ L298, 17.10.1989, p 23 as amended by Directive 97/36/EC (OJ L202, 30.7.1997, p 60)).
5. Council Directive 90/314/EEC of 13 June 1990 on package travel, package holidays and package tours (OJ L158, 23.6.1990, p 59).
6. Council Directive 92/28/EEC of 31 March 1992 on the advertising of medicinal products for human use (OJ L113, 30.4.1992, p 13).
7. Council Directive 93/13/EEC of 5 April 1993 on unfair terms in consumer contracts (OJ L95, 21.4.1993, p 29).
8. Directive 94/47/EC of the European Parliament and of the Council of 26 October 1994 on the protection of purchasers in respect of certain aspects of contracts relating to the purchase of the right to use immovable properties on a timeshare basis (OJ L280, 29.10.1994, p 83).
9. Directive 97/7/EC of the European Parliament and of the Council of 20 May 1997 on the protection of consumers in respect of distance contracts (OJ L144, 4.6.1997, p 19).
[10. Directive 1999/44/EC of the European Parliament and of the Council of 25 May 1999 on certain aspects of the sale of consumer goods and associated guarantees (OJ L171, 7.7.1999, p 12)](**)

(*) Directive Nos 1, 6, 7 and 9 contain specific provisions on injunctive actions.
(**) This Directive was added to the annex by Directive 1999/44/EC, Article 10.

APPENDIX G

Note: this is a sample GLO (see ch 3), followed by sample provisions on a costs-sharing order (see ch 8) which may or may not be made at the time at which a GLO is made. The directions which may be appropriate should be considered on a case-by-case basis and these provisions should not be treated as a blueprint.

<u>Case No. 2000 S No 1234 & other actions listed in Schedule 1 hereto</u>

<u>IN THE HIGH COURT OF JUSTICE</u>
<u>QUEEN'S BENCH DIVISION</u>
<u>IN THE MATTER OF THE GROUP LITIGATION</u>
<u>BEFORE MASTER</u>

BETWEEN

PAUL SMITH

<u>Claimants</u>

-and-

AB PLC

<u>Defendants</u>

GROUP LITIGATION ORDER

BEFORE Master   sitting at the Royal Courts of Justice on

UPON HEARING Counsel for the Claimants and the Defendants

IT IS ORDERED:

1. Group Litigation

1.1 There be a Group Litigation Order (GLO) in accordance with CPR, Rule 19.III in relation to all claims which include [one or more of] the GLO issues.
1.2 The GLO issues are:
    1.2.1
    1.2.2
    1.2.3
    1.2.4

2. Management Court

2.1 The management court shall be the Queen's Bench Division of the High Court, Royal Courts of Justice in London.

2.2 All actions which raise one or more of the GLO issues which are commenced after the date of this Order shall be commenced in the management court.

2.3 Any proceedings which are, as of the date of this Order, still proceeding in any other court shall be transferred to the management court forthwith.

3. The Group Register

3.1 ... shall be the lead solicitors for the Claimants and shall maintain the Group Register.

3.2 The Group Register shall contain the following information in respect of the Claimants within the Group:

    3.2.1 the full name, address and postcode of each Claimant;

    3.2.2 the full name, address and postcode of each Claimant's litigation friend;

    3.2.3 the date of birth of each Claimant;

    3.2.4 the name and address, postcode, telephone and facsimile numbers of the solicitors on the record for each Claimant;

    3.2.5 the case or action number for each Claimant;

    3.2.6 the number of the Community Legal Service Certificate issued (if appropriate);

    3.2.7 the names of all Defendants against whom the Claimant is proceeding;

    3.2.8 the date of issue and service of the Writ/Claim Form;

    3.2.9 the date of joining the Register.

3.3 The Claimants' solicitors shall serve on the Defendants' solicitors a copy of the updated Register at three monthly intervals, commencing on

3.4 The Defendants' solicitors shall inform the Claimants' solicitors within 28 days of the receipt of the latest copy of the Register if it does not conform with their understanding of the details of the Claimants bringing proceedings against their respective clients, identifying in what respects it does not do so.

3.5 A Claimant shall remain on the Register until such time as he/she serves Notice of Discontinuance or, if required, obtains leave to discontinue, or following an appropriate Order of the Court, in which event he/she will cease to be on the Register at the expiry of the quarter during which Notice of Discontinuance was served, or leave to discontinue was obtained or the appropriate Court Order made.

3.6 The Claimants' solicitors shall keep in a separate section of the Register details of those who leave the group, giving details within that section of the name of the Claimant, the action number of the claim which has been terminated and the date of the termination of the claim.

4. Joining the Register

4.1 Any claim which is subject to this GLO and gives rise to all of the GLO issues shall be included on the Group Register.

4.2 Forthwith upon receipt of a statement of case which shows that the criteria for entry of the claim on the Group Register have been met, the lead solicitors shall forthwith enter that claim on the Register.

4.3 Any solicitor who issues or has issued a claim which is subject to this GLO shall immediately send to the lead solicitors a copy of the issued Claim Form and statement of case, together with all the details listed in paragraph 4.2 above and a request for the claim to be entered on the Register.

4.4 Where a dispute arises between any of the parties as to whether a Claimant comes within the definition of those who are subject to this GLO, and/or as to whether his/her name should be entered on the Register, the Claimant's solicitors shall refer the matter to the Court.

Specimen GLO Directions

4.5 No claim may be added to the Group Register after   unless the management court gives permission.

5. Standard Minimum Requirements[1]

5.1 All claimants who are or become subject to this GLO shall serve on the Defendants' solicitors as soon as possible, the following:
  5.1.1 a Notice of the grant of public funding or of the existence of a conditional fee agreement and/or an insurance policy, as appropriate;
  5.1.2 a signed consent form in relation to his/her medical records, which form must be in the form set out in Schedule 1 hereto;
  5.1.3 such medical records (or copies thereof) as are in his/her possession;
  5.1.4 a completed individual claim notification form in the form set out in Schedule 3 hereto.

5.2
  5.2.1 As soon as possible after   the Defendants shall, by their solicitors, make proposals to the Claimants' solicitors as to the time for the service of a response to the Letters of Claim, and the provision of disclosure, as set out hereafter;
  5.2.2 In accordance with the timetable agreed between the parties' solicitors pursuant to sub-paragraph (5.2.1) above, or as directed by the Court, the Defendants shall respond to the Letters of Claim within the spirit of [paragraph 3.10 of the Pre-Action Protocol for Personal Injury Claims], including providing disclosure of documents material to the matters in issue identified in the letter of claim and the Defendants' response thereto, such disclosure to be upon the standard basis.

6. Sample Pleadings

6.1 The claimants do serve statements of case in x cases.

7. Further Directions

7.1 The parties to attend by their Clerks not later than   to fix a date for a further Case Management Conference not earlier than
7.2 The Court's consideration of the proposed costs-sharing order be adjourned to the further Case Management Conference.
7.3 The parties do lodge bundles for use at the further Case Management Conference 5 clear days beforehand, skeleton arguments 3 clear days beforehand, and bundles of authorities 2 clear days beforehand.

8. Costs-Sharing

Save as otherwise ordered:
(a) The liability of each party for and each party's entitlement to recover costs shall be several and joint.
(b) Individual costs are those costs and disbursements incurred for and/or in respect of any individual Claimant in relation to matters which are personal to each such Claimant, excluding costs and disbursements incurred for and/or respect of any claims which may hereafter be selected as lead cases.
(c) Common costs are all costs and disbursements other than individual costs.

---

[1] The court may also order, to the extent to which these have not already been served:
  (a) a letter of claim within the spirit of, for example, paragraph 3.1 of the Pre-Action Protocol for Personal Injury Claims setting out a summary of the facts upon which each claim is based and the nature of the injuries suffered and identifying the issues raised against each of the defendants so as to enable them to address such issues in response, and/or
  (b) statements of case.

(d) The common costs incurred in any quarter by the Claimants and each of the Defendants are to be divided by the number of Claimants pursuing their claims on the first day of the quarter.
(e) If in any quarter a Claimant compromises his/her claim with any one or more of the Defendants on terms which provide for such Defendants to pay that Claimant his/her costs then that Claimant shall be entitled to recover his/her individual costs and his/her several share of the common costs incurred by the Claimants up to the last day of that quarter.
(f) If in any quarter a Claimant discontinues his/her claim against any one or more of the Defendants or it is dismissed by an Order of the Court whereby that Claimant is ordered to pay such Defendants' costs, then he/she will be liable for his/her individual costs together with his/her several share of the common costs incurred by such Defendants up to the last day of that quarter.
(g) The first quarter under this costs-sharing order shall run from . . .
(h) Each of the Claimants shall for the purposes of this Order be treated as if he/she had been a Claimant in the actions as from . . .

9. Costs

9.1 Costs in the case.
9.2 Certificates for 2 Counsel to Claimants and Defendants.

Counsel for the Claimants ....
Counsel for the Defendants ....
Dated:

SCHEDULE 1
MEDICAL RECORDS CONSENT FORM

I,   , the parent/legal guardian of [CLAIMANT] (hereafter referred to as 'the Patient') hereby authorise the release and delivery to [SOLICITORS FOR DEFENDANT], solicitors for [DEFENDANT], of all medical records, reports, notes, documents (whether originals or copies or stored electronically) and other information relating to the Patient including but not limited to:

1. All general practitioner notes, records, other medical documents and material and correspondence to and from the general practitioner;
2. All hospital notes (inpatient and outpatient), records, reports, other documents and materials including but not limited to material relating to the Patient and his medical history, diagnosis, prognosis, progress, surgical procedures, anaesthetics, investigations, laboratory results and reports (including but not limited to haematology, histology, pathology and microbiology), medication and drug charts and records, nursing notes, consultants' notes, psychiatric notes, scans, results and reports from ECGs, EEGs, MRI, CAT scans and all other diagnostic techniques; and
3. All other documents, records, reports, photographs, correspondence, scans and medical materials (including clinical samples and specimens) relating to the examination, diagnosis or treatment of the Patient, whether medical, surgical, psychiatric or other.

This consent is conditional upon such information and materials not being used for any purpose except in connection with the action commenced by the Patient against [DEFENDANT] and presently proceeding in the Central Office, Royal Courts of Justice, save to the extent that any overriding requirements of law imposed upon [DEFENDANT] or its associated companies necessitate the supply of such information or materials to government regulatory authorities in connection with the reporting of possible adverse reactions.

This authority does not extend to the disclosure of any medical reports that may have been commissioned by the Patient or his parent/legal guardian or his solicitors for the purposes of this litigation.

Specimen GLO Directions

The name and address of the Patient's current general practitioner and of all physicians, surgeons, consultants or other health care practitioners whom the Patient has consulted in the United Kingdom or abroad are attached at schedule A.

I confirm that the patient's date of birth is..

Signed... Date...

Schedule A

Schedule of treating doctors and health care practitioners

The name and address of the Patient's current general practitioner and any other consultant or medical or other health care practitioner whom [**CLAIMANT**] has consulted in the United Kingdom or abroad is:

1. NAME
   ADDRESS

   DESCRIPTION (eg GP/surgeon/psychiatrist/etc)

2. NAME
   ADDRESS

   DESCRIPTION (eg GP/surgeon/psychiatrist/etc)

3. NAME
   ADDRESS

   DESCRIPTION (eg GP/surgeon/psychiatrist/etc)

FURTHER SCHEDULE FOR USE WITH MEDICINAL PRODUCT CLAIMS

INDIVIDUAL CLAIM NOTIFICATION

PERSONAL DETAILS

Name Claim number
Date of Birth NI number
Address Date claim issued
  LSC Certificate No Issue Date of SSC Cert

Name & Address Name & Address of
of Litigation Claimant('s) Solicitor
Friend
Age of Patient

PRODUCT DETAILS

Date Location
Batch number Type
  Brand Administered by Manufacturer

ADVERSE REACTION DETAILS

Date of first Development
reaction of reaction
Condition(s) Diagnosing doctor and date
diagnosed

APPENDIX H

Multi-Party Action Panel Arrangements 2000

These procedures are made by the Legal Services Commission. They apply with effect from 5 April 2000. They constitute amendments to the Legal Aid Board Multi-Party Action Arrangements 1999. They make substantially the same provision as those arrangements but with minor drafting amendments and with amendments to fit the provisions of the Access to Justice Act 1999 (including the replacement of the Legal Aid Board by the Legal Services Commission) and the Funding Code.

Part I Preliminary

Introduction

1. The MPA procedures in the Funding Code apply to MPA Contracts. Except so far as procedures are specified by the Funding Code, these MPA procedures 2000 set out the procedures which apply to multi-party actions under the Act.

2. Parts II and IV of these procedures deal with the procedures leading up to and including signing of an MPA Contract. In particular, firms seeking an MPA Contract must have regard to the requirements set out in Part III.

The procedures which will apply once an MPA Contract is in force are set out in Part V of these procedures. Unless the Commission otherwise specifies in any contract or otherwise, the provisions of Part V are incorporated into every contract entered into under these procedures.

Interpretation

3. In these procedures, unless the context otherwise requires:

'the Act' means the Access to Justice Act 1999;

'all-work contract' means an MPA Contract covering all work in the action (both generic work and individual work);

'Certificate' has the meaning set out in the Funding Code;

'the Commission' means the Legal Services Commission established under the Act and includes any person or body (including the MPA Unit) duly authorised to act on its behalf;

'client' means a person making a claim in a multi-party action with the benefit of a Certificate;

'contract work' means work of the type specified in an MPA Contract in accordance with paragraph 30;

'contracted firm' means any firm which has entered into an MPA Contract with the Commission, whether by itself or as one of a group of firms;

'firm' means a firm of solicitors or other legal representatives duly authorised under the Act to perform work within scope of the MPA Contract;

'Fund' means the Community Legal Service Fund established under section 5 of the Act;

'Funding Code' means the code established under section 8 of the Act;

'Funding Review Body' has the meaning set out in the Funding Code;

'generic work' has the meaning set out in the Funding Code;

'group of firms' means a pair, group, consortium or steering committee of firms which propose to enter into an MPA Contract;

Appendix H: MPA Procedures

'legal representation' has the meaning set out in the Funding Code;
'Legal Representative' has the meaning set out in the Funding Code;
'local firm' means any firm representing a client in respect of work which is not covered by an MPA Contract;
'MPA Committee' has the meaning set out in the Funding Code'
'MPA Contract' means an MPA Contract between one or more firms and the Commission entered into under these procedures;
'MPA Manager' means the member of the Commission's personnel responsible for the management of contracts with contracted firms;
'MPA Unit' has the meaning set out in the Funding Code;
'multi-party action' or 'MPA' has the meaning set out in the Funding Code;
'nominated contracted firm' means the firm specified in the contract as responsible for a particular obligation;
'panel' means the panel of firms established under paragraph 6;
'paragraph' means a numbered paragraph in these procedures;
'private client' means a person making a claim in a multi-party action without the benefit of a Certificate;
'Regional Director' has the meaning set out in the Funding Code (note that the Director of the Special Cases Unit may exercise any of the powers of a Regional Director in relation to cases referred to the Special Cases Unit and that the MPA Unit is part of the Special Cases Unit);
'regulations' means regulations under the Act;
'Special Cases Unit' has the meaning set out in the Funding Code;
'Support Funding' has the meaning set out in the Funding Code;
'termination' means termination of an MPA Contract.

Unless otherwise provided, words and phrases which are defined in the Act, regulations or Funding Code have those meanings in these procedures.

Part II Administration

4. The MPA Committee will operate in accordance with any guidance and directions issued by the Commission. The MPA Committee may co-opt additional members to serve on it for particular functions or for the purposes of a particular action. The Chairman of the MPA Committee may, if he or she thinks fit, refer any matter before the MPA Committee to the Chairman of the Commission or to the Commission.

5. When the MPA Committee is carrying out the following functions namely:
    (i) approving firms to join the panel under paragraph 8;
    (ii) removing firms from the panel under paragraph 10;
    (iii) selecting firms to enter into contracts under paragraph 26;
    (iv) terminating contracts under paragraph 71

the MPA Committee will include a nominee of The Law Society and a nominee of either the National Consumer Council or the Consumers' Association. The nominations will be vetted by the Commission to ensure that there is no conflict of interest.

6. The Commission may establish a panel of franchised firms which are approved for the purpose of tendering under these Procedures. The Commission may advertise or invite firms to join the panel and will set criteria for joining which may include any of the following:
    (i) proven recent experience in multi-party action work and complex, high value litigation;
    (ii) appropriate resources for complex multi-party litigation, both human resources and infrastructure;
    (iii) evidence of financial and corporate stability;
    (iv) a franchise in any category of work.

Appendix H: MPA Procedures

7. A firm applying to join the panel will be initially considered by the Commission and may be asked to supply additional information or be inspected by a Commission representative. The Commission may then appoint the firm to the panel.

8. Any firm not so appointed to the panel may appeal to the MPA Committee. A firm appealing under this paragraph may be invited to attend before the MPA Committee. The decision of the MPA Committee as to panel membership shall be final.

9. Firms on the panel must notify the Commission of any significant change in their structure or other material change which might be relevant to their membership of the panel. The Commission may audit panel firms from time to time and may require panel firms to be reconsidered by the MPA Committee on an annual or any other basis.

10. The MPA Committee may remove firms from the panel if in the view of the MPA Committee:
    (i) the criteria then applying for joining the panel are no longer satisfied or
    (ii) a panel firm has acted in any multi-party action (whether contracted or not) in a way which would justify termination of an MPA Contract under paragraph 71.

Part III Procedures Prior to Contract

11. As soon as a multi-party action or potential multi-party action has been identified the Commission will normally nominate the MPA Unit (but may nominate another office or make no nomination) to deal with all applications for funding and all certificates in that action. The Regional Director will appoint an MPA Manager to have overall responsibility for each nominated action.

12. When an action has been nominated under paragraph 11 the MPA Manager will prepare a report for the Commission including, insofar as information is available:
    (i) a brief description of the action;
    (ii) estimates of the present and likely future numbers of certificates and private clients;
    (iii) the suitability of the case for an MPA Contract;
    (iv) the suitability of the case for a generic work contract, an all work contract or for an other work contract;
    (v) details of any groups representing clients in the action;
    (vi) details of any other significant funders of claims within the action;
    (vii) details of any conditional fee agreements and the likelihood of any conditional fee agreement being available;
    (viii) the suitability of the case for Legal Representation or Support Funding.

13. The Commission may liaise with any other funders in the action with a view to considering joint tendering with such funders if it considers that it would be in the interests of clients to do so. The provisions of these procedures will be treated as modified so far as necessary to comply with any such joint tendering exercise.

14. If it appears to the Commission:
    (i) desirable for legal representation or support funding in the action to be provided under contract;
    but
    (ii) likely that it would cause undue delay or otherwise prejudice the interests of clients for there to be a competitive tender for the contract;
the Commission may seek to agree with firms involved in the action, procedures for the progression of the claims and for the pricing of work to be carried out.

15. If in the circumstances described under paragraph 14 it appears to the Commission that satisfactory terms can be agreed, the Commission may enter into an MPA Contract with some firms for the future conduct of the action and will amend as necessary any certificates in the action.

16. If it appears to the Commission desirable that there should be a tendering exercise, the Commission will normally place an advertisement in The Law Society's Gazette inviting tenders from firms wishing to apply for the contract.

17. Any advertisement under paragraph 16 will specify:
    (i) the name or a description of the multi-party action;
    (ii) work which the proposed contract will cover, whether generic work only (which will normally be the case) all work or such other work as may be specified;
    (iii) that tender packs will be sent to firms who request them;
    (iv) the date by which tenders must be submitted.

18. Subject to section 20 of the Act the Commission may request any firm which has carried out work in the action to prepare a brief report on the history of the case and the principal issues raised by the claims, with a view to that report being made available to any firm that wishes to tender. If a firm fails to provide a satisfactory report under this paragraph, the Commission may, if it thinks fit, exclude that firm from tendering in the action.

19. Tender packs will specify the information which should be contained in any tender. In general tenders will be required to include at least:
    (i) a case plan detailing how it is proposed the litigation be progressed, including the use of experts and counsel;
    (ii) price information;
    (iii) details of work already carried out in the action;
    (iv) proposals for how clients presently with other firms should be dealt with and proposals for dealing with clients geographically distant from the firm, whether through agency arrangements or otherwise;
    (v) the name of the proposed lead solicitor responsible for liaising with the MPA Unit.

20. In respect of tenders involving firms not on the panel the Commission will also require in respect of each such firm detailed information as to the systems, experience, expertise and stability of the firm.

21. Unless the Commission otherwise directs, a tender will be considered by the Commission provided, at the time the advertisement under paragraph 16 is placed or such other time as the Commission may specify, at least one of the firms involved in the tender is either:
    (i) on the panel; or
    (ii) already involved in the action.

A firm will be treated as already involved in the action if the Commission is satisfied that the firm has one or more certificates in the action or has carried out relevant work in the action (which may include work on behalf of private clients).

22. The Commission will conduct an initial sift of all tenders received and will make such enquiries as it considers appropriate and may require further information or arrange to visit any firm to verify or clarify information contained in a tender.

23. The Commission may reject any tender which it considers does not meet the Funding Code criteria or which it considers would not, if accepted, provide work to an appropriate standard. The Commission will notify tenderers so rejected. If there are no tenders of an appropriate standard the Commission will decide how best to proceed in the interest of the clients and may invite further tenders.

24. If only one tender is of an appropriate standard, the Commission may, if the proposals contained in the tender appear satisfactory or can be agreed, enter into an MPA Contract with the tenderer. If there is more than one such tender, the tenders will be referred to the MPA Committee. The Commission may shortlist tenders where it considers that it is impractical for the MPA Committee to consider all tenders. Tenderers may be invited to attend before the MPA Committee to answer questions or make presentations in support of their tenders.

25. The MPA Committee will consider tenders referred to it with a view to selecting the tender most likely to progress the claims efficiently and effectively, securing best possible value for money, in the interest of clients and the Fund. The MPA Committee will take into account, inter alia:
    (i) the tenders;

Appendix H: MPA Procedures

    (ii) any representations by the MPA Manager;
    (iii) the views of any clients or client groups (if known).

26. The MPA Committee may either:
    (i) select a tender;
    (ii) select a tender subject to agreement over price or any other aspect of the tender;
    (iii) invite firms to agree to a smaller/larger or different group of firms from that proposed, and if the chosen firms agree, select them;
    (iv) make no selection and invite further tenders; or
    (v) decide not to proceed to enter into an MPA Contract for the time being.

27. The MPA Committee may waive or dispense with any of the requirements of this Part of these procedures if it is of the opinion that to do so would be appropriate for a particular action and would not cause any significant prejudice to clients.

28. Nothing in these procedures shall oblige the Commission to call for tenders or enter into any contracts and the Commission may choose to limit the number of contracts in force at any time or restrict contracts to particular types of action.

Part IV Entry Into and Effects of Contracts

29. Where a tender has been selected the Commission may enter into an MPA Contract. The contract will be signed on behalf of the Commission by the chairman of the MPA Committee or by a Commission member or by the Regional Director and by each contracted firm.

30. MPA contracts will normally cover generic work only. However, each MPA Contract will specify the claims or types of claim to which it relates and will specify the work which it covers which will be either:
    (i) generic work only;
    (ii) all work;
    (iii) such other work as is specified in the MPA Contract.

31. When an MPA Contract has been entered into, all relevant certificates will be amended as required. Unless the Commission otherwise directs, contract work will be limited to work by contracted firms in pursuance of the contract. In the case of an all-work contract, unless the commission otherwise directs, all certificates will be transferred into the name of one of the contracted firms.

32. Normally, work in an action outside the scope of an MPA Contract will not be funded by the Commission. However, if it is, clients may be funded outside these procedures in respect of work which is not covered by the contract, so that if e.g. the contract covers only generic work, a client may choose a local firm as regards non-generic work.

33. While an MPA Contract is in force, the Commission may from time to time amend or clarify the scope of work covered by the contract. The contracted firms may also apply to the Commission for permission to add, substitute or remove firms from the group to meet the needs of the action as it progresses. Proposed changes in the nature of the work covered by the contract or in the contracted firms may be referred to the MPA Committee.

34. Except where any MPA Contract expressly provides otherwise, each MPA Contract entered into under these procedures shall contain and be subject to the provisions of Part V of these procedures.

35. The Commission may amend these procedures from time to time and unless the contrary is stated such amendments shall apply both to existing and future MPA Contracts

Part V Standard Contracting Provisions

General

36. Contracted firms will carry out only such work as is authorised by the MPA Manager and will comply with such limitations on contract work as the MPA Manager may from time to time impose. Contracted firms may appeal any decision of the MPA Manager as to the scope of the work permitted and as to price conditions to the MPA Committee.

37. The MPA Manager may refer any decision as to the scope or continuation of contract work directly to the MPA Committee whose decision shall be final.

38. Subject to any directions given by the MPA Manager:
    (i) contracted firms shall divide the contract work between them in accordance with the tender and may amend such division from time to time; but a major change of responsibilities within a group may only be made with the approval of the MPA Manager.
    (ii) each contracted firm shall individually record the contract work which it does:
    (iii) contracted firms may instruct counsel in respect of contract work but may not delegate or assign contract work to non-contracted firms without the approval of the MPA Manager.

39. A nominated lead solicitor in a contracted firm shall be primarily responsible for liaising with the Commission.

40. Contracted firms will perform the contract work in a timely manner and with all reasonable skill, care, diligence and accuracy. Where there is more than one contracted firm, they must work together harmoniously.

41. For the avoidance of doubt, all rights over contract work shall vest in the Commission and, subject to section 20 of the Act, the Commission will take into account information obtained pursuant to the contract for the purposes of discharging its functions under the Act. Contracted firms shall ensure that counsel, experts, solicitor agents and other persons carrying out contract work understand and agree the Commission's interest.

Monitoring Multi-Party Actions

42. A nominated contracted firm shall submit a report to the MPA Manager in a form prescribed by the Commission every six months or at such other times or period as the MPA Manager may require. Unless otherwise specified, reports under this paragraph must include:
    (i) an update to the case plan indicating significant developments and proposals for the future conduct of the litigation;
    (ii) updated price information and proposed price ceilings for negotiation or agreement;
    (iii) an assessment, incorporating counsel's opinion if appropriate of the merits and cost benefit of the litigation as a whole and of categories of individual claims.

43. If the nominated contracted firm fails to provide an adequate report the MPA Manager may:
    (i) withhold any payments on account pending submission of the report;
    (ii) limit work to submitting the report only;
    (iii) recommend to the MPA Committee termination of the contract.

44. The MPA Manager may during any action make enquiries of clients as to the standard of service they are receiving from contracted firms.

Remuneration

45. Remuneration will be determined by the contract.

46. Rates of remuneration and cost limitations under the contract shall govern only such costs as are payable from the Fund and shall not prejudice entitlement to, or the amount of, any recovery of costs inter partes.

47. Where, in accordance with the contract, costs fall to be assessed, such assessment shall be carried out by the Regional Director except where (because clients have an interest in the amount of costs and wish to make representations, or otherwise) the Commission requests the court to carry out a detailed assessment of costs.

Any assessment of contract costs by the Regional Director may, on application by the contracted firms, be reviewed by the MPA Committee which may (because clients have an interest in the amount of costs and wish to make representations, or otherwise) instead of reviewing the assessment direct that the court should be requested to carry out a detailed assessment. Any detailed assessment by the court of contract costs may be subject to rights of objection or appeals provided by regulations.

48. Unless otherwise agreed the MPA Contract will include:
    (i) a cost limitation for each step of contract work and for the contracted work as a whole;
    (ii) a breakdown of any such limitation into the three elements of profit costs, counsel's fees and disbursements;
    (iii) hourly rates fixed for specified levels of fee earner, or fixed in such other way as the Commission directs.

49. In any assessment (or detailed assessment by the court) of contract costs and on any objections hearing or appeal, contract terms (including those relating to hourly rates and costs limits) shall be binding.

50. Where it considers it appropriate, the Commission may approve specific items of expenditure under the MPA Contract.

51. Unless the terms of the contract provide otherwise or the Commission otherwise directs (in respect of counsel's fees or otherwise), all payments in respect of contract work will be made between the Commission and a nominated contracted firm and it will be for that firm to account to any other firms, counsel or others involved in the case.

52. The Commission may make payments on account in respect of contract work only as provided for by these procedures.

53. Contracted firms may apply to the MPA Manager for the payment of a sum on account of:
    (i) disbursements incurred or about to be incurred in connection with contract work;
    (ii) profit costs or counsel's fees in respect of contract work as soon as such work has been undertaken, including work in connection with contract work undertaken by them under a legal aid certificate issued prior to the date of the contract.

In relation to applications under sub-paragraph (ii) above the Commission will pay 75 per cent of what it considers to be a reasonable amount for work reasonably done. Payments on account will be made as soon as practicable, provided that sufficient details are submitted to enable the Commission to consider the reasonableness of the claim.

54. Where contract work is also carried out for the benefit of private clients the Commission will normally reduce the proportion of the work funded according to the proportion of private clients in the case.

Subject to paragraph 55, payments on account will be reduced by a percentage to take into account the current proportion of private clients in the action as a whole. For this purpose only private clients who have commenced proceedings or are otherwise clearly identified to the satisfaction of the MPA Manager will be taken into account, but contracting firms shall provide the MPA Manager with such information as he requires to enable a fair estimate of numbers to be given.

55. The Commission may, if it thinks fit, agree to payments on account being made as if there were fewer private clients or no private clients in the action. The Commission is likely to exercise this discretion where it is satisfied that:
    (i) reducing payments on account to take account of private clients might cause delay or otherwise prejudice the interests of clients; and
    (ii) contracting firms have taken all reasonable steps to obtain appropriate levels of funding from private clients in the action or have made appropriate arrangements for private clients to pursue claims with conditional fee agreements and insurance.

56. Contracted firms may apply to the MPA Manager for payment of the travelling costs of clients in connection with:
    (i) clients' meetings organised by contracted firms;
    (ii) MPA Committees organised by contracted firms which include client representatives.

The MPA Manager may approve such payments if the purpose of the meeting or MPA Committee is clear and is necessary to progress the conduct of the litigation, and the objectives of the meeting or committee cannot be achieved as effectively through other procedures. If such approval is given, the Commission will pay clients' reasonable travelling costs within the United Kingdom (equivalent to Second Class return rail fare) to contracted firms for distribution to clients, or reimburse contracted firms for any such reasonable sums as they have paid.

Contracted firms must explain to clients the effect of the statutory charge should damages be recovered and the contracted firms make any claim for payment from the Fund.

57. Where contracted firms have failed to comply with any relevant provision of the regulations, the Funding Code, these procedures or the MPA Contract:
   (i) payment on account may be deferred or suspended; and
   (ii) where as a result of such default or omission the Commission or any client incurs loss, such loss may be deducted from payment of profit costs in respect of contract work until the loss is recovered.

Keeping Clients and Local Firms Informed

58. Contracted firms will keep clients fully informed as to the preparation and prosecution of their claims.

59. Without prejudice to the obligation under paragraph 58, a nominated contracted firm shall make reports on at least a three-monthly basis to clients on the preparation and progress of their claims. Such reports may be sent via local firms to clients with an instruction that local firms should pass the reports on and deal with any queries from their clients. Reports sent to clients must be in language readily understandable to the layman.

60. Contracted firms will keep any local firms informed of the progress of the action and will given them sufficient guidance and information to enable them:
   (i) properly to advise and help their clients;
   (ii) to make representations on behalf of their clients on the conduct of the litigation;
   (iii) to assess so far as possible the likely impact of the statutory charge on claims of their clients;
   (iv) to progress the individual claims of their clients in accordance with the latest orders or directions from the court.

61. Nothing in these procedures shall oblige contracted firms to comply with all requests for information from local firms or clients or to disseminate information which in the opinion of contracted firms might prejudice the interest of clients in the action generally.

Complaints

62. Contracted firms shall issue details of their complaints procedure to clients and should ensure that, so far as possible, the following procedure is adopted in respect of obligations and procedures contained in these procedures:
   (i) clients should in the first instance complain to their own solicitors;
   (ii) unresolved complaints must be notified to the MPA Manager;
   (iii) complaints from other bodies, including solicitors' firms or counsel, about the conduct of the contracted firm must be made to the MPA Manager.

63. The MPA Manager will monitor and keep records of complaints. The MPA Manager will refer complaints to the MPA Committee where the complaints relate to the procedures themselves or where the volume or severity of the complaints might lead the MPA Committee to consider termination.

Advertising

64. Contracted firms may not advertise for clients without the consent of the Commission or the court. Firms may be required to submit proposed advertisements to the Commission prior to publication.

Appendix H: MPA Procedures

Conflicting Instructions and Compromises

65. Nothing in these procedures shall affect the normal professional duties of solicitors to their clients. Where, as a result of instructions received, contracted firms or local firms consider that they cannot reasonably be expected to act for any client they shall inform the MPA Manager and certificates may be amended or discharged as appropriate.

66. Where a contracted firm receives conflicting instructions (whether in relation to an offer of compromise or otherwise) and cannot resolve such conflict, it shall report the problem to the MPA Manager. The normal procedures as to amendment or discharge of certificates shall apply in such circumstances but where it appears to the MPA Manager that there may be grounds for terminating the contract or for dividing the clients into groups and entering into one or more new contracts, the MPA Manager will inform the MPA Committee and make appropriate recommendations.

Apportionment of Costs

67. In this and the remaining paragraphs of the procedures, 'costs' refers to all costs, counsel's fees and disbursements incurred in respect of contract work on behalf of clients, and 'generic costs' refers to such costs in respect of generic work. Costs will be apportioned between the accounts of clients by the Commission where required by regulations, the Funding Code or by the terms of an MPA Contract.

68. Contracted firms will keep such records and supply such information as is necessary to enable the Commission to carry out apportionment of costs. When lodging for detailed assessment by the court any bill of costs in respect of contract work, contracted firms will serve a copy of the bill on the MPA Manager.

69. When apportioning costs the Commission will seek to give effect to any costs sharing order made by the Court. Subject to any such order, and without prejudice to any inter partes costs order or agreement, the following principles will operate as guidelines only in the apportionment of costs claimed from the Fund:

    (i) subject to the following guidelines, generic costs will be divided equally between all clients and all other costs will be placed on the account of the individual client concerned;

    (ii) generic costs attributable to a particular group of clients will be divided equally between the members of that group. This would apply where there are issues in the action which relate only to that group, or where a group of clients continue with the action after others have discontinued or accepted offers of settlement;

    (iii) generic costs will be apportioned between clients ab initio, regardless of when they joined the action;

    (iv) clients who leave an action before it is concluded, whether by discontinuing, death, accepting an offer of settlement or otherwise ('early leavers') will be liable for their share of generic costs only up to the time they left, or up to the end of the next accounting period chosen for this purpose by the court or the Commission;

    (v) travelling costs to meetings paid under paragraph 56 will be placed on the account of the client concerned, travelling costs to MPA Committees under that paragraph will be treated as generic costs.

70. At the request of an early leaver the Commission may if it thinks fit specify a figure for that person's share of costs before the conclusion of the action. Any such determination shall then be binding on both the Commission and all clients, leaving the balance of the costs to be apportioned amongst the remaining clients at the conclusion of the action.

Termination

71. The Commission may terminate any contract, either in respect of a specific firm within a group or all firms, where in the opinion of the Commission:

(i) there has been a serious failure to comply with obligations under the regulations, the Funding Code, these procedures or the MPA Contract;
(ii) where any contracted firm has acted or is proposing to act in a way likely to cause substantial prejudice to clients or to the Commission, and the circumstances set out in the Schedule to these procedures shall be deemed to be potential grounds for termination;
(iii) information set out in the tenders or representations made by an MPA contracted firm in the tendering process are found to be inaccurate or misleading;
(iv) a firm which was on the panel when the contract was entered into no longer meets the criteria for panel membership;
(v) it is no longer possible to agree satisfactory price terms under the contract;
(vi) it is no longer appropriate to continue legal representation by means of an MPA Contract in the action;
(vii) a firm has colluded with another firm (which did not tender with it) in relation to any price element of a tender;
(viii) contracting firms (where there is more than one of them) or solicitors or other legal representatives within a contracting firm, are no longer able to work together harmoniously.

72. The Commission may terminate an MPA Contract from such date as it may specify where all work authorised by the contract had been completed or where the contracted firms all agree to termination.

73. The Commission may terminate immediately in case of urgency, otherwise:
(i) the MPA Manager will notify the contracted firm of the area of concern and ask for remedial steps to be taken within 21 days, or such other period as he may specify; and
(ii) if, having considered any representations by the contracted firms and the remedial steps taken since notice was served, the MPA Manager is of the opinion that the contract should be terminated, he will refer the contract to the MPA Committee to consider termination.

74. Where a termination has occurred the MPA Committee will consider how best to proceed in the interests of clients and the Commission may enter into a new contract or contracts without applying the procedures set out in Part III of these procedures.

75. Subject to paragraph 57, after termination a former contracted firm may apply for payment on account under paragraph 53 in respect of work done up to the date of termination. On termination, contracted firms will deliver up documents relating to contract work as required by the Commission and shall cooperate with the Commission and with firms continuing to perform work in the action with a view to minimising any disruption of the claims or prejudice to the clients.

Schedule
Grounds for Termination

1. Serious or persistent failure to comply with relevant provisions of regulations, the Funding Code, these procedures or the MPA Contract after appropriate notice of default. Examples include:
(i) unauthorised delegation of generic work;
(ii) failure to cooperate with other contracting or local firms, including failure to provide information needed for monitoring reports;
(iii) failure to comply with monitoring requirements including material non-disclosure which could substantially prejudice clients or the Commission;
(iv) failure to comply with any complaints procedure;
(v) failure to provide proper information to clients either as specifically required in the procedures or in response to reasonable requests;
(vi) failure to maintain accurate records of costs incurred as apportioned between clients.

2. Material alteration to partnership or team membership of any firm affecting ability to fulfil obligations to the Commission or to clients (eg. in the case of a split or merger in an MPA contract-

Appendix H: MPA Procedures

ing firm, the Commission may wish to terminate and enter new contracts if the team left its old firm and transferred to a new one which met the selection criteria. Alternatively as a result of the move neither firm might meet the criteria and a completely new firm might be required).

3. Failure properly to control the conduct and progress of the action.

4. Failure/inability to maintain adequate support services for the conduct of the action, ie. the breakdown of suitable secretarial, administrative and information technology facilities.

5. Poor quality of work and advice identified by the Commission.

6. Continuing substantiated complaints or an adverse adjudication by the OSS whether regarding work in the multi-party action or otherwise, including an adjudication on delay, or persistent discrimination against staff or clients.

7. Continuing excessive claims for payment, including for payments on account.

8. Major loss of confidence by clients.

9. The contracted firm being unable on ethical grounds to continue representing the clients.

10. The firm's financial condition being such that to continue might at worst lead to the bankruptcy of its partners, at best lead to diminished quality of work and advice.

11. Dishonesty or criminal conviction of relevant personnel.

12. Bankruptcy of partner members of the MPA Contract team.

Multi-Party Action Solicitors' Panel

1.0 Introduction
2.0 Operation of the Panel
3.0 Contract tendering procedure
4.0 Overview of Panel membership criteria
5.0 Firm membership criteria
6.0 Supervisor criteria
7.0 Notes for guidance
8.0 Glossary

Membership Criteria and Guidance

1.0 Introduction

1.1 On 16 July 1998, the Lord Chancellor announced the Government's commitment to the implementation of the proposals in *When the Price is High*, the Legal Aid Board's 1997 consultation paper on reforming policies and procedures in contracting multi-party actions (MPAs). In addition to the introduction of price tendering for contracts, and the imposition of cost limits on contract work, that report called for the establishment of a panel of solicitors with experience and expertise in group actions.

1.2 The rationale behind the MPA Solicitors' Panel is three-fold. First, we wish to ensure that tenders are received from those firms best able to conduct MPA work effectively and efficiently. Second, we wish to create an accredited group of firms whose members could be called upon at short notice to take over ongoing contracts in emergency circumstances. Finally, we wish to create a body of firms which could act as a consultative panel, alerting the Commission to emergent group actions at an early stage and raising any concerns about our contract and tender procedures.

1.3 As the legal aid scheme develops into a regime based largely on payment under contract, we will be contracting greater numbers of high cost cases, including MPAs. As has been the case since 1992, we will be contracting MPAs under individual case contracts. We will be letting contracts for MPAs following a standard procedure under revised Arrangements, a copy of which is included in this pack.

2.0 Operation of the Panel

2.1 Membership of the Panel will be open to any firm whose application is deemed by the Legal Services Commission's Head Office to meet the selection criteria, as set out at paragraphs 5.0 and 6.0 below. Firms will be free to apply to join the Panel at any time. Those firms wishing to be included in the initial Panel of members, to be announced when it is launched officially on 1 February 1999, will need to submit applications by 11 December 1998.

2.2 Firms which are not successful in their applications are entitled to appeal to the Multi-Party Actions (Operational) Committee. The Committee will consider both written and oral representations from firms. It may order an audit of an appellant firm. Its decision is final. However, firms may re-apply for membership at a future date if their circumstances change.

2.3 Firms on the Panel will have to notify the Commission of any significant change in their structure or other material change which might be relevant to their membership of the Panel. The Commission may audit Panel firms from time to time and may require Panel firms to be reconsidered by the Committee on an annual or any other basis.

2.4 The Committee may remove firms from the Panel if, in the view of the Committee, the criteria then applying for joining the Panel are no longer satisfied, or a Panel firm has acted in any MPA (whether contracted or not) in a way which would justify termination of a contract under the terms of the MPA Arrangements.

3.0 Contract tendering procedure

3.1 As under the MPA Arrangements 1992, any firms which have applied for, or been granted, legal aid by the set date under the 1999 Arrangements, will be able to tender for contracts. Those firms with private clients only will also be able to tender under the revised Arrangements. In other words, the MPA Panel will not be exclusive at this stage.

3.2 Panel members however, will be entitled to tender for *any* contract intended to be let by the Commission, whether or not they are involved in the action. In other words, they need not have any clients currently involved in the case. To assist Panel members wishing to tender for such contracts, the Commission will prepare a précis of the case. The précis will briefly outline the nature and history of the action, the stage it has reached in investigation or litigation, numbers of clients, both legally-aided and private (if known), the names of firms involved and of defendants in the action. On the basis of that information, it will then be left to the firm to make additional inquiries.

3.3 All firms will be required to submit costed case plans and a general plan for conducting the litigation. Non-Panel firms will be required to provide detailed information on their staffing, office resources, case experience, quality and complaints procedures and franchising status. However, Panel members will be treated as having satisfied the Commission's requirements in those areas. They will not, therefore, have to submit more than their case plan on tender and any information about changes in their firm since their Panel application.

4.0 Overview of Panel membership criteria

4.1 This document, and the accompanying MPA Panel application form, should be read in conjunction with the Legal Aid Board's Franchising Specification, (Second Edition, March 1995) or any document replacing it. Following the approach taken in the franchise specification, Panel membership criteria are divided into two categories. Criteria which the applicant firm as a corporate entity must meet are set out at paragraph 5.0 below. Criteria which must be met by fee-earners in the firm acting as supervisors in multi-party casework are set out at 6.0 below. We will also be considering additional information about the firm's record in conducting multi-party work, including outcomes of cases, time taken to progress cases and costs incurred.

4.2 The Panel is established under the authority of the Legal Aid Act 1988, the Multi-Party Action Arrangements 1999 and the Access to Justice Act 1999. The Arrangements set out, in general terms, the criteria for joining the Panel, the procedures for joining the Panel and the grounds for termination of Panel membership.

4.3 The Panel membership criteria are followed by brief notes for guidance, at paragraph 7.0 and a glossary of terms at paragraph 8.0. The criteria should be read in conjunction with those sections.

5.0 Firm membership criteria

(a) Possession of a Legal Services Commission franchise.
(b) Satisfactory record of: management of, or substantial involvement in, generic work in at least three MPAs involving complex issues in the last five years. One of the MPAs must have been of moderate size (at least 100 plaintiffs) and have reached a significantly advanced stage. We would usually expect this to involve the issue of proceedings and directions from the court
(c) Caseload demonstrating a satisfactory track record in complex and high value litigation in the last five years.
(d) Sufficient fee-earning and administrative staff to enable a moderately-sized MPA to be progressed without drawing in additional outside resources.
(e) Arrangements in place to call in additional resources from outside the firm if necessary.

(f) Access within the firm to appropriate data and information resources for conducting a moderately-sized MPA.
(g) Demonstrated financial stability.
(h) Demonstrated corporate stability.

6.0 Supervisor criteria

(a) Fee-earners supervising MPA casework must have a satisfactory record of: management of, or substantial involvement in, generic work in at least three MPAs involving complex issues in the last five years. One of the MPAs must have been of moderate size and have reached a significantly advanced stage. We would usually expect this to involve the issue of proceedings and directions from the court.
(b) In addition, fee-earners supervising MPA casework must be able to demonstrate a satisfactory track record of work in complex and high value litigation over the previous five years.

7.0 Notes for guidance

(a) Franchise requirement: We have not specified a franchise in any particular case category for two reasons. First, a growing number of MPAs are outside the personal injury field. Second, the Commission is simply looking for general assurance of an appropriate level of control of case and office management which a franchise is able to provide.
(b) MPA experience: The Commission is looking for evidence of direct involvement in running a moderately-sized MPA or in carrying out complex generic work. Firms whose MPA experience is confined to representing small numbers of individual clients will not therefore meet this requirement.
(c) Complex litigation experience: In terms of complexity, the Commission is looking for evidence of a firm's involvement in cases with multiple plaintiffs or defendants or cases involving issues of technical complexity. Specific case experience is not prescribed. In the personal injury field, complex litigation experience might be demonstrated through a record of handling medical negligence, industrial injury or environmental disputes. Outside personal injury, complex case experience might be shown through professional negligence or complex contract work.
(d) High value litigation experience: Firms and supervisors should be able to demonstrate experience in cases with estimated costs to trial of over £50,000.
(e) Staff resources: Applicants should be able to demonstrate that they have sufficient permanent staff to handle a moderately-sized MPA which we would define, by reference to data on MPAs we have funded over the past five years, to be one in which there are at least 100 plaintiffs. Applicants should also be able to demonstrate, by reference to recent cases, that they are able to supplement their staff complement at short notice in larger MPAs, or at points of particular pressure in the conduct of MPA litigation, such as discovery.
(f) Information/data resources: Applicants must demonstrate that they have the appropriate physical/information resources for handling a moderately-sized MPA. These would include: up-to-date reference materials including relevant journal holdings; internal e-mail; access to the Internet; case management software appropriate for large actions; an appropriate database including a list of relevant experts; mail merge facilities; appropriate information retrieval systems; appropriate office equipment including fax machines, photocopiers and modems. Applicant firms should demonstrate that they have sufficient storage space to accommodate the paper files involved in a moderately-sized MPA.
(g) Financial stability: The Commission will want to see profit and loss accounts, balance sheets, and quarterly variance analyses for the past three years. Applicants must also provide bankers' references.
(h) Corporate/firm stability: Because MPAs tend to be long-running cases, applicants should demonstrate that they are likely to remain intact as a corporate entity for at least the next five years. To do so, they will need to demonstrate that there are established working relationships

among the MPA specialists in the firm and that the firm itself has had a record of corporate continuity or stability, even if there have been occasional changes in the staff complement.
(i) The Commission will also want to consider the history of an applicant firm's involvement in MPAs, including: the outcome of cases, costs incurred, and time taken in progressing the case. We have not prescribed ideal outcomes, cost levels or speed of progressing these cases but are inviting firms to provide such information in outlining recent case experience. Where appropriate, we will consult with any Regional office solicitor about any MPA in which a firm had been involved.
(j) The Commission will be looking for evidence of systematic planning and organisation of casework: specifically, efficiency of approach in timetabling and allocating work. We will also be looking for objectivity in case management and willingness to abandon weak cases. Firms should be able to demonstrate capability of handling complex generic work through early identification of key technical and legal issues and planning for their investigation. They should be able to demonstrate a record of progressing and concluding cases within a reasonable period of time.
(k) Applicants for membership of the Commission's MPA Panel will be subject to standard status inquiries, including the Office for the Supervision of Solicitors, the Solicitors' Indemnity Fund and Legal Services Commission Accounts and Investigations Department.

8.0 Glossary

In this guidance, unless the context otherwise requires:
'the Act' means the Legal Aid Act 1988 or the Access to Justice Act 1999 as appropriate.
'the Board' and 'the Commission' means the Legal Aid Board established under the Act and includes any person or body duly authorised to act on its behalf. (Subsequently replaced by the Legal Services Commission persuant to the Access to Justice Act 1999).
'claimant' means a person making a claim in an MPA with the benefit of a certificate issued under the regulations.
'the Committee' means the MPA (Operational) Committee appointed to carry out functions under the MPA Arrangements 1999, including: approving firms to join the Panel; removing firms from the Panel; selecting firms to enter into contracts; and terminating contracts.
'contract' means a contract between one or more firms and the Commission entered into under the MPA Arrangements for the provision or representation under Part IV of the Act in a multi-party action;
'firm' means a firm of solicitors or other legal representatives duly authorised to provide representation under Part IV of the Act or under the MPA Arrangements;
'franchising' means a system of securing advice, assistance and representation under Parts III, IV and V of the Act from a solicitors' office in a franchised category of work.
'moderately-sized MPA' means one with at least 100 plaintiffs.
'Panel' means the group of firms appointed under paragraph 6 of the MPA Arrangements 1999.
'plaintiffs' means both legally-aided and privately-paying clients in a group action.
'private client' means a person making a claim in an MPA without the benefit of a certificate issued under the legal aid regulations or the Funding Code as appropriate.
'regulations' means the Civil Legal Aid (General) Regulations 1989 or The Funding Code as appropriate.
'supervisor' means the fee-earner nominated to guide and assist personnel in the conduct of multi-party work.

INDEX

abuse of process
  binding nature of orders and judgments 3.45
  striking out 7.25, 7.27, 7.29
Accident Line Protect 11.74
advertising 6.01–6.30, 9.17
  'ambulance chasing' 6.02
  Association of Personal Injury Lawyers Code of Conduct 6.20
  availability of product after 6.28
  bandwagon effect 6.02
  barristers 6.05
  benzodiazepine litigation 6.10, 6.11
  British Code of Advertising Practice 6.07, 6.08
  British Nuclear Fuels plc, litigation involving 24.08
  chambers, access to proceedings in 6.25
  Committee of Advertising Practice (CAP) 6.08
  consumer information 6.01
  copies, no requirement to keep 6.09
  costs 6.01
  court approval 6.15
  cut-off dates 6.23
  disaster cases 6.04
  early 6.02
  false expectations 6.02
  generic model 2.13
  Group Litigation Order (GLO) 6.29, 6.30
  health products 6.08
  impression created by 6.02
  inappropriate 6.15
  Independent Television Commission (ITC) 6.08
  issue 6.01–6.04
  issues, GLO 3.23
  judicial comments 6.10–6.28
    benzodiazepine litigation 6.10, 6.11
    'hangers on' 6.12
    tobacco litigation 6.12
  Law Society Working Party report 6.12, 6.14–6.18
  Lord Chancellor's Advisory Committee on Legal Education and Conduct 6.17
  loss of public confidence 6.03
  Marchioness litigation 6.19
  medicines, vulnerability of persons taking 6.07
  merits test, application of 6.02
  misleading advertisements 6.07
  MMR litigation 6.27
  non-broadcast advertising 6.08
  Norplant litigation 6.28
  Part 19.11, advertising under 6.29, 6.30
  pharmaceutical product litigation 6.12
  pre-approval mechanism 6.18
  pro-active campaigns 6.18
  public, effect on 6.03
  public funding 6.04
  regulatory controls 6.05–6.09
    barristers' rules 6.05
    British Code of Advertising Practice 6.07, 6.08
    Committee of Advertising Practice (CAP) 6.08
    copies, no requirement to keep 6.09
    health products 6.08
    Independent Television Commission (ITC) 6.08
    medicines, vulnerability of persons taking 6.07
    misleading advertisements 6.07
    non-broadcast advertising 6.08
    responsible 6.08
    solicitors' rules 6.05, 6.06
    therapies 6.08
    underestimation of potential for side effects 6.07
    unjustified prospects of success 6.07
    unnecessary disappointment, avoiding 6.08
  responsible 6.08
  safety issues 6.03
  solicitors' rules 6.05, 6.06
  surveys, evidence from 6.22
  therapies 6.08
  tobacco litigation 6.12, 6.26, 32.01–32.04
  underestimation of potential for side effects 6.07
  United States 6.09
  unjustified prospects of success 6.07
  unnecessary disappointment, avoiding 6.08
  vaccines 6.03
  Woolf Reforms 6.21, 6.24
advice lines, legal 10.04
aggregation of award 7.22

545

Index

AIDS cases 13.34–7, 19.03, 19.04
  see also HIV haemophilia litigation
'ambulance chasing' 6.02
application for Group Litigation Order
    3.07–3.15
  see also certification; Group Litigation Order
      (GLO)
  alternatives 3.10, 3.32
  Chancery Division 3.11
  claimant, by 3.07
  consultation with Law Society's Multi Party
      Action Information Service 3.10
  content 3.14, 3.15
  County Courts, to 3.11
  defendant, by 3.07
  form 3.14, 3.15
  High Court, to 3.11
  information included in 3.14, 3.15
  judges hearing application 3.12, 3.13
  Lord Chief Justice consent 3.08
  own initiative of court 3.08
  persons likely to be a party, by 3.08
  Practice Direction
    alternatives 3.10, 3.32
    hearing of application 3.15
    information to be included in application
        3.14, 3.15
    party making application 3.07
    preliminary steps 3.10–3.13
  preliminary steps 3.10
  referral of application 3.12
  Solicitors' Group, formation of 3.10
  specialist lists 3.11
  stage at which court controls 3.09
  timing 3.07
  to whom application made 3.11
  Vice-Chancellor consent 3.08
  written evidence in support 3.14
asbestos cases 13.21, 13.22
**Association of Personal Injury Lawyers Code of
    Conduct**
  advertising 6.20
  direct contact with potential client 6.20
Australia 15.01–15.83
  assessment of provisions 15.80–15.83
  Australian Competition and Consumer
      Commission, representative action by
      15.77–15.79
  certification 3.30
  class action 1.02, 1.04
    function of rules 1.12
  commonality 3.30
  consolidation 15.08, 15.16–15.20
  development of multi-party actions 15.01

  controversies 15.02
  financial services 15.02
  Gravigard IUD litigation 20.20, 20.21
  historical development 15.03
  issue estoppel 3.45
  joinder 15.08, 15.09–15.12
  liberalisation 15.04
  mass wrongs 15.02
  Part IVA FCA 1992 15.26–15.76
    commencement of proceedings 15.34, 15.35
    common issues arising from like
        circumstances 15.40–15.44
    costs 18.73–18.76
    drafting provisions 15.26
    further individual or group proceedings
        15.49
    generally 15.05, 15.26–15.33
    identification of applicants 15.36–15.39
    judgment 15.68–15.72
    non-common issues, determination of
        15.60–15.63
    notice 15.56–15.59
    opt out 15.05, 15.46–15.48
    order that proceedings not continue as
        representative proceedings 15.50–15.55
    requirements for representative action
        15.31–15.33
    same respondent, claim against 15.45
    settlement 15.64–15.67
    United States compared 15.27–15.30
  product liability 15.02
  recognition 15.03
  representative actions 15.08, 15.21–15.25
  statutory reforms 15.05
  test cases 15.08, 15.13–15.15
  toxic torts 15.02
  traditional mechanisms 15.08–15.25
    consolidation 15.08, 15.16–15.20
    joinder 15.08, 15.09–15.12
    representative actions 15.08, 15.21–15.25
    test cases 15.08, 15.13–15.15

bandwagon effect 6.02
barristers
  advertising 6.05
  conditional fee arrangements 11.62
BCCI case
  costs 8.25, 8.26
benzodiazepine litigation
  advertising 6.10, 6.11
  certification 3.34–3.38
  claims 22.08–22.12
  collapse of litigation 2.11
  common or related issues of fact or law 3.38

Index

benzodiazepine litigation (*cont.*):
  controlling 2.01
  costs 22.60–22.67
  course of litigation 22.19–22.30
  court's approach 22.13–22.18
  cut-off dates 5.43, 5.52, 22.54–22.59
  filtering cases 4.25
  funding 22.60–22.67
  generic model 2.13
  Group Register
    criteria 4.23, 4.24, 4.26
    financial viability 4.28
  investigation costs 2.11
  legal aid 22.60–22.67
  management of multi-party actions 2.01
  Master Statements of Claim 2.13, 4.41
  medical reports 7.13, 22.35–22.53
  pleadings 22.31–22.34
  preliminary issues 5.21
  products 22.01–22.07
  striking out 7.24, 7.30, 7.31, 22.68–22.82
  test cases 5.16, 5.21
  United States 3.36, 3.37
  weak cases 2.09, 4.26
British Coal *see* **respiratory disease litigation;**
    Vibration White Finger litigation
British Code of Advertising Practice 6.07, 6.08
British Columbia
  see also **Canada**
  certification 3.27
  class action 1.12
  preliminary tests 3.27
British Nuclear Fuels plc, litigation involving
    24.01–24.34
  advertising 24.08
  assigned judge 24.31
  discovery 24.26–24.30
  evidence 24.18–24.25
  facts of cases 24.04–24.06
  follow on cases 24.34
  Gardner study 24.03
  legal aid 24.09, 24.10
  plant's effects 24.02
  pleaded case 24.14–24.17
  procedural history 24.07
  selection of plaintiffs 24.11–24.13
  Sellafield 24.01–24.06
  trial 24.32, 24.33

Canada 14.01–14.47
  assessment of law in 14.47
  certification 3.24, 3.29, 3.38, 14.05–14.29
    cause of action 14.08
    class representative 14.27, 14.28

    common issues 14.13–14.17
    examples 14.29
    five part test 14.07
    identification of class 14.09–14.12
    motion to certify 14.06
    preferable procedure 14.18–14.26
    size of class 14.09–14.12
  damages 14.36
  discontinuance 14.32
  fees 14.37–14.45
  funding 14.37–14.45
  generally 14.01–14.04
  interlocutory motions 14.31
  issues, definition of 3.29
  judicial control 14.31–14.33
  limitation 14.46
  multi-party claims 1.04
  notice to class members 14.30
  provinces permitting class actions 14.01
  representation of class members 14.34
  resolution of individual issues 13.35
  scrutiny of class actions by court 14.33
  settlement 14.32
  United States 3.24
case studies 16.01–16.22
  see also individual case studies, e.g. pertussis
    vaccine litigation
  approach to management of actions 16.03
  focus 16.04
  funding 16.02
  future of group litigation 16.22
  generally 1.09
  historical context 16.01–16.04
  legal aid 16.05–16.09
  lessons to be learnt from 2.20–2.22
  management techniques 16.01, 16.04
  pharmaceutical product litigation
    16.16–16.21
  success rates 16.10–16.15
  table of 16.02
  underlying success rates 16.10–16.15
causation
  establishing 2.14
  generic model 2.14
  medicines 2.14
  Myodil litigation 21.20, 21.21
  product liability 2.14
certification
  Australia
    commonality 3.30
  benzodiazepine litigation 3.34–3.38
  British Columbia 3.27
  Canada 3.24, 3.29, 3.38, 14.05–14.29
    cause of action 14.08

Index

certification (*cont.*):
  Canada (*cont.*):
    class representative 14.27, 14.28
    common issues 14.13–14.17
    examples 14.29
    five part test 14.07
    identification of class 14.09–14.12
    motion to certify 14.06
    preferable procedure 14.18–14.26
    size of class 14.09–14.12
  common or related issues of fact or law 3.19, 3.20
  criteria 3.16–3.23
  discretion 3.16–3.23
  experience on criteria and discretion 3.24–3.38
  hearing 3.23
  informing superiors before 3.17
  issues, GLO 3.19, 3.22, 3.23
    see also issues, GLO
  jurisdiction 3.16–3.23
  Law Society Working Party 3.31
  number of claims 3.22
  Ontario 3.27
  overriding objective of CPR 3.18, 3.28
  pharmaceutical product litigation 3.38
  policy considerations 3.21
  Practice Direction 3.32
  preliminary tests 3.27
  product liability 3.38
  Quebec 3.26, 3.27
  same interest in claim 3.20
  superiors' decision 3.17
  United States 3.24–3.29
    adequacy 3.25, 3.28, 13.07
    adversely affecting parties' rights 3.28
    avoidance of inconsistent decisions 3.25, 3.28
    commonality 3.25, 3.28, 13.05, 13.06
    criteria 3.25
    Federal Rule 3.25
    investigation by court into merits of case 3.26
    numerosity 3.25
    predominance 3.25, 3.28, 3.29, 13.06, 13.08, 13.32
    preliminary tests 3.27
    representation 3.25, 3.29
    superiority 3.25, 3.28, 3.29, 3.33, 13.05, 13.08, 13.26–13.28
    typicality 3.25, 3.28, 3.29, 13.05
    usefulness of analysis 3.24
challenging GLO 3.54
champerty 11.01, 11.09

Chancery Division
  application for Group Litigation Order 3.11
Citizens Advice Bureaux (CAB) 11.82
Civil Justice Review 1988
  conditional fee arrangements 11.03
Civil Procedure Rules 1998 App. A
  drafting 1.07
  interpretation 2.32
  introduction 1.07
  overriding objective 3.18
  position before 1.07
  Practice Directions 1.07
  pre-action protocols *see* pre-action protocols
  Rule 19.III 1.08
CJD *see* **Creutzfeldt-Jakob disease litigation**
class action
  Australia *see* Australia
  British Columbia 1.12
  Canada *see* Canada
  meaning 1.02
  Netherlands 1.04
  Ontario 1.12
  Portugal 1.04
  Quebec 1.04
  United States *see* United States
CLS *see* **Community Legal Service (CLS)**
common or related issues of fact or law
  benzodiazepine litigation 3.38
  certification 3.19, 3.20
  commonality in United States compared 3.28
  jurisdictional requirement 3.19
  likely to be qualifying claims 3.21
  preliminary tests 3.27
  same interest in claim distinguished 3.20
  trigger for Part 19 9.01
Community Legal Service (CLS) 5.29, 12.01
  see also public funding
  contracts 12.35, 12.36
  costs protection 12.09–12.16
  criteria 12.06
  deployment of resources 12.02
  exclusions from funding 12.03, 12.28, 12.29
  funding 12.01
  Funding Code 12.06, 12.07
  payments 12.08
  prescribed costs threshold 12.07
  price tendering 12.35
  priorities for funding 12.02
  proscribed services 12.03, 12.04
  Schedule 2 services 12.03–12.05, 12.28, 12.29
  Solicitors Panel App. D, App. H2
Community Legal Service Fund 2.11, 2.32
conditional fee arrangements 11.01–11.83
  adverse selection 11.12

548

Index

conditional fee arrangements (*cont.*):
  agreement 11.08, 11.09
  availability 11.07
  background 11.01–11.06
  barristers 11.62
  challenge 11.43–11.48
  Civil Justice Review 1988 11.03
  client, risk for 11.24
  conflicts between lawyer and client
    11.63–11.72
  contents of agreement 11.08, 11.09
  costs 8.11, 8.19
  costs risk 11.18–11.22
  economic impact on defendants 11.82
  enabling legislation 11.04
  ethical considerations 11.13
  Europe, in 11.83
  expert witnesses 11.11
  financial implications 11.55–11.61
  guidance 11.13, 11.15
    small value claims 11.16
  historical development 11.01–11.06
  implementation of legislation 11.05
  indemnity principle 11.10
  industrial disease cases 11.57
  insurers, risk for 11.27, 11.28
  international issues 11.83
  investigation costs 11.29
  lawyers, risk for 11.25, 11.26
  lead solicitor 5.32
  Legal Aid Board, functions of 11.75, 11.76
  level of work undertaken by solicitor 11.58
  low value claims 11.59, 11.60
  maintenance of action 11.52
  Marre Committee 11.03
  matters to be drawn to attention of client
    11.08
  maximum uplift 11.05, 11.06, 11.13
  meaning 11.01
  medical negligence cases 11.54, 11.57
  MINELAS 11.03
  non-compliance with formalities 11.09
  notification 11.43–11.48
  number of policies issued 11.22
  other methods of funding, availability of
    11.17
  payment of insurance premiums 11.30–11.34
  percentage 11.04
  permitted conditional fees 11.07–11.12
  Personal Injury Panel 11.19–11.21
  preparation for case 11.68
  public funding 11.17, 12.17–12.20
  purpose 11.01
  recoverability of success fees and insurance
    premium 11.35–11.42
    amount of costs 11.38
    benefits of 11.40
    charging rates 11.39
    inflated insurance premiums 11.38
    payments on account, foregoing 11.37
    postponement of payment of fees/expenses
      11.37
    power of court 11.35
    problems 11.41, 11.42
    rates, lawyer's 11.39
    trade unions 11.36
  reduction of risk 11.01
  research into 11.57, 11.61, 11.73
  risk assessment 11.23–11.34
    accuracy 11.78
    client, risk for 11.24
    early 11.51
    front loading of investigation 11.51
    generally 11.23
    Handbook guidance 11.49
    insurers, risk for 11.27, 11.28
    investigation costs 11.29
    lawyers, risk for 11.25, 11.26
    maintenance of action 11.52
    multi-party actions 11.73–11.81
    need for 11.49–11.52
    payment of insurance premiums
      11.30–11.34
    personal injury claims 11.79
    pre-introduction of CFAs 11.50
    rationale 11.51
    responsibility for assessment 11.49
    review 11.49
    skills needed for 11.49
    tobacco litigation 11.52
    Woolf reforms 11.51
  road accident cases 11.54, 11.57
  Royal Commission on Legal Services 11.02
  South Africa 11.83
  specification of fee 11.04
  standard procedures, use of 11.57
  success fee 11.07, 11.12
    see also uplift *below*
  success rates 11.77
  surveys 11.54
  third party funder, agreements with 11.12
  tobacco litigation 2.28, 11.52, 11.80, 11.81,
    32.11, 32.12
  trade unions 11.36
  'try on' claims 11.59
  types of case
    financial implications of different
      11.55–11.61

549

Index

conditional fee arrangements (*cont.*);
  types of case (*cont.*);
    risks of different 11.53, 11.54
  undesirable practices 11.66
  unenforceable agreements 11.09
  unsuitable uses 11.56
  uplift
    challenging level 11.14
    degree of risk 11.13
    ethical considerations 11.13
    maximum 11.05, 11.06
    power to specify 11.13
    setting 11.13–11.17
    table for calculating 11.15
    writing reasons for setting success fee 11.14
  Woolf reforms 11.51
  work, accidents at 11.54, 11.57
  writing, agreement in 11.08
consolidation of claims 3.10
  precedence over GLO 3.33
consumer organisations 9.02
  injunctions,
    generally 1.10
contempt of court
  injunctions to protect collective interests of consumers 9.18
costs 8.01–8.34
  amount 8.01
  award 8.01
  BCCI case 8.25, 8.26
  benzodiazepine litigation 22.60–22.67
  circumstances to be considered 8.02
  common 8.03, 8.06–8.08
    liability of individuals 8.09–8.11
  common issues approach 8.16
  conditional fee agreements 8.11, 8.19
  cost-sharing arrangements 8.22, 8.23
  decisions on 8.24–8.34
    BCCI case 8.25, 8.26
    generally 8.24
    Nationwide case 8.31–8.34
    Watson Burton case 8.27–8.30
  discontinuance of claim 8.21
  discretion of court 8.01, 8.04
  environmental damage cases 25.30
  general rule 8.01
  generic model 2.08, 2.09, 2.14
  Group Litigation Order (GLO) 8.02–8.08, App. E
  Group Register 4.16
  individual 8.03–8.05
  individual case model 2.10, 8.16
  joining or leaving group 8.20, 8.21
  Law Society Report 8.10

  lead solicitors 8.12–8.15
    appointment, date of 8.13
    computerised records, uses of 8.14
    Marchioness litigation 8.15
    Practice Direction 8.12, 8.15
    preparatory work 8.14, 8.15
  Lockton litigation 27.19–27.35
  Marchioness litigation 8.15
  mixed winning and losing 8.16–8.19
  Nationwide case 8.31–8.34
  non-legally aided claimants, shielding 8.09
  Norplant litigation 8.18
  Opren litigation 8.09, 18.18, 18.19
  Practice Direction 8.05
  pre-action protocols 4.01
  proportionate share of overall costs, liability for 8.08–8.11
  protection for individual 8.19
  recovery
    European Commission proposals 1.10
  respiratory disease litigation 30.20, 30.21
  risks 1.11
  set-off, individual costs with 8.17
  several share of liability 8.07
  specimen costs sharing order 8.19, App. G
  timing of payment 8.01
  tobacco litigation 2.29, 8.18
  types 8.03
  Watson Burton case 8.27–8.30
  withdrawal of claim 8.21
Council of Bars and Law Societies of Europe (CCBE) 11.83
County Courts, to
  application for Group Litigation Order 3.11
Creutzfeldt-Jakob disease litigation 28.01–28.46
  assessment 28.40–28.46
  background 28.01–28.11
  costs 28.35–28.39
  generic model 2.24, 2.32, 28.17–28.19
    after trial 28.20–28.33
    complications of approach 28.34
  litigation 28.12–28.16
  management of multi-party actions 2.24
  test cases 5.20
cut-off dates 2.04, 5.39–5.57
  advertising 6.23
  approach 5.43–5.45
  basic rule 5.39
  benzodiazepine litigation 5.43, 5.52, 22.54–22.59
  communicating 5.46
  early dates 5.50–5.53
  investigation of claims 5.52

Index

cut-off dates (*cont.*):
  latecomers 5.53, 5.56
  limitation 5.54–5.57
    costs 5.55
    failure to observe 5.54
    interrelationship between 5.54
    latecomers 5.56
    Opren litigation 5.54
    public funding 5.56, 5.57
  Lloyd's litigation 5.47
  management of multi-party actions 2.04
  Myodil litigation 21.18, 21.19
  not imposing, reasons for 5.48, 5.49
  Opren litigation 5.54
  power to specify 5.39, 5.40
  Practice Direction 5.40, 5.41
  progress, proper 5.42
  publicity of group proceedings 5.46
  rationale for 5.42
  respiratory disease litigation 30.18
  selecting date 5.50
    early dates 5.50–5.53
  setting 5.46
  sub-groups 5.53
  sufficient number of cases in group 5.42
  targeted communication 5.46
  timing of date selected 5.50

directions 5.03–5.08
  case management 5.03
  discretion, managerial 5.03
  Group Particulars of Claim 4.40
  Group Register criteria 4.15, 4.18
  hearings initiated by managing judge 5.05
    examples 5.05
  indications of likely orders 5.05
  innovative proposals 5.04
  issues 5.06
  managing judge 5.03–8
    see also **directions**
  medical examination 5.07
  medical records 5.07
  meetings of representatives to discuss 5.05
  Norplant litigation 31.21–31.36
  personal injury cases 5.07
    medical examination 5.07
    medical records 5.07
  powers 5.03
  range 5.03
  regularity 5.05
  specimen App. G
Director General of Fair Trading
  injunctions to protect collective interests of consumers 9.21–9.23

disaster cases
  advertising 6.04
disclosure
  documentary evidence 7.02–7.07
discontinuance of claim
  costs 8.21
discovery
  British Nuclear Fuels plc, litigation involving 24.26–24.30
  documentary evidence *see* **documentary evidence**
  Opren litigation 18.17
  pertussis vaccine litigation 17.13
  pre-action *see* **pre-action discovery**
disposition of as many cases/issues as possible 5.11
Docklands nuisance class actions 26.01–26.30
  background 26.01–26.04
  Canary Wharf Ltd, proceedings issued against 26.22–26.25
  further representations 26.26–26.29
  judicial review 26.14–26.21
  LDDC, proceedings against 26.22–26.25
  relevant considerations 26.05–26.07
  representations, submission of 26.08–26.13
documentary evidence 7.02–7.07
  approaches to disclosure 7.03–7.05
  cost 7.05
  CPR, approach under 7.05
  CPR, under 7.06, 7.07
  disclosure 7.02–7.07
  Law Society Report 7.06
  lead cases 7.06
  limiting extent of disclosure 7.03
  Myodil litigation 7.05
  new approach 7.02
  pre-action disclosure 7.02
  preliminary issues 7.05
  preparatory work 7.05
  problems of 7.05
  reasonable search 7.02
  timing of disclosure 7.06
  undisputed issues 7.05

environmental damage cases 25.01–25.38
  background to proceedings 25.01–25.11
  costs 25.30
  evidence 25.24–25.29
  generic model 2.09
  group action 1.05
  legal aid 25.17–25.20
  nuisance 25.21–25.23
  procedural history 25.12–25.16
  settlement 25.32–25.38

Index

Europe
　multi-party actions 1.5
European Commission
　Directorate-General on Justice and Home Affairs 1.10
European Union 1.04
　developments 1.10
expert evidence 7.08–7.19
　core documents 7.10
　joint experts 7.09
　medical practitioner, evidence of 7.11
　medical reports 7.12–7.19
　　see also **medical reports**
　MMR litigation 7.09
　one expert, direction that evidence be given by 7.08
　organisation 7.10
　personal injury claims, in 7.11–7.19
　　medical practitioner, evidence of 7.11
　　medical reports 7.12–7.19; *see also* **medical reports**
　　pre-CPR position 7.12
　pertussis vaccine litigation 17.14
　research, conducting 7.09
　restriction 7.08
　vaccines litigation 7.09
expert witnesses
　conditional fee arrangements 11.11
　personal injury protocol 4.02

fees
　Group Register 4.16
financial services
　Australia 15.02
　Lockton litigation *see* **Lockton litigation**
Finland 1.04
framework for management of multi-party actions 1.08
France
　legal expenses insurance 10.02
frivolous claims 5.34
funding
　aspects 1.11
　benzodiazepine litigation 22.60–22.67
　Canada 14.37–14.45
　conditional fee arrangements *see* **conditional fee arrangements**
　costs *see* **costs**
　generally 1.11
　importance 1.11
　legal aid *see* **legal aid**
　legal expenses insurance *see* **legal expenses insurance**
　methods 1.06

　multi-party actions 1.06
　Norplant litigation 31.38–31.41
　public *see* **Community Legal Service (CLS); public funding**

generic model 2.08, 2.09, 2.13
　see also **tactical management issues**
　advertising 2.13
　assumptions 2.08, 2.09
　'bandwagon' effect 2.13
　benzodiazepine litigation 2.13
　causation 2.14
　CJD litigation 2.24, 2.32
　common issues 2.08
　costs 2.08, 2.09, 2.14
　Creutzfeldt-Jakob disease litigation 2.24, 2.32, 28.17–28.19
　　after trial 28.20–28.33
　　complications of approach 28.34
　criticisms 2.13
　environmental damage cases 2.09
　Gravigard litigation 2.13
　investigation costs 2.14
　'kitchen sink' pleading 2.13
　Law Society Report 2.16, 2.17
　Master Statements of Claim 2.13
　maximising number of claimants 2.14
　meaning 2.08
　media interest 2.13
　Norplant litigation 2.13, 2.25, 2.26, 2.32
　objectives 2.14
　Opren litigation 2.13
　pertussis litigation 2.13
　pleadings 2.13
　premises 2.09
　product liability 2.09, 2.13
　progression of cases 2.08
　proponents 2.14
　public funding 2.13
　respiratory disease litigation 2.32
　scrutiny of claims 2.13
　similarity 2.08
　speculative cases 2.09
　speculative claims 2.09
　tactical management issues 2.14, 2.16–2.19
　trial of generic issues 2.08
　validity 2.08, 2.09
　viability 2.08, 2.09
　Vibration White Finger case 2.32
　weak claims 2.09
Germany
　legal expenses insurance 10.02
GLO *see* **Group Litigation Order (GLO)**

Index

Gravigard IUD litigation 20.01–20.21
  allegations 20.05
  association with other devices 20.03, 20.04
  Australia 20.20, 20.21
  commentary on 20.12–20.19
  generic model 2.13
  Master Statements of Claim 2.13, 4.41
  procedural history 20.06–20.11
  product 20.01, 20.02
  weak cases 2.09
group action
  categories of cases 1.05
  environmental cases 1.05
  housing cases 1.05
  insurance protection claims 1.05
  investor protection 1.05
  meaning 1.02
  medical device products 1.05
  pharmaceutical products 1.05
  transport accidents 1.05
  United Kingdom 1.05
Group Litigation Order (GLO)
  advertising 6.29, 6.30
  application 3.07–3.15
    see also **application for Group Litigation Order**
  binding nature of orders and judgments 3.43–3.53
    abuse of process 3.45
    basic rule 3.43, 3.44
    issue estoppel 3.45–53; *see also* **issue estoppel**
    issues, GLO 3.44
  challenging 3.54
  collection of individual claims, as 5.11
  co-ordinatable group 3.04–3.06
  copy sent to Law Society 5.26
  costs 8.02–8.08, App. E
  discretion to make 3.16
    exercise 3.16
  effect 3.39–3.53
    binding nature of orders and judgments 3.43–53; *see also* **issue estoppel**
    management court *see* **management court**
  issues *see* **issues, GLO**
  likely claimants 3.06
  management court *see* **management court**
  meaning 1.02
  number of claims 3.04
  provisions for 3.01
  publicity 6.29, 6.30
  ten certificate rule 3.05
  theory underlying 3.01

Group Particulars of Claim 4.40–4.46
  see also **Master Statements of Claim**
  assumption underlying 4.40
  genuine summary of issues 4.46
  management court direction 4.40
  Practice Direction 4.40
  product liability 4.41
  schedule 4.40, 4.45
  summarising general allegations 4.40
Group Register 4.12–4.35
  adverse effect on case 4.15, 4.33
  amendments to claims 4.26
  application for entry onto 4.15
  benzodiazepine litigation
    criteria 4.23, 4.24, 4.26
    financial viability 4.28
  controls, requirement for 4.17
  costs 4.16
  criteria 4.17–4.27
    benzodiazepine litigation 4.23, 4.24
    direction by management court 4.15, 4.18
    importance 4.17, 4.21, 4.23
    investor protection 4.21
    issues, GLO 4.17
    Myodil litigation 4.24, 4.25
    personal injury cases 4.22
    questionnaires 4.19–4.22
    satisfaction 4.22
    setting 4.17
    transport accidents 4.21
    verification 4.20, 4.21
  details
    entered onto register 4.13, 4.14
    guidance 4.14
    not entered onto register 3.40
    verification of claims 4.14, 4.20
  direction by management court 4.15, 4.18
  establishment 4.13
  fees 4.16
  filtering 4.12, 4.20
  financial viability 4.28–4.31
    accuracy of evaluation 4.29
    benzodiazepine litigation 4.28
    conditional fee agreements 4.30
    funding mechanism 4.30
    legal aid 4.29
    proportionality 4.28
    reasonableness test 4.29
    United States 4.31
  investor protection 4.21
  issues, GLO 3.23, 4.17
  joining 4.32–4.35
    claim form 4.32, 4.35
    criteria, satisfaction of 4.33

553

Group Register (*cont.*):
  joining (*cont.*):
    different claims joining at different times 4.34
    limitation 4.35
    management court 4.33
    method 4.32
    new claims 4.34
    Practice Direction 4.32
    referral of claim to court 4.33
  lead solicitor 4.16
  limitation 4.35
  maintenance 4.15
  management court
    direction by 4.15, 4.18
    power 4.19
    questionnaires 4.19, 4.20
  manager 4.15, 4.16
  mechanism 4.12
  membership
    fact of 4.12
  Myodil litigation 4.24, 4.25
  new claims 4.34
  number identifying individuals 4.16
  order for details to be entered 4.15
  personal injury cases 4.22
  Practice Direction 4.14, 4.15
  purpose 4.12
  questionnaires 4.19–4.22
  refusal by management court to allow entry 4.15
  removal of case from 3.40, 4.14, 4.33
  request for documents 4.15
  solicitor maintaining 4.15
  transport accidents 4.21
  verification 4.14, 4.18, 4.20
    amendments to claims 4.26
    consequences of failure 4.26
    importance 4.20, 4.21
    investor protection cases 4.21
    questionnaires 4.19–4.22
    transport accident cases 4.21
  weak cases 4.26, 4.27
Guide for Use in Group Actions 5.27

haemophilia litigation *see* HIV haemophilia litigation
health products
  advertising 6.08
hearing
  certification 3.23
Hillsborough disaster litigation
  management of multi-party actions 2.03
historical development
  Civil Procedure Rules 1998 1.07
  litigation procedural rules 1.07
  Woolf reforms 1.07
HIV haemophilia litigation 19.01–19.27
  AIDS 19.03, 19.04
    effect on UK haemophiliacs 19.05, 19.06
  chambers, hearing in 5.05
  effect of AIDS on UK haemophiliacs 19.05, 19.06
  haemophilia 19.01, 19.02
  interlocutory hearings
    first 19.07–19.09
    second 19.10–19.15
    subsequent interlocutory orders 19.16–19.18
  medical negligence 19.26, 19.27
  public interest immunity 19.19–19.20
  publication of judicial observations in newspaper 19.21
  settlement encouraged by judge 5.05
  settlement of proceedings 19.22–19.25
  test cases 5.21
housing cases
  group action 1.05
human growth hormone litigation *see* Creutzfeldt-Jakob disease litigation
human rights
  determination of case within reasonable time 2.31
  management of multi-party actions 2.31

indemnity principle 11.10
Independent Television Commission (ITC) 6.08
independent trustee 5.33–5.38
  frivolous claims 5.34
  historical background 5.33–5.38
  problems creating need for 5.33, 5.34
  self-interested lawyers 5.33
  United States position 5.36
individual case model 2.10–2.12
  see also **tactical management issues**
  contemporary approach, as 2.32
  costs 2.10
  criticisms 2.12
  development 2.11
  filtering stage 2.10
  inappropriate uses 2.11
  Legal Aid Board 2.11
  meaning 2.10
  modification in current approach 2.32
  non-selected cases 2.12
  product liability 2.32
  proponents 2.14

individual case model (*cont.*):
  representative claims, assumption of 2.12
  tobacco litigation 2.27
  validation 2.12
industrial disease cases
  conditional fee arrangements 11.57
initial management of case 5.01–5.57
  cut-off dates *see* **cut-off dates**
  directions 5.03–5.08
    see also **directions**
  lead cases *see* **lead cases**
  managing judge 5.01, 5.02
  representation *see* **representation**
  test cases *see* **test cases**
initiation of action 3.01–3.54
  application for Group Litigation order *see*
    application for Group Litigation Order
  certification *see* **certification**
  effect of GLO 3.39–3.53
    see also under **Group Litigation Order (GLO)**; **management court**
  management court *see* **management court**
injunctions
  consumer organisations 1.10
    see also **injunctions to protect collective interests of consumers**
  protection of collective interests of consumers
    see **injunctions to protect collective interests of consumers**
injunctions to protect collective interests of consumers 9.09–9.26, App. F
  advertisements 9.17
  approved consumer organisation 9.09
  collective interests of consumers 9.25, 9.26
  consultation with qualified entity 9.17
  contempt of court 9.18
  co-ordination of investigations 9.21
  courts 9.17, 9.18
  damages 9.09
  designated courts competent to deal with 9.17, 9.18
  Director General of Fair Trading 9.21–9.23
  Injunctions Directive 9.10
    implementation 9.11
  introduction of mechanism 9.09
  Lead Body 9.21
  Named Bodies 9.13, 9.14, 9.20–9.22
  overview 9.09
  powers of qualified entities 9.15, 9.16
  private international law 9.24
  qualified entities 9.10–9.14
    consultation 9.16
    definition 9.12
    failure to exercise powers 9.13

    legitimate interest 9.12
    list of 9.15
    Named Bodies 9.13, 9.14
    objective criteria 9.13
    powers 9.15, 9.16
    private consumer organisations 9.14
    public consumer protection bodies 9.14
    publication of list of 9.15
    self-regulatory bodies 9.14
    trade associations 9.14
    trading standards departments 9.14
    utilities regulators 9.144
  quasi-regulator, organisations acting as 9.09
  remedies 9.19–9.24
  summary injunctions 9.18
  time limit to stop infringement 9.20
  undertakings to stop infringement 9.20
insurance
  companies, guaranteed annuity rates 2.32
  legal expenses *see* **legal expenses insurance**
  Lloyd's litigation *see* **Lloyd's litigation**
  protection claims 1.05
internal market 1.10
investigation
  costs *see* **investigation costs**
  cut-off dates 5.52
  discovery *see* **pre-action discovery**
  pre-action protocols *see* **pre-action protocols**
investigation costs
  conditional fee arrangements 11.29
  'front loading' 4.03
  generic model 2.14
  tobacco litigation 2.28
investor protection
  group action 1.05
  Group Register 4.21
Ireland
  pertussis vaccine litigation 17.25
issue estoppel 3.43–3.53
  Australia 3.45
  binding nature of orders and judgments 3.45–3.53
  extension of traditional rule 3.48–3.53
  meaning 3.45
  recognition of concept 3.45
  same parties, litigation between 3.45–3.47
  United States 3.45
issues, GLO 3.01
  advertising generating claims, where 3.23
  analysis 3.02
  certification 3.19, 3.22, 3.23
    hearing 3.23
  definition by court 3.22, 3.23
  examination by court 3.22, 3.23

Index

issues, GLO (*cont.*):
   freedom of choice 3.03
   Group Register 3.23, 4.17
   Lloyd's litigation 3.23
   misunderstandings over 3.23
   product liability 3.23
   similiarity 3.02
   transport accidents 3.23
   views on, differing 3.02
   wide 3.23
IUDs *see* Gravigard IUD litigation

Japan 1.04
joint experts 7.09
   see also expert evidence
judicial review
   Docklands nuisance class actions 26.14–26.21
   pertussis vaccine litigation 17.22–17.24
   public funding 12.38

'kitchen sink' pleading
   generic model 2.13

Law Society Report
   advertising 6.12, 6.14–6.18
   costs 8.10
   documentary evidence 7.06
   draft scenario 2.16
   generic model 2.16
   proposals 2.16, 2.17
Law Society's Multi Party Action Information Service
   consultation before application for GLO 3.10
LawAssist 11.74
lead cases
   see also test cases
   approaches, possible 5.15
   disposition of as many cases/issues as possible 5.11–5.14
   documentary evidence 7.06
   Lockton litigation 27.11–27.18
   Myodil litigation 21.17
   selection 5.10–5.23
   settlement of proceedings 7.20
   tobacco litigation 32.29–32.33
   Vibration White Finger litigation 5.12
lead solicitor 3.10, 5.24–5.32
   autonomy 5.37
   background to development of role 5.27–5.31
   co-ordination between firms 5.26
   complexity of litigation 5.25
   conditional fee agreements 5.32
   costs 8.12–8.15
      appointment, date of 8.13

      computerised records, uses of 8.14
      Marchioness litigation 8.15
      Practice Direction 8.12, 8.15
      preparatory work 8.14, 8.15
   dangers of 5.37
   differences of view between advisers 5.24, 5.37
   functions 5.24
   Group Register maintained by
      costs 4.16
   Lloyd's litigation 5.32
   Marchioness litigation 8.15
   nature of office 5.31
   need for 5.25
   office 5.31
   proper management and control 5.25
   relationship with other members of group 3.10
   role 3.10, 5.24, 5.31
leaving the group 7.01
   costs 8.21
legal advice lines 10.04
legal aid 16.05–16.09
   see also Community Legal Service; Public Funding
   benzodiazepine litigation 22.60–22.67
   British Nuclear Fuels plc, litigation involving 24.09, 24.10
   environmental damage cases 25.17–25.20
   reasonableness test 4.29
   tobacco litigation 32.05–32.10
Legal Aid Board 2.11
legal expenses insurance 10.01–10.09
   acceptance of cover 10.03
   advantage 10.04
   adverse selection 10.03
   aggregation of cover 10.01
   average premium 10.04
   choice of solicitor 10.07
   claims made basis 10.03
   commercial cover 10.02
   concealing information from insurer 10.08
   conduct of proceedings 10.08
   contractual terms 10.03
   cost 10.04
   disadvantages 10.05–10.08
   disputes resolution clauses 10.08
   duration of cover needed 10.03
   duty to advise on 10.01
   excess 10.03
   existence of cover 10.01
   France 10.02
   Germany 10.02
   gross written premium 10.02
   indemnity limit 10.05
   legal advice lines 10.04

Index

legal expenses insurance (cont.):
  liability for costs 10.09
  losing case 10.05
  market penetration 10.02
  merits test 10.06
  motoring risks 10.02
  non-party, costs awards against 10.09
  notification of loss 10.03
  number of policies in force 10.02
  occurrence based 10.03
  percentage of adults having cover 10.02
  personal accounts 10.02
  providers 10.03
  reasonable cost–benefit requirement 10.06
  recovery of premium 10.04
  sale of policies 10.01
  Sweden 10.02
  terms of contract 10.03
Legal Services Commission 12.01, App. H
LEI *see* **legal expenses insurance**
limitation
  Canada 14.46
  cut-off dates 5.54–5.57
    costs 5.55
    failure to observe 5.54
    interrelationship between 5.54
    latecomers 5.56
    Opren litigation 5.54
    public funding 5.56, 5.57
  Group Register, entry onto 4.35
  Lloyd's litigation 23.36–23.38
  Opren litigation 18.31–18.73
  respiratory disease litigation 30.18
  test cases 5.21
  tobacco litigation 32.52–32.58
litigation procedural rules
  Civil Procedure Rules 1998 *see* **Civil Procedure Rules 1998**
  consultation 1.08
  growth of multi-party actions due to 1.06
  historical development 1.07
Litigation Protection Limited 11.74
Lloyd's litigation 23.01–23.48
  adjournments 23.46, 23.47
  background 23.01, 23.02
  causes of action 23.06–23.18
    central fund litigation 23.17
    LMX spiral case 23.07
    long-tail cases 23.08–23.14
    personal stop loss cases 23.15
    portfolio selection cases 23.16
    reinsurance to close cases (RITC) 23.13, 23.14
    run-off contract cases 23.12

  causes of litigation 23.03
  central fund litigation 23.17
  Commercial Court administration 23.23–23.25
  cut-off dates 5.47
  defence 23.39
  issues, GLO 3.23
  law firm administration 23.33–23.35
  lead solicitor 5.32
  limitation 23.36–23.38
  LMX spiral case 23.07
  long-tail cases 23.08–23.14
  Outhwaite syndicates 23.19–23.22
  personal stop loss cases 23.15
  portfolio selection cases 23.16
  proceedings 23.26–23.478
  reinsurance to close cases (RITC) 23.13, 23.14
  settlement of proceedings 23.48
  summonses for directions 23.40–23.45
  syndicate 23.04, 23.05
  writs 23.26–23.32
Lockton litigation 27.01–27.35
  background 27.01, 27.02
  costs 27.19–27.35
  facts of case 27.03–27.05
  lead cases 27.11–27.18
  proposals for group action 27.06–27.10
Lord Chancellor's Advisory Committee on Legal Education and Conduct
  advertising 6.17
Lord Chief Justice
  consent for GLO 3.08

maintenance 11.01, 11.09
management court 3.39–3.42
  all claims to be commenced in 3.40
  binding nature of orders and judgments 3.43–3.53
  consequence of GLO 3.43
  directions 5.03–5.08
    see also directions
  Group Litigation Order (GLO) 3.39
  management directions 3.41, 3.42
    see also **directions**
  particulars of claim 4.39
  removal of case from Register 3.40
  specification 3.39
management directions
  management court 3.41–3.42, 5.03–5.08
    see also **directions**
management of multi-party actions
  adapting procedure 2.04
  advertising *see* **advertising**
  aggregation of award 7.22

557

management of multi-party actions (*cont.*):
  application for Group Litigation Order *see*
    application for Group Litigation order
  approach 2.06
    competing approaches 2.08–2.13
    contemporary 2.32–2.34
    generic model *see* **generic model**
    individual case model *see* **individual case model**
    suggested 2.33
  approach of court 2.05
  benzodiazepine litigation 2.01
  case histories, lessons to be learnt from 2.20–2.22
  certification
    see also certification
  CJD litigation 2.24
  contemporary approach 2.32–2.34
  context of action 2.34
  creativity 2.04
  Creutzfeldt-Jakob disease litigation 2.24
  cut-off dates *see* **cut-off dates**
  differences between cases 2.04
  directions *see* **directions**
  documentary evidence *see* **documentary evidence**
  documents discussing 2.22
  expert evidence *see* **expert evidence**
  fettering court's discretion 2.04
  flexibility 2.01–2.05, 2.34
  fundamental issues 2.06, 2.07
  general framework 2.04
  generally 1.10
  generic model *see* **generic model**
  Group Litigation Order *see* **Group Litigation Order (GLO)**
  Hillsborough disaster litigation 2.03
  historical development 2.01
  human rights 2.31
  individual case model *see* **individual case model**
  initial management *see* **advertising; cut-off dates; directions; initial management of group; lead cases; lead solicitor; managing judge; preliminary issues; representation; test cases**
  initiation of action *see* **application for Group Litigation Order; certification; Group Litigation Order (GLO); initiation of action**
  innovation, need for 2.02
  judicial discretion 2.01–2.05
  lead cases *see* **lead cases**
  leaving the group 7.01
  managing judge 5.01, 5.02
  MMR litigation 2.30

  need for case management principles 2.03
  Norplant litigation 2.25, 2.26
  options 2.34
  practical developments 2.23–2.31
    CJD litigation 2.24
    generally 2.23
    MMR litigation 2.30
    Norplant litigation 2.25, 2.26
    tobacco litigation 2.27–2.29
  pre-action protocols *see* **pre-action protocols**
  protocol approach 2.30
  reforms, effect of 1.13
  register *see* **Group Register**
  rights of individual litigants and 2.03
  settlement of proceedings 7.20, 7.21
  striking out 7.23–7.32
    see also **striking out**
  tactical positions 2.07, 2.14–2.19
  tactics *see* **tactical management issues**
  test cases *see* **test cases**
  tobacco litigation 2.27–2.29
managing judge 5.01, 5.02
  directions 5.03–5.08
    see also **directions**
  powers, management 5.03
Marchioness **litigation**
  advertising 6.19
  costs 8.15
  lead solicitor 8.15
Marre Committee
  conditional fee arrangements 11.03
Master Defence 4.41
Master Statements of Claim
  see also **Group Particulars of Claim**
  benzodiazepine litigation 2.13, 4.41
  generic model 2.13
  Gravigard litigation 2.13, 4.41
  individual statements and 4.41–4.43
  mechanism 4.41
  Norplant litigation 2.13, 4.43
  Opren litigation 2.13, 4.41
  pertussis litigation 2.13
  product liability 4.41
  rejection 4.42
  tobacco litigation 2.27, 4.44, 32.22, 32.23
  uses 2.13, 4.41, 4.42
medical device products
  group action 1.05
medical examination
  directions 5.07
  orders to attend 5.07
medical negligence cases
  conditional fee arrangements 11.54, 11.57
  HIV haemophilia litigation 19.26, 19.27

558

Index

medical records
  directions 5.07
  production 5.07
  tobacco litigation 2.28, 2.29, 32.13–32.15
medical reports
  benzodiazepine litigation 7.13, 22.35–22.53
  discretion to strike out 7.18
  extent 7.16
  limited use 7.16
  Opren litigation 18.20–18.23
  personal injury cases 5.07, 7.13–7.19
  service 7.18
  substantiating injury 7.15–7.18
  verification of complaints 7.14
medicines
  causation 2.14
MINELAS 11.03
misleading advertisements 6.07
MMR litigation
  advertising 6.27
  case management conference 4.05
  CPR approach 2.30
  expert evidence 7.09
  management of multi-party actions 2.30
  pre-action discovery 4.04, 4.09
  pre-action protocols 2.30, 4.04, 4.05
  preliminary hearings 4.04
  protocol approach 2.30, 4.04, 4.05
multi-district litigation procedure
  United States 1.03
multi-party actions
  alternatives to 9.01–9.31
  see also **injunction to protect collective interests of consumers; representative actions; representative parties**
  Australia 1.04, 15.01–15.83
    see also **Australia**
  Canada 1.04
  definition in *Funding Code* 3.01
  Europe 1.05
  European Union 1.04
  factors affecting rise in 1.06
  Finland 1.04
  funding 1.06
  group action as 1.02
  growth in 1.02, 1.06
  Japan 1.04
  management 1.01
  New Zealand 1.04
  Portugal 1.04
  public interest 3.01
  Quebec 1.04
  Spain 1.04
  Sweden 1.04
  United Kingdom 1.05
  United States 1.04
Myodil litigation 21.01–21.29
  action groups 21.29
  allegations, nature of 21.07–21.10
  causation 21.20, 21.21
  cut-off dates 21.18, 21.19
  documentary evidence 7.05
  generic and individual proceedings, relationship between 21.15, 21.16
  Group Register 4.24, 4.25
  lead cases 21.17
  Legal Aid Board 21.27, 21.28
  media, role of 21.29
  outline 21.11
  parties 21.01–21.03
  product 21.04–21.06
  registration of plaintiffs 21.22–21.26
  settlement of proceedings 21.12–21.14
  test cases 5.19
  trial of generic issue 21.17
  weak cases 2.09

Nationwide case
  costs 8.31–8.34
Netherlands
  class action 1.04
New Zealand 1.04
'no win no fee' arrangements 11.07
  see also **conditional fee arrangements**
Norplant litigation 31.01–31.44
  advertising 6.28
  aftermath of 31.44
  costs 8.18
  court control 31.14–31.20
  directions 31.21–31.36
  evidence 31.37
  funding 31.38–31.41
  generic model 2.13, 2.25, 2.26, 2.32
  management of multi-party actions 2.25, 2.26
  Master Statements of Claim 2.13, 4.43
  pre-litigation phase 31.04–31.13
  product 31.01–31.03
  transfer 31.14–31.20
  withdrawal of funding 31.38
nuclear fuel *see* **British Nuclear Fuels plc, litigation involving**
nuisance
  Docklands litigation *see* **Docklands nuisance class actions**
  environmental damage cases 25.21–25.23

Ontario
  see also **Canada**

559

Ontario (*cont.*):
　certification
　　preliminary tests 3.27
　class action 1.12
Opren litigation 18.01–18.73
　Action Group 18.06
　Arbitration report 18.28, 18.29
　background 18.04, 18.05
　costs 8.09, 18.18, 18.19
　cut-off dates 5.54
　discovery 18.17
　English litigation 18.08–18.73
　generic model 2.13
　limitation 18.31–18.73
　Master Statements of Claim 2.13, 4.41
　medical evidence 18.20–18.23
　product 18.01–18.03
　Randall v. Eli Lilly 18.27
　settlement 18.24–18.26
　test cases 5.16, 5.21
　timetable 18.11–18.16
　United States 18.07
overriding objective of CPR 3.18
　certification 3.18, 3.28
　settlement of proceedings 7.20

particulars of claim 4.36–4.46
　contents
　　discretionary 4.37
　　mandatory 4.36
　　personal injury claims 4.38
　　group 4.40–4.46
　　　see also **Group Particulars of Claim**
　management court powers 4.39
　normal position under CPR 4.36
　personal injury claims 4.38
　pre-action protocol 4.36
　requirement to serve 4.36
　statement of truth 4.20, 4.38
　verification 4.20, 4.38
payment into court
　test cases 5.18
penile prostheses 13.25–13.28
personal injury cases
　directions 5.07
　expert evidence 7.11–7.19
　　see also **expert evidence**
　Group Register 4.22
　medical reports 5.07, 7.13–7.19
　　see also **medical reports**
　particulars of claim 4.38
　protocol 4.02, 4.03
　　see also **pre-action protocols**
pertussis vaccine litigation 17.01–17.27
　assessment of 17.26, 17.27
　background 17.02–17.05
　co-ordination procedure 17.11
　discovery 17.13
　English cases 17.09–17.21
　evidence 17.17–17.21
　expert evidence 17.14
　generic model 2.13
　Ireland 17.25
　judgment 17.16
　judicial review 17.22–17.24
　litigation 17.06–17.21
　Master Statements of Claim 2.13
　Scotland 17.08
　test case 5.15, 5.16, 17.01–17.27
　trial 17.15
　United States 17.07
　Wellcome Foundation, role of 17.12
pharmaceutical product litigation
　advertising 6.12
　case studies 16.16–16.21
　certification 3.38
　difficulty in succeeding in 16.16–16.21
　group action 1.05
　Norplant *see* **Norplant litigation**
　Opren *see* **Opren litigation**
　pertussis vaccine litigation *see* **pertussis vaccine litigation**
pleadings
　generic model 2.13
police
　public funding of cases against 12.38
Portugal
　class action 1.04
Practice Direction App. B
pre-action discovery 4.09–4.11
　documentary evidence 7.02
　fishing expeditions 4.10
　formulation of claim 4.10
　general power to order 4.09
　justification 4.10
　Law Society Report 4.10
　MMR litigation 4.04, 4.09
　product liability 4.11
　rationale 4.11
　use 4.10
pre-action protocols 4.01–4.08
　application of approach 4.04
　conformity 4.01
　costs 4.01
　'front loading' of costs 4.03
　gathering evidence through 4.03
　importance 4.03
　MMR litigation 2.30, 4.04, 4.05

Index

pre-action protocols (*cont.*):
  non-compliance 4.01
  personal injury protocol 4.02
    denial of liability 4.02
    experts 4.02
    features 4.02
    gathering evidence 4.03
    insurer, identification of 4.02
    letter of claim 4.02
  risk assessment 4.03
  significance of CPR rules 4.01
preliminary issues
  see also **lead cases**; **test cases**
  documentary evidence 7.05
private international law
  injunctions to protect collective interests of consumers 9.24
product liability
  Australia 15.02
  benzodiazepine litigation *see* **benzodiazepine litigation**
  causation 2.14
  certification 3.38
  generic model 2.09, 2.13
  Group Particulars of Claim 4.41
  individual case model 2.32
  issues, GLO 3.23
  Master Statements of Claim 4.41
  Myodil *see* **Myodil litigation**
  pre-action discovery 4.11
protocol approach
  see also **pre-action protocols**
  application of approach 4.04
  management of multi-party actions 2.30
  MMR litigation 2.30, 4.04
public funding 12.01–12.71
  cessation of funding 12.27
  Community Legal Service (CLS) *see* **Community Legal Service (CLS)**
  conditional fee agreements 11.17, 12.17–12.20
  conduct of client 12.21
  costs protection 12.09–12.16
  defendants, representations by 12.64–12.71
  excluded services 12.03–12.05, 12.28, 12.29
  financial eligibility 12.21
  Full Representation 12.18, 12.22
  Funding Code 12.06, 12.07
  future restrictions 12.62, 12.63
  generic model 2.13
  Investigative Help 12.18, 12.20, 12.25
  Investigative Support 12.19, 12.20, 12.23
  judicial review 12.38
  Legal Services Commission *see* **Legal Services Commission**
  Litigation Support 12.19, 12.21
  multi-party actions 12.30–12.32
    applications 12.33
    control of funding 12.33
    procedures 12.33, 12.34
    scope of work 12.34
    Solicitors Panel App. H2, 12.36, App. D
    Unit 12.33, 12.34
  police, cases against 12.38
  private funding distinguished 12.17–12.27
  refusal of application 12.21
  Schedule 2 services 12.03–12.05, 12.28, 12.29
  service levels 12.17–12.27
  statutory framework 12.01–12.05
    generally 12.01
  Support Funding 12.26
  wider public interest cases 12.37–12.63
    benefits from case 12.43
    competing interests 12.58–12.61
    cost–benefit ratios 12.45–12.48
    definition 12.37
    examples 12.40
    financial eligibility 12.52
    fundamental rights 12.41
    future restrictions 12.62, 12.63
    general rule 12.37
    judicial review 12.38
    justification 12.39
    minimum number of people benefiting from case 12.43
    no cost–benefit ratio 12.45–12.48
    non-fundamental rights 12.41
    police, cases against 12.38
    potential to produce real benefits 12.38
    public bodies' failure to act 12.38
    public inquiry, not a 12.53–12.57
    Public Interest Advisory Panel 12.49–12.51
    success rate 12.42
    thresholds 12.42–12.44
    types of case 12.38
    valuing 12.45–12.48
  withdrawal 12.27
publicity of group proceedings
  see also **advertising**
  cut-off dates 5.46
  Group Litigation Order (GLO) 6.29, 6.30
  respiratory disease litigation 30.18

Quebec
  see also **Canada**
  certification 3.26, 3.27

561

Index

Quebec (*cont.*):
   class action 1.04
   preliminary tests 3.27
questionnaires
   Group Register 4.19–4.22

register *see* **Group Register**
reports
   medical *see* **medical reports**
representation
   development of law 5.27–5.30
   independent trustee *see* **independent trustee**
   lead solicitor 5.24–5.32
      see also **lead solicitor**
   two-tier system 5.27–5.31
representative actions
   see also **representative parties**
   Australia 15.08, 15.21–15.25
   meaning 1.10, 9.01
   proposals 9.27–9.31
   reform proposals 9.27–9.31
   trigger for 9.01
   use of procedure 3.10
representative organisations 9.02
representative parties 9.03–9.08, App. C
   see also **representative actions**
   common interest, grievance and relief 9.07
   compromise of claim 9.08
   CPR 9.03–9.05
   definition of group 9.08
   directing claim 9.08
   discontinuance of claim 9.08
   judgment 9.08
   permission to bring action 9.04
   restrictive approach 9.06, 9.07
   rules 9.03
   same interest in claim 9.03, 9.05, 9.06, 9.08
   sole control 9.08
   unincorporated associations 9.04
respiratory disease litigation 30.01–30.24
   background 30.01, 30.02
   case management 30.09–30.17, 30.22–30.24
   co-ordination of action 30.06–30.08
   costs 30.20, 30.21
   cut-off dates 30.18
   first cases 30.03–30.05
   generic model 2.32
   limitation 30.18
   publicity 30.18
   trial 30.19
risk assessment
   pre-action protocols 4.03
road accident cases
   conditional fee arrangements 11.54, 11.57

Royal Commission on Legal Services
   conditional fee arrangements 11.02

schedule
   Group Particulars of Claim 4.40, 4.45
Scotland
   Law Commission
      multi-party rule, rejection of 1.04
   pertussis vaccine litigation 17.08
   speculative fees 11.01
Sellafield leukaemia cases
   see also **British Nuclear Fuels plc, litigation involving**
   test cases 5.15
service
   medical reports 7.18
settlement of proceedings 7.20, 7.21
   advantages 7.20
   aggregation of award 7.22
   HIV haemophilia litigation 19.22–19.25
   lead cases 7.20
   Lloyd's litigation 23.48
   Myodil litigation 21.12–21.14
   Opren litigation 18.24–18.26
   overriding objective 7.20
   test cases 7.21
solicitor
   advertising 6.05, 6.06
      see also **advertising**
   lead *see* **lead solicitor**
   legal expenses insurance, duty to advise on 10.01
Solicitors' Group
   formation of 3.10
   lead solicitor 3.10
South Africa
   conditional fee arrangements 11.83
Spain 1.04
specialist lists
   application for Group Litigation Order 3.11
statement of truth
   particulars of claim 4.20, 4.38
striking out 7.23–7.32
   abuse of process 7.25, 7.27, 7.29
   benzodiazepine litigation 7.24, 7.30, 7.31, 22.68–22.82
   considerations 7.25
   cost–benefit analysis 7.23
   exercise of power 7.27
   frivolous, vexatious and bound to fail 7.24
   grounds 7.25
   impact of prolonged litigation 7.28
   matters that cannot be taken into account 7.26

Index

striking out (*cont.*):
 oppressive, vexatious and unjust proceedings 7.23
 viability of entire action 7.23
 work-related upper limb disorders 7.32
Sweden 1.04
 legal expenses insurance 10.02

tactical management issues 2.07, 2.14–2.19
 case histories, lessons to be learnt from 2.20–2.22
 defendant's, aims of 2.19
 generic model 2.14, 2.16–2.19
 motivation of claimants 2.15
 public inquiry, portrayal as 2.15
 reasons for failure of claims 2.18
test cases
 see also **lead cases**
 approaches, possible 5.15
 appropriate uses 5.10
 Australia 15.08, 15.13–15.15
 benzodiazepine litigation 5.16, 5.21
 collapse of case where small number selected 5.16
 compromise approach, as 68
 Creutzfeldt-Jakob disease litigation 5.20
 disposition of as many cases/issues as possible 5.11–5.14
 dropping out, case 5.17
 generic issues, trial of 5.20
 HIV litigation 5.21
 human growth hormone litigation 5.20
 individual cases, settlement of all 5.22
 limitation 5.21
 Myodil litigation 5.19
 Opren litigation 5.16, 5.21
 payment into court 5.18
 pertussis litigation 5.15, 5.16
 pertussis vaccine litigation 5.15, 5.16, 17.01–17.27
 power of court to manage 68
 preliminary issues 5.21
 selection 5.10–5.23
 Sellafield leukaemia cases 5.15
 settlement of proceedings 7.21
 tobacco litigation 5.21
therapies
 advertising 6.08
tobacco litigation 32.01–32.58
 advertising 6.12, 6.26, 32.01–32.04
 assignment of judge 32.18–32.21, 32.27, 32.28
 conditional fee agreements 2.28, 11.52, 11.80, 11.81, 32.11, 32.12
 costs 2.29, 8.18
 Court of Appeal 32.42–32.47
 debarring order 32.38–32.40
 early assignment of judge 32.18–32.21
 further directions 32.48–32.51
 further pleadings 32.34–32.37
 further proceedings 32.25, 32.26
 hearing before Senior Master 32.24
 individual case model 2.27
 investigation costs 2.28
 issue of proceedings 32.16, 32.17
 lead cases 32.29–32.33
 legal aid 32.05–32.10
 limitation 32.52–32.58
 management of multi-party actions 2.27–2.29
 Master Statements of Claim 2.27, 4.44, 32.22, 32.23
 media order 32.41
 medical records 2.28, 2.29, 32.13–32.15
 pre-Civil Procedure Rules 2.28
 significance 2.28
 speculative nature 2.09
 test cases 5.21
toxic shock syndrome 13.30
trade associations 9.02
trade unions 9.02
transport accidents
 group action 1.05
 Group Register 4.21
 issues, GLO 3.23
trial
 British Nuclear Fuels plc, litigation involving 24.32, 24.33
 pertussis vaccine litigation 17.15
 respiratory disease litigation 30.19
 Vibration White Finger litigation 29.12–29.23

unincorporated associations
 representative parties 9.04
United States
 advertising 6.09
 benzodiazepine litigation 3.36, 3.37
 certification 3.24–3.29
  adequacy 3.25, 3.28, 13.07
  adversely affecting parties' rights 3.28
  avoidance of inconsistent decisions 3.25, 3.28
  commonality 3.25, 3.28, 13.05, 13.06
  criteria 3.25, 13.04–13.13
  Federal Rule 3.25
  investigation by court into merits of case 3.26
  judicial time 13.09
  numerosity 3.25, 13.05

United States (*cont.*):
  certification (*cont.*);
    predominance 3.25, 3.28, 3.29, 13.06, 13.08, 13.32
    preliminary tests 3.27
    reluctance 13.23
    representation 3.25, 3.29
    requirements 13.04
    superiority 3.25, 3.28, 3.29, 3.33, 13.05, 13.08, 13.26–13.28
    typicality 3.25, 3.28, 3.29, 13.05, 13.25
    usefulness of analysis 3.24
  class action 1.02, 1.03, 1.12, 13.01–13.42
    Agent Orange litigation 13.38
    AIDS cases 13.34–13.37
    asbestos cases 13.21, 13.22, 13.40
    assessment 13.42
    cases used for 1.03
    certification 3.24–3.29; *see also* certification *above*
    criteria 3.25
    discrimination cases 13.14
    docket entries 13.10
    economies of scale 13.16
    effectiveness 13.14, 13.15
    exception to usual rule 13.01
    formal procedural rules 1.12
    function of rules 1.12
    generally 13.01–13.03
    investigation into merits of case 3.26
    judicial attitudes 1.03
    judicial time spent on 13.09
    large claims 13.34
    mass tort cases 13.03
    mini-trials 13.41
    nature 3.25
    notification 13.10–13.13
    penile prostheses 13.25–13.28
    practice, in 13.14–13.41
    product liability cases 13.16–13.19
    reluctance to certify 13.23
    suitable cases 13.02
    theory 13.04–13.13
    tobacco cases 13.31–13.33
    tort cases 13.15
    toxic shock syndrome 13.30
  contingency fee system 4.31
  fairly dealing and protecting interests of class 5.36
  issue estoppel 3.45
  lawyer, role of 5.36
  mini-trials 13.41
  multi-district litigation procedure 1.03
  Opren litigation 18.07
  pertussis vaccine litigation 17.07
  preliminary tests 3.27
  weak cases 4.27

vaccines
  advertising 6.03
  pertussis *see* **pertussis vaccine litigation**
Vibration White Finger litigation 29.01–29.26
  appeals 29.12–29.23
  generally 29.01–29.26
  generic model 2.32
  Group action 29.02–29.05
  handling agreement 29.24–29.26
  pre-trial phase 29.08–29.11
  selection of lead cases 5.12
  Steering Committee 29.06, 29.07
  trials 29.12–29.23
Vice-Chancellor
  consent for GLO 3.08

Watson Burton **case**
  costs 8.27–8.30
withdrawal of claim
  costs 8.21
witnesses
  expert *see* **expert evidence**
Woolf Reforms 1.07
  advertising 6.21, 6.24
  conditional fee arrangements 11.51
work, accidents at
  conditional fee arrangements 11.54, 11.57
work-related upper limb disorders
  striking out 7.32